THE PSYCHOLOGY OF WOMEN'S HEALTH

THE PSYCHOLOGY OF WOMEN'S HEALTH

PROGRESS
AND
CHALLENGES
IN RESEARCH
AND
APPLICATION

EDITED BY

ANNETTE L. STANTON

SHERYLE J. GALLANT

American Psychological Association
Washington, DC

First printing August 1995
Second printing April 1996

RA
564.85
.P895
1995

Published by the
American Psychological Association
750 First Street, NE
Washington, DC 20002

Copies may be ordered from
APA Order Department
P.O. Box 2710
Hyattsville, MD 20784

In the UK and Europe, copies may be ordered from
American Psychological Association
3 Henrietta Street
Covent Garden, London
WC2E 8LU England

Typeset in Minion by University Graphics, York, PA

Printer: Data Reproductions Corp., Rochester Hills, MI
Cover Designer: Anne Masters Design, Washington, DC
Technical/Production Editor: Sarah J. Trembath

Library of Congress Cataloging-in-Publication Data
Psychology of women's health: progress and challenges in research and
    application / edited by Annette L. Stanton and Sheryle J. Gallant.
        p.   cm.
    Includes bibliographical references and index.
    ISBN 1-55798-296-1 (alk. paper)
    1. Women—Health and hygiene—Psychological aspects.   2. Clinical
health psychology.   I. Stanton, Annette L.   II. Gallant, Sheryle J.
RA564.85P895   1995
613'.04244'019—dc20   95-10460
                                                             CIP

British Library Cataloguing-in-Publication Data
A CIP record is available from the British Library.

Printed in the United States of America

3220 2351

APA Science Volumes

Best Methods for the Analysis of Change: Recent Advances, Unanswered Questions, Future Directions

Cardiovascular Reactivity to Psychological Stress and Disease

The Challenge in Mathematics and Science Education: Psychology's Response

Cognition: Conceptual and Methodological Issues

Cognitive Bases of Musical Communication

Conceptualization and Measurement of Organism–Environment Interaction

Developmental Psychoacoustics

Emotion and Culture: Empirical Studies of Mutual Influence

Emotion, Disclosure, and Health

Examining Lives in Context: Perspectives on the Ecology of Human Development

Hostility, Coping, and Health

Organ Donation and Transplantation: Psychological and Behavioral Factors

The Perception of Structure

Perspectives on Socially Shared Cognition

Psychological Testing of Hispanics

Psychology of Women's Health: Progress and Challenges in Research and Application

Researching Community Psychology: Issues of Theory and Methods

Sleep and Cognition

Sleep Onset: Normal and Abnormal Processes

Studying Lives Through Time: Personality and Development

The Suggestibility of Children's Recollections: Implications for Eyewitness Testimony

Taste, Experience, and Feeding: Development and Learning

Temperament: Individual Differences at the Interface of Biology and Behavior

Through the Looking Glass: Issues of Psychological Well-Being in Captive Nonhuman Primates

APA expects to publish volumes on the following conference topics:

Attribution Processes, Person Perception and Social Interaction: The Legacy of Ned Jones

Changing Ecological Approaches to Development: Organism–Environment Mutualities

Conceptual Structure and Processes: Emergence, Discovery, and Change

Converging Operations in the Study of Visual Selective Attention

Genetic, Ethological, and Evolutionary Perspectives on Human Development

Global Prospects for Education: Development, Culture, and Schooling

Maintaining and Promoting Integrity in Behavioral Science Research

Marital and Family Therapy Outcome and Process Research

Measuring Changes in Patients Following Psychological and Pharmacological Interventions

Psychology of Industrial Relations

Psychophysiological Study of Attention

Stereotype Accuracy

Stereotypes: Brain–Behavior Relationships

Work Team Dynamics and Productivity in the Context of Diversity

As part of its continuing and expanding commitment to enhance the dissemination of scientific psychological knowledge, the Science Directorate of the APA established a Scientific Conferences Program. A series of volumes resulting from these conferences is produced jointly by the Science Directorate and the Office of Communications. A call for proposals is issued several times annually by the Science Directorate, which, collaboratively with the APA Board of Scientific Affairs, evaluates the proposals and selects several conferences for funding. This important effort has resulted in an exceptional series of meetings and scholarly volumes, each of which has contributed to the dissemination of research and dialogue in these topical areas.

The APA Science Directorate's conferences funding program has supported 35 conferences since its inception in 1988. To date, 24 volumes resulting from conferences have been published.

WILLIAM C. HOWELL, PHD
Executive Director

VIRGINIA E. HOLT
Assistant Executive Director

Contents

Contributors

Patricia L. Adams, University of Tennessee
Belinda Borrelli, University of Illinois
Betsy A. Butler, University of Pittsburgh, Pennsylvania
Joan C. Chrisler, Connecticut College
Sharon Danoff-Burg, University of Kansas
Paula S. Derry, Morgan State University, Maryland
Patricia M. Dubbert, University of Mississippi School of Medicine
Sheryle J. Gallant, University of Kansas
Margaret Gatz, University of Southern California
Diane L. Gressley, University of Tennessee
Lisa L. Harlow, University of Rhode Island
Jennifer R. Harris, The Karolinska Institute, Stockholm, Sweden
Stacey Hart, University of Southern California
Abby C. King, Stanford University Medical School, California
Bess H. Marcus, The Miriam Hospital and Brown University School of Medicine, Rhode Island
Marsha D. Marcus, Western Psychiatric Institute and Clinic, Pennsylvania
Robin J. Mermelstein, Prevention Research Center, Illinois
Beth E. Meyerowitz, University of Southern California
Patricia J. Morokoff, University of Rhode Island
Karin L. Parrett, Connecticut College
Bernardine M. Pinto, The Miriam Hospital and Brown University School of Medicine, Rhode Island
Kathryn Quina, University of Rhode Island
Sally A. Shumaker, The Bowman Gray School of Medicine, Wake Forest University, North Carolina

Teresa Rust Smith, The Bowman Gray School of Medicine, Wake Forest University, North Carolina
Annette L. Stanton, University of Kansas
Ruth H. Striegel-Moore, Wesleyan University, Connecticut
Cheryl B. Travis, University of Tennessee
Susan Turk-Charles, University of Southern California
Sharon C. Wilsnack, University of North Dakota School of Medicine
Rena R. Wing, University of Pittsburgh School of Medicine, Pennsylvania

Preface

Most of us who teach about the psychology of women's health are accustomed to questions about whether offering such a specialized course is advisable. Is there sufficient empirical content for such a course? Shouldn't such content be integrated into the general course curriculum? These questions represent relevant considerations for readers of this book also. Although much of the research on which this book is based has been conducted only within the past decade, the resultant empirical foundation is ample. Indeed, we were challenged to choose from a number of important areas of research. Thus, although there is much left to learn, the increasingly impressive quantity and quality of work that forms the research base in the psychology of women's health will be readily apparent to the reader.

Given that such content is available, should it be contained in a specialized volume or integrated into a more general text on health psychology? In our opinion, both options have merit. Our specialized approach provides a ready resource for students and researchers interested in an overview of psychological perspectives on women's health. Such an approach calls attention to empirical work that otherwise might be overlooked and to health issues that are specific to women. It illuminates crosscutting themes and assumptions in research about women. However, there also is merit in integrating material on women's health into more general publications in which documented gender differences and similarities, as well as mechanisms for gender-related effects are illustrated. In fact, we worry that audiences for specialized sources might not include scientists and practitioners whose research and thinking might most profit from specific information regarding women's health. However, material must be gathered and examined critically before synthesis can proceed; we hope that this volume will serve as a resource for those who wish to integrate findings and perspectives from these chapters into their teaching and research.

We have several goals for this book. Chapters are designed to delineate central health concerns of women from a psychosocial perspective. Authors review the most current research in their areas, which include topics in chronic disease, gynecologic health, health-related behaviors, and critical issues for the future (e.g., health of older women, health care policy). They portray the vital role of behavioral and psychosocial influences on women's health, and detail the impact of women's physical health on their psychological well-being. To the extent that pertinent research is available, chapter authors consider these issues within the context of women's diverse attributes and environments. Authors view the scientific literature with a critical eye, highlighting strengths and deficits in their research areas, suggesting ways in which assumptions about women have shaped the research agenda, and identifying methodological and conceptual concerns. Finally, they specify implications of extant research for promoting the health of women, and outline directions for future empirical activity and application.

Ultimately, our hope is that the chapters in this book provide a springboard for the next generation of research and application in psychosocial perspectives on women's health. Accordingly, we anticipate that the book will be of use to graduate students and researchers in psychology and other behavioral and social sciences, as well as to psychologists and other health care providers who are interested in an empirical foundation for offering effective services to women.

This book would not have seen completion but for the help of many supporters. Because we were interested in ensuring that the chapters provide the most incisive examination of the current empirical base, we enlisted the aid of many colleagues active in research to serve as reviewers for all chapters. Our gratitude goes to those who carefully reviewed original manuscripts, including Michael A. Andrykowski, Linda J. Beckman, Steven N. Blair, Helen L. Coons, Susan Czajkowski, Alice J. Dan, Lynda S. Doll, Denise Dougherty, Christine Dunkel-Schetter, Jean Endicott, Ellen R.

Gritz, Edith S. Lisansky Gomberg, Ian H. Gotlib, Jeannette R. Ickovics, Walter Kaye, Robert C. Klesges, Karen A. Matthews, Jan Moore, Michael W. O'Hara, C. Tracy Orleans, Marcia Ory, Tracey A. Revenson, Laurie Ruggiero, James F. Sallis, Catherine Shisslak, Ilene C. Siegler, Dawn Smith, and Richard S. Surwit. We especially wish to thank Timothy W. Smith, who provided important suggestions regarding the entire original manuscript. We gratefully recognize the patient good will of our chapter authors throughout the publication process, as well as the encouragement of the American Psychological Association editorial staff, including Susan Reynolds, Judy Nemes, and Sarah Trembath.

In part, this book was developed from a conference sponsored by the APA Science Directorate and the Clinical Psychology Program within the Department of Psychology at the University of Kansas in 1993. Five of the chapter authors (Gatz, Meyerowitz, Shumaker, Stanton, and Travis) were presenters at that conference. We are grateful to the Science Directorate staff and in particular Virginia Holt, the conference participants, the co-organizers (along with A. Stanton) of the conference, Charlene Muehlenhard and C. R. Snyder, and the University of Kansas Division of Continuing Education for their contributions to a successful meeting. In addition, Paul Forio, Nancy Hughes, Donna Flory, and many clinical faculty members and graduate students facilitated the activity of the conference. Finally, we thank the thousands of women and men who participated in the research cited herein. Their gracious willingness to share their experience made this book possible.

ANNETTE L. STANTON
SHERYLE J. GALLANT

PART ONE

Psychology of Women's Health—An Introduction

1

Psychology of Women's Health: Barriers and Pathways to Knowledge

Annette L. Stanton

A ttending a university reception with a colleague a few years ago, I re-acted strongly when he referred to a study regarding the link between caffeine consumption and heart disease, which had just received considerable media attention (Grobbee et al., 1990). "I guess our hearts are safe if we have a cup of coffee," he said. "*Your* heart may be safe; I have no idea about the safety of *my* heart! That study was conducted on over 45,000 men," came my retort. Thus began a discussion of how little the scientific community knew, from either a psychological or a biomedical perspective, concerning many facets of women's physical health. Indeed, had the chapters in this volume been written only a decade ago, their authors would have had much less to say. They would have devoted considerably more attention to exploring what was not known and why, rather than what was. Some topics would have been sufficiently devoid of content that they would not have been included at all.

Today, owing to the realization by researchers and practitioners that to understand women's health we need to study women and to include gender as a variable in conceptualizations of health and illness, the knowledge base in women's health is evolving rapidly. Witness the inclusion in scientific journals of special sections on gender-related issues in health (see, e.g., Baum & Grunberg, 1991 in *Health Psychology;* Grady & Lemkau, 1988 in *Psychology of Women Quarterly;* Stacey & Olesen, 1993 in *Social Science and Medicine*) and the creation of specialized outlets for scholarship in the area (e.g., *Journal of Women's Health, Women and Health, Women's Health Issues, Women's Health: Research on Gender, Behavior, and Policy*). Note also the recent volumes devoted to examining psychosocial issues in women's health (e.g., Adesso, Reddy, & Fleming, 1994; Blechman & Brownell, 1988; Travis, 1988). An additional marker of the growing interest in women's health is the development of scientific conferences dedicated to examining the most current research, theory, and policy issues (e.g., *Psychosocial and Behavioral Factors in Women's Health: Creating an Agenda for the 21st Century,* May, 1994; *Reframing Women's Health: Multidisciplinary Research and Practice,* October, 1992).

Sponsored by the Science Directorate of the American Psychological Association, one such conference (*Women's Psychological and Physical Health: A Scholarly and Social Agenda,* April, 1993) served as the impetus for this book. Along with other contributors to this volume, the conference presenters were asked to examine critically the most recent psychological research pertaining to specific topics in women's health and to present an agenda for the next generation of psychological research and application. Accordingly, our vision for this volume was that each chapter illuminate the most pressing health concerns of women from a psychosocial perspective and point the way toward the next decade of research in the area.

An overview of historical and recent developments in women's health will provide a context for examining subsequent chapters. Specifically, it is important to understand the criticisms that have been leveled against the prevailing body of thought regarding women's health, as well as to be aware of the exciting initiatives designed to redress some of the deficiencies in earlier models and policies. It is not the intent of this chapter to offer a comprehensive review of these areas, but rather to highlight limitations in traditional conceptualizations and research, and to describe some of the promising developments in the psychology of women's health.

WHAT IS A HEALTHY WOMAN? THE SOCIAL CONSTRUCTION OF WOMEN'S HEALTH

Observers of the literature on women's health have pointed out that concepts of health itself, and women's health in particular, are socially constructed phenomena (e.g., Corea, 1985; Ehrenreich & English, 1978; Travis, 1988). These writers argue that conceptualizations of women's health reflect prevailing sociocultural standards concerning women's proper place in the world. Lawrence and Bendixen (1992) illustrated this point through their analysis of depictions of male and female anatomy in medical texts. They first outlined two historical approaches to conceptualizing female and male anatomy: *hierarchy* and *difference*. Dominant from the time of the classical Greeks through the mid-seventeenth century, the hierarchical approach framed women and men as sharing similar basic biological structures, albeit in imperfect form in women. The authors quoted Aristotle's "For the female is, as it were, a mutilated male" (p. 926) to exemplify this understanding of female anatomy.

By contrast, post-seventeenth century writers began to present women's anatomy as quite distinct from that of men's. To illustrate the concept of difference, Lawrence and Bendixen (1992) quoted Sachs, a German physician, writing in 1830:

> The male body expresses positive strength, sharpening male understanding and independence, and equipping men for life in the State, in the arts and sciences. The female body expresses womanly softness and feeling. The roomy pelvis determines women for motherhood. The weak, soft members and delicate skin are witness of woman's narrower sphere of activity, of home-bodiness, and peaceful family life. (p. 926)

Other writers have pointed out that the scientists and physicians of the late 1800s used accepted scientific theories to promote the primacy of the maternal role for women (Travis, 1988). For example, Helmholtz's principle of energy conservation was used to support the proposition that, because women's most important function was reproduction, it followed logically that other biological structures, especially those involved in intellectual pursuits and physical activities, could not and should not function at maximum capacities in women (Travis, 1988). Further, the purported primacy of cyclic biology and hormonal function in women is illustrated by one physician's (Virchow, cited in Fausto-Sterling, 1985) statement in the late 1800s that "Woman is a pair of ovaries with a human being attached, whereas man is a human being furnished with a pair of testes" (p. 90). In addition, the exigencies of being a woman were used as a justification for female infirmity and for invalidism as an accepted role (Ehrenreich & English, 1978; Travis, 1988). Woven throughout these theories is the notion of woman and female qualities as not merely different but inferior.

Returning to the present day, Lawrence and Bendixen (1992) found in their analysis of medical texts between 1890 and 1989 that although 63% of anatomy illustrations in the medical texts they reviewed were not gender-specific and that text space devoted specifically to males had declined over the century, medical texts in 1989 still evidenced a disproportionate use of male-specific figures and descriptions. Further, male structures often were presented as the norm with female as the variation, and female-specific content was at times vague or inaccurate.

These findings illustrate two primary contentions of social constructionists—that scientific and professional treatments of women's health have served (a) to perpetuate the view of male as normative and female as deviation from the norm and (b) to promote a focus on women's reproductive function to the exclusion of other aspects of health. Some of the authors of the following chapters also argue that the social construction of women's health is apparent in researchers' selection of topics and in their interpretation of data. Fortunately, however, many researchers are investigating women's health concerns, are broadening their focus to encompass a host of areas other than reproductive health, and are framing answers to the question "What is a healthy woman?" in terms of women's own experience.

HOW SHOULD WOMEN BE TREATED? DIFFERENTIAL TREATMENT OF WOMEN'S HEALTH CONCERNS

According to a number of writers, medical treatment for women in the United States is a reflection of women's subordinate status, and many point out that differences exist in health care for women and men that cannot be completely explained by differences in morbidity or illness behaviors (e.g., Ehrenreich & English, 1978; Travis, 1988). An example of the first point comes from analyses of the history of childbirth in the United States, which increasingly became the province of the male-dominated medical system rather than a function of women and midwives (Scully, 1980; Wertz & Wertz, 1989). A consequence of this transition was an emphasis on the difficulties of childbirth and the necessity for medical experts and technologies to facilitate and control the process, with a concomitant decline in women's participation in informed decision-making regarding their own pregnancies and childbearing.

That the disadvantaged status of women contributes to inadequate health care is also evidenced by the fact that women, and particularly older women and women of color, are more likely to live in poverty and be unemployed than are men. A result is that women are less likely to have adequate health insurance and thus access to health care. Furthermore, lower socioeconomic status predicts less positive health outcomes, even when controlling for access to health care (Adler et al., 1994), rendering the disadvantaged status of women of particular importance.

Another consequence of gender inequality has been the historical lack of participation of women in the upper echelons of the medical profession and the behavioral sciences. Although women are now entering medical training in record numbers, women's relative nonparticipation is important because it may in part account for the lack of attention to women's health concerns and for less adequate treatment of women. For example, Lurie et al. (1993) found that male physicians were less likely to refer their female patients for cancer screening (i.e., Pap smears, mammograms) or to perform such tests than were female physicians. It is also notable that

13 of the 16 principal investigators for the vanguard centers of the Women's Health Initiative, the largest clinical trial ever performed in this country, are men. This is not to imply that competence as a scientist in studying women's health issues is linked to gender. However, increased entry of women into important roles as researchers and practitioners may serve to improve attention to and effective interventions for women's health concerns.

Differential treatment of women's health concerns is illustrated in a recent report of the Council on Ethical and Judicial Affairs of the American Medical Association (1991). The council reported gender disparities in access to kidney transplantation, diagnosis and treatment of cardiac disease, and diagnosis of lung cancer. Specifically, research was reviewed suggesting that (a) when age is controlled statistically, women are 25% to 30% less likely to receive cadaver kidney transplants than men are; (b) women are less likely to be referred for diagnostic testing for lung cancer than men, even when smoking status is taken into account; and (c) women are 6.5 times less likely to be referred for cardiac catheterization than are men, even when their radionuclide scans are abnormal. Further, physicians are more likely to attribute women's cardiac-related symptoms to psychosomatic or noncardiac factors. The report's authors suggested that biological differences, such as women's greater longevity and accompanying higher disease rate, may in part account for the gender disparities. However, they also posited that gender stereotypic attitudes may affect medical decision-making. Gender stereotypes may result in physicians' propensity to attribute women's health complaints to emotional rather than physical causes, and to view women's societal contributions as relatively unimportant and therefore their health concerns as less deserving of serious attention.

Many questions remain regarding differential treatment of women's health concerns. To what extent are gender disparities in specific medical diagnostic and treatment procedures accounted for by biomedical versus psychosocial factors? How often and in what contexts does a gender disparity reflect underattention to women's health or disproportionate attention to men's? Is it important to tailor medical and behavioral treatment strategies specifically for women, in such ways as gender-sensitive interventions for alcohol abuse or smoking? Should research and practice in women's health be established as a distinct specialty within medicine and health psychology, and should such activity be integrated into already existing structures, or should both integration and specialization be encouraged (Angell, 1993; Harrison, 1992; Rosser, 1993; Wallis, 1993)? Such questions are relevant to several chapters in this volume, and it is through addressing these that we will be able to answer questions regarding how women should be treated.

Where Are the Women? The Exclusion of Women as Participants in Research

Perhaps more than any other limitation, exclusion of women as research participants (Bennett, 1993; Johnson, 1992; Travis, 1988; U.S. General Accounting Office, 1990) has constrained progress in the area of women's health. This is most apparent in large clinical trials conducted solely on men, including those on the prophylactic effects of aspirin for cardiovascular disease, performed with over 22,000 men (The Steering Committee of the Physicians' Health Study Research Group, 1988) and on the identification of risk factors for coronary heart disease, in which over 300,000 men were screened and over 10,000 were included in the clinical trial (Multiple Risk Factor Intervention Trial [MRFIT]; e.g., Ockene, Kuller, Svendsen, & Meilahn, 1990). Examples from the psychosocial literature also exist, including the lack of research on Type A behavior, hostility, and other psychosocial risk factors for heart disease in women (Baker, Dearborn, Hastings, & Hamberger, 1984; Shumaker & Smith; Wenger, Speroff, & Packard, 1993, Chapter 2 of this volume). Furthermore, some have argued that the experience of and treatment for specific female-prevalent health conditions, such as osteoporosis and systemic lupus erythematosus, have been understudied as well (United States Public Health Service [USPHS], 1985).

Several purported barriers to inclusion of women in clinical studies have been identified (Bennett, 1993; USPHS, 1985). These include (a) the responsibility to protect the reproductive capacity of women in their childbearing years and to protect the fetuses of pregnant women; (b) the needs for convenient recruitment of participants and for easily identifiable cohorts (e.g., the Physicians' Health Study participants, who were recruited from the American Medical Association roster); (c) the potentially higher costs resulting from including women, given that women have lower mortality rates than men, and mortality often is the endpoint studied; (d) the need to recruit participants at high risk for the disease endpoints being examined (e.g., men's higher mortality rates for heart disease among particular age cohorts); (e) the goal of achieving homogeneity in a sample, thus not having to consider women's hormonal variation; and (f) the assumption that women are less likely than men to participate in clinical trials, to adhere to prescribed medical regimens, or to be willing to be subject to random assignment (note that there is no empirical evidence for this assumption).

Specific neglect of poor, ethnic minority, and older women is apparent in the literature on women's physical health (USPHS, 1985) and on aspects of women's psychological adjustment (Reid, 1993; Yoder & Kahn, 1993). This is of particular concern in light of the evidence that poor and ethnic minority women in general are at risk for greater morbidity and mortality than are their more affluent and White counterparts (USPHS, 1985). Moreover, older women are at risk for contracting multiple chronic conditions (i.e., comorbidities), may take multiple prescription medications, and, because of their greater likelihood of living in poverty than men, often are subject to inadequate health care (USPHS, 1985).

Of course, consequences of succumbing to the barriers against the inclusion of women as research participants are profound. We know less about biological and psychosocial risk and protective factors for diseases in women than in men. Generalization of findings from studies on men's health and disease has occurred in the absence of knowledge of the findings' applicability to women. Insufficient information is available on how endogenous and exogenous (e.g., oral contraceptives) hormones may interact with medications to affect the potency of medical treatments. Women (and sometimes fetuses in utero) are subject to pharmaceutical agents, medical treatments, and diagnostic procedures that are of undocumented safety and efficacy for them.

Not surprisingly, many authors of the following chapters cite the relative neglect of women in research on health concerns, with the possible exceptions of some facets of reproductive health and psychological adjustment to cancer. However, the numerous recent investigations cited in these chapters provide evidence that the barriers to inclusion of women in health research are crumbling. Positive changes in institutional and government policies will serve to create pathways to knowledge about women's health and will make asking the question, "Where are the women?" no longer necessary.

THE GOOD NEWS: TRENDS IN ATTENTION TO WOMEN'S HEALTH

Documented recognition that the health concerns of women require substantial empirical attention occurred at the federal level in 1985, with the publication of a report on the health status of American women by the Public Health Service Task Force on Women's Health Issues (USPHS, 1985). This was followed in 1986 by an announcement from the National Institutes of Health (NIH) that all researchers applying for NIH funding should consider the inclusion of women in clinical trials and that, when women are excluded, a clear rationale must be provided for doing so (p. XX). However, in 1990 the United States General Accounting Office (GAO), the investigative arm of Congress, found that few researchers were aware of this policy and that some scientific review panels had been instructed not to consider the inclusion of female participants as a criterion for evaluating the merit of a research proposal.

Along with other catalysts, the GAO report spurred the introduction in Congress of the Women's Health Equity Act of 1990. This act, developed by the Congressional Caucus on Women's Issues and introduced by Representatives Patricia Schroeder and Olympia Snowe, was designed to address deficiencies in women's health care in the areas of research, treatment, and prevention. Composed of 20 separate provisions, the bill proposed mechanisms for ensuring inclusion of women in study populations and bolstering empirical attention to women's health. Also proposed was authorization for funding of research, treatment, and prevention initiatives for women in specific areas including cancer, reproductive health, AIDS and sexually transmitted diseases, and osteoporosis, among others. Many of these provisions have seen favorable action in Congress, and others have been introduced under the Women's Health Equity Act of 1993.

Proposed in Congress and founded by the NIH in 1990, the establishment of the Office of Research on Women's Health represents another encouraging step in addressing women's health concerns. This office is charged with the coordination and oversight of efforts to enhance women's health research at the NIH by specifying pertinent research needs, supplementing extant funds for research on women's health, coordinating efforts among the various institutes, and promoting women's entry into and advancement in scientific careers. The office also monitors the inclusion of women in study populations, which now is mandated by the NIH unless a clear and compelling rationale for their exclusion is provided (NIH, 1994). Yet another stimulus for women's health research is the Food and Drug Administration's revision of a 16-year-old policy that excluded most women with childbearing potential from the initial phases of clinical trials. The FDA's formal statement to drug developers that women should be represented sufficiently in drug studies and that appropriate statistical analyses for sex-related effects should be undertaken (Merkatz et al., 1993) is also encouraging.

Federal attention to women's health set the stage for the development of the Women's Health Initiative, the largest clinical trial ever conducted in the United States. Following women aged 55 to 79 for up to 12 years, the initiative is designed to investigate contributors to and treatment for important causes of death and disability among women, including cardiovascular disease, breast and colorectal cancer, and osteoporosis. An observational component is included, and a randomized, controlled trial will test the efficacy of hormone replacement therapy and nutritional interventions in preventing these disorders. Psychosocial and behavioral factors will be examined, and the behavioral section charged with designing this component is headed by prominent health psychologists Karen

Matthews and Sally Shumaker. Results will carry implications for understanding several topics addressed in this volume.

Clearly, these promising developments at the federal level provide encouragement to researchers and practitioners with interests in women's health. For behavioral scientists, some additional good news is the increased attention to integrating psychosocial variables in biomedical studies. Several of this book's chapters illustrate the need to adopt a biopsychosocial model and examine the benefits to be gained in advancing our knowledge regarding women's health.

RESEARCH ON WOMEN'S HEALTH: THE NEED FOR A BIOPSYCHOSOCIAL APPROACH

The advantages of exploring interactions among biological, psychological, and social factors in order to understand health and disease have been documented for some time (Engel, 1977, 1980; Schwartz, 1982). The importance of assuming a biopsychosocial approach to research in women's health is underlined by Hamilton's (1993) contention that

> the social construction of gender implies that women's health can be understood only by a better appreciation of psychosocial aspects of women's lives, along with more integrative biological research. Indeed, every health discipline, with the notable exception of medicine, recognizes that psychology and the social sciences must be central to and at the very core of a woman-centered women's health movement. (p. 51)

Several lines of evidence converge to suggest that psychological and social factors are prominent determinants of the health of women.

One such line of evidence comes from research exploring sex-related differences in mortality and morbidity. Echoing the observations of many researchers (e.g., Rodin & Ickovics, 1990; Strickland, 1988; Verbrugge, 1990), Riley (1990) cited a "familiar but still puzzling paradox: in the United States today, on the average, at every age women report more illness and health care utilization than men, yet life expectancy is consistently higher for women than for men" (p. vii). Indeed, in all economically developed countries, females' mortality advantage increased during the twentieth century, particularly during the period of 1930 through 1970, in large part owing to males' increase in deaths from lung cancer and ischemic heart disease (Waldron, 1993). Although a decline in the mortality advantage for females in most age groups has been apparent since the 1970s, females currently live longer than males by an average of seven years (Nathanson, 1990). In this context of greater longevity, women appear to have higher rates of physical illness overall, especially acute illnesses and nonfatal chronic conditions; women have more disability days and physician visits, and use more prescription and nonprescription medication than do men (Rodin & Ickovics, 1990; Verbrugge, 1990; Verbrugge & Wingard, 1987). Exceptions to women's greater morbidity are men's greater rates of sensory/structural impairments, life-threatening chronic diseases, and major disabilities due to chronic conditions (Verbrugge, 1990). These exceptions are consistent with men's higher death rates.

Certainly, sex differences in mortality and morbidity are accounted for in part by biological influences. These include such factors as the lack of genetic redundancy on the Y chromosome and other chromosomal influences (e.g., Smith & Warner, 1990; Travis, 1988), the protective effect of estrogen with regard to heart disease (e.g., Hazzard, 1990), and sex-related differences in neuroendocrine and cardiovascular response to stressors (e.g., Matthews, 1989; Polefrone & Manuck, 1987). Psychological and social influences also play an important role. Health-related behaviors constitute one category of contributors. Changing sex differences in mortality, for example, can be attributed in part to changes in the behavior of cigarette smoking (Waldron, 1993). Although perhaps of lesser impact than smoking (Nathanson, 1990), other behaviors that confer health risk, including dietary practices, alcohol use, hazardous employment, unsafe sexual practices, lack of physical activity, reckless driving, and violent acts, also may produce differential impact on female and male morbidity and mortality (Verbrugge, 1990; Verbrugge & Wingard, 1987). Gender differences in illness and prevention orientation, including perception of symptoms, readiness to take preventive and curative actions, and health-reporting behaviors, also may contribute to morbidity and mortality differences (Verbrugge & Wingard, 1987). Furthermore, biological, behavioral, and social characteristics may interact to predict health risk in women and men (Matthews, 1989; Ory & Warner, 1990).

Other areas of inquiry also have illuminated the critical role of behavioral and psychosocial influences on women's health. For example, research has revealed the impact of sociodemographic transitions on health, such as the rapidly declining fertility rates in developing countries and the consequent decrease in maternal morbidity and mortality (Leslie, 1992). Also, although they reveal complex moderating and mediating factors, studies of women's social roles in general have demonstrated the relation of participation in multiple valued roles (e.g., worker, spouse, mother) to enhanced physical and psychological health and have suggested that paid employment may have particularly salutory effects (LaCroix & Haynes, 1987; Repetti, Matthews, & Waldron, 1989; Rodin & Ickovics, 1990; Waldron & Jacobs, 1989). Certainly, women's experiences of poverty and victimization also carry health consequences (Koss, Woodruff, & Koss, 1990; Plichta, 1992; USPHS, 1985). Thus, a number of sources of evidence indicate the crucial function of psychosocial variables in determining health outcomes. The following chapters provide numerous illustrations of this function.

Not only are psychosocial factors significant contributors to health end points, they also represent important end points in health research. Calls for increased empirical and applied attention to health-related quality of life have been issued in many arenas (e.g., Moinpour et al., 1989; Taylor & Aspinwall, 1990). Examples include consideration of quality of life variables in clinical trials and in research on chronic disease. Quality of life is a multidimensional construct that includes physical, psychological, and social functioning. Often, researchers in health psychology have relied on measures of psychological distress and life disruption to assess quality of life related to health and disease processes. More rarely examined is resilience, as indicated by life satisfaction or positive mood, for example. Functioning in social roles, such as return to paid employment after a heart attack, also requires attention. Several chapters illustrate the importance of exploring psychosocial factors in women's health, both as predictors and as consequences of women's health-related experiences. They also point to the importance of developing biopsychosocial models that focus on women's resilience and health to offset what traditionally has been a pervasive focus on distress and disease.

PLAN FOR THE BOOK

In the chapters that follow, you will find an examination of some of the most current research in psychological perspectives on women's health. We were happy to encounter difficult choices regarding which topics to include, given that this difficulty results from the burgeoning empirical interest in the area. Owing to page limitations, we were obliged to choose between rather narrow coverage of many topics or more intensive examination of a few. Because we did not want to shortchange the substantial new bodies of literature in several areas, we elected the latter strategy. This allowed inclusion of selected topics receiving intense empirical scrutiny in the areas of chronic disease, gynecologic health, and health-related behaviors, as well as consideration of central issues for the future.

This selectivity also meant that we were unable to include a number of important perspectives and topics. In some cases, our choices were guided by the availability of current references in other sources. We focused primarily on research on adult females, although the importance of viewing this work from a developmental perspective is outlined in the chapter by Gatz and colleagues (see also Berman & Ramey, 1982; Blechman & Brownell, 1995). We also requested that the authors address issues of ethnic and racial diversity in their chapters, although certainly a separate text devoted to examining issues regarding diversity in women's health is warranted.

With regard to topics addressed within the book's following four sections, the authors examine several leading causes of death and disability in the section on chronic diseases, but problems such as headache and chronic pain do not receive coverage (see Adesso et al., 1994; Blechman & Brownell, 1995, for reviews of some of these areas). In the section on gynecologic health, topics include psychosocial aspects of menstruation, menopause, pregnancy and the postpartum, infertility, and reproductive and birth-related technologies. We refer you to other excellent sources for work on abortion (Adler et al., 1990, 1992), contraception (O'Hara, Reiter, Johnson, Milburn, & Engeldinger, 1995; Travis, 1988), and hysterectomy and other gynecologic surgery (O'Hara et al., 1995; Travis, 1988). The section on health-related behaviors addresses smoking, physical activity, alcohol use, and disordered eating (bulimia nervosa and anorexia nervosa) in women. However, overeating and other unhealthy eating patterns, and abuse of substances other than alcohol are not explored (see Adesso et al., 1994; Blechman & Brownell, 1995). Finally, authors explore topics central to women's health concerns of the future, including research on older women and on health care policy. We close with an overview of major themes from the book's chapters and a discussion of directions for continued empirical examination of women's health concerns. Our hope is that this volume illuminates current progress and challenges in research and application regarding women's health, which in turn will spur future empirical activity directed toward the goal of understanding and promoting the health of women.

REFERENCES

Adesso, V. J., Reddy, D. M., & Fleming, R. (1994). *Psychological perspectives on women's health*. Washington, DC: Taylor & Francis.

Adler, N. E., Boyce, T., Chesney, M. A., Cohen, S., Folkman, S., Kahn, R. L., & Syme, S. L. (1994). Socioeconomic status and health: The challenge of the gradient. *American Psychologist, 49*, 15–24.

Adler, N. E., David, H. P., Major, B. N., Roth, S. H., Russo, N. F., & Wyatt, G. E. (1990). Psychological responses after abortion. *Science, 248*, 41–43.

Adler, N. E., David, H. P., Major, B. N., Roth, S. H., Russo, N. F., & Wyatt, G. E. (1992). Psychological factors in abortion. *American Psychologist, 47*, 1194–1204.

Angell, M. (1993). Caring for women's health—What is the problem? *Journal of the American Medical Association, 329*, 271–272.

Baker, L. J., Dearborn, M., Hastings, J. E., & Hamberger, K. (1984). Type A behavior in women: A review. *Health Psychology, 3*, 477–498.

Baum, A., & Grunberg, N. E. (Eds.). (1991). Special issue on gender and health. *Health Psychology, 10*(2).

Bennett, J. C., for the Board on Health Sciences Policy of the Institute of Medicine. (1993). Inclusion of women in clinical trials—Policies for population subgroups. *New England Journal of Medicine, 329,* 288–292.

Berman, P. W., & Ramey, E. R. (Eds.). (1982). *Women: A developmental perspective* (NIH Publication No. 82-2298). Bethesda, MD: National Institutes of Health.

Blechman, E. A., & Brownell, K. D. (Eds.). (1988). *Handbook of behavioral medicine for women.* New York: Pergamon.

Blechman, E. A., & Brownell, K. D. (Eds.). (1995). *Behavioral medicine for women: A comprehensive handbook.* Manuscript in preparation.

Corea, G., (1985). *The hidden malpractice: How American medicine mistreats women.* New York: Harper Colophon Books.

Council on Ethical and Judicial Affairs, American Medical Association. (1991). Gender disparities in clinical decision making. *Journal of the American Medical Association, 266,* 559–562.

Ehrenreich, B., & English, D. (1978). *For her own good: 150 years of the experts' advice to women.* Garden City, NY: Anchor Press/Doubleday.

Engel, G. L. (1977). The need for a new medical model: A challenge for biomedicine. *Science, 196,* 129–136.

Engel, G. L. (1980). The clinical application of the biopsychosocial model. *American Journal of Psychiatry, 137,* 535–544.

Fausto-Sterling, A. (1985). *Myths of gender: Biological theories about women and men.* New York: Basic Books.

Grady, K. E., & Lemkau, J. P. (Eds.). (1988). Women's health: Our minds, our bodies [Special issue]. *Psychology of Women Quarterly, 12*(4).

Grobbee, D. E., Rimm, E. B., Giovannucci, E., Colditz, G., Stampfer, M., & Willett, W. (1990). Coffee, caffeine, and cardiovascular disease in men. *New England Journal of Medicine, 323,* 1026–1032.

Hamilton, J. A. (1993). Feminist theory and health psychology: Tools for an egalitarian, woman-centered approach to women's health. *Journal of Women's Health, 2,* 49–54.

Harrison, M. (1992). Women's health as a specialty: A deceptive solution. *Journal of Women's Health, 1,* 101–106.

Hazzard, W. R. (1990). A central role of sex hormones in the sex differential in lipoprotein metabolism, atherosclerosis, and longevity. In M. G. Ory & H. R. Warner (Eds.), *Gender, health, and longevity: Multidisciplinary perspectives* (pp. 87–108). New York: Springer.

Johnson, K. (1992). Women's health: Developing a new interdisciplinary specialty. *Journal of Women's Health, 1,* 95–99.

Koss, M. P., Woodruff, W. J., & Koss, P. G. (1990). Relation of criminal victimization to health perceptions among women medical patients. *Journal of Consulting and Clinical Psychology, 58,* 147–152.

LaCroix, A. Z., & Haynes, S. G. (1987). Gender differences in the health effects of the workplace. In R. C. Barnett, L. Biener, & G. K. Baruch (Eds.), *Gender and stress* (pp. 96–121). New York: Free Press.

Lawrence, S. C., & Bendixen, K. (1992). His and hers: Male and female anatomy in anatomy texts for U.S. medical students, 1890–1989. *Social Science and Medicine, 35,* 925–934.

Leslie, J. (1992). Women's lives and women's health: Using social science research to promote better health for women. *Journal of Women's Health, 1,* 307–318.

Lurie, N., Slater, J., McGovern, P., Ekstrum, J., Quam, L., & Margolis, K. (1993). Preventive care for women: Does the sex of the physician matter? *New England Journal of Medicine, 329,* 478–482.

Matthews, K. A. (1989). Interactive effects of behavior and reproductive hormones on sex differences in risk for coronary heart disease. *Health Psychology, 8,* 373–387.

Merkatz, R. B., Temple, R., Sobel, S., Feiden, K., Kessler, P. A., & the Working Group on Women in Clinical Trials. (1993). Women in clinical trials of new drugs: A change in Food and Drug Administration policy. *New England Journal of Medicine, 329,* 292–296.

Moinpour, C. M., Feigl, P., Metch, B., Hayden, K. A., Meyskens, F. L., & Crowley, J. (1989). Quality of life end points in cancer clinical trials: Review and recommendations. *Journal of the NCI, 81,* 485–492.

Nathanson, C. A. (1990). The gender–mortality differential in developed countries: Demographic and sociocultural dimensions. In M. G. Ory & H. R. Warner (Eds.), *Gender, health, and longevity: Multidisciplinary perspectives* (pp. 3–23). New York: Springer.

National Institutes of Health. (1986). Inclusion of women in study populations. *NIH Guide for grants and contracts, 15* (22), 1.

National Institutes of Health. (1994). NIH guidelines on the inclusion of women and minorities as subjects in clinical research. *NIH Guide for Grants and Contracts, 23*(11), 2–10.

Ockene, J. K., Kuller, L. H., Svendsen, K. H., & Meilahn, E. (1990). The relationship of smoking cessation to coronary heart disease and lung cancer in the Multiple Risk Factor Intervention Trial (MRFIT). *American Journal of Public Health,* *80,* 954–958.

O'Hara, M. W., Reiter, R. C., Johnson, S. R., Milburn, A., & Engeldinger, J. (1995). *Psychological aspects of women's reproductive health.* New York: Springer.

Ory, M. G., & Warner, H. R. (Eds.). (1990). *Gender, health, and longevity: Multidisciplinary perspectives.* New York: Springer.

Plichta, S. (1992). The effects of woman abuse on health care utilization and health status: A literature review. *Women's Health Issues, 2,* 154–163.

Polefrone, J. M., & Manuck, S. B. (1987). Gender differences in cardiovascular and neuroendocrine response to stressors. In R. C. Barnett, L. Biener, & G. K. Baruch (Eds.), *Gender and stress* (pp. 13–38). New York: Free Press.

Reid, P. T. (1993). Poor women in psychological research: Shut up and shut out. *Psychology of Women Quarterly, 17,* 133–150.

Repetti, R. L., Matthews, K. A., & Waldron, I. (1989). Employment and women's health: Effects of paid employment on women's mental and physical health. *American Psychologist, 44,* 1394–1401.

Riley, M. R. (1990). Foreword: The gender paradox. In M. G. Ory & H. R. Warner (Eds.), *Gender, health, and longevity: Multidisciplinary perspectives* (pp. vii–xiii). New York: Springer.

Rodin, J., & Ickovics, J. R. (1990). Women's health: Review and research agenda as we approach the 21st century. *American Psychologist, 45,* 1018–1034.

Rosser, S. V. (1993). A model for a specialty in women's health. *Journal of Women's Health, 2,* 99–104.

Schwartz, G. E. (1982). Testing the biopsychosocial model: The ultimate challenge facing behavioral medicine? *Journal of Consulting and Clinical Psychology, 50,* 1040–1053.

Scully, D. (1980). *Men who control women's health: The miseducation of obstetrician gynecologists.* Boston: Houghton Mifflin.

Smith, D. W. E., & Warner, H. R. (1990). Overview of biomedical perspectives: Possible relationships between genes on the sex chromosomes and longevity. In M. G. Ory & H. R. Warner (Eds.), *Gender, health, and longevity: Multidisciplinary perspectives* (pp. 41–55). New York: Springer.

Stacey, M., & Olesen, V. (1993). Introduction [Special issue]. *Social Science and Medicine, 36*(1), 1–5.

The Steering Committee of the Physicians' Health Study Research Group. (1988). Preliminary report: Findings from the aspirin component of the ongoing Physicians' Health Study. *New England Journal of Medicine, 318,* 262–264.

Strickland, B. R. (1988). Sex-related differences in health and illness. *Psychology of Women Quarterly, 12,* 381–399.

Taylor, S. E., & Aspinwall, L. G. (1990). Psychological aspects of chronic illness. In P. T. Costa, Jr. & G. R. VandenBos (Eds.), *Psychological aspects of serious illness* (pp. 3–60). Washington, DC: American Psychological Association.

Travis, C. B. (1988). *Women and health psychology: Biomedical issues.* Hillsdale, NJ: Erlbaum.

United States General Accounting Office, Statement of Mark Nadel. (1990, June). *NIH: Problems in implementing policy on women in study populations.* Bethesda, MD: National Institutes of Health.

United States Public Health Service, Task Force on Women's Health Issues. (1985). *Women's health: Report of the Public Health Service Task Force on Women's Health Issues.* Washington, DC: U.S. Government Printing Office.

Verbrugge, L. M. (1990). The twain meet: Empirical explanations of sex differences in health and mortality. In M. G. Ory & H. R. Warner (Eds.), *Gender, health, and longevity: Multidisciplinary perspectives* (pp. 137–156). New York: Springer.

Verbrugge, L. M., & Wingard, D. L. (1987). Sex differentials in health and mortality. *Women and Health, 12*(2), 103–145.

Waldron, I. (1993). Recent trends in sex mortality ratios for adults in developed countries. *Social Science and Medicine, 36,* 451–462.

Waldron, I., & Jacobs, J. A. (1989). Effects of multiple roles on women's health: Evidence from a national longitudinal study. *Women and Health, 15*(1), 3–20.

Wallis, L. A. (1993). Why a curriculum in women's health? *Journal of Women's Health, 2,* 55–60.

Wenger, N. K., Speroff, L., & Packard, B. (1993). Cardiovascular health and disease in women. *New England Journal of Medicine, 329,* 247–256.

Wertz, R. W., & Wertz, D. C. (1989). *Lying-in: A history of childbirth in America.* New Haven: Yale University Press.

Yoder, J. D., & Kahn, A. S. (1993). Working toward an inclusive psychology of women. *American Psychologist, 48,* 846–850.

PART TWO

Chronic Diseases

2

Women and Coronary Heart Disease: A Psychological Perspective

Sally A. Shumaker and Teresa Rust Smith

Coronary heart disease (CHD) and other cardiovascular diseases (CVD) are the leading causes of death in women in the United States (Eaker, Johnson, Loop, & Wenger, 1992). Cardiovascular diseases (CVD) refer to all diseases related to the heart or blood vessels, including coronary heart disease (CHD), stroke, hypertension, and congestive heart failure. While it is well-known that these diseases are an important cause of morbidity in both women and men, ways in which women and men are differentially affected by CVDs are not well understood. Data from the Framingham Study, a prospective longitudinal study, show that CHD is significantly more age-related in women than men, with a 40-times increase in morbidity in the oldest ages (75 to 84 years) as compared with the youngest (35 to 44 years) patients (Lerner & Kannel, 1986). And, with the aging of our population, CHD is expected to become an increasingly serious problem in women. The gender differences that have been noted in morbidity, mortality, and recovery from CHD may be due to gender differences in the natural history or course of the disease, diagnosis and treatment, health behaviors, and psychosocial factors.

There are significant gender differences in the prevalence of heart diseases. Although heart disease is the leading cause of death in women, it is considerably more common in men (Eaker, Packard, Wenger, Clarkson, & Tyroler, 1987). Between the ages of 35 and 74, the death rate for CHD is 2.7 times higher among men than among women. The CHD death rate at all ages is higher in men than women, though this difference begins to narrow at about 60 years of age. However, because of the relatively large population of elderly women in the United States, in 1983 CHD accounted for a greater proportion of all deaths in women than in men (52% vs. 46%). Also, health care costs associated with heart disease are higher for women than for men.

The recognized onset of heart disease in women appears to lag about 10 years behind men (Eaker et al., 1987). Although a rise in CHD is sometimes associated with the menopause and postmenopause period, there is not a sharp rise in heart disease at this time in women's lives. Rather, the rise in heart disease in women is gradual, and by far most heart disease in both men and women occurs after the age of 65.

The prognosis of CVD for women is worse than for men with respect to both medical and surgical therapies (Wenger, Speroff, & Packard, 1993). Over 2.5 million U.S. women are hospitalized for CVD-related illnesses, and 500,000 die annually. Between the ages of 35 and 74, CVD accounts for 40% of all deaths in women (compared with 46% in men). In this age group, the largest component is CHD (54%), with another 24% due to other forms of heart disease and 17% due to stroke (cf. Blumenthal, Hamilton, & Sherwin, 1992; Lerner & Kannel, 1986; Wenger et al., 1993). Although women tend to fear breast cancer more than they do other diseases, there are 500,000 deaths in women due to CHD per year, compared with 90,000 deaths from stroke, 51,000 from lung cancer, and 44,500 from breast cancer (Eaker et al., 1992).

In spite of these dramatic figures, relatively little is known about CHD in women with respect to its normal course, effective diagnosis and treatment, and recovery. And, not surprisingly, far less is known about the role of psychosocial factors in heart disease in women. There are several factors that may help explain the dearth of information about women and CHD. One such factor is that women of childbearing age and older women have been systematically excluded from clinical research on CHD due to possible risks to the unborn child from maternal medication for the former group, and to the complexity of older age and coexisting conditions such as the hormonal changes associated with menopause with respect to the latter group (Gurwitz, Col, & Avorn, 1992; Wenger, 1992).

Historically, study of women's health issues has been limited primarily to factors associated with reproduction. Also, because many health researchers defined *normal* in terms of the healthy White male, physical processes that were particular to women such as menstruation, pregnancy, childbirth, and menopause were defined as inherently pathological (Ehrenreich & English, 1978). Illnesses of all kinds, both physical and mental, were attributed to a woman's uniquely female, and therefore pathological, physiology. As a result, symptoms that would have led to a diagnosis of CHD in a male patient might have been misattributed to "female trouble" in a woman. There is evidence that female heart patients are still treated differently than their male counterparts, with symptoms more often attributed to noncardiac causes in women and less aggressive measures being employed by physicians when coronary heart disease is diagnosed (Ayanian & Epstein, 1991; Shumaker & Czajkowski, 1993; Tobin et al., 1987; Young & Kahana, 1993).

Even when it was recognized that women suffer from many of the same diseases as do men, it was frequently assumed that women experienced these diseases in exactly the same way as men. Thus, although women were often excluded from research on CHD, findings were generalized to both women and men. Questions about physiological factors specific to women (e.g., pre-, peri-, and postmenopausal hormonal changes), as well as about psychosocial and behavioral gender differences (e.g., in the interpretation of symptoms, seeking of medical attention, and diet and lifestyle), were rarely addressed. This has resulted in a lack of data on all aspects of women and CHD. Although a number of studies have been initiated in recent years (e.g., the Post-menopausal Estrogen Progestin Investigation [PEPI]; the Women's Health Initiative [WHI]; and the Hormone Replacement Study [HRS]) to redress the inadequacy of data on women and CHD, currently available data are limited.

In the following pages, we discuss CHD in women with respect to known and possible risk factors. However, in order to understand what is known about the psychological aspects of women and CHD, it is critical first to understand the heart and heart diseases.

THE HEART AND HEART DISEASES

The heart is a muscular organ consisting of four chambers: the right and left atria, receiving chambers located at the top of the heart; and the right and left ventricles, the pumping chambers located at the bottom of the organ. The right atrium receives blood as it returns from the body, where it has exchanged oxygen for carbon dioxide. The blood then flows into the right ventricle, from which it is pumped to the lungs. After taking on oxygen in the lungs, the blood returns to the heart, from which it is pumped into the body. The vessels through which the blood must flow are flexible in order to accommodate differences in the amount of blood that passes through them. They vary in size from large arteries nearest to the heart to small capillaries connecting the veins to the arteries. The heart muscle itself, referred to as the *myocardium,* requires a constant supply of oxygenated blood to perform its essential pumping function. The coronary arteries carry this blood to the myocardium. If these arteries become blocked, heart function can be impaired. *Atherosclerosis* is the condition of gradual narrowing of the coronary arteries due to fatty deposits on the walls. When this process occurs, a myocardial infarction (MI), or "heart attack," can result. That is, if the artery becomes blocked, oxygen cannot be delivered to the myocardium and the heart muscle is damaged. If the blockage is less severe, myocardial ischemia (reduction in oxygen to the heart tissue) may not result in damage but may cause intermittent pain in the chest (angina pectoris). (Adapted from Lynch, 1979; see also Davidson, 1994.)

While causes of CHD are not fully understood, some risk factors for atherosclerosis have been identified. These risks include age, family history of the condition, hyperlipidemia, male gender, hypertension, diabetes, and cigarette smoking. The use of oral contraceptives is also a factor in heart disease (Cheitlin, Sokolow, & McIlroy, 1993).

Since the problem in CHD is the reduction in the flow of blood through the arteries, treatment consists of increasing the amount of blood that can pass through the arteries, either by thinning the blood to facilitate passage through the reduced diameter of the occluded vessels, or by enlarging or bypassing the narrowed vessels. Drug therapy is generally aimed at improving coronary blood flow and consists of three categories: beta-blocking agents, nitrates, and calcium entry blocking drugs. Widening the vessels, or Percutaneous Transluminal Coronary Angioplasty (PTCA), is a surgical procedure that employs a balloon catheter that is inserted into the affected vessel and inflated, thereby restoring blood flow. Coronary artery bypass graft (CABG) surgery is a procedure in which a vessel from some other part of the body (e.g., a vein from the leg) is grafted in place of the blocked vessel. This allows blood to flow around, or to bypass, the blocked area(s) of the heart.

In terms of post-MI treatment, antithrombolytic therapy (that is, therapy to prevent clotting, such as streptokinase), is used increasingly in patients seen early (i.e., within 6 hours) following an MI. Also, low dose aspirin as an antiplatelet is recommended for both men and women as a secondary prevention. It should be noted that although these drugs and others are beginning to be routinely used in the treatment of heart disease in women, their efficacy was assessed in randomized clinical trials[1] of predominantly male patient populations. A clinical trial assessing the efficacy of aspirin in primary prevention of heart disease in female nurses is currently underway. Trials to assess the efficacy of hormone therapy to prevent CHD in women (primary prevention; WHI) and to reduce recurrent heart disease in women (secondary prevention; HRS) are also underway.

PSYCHOSOCIAL ASPECTS OF CHD IN WOMEN

Until recently, most studies designed to assess the natural history of CHD, and the effects of primary or secondary treatments for CHD, restricted the dependent variables studied to relatively traditional indices of morbidity,

---

[1]Randomized clinical trials (RCTs) are studies in which patients are randomly assigned to treatment groups (e.g., active therapy vs. placebo).

mortality, and, in some cases, behaviorally based risk factors (e.g., smoking). However, there has been a marked change in this somewhat narrow approach to the study of CHD. In the past several years, some psychosocial variables have been routinely included in prospective observational studies, and clinical trials now often include health-related quality of life (HRQL) as a dependent variable in order to assess more fully the efficacy of various treatments. HRQL is a multidimensional hypothetical construct related to psychosocial factors in that it includes, at a minimum, perceived physical and role functioning, and emotional distress. Since the inclusion of HRQL and other psychosocial variables in CHD research is a recent phenomenon, however, the data on psychosocial factors and HRQL of women with CHD are limited. (See McDowell & Newell, 1987; Spilker, 1990; and Wilkin, Hallam, & Doggett, 1992 for a general overview of the HRQL literature.)

The Natural History or Course of CHD

Angina Pectoris

Angina pectoris—or chest pain—is the predominant initial presentation of CHD in women. There is some question, however, as to whether angina is evidence of atherosclerotic (thickening of the artery walls) disease in women, as it often is in men, since follow-up diagnostic data do not support this. For example, in the Coronary Artery Surgery Study (CASS), 50% of women presenting with chest pain had no artery narrowing, while this was true for only 17% of men.

Myocardial Infarction

MI is less often the initial manifestation of heart disease in women than in men (34% vs. 50%). However, initial episodes are more often fatal in women (39% vs. 31%). Also, women have more unrecognized MIs than men (35% vs. 27%) (Goldberg, Gore, Yarzebski, & Alpert, 1991; Greenland et al., 1991; Welty, 1991; Wenger et al., 1993). The gender difference in in-hospital mortality rates from MIs may be attributable to a number of factors. For example, women appear to seek care more slowly than men following the onset of symptoms for heart disease (Fiebach, 1991), so their condition is likely to be more serious at the time of hospital admission.

This is in contrast to women's usual health behaviors, which are often viewed as more vigilant and prevention-oriented than that of men (Wingard et al., 1992).

The difference in time for seeking care between men and women with heart disease symptoms may be related to the fact that women, their friends and family members, and their physicians appear to perceive CHD symptoms differently in men than in women (McKinlay, McKinlay, & Crawford, 1991; Moser, 1991; Schulman et al., 1992; Wingard, Cohn, Cirillo, Cohen, & Kaplan, 1992). That is, women and their physicians are less likely to attribute the same symptoms (e.g., chest pain), to heart disease in women than they are in men (McKinlay et al., 1991). Heart disease continues to be viewed as a disease of men, not women, and therefore is not expected to be seen in women. McKinlay and his colleagues (cf. Clark, Potter, & McKinlay, 1991; McKinlay, Crawford, McKinlay, & Sellars, 1993) referred to this phenomenon as the social construction of disease prevalence. That is, they argued that the "social context of decision making" influences diagnosis, leading to the "social construction of epidemiologic rates" (p. 1). Thus, the rates of women's heart diseases are, according to this model, based partially on "real" disease rates and partially on what the physicians and investigators expect to perceive. These rates, in turn, influence the interpretation, diagnostic follow-up, and treatment of symptoms.

Data on gender differences in long-term mortality rates following an acute MI are inconsistent (Blumenthal et al., 1992; Welty, 1991; Wenger, 1993). That is, some studies indicate that, after controlling for age and comorbid status, gender is not an independent predictor of mortality (Dittrich et al., 1988; Welty, 1991), while other investigations indicate that women are at an increased risk of dying even after adjusting for age and baseline clinical status (Fiebach, Viscoli, & Horwitz, 1990; Goldberg et al., 1991; Gomez-Martin et al., 1987; Greenland et al., 1991; Khan et al., 1990; Lerner & Kannel, 1986; Tofler et al., 1987; Wenger et al., 1993).

Women who experience an MI take longer to recuperate than men do and are less likely to return to work (Chirikos & Nickel, 1984; Murdaugh & O'Rourke, 1988). In addition, there is considerable evidence that more women than men undergo mood disturbances after an MI (Byrne, 1979;

Conn, Taylor, & Abele, 1991; Conn, Taylor, & Wiman, 1991; Guiry, Conroy, Hickey, & Mulcahy, 1987; Mayou, 1979). For example, Boogard and Brody (1985) found that following an MI, women patients were more depressed, less likely to return to work, and had greater impairment of sexual functioning than male patients. Stern, Pascale, and Ackerman (1977) also found that women were more likely to be depressed than men and less likely to return to work. On the other hand, Conn, Taylor, and Wiman (1991) found that although increased age was related to higher depression, lower HRQL, less social support, and poorer general health in post-MI patients, there were no gender differences in psychological status. However, women did report poorer health than men as reflected in reduced activity days, more chronic illnesses, and poorer perceived health (Shumaker & Czajkowski, 1993). Another study on post-MI patients indicated that women resume activities sooner than men, who take a longer time to recuperate (Boogaard, 1984).

Making sense of these conflicting data is difficult. For example, most studies to date do not adequately control for patients' clinical status or socioeconomic status; yet, both of these factors vary by gender and are known to affect post-MI morbidity, mortality, and HRQL. Women with CHD often present with worse clinical status and lower socioeconomic status than men. It is interesting to note, however, that in a study that was able to control for socioeconomic and clinical status prior to randomized treatment in a post-MI clinical trial (Schron, Pawitan, Shumaker, & Hale, 1991), significant gender differences in psychosocial status and HRQL remained, such that women had lower HRQL and psychosocial status (e.g., more depression, less social support) than men. These data suggest that the gender differences seen in mortality following the identification of CHD may be partially attributable to the psychological status of women. That is, poor psychosocial status may be a significant independent risk factor for CHD mortality in women.

The Diagnosis and Treatment of CHD

The major diagnostic procedures for heart disease include exercise stress tests and coronary angiography. Noninvasive procedures such as stress testing are less predictive for CHD in women than in men.

PTCA and CABG surgery are the primary nonpharmacological treatments for CHD, and women are less likely than men to be referred for either (Ayanian & Epstein, 1991; Becker, Corrao, & Alpert, 1982; Steingart et al., 1991; Tobin et al., 1987). The gender difference in approaches to treatment may be partially explained by the fact that women may receive less benefit from CABG surgery than do men. Also, a gender bias in surgery may represent a situation of over-intervening with men, rather than under-intervening in women (Shumaker & Czajkowski, 1993). Recent data suggest that reported gender biases in referral patterns for CABG surgery may actually represent more appropriate referral for women than men. That is, women may be less likely than men to be referred to CABG surgery when survival benefits are known to be negligible. However, there does appear to be a gender bias in physicians' estimates of risk for CHD (cf. McKinlay, McKinlay, & Crawford, 1991), and women may not receive as aggressive CHD preventive care as do men (Fiebach, 1991; Kahn et al., 1990; Steingart et al., 1991). Also, some studies suggest that women appear to have a higher mortality rate with CABG than do men (Kahn et al., 1990; Penckofer & Holm, 1990; Stanton, 1987), while others do not report such findings (King, Clark, & Hicks, 1992; King et al., 1993).

After controlling for the factors that influence referral practices such as the higher preoperative comorbid clinical status of women, their disease severity, and their older age at the time of surgery, there remains an independent gender-specific bias with respect to referral and the aggressive treatment of CHD in women (Fiebach, 1991; Kahn et al., 1990; Steingard et al., 1991). This difference, coupled with the lower overall rate of CHD in women, results in sparse data on the life quality and psychosocial aspects of women undergoing CABG surgery.

Other than the Coronary Artery Surgery Study (CASS) (Rogers et al., 1990), in which limited life quality data were collected, we are not aware of any completed clinical trials with bypass surgery patients that used HRQL measures and had women as subjects. However, there are observational studies that have investigated the impact of bypass surgery on the HRQL and psychosocial status of men and women. According to these studies, following bypass surgery, women are less likely to return to paid employment, take longer to recuperate from their surgery, and are more restricted in their activities and spend more days in bed, than men (Brown & Rawlinson, 1977; Stanton, Zyzanski, Jenkins, & Klein, 1982; Zyzanski, Rouse, Stanton, & Jenkins, 1982). Also, women who must retire from work after surgery have poorer emotional adjustment than do men (Zyzanski et al., 1982). In terms of both HRQL and psychosocial factors, comparing their status one year after surgery with their preoperative status, both women and men experience significant improvements in their perceptions of social support and general well-being. Also, the reported level of sexual activity increases postoperatively for both men and women (Stanton, 1987), although data on this are limited and often insensitive to sexual functioning issues specific to women (Shumaker & Czajkowski, 1993).

Some studies indicate that following surgery, women may be more anxious and depressed, and suffer from greater sleep disturbance, than men (Stanton, 1987). However, because of the retrospective and cross-sectional design of many of these studies, it is difficult to determine whether these differences are attributable to gender differences in the effects of surgery, or gender differences in the reporting of psychosocial factors and patients' status before surgery. In regard to presurgical status, some recent data support the position that women entering bypass surgery have poorer health status, are older, and have fewer economic and social resources when compared with men (Czajkowski et al., 1992).

In summary, data on the HRQL and psychosocial status of women who have undergone bypass surgery are limited. Studies indicate that both men and women experience some improvements in their HRQL for periods exceeding one year following bypass surgery. It is possible that observed gender differences in HRQL dimensions such as physical functioning and emotional well-being following surgery may be attributable to gender differences in the general population on these variables and have little or nothing to do with gender differences in the effects of surgery. There are several studies currently underway that are designed to disentangle these alternative hypotheses, and which also include adequate data on the clinical status of patients at the time of surgery. However, until these studies are concluded, it is difficult to determine whether many of the apparent gender differences in HRQL can be explained by the fact that women tend to be older and have higher rates of other kinds of health problems at the time of surgery than do men, or whether there are true gender differences in psychosocial status and HRQL.

As noted by Shumaker and Czajkowski (1993), the data on returning to work and productivity after surgery are complex. It is frequently reported that men are more likely than women to resume paid employment following surgery. However, when returning to work includes the resumption of homemaking activities, gender differences disappear. Data support a clear gender difference in the perceived benefit of surgery. However, the degree to which this difference reflects variations in postoperative clinical status versus reporting differences cannot be determined from available data. Finally, we should note that in a long-term study of HRQL in bypass patients conducted by Rogers et al. (1990), a sustained benefit of the surgery was demonstrated for neither women nor men.

Other consistent gender differences noted in the literature with respect to the treatment of CHD include differences in time between community hospital admission and transfer to tertiary care, with men being referred more rapidly than women (Sherwood et al., 1994); a less aggressive management approach pursued by physicians in women as compared with men with coronary artery disease (Bickell et al., 1992; Fiebach, 1991; Steingart et al., 1991; Wenger et al., 1993; Wingard et al., 1992); the older age and higher prevalence of comorbid conditions in women than in men (Greenland et al., 1991; Gurwitz, Col, & Avorn, 1992; Wenger, 1992); and the higher probability that women will develop congestive heart failure during the peri-infarction (MI) period (Kimmelstiel & Goldberg, 1990). Finally, there appear to be gender differences in critical psychological and sociological factors that may favor men. That is, women with identified CHD tend to be of lower education and economic status, and present with a profile of psychosocial factors that may put them at increased risk for a poor prognosis (e.g., depression, anxiety; Czajkowski et al., 1992; Eaker, 1989; Hallstrom, Lapidus, Bengtsson, & Edstrom, 1986; Matthews, Kelsey, Meilahn, Kuller, & Wing, 1989; Schron et al., 1991; Wingard et al., 1992).

RISK FACTORS AND HEALTH BEHAVIORS ASSOCIATED WITH CHD IN WOMEN

Nonpsychosocial risk factors for heart disease in women include family history of CHD, hypertension, diabetes, age, and oral contraceptive use. In addition, smoking, being overweight, and high serum cholesterol—factors that have both biological and behavioral aspects—are risk factors for CHD in women. And smoking acts synergistically with other risk factors, including cholesterol and oral contraceptive use. Diabetes is a much greater risk factor for CHD in women than men. The incidence of CVD, including CHD, is almost three times higher in diabetic versus nondiabetic women. In fact, diabetic women have the same risk of CHD as nondiabetic men.

Noncontraceptive hormone replacement therapy (HRT) in postmenopausal women may be protective against both the development of CHD and its worsening postdiagnosis. Assumptions regarding the protective aspects of HRT are based on prospective, cohort studies that are nonexperimental in design and restrict interpretation due to systematic biases in samples. For example, women who are healthier, thinner, and of higher socioeconomic status are more likely to take HRT than their counterparts. There are, however, several double-blind, clinical trials currently underway to assess the effects of HRT on risk factors associated with CHD (PEPI), incidence of CHD (WHI), and progression of disease in women with identified CHD (HRS).

Behavioral and Psychological Risks for CHD in Women

Psychosocial factors refer to such variables as an individual's personality, emotions, and social and personal relationships. It is well-known that psychosocial variables are related to physical health. Factors such as coronary-prone behavior (CPB) and response patterns, and stress-reactivity offer promising avenues of research in the area of coronary heart disease.

Coronary Prone Behavior

Since the 1970s, CPB has been associated with CHD in both women and men (Matthews et al., 1992). This behavior pattern and personality type is characterized by a sense of time-urgency, hostility, and impatience. One mechanism that has been proposed to explain the relationship between CPB and heart disease is stress-reactivity. That is, for individuals who exhibit this behavior pattern, being in stressful situations causes a physiological reaction, cardiovascular reactivity (CVR), that results in injury to the cardiovascular system and increases their susceptibility to CHD (Musante, Treiber, Davis, Strong, & Levy, 1992). Another hypothesized relational pathway between hostility and CHD includes an increased tendency for individuals who score high on hostility to engage in other behaviors that are associated with CHD, such as high dietary fat intake and cigarette smoking (Mustarte et al., 1992). After gaining wide acceptance, this hypothesis was called into question (Matthews & Haynes, 1986). Further investigations supported the relationship between coronary prone behavior and other risk factors in several specific instances. For example, the association was not supported in high-risk or patient populations but was supported in the general population. The relationship between coronary prone behavior and CHD was supported in all risk groups for the hostility component of the Type A complex. In addition, in some investigations the relationship of hostility and CHD was found to be stronger in women than in men (Helmers et al., 1993).

Social Isolation and Social Support

A number of studies have demonstrated a prospective relationship between social support, social integration, and CHD, independent of clinical status, age, and standard CHD risk factors (Berkman & Syme, 1979; House, Landis, & Umberson, 1988; Shumaker & Czajkowski, 1994; Shumaker & Hill, 1991). However, the protective relationship between supportive networks and morbidity and mortality appears to be weaker for women than men. This gender difference may play a role in the higher mortality rates found in women following an MI. The gender difference in the protective aspects of social support may be attributable to the fact that women experience more network strain, as well as support, than men (Rook, 1984; Shinn, Lehmann, & Wong, 1984). Similarly, women are more likely than men to occupy high responsibility, low control, and low social support jobs, a situation related prospectively to all-cause and cardiovascular-specific morbidity and mortality in men and women (Hall, 1989). (See Shumaker & Czajkowski, 1994, for a review of the relationship between social support and CHD.)

Diet and Exercise

Diet and exercise are related to the risk of CHD in women and in men. It has long been known that excess weight is related to the risk of heart disease. Excess weight is associated with high cholesterol levels, high blood pressure, and diabetes, all of which increase the risk of CHD. Recent evidence confirms that this relationship may be even more important for women. In a study of 115,886 nurses, it was found that being overweight was positively associated with CHD even in mildly to moderately overweight women, and women in the heaviest decile suffered MIs three times more often than women in the leanest quartile (Stefanick, 1993). Obesity is more common in women than in men in the United States, with 26.7% of White women and 50% of Black women at least 20% above their ideal weight (Stefanick, 1993).

Most exercise research has been conducted on males, so the specifics of the relationship between exercise and the risk of CHD in women are not well understood. It is well-known, however, that exercise is effective in weight control and has one of its potentially positive effects on cardiovascular health in this way. Exercise may also be related to stress-reactivity. Data suggest that exercise can reduce acute stress-reactivity in men and women (Rejeski, Thompson, Brubaker, & Miller, 1992). More research is needed to explore the effects of exercise on other risk factors associated with CHD (e.g., lipid profiles, depressive symptoms) at both the pre- and postmenopausal stages of life in women. It seems likely that exercise and other correlates of CHD exert their impact on risk by multiple and complex pathways.

Smoking

Historically, more men than women have smoked cigarettes, and a proportion of the gender difference in life expectancy can be attributed to the higher rate of cigarette smoking among men. Smoking contributes to mortality from CHD as well as from other conditions, such as lung diseases

(Douglas, 1989). Recently, however, gender differences in rates of smoking have narrowed. In 1991, 23.5% of U.S. women 18 and older smoked cigarettes, compared with 28.1% of men in the same age category (Ernster, 1993). And initiating of smoking behavior among adolescents and preadolescents is actually higher among girls than boys. Thus, we may see a narrowing of the gender gap in CHD mortality due to smoking in future years as the current cohort of smokers ages and the delayed health effects of smoking are manifest.

Changing gender roles have made it more acceptable for women and girls to smoke, and cigarette advertising is often directed specifically at women and girls. For example, tobacco ads that appear in women's magazines contain more romantic and erotic themes than ads that are placed in youth-oriented magazines, which have more risk and adventure themes (Altman, 1990). Although there is considerable public awareness of the negative effects of smoking, advertising associates smoking with sexual attractiveness, fitness, weight-control, and independence. These images are in direct contradiction to the reality—that smoking decreases the likelihood of maintaining these qualities (Ernster, 1993).

While quitting is by no means easy, smoking is a changeable risk factor in a way that one's family history of heart disease or one's age is not. However, studies show that rates of decrease are higher for men than for women and initiation rates are higher for women than for men, leading to a higher relative incidence of smoking among women than among men (Klesges & Shumaker, 1992). This may be partially attributable to the fact that the early smoking cessation programs focused on men, and it has not been until very recently that programs have been designed to fit the specific needs and smoking-related behaviors of women.

One factor that influences the motivation to quit smoking is the relationship between smoking and body weight. It is well-known that many people who quit smoking experience some weight gain. The actual magnitude of the gain is small, though most people assume the gain is large. On average people who quit smoking gain between four and eight pounds, with women tending to gain slightly more than men (Klesges & Shumaker, 1992). Although excess weight is a risk factor for CHD, the risk posed by gains associated with smoking-cessation is small when compared with the reduction of risk that results from stopping smoking. Cultural norms, which perpetuate the desirability of thinness for women, apparently exert considerable influence in the decision to initiate, continue, or resume smoking, especially in adolescent girls and young adult women (Grunberg & Greenwood, 1992). The desire to conform to the ideal body image seems to overshadow the concern to avoid risk factors for heart disease for some women and girls. To avoid short-term weight gain, they risk much more serious health consequences in the future.

Cardiac Rehabilitation

Women are less likely than men to participate in cardiac rehabilitation programs (Downing & Littman, 1991). The reasons for the lower participation rates of women are unknown but may reflect differences in physician recommendations; the degree to which programs are specifically tailored to meet the needs and schedules of men (King, 1994); the perceptions and expectations of women regarding the appropriateness of exercise programs for them; the degree to which family responsibilities, and in particular the more frequent caregiving role of women, limit their ability to attend such programs (Biegel, Sales, & Schulz, 1991; Shumaker & Hill, 1991); and the lower education and economic status of women (Wingard et al., 1992). When women do participate in rehabilitation programs, however, they gain benefits comparable to those achieved by men (Downing & Littman, 1991).

Depression

The relationship between depression, anxiety, and CHD in women has not been adequately researched. While there is considerable evidence that depression and anxiety are related to CHD in men, and women experience higher rates of depression in general than do men, depression as a risk factor for coronary mortality and morbidity in women has not been fully explored (Carney, et al., 1991). Because women report higher rates of depression than men in the general population, it is not clear whether higher rates of depression in women with CHD indicate a gender difference in the relationship of depression and CHD or simply reflect overall differences in depression between women and men. For women, greater anxiety and depression than men following an MI may be due to their generally poorer prognosis, their older age at onset of CHD, or differential treatment of women and men (Low, 1993). Anxiety related to sexuality is also a factor. Following an MI, women report more fears about the resumption of sexual activity, experience more symptoms during sexual activity, and receive less counseling about sexuality than do men. Women may also fear loss of attractiveness to their partners following an MI (Verbrugge, 1982). Studies that compare women who have had an MI with control groups of women who have not would provide useful information about the relationship of CHD, depression, and anxiety among women. Further research is needed to clarify the relationship, identify the causal mechanism(s), and develop interventions to reduce the risk of CHD in depressed women and to reduce the incidence of depression in women following an MI.

SUMMARY AND FUTURE DIRECTIONS

There is accumulating evidence that women differ from men in the presentation, diagnosis, treatment, and recovery from CHD. The degree to which these differences are related to the physiological process of the disease versus the social factors that affect health perceptions and behaviors is not clear. Additional research is needed to confirm the few findings on women and CHD, and to explore more fully the bases for gender differences in the disease. In order to begin to remedy the current lack of research on the psychosocial factors that affect women's experience with and recovery from CHD, several issues must be addressed. The inclusion of more women in clinical trials on CHD to be able to adequately assess the course of the disease and the effects of various treatments on women's HRQL and psychosocial status is critical.

In recent years, the limitation of data on women and CHD has become more apparent. In the past three years, hundreds of articles have appeared in medical journals reporting gender bias in the diagnosis and treatment of women for CHD and the systematic exclusion of women from clinical research. The response to this has been a substantial change in research funding policy at the federal level, the now-enforced mandate to include women in federally-funded clinical research, and a number of funded studies to look at the causes of CHD in women as well as the efficacy of various treatments (cf. Shumaker & Smith, 1994). Although a number of studies are currently underway that include women and psychosocial factors in CHD, it will be years before the results of these studies are known, thereby influencing clinical care of women.

Also, variables such as clinical status, socioeconomic status, and other demographic factors that are known to vary by gender must be accurately measured in order to separate these factors from the effects of the disease and its treatment. Outcomes such as HRQL must be measured with instruments that have been validated in populations of women.

Data on CHD and psychosocial factors in women are woefully inadequate. However, there are a number of activities currently underway to redress this problem, and within the next several years researchers' knowledge of women, CHD, and psychosocial factors will increase substantially. It is critical that social scientists become more invested in this process to ensure that appropriate psychosocial models and measures are integrated into this burgeoning research agenda.

REFERENCES

Altman, D. G. (1990). The social context and the case of tobacco. In S. A. Shumaker, E. B. Schron, & J. K. Ockene (Eds.), *Health behavior change* (pp. 241–269). New York: Springer.

Ayanian, J. Z., & Epstein, A. M. (1991). Differences in the use of procedures between women and men hospitalized for CHD. *New England Journal of Medicine, 325,* 221–225.

Becker, R. C., Corrao, J. M., & Alpert, J. S. (1982). Coronary artery bypass surgery in women: A review. *Clinical Cardiology, 11,* 443–448.

Berkman, L. F., & Syme, S. L. (1979). Social networks, host resistance, and mortality: A nine-year follow-up study of Alameda County residents. *American Journal of Epidemiology, 109,* 186–204.

Bickell, N. A., Pieper, K. S., Lee, K. L., Mark, D. B., Glower, D. D., Pryor, D. B., & Califf, R. M. (1992). Referral patterns for coronary artery disease treatment:

Gender bias or good clinical judgment? *Annals of Internal Medicine, 116,* 791–797.

Biegel, D. E., Sales, E., & Schulz, R. (1991). *Family caregiving in chronic illness* (Vol. 1). Newbury Park, CA: Sage.

Blumenthal, S. J., Hamilton, B. P., & Sherwin, B. (Eds.). (1992). *Forging a women's health research agenda.* Washington, DC: The National Women's Health Resource Center.

Boogaard, M. A. (1984). Rehabilitation of the female patient after myocardial infarction. *Nursing Clinics of North America, 19,* 433–440.

Boogaard, M. A., & Brody, M. (1985). Comparison of the rehabilitation of men and women post-myocardial infarction. *Journal of Cardiopulmonary Rehabilitation, 5,* 379–384.

Brown, J. S., & Rawlinson, M. E. (1977). Sex differences in sick role rejection and in work performance following cardiac surgery. *Journal of Health and Social Behavior, 18,* 276–292.

Byrne, D. (1979). Anxiety as state and trait following myocardial infarction. *British Journal of Social and Clinical Psychology, 18,* 417–423.

Carney, R. M., Freedland, K. E., Smith, L., Lustman, P. J., & Jaffe, A. S. (1991). Relation of depression and mortality after myocardial infarction in women. *Circulation, 84,* 1876–1877.

Cheitlin, M. D., Sokolow, M., & McIlroy, M. B. (1993). *Clinical cardiology* (6th ed.). Norwalk, CT: Appleton & Lange.

Chirikos, T. N., & Nickel, J. L. (1984). Work disability from coronary heart disease in women. *Women and Health, 9*(1), 55–71.

Clark, J. A., Potter, D. H., & McKinlay, J. B. (1991). Bringing social structure back into clinical decision making. *Social Science and Medicine, 32,* 853–866.

Conn, V. S., Taylor, S. G., & Abele, P. B. (1991). Myocardial infarction survivors: Age and gender differences in physical health, psychosocial state and regimen adherence. *Journal of Advanced Nursing, 16,* 1026–1034.

Conn, V. S., Taylor, S. G., & Wiman, P. (1991). Anxiety, depression, quality of life, and self-care among survivors of myocardial infarction. *Issues in Mental Health Nursing, 12,* 321–331.

Czajkowski, S. M., Lindquist, R., Hoogwerf, B., Dupuis, G., Shumaker, S. A., Terrin, M., & Knatterud for the Post-CABG Investigators. (1992). Women coronary artery bypass graft surgery patients are sicker and have fewer social and economic resources than men. *Circulation, 83* (Suppl. II), 674.

Davidson, D. M. (1994). An introduction to cardiovascular disease. In S. A. Shumaker & S. M. Czajkowski (Eds.), *Social support and cardiovascular disease* (pp. 3–19). New York: Plenum Press.

Dittrich, H., Gilpin, E., Nicod, P., Cali, G., Henning, H., & Ross, J., Jr. (1988). Acute myocardial infarction in women: Influence of gender on mortality and prognostic variables. *American Journal of Cardiology, 62*(1), 1–7.

Douglas, P. S. (1989). *Heart disease in women.* Philadelphia: Davis.

Downing, J., & Littman, A. (1991). Gender differences in response to cardiac rehabilitation. Paper presented at the Conference on Women, Behavior and Cardiovascular Disease, The National Heart, Lung and Blood Institute, Bethesda, MD.

Eaker, E. D. (1989). Psychosocial factors in the epidemiology of coronary heart disease in women. *Psychiatric Clinical Nursing, 12,* 167–173.

Eaker, E. D., Johnson, W. D., Loop, F. D., & Wenger, N. K. (1992). Heart disease in women: How different? *Patient Care,* February, 191–230.

Eaker, E. D., Packard, B., Wenger, N. K., Clarkson, T. B., & Tyroler, H. A. (Eds.). (1987). *Coronary heart disease in women: Proceedings of a NIH workshop.* New York: Haymarket-Doyma.

Ehrenreich, B., & English, D. (1978). *For her own good: 150 years of the experts' advice to women.* New York: Doubleday.

Ernster, V. L. (1993). Women and smoking. *American Journal of Public Health, 83,* 1202–1203.

Fiebach, N. H. (1991). Biobehavioral and psychosocial factors in the diagnosis and treatment of coronary disease in women. Paper presented at the Conference on Women, Behavior and Cardiovascular Disease, The National Heart, Lung and Blood Institute, Bethesda, MD.

Fiebach, N. H., Viscoli, C. M., & Horwitz, R. I. (1990). Differences between women and men in survival after myocardial infarction: Biology or methodology? *Journal of the American Medical Association, 263,* 1092–1096.

Goldberg, R. J., Gore, J. M., Yarzebski, J., & Alpert, J. S. (1991). Sex differences in the incidence and survival rates after myocardial infarction: A community-based perspective. Paper presented at the Conference on Women, Behavior and Cardiovascular Disease, The National Heart, Lung and Blood Institute, Bethesda, MD.

Gomez-Martin, O., Folsom, A. R., Kottke, T. E., Wu, S. C., Jacobs, D. R., Jr., Gillum, R. F., Edlavitch, S. A., & Blackburn, H. (1987). Improvement in long-term survival among patients hospitalized with acute myocardial infarction, 1970–1980. The Minnesota Heart Survey. *New England Journal of Medicine, 316,* 1353–1359.

Greenland, P., Reicher-Reiss, H., Goldbourt, U., Behar, S., & the Israeli SPRINT Investigators. (1991). In-hospital and 1–year mortality in 1,524 women after myocardial infarction. *Circulation, 83,* 484–491.

Grunberg, N. E., & Greenwood, M. R. C. (1992). Task Force 1: Mechanisms relevant to the relations between cigarette smoking and body weight. *Health Psychology, 11* (Suppl.), 4–9.

Guiry, E., Conroy, R. M., Hickey, N., & Mulcahy, R. (1987). Psychological response to an acute coronary event and its effect on subsequent rehabilitation and lifestyle changes. *Clinical Cardiology, 10,* 256–260.

Gurwitz, J. H., Col, N. F., & Avorn, J. (1992). The exclusion of the elderly and women from clinical trials in acute myocardial infarction. *Journal of the American Medical Association, 268,* 1417–1422.

Hall, E. M. (1989). Gender, work control, and stress: A theoretical discussion and an empirical test. *International Journal of Health Services, 19,* 725–745.

Hallstrom, T., Lapidus, L., Bengtsson, C., & Edstrom, K. (1986). Psychosocial factors and risk of ischemic heart disease and death in women: A twelve-year follow-up of participants in the population study of women in Gothenburg, Sweden. *Journal of Psychosomatic Research, 30,* 451–459.

Helmers, K. F., Krantz, D. S., Howell, R. H., Klein, J., Bairey, C. N., & Rozanski, A. (1993). Hostility and myocardial ischemia in coronary artery disease patients: Evaluation by gender and ischemic index. *Psychosomatic Medicine, 55,* 29–36.

House, J. S., Landis, K. R., & Umberson, D. (1988). Social relationships and health. *Science, 241,* 540–544.

Khan, S. S., Nessim, S., Gray, R., Czer, L. S., Chaux, A., & Matloff, J. (1990). Increased mortality of women in coronary artery bypass surgery: Evidence for referral bias. *Annals of Internal Medicine, 112,* 561–567.

Kimmelstiel, C., & Goldberg, R. J. (1990). Congestive heart failure in women: Focus on heart failure due to coronary artery disease and diabetes. *Cardiology, 77* (Suppl. 2), 71–79.

King, A. C. (1994). Biobehavioral variables, exercise and CVD in women. In S. M. Czajkowski, D. R. Hill, & T. B. Clarkson (Eds.), *Women, behavior, and cardiovascular disease: Proceedings of a conference sponsored by The National Heart, Lung and Blood Institute* (NIH No. 94-3309, pp. 69–88). Washington, DC: U.S. Department of Health and Human Services.

King, K. B., Clark, P. C., & Hicks, G. L. (1992). Patterns of referral and recovery in women and men undergoing coronary artery bypass grafting. *American Journal of Cardiology, 69,* 179–182.

King, K. B., Clark, P. C., Norsen, L. H., & Hicks, G. L., Jr. (1993). Coronary artery bypass surgery in older women and men. *American Journal of Critical Care, 1,* 28–35.

Klesges, R. C., & Shumaker, S. A. (1992). Understanding the relations between smoking and body weight and their importance to smoking cessation and relapse. *Health Psychology, 11* (Suppl.), 1–3.

Lerner, D. J., & Kannel, W. B. (1986). Patterns of coronary heart disease morbidity and mortality in the sexes: A 26–year follow-up of the Framingham population. *American Health Journal, 111,* 383–390.

Low, K. G. (1993). Recovery from myocardial infarction and coronary artery bypass surgery in women: Psychosocial factors. *Journal of Women's Health, 2,* 133–139.

Lynch, J. J. (1979). *The broken heart: The medical consequences of loneliness.* New York: Basic Books.

Matthews, K. A., & Haynes, S. (1986). Type A behavior pattern and coronary risk: Update and critical evaluation. *American Journal of Epidemiology, 123,* 923–960.

Matthews, K. A., Kelsey, S. F., Meilahn, E. N., Kuller, L. H., & Wing, R. R. (1989). Educational attainment and behavioral and biologic risk factors of coronary heart disease in middle-aged women. *American Journal of Epidemiology, 129,* 1132–1144.

Matthews, K. A., Woodall, K. L., Engelgretson, T. O., McCann, B. S., Stoney, C. M., Manuck, S. B., & Saab, P. G. (1992). Influence of age, sex, and family on Type A and hostile attitudes and behaviors. *Health Psychology, 11,* 317–323.

Mayou, R. (1979). Psychological reactions to myocardial infarction. *Journal of the Royal College of Physicians, 13,* 103–105.

McDowell, K., & Newell, C. (1987). *Measuring health: A guide to rating scales and questionnaires.* New York: Oxford University Press.

McKinlay, J. B., Crawford, S., McKinlay, S. M., & Sellers, D. E. (1993). On the reported gender difference in coronary heart disease: An illustration of the social construction of epidemiologic rates. New England Research Institute, Watertown, MA.

McKinlay, J. B., McKinlay, S. M., & Crawford, S. L. (1991). Does variability in physician behavior explain any of the gender difference in cardiovascular disease. Paper presented at the Conference on Women, Behavior and Cardiovascular Disease, The National Heart, Lung and Blood Institute, Bethesda, MD.

Moser, D. K. (1991). Gender differences in symptom recognition and health care seeking behaviors. Paper presented at the Conference on Women, Behavior and Cardiovascular Disease, The National Heart, Lung and Blood Institute, Bethesda, MD.

Murdaugh, C. L., & O'Rourke, R. A. (1988). Coronary heart disease in women: Special considerations. *Current Problems in Cardiology, 13,* 73–156.

Musante, L., Treiber, F. A., Davis, H., Strong, W. B., & Levy, M. (1992). Hostility: Relationship to lifestyle behaviors and physical risk factors. *Behavioral Medicine, 18,* 21–26.

Penckofer, S. M., & Holm, K. (1990). Women undergoing coronary artery bypass surgery: Physiological and psychosocial perspectives. *Cardiovascular Nursing, 26*(3), 13–18.

Rejeski, W. J., Thompson, A., Brubaker, P. H., & Miller, H. S. (1992). Acute exercise: Buffering psycho-social stress responses in women. *Health Psychology, 11,* 355–362.

Rogers, W. J., Coggin, C. J., Gersh, B. J., Fisher, L. D., Myers, W. O., Oberman, A., & Sheffield, L. T. (1990). Ten-year follow-up of quality of life in patients randomized to receive medical therapy or coronary artery bypass graft surgery: The coronary artery surgery study (CASS). *Circulation, 82,* 1647–1658.

Rook, K. S. (1984). The negative side of social interaction: Impact on psychological well-being. *Journal of Personality and Social Psychology, 46,* 1097–1108.

Schron, E. B., Pawitan, Y., Shumaker, S. A., & Hale, C. for the CAST Investigators. (1991). Health quality of life differences between men and women in a postinfarction study. *Circulation, 84* (Suppl. II), 976.

Schulman, K. A., Escarce, J. J., Eisenberg, J. M., Hershey, J. C., Young, M. J., McCarthy, D. M., & Williams, S. V. (1992). Assessing physicians' estimates of the probability of coronary artery disease: The influence of patient characteristics. *Medical Decision Making, 12,* 109–114.

Sherwood, J., Maclure, M., Mittleman, M., Goldberg, R. J., Tofler, G., & Muller, J. E. (1994). Women are referred later than men for tertiary care following myocardial infarction. In S. M. Czajkowski, D. R. Hill, & T. B. Clarkson (Eds.), *Women, behavior, and cardiovascular disease: Proceedings of a conference sponsored by The National Heart, Lung and Blood Institute* (NIH No. 94-3309, pp. 393–394). Washington, DC: U.S. Department of Health and Human Services.

Shinn, M., Lehmann, S., & Wong, N. W. (1984). Social interaction and social support. *Journal of Social Issues, 40,* 55–76.

Shumaker, S. A., & Czajkowski, S. M. (1993). A review of health-related quality of life and psychosocial factors in women with cardiovascular disease. *Annals of Behavioral Medicine, 15,* 149–155.

Shumaker, S. A., & Czajkowski, S. M. (1994). *Social support and cardiovascular disease.* New York: Plenum Press.

Shumaker, S. A., & Hill, D. R. (1991). Gender differences in social support and physical health. *Health Psychology, 10,* 102–111.

Shumaker, S. A., & Smith, T. R. (1994). The politics of women's health. *Journal of Social Issues, 50,* 189–202.

Spilker, B. (Ed.). *Quality of life assessments in clinical trials.* New York: Raven, 1990.

Stanton, B. A. (1987). Psychosocial aspects of coronary heart disease in women: Implications and expectations for rehabilitation. In E. D. Eacker, B. Packard, N. K. Wenger, T. B. Clarkson, & H. A. Tyroler (Eds.), *Coronary heart disease in women* (pp. 257–263). New York: Haymarket-Doyma.

Stanton, B. A., Zyzanski, S. J., Jenkins, C. D., & Klein, N. D. (1982). Recovery after major heart surgery: Medical, psychological, and work outcomes. In R. Becker, J. Catz, M. J. Polonius, & M. Speidel (Eds.), *Psychopathological and neurological dysfunctions following open-heart surgery* (pp. 217–226). Heidelberg: Springer-Verlag.

Stefanick, M. L. (1993). The roles of obesity, regional adiposity, and physical activity in coronary heart disease in women. In N. K. Wenger, L. Speroff, & B. Packard (Eds.), *Cardiovascular health and disease in women* (pp. 149–156). Greenwich, CT: Le Jacq Communications.

Steingart, R. M., Packer, M., Hamm, P., Coglianese, M. E., Gersh, B., Geltman, E. M., Sollano, J., Katz, S., Moye, L., Basta, L. L., Lewis, S. J., Gottlieb, S. S., Bernstein, V., McEwan, P., Jacobson, K., Brown, E. J., Kukin, M. L., Kantrowitz, N. E., & Pfeffer, M. A. (1991). Sex differences in the management of coronary artery disease. *New England Journal of Medicine, 325,* 226–230.

Stern, M., Pascale, L., & Ackerman, A. (1977). Life adjustment post-myocardial infarction. *Archives of Internal Medicine, 137,* 1680–1685.

Tobin, J. N., Wassertheil-Smoller, S., Wexler, J. P., Steingart, R. M., Budner, N., Lense, L., & Wachspress, J. (1987). Sex bias in considering coronary bypass surgery. *Annals of Internal Medicine, 107,* 19–25.

Tofler, G. H., Stone, P. H., Muller, J. E., Willich, S. N., Davis, V. G., Poole, W. K., Strauss, H. W., Willerson, J. T., Jaffe, A. S., Robertson, T., Passamani, E., Braunwald, E., & the MILIS Study Group. (1987). Effects of gender and race on prognosis after myocardial infarction: Adverse prognosis for women, particularly Black women. *Journal of the American College of Cardiology, 9,* 473–482.

Verbrugge, L. M. (1982). Sex differentials in health. *Public Health Reports—Hyattsville, 97,* 417–437.

Welty, F. K. (1991). Gender differences in survival and recovery following cardiovascular disease diagnosis and treatment. Paper presented at the Conference on Women, Behavior and Cardiovascular Disease, The National Heart, Lung and Blood Institute, Bethesda, MD.

Wenger, N. K. (1992). Exclusion of the elderly and women from coronary trials: Is their quality of care compromised? *Journal of the American Medical Association, 268,* 1460–1461.

Wenger, N. K., Speroff, L., & Packard, B. (1993). Cardiovascular health and disease in women. *New England Journal of Medicine, 329,* 247–256.

Wilkin, D., Hallam, L., & Doggett, M. (1992). *Measures of need and outcome for primary health care.* New York: Oxford Medical Publications.

Wingard, D. L., Cohn, B. A., Cirillo, P. M., Cohen, R. D., & Kaplan, G. A. (1992). Gender differences in self-reported heart disease morbidity: Are intervention opportunities missed for women? *Journal of Women's Health, 1,* 201–208.

Young, R. F., & Kahana, E. (1993). Gender, recovery from late life heart attack, and medical care. *Women and Health, 20,* 11–31.

Zyzanski, S. J., Rouse, B. A., Stanton, B. A., & Jenkins, C. D. (1982). Employment changes among patients following coronary bypass surgery: Social, medical and psychological correlates. *Public Health Reports—Hyattsville, 97,* 558–565.

3

Women and Cancer: Have Assumptions About Women Limited Our Research Agenda?

Beth E. Meyerowitz and Stacey Hart

Cancer is the second leading cause of death for women in the United States (Public Health Service, 1992). The American Cancer Society (1992) has estimated that approximately one in three Americans alive today will have cancer at some point during their lives. There are now over 8 million Americans who are living with or surviving cancer (American Cancer Society, 1994). Table 1 lists the estimated incidence of new cases and of cancer deaths for men and women in the United States (American Cancer Society, 1994).

The most common sites of cancer for men and women in 1994 are shown on Figure 1 (American Cancer Society, 1994). For women, breast, colorectal, and lung cancers have the highest incidence rates and are most likely to be causes of death, with lung cancer having recently surpassed breast cancer to become the leading cause of cancer deaths in women. Currently, the average relative five-year survival rate (the survival rate adjusted for normal life expectancy) for both genders and all cancers is es-

The authors thank Joanne Meyerowitz for her many helpful comments and suggestions at every stage of the writing of this chapter. We also are grateful to Annette Stanton, Sheryle Gallant, and Ellen Gritz, and to an anonymous reviewer for valuable input on an earlier draft of this chapter.

Table 1

Estimated Incidence of New Cancer Cases and Deaths in the United States in 1994*

	Women	Men	Total
New Cases	576,000	632,000	1,208,000
Deaths	255,000	283,000	538,000

*These figures exclude basal and squamous cell cancers and in situ carcinomas, except bladder. Data from *Cancer facts and figures—1994* (American Cancer Society, 1994, p. 6).

timated to be 53%. Clearly, millions of women and men are and will be living with cancer.

In this chapter we consider the ways in which medical and psychological researchers have studied women and cancer. Rather than providing a comprehensive summary of the findings of this extensive body of research, we attempt to take a step back from the literature and ask not only what researchers have found, but what they have looked for. Have researchers made assumptions about women that have limited the research agenda by leading them to consider only some possible questions? We describe findings from an analysis of articles in the medical and psychological literatures. Through this analysis, we attempt to describe when women have been studied and what questions have been asked. We focus on cancer patients and cancer survivors and on the research about the impact of cancer and its treatments on the lives of those affected by the disease.[1] We will be unable, in the space allotted, to address issues of cancer prevention and early diagnosis among women, although these topics deserve careful attention (see, for example, Reddy & Alagna, 1986).

WHICH WOMEN, WHICH CANCER?

It is almost impossible to make accurate statements about women and cancer without first asking "which women and which cancer?" Cancer is

---

[1]There also is a growing body of literature exploring psychological variables that may play a role in the onset and progression of cancer. Reviews of this literature are available for interested readers (e.g., see Levenson & Bemis, 1991 for a review).

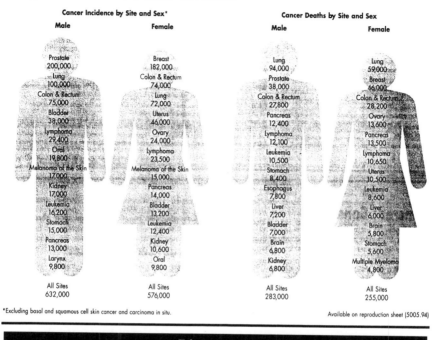

Leading Sites of Cancer Incidence and Death—1994 Estimates

*Excluding basal and squamous cell skin cancer and carcinoma in situ.

Available on reproduction sheet (5005.94)

Figure 1

Leading sites of cancer incidence and death—1994 estimates. From *Cancer Facts and Figures–1994* (p.11) by the American Cancer Society, 1994, Atlanta, GA: Author. Copyright 1994 by the American Cancer Society, Inc. Reprinted with permission.

a tremendously diverse illness. It can strike people of any age, race, socioeconomic level, or lifestyle. It can affect any part of the body. In a few cases cancer can be treated easily with simple outpatient procedures. In other cases it requires extraordinarily invasive treatments—surgery that can remove multiple body parts, chemotherapy and radiation therapy that can cause extreme side effects and toxicities, or bone marrow transplantation that can be painful and expensive. Some cancers are curable and will have no impact on life expectancy; patients with other cancers may have a life expectancy of only a few months after being diagnosed.

Not only do the sites, treatments, and prognoses of cancers differ, the causes and patterns of incidence vary as well. Some cancers have genetic links (e.g., some breast, ovarian, and colon cancers; King, Rowell, & Love, 1993); other cancers are clearly linked to lifestyle (as in the case of lung cancer and smoking) or to environmental or workplace exposures (as in the case of the link between mesothelioma and asbestos exposure; Selikoff, 1976). For other cancers, we have very little idea of what their causes might be.

Add to the heterogeneity of this disease the diversity among women. The women who get cancer are widely varied, therefore their reactions to the disease also vary. Several researchers have found that certain prediagnostic characteristics of women—such as younger age, prior stressful life events, psychiatric history, low sense of control, low perceived social support, and psychological distress—are predictive of poorer postdiagnostic coping and quality of life (e.g., Dean, 1987; Ell, Nishimoto, Morvay, Matell, & Hamovitch, 1989; Ganz, Schag, & Heinrich, 1985; Maunsell, Brisson, & Deschênes, 1992; Royak-Schaler, 1991; Taylor, Lichtman, & Wood, 1984). Stanton and Snider (1993), for example, reported recently that for breast cancer patients, "prebiopsy, psychosocial predictors accounted for 54% and 29% of the variance in negative and positive emotions, respectively. Prebiopsy variables also predicted postbiopsy and postsurgery mood" (p. 16).

These differences among women interact with differences across cancers because specific subgroups of women are at higher risk for certain cancers. A comparison of the epidemiologies of breast and cervical cancers demonstrates this point. Breast cancer is most prevalent in older (vs. younger) women, European/North American (vs. Asian or African) women, middle and upper class (vs. poor) women, highly educated (vs. less educated) women, and women who had children at an older (vs. younger) age (La Vecchia, Negri, & Franceschi, 1992; Marshall, 1993). By contrast, cervical cancer rates are highest by far in Latin America and, in the United States, are highest among Latina women (Peters, Thomas, Hagan, Mack, & Henderson, 1986). Increased risk of cervical cancer is also associated with lower socioeconomic status, earlier age at first intercourse, and lower level of education (La Vecchia, Negri, & Franceschi, 1992; Morris, Lusero, Joyce, Hannigan, & Tucker, 1989). In light of these demographics, it is difficult to attribute accurately any differences in reaction to breast versus cervical cancer because the site of disease is confounded with treatments, cultural/ethnic variables, education, socioeconomic status, family situation, and so forth.

The picture is further complicated by the fact that minority and poor women, who often have less access to adequate health care, are more likely to have cancer diagnosed at advanced stages and to have lower survival rates (Pierce, Fowble, Solin, Schultz, Rosser, & Goodman, 1992; Wells & Horm, 1992). In addition, the types of treatment that women receive for the same cancers vary by region of country, age, and race (Bain, Greenberg, & Whitaker, 1986; Nattinger, Gottlieb, Veum, Yahnke, & Goodwin, 1992). For example, Farrow, Hunt, and Samet (1992) compared the rates of breast-conserving (vs. radical) surgeries for breast cancer across nine regions in the United States. They found that the rates of breast-conserving surgery from 1985 to 1986 ranged from 41.5% in Seattle to 19.6% in Iowa.

Thus, different women are dealing with different cancers for which they are being prescribed different treatments for different stages of the disease. Clearly, psychosocial impacts are likely to vary based on the demographic and personal characteristics of the woman, and the nature of her disease and treatment.

SURVEY OF MEDICAL AND PSYCHOLOGICAL LITERATURE

In light of this great variety, we were curious to see if we could draw any general conclusions about the nature of women and cancer and about how women with cancer are dealt with in the medical and psychological literatures. We wondered what the story or stories are that the scientific literature tells about women when they have cancer (see Harding, 1987 for more about the "stories" told by sciences). How have we, as scientists, made sense of this very complex issue?

In order to address that question, we coded the gender distribution and content of empirical articles published in 1983 and 1992—the beginning and end of the decade preceding the year in which this chapter was initially written. Cancer incidence and death rates for those years are provided in Table 2. We have distinguished between rates of cancers that are specific to the breast or reproductive organs and rates of cancers at sites common to both women and men.[2] We make this distinction in order to explore the statement from NIH's Office of Research on Women's Health that "except for malignancies of the female reproductive system and breast, many biomedical studies have used men as models for the prototypical study population, with subsequent results applied to women as though such diseases or conditions would have the same natural history or response" (Pinn, 1992, p. 1921). Our strategies for identifying articles for coding were different for the medical and psychological literatures and are described in the sections below.

The Medical Literature

Because our primary interest was in the psychological literature, we did not attempt a comprehensive survey of the medical literature. Instead, we identified one well established, widely distributed oncology journal for review. We selected *Cancer,* the journal of the American Cancer Society, because it has the largest circulation rate of any refereed oncology journal (circulation rate for 1994–95 = 16,686; *Ulrich's International Periodicals Directory,* 1994). We recorded the site of disease and number of men and women studied for all articles that investigated cancer treatments in adults.[3] During 1983 and 1992, 768 and 759 articles were published in *Cancer,* of which 242 and 159 met our inclusion criteria, respectively.

Our results provide a picture of which cancers have been studied in women. Overall, women are not underrepresented as subjects in *Cancer* articles. In both 1983 and 1992 the total number of women included in

---

[2]We include breast cancer as a female-specific cancer, despite the fact that approximately 1,000 men per year contract the disease, constituting approximately .5% of breast cancer diagnoses. Researchers consider breast cancer almost exclusively a disease of women.

[3]In our survey of articles in *Cancer* we excluded animal research, studies about cell histology, research with children, and studies about prognosis, diagnosis, and prevention. In over 10% of articles in each year, the authors failed to provide the gender of the patients and therefore we were unable to code them. We also excluded those articles that were psychological in content (N = 3 in 1983 and 15 in 1992) and included them, instead, in the discussion of the psychological literature. It was not difficult to make a clear distinction between the medical and psychological literatures. Medical articles almost never dealt with patients' reactions to their illness or treatments, even when such considerations seemed relevant to the article's content. For example, physicians usually rated the side effects and toxicities of treatment themselves, rather than systematically obtaining patient self-report.

Table 2

Estimated Gender-specific and Gender-nonspecific New Cancer Cases and Deaths in the United States—1983 and 1992*

	1983		1992	
	Men	Women	Men	Women
Incidence of New Cases				
Gender-nonspecific Cancers	341,200	240,900	424,400	313,500
Reproductive Organ and/or Breast Cancers	81,300	191,600	140,600	251,500
Total	422,500	432,500	565,000	565,000
Deaths				
Gender-nonspecific Cancers	213,150	141,800	240,150	175,000
Reproductive Organ and/or Breast Cancers	25,350	59,700	34,850	70,000
Total	238,500	201,500	275,000	245,000

*These figures exclude carcinoma in situ and nonmelanoma skin cancers.
Data from *Cancer facts and figures—1983* (American Cancer Society, 1983, p. 10), and *Cancer facts & figures—1992* (American Cancer Society, 1992, p. 5).

the studies about cancer treatments exceeded the total number of men; 59.5% of the patients studied in both years were women. These findings are consistent with a recent report from the Agency for Health Care Policy and Research (as cited in Marwick, 1992). They reviewed the Public Health Service's grant program and found that 60% of the human subjects involved in extramural research projects were women (see Marwick, 1992).

Table 3 compares the numbers of men and women included in studies about cancers of the breast and reproductive organs versus studies about cancers of gender-nonspecific sites (i.e., cancers at sites other than the breast or reproductive organs). A substantial majority of the women studied in *Cancer* treatment articles, 69.1% in 1983 and 64.6% in 1992, had cancers of the breast or reproductive organs. In contrast, only 12.5% and 12.3% of the men studied in 1983 and 1992, respectively, had cancers of the reproductive organs.

Table 3

Total Number of Female and Male Patients Included as Subjects in Cancer Treatment Articles—1983 and 1992

	Women	Men
1983		
Gender-nonspecific Cancers	4240	8192
Breast and Reproductive Organ Cancers	9485	1165
1992		
Gender-nonspecific Cancers	2962	4984
Breast and Reproductive Organ Cancers	5402	700

As indicated in Figures 2 and 3, this attention to breast and reproductive organ cancers relative to gender-nonspecific cancers is inconsistent with the proportions of men and women who contract and die from these cancers. For women there is greater attention to breast and reproductive organ cancers (vs. gender-nonspecific cancers), whereas for men there is less research on these cancers than would be warranted by the gender distribution of cancer patients diagnosed with disease at these sites.

The reverse pattern holds for cancers that are not specific to gender. In 1983 and 1992, 41.4% and 42.5% of new gender-nonspecific cancers were diagnosed in women (see Table 2). The proportion of women (vs. men) studied in *Cancer* treatment articles, however, was 34.1% in 1983 and 37.3% in 1992. While approximately 56% of women who are diagnosed with cancers have gender-nonspecific diagnoses, only 30.9% in 1983 and 35.4% in 1992 of the women studied in *Cancer* had disease at these sites.

Totaling numbers of patients across studies does not tell the whole story because one or two heavily skewed studies could affect the results disproportionately. Therefore, we also counted the number of articles about gender-nonspecific cancers that had more men as subjects than women. Because the incidence of gender-nonspecific cancers in men is higher than in women, attending equally to men and women in research

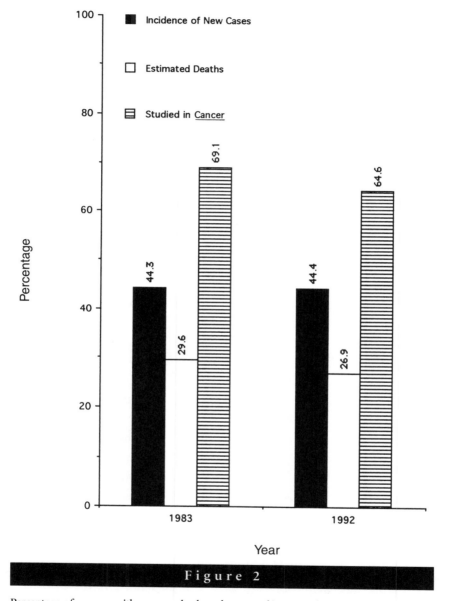

Figure 2

Percentage of women with cancer who have breast and/or reproductive cancers.

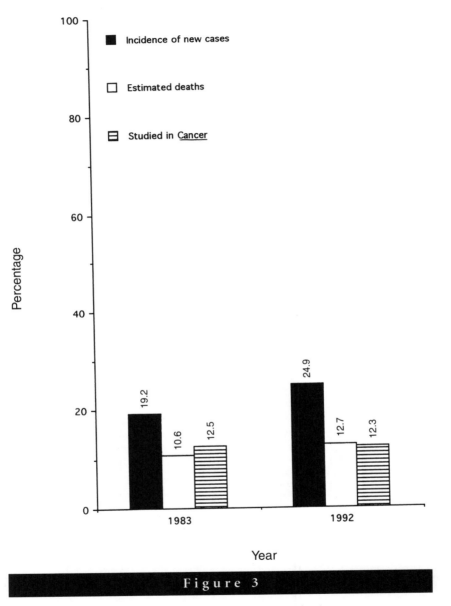

Figure 3

Percentage of men with cancer who have breast and/or reproductive cancers.

would yield studies with somewhat more men. We used a difference of over 20% as our cutoff, since men account for 57.5% of gender-nonspecific cancers.[4]

This analysis also demonstrated a discrepancy between men and women. In both 1983 and 1992 there was a preponderance of studies of gender-nonspecific cancers with over 20% more men than women (57.6% in 1983 and 62.2% in 1992). Almost all of the remaining studies had between 40% and 60% of subjects of each gender (31.4% in 1983 and 26.7% in 1992), with most of these studies also including more men than women.

These data must be interpreted very cautiously. We looked at only one journal and at only two years. We may be describing nothing more than chance findings or a short-lived editorial policy in one outlet. However, the reliability of findings across these two years, separated by a decade, is notable.

It appears that in oncology, as in other medical subspecialties, the focus of research on women is on breasts and genitals. Clearly, breast cancer is a major unsolved problem that deserves a great deal of attention in medical research. However, if topics for research were chosen solely on the basis of the magnitude of the problem, there also would be a focus on lung and colorectal cancers in women (see Figure 1). But, in 1992, only 5% of the women studied in *Cancer* had lung cancer and only 3.7% had colorectal cancers. Perhaps the link between smoking and lung cancer has led researchers to focus on prevention, rather than treatment of the disease. The inattention to colorectal cancers and prostate cancer in men remains unexplained, however.

Other possible explanations suggest that research topics may not always be chosen entirely on the basis of scientific need. Breast cancer, far more than any other cancers, has been the focus of advocacy groups that have worked hard and successfully to increase funding for breast cancer research. Their efforts, however, are unlikely to have influenced research focus and funding as early as 1983, when the proportion of studies about breast cancer was very similar to the focus in 1992. Another possible con-

---

[4]We excluded from these calculations case studies with 10 or fewer patients.

tributor to the interest in breast cancer may have to do with the demographics of the disease. As described earlier, well-educated, socioeconomically advantaged, White women are at greatest risk for the disease. In light of these risk factors, women who contract breast cancer are more likely to be in positions of power or to be the wives of men who are in positions of power (e.g., Betty Ford, Nancy Reagan). This power and visibility, coupled with the view that women are especially vulnerable to the psychological difficulties that might be associated with breast surgery, may subtly serve to increase attention to breast cancer.

In addition to wondering why breast and reproductive organ cancers are the focus of research on women, it is interesting to speculate about why reproductive organ cancers in men are understudied compared with cancers at other sites. Ageism may play a role in this lack of attention. Genital cancers in young men are fairly rare and often treatable. Prostate cancer, which has a high incidence rate, is primarily a disease of older men, with over 80% of diagnoses being made in men over 65 (American Cancer Society, 1994).

We suggest that another viable explanation may have to do with our society's interest in women as sex objects. A particular interest in women's breasts is far from unique to the medical literature. Perhaps it is not surprising that in a society in which women often are viewed as "other," the focus of interest in women will be on those physical attributes that most clearly distinguish them from men.

The possibility that women's bodies are dichotomized into reproductive and "all other" parts was the focus of a recent editorial in the *Journal of the American Medical Association*. Clancy and Massion (1992) pointed out that women are expected to seek regular preventive medical care from two different kinds of physicians and that only physicians specializing in women's reproduction (i.e., gynecologists) are likely to provide even basic pelvic examination. A study of women's use of preventive health services indicated that most women who had not had recent tests for breast and cervical cancer screening had had recent physician contact, presumably in which screening tests were not conducted (Makuc, Freid, & Kleinman, 1989). While we can only speculate about the possible mechanisms and beliefs underlying this apparent bias toward separating women's breasts and genitals from the rest of their bodies, the results are consistent with arguments claiming that sexual objectification of women's bodies can be subtle and widespread.

The preponderance of men in research on gender-nonspecific sites increases the possibility that the overall results will be more indicative of men's, rather than women's, response to treatment. This bias would not be especially problematic if treatment results were reported for men and women separately or if there were no gender differences in response to treatment. Unfortunately, neither of these possibilities is supported by research.

In our survey of articles from *Cancer* we found that fewer than 20% of the studies of gender-nonspecific cancers in either 1983 or 1992 reported a comparison of treatment results by gender, despite the fact that almost all studies included adequate numbers of men and women to allow for a comparison.[5] By analyzing results from men and women together, any gender differences become experimental noise. Indeed, it is precisely an expectation of gender differences that is often used as an argument in favor of excluding women from medical trials. It is curious, then, that when men and women are studied together, possible gender differences are overlooked. It is possible that data are regularly analyzed for gender differences but that nonsignificant results are not reported. If so, direct mention of that fact would seem essential to understanding treatment effects on women.

Data from oncology research suggests that we should not assume either that men and women are similar or that they are different. Both assumptions need to be tested explicitly. Ganz (1993), for example, pointed out, "the importance of considering gender as an important variable for planning and analyzing the results of lung cancer treatment trials" (p. 150). She cited evidence that women survive longer than men do with all types of lung cancers. Others have argued that special attention be paid to the role of hormonal variations in women, based on findings of differential

---

[5]We excluded from these calculations case studies with 10 or fewer patients.

63

effectiveness of breast surgery depending on the time in the menstrual cycle that treatment is received (Senie, Rosen, Rhodes, & Lesser, 1991).

Female hormones should not always be assumed to play a central role, however. The relationship between age at birth of first child and risk for colorectal cancer is an interesting case in point. Kune and his colleagues (Kune, Kune, & Watson, 1989) noted that "increasing parity and/or early age at birth of the first child [have been found to] protect females against large bowel cancer" (p. 533). They conducted an epidemiologic study of colorectal cancer and found that these variables were significant predictors of risk for men also. The authors concluded that "(s)ince the protection against colorectal cancer associated with having children and with earlier age at birth of the first child was found to be similar for both males and females in the Melbourne study, a life-style factor, as yet unidentified, rather than a female hormonal factor, is postulated as the mediator of these effects" (p. 533).

These findings underscore the importance of studying all cancers in both men and women. We certainly are not suggesting that any cancers be studied less. Careful attention to breast cancer is essential, especially in light of its high incidence rates and the only very modest improvements in treatment efficacy. Studying treatment effects in women with other cancers is also necessary, as is continuing research on male response to cancer treatments for gender-specific and gender-nonspecific sites of cancer. Moreover, when studies include both male and female patients, the possibility that men and women will respond differently to treatment should be tested empirically.

The Psychological Literature

To explore whether there is evidence of bias in what is studied psychologically about women and cancer, we undertook a more comprehensive review of the psychological literature in 1983 and 1992. Specifically, we conducted a computer search of the PsycLIT journal articles database, which abstracts over 1300 journals, using the terms *cancer* and *leukemia* for searches. We also searched the MEDLINE database, using the terms *psychology* or *quality of life* with *neoplasm*—the most all-encompassing term for cancer—to identify articles in the oncology literature that may not have been abstracted by PsycLIT.[6] The numbers of articles identified through each search in 1983 and 1992 are shown in Table 4.

We had predicted that the psychological literature would overrepresent women as subjects. The prediction, based on the frequent assumption that feelings and social interactions are more important for women than for men, was strongly supported in both years. Of the 8,248 subjects included in psychological research on cancer in 1983, 69.6% were women. In 1992, 70.1% of the 10,003 subjects were women.[7] In contrast, women represented 50.6% of all new cases of cancer in 1983, and 50% in 1992 (see Table 2).

It was not possible in the psychological literature, as it was in the medical literature, to make a clean distinction between articles about cancers of the breast and reproductive organs versus gender-nonspecific cancers. Studying cancer sites separately is not always necessary for answering important psychological questions. The subjects in many articles are heterogeneous with respect to site of disease; 48.9% of the articles in 1983 and 38% of the articles in 1992 include patients with cancers at a variety of sites.

It does appear, however, that female breast and reproductive organ cancers are widely studied in this literature, as in the medical literature.

---

[6]As with our review of the medical literature, we included only those articles that were about adult cancer patients or survivors. The following types of articles were excluded: research on children, research on cancer prevention or prognosis, research on purely medical side-effects of treatments, non-English language articles, review articles, nonempirical descriptive articles, animal experiments, and opinion or reply articles. In the MEDLINE search, we used only those articles that were in oncology journals or in major general medical journals (e.g., *Journal of the American Medical Association, Lancet,* and *New England Journal of Medicine*). Our search does not include articles from journals of other medical subspecialties or from the nursing or social work literature, unless those articles were in the journals abstracted by PsycLIT. This strategy allowed us to identify the literature specific to psychology and cancer.

In order to ensure that our search was comprehensive, we cross-checked identified articles in three ways. First, we compared the psychosocial articles that were identified in the MEDLINE search to the articles we had found through our survey of all *Cancer* articles. All of the psychosocial articles we found in *Cancer* were also identified by the MEDLINE search. Second, because MEDLINE and PsycLIT overlap in the journals that they abstract, we were able to compare the two searches, and in this fashion identified two articles on cancer and psychology through MEDLINE that had not been accessed through PsycLIT. Finally, we reviewed each paper published in two journals likely to contain articles on cancer and psychology—*Health Psychology* and *Journal of Psychosocial Oncology*—and confirmed that all relevant articles had been identified in the PsycLIT search.

[7]The results for articles published in medical journals and those published in psychology journals were very similar and, therefore, we do not report the findings separately.

Table 4

Number of Articles Identified Through PsycLIT and MEDLINE Computer Searches

	1983	1992
PsycLIT Search		
Total Number Identified	226	320
Number Meeting Inclusion Criteria	38	67
Number Not Providing Subject Gender	4	6
Number That Could Not Be Located	1	4
Total Articles Coded	33	57
MEDLINE Search		
Total Number Identified	35	82
Number Meeting Inclusion Criteria	16	37
Number Not Providing Subject Gender	2	2
Number That Could Not Be Located	—	—
Total Articles Coded	14	35

Of those studies that included only one cancer site, 62.5% in 1983 and 57.9% in 1992 focused on breast and reproductive organ cancers in women, approximately 90% of studies in both years being specific to breast cancer. By contrast, no studies in 1983 and 3.5% of those studies limited to only one cancer site in 1992 were specifically investigating reproductive organ cancer in men.

In the psychological research, even those studies that were not restricted to gender-specific cancers (but, in some cases, included patients with cancers at these sites) had a preponderance of women. In 1983, 62.3% of the patients in studies not limited to cancers of the breast or reproductive organs were women, and in 1992, 54.7% of the patients in these studies were women. Still, of the studies that were heterogeneous for site, 30.4% in 1983 and 48.6% in 1992 included more patients with breast cancer than cancer of any other site.

In addition to this emphasis on breast cancer, we found a relationship between the gender of the patients being studied and the topic of research.[8] Several areas of quality of life have been addressed in the psychosocial oncology literature, as listed in Exhibit 1 (see, e.g., Holland & Rowland, 1989).

We found that in 1992, 73 articles in our survey focused primarily on psychological state, social relationships, or both, whereas 19 articles had somatic and functional aspects of quality of life as their focus (see Exhibit 1 for examples of each area of quality of life). Of the subjects included in the articles addressing feelings and relationships, 77.1% were women. Women accounted for only 45.4% of the patients in articles about somatic discomfort and functional ability, however. This differential attention is consistent with the stereotype that women feel and men act. The relatively little attention that is paid to men in the psychosocial literature is largely concerned with whether they are able to continue performing their functions without undue interference from pain or treatment side effects.

Some examples from other years support this bias. Studies on employment in leukemia patients (Magid & Golomb, 1989) and work experiences in survivors of Hodgkin's disease (Bloom et al., 1988), for example, were among the few articles to include only men as subjects, despite the fact that both men and women get these diseases.[9] These studies provide important information about the impact of cancer on work in men, information that we also need about women. Studies on women focus on emotion, body image, and family functioning. Rarely is work, insurance, or fertility the primary focus of articles about women; rarely is body image or sense of manhood the focus of articles about men, although they would seem especially relevant to patients with cancers at sites such as the prostate.

Certainly, research on feelings in women and work in men is essential. It is possible that these aspects of quality of life are differentially im-

---

[8]Unfortunately, we were not able to determine if the gender of the researcher, as well as the subjects, was predictive of article content because some journals report only initials for first names and most have multiple authors.

[9]We do not mean to imply that social relationships and feelings are never studied in men (see, for example, Bloom et al., 1993; Gritz, Wellisch, Siau, & Wang, 1990).

Exhibit 1

Components of Quality-of-Life of Importance in Cancer Care

- Psychological State/Feelings
  Depression
  Anxiety/Nervousness/Irritability
  Anger
  Fears
  Body Image/Satisfaction With Appearance
  Enjoyment/Satisfaction/Positive Affect
  Sense of Masculinity/Femininity

- Social and Interpersonal Relationships
  Marital/Sexual
    Intimacy/Satisfaction
    Sexual Interaction/Enjoyment
  Family Functioning
  Time Spent With Family/Friends
  Enjoyment of Social Activities

- Somatic Discomfort
  Fatigue
  Pain
  Impact of Treatment Toxicities and Side Effects

- Physical and Occupational Functioning
  Ability to Work
  Ability to Perform Household Responsibilities
  Ability to Maintain Recreational Activities
  Cognitive Abilities
  Fertility
  Sexual Function

portant for men and women and, therefore, should receive additional focus. Unfortunately, we were unable to test this hypothesis because only a minority of the articles that included both female and male subjects (34.4% in 1983 and 47.4% in 1992) compared the findings by gender. Of those that did make this comparison, significant differences were found in 44.4% of the studies. These differences did not seem to follow a consistent pattern; in some cases greater impairment across areas of quality of life was reported by women and in some cases by men. We also considered the possibility that men and women differ in their willingness to participate in psychological research. Again, the evidence did not support this hypothesis. In 1992, only nine articles compared male and female participation rates. In no case were men found to be less willing to take part in research than women. Response rates for articles limited to only one gender also were comparable.

Our survey of the psychological literature indicates that women, particularly women with breast cancer, are the focus of much of the research on the psychological aspects of receiving treatment for and surviving cancer. Indeed, even medical clinical trials have been conducted with the primary intent of improving psychological, not medical, outcomes (e.g., studies of breast conserving surgeries). When men are studied in the psychosocial literature, the content of the research tends to be circumscribed symptom-management or assessment of functional and occupational capacity, not the more global aspects of emotional distress and social interaction, as is the focus with women. In the following section we discuss some of the assumptions that may have led to the targeting of breast cancer and the particular concern for women's psychosocial recovery following breast cancer treatment. We use the case of breast cancer to illuminate the role that gender-stereotypical assumptions can play in dictating the nature of questions asked in scientific research.

Breast Cancer: A Case Study

In our survey of the psychological literature, as with the medical literature, women with breast cancer seem to have been targeted for study. Why might breast cancer, as compared with cancers at other sites, be of such great interest?[10] First, five-year relative survival rates for breast cancer are approximately 77% according to the American Cancer Society (1992), which are higher than survival rates for many other cancers. These rates, coupled with the high incidence rates of breast cancer, assure that there are many breast cancer survivors available for participation in research. They also underscore the importance of identifying psychosocial issues likely to face the many women surviving breast cancer. In contrast, lung cancer, which also has a very high incidence rate, has a far worse prognosis (13% five-year relative survival rate). Studying lung cancer, in most cases, would mean studying late-stage disease and dying. Many other cancers are relatively infrequently diagnosed, making it more difficult to accrue sufficient numbers of patients for research and making specific findings relevant to a smaller population of patients.

However, survival and incidence rates do not fully explain the relative lack of attention to prostate and colorectal cancers. As indicated in Figure 1, both of these cancers have high incidence rates. Additionally, five-year relative survival rates are 56% and 74% for colorectal and prostate cancer, respectively (American Cancer Society, 1992), indicating that there are many people living with these cancers. Despite the fact that common sense would suggest that being diagnosed with and treated for prostate or colorectal cancer could have high psychosocial impact, we found only five articles in the two years searched that investigated psychological aspects of cancer at these specific sites. Three of these articles were reports of case studies, with fewer than five patients. Breast cancer, on the other hand, was the subject of 44 articles during those years. Clearly, incidence and survival rates alone cannot explain the focus on breast cancer in the psychological literature.

This focus may have resulted, in part, from the view that breast cancer is especially devastating psychologically. Some writers have asserted,

---

[10]The primary author of the present chapter acknowledges that much of her own research in psychosocial oncology focuses on quality of life in breast cancer. She has no intention of throwing stones from that glass house, nor does she mean to imply in any way that psychological reactions to breast cancer are overstudied or unimportant. There is much more to learn about the psychology of breast cancer. We are curious as to why other cancers have not also received attention in the psychosocial literature.

for example, that breast and gynecologic cancers are unique. As one stated, "they are different from other forms of the disease in that they possess the potential to devastate the patient by imposing a unique threat to her self-concept and psychological integration . . . through the destructive impact of the disease on the patients' body image and sexual identity" (Derogatis, 1980, p. 1). In another example, a nurse cautioned that women must be helped to "feel feminine" following mastectomy because patients feel that they no longer have any value as women (Anstice, 1970). The implicit assumption is that the breast is so central to womanhood that any assault to the breast will destroy women's psychological integrity.

This view of breast loss as psychologically devastating is relatively new and represents an attempt to be more sympathetic to the concerns of women. For many years radical mastectomy was the accepted treatment for breast cancer, with little concern shown for the removal of a very wide margin of healthy tissue. Nonetheless, overgeneralizations from either extreme are unhelpful, and in both cited examples, views were based on assumptions about women rather than on empirical evidence from patients.

In fact, there is very little research evidence to support either contention. Breast loss is clearly traumatic for many women, as amputation of any part of the body would be. However, psychological reactions to breast cancer are no more serious or intense than reactions to other cancers (see Meyerowitz, Chaiken, & Clark, 1988 for a review). Overall, breast cancer patients do not report greater psychological distress than women with cancer at other sites or than male cancer patients (e.g., Mendelsohn, 1990; Sneed, Edlund, & Dias, 1992). In addition, when mastectomy patients are asked to describe their greatest concerns, breast loss typically is not the most common. Zemore and his colleagues (Zemore, Rinholm, Shepel, & Richards, 1989), for example, found that the three most common concerns of mastectomy patients were difficulty engaging in strenuous physical activity, fear of cancer recurrence, and concern about receiving optimal medical care. The misperception that breast loss is central among mastectomy patients' concerns can lead patients to feel misunderstood and unsupported, especially by men, who have been found to hold this perception more strongly than women (Peters-Golden, 1982).

These comments are in no way meant to suggest that attention to women's concerns about breast loss or mutilation is unnecessary. Indeed, breast cancer patients have sparked some of the medical interest in identifying less invasive and disfiguring surgeries. Moreover, disruptions in some aspects of quality of life—for example, sexual functioning and partner communication (e.g., Schag et al., 1993)—have been found to be particularly relevant to some breast cancer survivors. The possibility that these problems may result in part from partners' reactions (in all studies, partners are either known or assumed to be male) rather than the patient's intrapsychic concerns, is suggested by the impact of husband's coping on wife's adjustment and by the delay in the development of some of these problems (Hannum, Giese-Davis, Harding, & Hatfield, 1991; Meyerowitz et al., 1988; Stalker, Johnson, & Cimma, 1989). Researchers should not assume how women will feel or what they will want and limit their research agenda on the basis of these assumptions, nor should they assume that reactions to breast cancer exist outside the social context of women's lives.

The difficulties inherent in making such assumptions are demonstrated by the dearth of systematic study of the use of external breast prostheses. Because of the assumption that breast loss would leave a woman feeling unwhole, several options have been made available to women (or to their physicians in the many cases where women have not been included in the decision-making process) to minimize the impact of breast surgery on physical appearance. Prior to the availability of conservative surgeries and breast reconstruction, use of external prosthetics was accepted without question in the medical literature as an essential step in the rehabilitation of women who had undergone mastectomy. The following quote demonstrates the assurance with which the benefits of prosthetic use were assumed: "An immediate and pressing need is to issue all mastectomy patients with a temporary prothesis as soon as possible after surgery" (Pendleton & Smith, 1986). While there is some anecdotal discussion in the literature about types of prostheses or strategies for recommending their use (e.g., Lee, 1991; Pendleton & Smith, 1986; Tanner, Abraham, & Llewellyn-Jones, 1983), the basic assumption that prostheses should be recommended continues to go untested and largely unquestioned.

The benefits of supplying prosthetics are not always as straightforward as these writers seem to believe. Certainly, some women are "very grateful indeed" to be supplied with prostheses while in the hospital (Brady, 1991, p. 1). By contrast, other patients, such as Audre Lorde (1980), have found that "[t]his emphasis upon the cosmetic after surgery reinforces this society's stereotypes of women, that we are only what we look or appear, so this is the only aspect of our existence we need to address" (p. 57). These contrasting examples demonstrate the dangers of making assumptions about what all women will want.

Unlike prosthetic use, breast conserving surgeries, which represent another attempt to minimize psychological distress by preserving a woman's sense of "wholeness" in the face of breast surgery, have been studied in the psychological literature. The strength of assumptions about the importance of the breast can be seen in the history of breast surgeries. When the breast was assumed to be unnecessary and superfluous after childbearing years, radical mastectomies were accepted as the treatment of choice, despite the absence of any data supporting the necessity of such mutilating surgery. As opinions shifted, major medical trials were mounted to determine whether more conservative surgery would be equally effective. Thus, substantial medical research was conducted not to increase survival or to delay recurrence, but to decrease presumed adverse impacts on quality of life. Controlled medical trials have found that for many breast cancers conservative surgery with local radiation is equivalent to radical surgery in efficacy, so that women no longer need to be subjected to unnecessary breast amputation (Fisher et al., 1985).

The strongly held belief that guided these medical trials was that women who had conservative surgery would report more positive quality of life than women with radical surgery. Subsequent psychosocial research has not substantiated this prediction. Most studies find that body image and, at times, sexual functioning are more positive in women who have had conservative surgery (Kiebert, de Haes, & van de Velde, 1991). However, conservative surgery does not regularly provide benefits in other aspects of quality of life or in overall emotional adjustment. Contrary to what many writers had expected, improved body image has not been consistently associated with the woman's assessment of her mood or quality of life (Ganz, Schag, Lee, Polinsky, & Tan, 1992). Body image does not appear to be as important to women's overall psychological well-being as some had assumed. Ability to choose between surgeries, when medically feasible, appears to be a stronger predictor of psychosocial outcome than the type of surgery chosen (Morris & Ingham, 1988).

In this section we have used breast cancer as an example of an area in which assumptions about women seem to have, at times, guided the research agenda. In some cases these assumptions have been modified on the basis of research, and in other cases the assumptions remain untested. The lack of empirical support for some strongly held assumptions (e.g., that breast conserving surgeries would greatly improve women's overall psychological well-being) demonstrates the necessity of making assumptions explicit so that they can be tested.

DIRECTIONS FOR FUTURE RESEARCH

Although the psychosocial literature on women who have been diagnosed with cancer may be limited, it has provided useful and important information in those areas on which it has focused. In general, researchers have found that most breast cancer patients experience increased emotional distress and physical disruption following surgery (e.g., Stanton & Snider, 1993). For most women who remain disease-free, these problems gradually decrease during the first postsurgical year to levels comparable to women who had not been diagnosed with cancer (Psychological Aspects of Breast Cancer Study Group, 1987). However, some women do not recover psychologically and most women continue to experience difficulties in some areas, such as sexual functioning (Schag et al., 1993). We suggest below two directions in which future research could expand on these findings.

Understudied Populations

Not all women with cancer have received attention in the psychosocial literature, as our survey documents. Patterns of psychosocial recovery following initial treatment for cancer and the areas in which problems are common or persistent may vary by site of disease and treatment protocol. For example, head and neck cancer patients receiving radiation, in contrast to radiation patients with cancer at other sites, reported difficulty eating sufficient amounts of food (Padilla et al., 1992). Future research should include longitudinal studies of quality of life and adjustment following the diagnosis and treatment of a wide range of cancers that have high incidence rates and are likely to be disruptive, such as colorectal cancers, head and neck cancers, and lung cancer.

A serious limitation of past research is that it has focused almost entirely on middle-class, non-Hispanic White women. We do not know whether findings from this literature can be generalized to women of color or to poor women. Several researchers have speculated on ways that culture and ethnicity might influence reactions to cancer and to typical medical interventions (see, e.g., Trill & Holland, 1993). Yet, almost no research has tested these hypotheses systematically. It is essential that future studies consider women of color and poor women, especially in light of the high incidence rates and poor survival rates for these women. We are not suggesting that women of color simply be compared to White women in standard research. Optimally relevant research will require the development of psychometrically sound assessment tools in multiple languages, that take into consideration the context of women's lives.

Most past research also has suffered from the apparent assumption that all women are heterosexual, and that good functioning occurs in the context of a heterosexual relationship. We recommend research that considers the possible influence of sexual orientation on quality of life and coping.

A final understudied group with whom we recommend research is the daughters of cancer patients. Although it is widely accepted that cancer affects patients' entire families, very few studies have considered the impact of the disease on patients' children. Such research is increasingly important in light of the identification of genetic and other technologies for screening women at high risk due to family history (Biesecker et al., 1993). Women at high risk for familial cancers will need to make decisions both about whether to receive genetic screening and about whether to undertake chemoprevention or prophylactic mastectomy if genetic susceptibility is indicated (Vogel, Yeomans, & Higginbotham, 1993). Very little research is available to guide women in making these decisions. Studies do indicate that the demand for genetic testing will be high and that psychologically vulnerable women may be more likely to elect testing (Lerman, Daly, Masny, & Balshem, 1994).

Interventions

By learning about the difficulties experienced by women from varied backgrounds as they cope with different cancers and treatments, we will be able to design and test interventions to alleviate distress and to speed psychological recovery. Researchers already have had some success in developing effective behavioral and counseling interventions (see Andersen, 1992 for a review). We recommend more research on psychological treatments that are effective in controlling symptoms, enhancing coping, and improving the delivery of medical services.

Controlling Symptoms

Cancer treatments are associated with a wide range of disruptive and distressing side effects. Controlled investigations of hypnosis, progressive muscle relaxation, and systematic desensitization have demonstrated that these interventions can be effective in alleviating treatment-related nausea, vomiting, pain, and dysphoria (Carey & Burish, 1988; Trijsburg, van Knippenberg, & Rijpma, 1992). Because the expanded research agenda previously recommended would allow researchers to identify other distressing reactions to treatment, behavioral interventions should be developed to help in controlling them. In addition to the direct advantages of gaining control over symptoms, patients who perceive themselves as having control are likely to experience better adjustment overall (Thompson, Sobolew-Shubin, Galbraith, Schwankovsky, & Cruzen, 1993).

Enhancing Coping

Researchers have identified coping strategies and styles that are associated with better adjustment and less emotional distress among cancer patients.

The most promising among these appear to be seeking and using social support, and being optimistic/focusing on the positive (for example, Carver et al., 1994; Dunkel-Schetter, Feinstein, Taylor, & Falke, 1992). There is some indication that the effectiveness of counseling (Greer et al., 1992) and social support (Fawzy et al., 1990a) interventions may result in part from enhancing these adaptive coping responses. More research is needed to determine the extent to which effective patterns of coping can be taught to patients through cost-effective interventions. We also need to determine if the same coping patterns and interventions would be optimally effective with multicultural patient populations. Coping may interact with aspects of cultural background in predicting adjustment.

There is some evidence from controlled investigations that psychotherapeutic interventions may improve medical, as well as psychosocial, outcomes (Richardson, Shelton, Krailo, & Levine, 1990; Spiegel, Bloom, Kraemer, & Gottheil, 1989). Researchers have suggested several explanations for this phenomenon, including increased adherence to medical recommendations and enhanced coping. Others have demonstrated links between immune activity, and both support group participation (Fawzy et al., 1990b) and active seeking of social support (Levy et al., 1990). Identifying the mechanisms by which coping may influence immune system functioning and other biological processes is a particularly intriguing area for future research. (See Andersen, Kiecolt-Glaser, & Glaser, 1994 for a review and proposal for a biobehavioral model for understanding the role of stress on disease course.)

Improving the Delivery of Medical Services

Research is needed to identify changes in the delivery of medical care that might increase quality of life and willingness to adhere to medical recommendations among women with cancer. Previous research has indicated that patients tend to be dissatisfied with the information they receive about treatment and symptom control (Wiggers, Donovan, Redman, & Sanson-Fisher, 1990), and that difficulties in patient–physician communication are common and disturbing (Lerman et al., 1993). Brief and inexpensive interventions that prepare patients for treatment can significantly decrease distress and improve coping (Burish, Snyder, & Jenkins,

1991). More information is needed about individual and cultural differences in preferred modes of communication and levels of knowledge.

CONCLUSIONS

In our survey of research about women and cancer, we found tendencies consistent with stereotypic categorizations of men and women, emphasizing functional capacities in men and body image and feelings in women. Much of what we know about women with cancer is about women with breast cancer. However, there is great variety in the types of cancer women contract and in the ways that they react to these cancers. For example, some women criticize a lack of attention to body image and disfigurement and other women are offended by a focus on women's bodies. This diversity of opinion is apparent now as women take an active role in trying to direct the federal research agenda on prevention of cancer in women. Women have strongly criticized the medical community for failing to conduct research on prevention of breast cancer. However, now that a large trial of tamoxifen as a possible preventive agent for high-risk women has been mounted, concern has been expressed about the use of women as guinea pigs in medical trials (Davidson, 1992).

So, what have we concluded about women and cancer? We conclude that there is no "woman's reaction." Different women have different opinions and concerns. Researchers should not try to simplify this complexity and diversity, and must instead try to avoid limiting their focus on the basis of preconceptions about either women or men. We are not suggesting that anything about women be studied less, but rather that everything should be studied. The ultimate goals of this endeavor can be both to understand the complexity of women and cancer, and to provide individual women and men with the information needed to make informed choices in their own best interests.

REFERENCES

American Cancer Society. (1983). *Cancer facts and figures—1983*. New York, NY: Author.

American Cancer Society. (1992). *Cancer facts and figures—1992*. Atlanta, GA: Author.

American Cancer Society. (1994). *Cancer facts and figures—1994*. Atlanta, GA: Author.

Andersen, B. L. (1992). Psychological interventions for cancer patients to enhance the quality of life. *Journal of Consulting and Clinical Psychology, 60,* 552–568.

Andersen, B. L., Kiecolt-Glaser, J. K., & Glaser, R. (1994). A biobehavioral model of cancer stress and disease course. *American Psychologist, 49,* 389–404.

Anstice, E. (1970). Coping after a mastectomy. *Nursing Times, 66,* 882–883.

Bain, R. P., Greenberg, R. S., & Whitaker, J. P. (1986). Racial differences in survival of women with breast cancer. *Journal of Chronic Diseases, 39,* 631–642.

Biesecker, B. B., Boehnke, M., Calzone, K., Markel, D. S., Garber, J. E., Collins, F. S., & Weber, B. L. (1993). Genetic counseling for families with inherited susceptibility to breast and ovarian cancer. *Journal of the American Medical Association, 269,* 1970–1974.

Bloom, J., Fobair, P., Gritz, E. R., Wellisch, D., Spiegel, D., Varghese, E., & Hope, R. (1993). Psychosocial outcomes of cancer: A comparative analysis of Hodgkin's disease and testicular cancer. *Journal of Clinical Oncology, 11,* 979–988.

Bloom, J. R., Hoppe, R. T., Fobair, P., Cox, R. S., Varghese, A., & Spiegel, D. (1988). Effects of treatment on the work experiences on long-term survivors of Hodgkin's Disease. *Journal of Psychosocial Oncology, 6*(3/4), 65–80.

Brady, J. (1991). The goose and the golden egg. In J. Brady (Ed.), *1 in 3 women with cancer confront an epidemic* (pp. 13–35). Pittsburgh, PA: Cleis Press.

Burish, T. G., Snyder, S. L., & Jenkins, R. A. (1991). Preparing patients for cancer chemotherapy: Effects of coping preparation and relaxation interventions. *Journal of Consulting and Clinical Psychology, 59,* 518–525.

Carey, M. P., & Burish, T. G. (1988). Etiology and treatment of the psychological side effects associated with cancer chemotherapy: A critical review and discussion. *Psychological Bulletin, 104,* 307–325.

Carver, C. S., Pozo-Kaderman, C., Harris, S. D., Noriega, V., Scheier, M. F., Robinson, D. S., Ketcham, A. S., Moffat, F. L., & Clark, K. C. (1994). Optimism versus pessimism predicts the quality of women's adjustment to early stage breast cancer. *Cancer, 73,* 1213–1220.

Clancy, C. M., & Massion, C. T. (1992). American women's health care: A patchwork quilt with gaps. *Journal of the American Medical Association, 268,* 1918–1920.

Davidson, N. E. (1992). Tamoxifen—panacea or Pandora's box? *The New England Journal of Medicine, 326,* 885–886.

Dean, C. (1987). Psychiatric morbidity following mastectomy: Preoperative predictors and types of illness. *Journal of Psychosomatic Research, 31,* 385–392.

Derogatis, L. R. (1980). Breast and gynecologic cancers: Their unique impact on body image and sexual identity in women. *Frontiers of Radiation Therapy and Oncology, 14,* 1–11.

Dunkel-Schetter, C., Feinstein, L. G., Taylor, S. E., & Falke, R. L. (1992). Patterns of coping with cancer. *Health Psychology, 11,* 79–87.

Ell, K., Nishimoto, R., Morvay, T., Mantell, J., & Hamovitch, M. (1989). A longitudinal analysis of psychological adaptation among survivors of cancer. *Cancer, 63,* 406–413.

Farrow, D. C., Hunt, W. C., & Samet, J. M. (1992). Geographic variation in the treatment of localized breast cancer. *New England Journal of Medicine, 326,* 1097–1101.

Fawzy, F. I., Cousins, N., Fawzy, N. W., Kemeny, M. E., Elashoff, R., & Morton, D. (1990a). A structured psychiatric intervention for cancer patients. *Archives of General Psychiatry, 47,* 720–725.

Fawzy, F. I., Cousins, N., Fawzy, N. W., Kemeny, M. E., Elashoff, R., & Morton, D. (1990b). A structured psychiatric intervention for cancer patients: II. Changes over time in immunology measures. *Archives of General Psychiatry, 47,* 729–735.

Fisher, B., Bauer, M., Margolese, R., Poisson, R., Pilch, Y., Redmond, C., Fisher, E., Wolmark, N., Deutsch, M., Montague, E., Saffer, E., Wickerham, L., Lerner, H., Glass, A., Shibata, H., Deckers, P., Ketzham, A., Oishi, R., & Russel, I. (1985). Five years of a randomized clinical trial comparing total mastectomy and segmental mastectomy with or without radiation in the treatment of breast cancer. *New England Journal of Medicine, 312,* 665–673.

Ganz, P. A. (1993). Age and gender as factors in cancer therapy. *Clinics in Geriatric Medicine, 9*(1), 145–155.

Ganz, P. A., Schag, C. A. C., & Heinrich, R. L. (1985). The psychosocial impact of cancer on the elderly: Is there a difference? *Journal of the American Geriatric Society, 33,* 429–435.

Ganz, P. A., Schag, C. A. C., Lee, J. J., Polinsky, M. L., & Tan, S. (1992). Breast conservation versus mastectomy. *Cancer, 69,* 1729–1738.

Greer, S., Moorey, S., Baruch, J. D. R., Watson, M., Robertson, B. M., Mason, A., Rowden, L., Law, M. G., & Bliss, J. M. (1992). Adjuvant psychological therapy for patients with cancer: A prospective randomised trial. *British Medical Journal, 304*, 675–680.

Gritz, E. R., Wellisch, D. K., Siau, J., & Wang, H. J. (1990). Long-term effects of testicular cancer on marital relationships. *Psychosomatics. 31*, 301–312.

Hannum, J. W., Giese-Davis. J., Harding, K., & Hatfield, A. K. (1991). Effects of individual and marital variables on coping with cancer. *Journal of Psychosocial Oncology, 9*(2), 1–20.

Harding, S. (Ed.). (1987). *Feminism and methodology.* Bloomington, IN: Indiana University.

Holland, J. C. & Rowland, J. H. (Eds.) (1989). *The handbook of psychooncology.* New York: Oxford University.

Kiebert, G. M., de Haes, J. C. J. M, & van de Velde, C. J. H. (1991). The impact of breast-conserving treatment and mastectomy on the quality of life of early-stage breast cancer patients: A review. *Journal of Clinical Oncology, 9*, 1059–1070.

King, M.-C., Rowell, S., & Love, S. M. (1993). Inherited breast and ovarian cancer: What are the risks? What are the choices? *Journal of the American Medical Association, 269*, 1975–1980.

Kune, G. A., Kune, S., & Watson, L. F. (1989). Children, age at first birth, and colorectal cancer risk: Data from the Melbourne colorectal cancer study. *American Journal of Epidemiology, 129*, 533–542.

La Vecchia, C., Negri, E., & Franceschi, S. (1992). Education and cancer risk. *Cancer, 70*, 2935–2941.

Lee, J. (1991). Everyday aids and appliances. *British Medical Journal, 302*, 43–44.

Lerman, C., Daly, M., Masny, A., & Balshem, A. (1994). Attitudes about genetic testing for breast–ovarian cancer susceptibility. *Journal of Clinical Oncology, 12*, 843–850.

Lerman, C., Daly, M., Walsh, W. P., Resch, N., Seay, J., Barsevick, A., Birenbaum, L., Heggan, T., & Martin, G. (1993). Communication between patients with breast cancer and health care providers: Determinants and implications. *Cancer, 72*, 2612–2620.

Levenson, J. L., & Bemis, C. (1991). The role of psychological factors in cancer onset and progression. *Psychosomatic Medicine, 32*, 124–132.

Levy, S. M., Herberman, R. B., Whiteside, T., Sanzo, K., Lee, J., & Kirkwood, J. (1990). Perceived social support and tumor estrogen/progesterone receptor status as predictors of natural killer cell activity in breast cancer patients. *Psychosomatic Medicine, 52*, 73–85.

Lorde, A. (1980). *The cancer journals.* San Francisco: Spinsters/Aunt Lute.

Magid, D. M., & Golomb, H. (1989). Effects of employment on coping with chronic illness among patients with hairy cell leukemia. *Journal of Psychosocial Oncology, 7*(1/2), 1–17.

Makuc, D. M., Freid, V. M., & Kleinman, J. C. (1989). National trends in the use of preventive health care by women. *American Journal of Public Health, 79,* 21–26.

Marshall, E. (1993). Search for a killer: Focus shifts from fat to hormones. *Science, 259,* 618–621.

Marwick, C. (1992). Women's health action plan sees first anniversary. *Journal of the American Medical Association, 268,* 1816–1817, 1821.

Maunsell, E., Brisson, J., & Deschênes, L. (1992). Psychological distress after initial treatment of breast cancer: Assessment of potential risk factors. *Cancer, 70,* 120–125.

Mendelsohn, G. A. (1990). Psychosocial adaptation to illness by women with breast cancer and women with cancer at other sites. *Journal of Psychosocial Oncology, 8*(4), 1–25.

Meyerowitz, B. E., Chaiken, S., & Clark, L. K. (1988). Sex roles and culture: Social and personal reactions to breast cancer. In M. Fine & A. Asch (Eds.), *Women with disabilities: Essays in psychology, culture, and politics* (pp. 72–89). Philadelphia: Temple University Press.

Morris, D. L., Lusero, G. T., Joyce, E. V., Hannigan, E. V., & Tucker, E. R. (1989). Cervical cancer, a major killer of hispanic women: Implications for health education. *Health Education, 20*(5), 23–28.

Morris, J., & Ingham, R. (1988). Choice of surgery for early breast cancer: Psychosocial considerations. *Social Science and Medicine, 27,* 1257–1262.

Nattinger, A. B., Gottlieb, M. S., Veum, J., Yahnke, D., & Goodwin, J. S. (1992). Geographic variation in the use of breast-conserving treatment for breast cancer. *The New England Journal of Medicine, 326,* 1102–1107.

Padilla, G. V., Grant, M. M., Lipsett, J., Anderson, P. R., Rhiner, M., & Bogen, C. (1992). Health quality of life and colorectal cancer. *Cancer, 70*(Suppl.), 1450–1456.

Pendleton, L., & Smith, A. (1986, June 4). Provision of breast prostheses. *Nursing Times, 82,* 37–39.

Peters, R. K., Thomas, D., Hagan, D. O., Mack, T. M., & Henderson, B. E. (1986). Risk factors for invasive cervical cancer among Latinas and non-Latinas in Los Angeles County. *Journal of National Cancer Institute, 77,* 1063–1077.

Peters-Golden, H. (1982). Breast cancer: Varied perceptions of social support in the illness experience. *Social Science and Medicine, 16,* 482–491.

Pierce, L., Fowble, B., Solin, L. J., Schultz, D. J., Rosser, C., & Goodman, R. L. (1992). Conservative surgery and radiation therapy in black women with early stage breast cancer. *Cancer, 69,* 2831–2841.

Pinn, V. W. (1992). Women's health research: Prescribing change and addressing the issues. *Journal of the American Medical Association, 268,* 1921–1922.

Psychological Aspects of Breast Cancer Study Group. (1987). Psychological response to mastectomy: A prospective comparison study. *Cancer, 59,* 189–196.

Public Health Service. (1992). *Health United States 1991 and prevention profile* (DDHS Publication No. PHS 92-1232). Hyattsville, MD: U.S. Government Printing Office.

Reddy, D. M., & Alagna, S. W. (1986). Psychological aspects of cancer prevention and early detection among women. In B. L. Andersen (Ed.), *Women with cancer: Psychological perspectives* (pp. 93–137). New York: Springer–Verlag.

Richardson, J. L., Shelton, D. R., Krailo, M., & Levine, A. M. (1990). The effect of compliance with treatment on survival among patients with hematologic malignancies. *Journal of Clinical Oncology, 8,* 356–364.

Royak-Schaler, R. (1991). Psychological processes in breast cancer: A review of selected research. *Journal of Psychosocial Oncology, 9*(4), 71–89.

Schag, C. A. C., Ganz, P. A., Polinsky, M. L. , Fred, C., Hirji, K., & Petersen, L. (1993). Characteristics of women at risk for psychosocial distress in the year after breast cancer. *Journal of Clinical Oncology, 11,* 783–793.

Selikoff, I. J. (1976). Lung cancer and mesothelioma during prospective surveillance of 1249 asbestos insulation workers, 1963–1974. *Annals of the New York Academy of Science, 271,* 448–456.

Senie, R. T., Rosen, P. P., Rhodes, P., & Lesser, M. L. (1991). Timing of breast cancer excision during the menstrual cycle influences duration of disease-free survival. *Annals of Internal Medicine, 115,* 337–342.

Sneed, N. V., Edlund, B., & Dias, J. K. (1992). Adjustment of gynecological and breast cancer patients to the cancer diagnosis; comparisons with males and females having other cancer sites. *Health Care for Women International, 13,* 11–22.

Spiegel, D., Bloom, J. R., Kraemer, H. C., & Gottheil, E. (1989). Effect of psychosocial treatment on survival of patients with metastatic breast cancer. *Lancet,* 888–891.

Stalker, M. Z., Johnson, P. S., & Cimma, C. (1989). Supportive activities requested by survivors of cancer. *Journal of Psychosocial Oncology, 7*(4), 21–31.

Stanton, A. L., & Snider, P. R. (1993). Coping with a breast cancer diagnosis: A prospective study. *Health Psychology, 12,* 16–23.

Tanner, R., Abraham, S. F., & Llewellyn-Jones, D. (1983). External breast prostheses: A survey of their use by women after mastectomy. *The Medical Journal of Australia, 1,* 270–272.

Taylor, S. E., Lichtman, R. R., & Wood, J. V. (1984). Attributions, beliefs about cancer, and adjustment to breast cancer. *Journal of Personality and Social Psychology, 46,* 489–502.

Thompson, S. C., Sobolew-Shubin, A., Galbraith, M. E., Schwankovsky, L., & Cruzen, D. (1993). Maintaining perceptions of control: Finding perceived control in low-control circumstances. *Journal of Personality and Social Psychology, 64,* 293–304.

Trijsburg, R. W., van Knippenberg, F. C. E., & Rijpma, S. E. (1992). Effects of psychological treatment on cancer patients: A critical review. *Psychosomatic Medicine, 54,* 489–517.

Trill, M. D., & Holland, J. (1993). Cross-cultural differences in the care of patients with cancer: A review. *General Hospital Psychiatry, 15,* 21–30.

Ulrich's International Periodicals Directory. (1994). New Providence, NJ: Reed Reference.

Vogel, V. G., Yeomans, A., & Higginbotham, E. (1993). Clinical management of women at increased risk for breast cancer. *Breast Cancer Research and Treatment, 28,* 195–210.

Wells, B. L., & Horm, J. W. (1992). Stage at diagnosis in breast cancer: Race and socioeconomic factors. *American Journal of Public Health, 82,* 1383–1385.

Wiggers, J. H., Donovan, K. O., Redman, S., & Sanson-Fisher, R. W. (1990). Cancer patient satisfaction with care. *Cancer, 66,* 610–616.

Zemore, R., Rinholm, J., Shepel, L. F., & Richards, M. (1989). Some social and emotional consequences of breast cancer and mastectomy: A content analysis of 87 interviews. *Journal of Psychosocial Oncology, 7*(4), 33–45.

4

Women With Diabetes: A Lifestyle Perspective Focusing on Eating Disorders, Pregnancy, and Weight Control

Betsy A. Butler and Rena R. Wing

INTRODUCTION

It is estimated that there are 6 million Americans with diagnosed diabetes mellitus, and probably an equal number who have the disease but do not know it (Harris, 1993). Diabetes mellitus is an endocrine disorder characterized by an inability to metabolize glucose. It is the seventh leading cause of death in the United States. Diabetes is associated with heart disease and is a major cause of kidney disease, amputations, and blindness. Recent data suggest that the direct and indirect costs of diabetes and its complications exceed $20 billion per year (Songer, 1992).

There are three major types of diabetes—insulin-dependent diabetes mellitus (IDDM) or Type I diabetes, which affects about 500,000 Americans; non-insulin dependent diabetes mellitus (NIDDM) or Type II diabetes, which is more prevalent, affecting over 5 million Americans; and gestational diabetes mellitus (GDM), which is diabetes that has its onset during pregnancy, after which it usually remits.

Insulin-Dependent Diabetes Mellitus

IDDM is usually diagnosed in individuals less than 30 years old. Individuals with IDDM are not able to produce insulin, which is required to enable the body to utilize glucose. Thus, they must give themselves insulin injections in order to survive. The amount of insulin and timing of injections must be coordinated with dietary intake and exercise. If these are not well balanced, the level of glucose in the blood can become too high or low. When blood glucose levels are too high, symptoms include intense thirst and hunger, and increased frequency of urination. On the other hand, when blood glucose levels fall below normal levels, the patient experiences symptoms of hypoglycemia, including trembling, sweating, headache, or confusion. Chronically uncontrolled glucose levels increase the risk of long-term complications including blindness; kidney disease; nerve disease (often involving pain or lack of sensation in the lower limbs, gangrene, or disturbances in the gastrointestinal autonomic nervous system); and coronary heart disease.

The treatment of IDDM has evolved in recent years to a point where the goal of therapy is not merely to prevent extremely high or extremely low blood glucose levels, but rather to maintain blood glucose as close to nondiabetic levels as possible. Several developments have led to this change. First, it has become possible for individuals with diabetes to accurately measure their own blood glucose levels (self-monitoring of blood glucose or SMBG). Second, a blood test is now available that indicates the overall level of blood glucose control during the most recent 2 to 3 months. This measure is called *glycosylated hemoglobin* (or HbA_1). Finally, a recent study, the Diabetes Control and Complications Trial (DCCT), demonstrated that maintaining blood glucose control as close to normal as possible was effective in delaying the onset of diabetic complications and decreasing the chance that complications will develop (DCCT Research Group, 1993).

Based on these developments, patients with diabetes are often treated with *intensive insulin therapy,* which requires multiple injections each day (i.e., 3 or more) or use of an *insulin infusion pump,* a device that delivers insulin continuously through an indwelling subcutaneous needle. The basic daily tasks of intensive insulin therapy are substantial. The patient self-monitors blood glucose before each meal. About 30 minutes before eating, she injects herself with insulin, after determining the correct dosage based on the current glucose level and the amount of food to be eaten. Meals are either prescribed to be consistent in carbohydrate, fat, and protein content from day to day, or the patient calculates the amount of glucose that will be produced by the meal and determines the appropriate insulin dosage. Daily exercise is important in maintaining normal glucose levels, but exercise lowers glucose levels, so it must be coordinated with meals and insulin to prevent hypoglycemia. The patient must be aware of the symptoms of low blood glucose, and must always carry a source of glucose, such as fruit juice or tablets of glucose. Thus, diabetes management places many demands on the patient, and adherence to this complex self-care regimen requires major behavioral changes to balance the many factors that affect blood glucose levels, including diet, exercise, and insulin.

In addition to the increased self-care demands on the patient, the efforts to maintain blood glucose at normal levels also increase the risk of hypoglycemia, the cost of medical supplies, and the possibility of weight gain due to the improvement in glucose metabolism. However, the benefits of intensive therapy—prevention or delay of diabetic complications—are believed to outweigh these risks.

Non-Insulin Dependent Diabetes Mellitus

NIDDM is usually diagnosed in adults, and in 60–80% of patients is accompanied by obesity (Fajans, 1990). NIDDM occurs disproportionately in minority groups; while 6% of Caucasians aged 20–74 have NIDDM, this disease affects approximately 10% of African Americans, 13% of Mexican Americans, and 30% of American Pima Indians in the same age group (Harris, 1991). Individuals with NIDDM are usually able to produce insulin, but there is resistance to the effects of insulin, resulting in elevated blood glucose levels. Insulin resistance can be reduced by decreasing dietary fat consumption, increasing exercise, and most important, by losing weight. However, these lifestyle interventions are often supplemented with oral hypoglycemic agents or insulin to improve glycemic control in individuals with NIDDM. In addition, some NIDDM patients monitor their glucose levels at home. NIDDM patients who use insulin often require less intense regimens than IDDM patients, because their bodies are still producing insulin. However, individuals with NIDDM are at risk for the same symptoms of high blood sugar and long-term complications of diabetes as described for IDDM.

Gestational Diabetes Mellitus

GDM is diabetes that has its onset during pregnancy. GDM occurs in 2–3% of the 3 million (or 90,000) women who give birth each year in the United States (Freinkel, Phelps, & Metzger, 1990). The rate is further increased in racial/ethnic-minority women and in those who are obese (Dooley, Metzger, & Cho, 1991). Control of blood glucose levels during pregnancy is very important to prevent complication to the baby and to prevent complications in delivery. GDM usually remits shortly after delivery, but women who develop GDM are at increased risk of developing NIDDM later in life (O'Sullivan, 1991).

Women and Diabetes

Diabetes affects men and women in similar proportions. In some studies, NIDDM has been shown to occur more frequently in women than men (Ostrander & Butler, 1982), but this usually reflects greater obesity among the women (Wing, Nowalk, & Guare, 1988). However, there are several aspects of diabetes that are of particular relevance to women. Three of these areas were selected as the focus of this chapter: the possible association between diabetes and eating disorders, the relationship between diabetes and pregnancy, and strategies for more effective weight-loss interventions in overweight women with NIDDM. Although there are many other aspects of diabetes that are relevant to women's health—such as the association of diabetes and depression, sexual problems in women with diabetes, and family issues surrounding diabetes—we have chosen to focus on the previously mentioned topics more thoroughly, rather than include all possible topics. Each topic will be presented and discussed in a developmental order: We begin with eating disorders, which are most common in adolescence and early adulthood; proceed to pregnancy; and end with weight loss and NIDDM, which is typically diagnosed in women older than 45 years.

EATING DISORDERS AND IDDM

From 1960 through the 1980s, there were numerous case reports of adolescents with diabetes who later developed eating disorders (see Marcus & Wing, 1990). These reports clearly documented the complexity of managing the two problems when they co-occurred, and their extremely negative effects on glycemic control and diabetic complications. These case studies raised the important question of whether eating disorders are more prevalent in diabetic subjects than in the general population, and if so, whether there are some aspects of the diabetic regimen that predispose patients to eating disorders. There was also concern about the effects of disordered eating on glycemic control in diabetic women. Recent research on these issues will be reviewed.

Diagnostic Criteria for Eating Disorders

The two major eating disorders are *anorexia nervosa* and *bulimia nervosa*. Anorexia nervosa is characterized by a low body weight, fear of gaining weight, disturbance in concept of body shape or weight, and amenorrhea (American Psychiatric Association, 1994). In the new revised *DSM–IV*, anorexia nervosa is divided into two types: *restricting anorexia* and *binge eating/purging anorexia*. The latter group of patients report binge eating during anorexic episodes, while those with the restricting type of anorexia do not. Estimates of the prevalence of anorexia among adolescent and young adult women range from 0.01 to 0.7% (Robins et al., 1984; Szmukler, 1985).

Bulimia nervosa is characterized by binge eating, lack of control over binge eating behavior, compensatory behaviors, and overconcern with shape and weight (American Psychiatric Association, 1994). In the *DSM–IV*, bulimia nervosa is divided into two types: *purging* and *nonpurging*. Patients with the purging type of bulimia nervosa use vomiting, laxatives, or diuretics as compensatory behaviors, and nonpurging bulimics use other compensatory behaviors, such as exercise or fasting. Bulimia nervosa is more common than anorexia nervosa, with reported rates ranging from 0.9% to 19% (Fairburn & Beglin, 1990) and the actual rate generally estimated as 5% (Johnson, Lewis, & Hagman, 1984; Johnson, Lewis, Love, Lewis, & Stuckey, 1984).

Vulnerability to Eating Disorders in IDDM Patients

Anorexia nervosa and bulimia nervosa are both more prevalent in women than men. In a comparative study (King, 1987), 0.5% of the males were diagnosed with an eating disorder, compared with 1.1% of the women. Both eating disorders usually begin in adolescence or young adulthood. Thus, studies of eating disorders in diabetic patients have focused on adolescent and young-adult females with IDDM, the groups at greatest risk. NIDDM patients are less at risk for these eating disorders because they are typically middle-aged, but a third eating disorder, *binge eating disorder,* is of particular concern in obese NIDDM patients, and is discussed in this chapter's section on obesity and NIDDM.

Two aspects of the diabetic regimen have been hypothesized to increase vulnerability to eating disorders in IDDM patients: dietary restraint and weight gain with insulin therapy. Polivy and Herman and their colleagues have proposed that binge eating results from a restrained eating style (i.e., chronic dieting) and the associated feelings of deprivation (Polivy & Herman, 1985; Polivy, Herman, Olmsted, & Jazwinski, 1984). Similarly, it has been suggested that the diabetic regimen, which places a great deal of emphasis on the types and quantity of foods consumed, may increase restraint and place the diabetic at risk for developing an eating disorder (Marcus & Wing, 1990; Stancin, Link, & Reuter, 1989).

Several studies have found that IDDM patients weigh significantly more than controls (Peveler, Fairburn, Boller, & Dunger, 1992; Steel, Young, Lloyd, & MacIntyre, 1989) and that insulin therapy leads to weight gain. A prospective study of 17 female IDDM patients found an average weight gain of 6.9 kg during the first year of insulin therapy, pushing all 17 women over their preferred weight (Steel, Lloyd, Young, & MacIntyre,

1990). Thus, the tendency to gain weight on insulin therapy may lead IDDM patients to search for ways to lose weight, such as binge eating without increasing insulin appropriately, which allows the extra calories to spill out in the urine, and vomiting.

Prevalence Research

The initial research on the prevalence of eating disorders in IDDM used self-report questionnaires to assess eating disorder symptomatology. These studies supported the conjecture that eating disorders are more frequent in IDDM than in the general population. High levels of eating disorder symptomatology were reported in 1.4% to 35% of IDDM patients (Birk & Spencer, 1989; Hudson, Wentworth, Hudson, & Pope, 1985; La Greca, Schwarz, & Satin, 1987; Powers, Malone, Coovert, & Schulman, 1990; Rodin, Craven, Littlefield, Murray, & Daneman, 1991; Rodin, Johnson, Garfinkel, Daneman, & Kenshole, 1986; Stancin et al., 1989; Steel, Young, Lloyd, & Clarke, 1987). These reported rates far exceeded the rates reported for the general population.

However, there were several problems with these studies. Most notable was the problem of using self-report questionnaires that classify behaviors appropriate for diabetes management as symptomatic of eating disorders. For example, the commonly used EAT-40 (Garner & Garfinkel, 1979) includes a question about avoiding foods with sugar, which is reasonable behavior for diabetic patients but can be associated with an eating disorder in nondiabetic subjects. Other problems with these early studies were lack of a nondiabetic control group and use of *DSM–III* criteria for diagnosis, which are less stringent and less objective than *DSM–III–R* criteria.

In contrast, more recent studies using more sophisticated methodology have found few differences in the prevalence of eating disorders in IDDM patients versus nondiabetic controls. Three recent studies have used the Eating Disorders Examination (EDE; Cooper, Cooper, & Fairburn, 1989)—a structured clinical interview that is the "gold standard" for eating disorder diagnosis—and compared individuals with IDDM to matched nondiabetic control groups. These studies found no differences in eating disorder symptomatology or in diagnosable eating disorders between IDDM patients and controls (Fairburn, Peveler, Davies, Mann, & Mayou, 1991; Peveler et al., 1992; Striegel-Moore, Nicholson, & Tamborlane, 1992).

Based on these studies, it seems appropriate to conclude that there probably is no difference in the rate of eating disorders in IDDM patients and matched controls. It should be noted, however, that these studies have relatively small sample sizes. Considering that the base rate of both eating disorders and IDDM is quite low, there is need for a definitive, large-sample study with appropriate statistical power to confirm whether or not IDDM increases the prevalence of eating disorders.

Subclinical Eating Disorders, Insulin Manipulation, and Glycemic Control

Although recent studies suggest that rates of eating disorders are not greater among IDDM patients than in the general population, there is still reason for concern regarding these problems because both clinical and subclinical eating problems strongly impact on glycemic control. Even small additions to an IDDM patient's diet that are not compensated for with additional insulin may cause elevated blood glucose levels. La Greca et al. (1987) found that 85% of female IDDM patients reported occasional binge eating, and Stancin et al. (1989) found that 17% of female IDDM patients reported binge eating at least once per week. Again, rates of sub-clinical eating disorders appear comparable in IDDM patients and non-diabetic controls (Robertson & Rosenvinge, 1990). However, subclinical eating disorders in IDDM patients are associated with poor glycemic control. For example, Wing, Nowalk, Marcus, Koeske, and Finegold (1986) found that level of eating disorder symptomatology was associated with glycemic control; patients with moderately elevated scores on the Binge Eating Scale had significant elevations in HbA_1 levels, indicating poor glycemic control over the previous 2 to 3 months. Similarly, La Greca and colleagues (1987) found that IDDM patients in good glycemic control reported 1.16 binge episodes per month, patients in fair control reported 7.0 episodes, and those in poor glycemic control reported 12.7 binge episodes per month.

In addition, some IDDM patients have discovered a particularly dangerous way to lose weight: manipulating insulin to intentionally worsen their glycemic control. Realizing that insulin injections are required to allow their body to use the food they eat, some patients omit or reduce their insulin, or fail to supplement their usual dose to accommodate binge episodes. Thus, glucose builds up in the blood, is filtered out by the kidneys, and the extra calories are eliminated in the urine. Insulin manipulation was described in 84% of early case studies of IDDM patients with eating disorders (Marcus & Wing, 1990). Insulin misuse has also been reported in IDDM patients not diagnosed with an eating disorder, with rates ranging from 6% (Rodin, Craven et al., 1991) to 18% (Birk & Spencer, 1989). In the *DSM–III–R*, IDDM patients who used insulin manipulation as their only compensatory behavior after binge eating could not be diagnosed with bulimia nervosa, but the *DSM–IV* criteria include use of "other medications," which allows for the bulimia nervosa diagnosis in such patients (American Psychiatric Association, 1994, p. 549).

Research Questions on Eating Disorders in IDDM

There are three research questions related to eating disorders in IDDM that we feel are of particular importance. The first is whether the increased concern about tight glycemic control in IDDM patients resulting from the findings of the DCCT study (DCCT Research Group, 1993) will affect the incidence of eating disorders in IDDM women. The DCCT study found that intensified diabetes treatment decreases the risk of long-term complications, but several studies have documented that tight glycemic control is associated with weight gain. In the DCCT, for example, patients went from 101.6% of ideal body weight at baseline to 109.2% after 1 year of intensive treatment (DCCT Research Group, 1988). This weight gain may be upsetting to women with IDDM and lead to increased efforts to lose weight via insulin manipulation. Likewise, the heightened emphasis on glycemic control may exacerbate concern with dietary intake and promote eating pathology. Alternatively, it can be argued that intensive insulin therapy provides patients with more flexibility in their dietary intake; they can adjust their insulin to match their planned meal. This flexibility could reduce eating disturbances in IDDM women. Thus, it will be very important to monitor the rates of eating disorder symptomatology in these patients as the approach to treatment changes.

Secondly, research is needed to develop better screening tools to detect clinical and subclinical eating disorders in IDDM patients. As noted above, current questionnaires include diabetes-appropriate behaviors as symptoms of an eating disorder. While it may be possible to disentangle these two in clinical interviews, simpler, less expensive techniques are needed for use in clinical settings to identify individuals with possible clinical and subclinical eating problems.

A third question that has received no research attention to date is the development of interventions for the treatment and prevention of eating disorders in IDDM patients. Cognitive–behavioral treatments and pharmacotherapy have been used for the treatment of anorexia nervosa and bulimia nervosa in nondiabetic subjects (Agras, 1987; Mitchell, Raymond, & Specker, 1993; Wilson & Fairburn, 1993) and in uncontrolled single case studies with diabetic subjects (Peveler & Fairburn, 1989; Peveler & Fairburn, 1992). To date, these approaches have not been systematically evaluated in patients with IDDM. There has also been some initial research on prevention of eating disorders in nondiabetic subjects. These studies have used cognitive–behavior therapy and body-size perception exercises to ameliorate body image distortions in females at high risk for the development of eating disorders (i.e., in those who demonstrate significant disturbance in body image; Rosen, Cado, Silberg, Srebnik, & Wendt, 1990). Similar prevention approaches should be applied to adolescent girls with IDDM.

PREGNANCY AND DIABETES

A second set of issues affecting women with diabetes are issues surrounding pregnancy. There are two situations in which pregnant women must cope with diabetes: (a) women with preexisting diabetes who become pregnant, and (b) women without diabetes who develop gestational diabetes during their pregnancy, which often remits postpartum. Diabetes is important in pregnancy because maternal glucose crosses the placenta.

High glucose levels during early pregnancy may cause malformations in fetal organ development. In later pregnancy, high glucose levels may cause the infant to be overweight (*macrosomia*), giving rise to problems with delivery, or may cause the fetus to compensate for the high blood glucose by producing high levels of insulin. This high insulin output may continue to be produced for up to 12 hours after birth, increasing the risk of neonatal hypoglycemia. In addition, normal glucose metabolism is disturbed during pregnancy even in nondiabetic women, with insulin resistance developing during later pregnancy (i.e., more insulin is needed to maintain normal glucose levels.) Women who are unable to secrete additional insulin may develop gestational diabetes, usually during the last trimester. This insulin resistance also increases insulin requirements in women with preexisting diabetes. Thus preexisting diabetes is a concern during the entire pregnancy, and gestational diabetes is a concern in later pregnancy. Different issues are involved in these two types of diabetes, and they will be discussed separately here.

Preexisting Diabetes and Pregnancy

Before the emphasis on good glycemic control, the risks of fetal and maternal morbidity and mortality were very high in diabetic pregnancies. For example, one study found a four-fold increase in the risk of congenital malformations in the infants of women with diabetes, with congenital heart defects and malformations of the central nervous system most prevalent (Landon & Gabbe, 1992). Macrosomia was found in 40–50% of infants born to diabetic mothers (Landon & Gabbe, 1992). Infants with macrosomia have normal size heads, but overweight bodies, which complicates delivery by increasing the risk of infant shoulder dislocation or asphyxia, and increases the need for cesarean section delivery. Consequently, in an attempt to reduce these risks, diabetic women have often been hospitalized during pregnancy for long periods of time to improve their glycemic control. As discussed in the introduction to this chapter, recent developments have improved diabetes care (e.g., self-monitoring of blood glucose, daily multiple insulin injections, and the HbA_1 assay to assess long-term glycemic control). With these developments, women with diabetes are now able to maintain good control throughout pregnancy without the need for hospitalization (Kitzmiller, 1993). Moreover, these techniques have allowed researchers to study the relationship between glycemic control and pregnancy complications. These studies have found that many of the complications of diabetic pregnancy occur prior to the seventh week of pregnancy, when vital fetal organs are forming (Mills, Baker, & Goldman, 1979), emphasizing the need to attain glycemic control prior to conception to reduce these complications.

Effect of Glycemic Control in the Early Months of Pregnancy and Preconception

Recent studies provide convincing evidence that improved glycemic control before conception and in early pregnancy can reduce the complications of diabetic pregnancies. For example, the Diabetes in Early Pregnancy Study examined the relationship between blood glucose levels and pregnancy complications in a multicenter observational study (no experimental intervention; Mills et al., 1983). One group of diabetic women was recruited before conception or within 21 days after conception and had glycemic control monitored throughout pregnancy; another group of diabetic women was recruited later in pregnancy. The malformation rate in infants of women who enrolled early was 4.9% versus 9.0% in infants of women who enrolled later. In nondiabetic controls, the rate was 2.1%. These results suggest that early care can reduce the rate of malformations.

In a recent preconception intervention study, Kitzmiller et al. (1991) compared the incidence of congenital malformations in infants born to diabetic women who began intensive treatment prior to conception and those who began treatment after they became pregnant (range = 6 to 32 weeks gestation). There were significantly fewer malformations in the preconception treatment condition (1.2% versus 10.9%), and these women had significantly lower HbA_1 levels at the first prenatal visit. For all women, the number of abnormalities was significantly associated with HbA_1 level, with 1.7% abnormalities in the lowest range of HbA_1 levels (indicating good glycemic control) and 25.0% for women with high HbA_1 levels (indicating poor glycemic control). Other preconception care studies are summarized in Table 1, and they convincingly argue the benefits of early preconception care.

Macrosomia and Glycemic Control in Later Pregnancy

Diabetic control throughout pregnancy, and particularly in late pregnancy, is also associated with improved outcomes and decreased risk of macrosomia. In the Diabetes in Early Pregnancy Study, macrosomia was present in 28.5% of infants of diabetic mothers versus 13.1% of infants of nondiabetic control mothers (Jovanovic-Peterson et al., 1991). The birth weight of infants was related to mothers' blood glucose levels after meals (when glucose levels are highest) and to her HbA$_1$ levels throughout pregnancy. This association was strongest for glucose levels after meals during the third trimester. Similar results were found by Combs, Gunderson, Kitzmiller, Gavin, and Main (1992); women whose infants had macrosomia reported significantly higher blood glucose levels after meals throughout pregnancy, and particularly during weeks 29–32.

Research Questions

The evidence that glycemic control is related to pregnancy outcome, and the need for good control in the very earliest weeks of pregnancy, raise

Table 1

Malformation Rates in Women Receiving Preconception Versus Postconception Care

Study	Preconception Care		Postconception Care		
	Total N	Malformation Rate	Total N	Malformation Rate	Significance
Furhmann et al., 1983	128	0.8%	292	7.5%	$p < .01$
Goldman et al., 1986	44	0.0%	31	9.6%	$p < .07$
Kitzmiller et al., 1991	84	1.2%	110	10.9%	$p = .01$
Steel et al., 1990	143	1.4%	96	10.4%	$p < .005$
Willhoite et al., 1993	62	1.6%	123	6.5%	none

several interesting areas of research for psychologists. First is the issue of getting women with diabetes to achieve good glycemic control prior to conceiving. The median time of the first prenatal visit in diabetic pregnancies has been eight weeks (as of 1984–1990; Gregory, Scott, Mohajer, & Tattersall, 1992). As previously noted, this is too late to avoid congenital malformations, which appear to be related to poor glycemic control during the first trimester. Efforts are needed to encourage women with diabetes to plan ahead for pregnancy and to use contraception until optimal glycemic control is achieved. There has been some controversy over the use of contraceptives in women with diabetes, because oral contraceptives may alter glucose metabolism and also increase risk of coronary heart disease, for which the diabetic woman is already at increased risk (Neinstein & Katz, 1986). Thus research in contraception use is even more critical.

Second, research is needed on ways to help diabetic patients maintain normal glucose levels throughout their pregnancies. Maintenance of normal glucose levels requires intensive self-care such as multiple daily injections, frequent monitoring of blood glucose, and meticulous attention to diet. This is particularly difficult during pregnancy because of the metabolic changes that women experience and problems such as vomiting during the first trimester. While it is often reported clinically that some women with diabetes adhere exceptionally well to this regimen during the 9 months of pregnancy, a recent review of the literature (Zayfert & Goetsch, 1992) raised questions about this assumption. These authors noted that adherence to blood glucose monitoring is rarely assessed in these studies. The notable exception is a study by Langer and Mazze (1986) in which 21 women with gestational diabetes and 13 women with pregestational diabetes monitored their blood glucose levels using meters with memory chips that recorded the time and blood glucose reading of each test. The women were studied from the 16th through the 39th gestational weeks and were asked to measure their glucose seven times per day. Results showed that 74% of subjects falsified blood glucose readings in their written diary; on average, 24% of the values recorded in the diary had not been determined by the meter. Likewise, 97% of the women omitted some readings from their self-report logs; on average, 23% of meter readings were omitted.

Moreover, the specific contribution of blood glucose monitoring to glucose control and pregnancy outcome are not well established. Retrospective studies suggest that blood glucose monitoring is associated with improved glycemic control, but two prospective randomized studies (Stubbs, Brudenell, Pyke, & Watkins, 1980; Varner, 1983) did not find differences in HbA_1 of pregnant diabetic women who were asked to self-monitor blood sugar versus those who monitored urine. In the Varner (1983) study, however, women who monitored blood glucose required fewer days in the hospital, thus reducing costs. Future research should focus not only on improving adherence to blood glucose monitoring, but also on teaching patients how to work with their physicians to effectively use the information obtained from blood glucose monitoring to modify other aspects of their diabetic regimen.

Gestational Diabetes

In the previous section, we discussed issues related to women with diabetes who become pregnant. There are also women who do not have diabetes prior to pregnancy, but who develop gestational diabetes (GDM) during the course of pregnancy.

GDM can have adverse effects both on the baby and the mother. Children of mothers with GDM have a 2 to 3-fold increased risk of macrosomia, and have an increased risk of later developing obesity and diabetes (Pettit et al., 1991; Silverman et al., 1991). Likewise, women with GDM are at increased risk of subsequently developing diabetes. Efforts to treat gestational diabetes are, therefore, needed.

GDM is usually diagnosed in later pregnancy, when insulin resistance is at its highest. At present, all women in the United States are screened for elevated blood glucose levels at 24–28 weeks gestation. Women whose blood glucose appears abnormal on this initial screen are then retested with a more intensive glucose tolerance test (Cousins et al., 1991). Those with elevated blood sugars are encouraged to self-monitor their glucose, to carefully watch their diet, and in some cases to start on insulin. Exercise also appears to be beneficial in maintaining normal blood sugar control. Evidence supporting each of these components of the GDM regimen is briefly described below.

Self-Monitoring of Blood Glucose

Evidence to support the use of SMBG comes from a study by Goldberg et al. (1986). One group of women was taught to monitor glucose before and after meals, whereas the control group members had their glucose measured only in the physician's office. All patients received diet therapy, and elevated blood glucose results were used as an indicator that insulin therapy should be initiated. Significantly more women were identified as needing insulin therapy in the SMBG group than in the control group (50% versus 21%, respectively). The mean weight of infants of women in the SMBG group was significantly less than in the control group, and less macrosomia was found in the SMBG group. Thus, women with gestational diabetes who are treated only with diet may benefit from performing SMBG in order to immediately identify the need for more intensive therapy.

Diet

Low-caloric diets are often used in patients with GDM because most of these women are overweight. However, there continues to be controversy about the use of such diets and the optimal level of calorie intake. The goal in treating women who develop diabetes during pregnancy is to achieve normal glucose levels, but to avoid the breakdown of fat into fatty acids called *ketones* because high levels of ketones in the blood are dangerous for the patient and the fetus. A recent study by Knopp and colleagues compared short periods of in-hospital caloric restriction and found evidence that reducing calorie intake by 33% produced normal glucose levels without *ketonuria* (presence of ketones in the urine), whereas a 50% reduction increased ketones (Knopp, Magee, Raisys, & Benedetti, 1991). Dornhurst et al. (1991) compared three groups of women: women with GDM who were treated with a low-calorie diet (1200–1800 kcal/day); women who had an abnormal initial GDM screening but were normal on the subsequent oral glucose tolerance test; and women who had normal screenings for GDM. The GDM women who were calorie-restricted fared comparably to the women with normal GDM screens and better than women who had abnormal screens and normal glucose tolerance tests. The calorie-restricted women gained less weight during pregnancy than both other groups, and had significantly less incidence of macrosomia than the women with abnormal screens. Thus, calorie restriction appeared to be beneficial to these women.

Exercise

Although exercise is a standard part of diabetes management, exercise has not been recommended as a treatment for GDM because some studies have suggested that exercise during pregnancy is associated with adverse effects, including lowering of fetal heart rate that indicates fetal distress, and increased uterine contractions that may induce premature labor (Jovanovic-Peterson & Peterson, 1992). However, because exercise is particularly effective in decreasing insulin resistance, recent studies have begun to investigate whether exercise may be useful in the treatment of women with GDM.

In a pilot study, Bung, Artal, Khodiguian and Kjos (1991) recruited women with GDM who did not have normal fasting blood glucose levels on diet treatment, and randomly assigned them to either exercise or standard insulin therapy. All women were sedentary prior to enrolling in the study, and bicycling was the prescribed activity. Exercise compliance was 90%, and women in the exercise group were able to attain normal glucose levels (94 mg/dl average blood glucose) similar to those of the insulin group (77 mg/dl). In each group, 11.7% experienced premature labor.

A 1990 study monitored uterine contractions in nondiabetic pregnant women during exercise on various machines (Durak, Jovanovic-Peterson, & Peterson, 1990). Bicycling resulted in uterine contractions 50% of the time, treadmill 40%, rowing machine 10%, and no contractions were associated with a recumbent bicycle or upper body exercise machine. Given the evidence that the latter types of exercise were particularly well suited for pregnant women, Jovanovic-Peterson and Peterson (1991) assigned women with GDM to an upper body exercise program or to a diet only. After six weeks, women in the exercise group had normal glucose levels both when fasting and after meals, and glycemic control in this group was significantly better than that in the diet group.

These studies suggest that exercise may be effective in maintaining glycemic control in women with GDM, with few adverse consequences to the fetus. However, exercise during pregnancy continues to be controversial, and should be implemented only under close medical supervision.

Insulin Treatment

Insulin therapy is recommended when standard diet therapy does not maintain normal fasting blood glucose levels (i.e., <106 mg/dl) and/or normal glucose levels two hours after meals (<120 mg/dl; Freinkel, 1985). However, recent research suggests that more aggressive use of insulin may further reduce the risks of macrosomia. Langer, Berkus, Brustman, Anyaegbunam, and Mazze (1991) found that women with GDM whose fasting blood glucose levels after a period of diet therapy were between 95 and 105 mg/dl had fewer complications if they were treated with insulin rather than diet only. At these moderately elevated glucose levels, the rate of macrosomia was 10.3% in infants of women treated with insulin, versus 28.6% in infants of women treated with diet. For women with fasting glucose levels less than 95 mg/dl, insulin therapy provided less benefit.

Coustan and Imarah (1984) compared pregnancy outcomes in women with GDM who (a) were treated by prophylactic insulin and diet; (b) were treated with diet only; and (c) received no treatment. Women in the prophylactic insulin group received insulin therapy regardless of fasting blood glucose level. Infants of mothers on insulin therapy weighed significantly less than others, with 7% macrosomia in the insulin condition versus 18.5% and 17.8% macrosomia in the diet and no-treatment conditions, respectively. However, it is important to note that condition was not random; rather, women were offered all treatments and were allowed to choose.

Research Questions

In the above review, we have noted several lifestyle interventions that appear beneficial in the treatment of GDM. We feel that additional controlled trials are needed to define the optimal level of caloric intake and the carbohydrate content of the diet, as well as the effect of exercise on ketone production. After identifying the ideal diet and exercise interventions, a large clinical trial is necessary to determine whether intensive lifestyle intervention and insulin therapy can reduce the acute perinatal abnormalities (such as macrosomia and neonatal hypoglycemia) and to determine the long-term effects of GDM on obesity and glucose intolerance in offspring.

In addition, a study by Ruggiero, Spirito, Bond, Coustan, and McGarvey (1990) found that adherence to diet and insulin regimens in patients with gestational diabetes treated with insulin was related to the level of social support. Low levels of stress ("hassles") were also related to adherence to the diet. More research is needed to determine whether social support is also related to regimen-adherence in women with preexisting diabetes who become pregnant, and to determine whether interventions to increase social support in pregnant women can improve adherence to the diabetic regimen and ultimately improve pregnancy outcomes.

Gestational diabetes is also an important risk factor for the subsequent development of diabetes in the mother. Although most women with GDM will return to normal glucose levels after pregnancy, even these women are at increased risk of developing GDM during subsequent pregnancies and of developing NIDDM in subsequent years. Although the literature on the conversion rates of GDM to NIDDM is difficult to summarize (due to differences in definitions of GDM and diabetes and in length of follow-up) it appears that approximately 5% of women with GDM will develop NIDDM each year. The risk of developing NIDDM is greatest in those with GDM who are also overweight (Metzger, Cho, Roston, & Radvany, 1993). To date, there have been no intervention studies to determine whether intensive lifestyle intervention (or perhaps lifestyle intervention plus drug treatment) can prevent the occurrence of GDM in subsequent pregnancies or reduce the risk of later NIDDM. Such research is clearly warranted.

OBESITY AND NIDDM

Among older women, the issues related to diabetes usually center around the treatment of obesity and NIDDM. The treatment of choice for obese patients with NIDDM is weight loss, because weight loss will improve glycemic control and reduce insulin resistance (Wing et al., 1987). Moreover, weight loss improves coronary heart disease risk factors, a benefit that may be of particular importance for women with NIDDM. Previous studies have shown that NIDDM entirely removes the female "advantage" in cardiovascular mortality; diabetic females have the same rate of mortality from coronary heart disease (CHD) as diabetic men (Kannel, 1978, 1982). Thus, efforts to improve CHD risk factors via weight loss may be particularly helpful for women with NIDDM. Moreover, in the United States, obesity is more prevalent in women than in men (Van Itallie, 1985), and more women enter treatment programs for their obesity. Thus, it is important to determine how best to treat obesity in women in general, and in those with diabetes in particular.

Weight Loss Strategies: Which Strategies Are More Effective For Women?

Three recent controlled studies have suggested that treatment interventions may be differentially effective for women versus men. One is a study by Wing and colleagues with 49 NIDDM patients (Wing, Marcus, Epstein, & Jawad, 1991). All participants had an overweight spouse who was also willing to participate in the treatment program. Participants were then randomly assigned to be treated alone or together with their overweight spouse. Subjects in the *alone* condition were given a standard 20-week behavioral treatment program. In the *together* condition, both the patient and spouse were targeted for weight loss—that is, both were taught to self-monitor their caloric intake; were given goals for weight, calorie intake, and exercise; and participated in all other aspects of the program. Moreover, in the *together* condition, both the patient and spouse were taught social support skills. Weight losses of patients treated alone or together did not differ significantly at posttreatment (19.9 versus 19.1 lb) or at 1 year follow-up (11.6 versus 7.0 lb). However, as shown in Figure 1, there was a significant interaction of treatment and gender; women did better when treated with their spouses whereas men did better when treated alone.

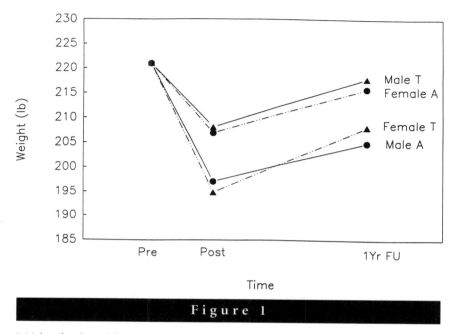

Figure 1

Weight of male and female patients in the together (T) and alone (A) conditions after adjusting for weight at baseline. Note: FU = follow up. Male T, $n = 8$; male A, $n = 10$; female T, $n = 12$; female A, $n = 13$.

This finding that women are more successful at weight loss when treated with their spouses deserves further investigation. Other studies of spouse support have typically used only female subjects, but a study by O'Neil et al. (1979) found no evidence that men and women differed in their response to a spouse-support intervention. It is unclear why different results were obtained in this study. Evidence that men and women may respond differentially to social support is also found in a study by Heitzmann and Kaplan (1984), where satisfaction with social support was associated with better glycemic control in women, but poorer control in men.

Another intervention that may be differentially effective for men and women is the combination of diet-plus-exercise versus diet-only. In a study of overweight nondiabetic men and women, Wood and colleagues (Wood, Stefanick, Williams, & Haskell, 1991) compared the effects of a diet low in calories, saturated fat, and cholesterol, used with or without exercise (walking and jogging). The subjects completing the 1-year study were 119 men and 112 women. In men, there was a significant difference between the diet-only and the diet-plus-exercise condition for weight-loss (-5.1 versus -8.7 kg) and fat-loss (-4.3 versus -7.8 kg). In contrast, among women, both interventions did better than a no-treatment control group, but diet-only and diet-plus-exercise produced similar weight losses (-4.1 versus -5.1 kg) and loss of fat weight (-4.0 versus -5.5).

Moreover, Wing et al. suggest that it is women who benefit most from very low calorie diets (VLCDs of less than 800 calories per day; Wing, Blair, Marcus, Epstein, & Harvey, 1994). In their study, 93 obese diabetic subjects were randomly assigned to a year-long behavioral treatment that used either a balanced 1000–1200 calorie/day diet throughout or included two 12-week periods of VLCD. The VLCD consisted of lean meat, fish, or fowl, with liquid formula used for occasional meals. In this study, men lost large amounts of weight on both treatment regimens with no difference between the two diets (-15.4 kg for VLCD versus -15.5 kg for low calorie diet); in contrast, for women, use of the VLCD markedly improved their weight loss (-14.1 kg on VLCD, versus -8.6 kg on low calorie diet, $p < .023$).

Additional research is needed to determine whether these gender differences are replicable across studies and if so, to begin to understand the mechanisms responsible for these differences. It may be that the most effective intervention for women is one that focuses more on the dietary aspects of obesity and uses social support to help maintain these changes.

Binge Eating Disorder

Obese women with NIDDM may also report significant problems with binge eating and may meet criteria for a new eating disorder named *binge eating disorder*, which is included in the appendix of the *DSM–IV*. Binge eating disorder is characterized by recurrent episodes of binge eating and feelings of loss of control, but not the compensatory techniques present in bulimia nervosa. Wing, Marcus, Epstein, Blair, and Burton (1989) examined the extent of binge eating among obese NIDDM patients presenting for treatment in a behavioral weight loss program and found that significantly more women than men had serious problems with binge eating (21% of females versus 9% of males). They found that binge eating was associated with depressive symptomatology, but was unrelated to glycemic control.[1] A previous study (Marcus, Wing, & Hopkins, 1988) indicated that binge eating in nondiabetic obese women affects response to weight loss treatments; although binge eaters lost weight at the same rate as nonbingers, the bingers were more likely to drop out of treatment and to regain weight more rapidly after treatment. To date, there has been no research on treatment outcome in obese diabetic patients with binge eating problems. With the publication of the *DSM–IV* and the standardization of diagnostic criteria for binge eating disorder, we hope there will be increased research on the prevalence of binge eating disorder in women with NIDDM and its effect on weight-loss treatments.

Research Needs

The most pressing research need in this field is for the development of an effective weight loss program for obese patients with diabetes. Previous studies have shown that even modest weight loss, if maintained, can significantly improve glycemic control and cardiovascular risk factors in overweight patients with diabetes (Wing et al., 1987). However, the problem is that most obese diabetic patients, like obese patients in general, are unable to maintain their weight loss over time. Moreover, recent data suggest that maintenance of weight loss may be even poorer in diabetic women than in nondiabetics of comparable age and weight (Guare, 1991). As noted, more research on very low calorie diets, spouse support, and binge eating disorder may be helpful in the development of a more effective weight loss program for women with NIDDM. In addition, given the increased prevalence of NIDDM in minority-group populations, additional research should investigate whether behavioral therapies can be tailored

[1]In IDDM patients, binge eating is associated with poor glycemic control, as discussed in this section; the present study assessed NIDDM patients who continue to produce some insulin and who may have less dramatic blood glucose elevations after binge eating

for these subgroups, and whether there are cultural differences in lifestyle that may increase the risk of NIDDM in these subgroups.

CONCLUSIONS

In this chapter we have reviewed the diabetes research related to eating disorders, pregnancy, and weight loss—areas that are clearly of special concern in women. In general, diabetes research has not focused on women, nor has it examined gender differences in issues related to diabetes. Consequently, there are other areas that may benefit from a women's-health perspective. For example, epidemiological studies indicate that diabetics are at increased risk for depression (Gavard, Lustman, & Clouse, 1993), and this may be particularly true among women. Additional research examining gender differences in the onset and course of depression, and the effect of depression on adherence to diabetes treatment, is clearly needed.

Although diabetes is more prevalent in some ethnic minority populations (i.e., African Americans, American Pima Indians, Mexican Americans), there has been very little research to investigate cultural differences in the lifestyles of members of these subgroups, or differences in adherence, adaptation, or treatment efficacy.

Likewise, to date, there has been little attention to differences between mothers and fathers in their response to the onset of diabetes in young children, roles in managing the care of a diabetic child, or reaction to finding out that their child is at risk for developing diabetes (Johnson, Riley, Hansen, & Burick, 1990). Furthermore, previous studies have also shown gender differences in the prevalence of diabetic complications (Orchard et al., 1990); severe retinopathy and nephropathy have been shown to be more common in women with diabetes of short duration, and peripheral vascular disease is particularly common in women after 30 years duration of diabetes (>30% of women versus 11% of men). The factors associated with gender differences in the occurrence of complications should be studied further, along with gender differences in the psychological reactions to the development of complications.

These examples indicate that gender differences in diabetes have not been fully explored. There are clearly a large number of women with diabetes, and they may experience this disease and its treatment differently from men. Focusing on issues related to women's health might add substantially to our understanding of diabetes and increase the quality of the lives of women living with diabetes.

REFERENCES

Agras, W. S. (1987). *Eating disorders: Management of obesity, bulimia, and anorexia nervosa* (pp. 90–105). New York: Pergamon.

American Psychiatric Association. (1987). *Diagnostic and statistical manual of mental disorders* (3rd ed., rev.). Washington, DC: Author.

American Psychiatric Association. (1994). *Diagnostic and statistical manual of mental disorders* (4th ed.). Washington, DC: Author.

Birk, R., & Spencer, M. L. (1989). The prevalence of anorexia nervosa, bulimia, and induced glycosuria in IDDM females. *Diabetes Educator, 15,* 336–341.

Bung, P., Artal, R., Khodiguian, N., & Kjos, S. (1991). Exercise in gestational diabetes: An optional therapeutic approach? *Diabetes, 40* (Suppl. 2), 182–185.

Combs, C. A., Gunderson, E., Kitzmiller, J. L., Gavin, L. A., & Main, E. K. (1992). Relationship of fetal macrosomia to maternal postprandial glucose control during pregnancy. *Diabetes Care, 15,* 1251–1257.

Cooper, Z., Cooper, P. J., & Fairburn, C. G. (1989). The validity of the Eating Disorder Examination and its subscales. *British Journal of Psychiatry, 154,* 807–812.

Cousins, L., Baxi, L., Chez, R., Coustan, D., Gabbe, S., Harris, J., Landon, M., Sacks, D., & Singh, S. (1991). Screening recommendations for gestational diabetes mellitus. *American Journal of Obstetrics and Gynecology, 165,* 493–496.

Coustan, D. R., & Imarah, J. (1984). Prophylactic insulin treatment of gestational diabetes reduces the incidence of macrosomia, operative delivery, and birth trauma. *American Journal of Obstetrics and Gynecology, 150,* 836–842.

Diabetes Control and Complications Trial (DCCT) Research Group. (1988). Weight gain associated with intensive therapy in the Diabetes Control and Complications Trial. *Diabetes Care, 11,* 567–573.

DCCT Research Group. (1993). The effect of intensive treatment of diabetes on the development and progression of long-term complications in insulin-dependent diabetes mellitus. *New England Journal of Medicine, 329,* 977–986.

Dooley, S. L., Metzger, B. E., & Cho, N. H. (1991). Gestational diabetes mellitus: Influence of race on disease prevalence and perinatal outcome in a U.S. population. *Diabetes, 40* (Suppl. 2), 25–29.

Dornhurst, A., Nicholls, J. S. D., Probst, F., Paterson, C. M., Hollier, K. L., Elkeles, R. S., & Beard, R. W. (1991). Calorie restriction for treatment of gestational diabetes. *Diabetes, 40* (Suppl. 2), 161–164.

Durak, E. P., Jovanovic-Peterson, L., & Peterson, C. M. (1990). Comparative evaluation of uterine response to exercise on five aerobic machines. *American Journal of Obstetrics and Gynecology, 162,* 754–756.

Fairburn, C. G., & Beglin, S. J. (1990). Studies of the epidemiology of bulimia nervosa. *American Journal of Psychiatry, 147,* 401–408.

Fairburn, C. G., Peveler, R. C., Davies, B., Mann, J. I., & Mayou, R. A. (1991). Eating disorders in young adults with insulin dependent diabetes mellitus: A controlled study. *British Medical Journal, 303,* 17–20.

Fajans, S. S. (1990). Classification and diagnosis of diabetes. In H. Rifkin & D. Porte, Jr. (Eds.), *Diabetes mellitus: Theory and practice* (4th ed., pp. 346–356). New York: Elsevier Science.

Freinkel, N. (Ed.). (1985). Proceedings of the Second International Workshop–Conference on Gestational Diabetes Mellitus. *Diabetes, 34* (Suppl. 2), 123–126.

Freinkel, N., Phelps, R. L., & Metzger, B. E. (1990). The mother in pregnancies complicated by diabetes. In H. Rifkin & D. Porte, Jr. (Eds.), *Diabetes mellitus: Theory and practice* (4th ed., pp. 634–650). New York: Elsevier Science.

Furhmann, K., Reiher, H., Semmler, K., Fischer, F., Fischer, M., & Glockner, E. (1983). Prevention of congenital malformations in infants of insulin-dependent diabetic mothers. *Diabetes Care, 6,* 219–223.

Garner, D. M., & Garfinkel, P. E. (1979). The Eating Attitudes Test: An index of the symptoms of anorexia nervosa. *Psychological Medicine, 9,* 273–279.

Gavard, J. A., Lustman, P. J., & Clouse, R. E. (1993). Prevalence of depression in adults with diabetes: An epidemiological evaluation. *Diabetes Care, 16,* 1167–1178.

Goldberg, J. D., Franklin, B., Lasser, D., Jornsay, D. L., Hausknecht, R. U., Ginsberg-Fellner, F., & Berkowitz, R. L. (1986). Gestational diabetes: Impact of home glucose monitoring on neonatal birth weight. *American Journal of Obstetrics and Gynecology, 154,* 546–550.

Goldman, J. A., Dicker, D., Feldberg, D., Yeshaya, A., Samuel, N., & Karp, M. (1986). Pregnancy outcome in patients with insulin-dependent diabetes mellitus with preconceptional diabetic control: A comparative study. *American Journal of Obstetrics and Gynecology, 155,* 293–297.

Gregory, R., Scott, A. R., Mohajer, M., & Tattersall, R. B. (1992). Diabetic pregnancy 1977–1990: Have we reached a plateau? *Journal of the Royal College of Physicians of London, 26,* 162–166.

Guare, J. C. (1991). *Response of obese nondiabetic and diabetic women to behavioral weight loss therapy.* Unpublished doctoral dissertation, University of Pittsburgh, Pittsburgh, PA.

Harris, M. I. (1991). Epidemiological correlates of NIDDM in Hispanics, Whites, and Blacks in the U.S. population. *Diabetes Care, 14,* 639–648.

Harris, M. I. (1993). Undiagnosed NIDDM: Clinical and public health issues. *Diabetes Care, 16,* 642–652.

Heitzmann, C. A., & Kaplan, R. M. (1984). Interaction between sex and social support in the control of type II diabetes mellitus. *Journal of Consulting and Clinical Psychology, 52,* 1087–1089.

Hudson, J. I., Wentworth, S. M., Hudson, M. S., & Pope, H. G. (1985). Prevalence of anorexia nervosa and bulimia among young diabetic women. *Journal of Clinical Psychiatry, 46,* 88–89.

Johnson, C., Lewis, C., & Hagman, J. (1984). The syndrome of bulimia: Review and synthesis. *Psychiatric Clinics of North America, 7,* 247–273.

Johnson, C., Lewis, C., Love, S., Lewis, L., & Stuckey, M. (1984). Incidence and correlates of bulimic behavior in a female high school population. *Journal of Youth and Adolescence, 13,* 15–26.

Johnson, S. B., Riley, W. J., Hansen, C. A., & Burick, M. A. (1990). Psychological impact of islet cell-antibody screening: Preliminary results. *Diabetes Care, 13,* 93–97.

Jovanovic-Peterson, L., & Peterson, C. M. (1991). Is exercise safe or useful for gestational diabetic women? *Diabetes, 40* (Suppl. 2), 179–181.

Jovanovic-Peterson, L., & Peterson, C. M. (1992). Pregnancy in the diabetic woman: Guidelines for a successful outcome. *Endocrinology and Metabolism Clinics of North America, 21,* 433–456.

Jovanovic-Peterson, L., Peterson, C. M., Reed, G. F., Metzger, B. E., Mills, J. L., Knopp, R. H., Aarons, J. H., and the National Institute of Child Health and Human Development—Diabetes in Early Pregnancy Study. (1991). Maternal postprandial glucose levels and infant birth weight: The Diabetes in Early Pregnancy study. *American Journal of Obstetrics and Gynecology, 164,* 103–111.

Kannel, W. B. (1978). Role of diabetes in cardiac disease: Conclusions from population studies. In S. Zoneraich (Eds.), *Diabetes and the Heart* (pp. 97–112). Springfield, IL: Charles C. Thomas.

Kannel, W. B. (1982). Diabetes as a risk factor for atherosclerotic cardiovascular disease. In B. N. Brodoff & S. J. Bleicher (Eds.), *Diabetes mellitus and obesity* (pp. 735–740). Baltimore: Williams & Wilkins.

King, M. B. (1987). Eating disorders in a general practice population: Prevalence, characteristics and follow-up at 12 to 18 months. *Psychological Medicine Monograph Supplement, 14,* 1–34.

Kitzmiller, J. L. (1993). Sweet success with diabetes: The development of insulin therapy and glycemic control for pregnancy. *Diabetes Care, 16,* 107–121.

Kitzmiller, J. L., Gavin, L. A., Gin, G. D., Jovanovic-Peterson, L., Main, E. K., & Zigrang, W. D. (1991). Preconception care of diabetes: Glycemic control prevents congenital abnormalities. *Journal of the American Medical Association, 265,* 731–736.

Knopp, R. H., Magee, M. S., Raisys, V., & Benedetti, T. (1991). Metabolic effects of hypocaloric diets in management of gestational diabetes. *Diabetes, 40* (Suppl. 2), 165–171.

La Greca, A. M., Schwarz, L. T., & Satin, W. (1987). Eating patterns in young women with IDDM: Another look. *Diabetes Care, 10,* 659–660.

Landon, O., & Gabbe, R. S. (1992). Diabetes mellitus and pregnancy. *Obstetrics and Gynecology Clinics of North America, 19,* 633–654.

Langer, O., Berkus, M., Brustman, L., Anyaegbunam, A., & Mazze, R. (1991). Rationale for insulin management in gestational diabetes mellitus. *Diabetes, 40* (Suppl. 2), 186–190.

Langer, O., & Mazze, R. S. (1986). Diabetes in pregnancy: Evaluating self-monitoring performance and glycemic control with memory-based reflectance meter. *American Journal of Obstetrics and Gynecology, 155,* 635–637.

Marcus, M. D., & Wing, R. R. (1990). Eating disorders and diabetes. In C. S. Holmes (Ed.), *Neuropsychological and behavioral aspects of insulin- and non-insulin dependent diabetes* (pp. 102–121). New York: Springer–Verlag.

Marcus, M. D., Wing, R. R., & Hopkins, J. (1988). Obese binge eaters: Affect, cognitions, and response to behavioral weight control. *Journal of Consulting and Clinical Psychology, 56,* 433–439.

Metzger, B. E., Cho, N. H., Roston, S. M., Radvany, R. (1993). Pre-pregnancy weight and antepartum insulin secretion predict glucose tolerance five years after gestational diabetes mellitus. *Diabetes Care, 16,* 1598–1605.

Mills, J. L., Baker, L., & Goldman, A. S. (1979). Malformations in infants of diabetic mothers occur before the seventh gestational week: Implications for treatment. *Diabetes, 28,* 292–293.

Mills, J. L., Fishl, A. R., Knopp, R. H., Ober, C. L., Jovanovic, L. G., Polk, B. F., & the NICHD—Diabetes in Early Pregnancy Study. (1983). Malformations in infants of diabetic mothers: Problems in study design. *Preventive Medicine, 12,* 274–286.

Mills, J. L., Knopp, R. H., Simpson, J. L., Jovanovic-Peterson, L., Metzger, B. E., Holmes, L. B., Aarons, J. H., Brown, Z., Reed, G. F., Bieber, F. R., Van Allen, M., Holzman, I., Ober, C., Peterson, C. M., Witham, M. J., Duckles, A., Mueller-Heubach, E., Polk, B. F., & the National Institute of Child Health and Human Development Diabetes in Early Pregnancy Study. (1988). Lack of relation of increased malformation rates in infants of diabetic mothers to glycemic control during organogenesis. *New England Journal of Medicine, 318,* 671–676.

Mitchell, J. E., Raymond, N., & Specker, S. (1993). A review of the controlled trials of pharmacotherapy and psychotherapy in the treatment of bulimia nervosa. *International Journal of Eating Disorders, 14,* 229–247.

Neinstein, L. S., & Katz, B. (1986). Contraceptive use in the chronically ill adolescent female: Part I. *Journal of Adolescent Health Care, 7,* 123–133.

O'Neil, P. M., Currey, H. S., Hirsch, A. A., Riddle, F. E., Taylor, C. I., Malcolm, R. J., & Sexauer, J. D. (1979). Effects of sex of subject and spouse involvement on weight loss in a behavioral treatment program: A retrospective investigation. *Addictive Behaviors, 4,* 167–177.

Orchard, T. J., Dorman, J. S., Maser, R. E., Becker, D. J., Drash, A. L., Ellis, D., LaPorte, R. E., & Kuller, L. H. (1990). Prevalence of complications in IDDM by sex and duration: Pittsburgh Epidemiology of Diabetes Complications Study–II. *Diabetes, 39,* 1116–1124.

Ostrander, L. D., & Butler, W. J. (1982). Diabetes and blood glucose: The Tecumseh study. In E. Eschwege (Ed.), *Advances in diabetes epidemiology* (pp. 57–64). New York: Elsevier Biomedical.

O'Sullivan, J. B. (1991). Diabetes mellitus after GDM. *Diabetes, 29* (Suppl. 2), 131–135.

Pettit, D. J., Bennett, P. H., Saad, M. F., Charles, M. A., Nelson, R. G., & Knowler, W. C. (1991). Abnormal glucose tolerance during pregnancy in Pima Indian women: Long-term effects on offspring. *Diabetes, 40* (Suppl. 2), 126–30.

Peveler, R. C., & Fairburn, C. G. (1989). Anorexia nervosa in association with diabetes mellitus—a cognitive–behavioural approach to treatment. *Behaviour Research and Therapy, 27,* 95–99.

Peveler, R. C., & Fairburn, C. G. (1992). The treatment of bulimia nervosa in patients with diabetes mellitus. *International Journal of Eating Disorders, 11,* 45–53.

113

Peveler, R. C., Fairburn, C. G., Boller, I., & Dunger, D. (1992). Eating disorders in adolescents with IDDM. *Diabetes Care, 15,* 1356–1360.

Polivy, J., & Herman, C. P. (1985). Dieting and binging: A causal analysis. *American Psychologist, 40,* 193–201.

Polivy, J., Herman, C. P., Olmsted, M. P., & Jazwinski, C. (1984). Restraint and binge eating. In R. C. Hawkins, W. J. Fremouw, & P. F. Clement (Eds.), *The binge–purge syndrome: Diagnosis, treatment, and research* (pp. 104–122). New York: Springer.

Powers, P. S., Malone, J. I., Coovert, D. L., & Schulman, R. G. (1990). Insulin-dependent diabetes mellitus and eating disorders: A prevalence study. *Comprehensive Psychiatry, 31,* 205–210.

Robertson, P., & Rosenvinge, J. H. (1990). Insulin-dependent diabetes mellitus: A risk factor in anorexia nervosa or bulimia nervosa? An empirical study of 116 women. *Journal of Psychosomatic Research, 34,* 535–541.

Robins, L. N., Helzer, J. E., Weissman, M. M., Orvaschel, H., Gruenberg, E., Burke, J. D., Jr., & Regier, D. A. (1984). Lifetime prevalence of specific psychiatric disorders in three sites. *Archives of General Psychiatry, 41,* 949–958.

Rodin, G. M., Craven, J., Littlefield, C., Murray, M., & Daneman, D. (1991). Eating disorders and intentional insulin undertreatment in adolescent females with diabetes. *Psychosomatics, 32,* 171–176.

Rodin, G. M., Johnson, L. E., Garfinkel, P. E., Daneman, D., & Kenshole, A. B. (1986). Eating disorders in female adolescents with insulin dependent diabetes mellitus. *International Journal of Psychiatry in Medicine, 16,* 49–57.

Rosen, J. C., Cado, S., Silberg, N. T., Srebnik, D., & Wendt, S. (1990). Cognitive behavior therapy with and without size perception training for women with body image disturbance. *Behavior Therapy, 21,* 481–498.

Ruggiero, L., Spirito, A., Bond, A., Coustan, D., & McGarvey, S. (1990). Impact of social support and stress on compliance in women with gestational diabetes. *Diabetes Care, 13,* 441–443.

Silverman, B. L., Rizzo, T., Green, O. C., Cho, N. H., Winter, R. J., Ogata, E. S., Richards, G. E., & Metzger, B. E. (1991). Long-term prospective evaluation of offspring of diabetic mothers. *Diabetes, 40* (Suppl. 2), 121–125.

Songer, T. J. (1992). The economic costs of NIDDM. *Diabetes Metabolism Review, 8,* 389–404.

Stancin, T., Link, D. L., & Reuter, J. M. (1989). Binge eating and purging in young women with IDDM. *Diabetes Care, 12,* 601–603.

Steel, J. M., Johnstone, F. D., Hepburn, D. A., & Smith, A. F. (1990). Can prepregnancy care of diabetic women reduce the risk of abnormal babies? *British Medical Journal, 301,* 1070–1074.

Steel, J. M., Lloyd, G. G., Young, R. J., & MacIntyre, C. C. A. (1990). Changes in eating attitudes during the first year of treatment for diabetes. *Journal of Psychosomatic Research, 34,* 313–318.

Steel, J. M., Young, R. J., Lloyd, G. G., & Clark, B. F. (1987). Clinically apparent eating disorders in young diabetic women: Associations with painful neuropathy and other complications. *British Medical Journal, 294,* 859–862.

Steel, J. M., Young, R. J., Lloyd, G. G., & MacIntyre, C. C. A. (1989). Abnormal eating attitudes in young insulin-dependent diabetics. *British Journal of Psychiatry, 155,* 515–521.

Striegel-Moore, R. H., Nicholson, T. J., & Tamborlane, W. V. (1992). Prevalence of eating disorder symptoms in preadolescent and adolescent girls with IDDM. *Diabetes Care, 15,* 1361–1368.

Stubbs, S. M., Brudenell, J. M., Pyke, D. A., & Watkins, P. J. (1980). Management of the pregnant diabetic: Home or hospital, with or without glucose meters? *Lancet, 1,* 1122–1124.

Szmukler, G. I. (1985). The epidemiology of anorexia nervosa and bulimia. *Journal of Psychiatric Research, 19,* 143–153.

Van Itallie, T. B. (1985). Health implications of overweight and obesity in the United States. *Annals of Internal Medicine, 103,* 983–988.

Varner, M. W. (1983). Efficacy of home glucose monitoring in diabetic pregnancy. *American Journal of Medicine, 75,* 592–596.

Willhoite, M. B., Bennert, H. W., Jr., Palomaki, G. E., Zaremba, M. M., Herman, W. H., Williams, J. R., & Spear, N. H. (1993). The impact of preconception counseling on pregnancy outcomes: The experience of the Maine Diabetes in Pregnancy Program. *Diabetes Care, 16,* 450–455.

Wilson, G. T., & Fairburn, C. G. (1993). Cognitive treatments for eating disorders. *Journal of Consulting and Clinical Psychology, 61,* 261–269.

Wing, R. R., Blair, E., Marcus, M., Epstein, L. H., & Harvey, J. Year-long weight loss treatment for obese patients with type II diabetes: Does including a very-low-calorie diet improve outcome? *American Journal of Medicine, 97,* 354–362.

Wing, R. R., Koeske, R., Epstein, L. H., Nowalk, M. P., Gooding, W., & Becker, D. (1987). Long-term effects of modest weight loss in type II diabetic patients. *Archives of Internal Medicine, 147,* 1749–1753.

Wing, R. R., Marcus, M. D., Epstein, L. H., Blair, E. H., & Burton, L. R. (1989). Binge eating in obese patients with type II diabetes. *International Journal of Eating Disorders, 7*, 671–679.

Wing, R. R., Marcus, M. D., Epstein, L. H., & Jawad, A. (1991). A "family-based" approach to the treatment of obese type II diabetic patients. *Journal of Consulting and Clinical Psychology, 59*, 156–162.

Wing, R. R., Nowalk, M. P., & Guare, J. C. (1988). Diabetes mellitus. In E. A. Blechman & K. D. Brownell (Eds.), *Handbook of behavioral medicine for women* (pp. 236–252). New York: Pergamon.

Wing, R. R., Nowalk, M. P., Marcus, M. D., Koeske, R., & Finegold, D. (1986). Subclinical eating disorders and glycemic control in adolescents with type I diabetes. *Diabetes Care, 9*, 162–167.

Wood, P. D., Stefanick, M. L., Williams, P. T., & Haskell, W. L. (1991). The effects on plasma lipoproteins of a prudent weight-reducing diet, with or without exercise, in overweight men and women. *New England Journal of Medicine, 325*, 461–466.

Zayfert, C. & Goetsch, V. L. (1992). Self-monitoring of blood glucose: Impact and adherence during diabetic pregnancy. *Annals of Behavioral Medicine, 14*, 292–301.

5

Women and AIDS

Patricia J. Morokoff, Lisa L. Harlow, and Kathryn Quina

A cquired immune deficiency syndrome (AIDS) and the human immunodeficiency virus (HIV) that causes AIDS, have had a powerful effect on women's lives. HIV is the fourth leading cause of death in women 25–44 years of age in the United States, and the only infectious disease among the leading causes of death. However, among women of color, poor women, and women using drugs, the risk is substantially greater. The scientific community has been slow to address issues for women and HIV infection or AIDS, both with respect to the natural course of the disease and with respect to prevention efforts targeted at women (Squire, 1993). Prevention for women is not the same as prevention for men, because the primary method for preventing sexual transmission among sexually active individuals is condom use, a male-controlled method. AIDS also affects women differently from men in that women can pass the infection to a baby during pregnancy, delivery, or breastfeeding. Thus AIDS has a central effect on women's sexual and reproductive decision-making, especially for those women who perceive themselves to be at high risk.

The purposes of this chapter are to review our current knowledge of behavioral factors in prevention of HIV and AIDS in women, to discuss primary prevention programs, to reach conclusions concerning the most effective strategies for primary prevention of HIV/AIDS, and to propose an agenda for psychological research. In order to do so, it is important to review the demographics of HIV and AIDS in women and the role of HIV/AIDS knowledge and cultural values for women. Analysis of prevention issues will receive a heavy emphasis in this chapter because of psychology's contribution to AIDS prevention, the area in which the bulk of research has been focused. In addition, this chapter will address diagnosis of AIDS in women, psychosocial needs of women with HIV/AIDS, and special issues for women confronting this disease including discrimination and reproductive rights. Throughout, areas that require further research or that have been neglected in current research will be identified, as will methodological and conceptual issues.

EPIDEMIOLOGICAL TRENDS

HIV Infection and AIDS Worldwide

It is estimated that by the end of 1992 about 4.4 million women worldwide were infected with HIV (Chin, 1990). The World Health Organization (WHO) has described several distinct epidemiological patterns of HIV/AIDS transmission (Chin & Mann, 1988): Ninety percent of these women are in *Pattern II areas,* which include sub-Saharan Africa and some Carribean countries. In Pattern II areas the predominant modes of HIV transmission are heterosexual intercourse and perinatal transmission. In *Pattern I areas,* such as North America, Western Europe, and Oceania, the primary population groups affected are gay men, intravenous drug users, and their sexual partners. The World Health Organization estimates that in 1990, there were about 500,000 cases of AIDS in women and children globally.

HIV Infection in the United States

Prevalence of HIV Infection

Seroprevalence among childbearing women, based on serosurveys conducted in 44 states, was .17% in 1991–1992. African American women were 3 to 28 times more likely to be seropositive than White women, and accounted for 63% of all seropositive women in the 21 states that collected data on race/ethnicity. In five states, more than 1% of African American childbearing women were seropositive (Centers for Disease Control and Prevention [CDC], 1994b).

Serosurveys among Job Corps entrants reveal additional interesting information concerning adolescent women (aged 16 to 21). In 1991–1992, seroprevalence was higher among young women (.35%) than among young men (.23%). This difference was primarily accounted for by the high seroprevalence among African American young women (.60%) compared with African American young men (.38%). As the authors of the Serosurveillance Summary note, these trends suggest a prominent role of heterosexual transmission in this group: "Because young women tend to have sex with older men, rates of sexually transmitted diseases are generally higher among women than among men in the youngest age groups" (CDC, 1994b, p. 10). There are important implications of these findings for prevention efforts and public policy.

Testing for HIV Antibody

While surveys of childbearing women and Job Corps entrants provide precise information on seroprevalence trends in these samples, it is very difficult to estimate seroprevalence in the larger population. There are many barriers to serotesting for women, including the failure of physicians to refer women for testing in spite of relevant symptoms; women's fears of disclosing serostatus; limited access to testing sites; and concerns over negative consequences with respect to jobs, children, and other aspects of life (Berrios et al., 1993). Data also suggest that fewer women report having been tested for HIV antibodies than men. In a nationwide, population-based telephone survey of over 13,000 men and women, 25% of men compared with 16% of women reported having been tested. Among women who had more than 10 partners in their life and were between the ages of 21 to 34, only 38% had been tested for HIV antibody.

AIDS in U.S. Women

As of the end of December 1993, 44,357 female adults and adolescents had been diagnosed with AIDS in the United States. This represents over 12%

of the total of adults and adolescents in the United States diagnosed with AIDS (CDC, 1994a). This cumulative figure reflects the fact that over the years, the number of AIDS cases in women is an increasing percentage of total adult AIDS cases (e.g., 6.6% in 1985, 11.5% in 1991, 15% for October 1992 to September 1993; Ellerbrock, Bush, Chamberland, & Oxtoby, 1991; CDC, 1993a). The rate of increase in diagnosed AIDS cases from 1992 to 1993 was 2.4 for women, compared to 2.05 for men. As previously mentioned, HIV infection is the fourth leading cause of death in the United States for women aged 25–44 (CDC, 1993a).

Over half of American women with AIDS are African American (53%), while one quarter are White and one fifth are Hispanic. Among African American women aged 25–44, HIV infection became the second leading cause of death in 1992, accounting for 16.5% of deaths. Among Hispanic women, HIV infection became the third leading cause of death, accounting for 12.5% of deaths. For White women, HIV infection was the sixth leading cause of death, accounting for 3.8% of deaths in 1992. The death rate from HIV infection for those aged 25–44 was 12 times as high for African American women (38 per 100,000) as for White women (3.3 per 100,000) (CDC, 1993a).

It has been reported that .8% of women with AIDS are lesbian (Chu, Buehler, Fleming, & Berkelman, 1990). The criteria used for designating a woman as lesbian required that she had had sex only with a female partner since 1977. Bisexual women—those who had sex with both men and women since 1977—accounted for an additional 1% of cases of women with AIDS. The definitions used to categorize lesbians have been critiqued, however, suggesting that these figures underestimate the incidence of AIDS in lesbians (Stevens, 1993). Furthermore, evidence suggests that certain populations of lesbian and bisexual women are currently at much greater risk than was suggested in the Chu et al. paper. In a study conducted by Magura, Kang, Shapiro, and O'Day (1993) on a prison sample of women, 43% of whom were HIV seropositive, 30% identified themselves as exclusively lesbian while another 23% identified themselves as bisexual.

Route of Transmission

Almost half of women diagnosed with AIDS are reported by the CDC to have been exposed through injection-drug use, while 35% are classified as having been exposed through heterosexual transmission (CDC, 1994a). Of women exposed through heterosexual contact, 55% were exposed through sex with an injection-drug user and an additional 25% were exposed through sex with an HIV-infected person (risk not specified). The next most likely mode of heterosexual transmission is sex with a bisexual male (8%). Other categories of exposure include receipt of blood transfusion (6%) and unidentified risk (8%). Hispanic women are somewhat less likely than other women to have been infected through injection drug use (49%), and are more likely than other women to have been infected through heterosexual contact (41%). Among Hispanic women infected through heterosexual contact, 69% were infected through sex with an injection-drug user.

Risk Factors for Transmission

The percentage of women infected through heterosexual contact (37%) is much higher than that for men (3%). In fact, women represent 65% of all individuals diagnosed with AIDS who were exposed through heterosexual contact. Two primary reasons for women's greater rate of AIDS through heterosexual contact have been proposed. One is that because there are many more men infected with HIV, the risk for a heterosexual woman in any given unprotected sexual encounter is much greater than for a man. Second, the risk from penile penetration of a woman by an HIV-infected man is believed to be 12 times more likely than from an HIV-infected woman to a man who penetrates her (Padian, Shiboski, & Jewell, 1990). Other risk factors for women include anal intercourse, history of sexually transmitted diseases (STDs), and a male sexual partner who has recently seroconverted or who is in late stages of AIDS (because at these times his viral load will be greatest) (European Study Group, 1989; Ickovics & Rodin, 1992).

Few studies have been conducted to determine predictors of HIV-positive serostatus in women. One exception is the study conducted by Magura et al. (1993). They evaluated predictors of HIV status in 165 female injection-drug users incarcerated at Rikers Island in New York City. The overall seropositivity rate for the sample was 43%. A multivariate analysis of potential risk variables showed that the following variables were associated with HIV-positive serostatus: cocaine injection frequency, lifetime injection risk behavior, performing oral sex on men who were high on crack, and Hispanic ethnicity. These variables together correctly classified 72% of cases.

HIV/AIDS KNOWLEDGE AND CULTURAL VALUES

Knowledge about HIV and AIDS, especially differential risk based on factors such as racial/ethnic status, geographic region, and risk behaviors, is necessary for women to accurately evaluate their infection risk. Knowledge of such risk factors can potentially motivate women to take action to protect themselves (Fisher & Fisher, 1992). Numerous studies, however, have demonstrated that women's knowledge level is not predictive of engagement in protective behaviors (Baldwin & Baldwin, 1988; Flaskerud & Nyamathi, 1990; Harlow, Quina, Morokoff, Rose, & Grimley, 1993).

Facts concerning disease and prevention of disease do not exist in a cultural vacuum, and women's knowledge of HIV/AIDS and attitudes toward adopting risk reduction behaviors will be strongly influenced by a multitude of factors (Mays & Cochran, 1988). The majority of women with AIDS are African American and poor. It is essential to understand the context of these women's lives and cultural values before reaching conclusions about what behavior changes to recommend. In this section we will first review research on women's knowledge about HIV and AIDS, focusing on women who engage in risky behaviors. We will then discuss beliefs concerning AIDS as genocide or a human-made conspiracy.

Quinn (1993) studied AIDS knowledge among 170 African American women seeking health care services in a community health clinic located in a low-income, public housing complex in Washington, DC. On average, the AIDS knowledge was only 50% correct, less than the 80% correct that researchers believed would reflect a satisfactory knowledge level. In particular, only 11% of women knew that the majority of children with AIDS are African American, and only 10% knew that most women with AIDS are African American. Only 35% of women knew that cleaning drug injection needles with bleach can reduce the risk of spreading AIDS (see also Harrison et al., 1991). Minority women have also been shown to have lower perceived risk for AIDS. Women at a mass transit waiting area ($N =$ 272) in Chicago were surveyed (Kalichman, Hunter, & Kelly, 1992). Minority women, most of whom were African American, indicated less concern than their nonminority counterparts that an acquaintance would get AIDS. Furthermore, nonminority women who reported engaging in risk behaviors indicated greater concern about both themselves and someone else getting AIDS than all other groups, including minority women at high risk. Minority women estimated themselves to be at lower risk than nonminority women.

Quinn (1993) suggests that this lower level of concern may be due to the misconception that AIDS is a gay, White man's disease. Quinn also suggests that AIDS prevention programs have not reached African American or Hispanic women in a culturally sensitive manner. Additional reasons why poor ethnic women may not perceive their personal risk for HIV/AIDS to be high are suggested by Mays and Cochran (1988). These authors emphasize that for poor ethnic-minority women, HIV/AIDS is one more risk with which to be concerned and may be a less pressing risk than exposure to the elements, care of dependent children, hunger, drug withdrawal, acute illness or trauma associated with physical or sexual assault, threat of withdrawal of financial support, or loss of loved ones.

Traditional health beliefs among African American women may also influence knowledge and beliefs about AIDS. Focus group sessions were conducted with 22 African American women in Los Angeles (Flaskerud & Rush, 1989). All participants believed that "you get AIDS from sex with the wrong people or from needles when you're using drugs" (p. 212). However, only three participants believed that these were the only ways to get AIDS. The authors report that there was a generalized belief that a person can get AIDS from lowered resistance due to impurities, poor health habits, exposure to cold, cyclical weaknesses, and improper nutrition. It is evident that some of these beliefs are consistent with a dominant culture understanding of the causes of illness and thus with public health AIDS prevention messages, while others are not. Although this study is not based on a representative sample, it makes clear that AIDS prevention programs need to be sensitive to cultural beliefs about the nature and causes of illness in order to make sense to some community members.

Furthermore, there is evidence that Latina women who are less acculturated to the dominant cultures may have less knowledge of HIV/AIDS. Nyamathi, Bennett, Leake, Lewis, and Flaskerud (1993) compared AIDS knowledge in African American women, high-acculturated Latinas, and low-acculturated Latinas. While knowledge was equivalent for many items, low-acculturated Latinas were more likely than the other groups to believe that HIV could be transmitted through food, sneezing, or use of toilet seats. Low-acculturated Latinas also had a lower perceived risk of getting AIDS than the other groups and in fact were least likely to engage in illegal drug use and sexual activity with multiple partners. Only a third of African American women and high-acculturated Latinas in this sample believed they had no chance of contracting HIV compared to 50% of low-acculturated Latinas. In another study, Hispanic men and women who were low in acculturation reported more machismo beliefs,[1] less fear of AIDS, and more willingness to believe in fate (Mikawa et al., 1992).

An important misconception some women may hold concerning HIV/AIDS is that there is a government policy promoting selective genocide and that the AIDS virus is a human-made agent of genocide. This viewpoint may make sense in the context of groups that have a history of oppression, such as gays and African Americans (Croteau, Nero, & Prosser, 1993). African Americans have specific reasons for mistrust of the health care system, such as the Tuskegee Syphilis Study that was conducted from 1932 to 1972. As described by Jones (1993), 412 African American men participated in a study of the natural history of syphilis. They were never educated about syphilis and were not treated even after penicillin became available. This experiment may help to explain the fears of some individuals that the government and medical research establishment could act in an unethical manner to the detriment of African Americans.

---

[1]Examples of machismo beliefs related to AIDS risk were endorsement that it is a woman's job to be responsible for birth control, that no woman should tell a man that he has to use a condom, and that a woman who carries condoms in her purse is loose.

A survey was conducted to determine HIV education needs among African American church members in five cities (Thomas & Quinn, 1991). Results indicated that 35% of respondents agreed with the statement "I believe AIDS is genocide against the African-American race," with an additional 30% feeling unsure and 35% disagreeing. Similarly, 34% agreed with the statement "I believe AIDS is a manmade virus;" 44% were unsure, and only 22% disagreed. Only 21% of respondents agreed with the statement "I believe the government is telling me the truth about AIDS." While it is clear that many African Americans do not report mistrust of the government, when planning public health appeals and interventions it is important to acknowledge the mistrust that does exist.

In summary, research results indicate that among specific populations, knowledge of AIDS risk factors and transmission routes is lower than levels set as acceptable by researchers. It furthermore appears that minority women report less concern about risk than nonminority women and that women who are less acculturated have less accurate knowledge in some areas than more acculturated women. Significant methodological issues in this research area, however, exist in relation to sampling techniques and representativeness of samples. No study reviewed here used probability sampling techniques or stratified the sample by income or education level. It is critical to evaluate knowledge, beliefs, and attitudes in the populations most at risk because this information will assist in developing intervention strategies. However, in comparing racial/ethnic groups it is imperative to determine whether any observed differences are due to demographic variables.

PRIMARY PREVENTION OF HIV INFECTION

Primary prevention of HIV infection requires that individuals modify the behaviors that put them at risk. The predominant behaviors that put women at risk are sharing drug-injection equipment and having unprotected sex with HIV-infected men. Most often these men are injection drug users themselves. While HIV transmission is preventable, prevention relies on our ability to decrease women's exposure both to shared drug injection equipment and to unprotected sex. Realistic assessment needs to be made of our capacity to develop effective programs to reduce risk.

Can Risk of Transmission From Needles Be Reduced?
Gender Differences in Injection Behavior

The most prevalent manner in which women are exposed to HIV/AIDS is through injection drug use. Women are exposed directly to risk of HIV infection by sharing needles and other drug-injection paraphernalia. Drug injection carries a high risk of infection because a user draws her blood into the syringe to be mixed with injectable drugs before injecting herself or another user. Paraphernalia such as drug cookers used to melt heroin in water before use, cotton used to filter drugs, and rinse water used to unclog needles, may also come in contact with blood and therefore serve to transmit infection (Singer, 1991). Evidence suggests that the majority of women who inject drugs share needles and are therefore exposed to risk of HIV transmission. Data on 6,609 women who had injected drugs at least once in the past 6 months were collected through the National AIDS Demonstration Research (NADR) program between 1988 and 1990. These data showed that 58% of women reported having had two or more partners with whom they had shared needles (Brown & Weissman, 1993). Only 18% of women in the sample reported no needle-sharing, and even fewer said they did not share drug cookers, cotton, or needle rinse water. Of the women in this sample, 66% had borrowed or rented used needles in the past 6 months.

Furthermore, gender differences in this sample suggested that women injection-drug users were more at risk for HIV disease than men (Brown & Weissman, 1993). This conclusion reflects not only the amount of needle-sharing that women engage in, but their pattern of injection and sexual behaviors. It is important to realize that women intravenous drug users (IDUs) are more likely than men IDUs to have an injection-drug using partner. In fact, most male sexual partners of IDU women are also IDUs. While a NADR study in Cleveland found that 93% of male and 91% of female IDUs reported having at least one sexual partner in the previous 6 months, men were much more likely to report at least one non-IDU partner (88%) than women (45%) (Feucht, Stephens, & Roman, 1990). This supports a previous report indicating that while women drug users typically have a partner who is also a drug user, 80% of male drug users have partners who do not use drugs (Mondanaro, 1987). These data suggest a higher HIV-risk associated with engaging in sexual behaviors for IDU women than for IDU men.

The data on injection-drug use indicate that women are more likely than men to have only one needle-sharing partner (24% of women compared to 17% of men; Brown & Weissman, 1993). Additional data suggest that that one needle-sharing partner is often a sex partner. For example, more women than men IDUs lend needles to sex partners, and they do so more frequently (Stephens, Feucht, & Gibbs, 1993). Furthermore, women report using drugs at home more frequently than men do (Stephens et al., 1993). In addition, more women than men report that when they shoot drugs they are always alone with a sex partner (Brown & Weissman, 1993). It is also of interest that among 39 heterosexual couples in a methadone maintenance clinic, women commonly used injection equipment after men (Clark, Calsyn, Saxon, Jackson, & Wrede, 1992 as cited in Castro, Valdiserri, & Curran, 1992). These data suggest that women may be uniquely vulnerable to risk of HIV transmission because they tend to share needles and have sex with their IDU partners.

Although the studies discussed here provide important information on gender differences in injection behaviors, continuing study is crucial because patterns of behavior are changing. For example, the use of crack cocaine, which is smoked rather than injected, may decrease the risk from needle sharing, but increase the risk from sexual behaviors. Furthermore, little is currently known about women's injection behaviors. Current evidence is consistent with the interpretation that women's gender role prescribes sharing injection paraphernalia, but this has not been directly tested. It is important to determine how power in women's relationships with IDU partners affects needle-sharing and sexual behaviors.

Needle Exchange Programs

Public policy changes could reduce the risk of HIV transmission through needle-sharing. A recent study found that a syringe and needle exchange program (NEP) was rapidly accepted by male and female IDUs in San Francisco (Watters, Estilo, Clark, & Lorvick, 1994). Over the study period, an increasing proportion of community IDUs indicated they usually obtained syringes from the exchange program (45% at the end of the study period). Furthermore, syringe sharing decreased from 66.3% in 1987 to 35.5% in 1992. There was no decline in syringe sharing among IDUs who did not use the syringe exchange program. From 1991 to 1992, 39% of women reported sharing syringes compared to 34% of men. A random sample of syringes returned in the exchange program revealed that 7% contained HIV antibodies. The authors calculate that 3,600 contaminated syringes were recovered during one month of random testing alone. Furthermore, the results did not suggest that the exchange program led to increases in drug injection, because there was a decline in self-reported frequency of injection during the 5.5-year study period. This may have been in part due to the coincidental increased popularity of crack cocaine, which is smoked rather than injected.

As of September 1993, there were 37 active NEPs in the United States (CDC, 1993b). Only about half of the programs were legal, however, because some states have laws precluding the purchase of a syringe without a prescription. In a review of 26 evaluations of the effect of NEPs on HIV drug and sex risk-behavior, the authors conclude that the majority of studies of NEP clients demonstrate decreased rates of HIV drug risk behavior but not sex risk behavior (CDC, 1993b). It is of interest to know whether NEPs have produced a decrease in HIV infection rates. Such a decrease has not been demonstrated, primarily because the need for large sample sizes and impediments to randomization make adequate research designs difficult to achieve. However, model estimates of NEP impact suggest that such programs can prevent significant numbers of infections among clients of programs, their partners, and their children (CDC, 1993c). Overall, results support the need for public health policies that minimize potential for syringe and needle sharing through increased availability of clean needles and syringes.

It is of special interest to ascertain the extent to which women are able to take advantage of NEPs that exist in their communities. Data on well funded NEPs suggest they have the capacity to impact a large proportion of local IDU populations. For example, the first legal NEP in the country, established in New Haven, Connecticut, is estimated to have reached between 49% and 68% of local IDUs (CDC, 1993b). However, the same report indicates that on average, programs in the United States and Canada have had contact with only 14% of the estimated number of IDUs in their areas. Furthermore, evidence suggests that compared to nonclient samples, needle exchange clients are slightly more likely to be male (CDC, 1993b).

It is important for future research to identify barriers to women's participation in NEPs. Data from focus groups, which were not broken down by gender, indicate that factors influencing use of NEPs include fear of arrest or harassment by police, convenience of the location and hours of the program, staff attitudes, desire to not be identified as an IDU, and the existence of alternative sources of sterile syringes (CDC, 1993b). It is likely that some of these factors are especially significant for women IDUs who are more likely than men IDUs to have children and thus childcare responsibilities, to be unemployed and therefore have greater financial constraints on travel to program sites, and to be more often physically ill than men, making participation in a program more difficult (Brown & Weissman, 1993). It is important that future studies explore potential barriers to women's participation as well as the effects of design features of NEPs on women's usage, drug treatment referrals, and other variables. Despite potential barriers, it is important to emphasize that where programs are available, many women will take advantage of them and benefit by them, as evidenced by the decrease in women's syringe sharing in the Watters et al. (1994) study.

Drug Treatment Programs

A second strategy for containment of HIV transmission is drug treatment. This is a long-range strategy that involves making drug treatment programs available to women and providing early interventions designed to help prevent drug use. Unfortunately, women's access to drug treatment has historically been severely restricted. It has been estimated that for every drug dependent person in treatment, there may be seven who are not in treatment (Mondanaro, 1987). The problem is especially acute for women because many treatment programs were designed for men and restrict access of women. Many chemical dependence treatment programs do not accept women. For example, a 1990 position paper for the U.S. House of Representatives Select Committee on Children, Youth and Families indicated that of California's 366 publicly funded drug treatment programs, only 67 treat women and only 16 can accommodate children (Kennedy, 1990). Most drug treatment programs have historically not provided childcare and have discouraged visitation of children younger than 12 (Karan, 1989). It is an unreasonable burden to expect that a woman will be able to separate from children who live with her for a month or more of detoxification and treatment (Morokoff, 1992). In recent years, a large number of demonstration projects of comprehensive drug treatment for women have been funded. It is encouraging to note that a recent study found no differences in the number of IDU men and women who had been in drug treatment (57% of men and 59% of women). It is clear, however, that a large percentage of IDUs have never been in a formal drug treatment program.

Treatment options for pregnant substance-users are especially problematic. The vast majority of treatment programs will not assume medical responsibility for a pregnant women and thus will not admit her (Karan, 1989). Of 78 drug treatment programs surveyed in New York City in 1989, 54% excluded all pregnant women, 67% would not accept pregnant women who were Medicaid beneficiaries, and 87% would not accept pregnant crack-addicted women who were Medicaid beneficiaries (Chavkin, 1989). It was reported that there were only 51 treatment beds for pregnant, drug-abusing women in the state of Massachusetts, yet there are several thousand such women at any time (Kumpfer, 1991). These severe restrictions are in part due to medical uncertainty over the optimal medical management during pregnancy, exacerbated by potential legal liabilities. According to Chavkin (1990), physicians initially feared that detoxification during pregnancy could lead to stillbirth or fetal compromise. Subsequently it has been reported that methadone maintenance during pregnancy is associated with improved pregnancy outcomes for women receiving treatment compared to heroin or methadone addicts not undergoing substance abuse treatment (Deren, 1986).

Another barrier to women's use of drug treatment programs is the increasing trend toward criminal liability for women who use drugs during pregnancy. According to the American Civil Liberties Union, as of 1990, over 30 American women have been criminally charged for drug use during pregnancy resulting in the delivery of drugs to a minor (Kennedy, 1990). This trend toward criminalization of drug use during pregnancy makes some programs less likely to accept pregnant drug users and women less likely to want to reveal their drug use in publicly funded programs.

In spite of such issues, there has been an increase in methadone maintenance programs providing specialized services for pregnant and postpartum women in recent years. This may account for the fact that women IDUs report greater use of methadone maintenance programs than men (Brown & Weissman, 1993).

In addition to drug treatment, many other issues arise in providing comprehensive care to drug using women. In NADR projects, many types of services have been provided to women, including rape counseling, suicide prevention, home visits, medical and legal advocacy, and pediatric care in mobile medical vans (Weissman & NARC, 1991). Comprehensive care for these women involves addressing not only drug use, but also homelessness, lack of financial support, job training, relationships, legal problems, health problems, and violence. Women who use drugs may be perceived by men as more sexually available, and men may therefore rape or physically abuse women who do not consent to sex (Karan, 1989). Even if these women do not risk HIV exposure from needle-sharing, they are vulnerable to infection from sexual experiences.

Can Risk From Sexual Behaviors Be Reduced?

IDU Women and Female Sex Partners of IDU Men: Comparability of Populations

While it might at first seem that reduction of HIV/AIDS risk focused on a sexual transmission route is unconnected to risk programs focused on drug use, the evidence suggests otherwise. Women at highest risk for sexual transmission of HIV are female sex partners of male IDUs. Female sex partners of male IDUs were studied through the NADR program sponsored by the National Institute on Drug Abuse (NIDA) (Weissman & NARC, 1991). Over two thirds of these women were IDUs, which permitted a comparison of women IDUs to non-IDUs. Data on 3,272 IDU women and 1,913 non-IDU women were compared. An important finding from this study was that the two groups were similar in many respects. One area of similarity was in noninjection drug use. For example, marijuana was used daily by comparable percentages of the IDU and non-IDU groups (15% and 13% respectively). Daily cocaine use was reported by one quarter of each group. Daily alcohol use was reported by about one quarter of the IDU and about one fifth of the non-IDU group. A mere 15% of the non-IDU group had not engaged in any substance use in the previous 6 months. It is clear that drug use was an important part of the lives of both the IDUs and the non-IDU women. This was the case despite the fact that the non-IDU group was frequently recruited through community outreach and from door to door solicitation rather than through a drug-treatment program of the male partner.

In addition to drug use, there were other ways in which IDUs and non-IDU women were similar. For example, among women in each group who used crack, about a third traded sex for drugs. If women did not use crack, they were less likely to trade sex for drugs, regardless of group. Over half of IDUs were unemployed, as were 49% of non-IDUs. Many of these women had children living with them, and a subset of each group had been in jail during the previous 6 months (although this percentage was higher for IDUs [29%] than non-IDUs [13%]). While certainly the groups are not identical, it would be a mistake to conclude that women who are exposed to AIDS through injection drug use represent a completely separate population from those who are exposed to AIDS through sexual behavior. In many ways the similarities outweigh the differences. Looking at both women with AIDS who were exposed via injection-drug use and women who are sexual partners of male IDUs reveals that 69% of women diagnosed with AIDS have a drug-related exposure route (CDC, 1994a).

Compared to women of various ethnic backgrounds, the greatest percentage of Hispanic women with AIDS were exposed through a drug-related exposure route (76%), followed by African American women with AIDS (71%), and White women with AIDS (61%) (CDC, 1994b).

The similarities between women who inject drugs and female sex partners of men who inject drugs suggest that drugs and the drug culture play a central role in the heterosexual transmission of HIV/AIDS. The implications are that it is crucial to determine the prevalence of sexual risk behaviors such as unprotected sexual intercourse, to identify realistic ways of increasing protective behaviors, and to evaluate the efficacy of programs directed toward these populations.

Sexual Behaviors

In order to evaluate risk of women in the general population, women who inject drugs, or those who are partners of men who inject drugs, it is important to assess the extent to which women in these groups are sexually active and protect themselves during sex. We will begin by discussing sexual behaviors of women and men, then condom use, and finally other methods of preventing transmission of HIV. Because of the need to identify risks for ethnic racial and minority women, information on relevant risks for ethnic groups will be provided when possible.

Intercourse

A national probability sample of 8,450 women was conducted in the United States as part of the National Survey of Family Growth (NSFG), Cycle IV. Women aged 15–44 were sampled in 1988. Data indicated that 89% of women had had intercourse in the preceding 3 months (Seidman, Mosher, & Aral, 1992). Because this data set includes teenage women, the percent of women who were sexually active in the three month period is lower than it would be if the sample had been restricted to adult women.

In the NADR study, over 90% of female sex partners of injection-drug using men ($N = 5,192$) had engaged in vaginal sex in the past 6 months. About 15% had engaged in anal sex in the past 6 months (Weissman & NARC, 1991). Another study of 137 female sex partners of male IDUs was reported by Corby, Wolitski, Thornton-Johnson, and Tanner (1991). Vaginal intercourse without a condom was reported in the past six months by 96% of African American women, 94% of Hispanic women, and 93% of White women. Anal intercourse without a condom was reported by 4% of African American women, 6% of Hispanic women, and 15% of White women. Overall, these data make clear that the vast majority of women are engaging in vaginal intercourse, and in particular that women who are IDUs themselves or who are sex partners of IDUs are engaging in intercourse at the same rate as the general population. Although engaged in much less frequently, unprotected anal intercourse is a riskier behavior than unprotected vaginal intercourse, and thus is a health concern.

Number of Sexual Partners

In a nationally representative sample of the general population, Seidman et al. (1992) reported that of sexually active women (women who have had sexual intercourse in the preceding year), 3.4% of women reported having sexual intercourse with two or more men in the previous three months. Only 0.4% of the total sample of married women reported multiple partners in the preceding 3 months, but 8% of never-married women and 9.5% of divorced/separated women reported multiple partners within the three-month time period.

A random-digit-dialing study of women in 23 high-risk urban areas in the United States was conducted on 3,482 women to assess extent of sexual risk for HIV-infection (National AIDS Behavioral Surveys) (Grinstead, Faigeles, Binson, & Eversley, 1993). Multiple partners were defined as having two or more partners in the past 12 months. Overall, 6.7% of women reported multiple partners. Single women were again more likely than married or cohabiting women to report multiple partners. Predictors of multiple partners differed across ethnic groups. Among White women, those with more than 12 years of education were more likely to have multiple partners. Among African American and Hispanic women, younger women were more likely than older women to have multiple partners.

Considerably higher percentages of women with multiple partners have been reported for specific populations. For example, Calsyn, Saxon, Wells, and Greenberg (1992) studied a group of 225 male and 88 female

IDUs recruited at drug treatment programs. Before an AIDS intervention, 36% of women and 43% of men reported having multiple sexual partners in the preceding 12 months. In a study of 1,173 minority women recruited from homeless shelters or drug recovery programs (Nyamathi et al., 1993), it was reported that 49% of African American women, 31% of high-acculturated Latina women, and 13% of low-acculturated Latina women (of whom significantly more were married than the other two groups) had more than one sex partner in the previous six months. Corby et al. (1991) report that among 137 female sex partners of male IDUs, 33% of the women re-ported more than one sex partner in the past 6 months. It is clear from these data that subsections of the population have considerably higher frequencies of multiple partners than the general population. These subsamples appear to be groups among whom higher rates of AIDS or HIV seroprevalence have been identified (e.g., IDUs and homeless women). The number of sexual partners an individual has may relate not only to individual factors but also to larger social conditions; this is suggested by Bassett and Mhloyi (1991) in their analysis of the consequences of European colonization in Zimbabwe, and by Fullilove, Fullilove, Haynes, and Gross (1990) in their analysis of eco-nomic factors affecting the African American population.

Partner Risk

The National AIDS Behavioral Surveys found that 5% of women surveyed reported having a *risky primary sexual partner* (defined as someone who is HIV-positive, is an injection drug user in the past 5 years, has been non-monogamous in the past 5 years, has been a transfusion recipient between 1978 and 1985, or is a hemophiliac) (Grinstead et al., 1993). Predictors of having had a risky partner differed by ethnic group. Among Hispanic women, more education was associated with increased likelihood of hav-ing a risky partner. For White women this effect was reversed: White women with less than a high school education were three to four times more likely than those with at least a high school education to have had a risky main sexual partner.

An additional group of women who may be at risk are those who do not know their partner's risk status. In the Grinstead et al. (1993) study, 17% of women who reported no risk behavior of their own said they were unsure if their partners were at risk. Minority women, older women, and less educated women were disproportionately represented in this group. Some female sex partners of IDU men are not aware they are at risk because they are unaware of their partner's drug use (Cohen, Hauer, & Wofsy, 1989; Mondanaro, 1987). Half of male IDUs who were in relationships with one or more non-IDU partners reported that their partners did not know about their injection drug use. Even among IDU men who were monogamous, 17% believed their non-IDU partner was unaware of their drug use (Rhodes et al., 1990).

Use of condoms. In order to assess the behavioral risk of sexual activity, it is important to determine frequency of condom use. Condoms are the most effective method for prevention of HIV transmission, but are a male-controlled method. As can be seen in Table 1, studies indicate that women face substantial risk from unprotected sex. Seven of the studies in Table 1 provide a percentage distribution of women by frequency of condom use (all except Harrison et al., 1991; Mosher and Pratt, 1990; and Osmond et al., 1993). Of these seven, five found that 14% or fewer of women reported that a partner "always" used condoms during sex. Grinstead et al.'s (1993) study focused on women at risk due to either multiple partners or a risky partner. Of women who had multiple partners, 19% had sex in which condoms were always used; Hingson et al. (1990) found that 26% of women aged 16–19 had sex in which condoms were always used.

Many studies are flawed by inadequate measurement of condom use. It is virtually meaningless to classify women only as having sex in which condoms are used without estimating frequency of condom use. Many studies have categorized condom use according to a three-point scale of *always, sometimes,* or *never.* The validity of these categories may be dependent on the way in which women are asked to recall their experience, however. For example, interviewers or questionnaires often request that a participant estimate these categories for sexual experiences over a designated time-frame. If this period is longer than a few weeks, it is likely that respondents will use some form of estimation rather than remembering specific experiences. Retrospective bias enters such estimates. As suggested by Catania, Gibson, Chitwood, and Coates (1990), a better method may involve a partner-by-partner approach to help respondents recall sexual behaviors when they have multiple partners. This approach was employed by Grinstead et al. (1993), whose data were collected as part of the National AIDS Behavioral Surveys (Catania, Coates, Stall, et al., 1992).

Because their data were collected in national probability surveys, the studies by Mosher and Pratt (1993) (for which data were collected in 1990), and Grinstead et al. (1993) (for which data were collected from June 1990 to February 1991) provide the most accurate picture of women's level of risk from unprotected sexual experiences. Although not based on a representative sample, Brown and Weissman's (1993) study of 6,609 women IDUs, for which data were collected between June 1988 and September 1990, represents a massive effort and reveals the high risk-level of this vulnerable population.

Following is a list of predictors of condom use. It is important to look at these factors in order to identify appropriate targets for intervention.

Marital status. Unmarried women are more likely to have partners who use condoms than married women. Mosher and Pratt (1993) found that 14% of unmarried women and only 1% of married women had partners who always used condoms for disease prevention.

Gender. Studies have found that heterosexual men report significantly more condom use than heterosexual women report their male partners to be practicing. Catania, Coates, Stall, et al. (1992) report, for example, that only 45% of African American men say they never use condoms compared to 68% of African American women who say their partners never use condoms. Hingson et al. (1990) report that 34% of male adolescents indicated they always use condoms while only 26% of female adolescents indicated their male partners always use condoms. Basen-Engquist (1992) found that male status was a significant predictor of condom use.

If it is assumed that male and female partners are drawn from the same population, it is not easy to explain the difference in reporting rate for men and women. A viable hypothesis is that social desirability or other reporting biases lead women to be more willing to report lower rates of condom use and encourages men to report higher condom use rates.

Table 1

Condom Use in Studies of HIV Risk-Behaviors in Women

Study	Participants	Design	Measurement of Condom Use	Results: Condom Use Frequency
Brown & Weissman, 1993	6,609 women IDUs who injected in past 6 months	Community outreach interview	Interviewer assessment of CU on 3-pt. scale	13.5% always 29% sometimes
Catania, Coates, Kegeles, et al., 1992	580 sexually active women in San Francisco	Probability study questionnaires	Frequency of CU in past year with all partners (3-pt. scale)	9% always 30% sometimes 61% never
Corby et al., 1991	137 female sex partners of IDU men	Community outreach (interviews)	No use, inconsistent use, or always use	5% always 30% inconsistent 65% never
Grinstead et al., 1993	3,482 women aged 18–49	National probability sample of high-risk cities	Telephone interview rating of CU on a 3-pt. scale	Always: 25% mult. P.[1] 13% risky P.[2] 34% 2nd p.[3]
Harrison et al., 1991	620 nonpregnant South Florida women recruited from jails, etc.	Community outreach (interviews)	Determination of percent who had unprotected sex	66% had unprotected sex with main partner
Hingson et al., 1990	1,050 sexually active male and female adolescents 16–19 years old	Random digit dialing telephone survey	CU rated on a 3-pt. scale	Females: 26% always; Males: 34% always
Mosher & Pratt, 1990	8,450 women aged 15–44	National probability sample	Determination of percent using condoms as contraception	12% of sexually active; 10% of all women

Table 1 (cont.)

Study	Participants	Design	Measurement of Condom Use	Results: Condom Use Frequency
Mosher & Pratt, 1993	2,832 women aged 15–44	Follow-up telephone survey of 1990 study	CU frequency in past 3 months rated on a 3-pt. scale	10% of sexually active (sex in past month): always
Weissman & NARC, 1991	3,272 female IDUs & 1913 female non-IDUs	Community outreach	Interview assessment of percent always using condoms	10% IDUs always; 8% non-IDUs always
Osmond et al., 1993	268 women with a main sex partner	Agency recruitment	Determination of percent time condoms used	Condoms used 26% time with main partners

CU = condom use; IDU = intravenous drug user
[1]mult. p. = among women reporting multiple partners, CU with primary partner
[2]risky p. = among women reporting a risky partner, CU with that partner
[3]2nd p. = among women reporting multiple partners, CU with a secondary partner

Age. In their study of 16–19 year old adolescents, Hingson et al. (1990) found that more 19-year-olds than 16-year-olds always used condoms. However, Mosher and Pratt (1993) found that beyond the teenage years, the proportion of women indicating that they made a behavior change to avoid AIDS declined sharply with age.

Education. Clear differences in condom use by education level were found in Mosher and Pratt's (1993) national probability study. Among unmarried women who had less than a high school education, only 4% reported that their partner always used condoms, compared to 11% of women who were high school graduates and 21% of women with college educations.

Race/ethnicity. Mosher and Pratt (1993) found that the percentage of women reporting that their partners always use condoms was about the same for White, African American, and Hispanic women. However, a lower percentage of African American women (64%) reported their partners never using condoms, compared to White women (81%) or Hispanic women (76%). Data supporting the greater use of condoms by sex partners of African American women were also provided by Osmond et al. (1993). However, Catania, Coates, Kegeles, et al. (1992) found that unmarried Hispanic and African American women in San Francisco were less likely than White women to have sexual partners who always use condoms. This was the case after controlling for other variables studied. It is not immediately evident how to reconcile this finding with that of Mosher and Pratt (1993). However, a difference between the studies is that the Catania study was based on a survey of 16 census tracts characterized by high rates of sexually transmitted diseases and admission to drug programs. It is reasonable to expect that individuals in this sample would perceive their HIV risk to be higher than those in the national sample, making the samples nonequivalent. Furthermore, education level, which did predict condom use in Mosher and Pratt's data, was not measured by Catania, Coates, Kegeles, et al. (1992) and may potentially differentiate the two samples.

Number of sex partners. A trend across studies indicates that among women who have multiple partners, condoms are used more often than among women who report only one partner. Mosher and Pratt (1993) report that although the always use category was not different for women with multiple partners, the sometimes use category was. Of the women with multiple partners, 44% reported using a condom some of the time, compared to 22% of women with only one partner. Grinstead et al. (1993) found that consistent condom use with a primary partner was more common among women with multiple partners than among monogamous women who were at risk because their partner met a risk criterion. Corby et al. (1991) found that women with multiple partners were more likely than those with one partner to report having used condoms at least once (51% vs. 20%).

Exchange of sex for drugs or money. Osmond et al. (1993) found that women reported condom use with clients 70% of the time, compared with 26% of the time with main partners. Weissman and the National AIDS Research Consortium (NARC) (1991) report that condoms were used more frequently by partners of women who exchanged sex for money or drugs than partners of women who didn't.

Condom use decision-making. Osmond et al. (1993) asked women to indicate who made the decision to use condoms: Categories were *self, partner, both,* or *never discussed.* The *never discussed* variable alone accounted for 20% of variance in frequency of condom use. Among those who never discussed condom use, none used condoms more than half the time. If the partner decided, only 12% used condoms more than half the time. However, for women who made the decision themselves, 49% reported condom use more than half the time, and if both decided, 32% used condoms more than half the time. In this study, one third of women reported that either their partner made the decision or condom use was never discussed. Both groups reported low condom use. These results are consistent with results from a study of condom use among Hispanic men and women (Mikawa et al., 1992). The authors reported that the use of condoms appeared to be a male prerogative rather than a female one, with men being much more likely than women to buy and initiate use of condoms. Whether or not condoms are used seems to depend on "how well males took charge of obtaining condoms and fulfilled certain aspects of the machismo role" (p. 430).

Alcohol use. Hingson et al. (1990) found that male and female respondents who drank five or more drinks per day were less likely to use condoms than those who abstained.

Enjoyment of condom use. Enjoyment of condom use has also been found to be related to condom use. Condom use in adolescent women attending a family planning clinic was found to be predicted by enjoyment of condom use and willingness to request that partners use a condom (Catania et al., 1989). Additionally, condom use in women in San Francisco living in census tracts characterized by high rates of sexually transmitted diseases and admission to drug programs was found to be predicted by greater enjoyment of condom use (Catania, Coates, Kegeles et al., 1992). In this study, enjoyment of condom use was measured by self-report of the degree to which respondents enjoyed vaginal or anal intercourse when they used a condom, or, if respondents had never used condoms, how much they expected to enjoy intercourse with condoms.

Perceived risk. Catania, Coates, Stall et al. (1992) did not find that perceived susceptibility (perceived likelihood of contracting the AIDS virus in the next year) or AIDS anxiety (degree of concern over the possibility of contracting the AIDS virus) were predictive of condom use in women. However, Hingson et al. (1990) found that respondents (male and female adolescents combined) were more likely to always use condoms if they felt susceptible to AIDS. While these cross-sectional studies provide information concerning current attitudes and behaviors, longitudinal research is important to know whether women change sexual safety behaviors as their perceptions of risk change (Moore, Harrison, & Doll, 1994). Furthermore, it is of interest whether there are generational changes in women's willingness to take protective measures in the face of risk.

Test of models. Variables associated with the health belief model, the theory of reasoned action, and theories of cognitive coping style were tested on 275 undergraduate students (Basen-Engquist, 1992). College students' use of condoms was predicted by intention to use condoms, male gender, lower social support, and a cognitive style referred to as *blunting*, in which an individual copes with anxiety by blocking out stressors. Perceived susceptibility to the disease and perceived barriers to preventive behavior were related to intention to use condoms. The Basen-Engquist model accounted for 35% of variance.

A different model of the practice of unprotected sex by college women was tested by Harlow et al. (1993). A structural model was evaluated. Predictors of unprotected vaginal sex included greater sexual experience, anticipation of negative reaction by partner to condom use, and self-efficacy for AIDS prevention (see also Goldman & Harlow, 1993). Seventy percent of variance was explained in unprotected vaginal intercourse. A separate dependent variable in this model was unprotected anal intercourse. Predictors of this variable were less sexual foreplay experience, greater sexual experience, and less sexual assertiveness with respect to pregnancy/STD prevention. Forty-one percent of variance for this dependent variable was explained. A third dependent variable evaluated in the model was identified as partner risk. This composite variable included both number of partners and risk characteristics of partners. Significant predictors of partner risk were greater alcohol use, less use of other drugs, history of adult sexual victimization, ability to refuse sex, a composite measure of psychosocial functioning (including measures of hopelessness, demoralization, meaninglessness, and perceived stress), and self-efficacy for AIDS prevention. Of the variance in this dependent variable, 64% was explained.

In summary, these data suggest that unmarried women who have multiple partners, are better educated, abstain from alcohol, have sex with a client rather than a main partner, believe they can protect themselves from sexually transmitted disease, enjoy using condoms, or have control over condom decision-making are more likely to use condoms during sex. For some of these variables it appears that women who perceive their risk to be higher (e.g., due to having multiple partners or being involved in the exchange of sex for money) use condoms more often. As previously indicated, some empirical support exists for an association between perceived risk and condom use. This indicates the need to educate women with respect to their personal level of risk. Education may also help women to feel more efficacious concerning their ability to protect themselves sexually. However, perceptions of AIDS prevention efficacy relate to specific characteristics of relationships, as in the case of the women in Osmond et al.'s (1993) study who perceived having no input in condom use decision-making. Future research on predictors of condom use and other sexual behaviors should address the interpersonal aspects of condom use. For example, decision-making in a variety of relationship domains such as child-care or household decisions may be related to condom use and other sexual decisions. In further exploration of the characteristics related to condom use decision-making, it is important to have estimates of relationship variables from both female and male partners.

Psychoeducational Interventions to Reduce HIV/AIDS Risk

Given the findings that the great majority of women do not always use condoms and that a substantial percentage do not have a role in making the decision about whether condoms will be used, the question arises of whether programs can be implemented to increase women's ability to ne-

Table 2

Interventions to Decrease HIV Risk in Women

Study	Participants	Design	Results
Deiter, 1993	90 undergraduate women	4-week sexual assertiveness vs. general assertiveness control vs. no-intervention control	No significant differences in condom use or assertiveness
Franzini et al., 1990	41 undergraduate women; 38 undergraduate men	3 1-hr. groups on sexual assertiveness vs. control	Women: control group showed more assertiveness when condom use was role-played at posttest; Men: experimental group more assertive at posttest
Gallagher et al., 1991	60 undergraduate women	Cognitive–behavioral rehearsal (including role plays) vs. AIDS information alone	Experimental group: condom use increased from 13% to 27% at 1 mo. follow-up
Gallagher & Lang, 1993	60 undergraduate women	Follow-up to Gallagher (1991) at 1 year	No difference between experimental and control groups
Jemmot et al., 1992	19 adolescents	105 minute social/cognitive program vs. AIDS info. alone vs. general health promotion	Social/cognitive: Increased intentions to use condoms; increased self-efficacy for condom use
Kavanagh et al., 1992	9 women on methadone maintenance	Program of 8 2-hour sessions. No control.	Changes reported in increased condom use and use of bleach to clean needles

Table 2 (cont.)

Study	Participants	Design	Results
Kelly et al., 1994	197 inner-city women	HIV/AIDS risk reduction group (4 sessions) vs. health education control (3 sessions) + follow-up	Experimental group: condom use increased from 26% to 56%; no change for control group
Rhodes et al., 1992	53 female sex partners of male IDUs	Four session program focusing on condom use/ needle cleaning, making a commitment to change, and reducing barriers to change	Changes reported in discussing condom use with partner, stopping drug use, cleaning needles, and asking partner to leave

gotiate condom use with their male partners. Table 2 summarizes the results from representative studies in the literature that evaluated intervention programs. The most promising program (Kelly et al., 1994) describes a four-session intervention that included detailed information about HIV risk, role-playing on initiating discussion of AIDS concerns and condom use, and role-playing on how to decline sex from men whose risk history was unknown or with whom the woman did not want to have sex. Random assignment was made to either an HIV/AIDS risk-reduction intervention or to a comparison intervention dealing with health topics unrelated to AIDS. Results indicated a significant increase in condom use and an increase in both sexual communication and negotiation skills at three-month follow-up in the HIV/AIDS risk reduction group but not the comparison group. An increase in condom use was also reported by Gallagher, Morokoff, Quina, and Harlow (1991) following a five-session small group intervention with college women; however, a subsequent study (Gallagher & Lang, 1993) revealed that condom use had decreased to a level below that of the control group after one year. This study emphasizes the importance of long-term follow-up in evaluating the success of programs. Other programs presented in Table 2 either did not employ a control group or did not demonstrate improvements in condom use or sexual assertiveness.

Other studies have also reported negative results. For example, a study presented at the Ninth International Conference on AIDS (Lubega, 1993) described a program to provide AIDS education in the workplace in order to help Ugandan women introduce condom use to their spouses. Role-play and negotiation training were included. The authors report that 90% of women still feared introducing condoms to their sexual partners after the program because they did not want to appear unfaithful or lose their husbands to more cooperative sexual partners. A program in Nairobi Kenya also reported at the conference involved weekly educational outreach to women over a period of more than three months (Kiuri, Awuor, Onyango, & Adhiambo, 1993). The program coordinators found that educational programs worked best when alternative economic support was also provided to economically disadvantaged women.

Negative results with women are in sharp contrast to efforts to teach condom use to men, which appear to be more uniformly successful. For example, clinical outcome studies have documented the effectiveness of short-term small group sessions on AIDS-risk reduction behavioral skills training for gay and bisexual men (Kelly, St. Lawrence, Hood, & Brasfield, 1989; Kelly, St. Lawrence, Betts, Brasfield, & Hood, 1990; Valdiserri et al., 1989). These studies have shown that analog practice in condom use and role-play of sexually assertive behaviors are effective in increasing knowledge and behavioral skills while decreasing risky sexual behaviors.

The model for AIDS-risk reduction proposed by Fisher and Fisher (1992) posits that there are three fundamental determinants of AIDS-risk reduction: information, motivation, and behavioral skills. Certainly these components are necessary for women to insist on condom use or to ask for information concerning sexual history. However, women do not wear condoms, and ending a relationship may be a woman's ultimate threat if her partner doesn't wish to use condoms. Can women be motivated to end relationships if partners won't use condoms? It is unrealistic to imagine that all women can be convinced that protecting their health is the only important thing in life. Therefore, women may not always choose to end a relationship if their partners refuse to use condoms, especially when they rely on that partner for financial support, parenting, or love. As discussed by Aggleton, O'Reilly, Slutkin, and Davies (1994), the models of health behavior commonly used today, including the health belief model, the theory of reasoned action, and social learning theory, make the basic assumption that individuals make decisions about and potentially have control over their health behavior. It is critical to integrate social/gender factors into such models.

For some women, such as those described by Osmond et al. (1993),

> Safer sex appears to be a remote concern for the majority in the sample, who are impoverished, single heads of households with young children dependent on them for emotional and financial support. To many, sex is the major source of income. To most, sex is a means to establish intimacy in relationships or a means of simply getting tangible supports that are generally short in supply. They are keenly aware that they can expect little assistance from public agencies, where their needs compete with pregnant teenagers, cocaine addicts, adolescent runaways, and men as well as women who need medical assistance and jobs. They are constantly fearful of driving away a partner who may not be only the father of their children but also their only source of emotional support. (p. 115)

Findings such as these lead us to address again the question of whether the most effective HIV/AIDS risk-reduction strategy should focus on teaching women to get their partners to use condoms. Can we serve women best by expecting them to talk their partners into using condoms, or should we focus on interventions teaching men to use condoms, which research indicates is a more effective strategy? Alternatively, we can focus on AIDS prevention methods other than using condoms.

Exploring Other Prevention Methods

Female-controlled Versus Male-controlled Methods

Experience from the family planning literature indicates that when types of contraceptives that can be controlled by women are available, they are often used (Rosenberg & Gollub, 1992). When types of contraception traditionally controlled by men are relied on, they are not used as often. A distinction can be drawn between *efficacy of condoms*, defined as the reduction in HIV transmission achieved on each occasion that a condom is used correctly, and the effectiveness of a disease prevention program based on condom use. The efficacy of condoms is somewhat established. Two reviews of the use of latex condoms among serodiscordant heterosexual couples document that using latex condoms substantially reduces the risk for HIV transmission (Cates & Stone, 1992; Weller, 1993). In an editorial note to a report on the efficacy of barrier protection, it is stated that "latex condoms are highly effective for preventing HIV infection and other STDs when used consistently and correctly" (CDC, 1993c, p. 590).

Effectiveness relies on acceptability of and compliance with a method as well as its efficacy, however. In order for condoms to be effective, a woman must be able to make decisions with regard to their use. These issues have led some to suggest that public health officials should advocate use of spermicides to prevent HIV and other STDs. Although the efficacy of spermicides does not match that of the condom, if spermicides are used more often they may actually be more effective. Rosenberg and Gollub (1992) reviewed ten observational studies that compared the effect of condoms, diaphragms, and spermicides on the risk of STDs (not including HIV). Nine of the ten studies found lower risk among users of female-controlled devices than among condom users. The largest study (Rosenberg, Davidson, Chen, Judson, & Douglas, 1992) found a significantly greater risk for male-controlled (condoms) than female-controlled (spermicide or diaphragm) methods. It should be noted that the recommendation to use spermicides to prevent HIV infection has not gained widespread acceptance. It may, however, stimulate research into microbicides that have a high rate of efficacy against HIV and other STDs.

The Need for a Microbicide

As pointed out by Stein (1990), the sole physical barrier presently promoted for the prevention of sexual transmission of HIV is the condom. Active male cooperation is required for use. Thus Stein argues for the necessity of empowering women, not by training them to be more assertive with male partners, but by giving them the tools to protect themselves such as a virucide or microbicide.

The World Health Organization (WHO) has now adopted a strategy of identifying a safe and effective substance that kills HIV that can be inserted into the vagina in a foam, gel, or sponge. This strategy was discussed at a meeting in November 1993 in Geneva. Ability to develop a vaginal microbicide appears to be within technological grasp. Altman (1993) quotes Michael H. Merson, executive director of the WHO's AIDS program as saying "If scientific and pharmaceutical communities set their minds to it and made the needed investments, such a product could rapidly be developed" (p. C3). According to Potts (1994), however, an appropriately funded research program is not yet in existence. Some of the issues that need to be addressed to develop an effective vaginal microbicide are whether all cells in the female reproductive tract are susceptible to HIV and what effect the microbicide would have on sperm or beneficial organisms that live in the vagina.

The Female Condom

A polyurethane intravaginal pouch, the *female condom*, has now received approval from the Food and Drug Administration (FDA) and is being now marketed to the general public soon. Laboratory studies indicate that it is an effective mechanical barrier to viruses, including HIV. Pilot testing indicates that women are not yet completely accepting of the device. For example, Latin American women felt they would need complete assurance that the pouch would be used by peers in order to adopt it on a regular basis with their main partners. They also lacked confidence in their own ability to use the pouch correctly and were not completely convinced that the pouch would protect them from pregnancy or disease (Bond, Quinonez, & Chavez, 1993). The authors also suggest that both the size of the pouch and its cost might be barriers to use. Furthermore, it is not clear that the pouch will empower women to protect themselves in the same way that a microbicide would, because it is obtrusive and thus might still require negotiation with a partner for use.

Recommendations Concerning Primary Prevention

An important strategy that could be implemented to reduce HIV transmission in women is the needle exchange program. Current data show such programs to be effective, although special effort is required to make existing programs more available to women. Treatment programs to help women stop using injection drugs are a longer range strategy that is important for multiple reasons, many of which go well beyond HIV risk alone. There is scant available evidence, however, concerning the effectiveness of such programs for women. Even if such programs can be demonstrated to be highly effective, there currently are barriers to provision of adequate treatment of women in chemical dependence programs.

Evidence suggests that it is difficult to increase use of condoms, an essentially male behavior, through interventions targeted at women. Programs directed specifically toward men appear more successful. However, heterosexual men's motivation to participate in such programs may be limited in part by their lower level of vulnerability to HIV infection from unprotected vaginal intercourse. As suggested by Holland, Ramazanoglu, Scott, Sharpe, and Thomson (1990), "Public health campaigns have followed convention in expecting women to take responsibility not only for their own reputations, and their own bodies, but also for policing their partners' male sex drive. Health education has not yet addressed the need to change the behaviour of heterosexual men" (p. 347). Thus, a danger in directing programs solely at women is adoption of the gender stereotype that views women as responsible not only for their own sexual behaviors but for their male partners' behaviors as well.

In addition to developing programs to change heterosexual men's behavior, the most important single effort toward the goal of primary prevention in women at this point is the development of a woman-controlled microbicide that would inactivate HIV without harming sperm (Potts, 1994). Evidence indicates that when women have decision-making power over use of a sexually protective product, it is more likely to be used.

Programs designed to empower women and to help them end relationships in which partners refuse to use condoms are important (Morokoff & Harlow, 1993). Again, these are a longer range strategy to reducing the threat of HIV/AIDS. Some of the programs reviewed here had positive effects that went well beyond whether or not partners used condoms. In designing programs, several issues suggested by Croteau et al. (1993)

need to be kept in mind: (a) Targeted group members should be included as full partners in planning and developing programs. For instance, if a program is to be planned for African American women, the messages need to be controlled by African American women. (b) Peer leaders need to be involved in implementing the program. Research suggests that programs may be more successful when the message is delivered by a member of the targeted group. (c) It is essential to include culturally relevant content, media, and settings. Successful programs are those that incorporate culturally relevant material (Kalichman, Kelly, Hunter, Murphy, & Tyler, 1993). (d) It is important to foster group pride. This strategy was highly successful in empowering gay men to make changes in their sexual behaviors. (e) It is important to make the target group as specific as possible. For example, a program incorporating culturally sensitive messages for Puerto Rican women may not be optimal for Cuban women, because the term *Hispanic* is an umbrella term applying to groups characterized by historical, social, and economic differences (Amaro, 1988). The most effective programs will include women from the target group at all phases of program delivery.

GENDER-SPECIFIC ISSUES FOR HIV-SEROPOSITIVE WOMEN AND WOMEN WITH AIDS

AIDS Case Definition

Numerous authors have discussed discrimination toward women in the CDC case definition for AIDS (e.g., Quinn, 1993; Rosser, 1991). This criticism is primarily based on the fact that HIV infection can produce disorders of a woman's reproductive system independent from other diseases on the CDC list—a list originally developed from observations of conditions associated with HIV in men. A number of disorders of the female genital tract appear to be made worse by HIV infection, including vaginal yeast infections (*candidiasis*) and *human papilloma virus* (HPV), the virus that is related to cervical cancer and precancerous cervical lesions (Mitchell, Tucker, Loftman, & Williams, 1992). It is difficult to establish whether these disorders are AIDS-defining, however, because of their high base-rates, especially in the population of women most at risk for HIV infection. The failure to identify appropriate gynecologic conditions for inclusion in the AIDS case definition has contributed to late diagnoses of women with AIDS, who are therefore not able to receive early treatment or participate in clinical trials. A revised classification system for HIV infection and an expanded surveillance case definition for AIDS in adolescents and adults went into effect January 1993 (CDC, 1992). The revised system categorizes individuals based on both clinical conditions and on immune function parameters, specifically CD4+T-lymphocyte counts. The previous system which did not include criteria related to CD4+T-lymphocyte counts was developed before testing for CD4+T-cells was common. In addition, three clinical conditions were added to the clinical conditions: pulmonary tuberculosis, recurrent pneumonia, and invasive cervical cancer. These changes will help in diagnosis of women, although other gynecological conditions may also be early signs of advancing HIV infection.

Health Care and Support Systems for Women With HIV/AIDS

Early retrospective evidence suggested that women who were diagnosed with AIDS survived for less time than men diagnosed with AIDS (Rothenberg et al., 1987). However, more recent prospective data in which health care, stage of disease, and zidovudine (AZT) use were controlled for demonstrated that survival times of HIV-infected women and men were comparable (Castro, Valdiserri, & Curran, 1992; Szabo et al., 1992). Sex differences in earlier studies may have been due to diagnosis occurring at a later disease stage for women than men. Later diagnosis could result from the previously described lack of awareness of the natural history and manifestation of symptoms in women compared with men. Furthermore, early results may have been affected by the fact that women have had less access to health care than men.

Psychosocial Support

Women in the United States with HIV encounter specific obstacles to obtaining treatment. Chung and Magraw (1992) indicate that there is underrecognition by the public and health professionals of the extent of HIV/AIDS in women. It is also the case that HIV/AIDS predominantly affects poor women (Zuckerman & Gordon, 1988). It is worth remembering that the majority of women with AIDS were infected as a result of injection-drug use or sexual contact with an IDU partner. Many of these women lack social support, and financial, medical, and legal resources to deal effectively with the disease. Numerous studies have documented the psychological symptoms reported by HIV-infected men, including anxiety, depression, anger, insomnia, loss of libido, and memory or concentration loss (Coates & Lo, 1990; LaPerriere, Schneiderman, Antoni, & Fletcher, 1990). Fewer studies have looked at psychosocial problems encountered by HIV-infected women.

One investigation looked at issues for a group of White, lower-middle class women who participated in support groups (Chung & Magraw, 1992). A common problem identified by women was isolation. The authors report that before entering the support group, most of the women had never met another woman with HIV infection. Many women felt alone with the illness, and believed that most support services were designed for gay men. Women also felt stigmatization and shame due to their illness. Women were able to provide support to each other with respect to symptoms that may be discounted by physicians. Women had concerns about transmitting HIV to other family members. They also reported that family members expected them to be caretakers of others even though they were sick. This phenomenon is pervasive across categories of chronic disease when gender expectations require women to be caretakers (Gallant, Coons, & Morokoff, 1994). When women are sick there is often no one to provide care for them. Disclosing HIV status to children is another problem faced by women, who must help their children confront their own death.

Psychosocial Sequelae to HIV/AIDS Diagnosis

Research suggests that women experience depression, apprehension, sadness, helplessness, anger, and fear in confronting an HIV/AIDS diagnosis (Coons et al., 1993; Eversley, 1993). In interviews with HIV-infected women in the San Francisco Bay area, Eversley found that women may be fearful of disclosing their HIV-infection to others, in part due to concerns of stigmatization, loss of existing social support, and fear of losing their children. Lack of disclosure may prevent women from receiving needed medical care. Eversley reports that the presence of a psychotherapist, social worker, or other provider of support can enhance the ability of HIV-positive women to seek and maintain appropriate medical care.

Cleary et al. (1993) studied depression and other psychological factors in women and men blood donors who had to be notified that they were HIV-positive. The authors report that the average depressive symptom scores for both women and men in this study were substantially higher than those of persons in the general population following notification. A study of pregnant women who were HIV-positive found that all had a psychiatric disturbance and most elected to continue their pregnancy (James, 1988).

However, a study conducted in Italy in which HIV-positive women were compared to seronegative controls who had requested HIV testing revealed little difference in psychological status between the two groups (Pergami et al., 1993). Where differences did exist (e.g., in subscales of the Symptoms Checklist [SCL]-90 measuring depression, anxiety, hostility, paranoid ideation, and the global severity index), it was the seronegative group who had the poorer level of functioning. These results underscore the need for awareness of the complexity of stressors affecting both HIV seropositive women and women who are at risk for HIV infection due to such factors as their own or a partner's drug use.

Reproductive Rights

Another salient issue for HIV-infected women concerns reproductive choices. A set of recommendations was released by the CDC in 1985 concerning prevention of perinatal transmission of HIV. It is recommended that certain categories of pregnant women be offered counseling and testing. For seropositive women, the report indicates that they "should be advised to consider delaying pregnancy until more is known about perinatal transmission of the virus" (CDC, 1985). While there may be compelling reasons for some women to delay childbearing, as suggested by the CDC, for others there may be compelling reasons not to delay childbearing, in spite of risks to the child. The risk of perinatal transmission of HIV is about 1 in 4 (Altman, 1994; Arras, 1990). Most HIV-infected women and women with AIDS are poor women of color. In order to understand the impact of delayed childbearing for these women, one must look at their lives and cultural values. As discussed by Carovano (1991), in many cultures there may be no social place for women who do not have children. Where women's opportunities for personal goals or professional opportunities are severely restricted, children may become the goal of their existence. An HIV-infected woman was quoted by Levine and Dubler (1990), "I really wanted something of mine, you know, mine, mine. I don't have nothing in this world ... nothing that I really care about" (p. 335). Women's reproductive decisions may also be influenced by many factors including loss of previous children.

Even if a poor HIV-infected woman desires an abortion, she may not be able to get one. In a study conducted by the AIDS Division of the New York City Commission on Human Rights, 20 of the 30 clinics and private doctors called would not keep an appointment after learning that the patient was HIV-infected (Levine & Dubler, 1990). Poor women are in the no-win situation of being held responsible for spreading HIV/AIDS without being provided with resources to limit reproduction (Quinn, 1993).

Recent data indicate that the risk of perinatal transmission of HIV can be substantially reduced if HIV-infected women take AZT during pregnancy. In a placebo controlled evaluation of the use of AZT during pregnancy (CDC, 1994c), 26% of women receiving a placebo bore children infected with HIV. For those taking AZT, only 8% (a two-thirds reduction) of babies were HIV-infected. This new finding underscores the need for inclusion of women, in this case pregnant women, in relevant drug trials. Availability of an effective preventive treatment raises the need for equitable access to treatment. As usual, poor women who are most in need of this treatment may not be able to receive it.

Society's response to HIV/AIDS must go beyond instructing an individual to be responsible for her own actions. Our response must combine respect for the individual's motivation and ability to make changes in her life with knowledge of barriers that may exist toward fulfillment of her goals. As Levine and Dubler (1990) pointed out

> A society that permits poverty, drugs, and economic dislocation, spends proportionately less for education of the poor while overlooking truancy and dropouts, and perpetuates neighborhoods with inferior health care and social services bears at least some moral responsibility for the consequences of these unleashed societal forces. (p. 337)

If a society casts HIV/AIDS prevention exclusively as the responsibility of individuals, especially given that those at greatest risk for HIV infection are the poorest members of society, then society is placing a heavy burden on those with the least resources.

CONCLUSIONS

Most women with AIDS and most women at risk for HIV infection are poor ethnic minority women who are involved with injection-drugs, either through their own use or through a partner's. This does not discount the very real level of risk confronting nonminority women, and women who do not live in neighborhoods where HIV/AIDS is prevalent, inject drugs, or are not involved with partners who inject drugs. The level of risk, however, is lower. Primary prevention efforts must take into account the demands on poor women's lives and their potential lack of autonomy in sexual decision-making. Secondary prevention involving access to appropriate medical care must also take into account the reality of women's lives. At-risk women have been advised to make difficult changes in their lives such as refusing to share needles, abstaining from drugs, insisting on condom use for sex, practicing sexual abstinence, or foregoing childbearing if they are HIV-infected. Resources are not made available to women which would help protect them against HIV infection. A needle exchange program is a resource that would help women be protected against disease transmission through needle-sharing. Needle exchange is currently not available to women in many cities, often on the grounds that drug use is immoral.

A microbicide that women can use is another resource that would protect women in sexual encounters without challenging sexual power in relationships. One reason a microbicide has not been developed may be because women's health needs have been overlooked both in the AIDS epidemic and in other health areas. Another reason may be because gender-based power differences in sexual relationships are fully not understood. If we fail to acknowledge that women cannot easily influence or control men's sexual behavior, then it will be assumed that condom use, which is under men's control, will adequately protect women.

The Challenge of HIV/AIDS to Society

The HIV/AIDS epidemic has had, and will continue to have, a profound effect on society. Because in many cities the majority of women with HIV are poor, researchers must carefully examine societal barriers to health care for these women. According to Mitchell et al. (1992), access to care and services is directly related to whether women are minority members, whether they are poor, and whether they are drug users. The norm of economic opportunity based on race ensures a society in which oppressed groups are at risk. Greater equal economic opportunity that enhances stability of family relationships, educational opportunities, and access to health care and other societal benefits would immensely improve efforts to prevent the spread of HIV/AIDS.

At the same time, our societal response to addictions is being challenged. Data indicate that the most effective approaches to reducing the spread of HIV through needles are adoption of needle exchange programs, drug education to prevent injection drug use, and availability of substance abuse treatment. Many communities have resisted needle exchange programs because they appear to support drug use. Many resist taking money away from law enforcement of drug use to put it into prevention and treatment. Redirection of public resources to such programs would entail a significant societal reevaluation.

The public health construct of safer sex calls for several significant changes in the traditional ideals for heterosexual behavior. First, it is based on the idea that two people enter voluntarily into consensual sexual ac-

tivity. The reality of gendered power relations in sexuality has forced, perhaps for the first time, a growing public recognition that women are not
equals to men in sexual decision-making. Second, this construct places a
positive value on nonpenetrative sex. This redefinition of sex from penile–vaginal penetration is not trivial, because it shifts the concept of sex
from what is commonly perceived as the male sexual objective to something different. Third, safer sex focuses on communication between partners. The traditional ideal of an implicit understanding of what is sexually expected must give way not only to a discussion between partners of
past sexual experience, but also to a negotiated agreement of what should
be included in the present sexual encounter. Ultimately, the message of
safer sex requires a new sexual revolution: one in which sex is shifted from
the ideal of male dominance/female submission to an ideal of gender
equality in heterosexual relationships.

The Role of Psychology

Psychology can play a crucial role in making the case to society at large of
the need for more resources for women at risk. Psychologists can help to
document the reality of women's lives, which will provide necessary information concerning development of prevention programs. This would
include such topics as the prevalence of needle-sharing; the relation between power in women's relationships with IDUs and needle-sharing; the
effect of differential patterns of injection-equipment use on disease risk;
predictors of women's risky sexual behaviors, including interpersonal factors predicting condom-use decisions; and social factors that limit
women's ability to lead healthful and less risky lives. This information can
be effectively used to make the case for more resources for women's health.

In addition, information from studies of factors in women's lives can
be used to develop urgently needed programs for women. Documentation
of the effectiveness of demonstration needle exchange projects is already
underway. Demonstration projects of comprehensive drug treatment programs for women and their children have also been developed and implemented in a number of cities, but more and better programs and evaluations of programs are needed. Some programs have attempted to teach
sexual assertiveness and AIDS protection to women at risk. Evaluation of

such programs is needed. Women need support groups for people with HIV, confidential HIV testing programs, and counseling for HIV-infected women. Women also need access to drug trials, medications, and other available treatment for AIDS.

Data are now available from women concerning their partners' use of condoms. There is less information collected from heterosexual men on their use of condoms. This is unfortunate because evidence indicates that men's condom use behavior can be more easily modified through direct intervention than it can through teaching women to be more sexually assertive. Data on predictors of heterosexual men's use of condoms would help in developing urgently needed programs to teach heterosexual men about the risks of STDs and preventing STDs through condom use. It is also important to determine whether interventions to change condom use are best targeted at heterosexual women, men, or both partners of a couple.

The psychological effect of HIV/AIDS on women has barely been studied. Effects on psychological functioning, special problems that various populations of women face in coping with HIV/AIDS, issues in undergoing serostatus testing, and problems such as disclosing test results and obtaining medical care are topics on which little research has been conducted. As more women become sick, these problems will become more acutely perceived. While methodologically rigorous research is often difficult, at this stage of our knowledge it is important simply to begin to understand the phenomena.

AIDS has presented researchers and practitioners with many challenges, which are all the more urgent because of the deadly nature of the disease. We are challenged to find ways to help women protect themselves from sexually transmitted disease, even though in many ways this requires a realignment of gender roles. We are challenged to help women protect themselves from disease transmitted through injection-drug use. We are challenged to understand the psychological effects of diagnosis and symptoms and to understand women's medical needs, especially when they are different from men's. And we are challenged to help even the poorest members of society obtain medical care. Finally, as researchers and practitioners, it is our responsibility to accept these challenges and to respond to the crisis of AIDS.

REFERENCES

Aggleton, P., O'Reilly, K., Slutkin, G., & Davies, P. (1994). Risking everything? Risk behavior, behavior change, and AIDS. *Science, 265,* 341–345.

Altman, L. K. (1993, November 2). New strategy backed for fighting AIDS. *The New York Times,* pp. C1, C3.

Altman, L. K. (1994, February 21). Drug dramatically cuts infection of HIV in newborns, study says. *The New York Times,* pp. A1, A13.

Amaro, H. (1988). Considerations for prevention of HIV infection among Hispanic women. *Psychology of Women Quarterly, 12,* 429–443.

Arras, J. (1990). AIDS and reproductive decisions: Having children in fear and trembling. *Milbank Quarterly, 68,* 353–382.

Baldwin, J. D., & Baldwin, J. I. (1988). Factors affecting AIDS-related sexual risk-taking behavior among college students. *Journal of Sex Research, 25,* 181–196.

Basen-Engquist, K. (1992). Psychosocial predictors of "safer sex" behaviors in young adults. *AIDS Education and Prevention, 4,* 120–134.

Basset, M. T., & Mhloyi, M. (1991). Women and AIDS in Zimbabwe: The making of an epidemic. *International Journal of Health Services, 21,* 143–156.

Berrios, D. C., Hearst, N., Coates, T. J., Stall, R., Hudes, E., Turner, H., Eversely, R., Catania, J. (1993). HIV antibody testing among those at risk for infection. *Journal of the American Medical Association, 270,* 1576–1580.

Bond, L., Quinonez, A., & Chavez, G. (1993, June). Exploratory study on attitudes and behavior toward the use of the female pouch—implications for HIV/STD transmission prevention. *Proceedings of the IXth International Conference on AIDS.* Abstract No. PO-D03-2494, p. 800.

Brown, V., & Weissman, G. (1993). Women and men injection drug users: An updated look at gender differences and risk factors. In B. S. Brown & G. M. Beschner (Eds.), *Handbook on risk of AIDS: Injection drug users and sexual partners* (pp. 173–194). Westport, CT: Greenwood Press.

Calsyn, D. A., Saxon, A. J., Wells, E. A., & Greenberg, D. M. (1992). Longitudinal sexual behavior changes in injecting drug users. *AIDS, 6,* 1207–1211.

Carovano, K. (1991). More than mothers and whores: Redefining the AIDS prevention needs of women. *International Journal of Health Services, 21,* 131–142.

Castro, K. G., Valdiserri, R. O., & Curran, J. W. (1992). Perspectives on HIV/AIDS epidemiology and prevention from the Eighth International Conference on AIDS. *American Journal of Public Health, 82,* 1465–1470.

Catania, J. A., Coates, T. J., Kegeles, S., Fullilove, M. T., Peterson, J., Marin, B., Siegel, D., & Hulley, S. (1992). Condom use in multi-ethnic neighborhoods of San Francisco: The population-based AMEN (AIDS in Multi-Ethnic Neighborhoods) study. *American Journal of Public Health, 82,* 284–287.

Catania, J. A., Coates, T. J., Stall, R., Turner, H., Peterson, J., Hearst, N., Dolcini, M. M., Hudes, E., Gagnon, J., Wiley, J., & Groves, R. (1992). Prevalence of AIDS-related risk factors and condom use in the United States. *Science, 258,* 1101–1106.

Catania, J. A., Dolcini, M. M., Coates, T. J., Kegeles, S. M., Greenblatt, R. M., Puckett, S., Corman, M., & Miller, J. (1989). Predictors of condom use and multiple partnered sex among sexually-active adolescent women: Implications for AIDS-related health interventions. *Journal of Sex Research, 26,* 514–524.

Catania, J. A., Gibson, D. R., Chitwood, D. D., & Coates, T. J. (1990). Methodological problems in AIDS behavioral research: Influences on measurement error and participation bias in studies of sexual behavior. *Psychological Bulletin, 108,* 339–362.

Cates, W., & Stone, K. M. (1992). Family planning, sexually transmitted diseases, and contraceptive choice: A literature update. *Family Planning Perspective, 24,* 75–84.

Centers for Disease Control. (1985, December 6). Recommendations for assisting in the prevention of perinatal transmission of HTLV-III/LAV and acquired immunodeficiency syndrome. *Morbidity and Mortality Weekly Report, 32,* 721–732.

Centers for Disease Control and Prevention. (1992, December 18). 1993 revised classification system for HIV infection and expanded surveillance case definition for AIDS among adolescents and adults. *Morbidity and Mortality Weekly Report, 41,* 1–19.

Centers for Disease Control and Prevention. (1993a). Update: Mortality attributable to HIV infection among persons aged 25–44 years—United States, 1991 and 1992. *Morbidity and Mortality Weekly Report, 42,* 869–872.

Centers for Disease Control and Prevention. (1993b). *The public health impact of needle exchange programs in the United States and abroad.* Atlanta, GA: Author.

Centers for Disease Control and Prevention. (1993c, August 6). Update: Barrier protection against HIV infection and other sexually transmitted diseases. *Morbidity and Mortality Weekly Report, 42,* 589–591.

Centers for Disease Control and Prevention. (1994a) *HIV/AIDS surveillance report (through December 30, 1992).* Atlanta, GA: Author.

Centers for Disease Control and Prevention. (1994b). *National HIV serosurveillance summary: Results through 1992.* (Vol. 3). Atlanta, GA: U.S. Department of Health and Human Services.

Centers for Disease Control and Prevention. (1994, April 6). Zidovudine for the prevention of HIV transmission from mother to child. *Morbidity and Mortality Weekly Report, 43,* 285–287.

Chavkin, W. (1989, July 18). Help, don't jail addicted women. *New York Times,* p. A21.

Chavkin, W. (1990). Drug addiction and pregnancy: Policy crossroads. *American Journal of Public Health, 80,* 483–487.

Chin, J. (1990). Current and future dimensions of the HIV/AIDS pandemic in women and children. *Lancet, 336,* 221–224.

Chin, J., & Mann, J. M. (1988). Global patterns and prevalence of AIDS and HIV infection. *AIDS, 2,* (Suppl. 1), S247–S252.

Chu, S. Y., Buehler, J. W., Fleming, P. L., & Berkelman, R. L. (1990). Epidemiology of reported cases of AIDS in lesbians, United States 1980–89. *American Journal of Public Health, 80,* 1380–1381.

Chung, J. Y., & Magraw, M. M. (1992). A group approach to psychosocial issues faced by HIV-positive women. *Hospital and Community Psychiatry, 43,* 891–894.

Clark, L. L., Calsyn, D. A., Saxon, A. J., Jackson, T. R., & Wrede, I. A. F. (1992, July). HIV risk behaviors of heterosexual couples in methadone maintenance. *Proceedings of the VIIIth International Conference on AIDS,* Abstract No. PoC4656, p. 352.

Cleary, P. D., Van Devanter, N., Rogers, T. F., Singer, E., Shipton-Levy, R., Steilen, M., Stuart, A., Avorn, J., & Pindyk, J. (1993). Depressive symptoms in blood donors notified of HIV infection. *American Journal of Public Health, 83,* 534–539.

Coates, T. J., & Lo, B. (1990). Counseling HIV seropositive patients: An approach for medical practice. *Western Journal of Medicine, 153,* 629–634.

Cohen, J., Hauer, L., & Wofsy, C. (1989). Women and IV drugs: Parenteral and heterosexual transmission of human immunodeficiency virus. *Journal of Drug Issues, 19,* 39–56.

Coons, H. L., McGowan, W. G., Koffler, S. P., Spence, M. R., Helz, J. W., Walch, S. E., Malloy, C. D., Campbell, E. H., & Smith, J. L. (1993, August). Psychosocial aspects of HIV and AIDS in women. In P. J. Morokoff (Chair), *Primary and secondary prevention of AIDS in women.* Symposium conducted at the meeting of the American Psychological Association, Toronto, Canada.

Corby, N. H., Wolitski, R. J., Thornton-Johnson, S., & Tanner, W. M. (1991). *AIDS Education and Prevention, 3,* 353–366.

Croteau, J. M., Nero, C. I., & Prosser, D. J. (1993). Social and cultural sensitivity in group-specific HIV and AIDS programming. *Journal of Counseling and Development, 71,* 290–296.

Deiter, P., & Quina, K. (1993, August). Sexual assertiveness training for college women. In P. J. Morokoff (Chair), *Sexual assertiveness and AIDS risk reduction in women.* Roundtable conducted at the annual meeting of the American Psychological Association, Toronto, Canada.

Deren, S. (1986). Children of substance abusers: A review of the literature. *Journal of Substance Abuse Treatment, 3,* 77–94.

Ellerbrock, T., Bush, T. J., Chamberland, M. E., & Oxtoby, M. J. (1991). Epidemiology of women with AIDS in the United States, 1981 through 1990: A comparison with heterosexual men with AIDS. *Journal of the American Medical Association, 265,* 2971–2975.

European Study Group. (1989). Risk factors for male to female transmission of HIV. *British Medical Journal, 298,* 411–415.

Eversley, R. B. (1993, August). Social support and access to health care in HIV-infected women. In P. J. Morokoff (Chair), *Primary and secondary prevention of AIDS in women.* Symposium conducted at the meeting of the American Psychological Association, Toronto, Canada.

Feucht, T., Stephens, R., & Roman, S. (1990). The sexual behavior of intravenous drug users: Assessing the risk of sexual transmission of HIV. *The Journal of Drug Issues, 20,* 195–213.

Fisher, J. D., & Fisher, W. A. (1992). Changing AIDS-risk behavior. *Psychological Bulletin, 111,* 455–474.

Flaskerud, J., & Nyamathi, A. (1990). Effects of an AIDS education program on the knowledge, attitudes and practices of low income Black and Latina women. *Journal of Community Health, 1990, 15,* 343–355.

Flaskerud, J. H., & Rush, C. E. (1989). AIDS and traditional health beliefs and practices of Black women. *Nursing Research, 38,* 210–215.

Franzini, L. R., Sideman, L. M., Dexter, K. E., & Elder, J. P. (1990). Promoting AIDS risk reduction via behavioral training. *AIDS Education and Prevention, 2,* 313–321.

Fullilove, M. T., Fullilove, R. E., Haynes, K., & Gross, S. (1990). Black women and AIDS prevention: A view towards understanding the gender rules. *Journal of Sex Research, 27,* 47–64.

Gallagher, P. L., & Lang, M. (1993, August). AIDS risk reduction training plus 1 year follow-up. In P. J. Morokoff (Chair), *Sexual assertiveness and AIDS risk reduction in women.* Roundtable conducted at the meeting of the American Psychological Association, Toronto, Canada.

Gallagher, P., Morokoff, P. J., Quina, K., & Harlow, L. L. (1991, August). AIDS risk reduction training among college women. In K. Quina (Chair), *Preventing AIDS in women.* Symposium conducted at the meeting of the American Psychological Association, San Francisco.

Gallant, S. J., Coons, H. D., & Morokoff, P. J. (1994). Psychology and women's health: Some reflections and future directions. In V. Adesso, D. Reddy, & R. Fleming (Eds.), *Psychological perspectives on women's health.* Washington, DC: Hemisphere.

Goldman, J., & Harlow, L. L. (1993). Self-perception variables that mediate AIDS-preventive behavior in college students. *Health Psychology, 12,* 489–498.

Grinstead, O. A., Faigeles, B., Binson, D., & Eversley, R. (1993). Sexual risk for human immunodeficiency virus infection among women in high-risk cities. *Family Planning Perspectives, 25,* 252–256, 277.

Harlow, L. L., Quina, K., Morokoff, P. J., Rose, J. S., & Grimley, D. M. (1993). HIV risk in women: A multifaceted model. *Journal of Applied Biobehavioral Research, 1,* 3–38.

Harrison, D. F., Wambach, K. G., Byers, J. B., Imershein, A. W., Levine, P., Maddox, K., Quadagno, D. M., Fordyce, M. L., & Jones, M. A. (1991). AIDS knowledge and risk behaviors among culturally diverse women. *AIDS Education and Prevention, 3,* 79–89.

Hingson, R. W., Strunin, L., Berlin, B. M., & Heeren, T. (1990). Beliefs about AIDS, use of alcohol and drugs, and unprotected sex among Massachusetts adolescents. *American Journal of Public Health, 80,* 295–299.

Holland, J., Ramazanoglu, C., Scott, S., Sharpe, S., & Thomson, R. (1990). Sex, gender, and power: Young women's sexuality in the shadow of AIDS. *Sociology of Health and Illness, 12,* 336–350.

Ickovics, J. R., & Rodin, J. (1992). Women and AIDS in the United States: Epidemiology, natural history, and mediating mechanisms. *Health Psychology, 11,* 1–16.

James, M. E. (1988). HIV seropositivity diagnosed during pregnancy: Psychosocial characterization of patients and their adaptation. *General Hospital Psychiatry, 10,* 309–316.

Jemmott, J. B., Jemmott, L. S., Spears, H., Hewitt, N., & Cruz-Collins, M. (1992). Self-efficacy, hedonistic expectancies, and condom-use intentions among inner-city Black adolescent women: A social cognitive approach to AIDS risk behavior. *Journal of Adolescent Health, 13,* 512–519.

Jones, J. H. (1993). *Bad blood: The Tuskegee syphilis experiment.* New York: Free Press.

Kalichman, S. C., Hunter, T. L., & Kelly, J. A. (1992). Perceptions of AIDS susceptibility among minority and nonminority women at risk for HIV infection. *Journal of Consulting and Clinical Psychology, 60,* 725–732.

Kalichman, S. C., Kelly, J. A., Hunter, T. L., Murphy, D. A., & Tyler, R. (1993). Culturally tailored HIV–AIDS risk-reduction messages targeted to African-American urban women: Impact on risk sensitization and risk reduction. *Journal of Consulting and Clinical Psychology, 61,* 291–295.

Karan, L. D. (1989). AIDS prevention and chemical dependence treatment needs of women and their children. *Journal of Psychoactive Drugs, 21,* 395–399.

Kavanagh, K. H., Harris, R. M., Hetherington, S. E., & Scott, D. E. (1992). Collaboration as a strategy for acquired immunodeficiency syndrome prevention. *Archives of Psychiatric Nursing, 6,* 331–339.

Kelly, J. A., Murphy, D. A., Washington, C. D., Wilson, T. S., Koob, J. J., Davis, D. R., Ledezma, G., & Davantes, B. (1994). Effects of HIV/AIDS prevention groups for high-risk women in urban primary health care clinics. *American Journal of Public Health, 84*(12), 1918–1922.

Kelly, J. A., St. Lawrence, J. S., Betts, R., Brasfield, T. L., & Hood, H. V. (1990). A skills-training group intervention model to assist persons in reducing risk behaviors for HIV infection. *AIDS Education and Prevention, 2,* 24–35.

Kelly, J. A., St. Lawrence, J. S., Hood, H. V., & Brasfield, T. L. (1989). Behavioral intervention to reduce AIDS risk activities. *Journal of Consulting and Clinical Psychology, 57,* 60–67.

Kennedy, M. (1990). *Women, addiction, and perinatal substance abuse: Fact sheet.* U.S. House of Representatives, Select Committee on Children, Youth, and Families.

Kiuri, A. N., Awuor, L., Onyango, D. O., & Adhiambo, S. O. (1993, June). Educating women, women sex workers and women's groups on HIV and AIDS to help bring sexual behaviour change. *Proceedings of the IXth International Conference on AIDS.* Abstract No. PO-D03-3510, p. 803.

Kumpfer, K. L. (1991). Treatment programs for drug-abusing women. *The Future of Children, 1,* 50–60. (Available from The David & Lucille Packard Foundation, 300 Second Street, Suite 102, Los Altos, CA 94022).

LaPerriere, A., Schneiderman, N., Antoni, M. H., & Fletcher, M. A. (1990). Aerobic exercise training and psychoneuroimmunology in AIDS research. In L. Temoshok & A. Baum (Eds.), *Psychosocial perspectives on AIDS* (pp. 259–286). Hillsdale, NJ: Lawrence Erlbaum Associates.

Levine, C., & Dubler, N. N. (1990). Uncertain risks and bitter realities: The reproductive choices of HIV-infected women. *The Millbank Quarterly, 68,* 321–351.

Lubega, C. N. (1993, June). The problems faced by working women in introducing safer sex to their spouses—A case study. *Proceedings of the IXth International Conference on AIDS.* Abstract No. PO-D03-3481.

Magura, S., Kang, S., Shapiro, J., & O'Day, J. (1993). HIV risk among women injecting drug users who are in jail. *Addiction, 88,* 1351–1360.

Mays, V. M., & Cochran, S. D. (1988). Issues in the perception of AIDS risk and risk reduction activities by Black and Hispanic/Latina women. *American Psychologist, 43,* 949–957.

Mikawa, J. K., Morones, P. A., Gomez, A., Case, H. L., Olsen, D., & Gonzales-Huss, M. J. (1992). Cultural practices of Hispanics: Implications for the prevention of AIDS. *Hispanic Journal of Behavioral Sciences, 14,* 421–433.

Mitchell, J. L., Tucker, J., Loftman, P. O., & Williams, S. B. (1992). HIV and women: Current controversies and clinical relevance. *Journal of Women's Health, 1,* 35–39.

Mondanaro, J. (1987). Strategies for AIDS prevention: Motivating health behavior in drug dependent women. *Journal of Psychoactive Drugs, 19,* 143–149.

Moore, J. S., Harrison, J. S., & Doll, L. S. (1994). Interventions for sexually active, heterosexual women in the United States. In R. D. DiClemente and J. L. Peterson (Eds.). *Preventing AIDS: Theories and methods of behavioral interventions* (pp. 243–265). New York: Plenum.

Morokoff, P. J. (1992, August). AIDS prevention in women: Behavioral change efforts and public policy. In S. M. Czajkowski (Chair), *Biobehavioral influences on women's health: Research and policy perspectives.* Symposium conducted at the meeting of the American Psychological Association, Washington, DC.

Morokoff, P. J., & Harlow, L. L. (1993, August). The role of sexual assertiveness in the primary prevention of AIDS in women. In P. J. Morokoff (Chair), *Primary and secondary prevention of AIDS in women*. Symposium conducted at the meeting of the American Psychological Association, Toronto, Canada.

Mosher, W. D., & Pratt, W. F. (1990, March 20). Contraceptive use in the United States, 1973–88. *Advance Data from Vital and Health Statistics of the National Center for Health Statistics, 182.*

Mosher, W. D., & Pratt, W. F. (1993, December 22). AIDS-related behavior among women 15–44 years of age: United States, 1988 and 1990. *Advance Data from Vital and Health Statistics of the National Center for Health Statistics, 239.*

Nyamathi, A., Bennett, C., Leake, B., Lewis, C., & Flaskerud, J. (1993). AIDS-related knowledge, perceptions, and behaviors among impoverished minority women. *American Journal of Public Health, 83,* 65–71.

Osmond, M. W., Wambach, K. G., Harrison, D. F., Byers, J., Levine, P., Imershein, A., & Quadagno, D. M. (1993). The multiple jeopardy of race, class, and gender for AIDS risk among women. *Gender & Society, 7,* 99–120.

Padian, N. S., Shiboski, S. S., & Jewell, N. (1990, June). The relative efficiency of female-to-male HIV sexual transmission. *Proceedings of the VIth International Conference on AIDS.* Abstract No. Th.C.101, p. 159.

Pergami, A., Gala, C., Burgess, A., Durbano, G., Zanello, D., Riccio, M., Invernizzi, G., & Catalan, J. (1993). The psychosocial impact of HIV infection in women. *Journal of Psychosomatic Research, 37,* 687–696.

Potts, M. (1994). The urgent need for a vaginal microbicide in the prevention of HIV transmission. *American Journal of Public Health, 84,* 890–891.

Quinn, S. C. (1993). AIDS and the African American woman: The triple burden of race, class, and gender. *Health Education Quarterly, 20,* 305–320.

Rhodes, F., Corby, N. H., Wolitski, R. J., Tashima, N., Crain, C., Yankovich, D. R., & Smith, P. K. (1990). Risk behaviors and perceptions of AIDS among street injection drug users. *Journal of Drug Education, 20,* 271–288.

Rhodes, F., Wolitski, R. J., & Thornton-Johnson, S. (1992). An experiential program to reduce AIDS risk among female sex partners of injection-drug users. *Health and Social Work, 17,* 261–272.

Rosenberg, M. J., Davidson, A. F., Chen, J. H., Judson, F. N., & Douglas, J. M. (1992). Barrier contraceptives and sexually transmitted diseases in women: A comparison of female-dependent methods and condoms. *American Journal of Public Health, 82,* 669–674.

Rosenberg, M. J., & Gollub, E. L. (1992). Commentary: Methods women can use that may prevent sexually transmitted disease, including HIV. *American Journal of Public Health, 82,* 1473–1478.

Rosser, S. V. (1991). AIDS and women. *AIDS Education and Prevention, 3,* 230–240.

Rothenberg, R., Woelfel, M., Stoneburner, R., Milberg, J., Parker, R., & Truman, B. (1987). Survival with the acquired immunodeficiency syndrome. *New England Journal of Medicine, 317,* 1297–1302.

Seidman, S. N., Mosher, W. D., & Aral, S. O. (1992). Women with multiple sexual partners: United States, 1988. *American Journal of Public Health, 82,* 1388–1394.

Singer, M. (1991). Confronting the AIDS epidemic among IV drug users: Does ethnic culture matter? *AIDS Education and Prevention, 3,* 258–283.

Squire, C. (1993). *Women and AIDS: Psychological perspectives.* Newbury Park, CA: Sage.

Stein, Z. A. (1990). HIV prevention: The need for methods women can use. *American Journal of Public Health, 80,* 460–462.

Stephens, R. C., Feucht, T. E., & Gibbs, B. H. (1993). Needle use behavior. In B. S. Brown & G. M. Beschner (Eds.), *Handbook on risk of AIDS.* Westport, CT: Greenwood.

Stevens, P. E. (1993). Lesbians and HIV: Clinical, research and policy issues. *American Journal of Orthopsychiatry, 63,* 289–294.

Szabo, S., Miller, L. J., Sacks, H. S., et al. (1992, June). Gender differences in the natural history of HIV infection. *Proceedings of the VIIIth International Conference on AIDS.* Abstract No. MoC0030, 10.

Thomas, S., & Quinn, S. (1991). The Tuskegee Syphilis Study 1932–1972: Implications for HIV education and AIDS risk reduction programs in the African American community. *American Journal of Public Health, 81,* 1498–1505.

Valdiserri, R. O., Lyter, D. W., Leviton, L. C., Callahan, C. M., Kingsley, L. A., & Rinaldo, C. R. (1989). AIDS prevention in homosexual and bisexual men: Results of a randomized trial evaluating two risk reduction interventions. *AIDS, 3,* 21–26.

Watters, J. K., Estilo, M. J., Clark, G. L., & Lorvick, J. (1994). Syringe and needle exchange as HIV/AIDS prevention for injection drug users. *Journal of the American Medical Association, 271,* 115–120.

Weissman, G., & The National AIDS Research Consortium. (1991). AIDS prevention for women at risk: Experience from a National Demonstration Research Program. *The Journal of Primary Prevention, 12,* 49–63.

Weller, S. C. (1993). A meta-analysis of condom effectiveness in reducing sexually transmitted HIV. *Social Science and Medicine, 36,* 1635–1644.

Zuckerman, C., & Gordon, L. (1988). Meeting the psychosocial and legal needs of women with AIDS and their families. *New York State Journal of Medicine, 88,* 619–620.

6

Women and Autoimmune Disorders

Joan C. Chrisler and Karin L. Parrett

A utoimmune disorders are those in which the immune system creates antibodies that attack and destroy healthy tissue and organs. These disorders represent a significant portion of the total incidence of chronic disease and remain a major health problem that disproportionately impacts on women. Autoimmune disorders should be of concern to those interested in women's health because women more often experience these conditions. The disorders are characterized by diffuse symptoms, which make them difficult to diagnose. Various autoimmune disorders are often mistaken for one another, and patients may have a long wait until a differential diagnosis can be made. The course of the disorders is unpredictable and idiosyncratic; some patients experience mild symptoms with little progression, whereas others experience severe symptoms that result in increasing pain and progressive physical deterioration and disability. Treatments are palliative rather than curative, and some are associated with dangerous side effects. Patients must expect periods of active disease, which alternate with spontaneous improvement or even remission of symptoms. The unpredictability, the knowledge that the disorders are progressive and incurable, the possibility of deleterious treatment side effects, and the public's unfamiliarity with autoimmune disorders can make living with one a frustrating and isolating experience.

Because women are more likely than men to experience an autoimmune disorder, a gender-sensitive approach is essential. Such a perspective affords an opportunity to explore the role of gender in the disease process and the potential differential impact of these conditions on quality of life for women. Gender role socialization and stereotyping can affect the diagnostic process and the recommendations women receive from their physicians. Coping with the disorder may require changes in women's multiple roles and dealing with body image and sexuality concerns. Ability to cope may be affected by family reactions and access to social support.

In this chapter we will briefly introduce autoimmune disorders, give descriptions of three of the more common ones, review some of the available health psychology literature, and suggest directions for future research. These will be done with women's unique needs in mind.

WHAT ARE AUTOIMMUNE DISORDERS?

The immune system is responsible for protecting the body against infection and disease by recognizing foreign antigens and destroying or eliminating them. Autoimmune disorders result when the immune system fails to discriminate between self and non-self, and thus attacks the body's own cells.

Many *inflammatory* (e.g., rheumatoid arthritis, systemic lupus erythematosus), *granulomatous* (e.g., glomerulonephritis), *degenerative* (e.g., multiple sclerosis), and *atrophic* (e.g., Sjorgren's syndrome) disorders are now attributed to probable or possible autoimmune reactions. Genetic factors are thought to play a role in the development of these disorders because relatives of patients with autoimmune disorders show a higher than expected incidence of similar autoantibodies, and the concordance rate is higher in monozygotic than in dizygotic twins (Merck Research Laboratories, 1992). The genetic contribution is believed to be by a predisposition through which an environmental agent (e.g., virus, drug, toxin, or tissue injury) could provoke the onset of disease. The greater frequency of most autoimmune disorders in women and age distributions showing increased incidence coinciding with periods of marked alterations in endocrine functioning have led researchers to suggest that sex hormones may be involved because of their influence on aspects of immunity (Kiecolt-Glaser & Glaser, 1988).

Systemic Lupus Erythematosus

Systemic Lupus Erythematosus (SLE) is a chronic inflammatory disease of the connective tissue. It was once thought to be a rare disorder, but better diagnostic procedures developed in the past 40 years have demonstrated SLE to be relatively common (Reiter & Penzel, 1983). An estimated 500,000 Americans have been diagnosed with SLE, which occurs 5 to 10 times more often in women than in men. Black women are three times more likely than White women to have SLE (Carr, 1986). Epidemiological evidence also suggests racial differences in morbidity and mortality. For example, Blacks tend to experience earlier onset and more severe manifestations of the disease (Liang, Partridge, Daltroy, Straaton, Galper, & Holman, 1991). Blacks with SLE tend to die sooner than Whites, which may be due as much to socioeconomic status and access to quality health care as to genetic differences.

SLE is a multisystemic disease that may affect one or a combination of tissue and organ systems (e.g., dermatological, gastrointestinal, renal, neurological, musculoskeletal) at any given time. SLE can strike at any age, but usually begins during the reproductive years. In addition to the higher female incidence of SLE, there are several other factors pointing to a role for estrogenic hormones, such as the facts that oral contraceptives can exacerbate symptoms, flare-ups are common during the postpartum, and both men and women with disorders involving excessive estrogen exposure are at increased risk (Achterberg-Lawlis, 1988; Kiecolt-Glaser & Glaser, 1988). Manifestations of SLE may be relatively mild, with only minor joint pain and dermatologic outbreaks, or they may be severe and potentially life-threatening, with involvement of vital organs such as the kidneys or central nervous system (Carr, 1986; Reiter & Penzel, 1983; Robinson, 1988). Kidney failure is the most frequent cause of death in SLE patients (Alexander & LaRosa, 1994). Periods between disease flare-ups may last for weeks, months, or even years.

Because its symptoms resemble those of more than 20 other diseases, SLE has been called "the great impostor." There is no single test or diagnostic procedure that can definitively determine whether an individual has SLE (Carr, 1986). Individuals must cope with exacerbation and remission of symptoms, unsuccessful treatment regimens (Cornwell & Schmitt, 1990), side effects of medications, and the often lengthy phase of uncertain diagnoses.

Rheumatoid Arthritis

Rheumatoid Arthritis (RA) is a chronic disorder that is characterized by nonspecific, usually symmetric inflammation of the peripheral joints that results in pain, swelling, stiffness, and the progressive destruction and deformity of the joints (Merck Research Laboratories, 1992; Young, 1992). As the disease progresses, the range of body systems affected often expands to include the heart, lungs, skin, and blood vessels in addition to the joints. RA is considered to be the most disabling and painful form of arthritis. RA is not an uncommon condition; it affects approximately 1% of the population, although the rate is higher in some Native American groups, such as Chippewa and Yakima (Weiner, 1991). Women are 2 to 3 times more likely than men to be diagnosed with RA (Lawrence et al., 1989; Merck Research Laboratories, 1992). Although the onset may occur at any age—a juvenile form of RA affects about 250,000 children in the United States—it most often begins between the ages of 25 and 50 (Achterberg-Lawlis, 1982; Merck Research Laboratories, 1992). A role for ovarian steroids in RA among women is suggested by several factors, including an increased incidence of RA at menopause, the link between pregnancy and disease remission, the association of postpartum and RA flare-up, and the finding that use of oral contraceptives can ameliorate symptoms and slow progression of the disease (Alexander & LaRosa, 1994; Kiecolt-Glaser & Glaser, 1988).

The onset of RA may be abrupt, with simultaneous inflammation in several joints. More commonly, it may be insidious, with progressive involvement from single to multiple joints. Tenderness and swelling are the most typical physical signs of RA. Stiffness lasting more than 30 minutes after arising in the morning or after prolonged inactivity is another common sign. Early afternoon fatigue and malaise also may be reported. Joints commonly affected include the knees, hips, fingers, toes, wrists, elbows, and ankles. Most RA patients (about 70%) experience unpredictable remissions and exacerbations of disease activity (Young, 1992).

Symptoms of a number of other diseases, such as SLE, Lyme disease, Sjorgren's syndrome, and gout, overlap with RA, and each of these must be ruled out before a treatment plan is set (Merck Research Laboratories, 1992). Women and men with RA must cope with chronic pain, functional impairment, side effects of medication, and possible surgical joint replacement (Young, 1992).

Multiple Sclerosis

Multiple Sclerosis (MS) is a progressive, degenerative disorder of the central nervous system characterized by scattered areas of demyelination in the brain and spinal cord that result in various neurological signs and symptoms (Merck Research Laboratories, 1992). It is the most common neurological illness among young adults (Thornton & Lea, 1992), with a typical age of onset between 20 and 40 years. MS tends to run in families and has the most equitable gender distribution of the autoimmune disorders, with a female-to-male ratio of 1.4 to 1 (Matthews, 1982). Its incidence is about five times more frequent in temperate than in tropical climates (Merck Research Laboratories, 1992), but the reasons for this are unknown.

The onset of the disease is usually insidious. The most frequent early signs of MS are numbness or tingling in the extremities, trunk, or face; weakness or clumsiness of a hand or leg; and visual disturbances. Also common are brief ocular palsy, unusual fatigability of a limb, minor gait disturbances, difficulties with bladder control, vertigo, and emotional lability. Such symptoms may first appear months or even years before the disease is diagnosed (Merck Research Laboratories, 1992). MS has been called the "malignant uncertainty" (Weeks, 1980) because in some patients it is relatively benign and results in only mild neurological dysfunction with long periods of remission, whereas others experience short remissions and severe exacerbations that cause multiple neurological losses and result in total disability (Wineman, 1990).

Diagnosis of MS is indirect and generally cannot be made during the first attack. A history of exacerbations and remissions, evidence of demyelination from MRI (magnetic resonance imaging) or CAT (computerized axial tomography) scans, and the ruling out of disorders with overlapping symptoms (e.g., SLE, pernicious anemia, syphilis, brain tumors) enable a physician to make a firm diagnosis. There is no specific therapy for MS, and the spontaneous remissions make it difficult to evaluate the effectiveness of various medications. Individuals with MS must cope with the uncertainty of a disease whose course is difficult to predict (Wineman, 1990), functional impairment that often results in unemployment (Kornblith, LaRocca, & Baum, 1986), and the fears and misconceptions of their families and friends (Thornton & Lea, 1992).

DO PSYCHOSOCIAL FACTORS CONTRIBUTE TO AUTOIMMUNE DISEASE ACTIVITY?

Stress has repeatedly been shown to compromise immune functioning (see Kiecolt-Glaser & Glaser, 1991 for a review), but whether stress-related immunosuppression is associated with the etiology of autoimmune disorders is unknown. This uncertainty is partly due to the relative paucity of research on behavioral and psychosocial components of autoimmune disorders. Furthermore, studies indicating a link between stressful events and the onset or course of autoimmune disorders typically have not employed designs appropriate for evaluating the causal influence of stress. Nevertheless, some findings suggest the importance of certain psychosocial factors and underscore the need for additional research.

A recent study (Zautra, Burleson, Matt, Roth, & Burrows, 1994) that compared the reactions to interpersonal conflict of women with RA to women with osteoarthritis (OA), which is not classified as an autoimmune disorder, found interesting differences between them. Conflict accounted for more than twice as much of the variance in depression in women with RA than those with OA. Furthermore, RA patients' levels of immune-stimulating hormones (estradiol and prolactin) were significantly positively correlated with depression, conflict, ineffective coping, and physician ratings of disease activity. These results suggest differences in stress reactivity between RA and OA patients that may have implications for disease onset and progression, and they raise the question of whether such patterns of reactivity might be found in women with other autoimmune disorders.

Poverty and factors associated with it predict worse outcome in many chronic diseases, including autoimmune disorders. For example, in one study (Guevarra, Ouelette, Goldin, & Mizrahi, 1993) White women with higher incomes had lower depression scores and lower physician-rated SLE activity than women of color with lower incomes. Research designed to take into account possible interactions among gender, race, socioeconomic status, stress level, and access to health care would make important contributions to our understanding of the etiology and course of autoimmune disorders in subgroups of women. An example is the differences between Black and White women in incidence rates and severity of these disorders. Although genetic or physiological differences may account for some of the disparity in disease patterns, more research is needed on the role of psychological and sociocultural factors. Continual struggles to survive despite poverty, racism, and sexism mean that many women of color in the United States live in a state of chronic psychological stress (Davis, 1990). Future research should address the ways in which these contextual and lifestyle differences may mediate disease manifestations.

In addition to possibly having a role in disease onset, stress has been identified as a potential triggering factor in autoimmune disorders (Achterberg-Lawlis, 1982), causing exacerbation of symptoms or trigger flares. Wekking, Vingerhoets, van Dam, Nossent, and Swaak (1991) found that as the number of reported stressors increased, the physical ability of women and men with SLE decreased, although the same relationship did not hold for RA patients. In a study of self-care in women and men with SLE, Kinash (1983) found that patients were aware of the effects of stress on their functioning. Among the activities important for their health, they reported adequate rest and sleep, control of physical and mental stress, moderation in work and exercise, and a positive mental attitude. Although evidence of triggering effects in humans is limited to reports of stressful events preceding the flares of SLE and RA, support for Kinash's findings has been shown in animal studies that have directly assessed the effect of different stressors on severity of arthritis (Achterberg-Lawlis, 1988).

Environmental toxins have also been theorized to be partially responsible for the development of autoimmune disorders, but more research should be focused on the possible effects of substances to which women are more likely to be exposed. For example, women of color, who are at higher risk for SLE than White women, are overrepresented in occupations that carry high risk of exposure to chemicals, such as laundering and hairdressing (Stellman, 1988). Among suspected toxins currently under investigation are hair dyes (Liang et al., 1991) and silicone breast implants (Coleman, Lemon, Rudick, Depuy, Feuer, & Edwards, 1994).

In sum, although current research is suggestive of an important role for psychosocial factors in the onset and course of autoimmune disorders, much remains to be learned. No specific behavioral or psychological risk factors have been identified in women or men, and we presently know little of the pathways through which psychosocial variables may influence autoimmune disorders. Longitudinal studies using sophisticated methodologies are needed to evaluate the contributions of psychological, social, and environmental factors in relation to the genetic and biological aspects of these diseases.

WHAT ARE THE PSYCHOSOCIAL CONSEQUENCES OF AUTOIMMUNE DISORDERS?

In addition to a possible role in disease onset and course, there has been interest in the potential psychosocial sequelae of autoimmune disorders. Here again research is limited, and the implications for women are sometimes difficult to discern because studies too often do not address the role of gender specifically, and occasionally do not even state whether or how many women were included in their samples. Nevertheless, some findings suggest that autoimmune disorders can significantly impact upon psychological well-being and functioning, and point to important directions for future research.

Elevated depression scores have been found in individuals with SLE, RA, and MS (Schiffer & Hoffman, 1991; Weiner, 1991). Giang (1991) compared depression scores of SLE and RA patients, found the SLE group to be significantly more depressed, and concluded that organic effects must be largely responsible for the difference. However, in other studies pain, learned helplessness (Nicassio, Radojevic, & Tayer, 1993), social support, coping style (Chrisler & Parrett, 1993), and medication side effects (Joffe et al., 1988) have been found to predict depression scores in women with SLE. Depression in women and men with RA has been associated with pain, active disease (Affleck, Tennen, Urrows, & Higgins, 1991), duration of illness, marital status (Katz & Yelin, 1993), functional decline, and poor clinical status (Katz & Yelin, 1993; Wolfe & Hawley, 1993). One study (Millefiorini et al., 1992) of MS patients assessed brain functioning by MRI and examined depression scores, physical disability, and cognitive functioning. Results indicated that, at least in the early stages of MS, depression is more related to physical disability than to brain pathology. Pain severity and an avoidant coping style have also been found to predict depression scores in women and men with MS (Sullivan, Edgley, Mikail, Dehoux, & Fisher, 1992).

Although psychological research on body-image concerns has been largely confined to studies of adolescents and disordered eaters (Chrisler & Ghiz, 1993), body-image disorders can occur at any age and are likely to be associated with chronic, debilitating illnesses. Given some women's high levels of appearance anxiety and the interest of upper and middle class women in physical fitness, body-image issues should be expected to surface among women with autoimmune disorders as increasing fatigue, weakness, and joint deformity alter appearance and mobility. Changes in activity level due to symptom severity may lead to weight gain, which can also trigger body image issues. Little work has been done in this area, but one study (Vamos, 1990) did find that body-image concerns (e.g., judgments of hand attractiveness and behaviors related to the adornment or concealment of the hands) predicted the willingness of women with RA to undergo hand surgery. Negative changes in self-esteem, self-concept, and body-image scores of women with SLE were considerably lower than those of women with RA (Cornwell & Schmitt, 1990). It would be useful for clinicians to know how body-image concerns of women with autoimmune disorders influence depression, sexuality, quality of life, and willingness to maintain role obligations or to seek social support.

Sexual dysfunctions have been found to occur frequently in MS patients; up to 56% of women and 75% of men may be affected (Bezkor & Canedo, 1987). In a study conducted in Denmark (Stenager, Stenager, Jensen, & Boldsen, 1990), 117 MS patients were interviewed about changes in sexual functioning since the onset of the disease. About half (55%) had experienced changes in sexual functioning; increased sexual dysfunction was correlated with increased disability. Women with MS appear to be most troubled by fatigue, decreased sensation and libido, infrequent orgasm, and low arousability. A study (Ferguson & Figley, 1979) of 100 patients with RA and SLE found that about half (54%) reported concerns about changes in sexual functioning. The women most commonly mentioned pain or weakness, fatigue, and problems with their partners, such as partner's lack of interest, as causes. A more recent study (Curry, Levine, Jones, & Kurit, 1993) of women with SLE found that poor sexual adjustment was related to more severe disease, poor premorbid sexual adjustment, and poor relationship quality. Sexual problems were found most frequently in older White women.

The literature on sexuality has limited its samples to heterosexuals or assumed without inquiring that all participants are heterosexual. Women with SLE have complained that their physicians seem preoccupied with pregnancy and spend time assuring them that they can have children without asking whether they want to have them (Whitehead, 1992). In addition, health care practitioners seem to emphasize a woman's ability to be an effective sexual partner for a man, and a man's ability to maintain an erection. There is more to sexuality than penile penetration, and better designed studies of how women with autoimmune disorders express themselves sexually may be helpful in counseling others with chronic illnesses. Furthermore, little attention has been given by researchers to how women's concerns about becoming pregnant alter their sexual functioning. The role of pregnancy itself is complex and in need of further study; findings suggest that pregnancy can ameliorate or exacerbate the symptoms of autoimmune disorders. For example, remissions of SLE are extremely unlikely during pregnancy or for several months postpartum (Merck Research Laboratories, 1992); however, pregnancy is associated with amelioration of symptoms in RA patients and may play a role in the prevention of the disease (Alexander & LaRosa, 1994; Kiecolt-Glaser & Glaser, 1988). Fertility may be decreased and the menstrual cycle altered in other ways by hormonal changes caused either by SLE or by the medications used to treat it. These areas have not received appropriate attention from researchers.

The flares and remissions of chronic disease impact women's ability to carry out their multiple roles. Interference with role functioning affects women's relationships with family, friends, and coworkers, as well as their sense of well-being and quality of life. Increasing disability may eventually result in the loss of valued roles, but well-meaning physicians and relatives may urge women to give up work or other social roles too soon (Karasz, Bochnak, & Ouellette, 1993).

Disabled men are more likely than disabled women to be in the workforce (Asch & Fine, 1988); Kornblith, LaRocca, and Baum (1986) found that the employment rate of women with MS is 12.5% lower than that for men. This lower employment rate is due in part to the fact that more men than women were working before their MS diagnoses, but gender roles do affect medical advice on work and disability (Russell, 1989). Physicians and patients alike may be influenced by the prevailing attitude that employment is more important for the self-esteem of men than women. Among the variables that have been found to predict continued employment for people with MS are educational level, social support, coping variables, and the willingness of employers to adjust job requirements and work environments (Gulick, 1992). Patients with RA are more likely to remain employed when they work in jobs where they can control the pace and conditions of their work (Yelin, Meenan, Nevitt, & Epstein, 1980). The results of these studies suggest that educated, skilled workers in white-collar occupations, which are less often occupied by women of color, are more likely to remain employed.

Chronic illness also affects parenting and homemaking roles, but few researchers have considered this. Reisine, Goodenow, and Grady (1987) studied women with RA and found that although women employed outside the home were less disabled than those who were not, all continued to assume primary responsibility for homemaking. Allaire (1992) found that little paid household help is used by RA patients, even among those with high incomes. The household tasks most commonly affected by RA flares include cleaning, straightening up, laundry, shopping, and cooking (Reisine et al., 1987). Mothers with RA worry that their symptoms will interfere with parenting, especially with making arrangements, maintaining family ties, and caring for sick children (Reisine et al., 1987). Women report considerable emotional distress when illness affects parenting (Lanza & Revenson, 1993a). As it becomes increasingly difficult for women with severe RA to attend to family and household responsibilities, these are displaced onto family (Allaire, 1992) and friends, causing stress and possibly leading to guilt and anger.

Because the presence of someone with a chronic illness changes family interactions in many ways, the whole family should be addressed by health care professionals (Roth & Robinson, 1992). Family members may be unfamiliar with disorders such as SLE and MS, and may not know how to treat the patient. It has been noted that families who deny the seriousness of SLE and refuse to give attention or consideration to the ill person's needs as well as those who overemphasize the severity of SLE and infantilize the ill person equally detract from a patient's quality of life (Rose-Itkoff, 1987). Also, young children may be frightened by their mother's reaction to symptom flares or worry that she is going to die. Older children, spouses, and significant-others may feel burdened by caring for the ill woman and taking on her "duties." Living with someone who has an unpredictable disease and worrying about her pain and disability is stressful, and spouses with better social support networks are less depressed and better able to cope (Revenson & Majerovitz, 1991). Caring for a disabled wife is a role reversal for a man who entered marriage expecting that she would be taking care of his needs. Asch and Fine (1988) have written that a disabled woman evokes pity that is generalized to her partner. The public often assumes that the disabled woman is a "burden," and that any man associated with her is either a "saint" or a "loser". Such assumptions may contribute to the fact that women with MS have a higher divorce rate than men with MS (Russell, 1989). Russell (1989) found that the women whose marriages lasted tended to be older, have marriages of longer duration, be diagnosed with MS at a later age, and be less seriously disabled.

Progressive disability also may affect women's friendships with nondisabled women because nondisabled people often do not associate with the disabled. Friends may have to alter their interactions or actively negotiate in order to maintain reciprocity so that both parties think that what they contribute to the friendship and what they receive are balanced. Because a nondisabled friend may be running errands or providing physical help, the disabled individual may have to become especially attentive and emotionally supportive (Fisher & Galler, 1988). Friends are an important part of any social support network, yet the impact of chronic illness on friendships has not received much attention.

In sum, research suggests a broad array of psychosocial concomitants of autoimmune disorders including increased depression, body-image concerns, sexual dysfunctions, and potential disruption of work, family, and social roles. More research is needed that focuses specifically on the psychosocial consequences for women and rarely studied subgroups of women.

WHAT PSYCHOSOCIAL FACTORS PREDICT ADJUSTMENT TO AUTOIMMUNE DISORDERS?

Social Support

Adaptation to life with a chronic illness is facilitated by a network of interpersonal relationships on which one can depend for both practical help and emotional support (Lanza & Revenson, 1993b). Social support refers not only to emotional sustenance, but also to information about the disorder, and suggestions on how to cope with various symptoms and perform tasks that have become difficult. Social support also refers to practical advice about such topics as devices and services to make life easier (e.g., clothing with front openings that fasten with velcro or snaps to facilitate dressing for the arthritic, or pet-walking services, grocers, and dry cleaners that deliver; Cone, 1984).

There are associations that have been organized to promote understanding and treatment of SLE, RA, and MS. These organizations also serve as major sources of information and support, especially for the newly diagnosed. Support groups, which often are run by local branches of the associations, hospitals, or other health-related agencies, can provide opportunities for the exchange of all types of social support. However, one study (Paine, Suarez-Balcazar, Fawcett, & Borck-Jameson, 1992) found that MS support groups tend to focus more on information transmittal than encouragement of self-disclosure. Futhermore, most users of support groups are White and middle class, which indicates that to increase their effectiveness groups may need to engage in better outreach efforts and become more culturally sensitive (Robbins, Allegrante, & Paget, 1993).

Thornton and Lea (1992) interviewed 40 women with MS about their use of support groups. They found that about one third of the sample had attended a support group, usually about two years after initial diagnosis. Most of the women thought that there had been times when they needed social support but had not received it, yet they were uncertain that a formal support group would fill their needs. Some were anxious about seeing others whose symptoms were worse than their own while others were resentful of those whose symptoms were milder, but all thought that the information they received from group leaders had been beneficial. Despite concerns about being in a group with others with varying symptom severity, there is evidence that individuals tend to extract self-enhancing information from any comparison. In a study of women with RA who watched a videotape of a woman with RA who coped either well or poorly with her illness, the subjects who viewed good coping did not later denigrate their own coping efforts (DeVellis, Blalock, Holt, Renner, Blanchard, & Klotz, 1991).

Research using the Quality of Social Support Scale (Goodenow, Reisine, & Grady, 1990), which measures information and feedback, task assistance, opportunity for confiding, physical affection, and affirmation/ego support, has found that low levels of social support predict depression in women with RA (Goodenow, Reisine, & Grady, 1990) and SLE (Chrisler & Parrett, 1993). Older people with more satisfactory relationships are more likely to engage in health-promoting behaviors (Hawley & Klauber, 1988), and supportive social interactions are predictive of good adaptation in older MS patients (Wineman, 1990). Patients with SLE have reported that what they most need is support, understanding, and information about the disease (Kinash, 1983). Individuals with MS who live in rural areas have reported lower perceptions of (and fewer opportunities for) social support than those who live in urban areas (Long & Weinert, 1992).

Spouses are an important source of social support. In one study (Reisine, 1993), married RA patients reported that they experienced more physical affection, had a greater sense that they were needed by others, and had more help with household tasks than did the unmarried. Druley, Parris Stephens, and Coyne (1993) recently reported that having a supportive partner with whom to discuss emotional reactions to SLE was associated with greater well-being. However, talking to one's partner about the symptoms did not appear to be an effective coping strategy. Futhermore, patients with spouses who made critical remarks about their illness and their degree of functioning have been found to have poorer psychological adjustment to RA than did those whose spouses were perceived as supportive (Manne & Zautra, 1989). Social support may not only enhance personal well-being, but also be necessary for women to continue giving social support to others, as many women believe is their role (Goodenow, Reisine, & Grady, 1990).

Helplessness and Efficacy

Higher self-efficacy has been found to be related to the expression of fewer pain behaviors in a sample of men with RA (Buescher et al., 1991), and helplessness accounted for a significant proportion of the variance in a study of physical functioning in men and women RA patients (Lorish, Abraham, Austin, Bradley, & Alarcon, 1991). Inspired by the learned helplessness model, Schiaffino and Revenson (1992) recently examined the role of self-efficacy, perceived control, and causal attributions on adaptation in individuals with RA. They found that when RA controllability and self-efficacy were perceived as low, internal, stable, and global attributions for the cause of symptom flare-ups were made and depression scores were greater. Similar studies should be conducted with SLE and MS patients because such results would be useful in designing better cognitive–behavioral interventions for individuals with autoimmune disorders.

Efficacy and helplessness have been hot topics of research and theory in both health psychology and the psychology of women. Yet, little has been done at the intersection of these two fields. Researchers ought to look more closely at how these topics affect women's health behaviors and adaptation to chronic illness, and practitioners should consider developing and testing interventions to increase efficacy in women patients.

Coping Strategies

Most of the studies of coping have examined the use of various strategies to manage pain in RA and SLE patients. In her sample of 92 women with RA, Lambert (1985) found that pain and difficulty in performing tasks were negatively correlated with psychological well-being. The women spoke in interviews about the frustration that pain and stiffness caused them, and told about having to plan their days around their pain. When joint pain was lessened they could "make up for lost time" (p. 53) by completing tasks they could not do at other times.

Strategies focused on both cognitions and emotions have been found to be useful in coping with the pain of arthritis (Stewart & Knight, 1991). Relaxation strategies (Affleck, Urrows, Tennen, & Higgins, 1992) and low impact aerobic activities (Minor, 1991; Minor & Sanford, 1993) have been found to benefit RA patients, as have positive self-statements about the pain (Stewart & Knight, 1991). In a study of coping with SLE (Chrisler & Parrett, 1993), positive reappraisal was associated with low depression scores.

Jordan and Lumley (1993) compared coping strategies of Black and White RA patients whose average scores on measures of disease duration, disability, and pain severity did not differ. They found that lower income Blacks had greater psychological distress and were less physically active than Whites or higher income Blacks. Perceived pain control did not differ significantly between these racial groups; ignoring the pain and making positive self-statements appeared to be the most successful coping strategies. Black patients reported more frequent use of praying and hoping the pain would diminish, but these strategies were not associated with psychological adjustment or activity level.

FUTURE DIRECTIONS

Given the fact that SLE, RA, and MS are all more likely to occur in women, it is surprising how small a role gender has played in the research on these disorders. In fact, some studies (e.g., Giang, 1991; Hall, Stickney, & Gardner, 1981) published in the medical literature did not even describe the gender composition of their samples. Research conducted by nurses and rehabilitation therapists was more likely than that by psychologists and physicians to focus on women and issues that primarily concern women, such as body image (Cornwell & Schmitt, 1990).

Although SLE is more common among Black women and RA may be more common among Native American women, little work has been done with women of color. Except for the few studies that explicitly focus on racial differences (e.g., Jordan & Lumley, 1993; Liang et al., 1991), it is difficult to find information about how women of color are affected by and cope with autoimmune disorders. Most of the studies reviewed for this chapter did not specify the racial composition of their samples. Nursing researchers appear to be more successful than others in recruiting diverse samples. It would be useful in future work to examine how race and age interact with gender in relation to disease onset and course.

Most of the coping research focuses on how patients cope with one illness or another, yet older women often have more than one chronic illness, such as arthritis and diabetes. We know little about adaptation to multiple conditions or how people cope when one illness is under control and the other isn't. More sophisticated studies that can take multiple physical conditions into account could provide helpful information that might impact the lives of older women.

The attitudes of physicians directly affect the quality of care women receive as well as women's ability to make informed decisions about their health (Chrisler & Hemstreet, 1995). Investigation of women's satisfaction with the doctor–patient relationship is another area that requires attention. The ability of physicians to listen carefully to patients and to see them as experts on their own conditions may be particularly important when patients have autoimmune disorders, which are so difficult to diagnose. Physicians' beliefs that women over-report pain (Lack, 1982) may lead them to dismiss women's complaints, thus further delaying proper diagnosis. Consultation and acknowledgment of patient expertise requires power sharing, which may be especially unlikely to occur with SLE because the physician is usually a White male and the patient usually a woman of color (Whitehead, 1992). Many of the women with MS in Thornton and Lea's (1992) study complained that their relationships with their physicians were not sufficiently supportive. Nearly half believed that their diagnosis had been withheld from them initially. Others reported that their physicians were not well informed about medication side effects or were uncomfortable working with patients with incurable illnesses. Studies of factors that enhance physicians' ability to communicate effectively and counsel women with autoimmune disorders could provide a valuable service by educating physicians about women's needs.

A review of the self-help literature available to women with autoimmune disorders also might prove instructive. What gender role stereotypes might it be promoting? Whitehead (1992) has noted the ubiquitous references to women with SLE as "victims" and "sufferers" in pamphlets given to the newly diagnosed. Such language is disappearing from the literature on other disorders; perhaps it has not yet happened here because it is more comfortable to see women as victims than it is to see men so labeled.

There is a pressing need for more research on the biopsychosocial contributors to disease onset and course. Autoimmune disorders remain prevalent, and their negative impact on quality of life and lifestyle is significant and falls disproportionately upon women in part because they are more likely than men to experience these disorders. Current information on the role of biopsychosocial factors is limited for a variety of reasons including that most of the research has been on small samples and has not been designed with a time-frame adequate to assess the causal influence of such factors. The possible role of hormonal factors, particularly ovarian steroids, and their potential interaction with ethnicity and age is worthy of further careful study as one set of factors that may put women at greater risk. Because at present there is no way to prevent autoimmune disorders and no curative remedies, expanding our knowledge of the role of psychosocial factors and their interactions with biological aspects of the disease process offers the promise of developing more effective interventions to reduce discomfort and limit disability.

Finally, there is a need for public policy work to make certain that the high quality health care necessary for the diagnosis and treatment of chronic illnesses is available to all women. Pregnant women with SLE should be able to find obstetricians and midwives who are willing to work with a high-risk delivery. Adequate funding of research and delivery of both medical and psychosocial interventions are essential to ensure a good quality of life for women with autoimmune disorders.

REFERENCES

Achterberg-Lawlis, J. (1982). The psychological dimensions of arthritis. *Journal of Consulting and Clinical Psychology, 50,* 984–992.

Achterberg-Lawlis, J. (1988). Musculoskeletal disorders. In E. A. Bleckman & K. D. Brownell (Eds.), *Handbook of behavioral medicine for women* (pp. 222–235). New York: Pergamon Press.

Affleck, G., Tennen, H., Urrows, S., & Higgins, P. (1991). Individual differences in the day-to-day experience of chronic pain: A prospective daily study of rheumatoid arthritis patients. *Health Psychology, 10,* 419–426.

Affleck, G., Urrows, S., Tennen, H., & Higgins, P. (1992). Daily coping with pain from rheumatoid arthritis: Patterns and correlates. *Pain, 51,* 221–229.

Alexander, L. L., & LaRosa, J. H. (1994). *New dimensions in women's health.* Boston: Jones and Bartlett.

Allaire, S. H. (1992). Employment and household work disability in women with rheumatoid arthritis. *Journal of Applied Rehabilitation Counseling, 23,* 44–51.

Asch, A., & Fine, M. (1988). Introduction: Beyond pedestals. In M. Fine & A. Asch (Eds.), *Women with disabilties: Essays in psychology, culture, and politics* (pp. 1–37). Philadelphia: Temple University Press.

Bezkor, M. F., & Canedo, A. (1987). Physiological and psychological factors influencing sexual dysfunction in multiple sclerosis. *Sexuality and Disability, 8,* 143–146.

Buescher, K. L., Johnston, J. A., Parker, J. C., Smarr, K. L., Buckelew, S. P., Anderson, S. K., & Walker, S. E. (1991). Relationship of self-efficacy to pain behavior. *Journal of Rheumatology, 18,* 968–972.

Carr, R. (1986). *Lupus erythematosus: A handbook for physicians, patients and their families.* Rockville, MD: Lupus Foundation of America.

Chrisler, J. C., & Ghiz, L. (1993). Body image issues of older women. *Women & Therapy, 14*(1/2), 67–75.

Chrisler, J. C., & Hemstreet, A. H. (1995). The diversity of women's health needs. In J. C. Chrisler, & A. H. Hemstreet (Eds.), *Variations on a theme: Diversity and the psychology of women* (pp. 1–28). Albany, NY: State University of New York Press.

Chrisler, J. C., & Parrett, K. L. (1993, August). *Coping, social support, and women's adjustment to systemic lupus erythematosus.* Paper presented at the meeting of the American Psychological Asociation, Toronto, Canada.

Coleman, E. A., Lemon, S. J., Rudick, J., Depuy, R. S., Feuer, E. J., & Edwards, B. K. (1994). Rheumatic disease among 1167 women reporting local implant and systemic problems after breast implant surgery. *Journal of Women's Health, 3,* 165–177.

Cone, D. M. (1984). Clothing needs of the elderly arthritic women. *Educational Gerontology, 10,* 441–448.

Cornwell, C. J., & Schmitt, M. H. (1990). Perceived health status, self-esteem, and body image in women with rheumatoid arthritis or systemic lupus erythematosus. *Research in Nursing and Health, 13,* 1187–1196.

Curry, S. L., Levine, S. B., Jones, P. K., & Kurit, D. M. (1993). Medical and psychosocial predictors of sexual outcome among women with systemic lupus erythematosus. *Arthritis Care and Research, 6,* 23–30.

Davis, A. Y. (1990). Sick and tired of being sick and tired: The politics of black women's health. In E. C. White (Ed.), *The black women's health book: Speaking for ourselves* (pp. 18–26). Seattle: Seal Press.

DeVellis, R. F., Blalock, S. J., Holt, K., Renner, B. R., Blanchard, L. W., & Klotz, M. L.

(1991). Arthritis patients' reactions to unavoidable social comparisons. *Personality and Social Psychology, 17,* 392–399.

Druley, J. A., Parris Stephens, M. A., & Coyne, J. C. (1993, August). *Couples coping with lupus: The role of illness-related self-disclosure.* Paper presented at the meeting of the American Psychological Association, Toronto, Canada.

Ferguson, K., & Figley, B. (1979). Sexuality and rheumatic disease: A prospective study. *Sexuality and Disability, 2,* 130–138.

Fisher, B., & Galler, R. (1988). Friendship and fairness: How disability affects friendship between women. In M. Fine & A. Asch (Eds.), *Women with disabilities: Essays in psychology, politics, and culture* (pp. 172–194). Philadelphia: Temple University Press.

Giang, D. W. (1991). Systemic lupus erythematosus and depression. *Neuropsychiatry, Neuropsychology, and Behavioral Neurology, 4,* 78–82.

Goodenow, C., Reisine, S. T., & Grady, K. E. (1990). Quality of social support and associated social and psychological functioning in women with rheumatoid arthritis. *Health Psychology, 9,* 266–284.

Guevarra, J. S., Ouellette, S. C., Goldin, J., & Mizrahi, K. (1993, August). *Psychosocial factors, race, and SLE.* Paper presented at the meeting of the American Psychological Association, Toronto, Canada.

Gulick, E. E. (1992). Model for predicting work performance among persons with multiple sclerosis. *Nursing Research, 41,* 266–272.

Hall, R. C. W., Stickney, S. K., & Gardner, E. R. (1981). Psychiatric symptoms in patients with systemic lupus erythematosus. *Psychosomatics, 22,* 15–24.

Hawley, P. J., & Klauber, M. R. (1988). Health practices and perceptions of social support in persons over age 60. *Journal of Applied Gerontology, 7,* 205–230.

Joffe, R. T., Denicoff, K. D., Rubinow, D. R., Tsokos, G., Balow, J. E., & Pillemer, S. E. (1988). Mood effects of alternate day corticosteroid therapy in patients with systemic lupus erythematosus. *General Hospital Psychiatry, 10,* 56–60.

Jordan, M. S., & Lumley, M. A. (1993, August). *Pain and coping in African American and Caucasian rheumatoid arthritis patients.* Paper presented at the meeting of the American Psychological Association, Toronto, Canada.

Karasz, A. K., Bochnak, E., & Ouellette, S. C. (1993, August). *Role strain and psychological well being in lupus patients.* Paper presented at the meeting of the American Psychological Association, Toronto, Canada.

Katz, P. P., & Yelin, E. H. (1993). Prevalence and correlates of depressive symptoms among persons with rheumatoid arthritis. *Journal of Rheumatology, 20,* 790–796.

Kiecolt-Glaser, J. K., & Glaser, R. (1988). Immunological competence. In E. A. Bleckman & K. D. Brownell (Eds.), *Handbook of behavioral medicine for women* (pp. 195–205). New York: Pergamon Press.

Kiecolt-Glaser, J. K., & Glaser, R. (1991). Stress and immune function in humans. In R. Ader, D. Felten, & N. Cohen (Eds.), *Psychoneuroimmunology* (pp. 849–867). New York: Academic Press.

Kinash, R. G. (1983, June). Systemic lupus erythematosus: The psychological dimension. *Canada's Mental Health, 31,* 19–22.

Kornblith, A. B., LaRocca, N. G., & Baum, H. M. (1986). Employment in individuals with multiple sclerosis. *International Journal of Rehabilitation Research, 9,* 155–165.

Lack, D. Z. (1982). Women and pain: Another feminist issue. *Women and Therapy, 1*(1), 55–64.

Lambert, V. A. (1985). Study of factors associated with psychological well being in rheumatic arthritic women. *Image, 17*(2), 50–53.

Lanza, A. F., & Revenson, T. A. (1993a, August). *Rheumatic diseases, social roles, and the social support matching hypothesis.* Paper presented at the meeting of the American Psychological Association, Toronto, Canada.

Lanza, A. F., & Revenson, T. A. (1993b). Social support interventions for rheumatoid arthritis patients: The cart before the horse? *Health Education Quarterly, 20,* 97–117.

Lawrence, R. C., Hochberg, M. C., Kelsey, J. L., McDuffie, F. C., Medsger, T. A., Felts, W. R., & Schulman, L. E. (1989). Estimates of the prevalence of selected arthritic and musculoskeletal diseases in the United States. *Journal of Rheumatology, 16,* 427–441.

Liang, M., Partridge, A., Daltroy, L., Straaton, K., Galper, S., & Holman, H. (1991). Strategies for reducing excess morbidity and mortality in blacks with systemic lupus erythematosus. *Arthritis and Rheumatism, 34,* 1187–1196.

Long, K. A., & Weinert, C. (1992). Descriptions and perceptions of health among rural and urban adults with multiple sclerosis. *Research in Nursing and Health, 15,* 335–342.

Lorish, C. D., Abraham, N., Austin, J., Bradley, L. A., & Alcarcon, G. S. (1991). Disease and psychosocial factors related to physical functioning in rheumatoid arthritis. *Journal of Rheumatology, 18,* 1150–1157.

Manne, S. L., & Zautra, A. J. (1989). Spouse criticism and support: Their association with coping and psychological adjustment among women with rheumatoid arthritis. *Journal of Personality and Social Psychology, 56*, 608–617.

Matthews, W. B. (1982). *Diseases of the nervous system*, 4th ed. Oxford: Blackwell.

Merck Research Laboratories. (1992). *The Merck manual of diagnosis and therapy* (16th ed.). Rahway, NJ: Merck & Co.

Millefiorini, E., Padovani, A., Pozzilli, C., Loriedo, C., Bastianello, S., Buttinelli, C., DiPiero, V., & Fieschi, C. (1992). Depression in the early phase of MS: Influence of functional disability, cognitive impairment, and brain abnormalities. *Acta Neurologica Scandinavica, 86*, 354–358.

Minor, M. A. (1991). Physical activity and the management of arthritis. *Annals of Behavioral Medicine, 13*, 117–124.

Minor, M. A., & Sanford, M. K. (1993). Physical interventions in the management of pain in arthritis. *Arthritis Care and Research, 6*, 197–206.

Nicassio, P. M., Radojevic, V., & Tayer, W. G. (1993, August). *Physical and psychosocial correlates of depession in systemic lupus erythematosus.* Paper presented at the meeting of the American Psychological Association, Toronto, Canada.

Paine, A. L., Suarez-Balcazar, Y., Fawcett, S. B., & Borck-Jameson, L. (1992). Supportive transactions: Their measurement and enhancement in two mutual-aid groups. *Journal of Community Psychology, 20*, 163–180.

Reisine, S. (1993). Marital status and social support in rheumatoid arthritis. *Arthritis and Rheumatism, 36*, 589–592.

Reisine, S. T., Goodenow, C., & Grady, K. E. (1987). The impact of rheumatoid arthritis on the homemaker. *Social Science and Medicine, 25*, 89–95.

Reiter, H., & Penzel, F. (1983). Psychological aspects of systemic lupus erythematosus. *Asian Journal of Psychology and Education, 11*, 5–18.

Revenson, T. A., & Majerovitz, S. D. (1991). The effects of chronic illness on the spouse: Social resources as stress buffers. *Arthritis Care and Research, 4*, 63–72.

Robbins, L., Allegrante, J. P., & Paget, S. A. (1993). Adapting the Systemic Lupus Erythematosus Self-Help (SLESH) course for Latino patients. *Arthritis Care and Research, 6*, 97–103.

Robinson, D. (1988). Systemic lupus erythematosus. *Scientific American, 15*, 1–15.

Rose-Itkoff, C. (1987). Lupus: An interactional approach. *Family Systems Medicine, 5*, 313–321.

Roth, S. L., & Robinson, S. E. (1992). Chronic disease in women: The role of the mental health counselor. *Journal of Mental Health Counseling, 14*, 59–72.

Russell, S. (1989). From disability to handicap: An inevitable response to social constraints? *Canadian Review of Sociology and Anthropology, 26,* 276–293.

Schiaffino, K. M., & Revenson, T. A. (1992). The role of perceived self-efficacy, perceived control, and causal attributions to rheumatoid arthritis: Distinguishing mediator from moderator effects. *Personality and Social Psychology Bulletin, 18,* 709–718.

Schiffer, R. B., & Hoffman, S. A. (1991). Behavioral sequelae of autoimmune disease. In R. Ader, D. Felton, & N. Cohen (Eds.), *Psychoneuroimmunology* (pp. 1037–1066). New York: Academic Press.

Stellman, J. M. (1988). The working environment of the working poor: An analysis based on worker's compensation claims, census data, and known risk factors. In C. A. Perales, & L. S. Young (Eds.), *Too little, too late: Dealing with the health needs of women in poverty* (pp. 83–101). New York: Harrington Park Press.

Stenager, E., Stenager, E. N., Jensen, K., & Boldsen, J. (1990). Multiple sclerosis: Sexual dysfunctions. *Journal of Sex Education and Therapy, 16,* 262–269.

Stewart, M. W., & Knight, R. G. (1991). Coping strategies and affect in rheumatoid and psoriatic arthritis: Relationship to pain and disability. *Arthritis Care and Research, 4*(3), 116–122.

Sullivan, M. J., Edgley, K., Mikail, S., Dehoux, E., & Fisher, R. (1992). Psychological correlates of health care utilization in chronic illness. *Canadian Journal of Rehabilitation, 6,* 13–21.

Thornton, H. B., & Lea, S. J. (1992). An investigation into the needs of people living with multiple sclerosis and their families. *Disability, Handicap, & Society, 7,* 321–338.

Vamos, M. (1990). Body image in rheumatoid arthritis: The relevance of hand appearance to desire for surgery. *British Journal of Medical Psychology, 63,* 267–277.

Weeks, C. C. (1980). MS: The malignant uncertainty. *American Journal of Nursing, 80,* 298–299.

Weiner, H. (1991). Social and psychobiological factors in autoimmune disease. In R. Ader, D. Felton, & N. Cohen (Eds.), *Psychoneuroimmunology* (pp. 955–1011). New York: Academic Press.

Wekking, E. M., Vingerhoets, A. J., van Dam, A. P., Nossent, J. C., & Swaak, A. J. (1991). Daily stressors and systemic lupus erythematosus: A longitudinal analysis—first findings. *Psychotherapy and Psychosomatics, 55,* 108–113.

Whitehead, K. (1992). Systemic lupus erythematosus: Another woman's problem? *Feminism & Psychology, 2,* 189–195.

Wineman, N. M. (1990). Adaptation to multiple sclerosis: The role of social support, functional disabiltiy, and perceived certainty. *Nursing Research, 39*, 294–299.

Wolfe, F., & Hawley, D. J. (1993). The relationship between clinical activity and depression in rheumatoid arthritis. *Journal of Rheumatology, 20*, 2032–2037.

Yelin, E. , Meenan, R., Nevitt, M., & Epstein, W. (1980). Work disability in rheumatoid arthritis: Effects of disease, social, and work factors. *Annals of Internal Medicine, 93*, 551–556.

Young, L. D. (1992). Psychological factors in rheumatoid arthritis. *Journal of Consulting and Clinical Psychology, 60*, 619–627.

Zautra, A. J., Burleson, M. H., Matt, K. S., Roth, S., & Burrows, L. (1994). Interpersonal stress, depression, and disease activity in rheumatoid arthritis and osteoarthritis patients. *Health Psychology, 13*, 139–148.

PART THREE

Gynecological Health

7

Menarche, Menstruation, and Menopause: Psychosocial Research and Future Directions

Sheryle J. Gallant and Paula S. Derry

The biological aspects of women's menstrual life—of menarche, menstruation, and menopause—are the same in different cultures, but the contexts differ and contribute to a diversity of personal experience. In Western culture, menarche is given little formal recognition; there are no ceremonies, celebratory rituals, or symbols. It is considered a major biological event, but its psychological significance is largely ignored. In contrast, considerable psychological significance is attributed to menstruation and menopause, as is evident from cultural stereotypes about how these processes affect women emotionally. These events also occur in different life stages. Menarche occurs during early adolescence, when the girl is beginning to separate from her family, formulate life goals relating to careers and relationships, and grapple with her sexuality. Menstruation begins in adolescence and spans the adult years, when decisions about marriage, childbearing, caretaking, and career options are potential sources of conflict. Menopause occurs in conjunction with such midlife issues as beginning to be aware of bodily changes that are the first visible signs of aging and confronting the cultural bias favoring youth and devaluing older women. Thus, to understand women's experience of menstrual events, social and psychological contexts must be taken into account.

In this chapter, we review research addressing psychosocial factors associated with menstrual events. Our view is health focused, and we define health as a woman's ability to maximize positive experiences and cope with symptoms by using her psychosocial resources. We discuss symptoms that may be related to the menstrual cycle, such as those of premenstrual syndrome (PMS) and hot flashes. However, we also assume that health involves both positive feelings about oneself and one's body and the positive negotiation of life-cycle-related changes. We see this as an important counterweight to the widely accepted disease model, which narrowly focuses on biological mechanisms and overemphasizes the negative aspects of reproductive life transitions. Our broader goal in this chapter is to provide a review of psychosocial research on menstrual-related health issues as a step toward integrating biomedical and psychosocial perspectives.

MENARCHE
Biological Context

Menarche, the first occurrence of menstruation, is one of the later events of puberty. It is preceded by the peak growth spurt and the emergence of secondary sex characteristics, including the beginnings of breast development, growth of axillary and pubic hair, weight gain and increase in body fat, and feminizing changes in body contours (Tanner, 1969; M. P. Warren, 1983). The current average age of menarche in the United States is 12.3 years (Tanner, 1991), but there is substantial individual variation (Eveleth & Tanner, 1990). Two important determinants of age of menarche appear to be skeletal growth and reaching minimum weight for one's height. These may be influenced by genetic factors, endocrine function, and environmental conditions, including nutrition and physical activity (Brooks-Gunn, 1991b; Brooks-Gunn & Reiter, 1990). The last two factors have been of particular interest in observations of delayed menarche and menstrual problems (e.g., amenorrhea, irregular cycles, and anovulatory cycles) in some highly trained athletes and ballet dancers (e.g., Frisch, 1983; Frisch et al., 1981; Frisch, Wyshak, & Vincent, 1980; M. P. Warren, 1980). In unselected samples, both low weight and strenuous physical activity have been shown to predict delayed menarche and to have additive effects (e.g., Vandenbroucke, Van Laar, & Valkenburg, 1982). Physical exercise training initiated before puberty may have a direct causal influence on later menarche (Frisch, 1983). This remains open to question however, because of potential sampling bias in the quasi-experimental designs used (Stager, Wigglesworth, & Hatler, 1990) and because the physical characteristics associated with delayed menarche may be those that increase a girl's suitability for sports participation (Brooks-Gunn, 1988). Dieting has also been associated with delayed menarche (e.g., Brooks-Gunn, Warren, & Hamilton, 1987), but the importance of various aspects of nutrition and nutrient intake have not been extensively studied. Furthermore, the relative importance of dieting versus nutrition versus intensity and duration of physical activity on menarcheal age remains to be clarified, as does the interaction of these variables with the complex sequence of biological changes that constitute puberty.

Psychological Aspects of Menarche

Research on the psychological aspects of menarche has examined the feelings and attitudes of pre- and postmenarcheal girls and the impact of menarche on self-perceptions and body image, symptom experience, and behavior. One striking characteristic of this research, however, has been its focus on White, middle-class groups. A few studies have used samples of Black women (e.g., Jackson, 1992) or adolescent girls (e.g., Scott, Arthur, Panizo, & Owen, 1989), but there is virtually no research on other ethnic minorities or low-income groups. Thus, generalizations to these groups should be made cautiously.

Given the pervasive negative stereotypes about menstruation in Western culture, it is not surprising that researchers have found girls to express negative and ambivalent feelings about beginning to menstruate. However, early reports of the psychological impact of menarche (e.g., Kestenberg, 1967; Whisnant & Zegans, 1975) were constrained by having been conducted on small and often clinical samples, from which emerged an exaggerated view of menarche as a potentially traumatic event. A more balanced view has been revealed in the work of Ruble and Brooks-Gunn

(1982, 1987; Brooks-Gunn & Ruble, 1982), who conducted a large, methodologically sophisticated study using a cross-sectional and longitudinal design. Their results indicated that strong negative reactions to menarche were infrequent. The most common response was an experience of both positive and negative feelings, some short-lived concern with secrecy, and symptoms of moderate intensity. There was no evidence of a broad impact of menarche on self-concept, and the strongest beliefs were about menstruation as a normal and natural event.

The complexity of girls' reactions was reflected in the seemingly paradoxical finding that longer experience with menstruation resulted in less embarrassment and worry about normalcy but more negative feelings and symptoms. Expectations were found to be a defining feature of later experience. As early as fifth grade, girls had expectations of menstrual and premenstrual symptoms. Actually beginning to menstruate tended to ameliorate feelings and attitudes and to reduce symptom reports. For example, postmenarcheal girls reported less pain and viewed menstruation as less debilitating than the premenarcheal girls anticipated. This is similar to findings in some other studies (e.g., McGrory, 1990), but not all (cf. L. R. Williams, 1983). Importantly, by examining longitudinal data, Ruble and Brooks-Gunn (1987) were able to separate the effects of age and menarcheal status and show that negative evaluations increased with age but not menarcheal status per se. This may account for some of the different findings across studies and highlights the value of longitudinal investigations, because age and menarcheal status are often confounded in cross-sectional research.

In addition to evaluating attitudes and menstrual symptoms, researchers have examined whether menarche precipitates changes in self-esteem or body image. Results for self-esteem have been mixed but, predominantly, have not yielded significant effects (e.g., McGrory, 1990; Simmons, Blyth, & McKinney, 1983). Although Ulman (1992) found self-esteem to be higher in girls who had been menstruating longer, it is not clear if the potential confounding effects of age were taken into account. Findings are more consistent for body image. Similar results have been reported using various methodologies, including interviews (Whisnant &

Zegans, 1975), recognition of photographs of one's own body (Collins & Propert, 1983), and projective techniques (e.g., Koff, 1983; Koff, Rierdan, & Silverstone, 1978). The best known work is that of Koff and colleagues that was based on human figure drawings. Postmenarcheal girls produced drawings that were more sexually differentiated than age-matched pre-menarcheal peers, and a significant change was observed in girls who attained menarche during the 6 months of the study, with their later drawings depicting a more mature female with breasts and body curves (Koff et al., 1978). Subsequent research (Koff, Rierdan, & Jacobson, 1981) confirmed that girls viewed menarche as increasing bodily maturity and femininity, but that this did not necessarily equate with greater body satisfaction (Koff & Rierdan, 1991).

Most studies have focused on the menarcheal girl in isolation. An exception is the recent study by Paikoff, Brooks-Gunn, and Carlton-Ford (1991) that examined the interplay of mother's age, mother's menstrual status, and daughter's age at menarche on aspects of family functioning and the well-being of mothers and daughters. For daughters, none of the variables examined, including menarcheal timing, were significantly related to well-being. However, mother's menstrual status interacted with daughter's age at menarche with respect to dieting behavior: Daughters who achieved menarche early and whose mothers were premenopausal dieted less than both (a) those whose mothers were postmenopausal and (b) those who experienced menarche "on time" (vs. early) whose mothers were premenopausal. This was an interesting study design because it allowed examination of psychological well-being in relation to menstruation within contextual (family) and life-span (menstrual-status) perspectives.

Contextual Determinants of Reactions to Menarche

Preparation

Researchers have found that those who felt unprepared for their first menstruation experienced more negative reactions to menarche (e.g., Ruble & Brooks-Gunn, 1982). In most studies, only a small percentage of women claimed to have been completely unprepared; however, many did report that their preparation was inadequate, and these rates were nearly twice as high among Black women and girls as among White samples (Jackson, 1992; Scott et al., 1989). Optimal preparation has been described as involving not only basic knowledge about menstrual physiology and hygiene but also information about positive and potential negative aspects (e.g., embarrassment, messiness, and inconvenience) to assist the girl in forming a balanced but realistic view (Rierdan, 1983). The effectiveness of preparation has been evaluated by Rierdan and Koff (1990) and by Rierdan, Koff, and Stubbs (1989) using a prospective design. Girls who were better prepared rated their emotional responses as more positive, independent of personality attributes and the timing of their menarche. One can thus speculate that adequate preparation enhances a girl's feelings of control over her body and the changes she is experiencing.

Menarcheal Timing

A number of studies have reported negative psychological effects from beginning to menstruate early (e.g., Brooks-Gunn, 1991a; Ruble & Brooks-Gunn, 1982; Simmons & Blyth, 1987; Tobin-Richards, Boyer, & Petersen, 1983), including negative attitudes toward menstruation, more reporting of symptoms, lower self-esteem, poorer body image, and—for those who began very early—greater experience of depressive affect (Rierdan & Koff, 1991). However, it is not clear to what extent these effects resulted from early menarche per se versus a lack of preparedness or the reactions of others to the early maturing girl. Citing social comparison needs and conformity pressures, Ruble and Brooks-Gunn (1982) suggested that early menarche sets a girl apart and thus generates feelings of insecurity.

In addition to significant psychological consequences, early menarche has been associated with behaviors that may disadvantage girls. Those who mature early are more likely to date, to engage in petting, and to have sexual intercourse at an earlier age (e.g., Helm & Lidegaard, 1989; Magnusson, Strattin, & Allen, 1985; Strattin & Magnusson, 1990; Udry & Cliquet, 1982). Causal determinants for this remain to be clarified, but it is likely that social pressure is exerted by others who attribute greater maturity to certain girls because of physical maturation than is warranted on the basis of chronological age (Caspi & Moffitt, 1991).

Risk for serious psychological and behavior problems among girls who reach menarche early was evaluated by Caspi and Moffitt (1991), using data from a large longitudinal cohort of New Zealand adolescent girls followed from birth. Measures in this study were sophisticated and included parents' reports and girls' self-reports of behavior problems as well as responses to the Diagnostic Interview Schedule for Children (DISC–C; Costello, Edelbrock, Kalas, Kessler, & Klaric, 1982). Only early maturing girls demonstrated significant negative effects because of their change in menarcheal status, and, in particular, early menarche was a significant risk factor for adjustment difficulties throughout adolescence among those with a history of behavior problems in childhood.

Methodological issues persist in this research because of the variable criteria used to define early versus late maturation and because of the need to investigate menarcheal timing effects within the broader context of the adolescent girl's life (Brooks-Gunn, 1988; Brooks-Gunn, Petersen, & Eichorn, 1985), such as her grade in school, which often shows larger effects than timing per se (Peterson & Crockett, 1985). Furthermore, the potential moderating effects of context have only rarely been explored (e.g., Brooks-Gunn & Warren, 1985). A case in point is "on-time" ballet dancers (Brooks-Gunn, 1991b), that is, girls who desire to excel at ballet who experience menarche at the normative age. From a strict timing perspective, these girls would not be anticipated to experience problems because they are not early maturers. However, the very fact of having attained menarche increases the likelihood that, for some, their physical characteristics (e.g., body weight or percentage of body fat) will not match the ideal requirements of the ballet world, and this contextual incongruency may be a significant source of stress.

Family Relationships

Although there is substantial literature on family relationships during puberty and adolescence, only a small body of research has examined how the experience of menarche may be influenced by the familial context in which it occurs or how interactions within the family may be altered by menarche. An example of the latter approach is a study by Danza (1983), examining mother–daughter and father–daughter interactions in a sample of age-matched pre- and postmenarcheal girls. Results suggested a definite change in family interactions after menarche, with differences between the groups in limit setting, personal responsibility, closeness, and amount of conflict. In comparison with premenarcheal peers, postmenarcheal girls reported more conflict and less closeness with parents; more reluctance to discuss such emotionally laden issues as love, sex, drugs, and alcohol; and a more negative view of their parents' marriage. Parents, in turn, reported more mature expectations for the postmenarcheal girls. Similar findings were reported by Ulman (1992); however, in this study, the parents' reports showed a curvilinear relationship as a function of time since menarche, with greater conflict and less closeness in relationships with daughters menstruating for less than 2 years in comparison with the premenarcheal girls or those who had been menstruating longer than 2 years. Unfortunately, it was not clear if this was a function of menarcheal status or age, because it appeared that the postmenarcheal girls who had been menstruating longer were older.

Hill and colleagues have also studied interaction patterns (Hill, 1988; Hill, Holmbeck, Marlow, Green, & Lynch, 1985; Holmbeck & Hill, 1991). Seventh-grade girls were divided into four groups: premenarcheal, menarche within the previous 6 months or 12 months, and menstruating for more than 1 year. Menarche appeared to initiate a lasting change in girls' relationships with their fathers, in that girls in all three postmenarcheal groups rated their fathers as less accepting and as having less influence over them than did those in the premenarcheal group. There were similar changes in interactions with mothers, but these were short lived—except for the early maturing group, in which the effects appeared to be long lasting. Paikoff et al. (1991) also found changes in mother–daughter interactions following menarche, but the direction of change was not consistent with that suggested by Hill and colleagues, in that mothers of early maturers reported less family conflict than those whose daughters had experienced menarche on time or late. Paikoff et al. speculated that the inconsistency may have reflected the fact that the early maturing girls in their study had experienced significantly more years since menarche in comparison with the other two groups; thus, increases in family conflict around the time of menarche had had more time to subside. These findings were similar to Ulman's (1992), suggesting that the risk of increased family conflict is greatest during the initial period after menarche. Paikoff et al. pointed out that their results argue against the idea that early maturers are at greater risk for family conflict throughout adolescence in comparison with on-time or late maturers.

In a rare (for this literature) observational study (Hill, 1988; Holmbeck & Hill, 1991) pre- and postmenarcheal girls and their parents participated in a structured family interaction task that was videotaped and coded for a number of variables, including agreement, number of interruptions, and decision influence. Different patterns were observed in the father–daughter and mother–daughter dyads as a function of menarcheal status. In comparison with those in the premenarcheal group, postmenarcheal father–daughter dyads exhibited less agreement and more frequent interruptions of daughters by fathers, with the frequency being highest in the newly postmenarcheal group. Daughters did not show a change in interruptions as a function of menarche, but those in the postmenarcheal groups did yield less to their father's attempts at interruption. In the mother–daughter dyads, there were no differences between the groups for agreement or yielding in the face of interruptions, but there was a higher frequency of interruptions by both mothers and daughters in the newly postmenarcheal group as opposed to the other groups. Overall, it is difficult to resolve conflicting findings or judge the overall significance of this research because of the very limited number of studies and the lack of longitudinal data, which are needed to draw inferences about the causal nature and direction of relationships observed between menarcheal timing and patterns of family interaction.

In approaching the converse question—Does the family context influence the experience of menarche?—researchers have focused on the role of family conflict and family composition in relation to the timing of menarche. Moffitt, Caspi, Belsky, and Silva (1992) tested a model put forth by Belsky, Steinberg, and Draper (1991) that sought to account for differences in maturational timing in terms of stressful childhood experiences. The model hypothesizes that children who experience family stress, such as family conflict and marital instability, develop psychologically and behaviorally in ways that precipitate earlier puberty and reproductive readiness. Using longitudinal data from the New Zealand sample described earlier, Moffitt et al. examined the influence of socioeconomic status, weight, behavior problems in childhood, family conflict, and marital instability (operationalized as father's absence) on age at menarche. Usable data were available for 416 girls, which represented 83% of the original sample. The best single predictor of age at menarche was weight at age nine. Correlations of menarcheal age with socioeconomic status and childhood behavior problems were not significant. However, family conflict showed a significant negative, although modest, correlation with menarcheal age. Furthermore, rates of father's absence were significantly higher for early maturers versus on-time and later maturers, and among the girls whose fathers were absent before age 11, menarcheal age was negatively associated with number of years the father had been absent. Family conflict and father absence contributed to the timing of menarche over and above the effect of weight and, in combination with weight, showed evidence of additive effects.

Drawing on research in nonhuman mammals suggesting that social factors—including stress and the presence of related versus unrelated conspecifics—can influence the timing of reproductive maturation, Surbey (1990) examined the effects of stress and family composition (i.e., father absence or mother absence vs. intact family) on girls' age at menarche in a large retrospective study. Girls who experienced father or mother absence did not differ from those raised with both parents in family size, birth order, socioeconomic status, weight, height, or weight for height. Stress, measured as the sum of negative life events in the girl's first 10 years weighted by severity, showed a significant negative correlation with menarcheal age. Furthermore, girls who experienced father absence attained menarche an average of 4 to 5 months earlier than those living with both parents, with no significant relationship observed for mother absence. Although girls who experienced father absence scored higher on life-events stress, both stress and father absence appeared to influence menarcheal age. These findings are suggestive; however, the data also revealed a significant correlation between mother's and daughter's menarcheal age. Surbey speculated that mothers who matured earlier not only have daughters who do also, but the mothers are also likely to marry at younger ages and to have less stable relationships. However, this question cannot be answered on the basis of retrospective data, and there was also some ambiguity about the age of subjects at the time of this study. Even though reports of age at menarche are often reliable, the greater the number of intervening years, the more error that is likely to be introduced.

It is important to examine menarche and family context, but this area of inquiry has exhibited weaknesses similar to those in other areas of research on menarche. Paikoff and Brooks-Gunn (1991) have pointed out the need for more diversity in race, ethnicity, and socioeconomic status in sample populations and for longitudinal investigations that begin before puberty to provide adequate characterization of baseline family processes. They have also pointed out the need to broaden the context beyond the parent–child dyad to the family system. We would add that the impact of menarche on relationships outside the family is also of interest. Research has suggested that the postmenarcheal girl views herself and is viewed by others as more sexually mature. Sexual maturation affords girls access to a source of interpersonal power that was previously unavailable. Therefore, it would be valuable for researchers to address how the postmenarcheal girl negotiates this change in status relative to gender-role expectations and what personal and contextual variables may influence this transition.

MENSTRUATION

Background

There is a voluminous literature on menstruation, encompassing studies of both normal menstrual experience and such problems as PMS, dysmenorrhea, amenorrhea, and menorrhagia. Only a small portion of this literature has examined the role of psychosocial factors, yet the range of topics has been broad and diverse, and include the effects of stress on menstrual cycle function; patterns of sexual arousal and behavior across the menstrual cycle; cognitive performance, perceptual-motor, and sensory responses in different cycle phases; cross-cultural research on attitudes and

GALLANT AND DERRY

behaviors relating to menstrual symptoms; behavioral approaches to treating menstrual disorders (e.g., dysmenorrhea and menstrual migraine); and the role of psychological factors in such problems as PMS and amenorrhea. We chose to focus on PMS because it is a topic that has generated considerable controversy and because there has been a lack of consensus concerning the role of psychosocial and behavioral factors in PMS. Readers desiring information on other psychosocial aspects of menstruation can consult several volumes for comprehensive reviews (e.g., Asso, 1983; Friedman, 1982; Gannon, 1990; Golub, 1992; Snowden & Christian, 1983) as well as other relevant articles and book chapters (e.g., Klebanov & Ruble, 1994; Parlee, 1983; Sommer, 1973).

Traditional biomedical research on PMS has focused on identifying the biological defect or defects responsible for PMS symptoms. A broad range of physiological parameters has been studied, including possible hormonal dysfunctions, neuroendocrine changes, neurotransmitter abnormalities, and vitamin deficiencies (see reviews by Bancroft & Backstrom, 1985; Halbreich, Alt, & Paul, 1988; Parry, 1994; Reid & Yen, 1981; Severino & Moline, 1989). Relevant studies include those that have examined biological differences directly as well as treatment studies addressing putative biological factors. Evaluation of this literature is complicated by methodological differences among studies in sample selection, criteria for establishing PMS, and study design. Nevertheless, it is clear that there is a lack of empirical support for many hypothesized biological determinants (e.g., Rubinow et al., 1988). Research is continuing into whether some women may have a biological "vulnerability" to PMS on the basis of findings of lower levels of serotonin premenstrually in women with PMS in comparison with controls (Ashby, Carr, Cook, Steptoe, & Frank, 1988; Rapkin et al., 1987) and because of indications that women with PMS have heightened sensitivity to induction of intense anxiety and panic attacks by carbon dioxide inhalation or lactate infusion (Facchinetti, Romano, Fava, & Genazzani, 1992; Harrison et al., 1989). Interest in biological factors has also been supported by research showing certain medical treatments for PMS (e.g., alprazolam) to be superior to placebo (see review by Rivera-Tovar, Rhodes, Pearlstein, & Frank, 1994). Overall however, the lack of support for a unidimensional biological explanation of PMS has given rise to more complex models that address psychological and social variables and their potential interactions with biological factors (e.g., Bancroft, 1994; Bancroft, Williamson, Warner, Rennie, & Smith, 1993; Keye & Trunnell, 1986). Severino and Moline (1989) stated that to explain PMS it is necessary to "understand what particular biological events trigger symptoms . . . how the woman understands what is happening to her and . . . the impact of the social setting on how [she] labels her experience" (p. 93). In seeking to contextualize women's experience of premenstrual symptoms within both biological and social domains, these models offer a new and potentially promising direction for future research.

In this section, we review research examining psychosocial variables related to PMS. We first discuss some methodological and measurement issues that should be considered in making judgments about research findings. In addition, to reduce ambiguity, we specify at the outset the basis for using certain terms. The term *premenstrual symptoms* is used in descriptions of studies of nonclinical populations unless specific symptom clustering and severity criteria were used to establish a diagnosis of PMS. *PMS* is used for studies of women seeking treatment for what they define as severe symptoms, with a further distinction between self-identified PMS and PMS diagnosed on the basis of prospective daily ratings of moods and symptoms thought to be associated with the premenstrual phase. An exception is that, when the diagnosis of Late Luteal Phase Dysphoric Disorder (LLPDD) from the *Diagnostic and Statistical Manual of Mental Disorders* (3rd ed., revised; American Psychiatric Association, 1987) was used, we used this more specific term. This diagnosis requires the presence of at least five symptoms, one of which must be affective, during the premenstrual phase of most menstrual cycles over the previous year. Symptoms must be associated with a significant impairment in social or occupational functioning and must be confirmed by two cycles of prospective daily self-ratings.

Nature and Assessment of Symptoms

There is general consensus that PMS refers to the cyclical recurrence of emotional, behavioral, and physical symptoms—such as anger, irritability, fatigue, and tearfulness—during the premenstrual phase that are severe enough to be distressing and to impair normal functioning. Operationally, however, there continues to be variability among studies in the nature, type, and number of symptoms assessed; in how severity is defined and measured; and in the definition and the length of premenstrual phase, with very few studies defining the premenstrual phase in terms of hormonal parameters (cf. Schachter, Bachman, Vaitukaitis, Phillips, & Saperstein, 1989).

There is a strong consensus that a diagnosis of PMS should be based on daily symptom ratings rather than on retrospective ratings, which amplify negative changes. When daily ratings are used, a woman records her experience of moods and symptoms each day on a scale ranging from, say, 0 (*none*) to 5 (*severe*). The presence of PMS is determined by comparing a woman's premenstrual ratings with ratings in the rest of her cycle (most often with ratings in the early follicular phase). Nevertheless, use of daily ratings is complicated because there is no standard rule for just how much ratings must increase premenstrually to justify a diagnosis (Schnurr, 1989). For example, the LLPDD diagnosis uses descriptors of "marked" or "persistent" in relation to symptom intensity and states that symptoms must seriously interfere with normal functioning, but it does not quantify the level that symptoms must achieve for a diagnosis to be appropriate. The result of not having an accepted standard is that studies have used different degrees of change criteria—some extremely liberal and others quite conservative—which reduces the ability to integrate this literature and resolve conflicting findings.

Fundamental to adopting degree of change in daily ratings as the "gold standard" for identifying PMS is the assumption that they allow a valid and reliable identification of those women who should and should not be diagnosed with PMS or LLPDD. This appears open to question. Gallant, Popiel, Hoffman, Chakraborty, and Hamilton (1992a) examined the five degree-of-change criteria used most often in research to establish a diagnosis of PMS on the basis of daily ratings. None were found to distinguish those women who claimed to experience severe symptoms and who met *DSM-III-R* criteria for a provisional diagnosis of LLPDD from those women who reported no premenstrual symptomatology. A similar nondiscriminatory pattern was reported by McFarlane and Williams (1994), who found, using conservative criteria, that 11% of a self-identified PMS group and 12.5% of a self-identified symptom-free group could be diagnosed with PMS on the basis of their daily ratings; rates rose to 19.4% versus 16.6%, respectively, for more liberal criteria. Diagnosing PMS on the basis of daily ratings has been considered a safeguard against misdiagnosis. However, if the ratings cannot reliably distinguish women who are troubled by their symptoms to the point of seeking treatment from those who see themselves as having no troubling symptoms, then this suggests that such ratings are not adequate for making a diagnosis. Furthermore, studies have rarely even attempted to quantify or prospectively confirm the criterion of a significant impairment in social or occupational functioning (cf. Gallant et al., 1992b). Yet, this severity criterion is an important component of LLPDD that distinguishes it from premenstrual symptoms that are distressing but not debilitating, and it should thus be confirmed before this diagnostic label is applied legitimately.

Given the foregoing facts, it should not be surprising that there has been, and continues to be, significant controversy over the inclusion of a PMS diagnostic category in the *DSM*. Proponents have asserted that such a diagnosis will improve treatment and advance research by providing a uniform set of criteria. Critics, while acknowledging that a standard set of criteria is essential to developing a solid research base, have argued that inclusion in the *DSM* is premature at best, given the equivocal nature of the current reliability and validity data. The decision was made to retain the diagnosis in the *DSM-IV* in the research appendix, which specifies criteria sets in need of further study. The name has been changed to *Premenstrual Dysphoric Disorder* (PDD).

Part of the problem is that the LLPDD–PDD diagnosis, like others in the *DSM* nosology, is merely a description of symptoms, which, by itself, reveals nothing about the relationships among the symptoms identified or about the nature of the underlying biological or psychosocial causal processes (Persons, 1986). It is clear that in the recent literature on PMS there has been a strong emphasis on methodological rigor, yet much less attention has been paid to the need for such rigor in conceptualization. Even though there has been criticism of the state of theorizing in the field (e.g., Parlee, 1988, in press), these views have not as yet had a major impact on etiological models or research. Given the history of methodological problems in research on PMS, this emphasis on methodology is understandable. However, there is a need for research that is both methodologically sound and conceptually sophisticated, and this will require renewed attention to developing an integrative theory of premenstrual emotional experience that is grounded in the psychosocial as well as the biological reality of women's lives and within which the appropriate questions can be framed. If one's interest is in determining the biological correlates of premenstrual symptoms, it may make sense to study women who show significant mood and behavior changes regardless of whether or not they discern the cyclical nature of these changes or perceive themselves to be suffering from PMS. However, if the goal is to gain an understanding of the "problem" of PMS, it is not sufficient to focus only on the cyclicity of symptoms. Research indicating that some women identify themselves as having a severe problem whereas other women with a similar pattern of mood changes do not suggests that researchers need to broaden their focus to encompass the ways that defining oneself as "having PMS" is meaningful in a woman's life. Some of the newer models mentioned briefly at the beginning of this section appear to be moving in this direction, but it remains to be seen whether they will become the dominant paradigm. We now move to reviewing research on psychological and social factors and PMS, but we hope that readers will keep in mind that the question of what is central to the experience of PMS has yet to be fully determined.

Psychology of PMS

Psychological Disturbance

Although the traditional biomedical model of PMS has sought a physiological abnormality as the basis of symptoms, the corresponding psychological model has focused on the role of psychological disturbance. Both viewpoints assume that the primary cause of PMS resides within each woman, that is, that PMS reflects pathological functioning of the body or mind. Ideas about the role of psychological disturbance in PMS have a long history and remain a focus of research. Early writings linked PMS to disturbances in feminine identity or role acceptance. Research did not support this, however (e.g., Slade & Jenner, 1980), and rather than lack of acceptance, recent studies have suggested that women seeking treatment for PMS evidence strong endorsement of the traditional feminine role (Freeman, Sondheimer, & Rickels, 1987; Stout & Steege, 1985).

PMS continues to be examined in relation to psychopathology, particularly neuroticism and anxiety (e.g., Bancroft et al., 1993; Mira, Vizzard, & Abraham, 1985; Mohan & Chopra, 1987). Findings for neuroticism have been mixed, with some studies showing a significant relationship to symptom severity or PMS status and others showing none (cf. Mira et al., 1985; Mohan & Chopra, 1987). Discrepant findings do not simply reflect different methodologies, because findings are not consistent, even among studies that used the same criteria (e.g., prospective assessment). Findings have been more consistent for anxiety with several recent studies (e.g., Giannini, Price, Loiselle, & Giannini, 1985; Halbreich & Kas, 1977; Mira et al., 1985)—although not all (cf. Christensen, Board, & Oei, 1992; Kuczmierczyk, Labrum, & Johnson, 1992) reporting higher trait anxiety and greater increases in anxiety from follicular to luteal phases in women with PMS (whether self-identified or diagnosed on the basis of prospective ratings) in comparison with controls.

Although women with PMS may be anxiety prone, the reporting of global scores has not been informative about particular aspects of this anxiety. For example, it would be interesting to know if women with PMS are more attuned, in general or premenstrually, to the physiological correlates of anxiety. Examining responses to such measures as the Anxiety Sensitivity Index (R. A. Peterson & Reiss, 1987) or the Body Consciousness Scale (Miller, Murphy, & Buss, 1981) would allow an assessment of a woman's tendency to be aware of such bodily sensations and of a potential mechanism through which greater anxiety may be experienced.

Several studies have examined Minnesota Multiphasic Personality Inventory (MMPI) scores of women with PMS (variously defined), sometimes including a comparison sample of asymptomatic women (also variously defined). Here again, results have been mixed, with some studies (e.g., see Mortola, 1992; Stout & Steege, 1985) finding little evidence of psychopathology, whereas others (e.g., Chuong, Colligan, Coulom, & Bergstralh, 1991; Freeman et al., 1987; Hammond & Keye, 1985; Trunnell, Turner, & Keye, 1988) found significantly higher luteal phase scores on many of the MMPI clinical scales in the PMS group in comparison with controls and a significant difference in phase scores in the PMS group. The meaningfulness of these results is questionable given that the data are typically presented as group mean scores, from which nothing can be discerned except the presence of higher symptom endorsement (or the lack thereof) between groups or phases. It seems a monumental waste to have women complete this 500-plus item inventory and then not use the test as it was intended. The power and validity of the MMPI is in the pattern of individual profiles that it reveals. However, none of these studies reported whether certain high-point pairs or code types (which provide information about specific areas of disturbed functioning) differentiated women with PMS from controls or women whose PMS was confirmed from those whose PMS was not confirmed. One study (Keye, Hammond, & Strong, 1986) gave a lengthy and very negative characterization of women seeking treatment for PMS, but no profile data were presented from which one could evaluate the conclusions drawn.

Evidence for some kind of link between PMS and psychopathology has been found in research on life-time risk for psychiatric illness, which has consistently found that women with PMS are at increased risk relative to the general population. For example, Hurt, Williams, Severino, and Anderson (1986) found that 60% of a sample of self-identified PMS sufferers had experienced at least one occurrence of a psychiatric disorder, and comparable rates have been reported for women whose PMS was diagnosed on the basis of prospective ratings (e.g., DeJong et al., 1985; Pearlstein et al., 1990; Severino, Hurt, & Shindledecker, 1989). Particular attention has been focused on the risk of affective disorders, and a number of studies have found that women with PMS have a higher incidence of affective illness (e.g., DeJong et al., 1985; Dennerstein, Morse, & Varnanides, 1988; Endicott & Halbreich, 1988; Hurt et al., 1986; Pearlstein et al., 1990; P. Warner, Bancroft, Dixson, & Hampson, 1991), especially depression and anxiety.

Little can be concluded from this line of research beyond that, for reasons as yet unclear, women with PMS appear to be vulnerable to disorders of depression and anxiety. Useful information regarding causality might be gained if women with PMS were studied longitudinally through repeated assessments of psychological functioning in relation to potentially important social (e.g., stress, career and family roles) and biological variables.

Personality, Attitudes, and Expectations

Personality. Given the traditional biomedical conceptualization of PMS and its emphasis on psychiatric illness, it is not surprising that there is only a small literature on PMS and "normal" personality variables. This research is not only scant but also suffers from the lack of a developed theory about the role of personality in PMS. Recent studies have examined differences related to locus of control, attributional style, and self-esteem—all variables reported in the literature on depression to be important. For example, O'Boyle, Severino, and Hurt (1988) examined locus-of-control scores for women diagnosed with PMS and found them to be higher than in a no-PMS group, indicating a stronger belief among the PMS group that outcomes are determined by external forces beyond their control. The same was reported by Christensen et al. (1992), although locus-of-control scores did not differ between women whose symptoms were confirmed by prospective ratings and those not confirmed. Studies examining attributional style (e.g., Trunnell et al., 1988) have used the Attributional Style Questionnaire (e.g., C. Peterson et al., 1982). Unlike in studies of depression, however, no specific attributional style has been found to characterize women with PMS or to differentiate them from asymptomatic women. This seems somewhat surprising given the higher locus-of-control scores in women with PMS, which would lead to an expectation of higher scores for external attributions.

With regard to self-esteem, Woods, Mitchell, and Lentz (1993), using a large population-based sample, compared self-esteem scores for women confirmed to have PMS, *premenstrual magnification* (PMM; Harrison,

1982), where symptoms were present over the cycle but increased significantly during the premenstrual phase, or low symptoms on the basis of 3 months of prospective ratings. Self-esteem was lowest in the PMM group and significantly lower in both the PMM and PMS groups than in the low-symptom group. Similar findings have been reported in other studies (e.g., Maddocks & Reid, 1992), suggesting that women with PMS and those who are more chronically symptomatic are vulnerable to negative self-appraisals. However, cause and effect have not been disentangled, and a bidirectional relationship appears likely.

The importance of personality in PMS is unclear at this point. There are too few studies, and the range of variables examined has been narrow. However, given that there are now several psychometrically sound instruments that measure multidimensional aspects of personality, it would not be difficult to more thoroughly examine personality traits in women with PMS. The bigger challenge is to develop a theory that integrates findings and guides research.

Attitudes. The relationship of PMS to menstrual attitudes has been examined in a number of studies, although typically in nonclinical populations, such that the generalizability to women reporting severe symptoms is unclear. Furthermore, most studies have not tested any causal influence of these variables on symptom experience. Some comparability is afforded because most studies have used the Menstrual Attitudes Questionnaire (Brooks-Gunn & Ruble, 1980). Stronger relationships have been observed when symptoms are assessed retrospectively than according to daily ratings, but significant correlations have been reported for both (e.g., Gallant, Hamilton, Popiel, Morokoff, & Chakraborty, 1991; Klebanov & Jemmott, 1992; Ruble & Brooks-Gunn, 1987). For example, Klebanov and Jemmott found that greater premenstrual distress (assessed retrospectively) was associated with viewing menstruation as more debilitating and predictable and with less denial of effects of menstruation. The potential bidirectional nature of these relationships seems intuitive; that is, more negative attitudes may lead a woman to construe her psychological state in terms of symptoms and, conversely, experiencing distressing symptoms may create negative attitudes.

Expectations. Research has suggested that women are socialized to expect negative emotional, physical, and behavioral states to occur premenstrually (e.g., Delaney, Lupton, & Toth, 1976; Ruble & Brooks-Gunn, 1979), which may lead to interpreting any such psychological or physical states in terms of their menstrual status rather than attributing them to situational or other factors. The findings of Brooks-Gunn and Ruble (1982) underscored that even young girls have expectations about premenstrual symptoms that are consistent with stereotypes and correlate with symptom reporting. In her classic study of adults, Ruble (1977) examined the influence of expectancies by manipulating perceptions of cycle phase. Some subjects were told that they were premenstrual and others that they were intermenstrual, when, in actuality, all were premenstrual. Those who thought they were intermenstrual reported fewer symptoms of pain and water retention; but it is noteworthy that there were no differences for negative affect, concentration, or behavior change. Using a similar methodology, Klebanov and Jemmott (1992) conducted two studies to replicate and extend Ruble's findings. Results differed in the two studies, but overall they provided only weak support for an effect of expectancies. In the first study, women were tested only during their premenstrual phase. Those who had previously reported greater premenstrual distress on a retrospective questionnaire were found subsequently to report more symptoms in the lab regardless of whether they were led to believe they were premenstrual or intermenstrual. In the second study, symptoms were assessed both premenstrually and intermenstrually. Women who were led to believe they were premenstrual reported more symptoms than women who thought they were intermenstrual, but subscale analysis revealed that this effect was significant only for pain, not for reports of negative affect, water retention, or autonomic reactions.

In a related approach, Bains and Slade (1988) attempted to replicate in an older, less homogenous, female sample the often-cited findings of Koeske (Koeske, 1980; Koeske & Koeske, 1975) that college students use information about cycle phase to explain negative premenstrual moods even when other plausible explanatory factors are present. Consistent with earlier findings, negative moods that occurred premenstrually were attributed to cycle phase, whereas the same moods occurring intermenstrually were explained in terms of work and personality factors. These findings indirectly support the expectancy hypothesis. However, the methodology introduced a demand characteristic that may have influenced results: Each woman responded to four vignettes that varied only in information about menstrual cycle phase and mood, which may have raised the salience of the menstrual cycle as an explanatory category.

Indirect support for the role of expectancies has come from several studies showing that women report more premenstrual symptoms if they are aware that they are participating in a menstrual cycle study than if they are kept blind to the study's focus (e.g., AuBuchon & Calhoun, 1985; Englander-Golden, Sonleiter, Whitmore, & Corbley, 1986; Englander-Golden, Whitmore, Dienstbier, 1978). However, these findings were in young college students. Research on an older, nonstudent sample found only a weak effect of such a demand characteristic (Gallant et al., 1991), and no effect was found for women who self-identified as having severe PMS (Gallant et al., 1992b).

More direct tests of the expectancy hypothesis have been provided in studies that manipulated subjects' beliefs about menstrual cycle effects. Olasov and Jackson (1987) found that women exposed to information to heighten their expectations of menstrual-cycle effects on moods subsequently reported more negative daily moods in comparison with women whose expectancies were experimentally decreased. However, this effect was not specific to the premenstrual phase but was evident across all phases. Fradkin and Firestone (1986) manipulated beliefs about PMS as biologically or psychologically based (i.e., resulting from negative social myths) and compared symptom reports for these two groups and a control group. Women in the PMS–psychological group showed a significant decrease in their belief in biological attribution, had lower symptom expectations in comparison with expectations at the premanipulation level, and reported less negative moods when tested premenstrually and retrospectively at the end of the cycle than the other two groups. These results should be interpreted conservatively, however, because subjects were not naive to the focus of the study, and this may have introduced a demand characteristic.

In summary, the role of expectations and related cognitive factors in PMS as envisioned by Ruble and Brooks-Gunn (1979) and by Koeske (1980) remains unresolved. Both theories focus centrally on these variables, and, although formulated more than 10 years ago, they remain the only detailed models of PMS from a predominately psychosocial perspective. Neither, however, has received sufficient careful evaluation to date. Overall, findings in nonclinical populations have been equivocal concerning the expectancy hypothesis of PMS, with results from some studies difficult to evaluate because of methodological flaws.

The only studies of women with PMS that are relevant to the expectancy hypothesis have involved women who have undergone a hysterectomy with conservation of the ovaries (e.g., Metcalf et al., 1991; Osborn & Gath, 1990). It had been assumed that the loss of menstruation would be accompanied by the loss of a physical marker that serves to anchor expectations about symptom experience. Thus, to the extent that symptoms are the products of expectations, they should be resolved among women who have hysterectomies, despite the continued presence of underlying hormonal fluctuations. Gath and Iles (1988), in a brief report on the postoperative responses of 40 women with PMS who underwent hysterectomies, indicated that symptoms resolved in two thirds and were significantly ameliorated in the remaining one third of the sample. Similar dramatic reductions in both premenstrual psychological (59%) and physical symptoms (72%) were reported in a subsequent study (Osborn & Gath, 1990). One particularly noteworthy study (Metcalf, Braiden, Livesey, & Wells, 1992) found not only that the severity of premenstrual symptoms declined dramatically (66%) but also that the decline could not be attributed to any of several alternative explanations, including that the decrease in symptoms was due to compromised ovarian functioning resulting from damage to the ovaries during surgery, or to the "tonic" effect of hysterectomy (i.e., improved physical well-being of women who were unwell before surgery). Thus, these findings provide strong indirect support for the idea that PMS reflects symptom reporting based on expectancies rather than on hormonal fluctuations.

One final study (Schmidt et al., 1991) deserves comment because it has received a great deal of attention and is relevant to the question of expectations. This study administered the drug mifepristone (RU-486) in combination with human chorionic gonadotropin (HCG) or placebo to chemically manipulate menstrual-cycle phase in a small group of women diagnosed with PMS. The symptom reports of this group were compared with those from a similar group of women who received only placebo. The women who received RU-486 and either HCG or placebo had their luteal phase truncated and experienced a bleeding episode. The results indicated no difference in the timing or intensity of symptom reports between the women with PMS whose premenstrual phase was hormonally reset to levels characteristic of the early follicular phase, those whose plasma progesterone levels were maintained by HCG, and those who only received placebo and, therefore, had their normal premenstrual phase. Although these findings can be taken as directly negating the role of luteal-phase endocrine events in the etiology of PMS, they also indirectly negate the role of expectations, because women who expect to have symptoms premenstrually should expect to be symptom-free once menstruation has occurred. Thus, the reporting of symptoms after having menstruated appears inconsistent with an expectancy hypothesis. Unfortunately, it is difficult to evaluate this fully, because no information was provided about what subjects were told concerning the purpose of the study or whether they thought the bleeding episode was a "real period." Furthermore, as discussed by J. A. Hamilton and Gallant (1993), the study has been criticized because the hormonal manipulation that was used complicates interpretation of the findings.

Stress, Coping, and Interpersonal Relationships

An alternative to the biomedical–psychiatric conceptualization of PMS is the view that there are perhaps differences in the life circumstances of women who experience severe premenstrual symptoms. Research from this perspective has examined stress, coping responses, and the quality of interpersonal relationships in women with PMS.

Stress. A number of studies have found that stress correlates with reports of premenstrual symptoms, particularly mood symptoms, and that women with PMS report a higher degree of life stress than asymptomatic women (e.g., Gallant et al., 1992b; Maddocks & Reid, 1992; R. Warner & Bancroft, 1990). For example, N. A. Williams, Severino, Hurt, and Anderson (1986) reported that nearly 80% of their sample of self-identified PMS sufferers stated that some type of stress—primarily problems in close relationships, with children, or at work—was a major factor in their life and increased their symptoms. Similarly, Mills (1991) studied 100 women with chronic "medically diagnosed" PMS. Over 60% of the women and nearly 50% of their male partners attributed increases in PMS severity to greater stress in relation to workload, financial difficulties, and scheduling problems.

It is assumed that stress causes or exacerbates symptoms or makes a woman less able to cope with them. However, this is a complicated issue, because premenstrual symptoms may themselves be a significant source of stress, and some studies have used measures of stress that confound the two (e.g., Heilbrun & Frank, 1989). Furthermore, even methodologically sound studies have presented varied findings. Some (e.g., Schmidt, Grover, Hoban, & Rubinow, 1990) have found that women diagnosed with PMS experienced more negative and fewer positive life events, particularly during the premenstrual phase, in comparison with controls, whereas other studies have found no relationship between reports of symptom severity and ratings of daily stress or frequency of major life events (e.g., Woods, Most, & Longnecker, 1985). Discrepant findings may in part reflect the contribution of premenstrual symptoms to the experience of stress. Beck, Gevirtz, and Mortola (1990) found that stress ratings increased premenstrually in a sample of women diagnosed with PMS. However, when the contribution of symptoms was removed through covariance analysis, stress was not found to be greater premenstrually than in other cycle phases. Likewise, the frequency of stress of various types (e.g., work, family, or financial) was not different premenstrually in comparison with other phases, and stress level in a particular cycle did not predict the severity of PMS experienced. Thus, although women with PMS often rank stress as a major factor in their symptom experience, empirical support for this is weak.

Research by Woods et al. (1993) has suggested that stress may be a more important factor in PMM than in PMS, underscoring the importance of distinguishing between these symptom patterns. The work of Woods and colleagues (e.g., Woods et al., 1985, 1993) is of particular note because it was based on a large multi-ethnic community sample that included low-income populations, in contrast with most studies that have been conducted on predominately White and upper-income samples. In addition, these researchers (e.g., Taylor, Woods, Lentz, Mitchell, & Lee, 1991) have formulated a model of PMS and evaluated its fit to empirical data with statistical techniques (structural equation modeling) that facilitate the testing of causal hypotheses with correlational data.

In the stress research area, a recent focus has been on PMS in relation to family and work roles. Coughlin (1990) compared a large sample of married women who had mild, moderate, or severe PMS. The "severe" group had their symptoms evaluated by history, interview, and prospective charting, and the others were evaluated from retrospective symptom reports. Marital dissatisfaction was found to relate to premenstrual distress after the influence of general life stress was controlled for. Furthermore, women who worked outside the home reported greater premenstrual distress than did homemakers. However, choice appeared to be a key variable for these results: Women who reported being homemakers by choice had the lowest symptom ratings, whereas those who reported that they were working not by choice had the highest. Finally, Kuczmierczyk et al. (1992) compared family and work characteristics of a sample of women diagnosed with PMS and a group of routine gynecological patients. Those with PMS reported more conflict in their families, greater religious emphasis, less direct expression of feelings, and less autonomy. They also reported more work pressure and job monotony. The authors interpreted their findings as suggesting that women with PMS experience more work stress and have families that tend toward a rigid, enmeshed structure.

Coping. Researchers have only recently examined the potential role of coping in PMS. Results have suggested that women with PMS tend to use more indirect coping strategies that may be less effective (e.g., C. J. Warren & Baker, 1992; Woods et al., 1993). For example, Gallant et al. (1994) found higher scores for avoidance and wishful thinking and lower scores for problem-focused and social support coping in women with PMS (self-identified) in comparison with asymptomatic controls. The pattern of findings does not suggest that women with PMS have deficits in coping resources per se, but that they tend to underuse those coping strategies that have been found to show the strongest relationships to health and well-being. The same conclusion can be drawn from studies that have examined the coping resources of both women with PMS and their partners. Ornitz and Brown (1993) studied couples in which the women were divided into high- and low-symptom groups on the basis of retrospective ratings. The biggest difference between the groups was the less frequent use of social support and a greater reliance on religion and spirituality (e.g., having faith in God) in the high-symptom group. T. A. Hamilton (1986) found both group and phase differences in coping strategies reported by women with PMS and their partners. The women were categorized as high or low PMS on the basis of criteria established by Abraham (1980). Use of rationalization–avoidance (an indirect coping strategy) was reported more by the men than by women in both groups, but more so by the male partners of women in the high-symptom group, and particularly in the premenstrual phase. Direct action to solve a problem was reported more by women in the low- than high-symptom group and more by male partners of women in the high-symptom group. Finally, coping by appeasement, active conflict, or withdrawal were more frequent in the high- than the low-symptom group, especially during the premenstrual phase. These data are consistent in suggesting less than optimal coping both by women with PMS and by their male partners; however, more detailed studies with longitudinal designs are needed.

Interpersonal functioning. Many women complaining of PMS report that their symptoms negatively affect their relationships with others, particularly with intimate partners and family members. This is often described as one of the most distressing aspects of "having PMS," and for many women, it is a strong factor in the decision to seek treatment. The belief that PMS impairs a woman's ability to relate to others appears to be widespread. It has been reflected in clinical reports linking severe PMS with marital and family discord (e.g., Dalton, 1984; Norris & Sullivan, 1983). For example, Norris and Sullivan reported that, among the nearly

25% of their PMS patients who were divorced, all claimed that their PMS was the primary cause, and this belief was shared by the husbands as well. There have also been several large survey studies (e.g., Corney & Stanton, 1991; Futterman, Jones, Miccio-Fonseca, & Quigley, 1992), and studies of clinical patients (e.g., Keye et al., 1986; Stout & Steege, 1985) in which reports of severe PMS were associated with lower ratings of marital or relationship satisfaction. For example, Keye et al. found that women seeking treatment for PMS reported less marital satisfaction than other gynecology patients and that their scores were similar to women seeking marital and sex therapy. Furthermore, studies that have examined men's as well as women's perceptions have suggested that both genders attribute a variety of relationship problems to PMS (e.g., Brown & Zimmer, 1986). In one such study, Brown and Zimmer administered a questionnaire—a portion of which assessed beliefs about the impact of PMS on family life—to a sample of men and women attending a lecture on PMS. Fifty-seven percent of the women reported severe disruption of their interpersonal or family life premenstrually, whereas 32% reported moderate disruption. Seventy-six percent of the men reported that their lives were moderately or greatly disrupted by their partner's symptoms. The most frequently reported negative effects were increased conflict, less time spent in enjoyable family activities, decreased performance of household tasks by the woman, and lower family cohesiveness. In a subsequent study (Brown & Zimmer, 1987)—one of the few in which symptoms were assessed during the premenstrual phase rather than retrospectively—data were collected on 104 families divided into two groups based on the women's high or low premenstrual symptoms. The more symptomatic women reported lower marital quality and less perceived support from their partner premenstrually in comparison with postmenstrually, but no such differences were reported in the low-symptom group. Furthermore, husbands of the more symptomatic women rated themselves as less satisfied with the functioning of their families, both premenstrually and postmenstrually, in comparison with the spouses of women in the low-symptom group.

Given the apparent pervasive belief in the potential of PMS to cause relationship problems and the observed association between PMS and relationship dissatisfaction, it is surprising that there has been so little careful study of this question. Most of the research has been limited to correlating retrospective symptom reports with global ratings of relationship or marital satisfaction, which is uninformative about causal processes or other specifics. Studies in which more detailed aspects have been examined have suggested that PMS is associated with an array of negative interpersonal features, including increased conflict, poor communication and problem solving, less positive quality time together, and greater sexual dissatisfaction (e.g., Brown & Zimmer, 1986; Cohen, 1986; T. A. Hamilton, 1986). However, these studies have also had serious methodological weaknesses that make it impossible to draw firm conclusions. For example, they failed to control for possible psychiatric problems in the PMS subjects or their partners, such as anxiety, depression, or personality disorders that could be expected to interfere with relating to others. Although it is believed that PMS can coexist with other psychiatric conditions, care should be taken to avoid misidentifying women as having PMS who actually have another psychiatric problem, such as depression. Given the overlap in emotional and physical symptoms reported by women with PMS and by individuals with a depressive disorder and the fact that depression has been associated with increased marital distress (e.g., Monroe, Bromet, Cornell, & Steiner, 1986), future studies should screen carefully to exclude those with depression and other psychological problems from PMS studies.

The design of the aforementioned studies does not allow inferences regarding the causal direction of observed relationships. Despite this, the most common interpretation from them has been that PMS causes marital and family disturbance. An alternative hypothesis has been suggested by Siegel (1986), however. She proposed that the negative emotionality stereotypically associated with PMS allows a woman to express feelings of tension, anger, and frustration that have been building up over the cycle in response to important relationship issues that have not been addressed to her satisfaction. Because the expression of these feelings can be blamed on having PMS, they are excused, yet they ultimately lose credibility as legitimate complaints about the relationship or family life. This in turn works to perpetuate a cycle of dysfunctional relating in the couple. This is an interesting model of

PMS because it seeks to explain a woman's symptom experience within the broader context of the couple's relationship and draws attention to issues of power and control that have been infrequently studied. To test such a model requires an in-depth look at the nature and quality of the interactions that occur in couples over the whole cycle, not just premenstrually. It also requires collecting data over several cycles so that the magnitude and causal direction of effects can be examined by using statistical procedures that are appropriate for making causal inferences on the basis of correlational data. Furthermore, a well-established methodology for investigating conflict resolution in couples already exists, and it could be adapted to the study of these couples. The fact that there may be bidirectional causality between PMS severity and relationship problems makes it all the more important to design studies in a way that will clarify the relative importance of each.

Summary

Research on the psychological aspects of PMS covers a broad spectrum and includes studies of the link between PMS and psychopathology; the influence of personality, coping strategies, attitudes and expectations; and the role of stress and interpersonal relationships in the experience of symptoms. This literature is difficult to integrate because it is so heterogeneous and, to a large extent, represents discrete areas that are not tied to a common model or paradigm. Furthermore, regardless of the approach, many studies suffer methodological limitations that restrict confidence in their results, and even methodologically sound studies frequently do not approach the level of sophistication necessary for issues of causality to be addressed. Although research findings are suggestive concerning the role of psychological variables in PMS, understanding of interrelationships among these factors and pathways of influence is truly meager. Stronger evidence could likely be obtained from multidimensional models that conceptualize women's experience of PMS within a biosocial context and use appropriate prospective and longitudinal designs.

MENOPAUSE

Menopause is the cessation of menstruation associated with loss of ovarian activity (World Health Organization, 1981). However, this is not a discrete event: Natural menopause is a process that typically occurs over a period of years. There is a gradual decrease in ovulatory cycles, characterized by steadily increasing levels of luteinizing hormone and follicle stimulating hormone and decreasing levels of estrogen (manifested in irregular bleeding) until menstruation ceases (Gannon, 1990).

How best to choose markers that define the important phases of the menopausal process has been a methodological problem (see below). The emerging standard for menopause as a physiological process is its definition as a period of 12 months with no menstrual bleeding; an additional measure is sometimes an elevated FSH level (above 30 international units). Women whose menstrual cycles are regular are defined as *premenopausal.* Those in between—that is, those with irregular bleeding or a cessation of menstruation of less than 12 months—are defined as being in the *perimenopause* stage. Asking whether women define themselves as being menopausal is an additional criterion that is sometimes included, especially when the psychological effects of menopause are being researched.

The traditionally dominant view of menopause, the biomedical view, has involved a set of assumptions that have exerted important constraints on the research agenda. First, this view assumes the existence of a "menopausal syndrome" that includes hot flashes, profuse sweating, headaches, weight increase, dryness and thinning of the vaginal walls, increased incidence of vaginal infections, loss of breast firmness, dizziness, sensations of cold in the hands and feet, irritability, depression, insomnia, pruritus of the sex organs, constipation, atherosclerosis, and osteoporosis (Gannon, 1990). However, research has typically failed to uphold the existence of such a menopausal syndrome. Symptoms do not typically co-occur or are not more common in menopausal, in comparison with other, women, with the exception of vaginal changes (such as dryness), hot flashes (sensations of heat, especially in the face, neck, and chest, and sometimes associated with profuse sweating), and, perhaps, osteoporosis (Ballinger, 1975; S. McKinlay & McKinlay, 1973).

A second aspect of this biomedical view of menopause is that menopausal symptoms are assumed to result directly from the lowered levels of estrogen defining menopause. The underlying assumption is that menopause is an *endocrinopathy*—an abnormal withering or malfunction of the ovaries (Martin, 1987; Wilson & Wilson, 1963). This ovarian "failure" then results in other associated problems or symptoms, such as hot flashes or clinical depression. Treating these symptoms requires the restoration of premenopausal levels of estrogen. Thus, estrogen replacement therapy (ERT), or treatment with estrogen combined with progesterone (hormone replacement therapy, or HRT) have been preferred treatments for such symptoms. Other causal mechanisms or other treatment modalities, whether physiological or psychosocial, have been relatively understudied. For example, HRT has often been prescribed to alleviate hot flashes, which are one of the more common disturbing physical symptoms of menopause. Although HRT does appear to be effective as a treatment, research has been inconclusive as to whether hot-flash frequency or intensity are causally determined by estrogen levels (Ballinger, Browning, & Smith, 1987; Casper, Yen, & Wilkes, 1979).

A more recent viewpoint, in contrast to the view that menopause is an endocrinopathy, is the view that menopause is a physiologically normal period of feminine development (e.g., Voda, 1992). In this view, menopause is a lawful process, not a breakdown phenomenon. Those who hold this perspective might interpret the endocrinopathy view as misogynistic (Martin, 1987; McCrae, 1983). This viewpoint encourages one to seek causal mechanisms that are broader than simply restoring premenstrual estrogen levels and, therefore, a broader range of interventions to control symptoms. Furthermore, this perspective is more consistent with investigating psychosocial factors that are part of the menopausal process. Regarding hot flashes, for example, it is only relatively recently that causal mechanisms other than estrogen deficiency (such as hypothalamic changes and lower levels of endogenous opioids) and other treatments (such as biofeedback or stress management) have been considered (Gannon, 1990). The psychosocial context is a relatively recent area of study, including whether frequency of flashes is influenced by stress (Gannon, 1988), whether the problematic quality of flashes is influenced by whether flashes are expected or not, and whether they create problems such as avoidance of social contact (Schmidt & Rubinow, 1991). Why cross-cultural differences (e.g., Beyenne, 1986) exist in the frequency of flashes is also a recent area of study.

Psychology of Menopause

Depression

The interplay of these conceptual frameworks has been seen in research on the psychology of menopause. Until relatively recently, this research was dominated by the question of whether menopause is associated with psychological distress, especially depression. The traditional biomedical view has listed depression as a symptom within the menopausal syndrome, resulting from lowered estrogen levels. Indeed, estrogen has been advocated as a treatment for such depression. Schmidt and Rubinow (1991), for example, suggested that if women have a first episode of severe depression during the early menopausal years, accompanied by menopausal symptoms, then estrogen replacement should be the treatment of choice. The overriding focus on the question of whether or not women are at increased risk for depression during menopause—and, relatedly, whether women commonly are depressed as a consequence of menopause—and whether or not such depression during the midlife years is a consequence of lowered estrogen levels or other causes has constrained psychological research on menopause for many years. It is only recently that a broader range of questions about the psychology of menopause has become a focus of research.

The earliest research in this area supported the concept of a link between menopause and depression (e.g., Smith, 1971). However, this research was criticized on the grounds that it was based on patient populations and did not control for such factors as self-selection into hormone-replacement versus control groups and inflated levels of menopausal problems among those with previous psychiatric histories. During the 1970s, a series of cross-sectional studies were conducted with epidemiological populations. Most of these studies (e.g., S. McKinlay & Jeffreys, 1974) failed to show a link between menopause and depression among general population groups. However, these studies were in turn criticized for such methodological problems as using retrospective accounts of symptoms as well as the intrinsic inability to make causal inferences from correlational studies.

During the 1980s, a series of prospective epidemiological studies (Hunter, 1990; Kaufert, Gilbert, & Tate, 1992; Matthews, 1992; Matthews et al., 1990; J. McKinlay, McKinlay, & Brambilla, 1987) were conducted to evaluate whether causal, as opposed to correlational, relationships existed between menopause and depression. These studies typically involved interviewing a large cohort of women (at least 500) from the general population who were premenopausal and interviewing them again after a change in menopausal status (using either one postmeasure or a series of follow-up interviews). Baseline measures of mood as well as other variables could then be compared with later measures. Usually, data were analyzed through multiple regression analysis, in which menopausal status as well as other physical and psychosocial variables were predictors of distress. An additional method was to identify women who changed from baseline to later measures in a variable of interest, such as depression, and then isolate variables that distinguished those who changed from those who did not.

Although differing among themselves in the specifics of the methodologies used, these studies consistently showed that, of the symptoms in the traditional menopausal syndrome, only hot flashes and vaginal problems such as dryness were reliably linked to menopausal status. Risk of depression did not increase for women experiencing natural (as opposed to surgical) menopause above their likelihood for depression before the onset of menopause. The one exception was found in a study by Hunter (1990). However, Hunter's study differed from the others in that her sample was quite small (only 6 subjects were premenopausal, 10 were postmenopausal, and 31 were perimenopausal), and there were methodological problems (no controls for aging, collapsing of peri- and postmenopausal women into one group, no use of a standard depression scale, regression analysis with several predictor variables used with a small sample size that included only six cases of depression). In any event, the effect that she obtained was quite small.

The longitudinal studies demonstrated that increased risk of depression was associated with such psychosocial variables as stressors and previous history of depression, as well as with problematical health-related variables, rather than with menopausal status. This finding that a stress and coping model and previous history of psychopathology predicted depression is consistent with current understanding of the nature of depression. For this age group, stressors included psychosocial stressors and physical health variables.

In the aforementioned studies, depression was associated with measures of interpersonal stress. However, results did not support the view that risk of depression is a consequence of interpersonal loss, except when loss was a psychosocial stressor. J. McKinlay et al. (1987), for example, found that having had a child leave home was not associated with increased risk of depression; on the other hand, having a child who had previously left home return home did predict increased risk. Similarly, Kaufert et al. (1992) found that death of a family member was not associated with increased risk of depression; the majority of deaths (84%) were of parents and, the authors suggested, were "presumably expected." One can speculate that these deaths were also associated with reduction in the stress of caretaking and seeing elderly parents suffer.

Health problems, especially the onset of chronic health problems such as diabetes or arthritis, have also been associated with increased risk of depression. One can speculate, again, that these constituted long-term stressors. Interestingly, both Kaufert et al. (1992) and J. McKinlay et al. (1987) found that paid employment was protective against the onset of depression: McKinlay et al. reported that the effect of stressors on risk of depression held only for nonemployed women. Also consistent with the view that depression in midlife is associated with coping with stressors was Matthews's (1992) finding that in a sample of healthy midlife women, rates of depression were elevated during perimenopause rather than during menopause. This is significant because it is during perimenopause that a transition occurs. McKinlay et al. suggested that if a woman complains of depression, it is most likely a coincidence that she is also menopausal.

The longitudinal studies did identify risk factors for depression in midlife women. Although research has shown that depression is not a common effect of menopause, it has also revealed that women who have a history of depression, who experience surgical menopause, or who are experiencing social stress are at increased risk of developing depression during their menopausal years.

Although, in previous research, women with surgical and natural menopause had most often been collapsed into one group for study (because, if the key factor in menopause is lowered levels of estrogen, then the cause of menopause should be irrelevent), the longitudinal studies (Kaufert et al., 1992; J. McKinlay et al., 1987) found that surgical, but not natural, menopause was a risk factor for developing depression. This is an important finding; however, further research is needed to ascertain the degree to which women with preexisting depressions are also more likely to have been recommended surgery by their physicians, the degree to which surgery is a psychosocial stressor increasing vulnerability to depression, and whether the acute change in physiology associated with abrupt menopause may be associated with depression (by directly affecting mood or indirectly affecting mood by increasing troublesome physical symptoms, such as hot flashes). At this point it is unclear whether the effect of surgical menopause may be due to a rapidly changing endocrine environment, the trauma of surgery, the greater likelihood that depressed or otherwise vulnerable women will receive hysterectomies, or some combination of these factors.

Further research also is needed to determine the dynamics underlying the finding that women who have histories of depression (e.g., Matthews, 1992; Matthews et al., 1990) are more vulnerable to developing a recurrence in midlife. Are these women more vulnerable to the psychosocial stressors, more depressed because they are more likely to have been referred for surgical menopause, or more vulnerable to reacting to the physical effects of menopause (e.g., discomfort caused by vasomotor symptoms or change in hormone picture)?

Although the longitudinal studies established that depression is not a normal part of menopause, there is continued debate about whether subpopulations of women exist for whom this relationship holds (Schmidt & Rubinow, 1991). Some researchers have suggested that HRT can improve mood for certain depressed women. However, this research is inconclusive, in part because it is not clear whether the improvement in mood (if any) is secondary to improvement in physical symptoms, such as hot flashes, that have been the source of distress.

Midlife

It is only recently that a range of questions about the psychology of midlife, including menopause, are being asked that go beyond whether or not menopause is associated with depression or is in some other way problematic. In an adult-developmental perspective, important issues include understanding whether there are typical tasks and transitions during this period, whether there are positive experiences associated with this period, and whether menopause is a biological marker around which developmental issues emerge or are thought about. Anthropological studies have previously demonstrated qualitatively that menopausal experience varies cross-culturally. However, it is only recently that researchers have tried to identify what dimensions of midlife experience are important to understand among groups of Western women.

One question raised by an adult-developmental perspective is whether there is a redefinition of the self and its relationship to the social context during midlife. This suggests the need for studies of positive experiences, such as feelings of power, satisfaction with oneself, and changes in one's orientation to pleasing others versus oneself. Helson and Wink (1992) have provided data suggesting that the self-definition of midlife women may change in these directions. Recent qualitative studies (e.g., Cooksey, Imle, & Smith, 1991; Quinn, 1991) as well as health-related surveys (e.g., Mansfield, Theisen, & Boyer, 1992) have suggested parameters that are areas for further research. Both Quinn and Cooksey et al. (1991) have suggested that menopause is a passage or transition, rather than inherently a crisis. Although identifying somewhat different categories within which to understand this transition, both studies suggest a period of initial uncertainty about whether one is experiencing menopause, a process of sorting out issues and feelings, and an integrative stage. Quinn's stages include initial uncertainty about whether physical experiences are due to menopause or aging; a paradox of feelings, including conflicting feelings about aging, reproduction, physical vulnerability, and uncertainty versus looking forward to changes; arriving at a meaning of menopause (Is it natural? Will I still be attractive?); and making adjustments, such as changes in lifestyle to maximize health. Cooksey et al. found that, across diverse life circumstances, a similar underlying process occurred of sorting out, searching for meaning, and integrating menopause into a concept of oneself.

These qualitative studies suggest that menopause can be a marker for broader issues of the transition into midlife. For example, vulnerability to disease emerges as an issue. More broadly, a developmental task is developing a positive self-concept as a midlife woman. The role of women has changed in the last 30 years, in ways that would lead us to expect cohort effects for psychological issues during midlife. Increased life span and the recent distinction made between the "young old" and the "old old," suggest that the importance of midlife to one's sense of self as being old may differ from its importance 30 years ago. The social circumstances of midlife women are in general more variable: Some women are looking forward to retirement, whereas others are beginning school and changing jobs, and some women are becoming grandmothers, whereas others still have pre-teenaged children living at home. These social changes, with the consequent lack of a consensual social definition of midlife, all suggest the need for women to arrive at a positive self-concept of what it means to be a midlife woman.

An additional developmental task and an important health issue is how to cope with menopause itself. Recent research (e.g., Gannon & Ekstrom, 1993; Matthews, 1992) has suggested that a woman's expectations influence her experience of menopause. In addition, a woman in the initial stages of menopause may be confused about whether menstrual changes are normal or are symptoms of disease. For example, Cooksey et al. (1991) reported that women did not always realize at first that the physical symptom they were experiencing was a hot flash, as opposed to, say, anxiety. Other authors have suggested that normal changes might be misinterpreted both by a woman and her physician as symptoms of disease, as when normal changes in menstrual flow are interpreted as possible signs of cancer. Women need to be educated about what to expect during menopause (Mansfield et al., 1992). Whether uncertainty associated with menopausal changes may contribute to distress is a question worthy of study: Matthews's (1992) finding that depression increased during perimenopause is consistent with this idea. In addition, health research should continue to document normal menopausal changes, with their individual variations.

Menopause is associated with an increased risk of uncomfortable physical symptoms, such as hot flashes. Although HRT is an effective treatment for these physiological symptoms, it carries possible health risks. Additional research is needed on whether behavioral treatments are as effective in controlling these symptoms. Furthermore, whether hot flashes are directly affected by such techniques as relaxation or whether their aversiveness is affected indirectly by change in attitudinal variables should also be investigated.

Other Health Issues

During the midlife years, there is an increase in the incidence of such chronic diseases as cardiovascular disease and osteoporosis in women. A recent area of great research interest has been to investigate if the physiological changes accompanying menopause may increase vulnerability to these conditions. Much of this research has focused on identifying how estrogen physiologically affects such risk factors as cholesterol levels or how HRT may be related to disease outcomes.

Cardiovascular disease—long considered a disease primarily affecting men—is the leading cause of death among older women (Eaker, Packard, Werger, Clarkson, & Tyroler, 1986). Understanding risk factors and the psychosocial context of heart disease in women is a complex and understudied area (National Heart, Lung, and Blood Institute, 1992). The risk of cardiovascular disease among young women is lower than that among young men, but the disease risk increases and the differential risk between women and men decreases beginning in midlife. Researchers have begun to explore whether the presence of estrogens, which differentiate the sexes during the time that women are protected against heart disease, might be related to the observed differences in rates of disease. The best evidence that estrogen is protective has come from a number of observational and correlational studies (reviewed by Stampfer & Colditz, 1991), in which menopausal women for whom ERT was prescribed were compared with nonhormone users. These studies typically have demonstrated that estrogen users have a substantially lower risk of heart disease than do nonusers—and most commonly cited as one half the risk. Also suggested, but less well studied, is that women using an estrogen–progestin combination (to protect against estrogen causing an increased risk of uterine cancer) may be similarly protected if levels of progestin are kept low.

One important mechanism thought to underlie the protection afforded by estrogen is its effect on lipoprotein levels. Estrogen users typically have higher levels of high-density lipoproteins ("good" cholesterol) and lower levels of low-density lipoprotein ("bad" cholesterol). Other possible effects of estrogen on the cardiovascular system (e.g., on clotting factors) are also being examined. Research on whether endogenous levels of estrogens are related to cardiovascular risk factors is far less developed than that on exogenous hormones, although Matthews, Kuller, Wing, and Meilahn (1994) have presented evidence that lipid levels vary with endogenous estrogen levels following menopause. However, notwithstanding the relationship between estrogen and physiological measures, it appears that the relationship of estrogen to cardiovascular risk is not a simple linear one. Estrogen in the form of birth control pills may increase risk; men with cardiovascular disease have shown higher levels of estrogen; and exogenously given estrogen has been shown to increase cardiovascular risk in men (Matthews, 1989). Matthews suggested that reproductive hormones do not produce simple main effects but, instead, interact with behavioral characteristics. For example, she presented evidence that cardiovascular reactivity to stressors may be greater among menopausal women and that menopausal status may interact with such behavioral characteristics as adherence to a traditional feminine gender role in determining cardiovascular response.

The studies of ERT and HRT users are compelling because of the consistency and magnitude of their results. However, because they have typically studied women who chose these treatments, self-selection into user versus nonuser groups and preexisting differences between groups that account for both hormone use and heart disease incidence cannot be ruled out as alternative explanations for at least part of the obtained differences between groups. Researchers (e.g., see Barrett-Connor & Bush, 1991; Matthews, Kuller, Wing, Meilahn, & Bromberger, 1993) have reported hormone replacement users to be better educated and healthier than nonusers as well as more aggressive about obtaining medical care; Barrett-Connor and Bush pointed out that it is difficult to control statistically for these factors. Matthews et al. found that users were more physically active and had higher levels of high-density lipoproteins prior to hormone use. As we describe below, randomized double-blind studies of the relationship of hormone use to cardiovascular risk designed to eliminate the problem of self-selection are currently under way.

Osteoporosis is a second chronic disease whose incidence is thought to be related to menopausal status. Osteoporosis refers to a condition in which decreased bone mass leads to a vulnerability to fracture. Bone is always being formed and existing bone absorbed; as both men and women age, the rate of absorption exceeds that of formation, and bone mass therefore decreases (Gannon, 1990). When there is a high rate of bone loss, and fracture has occurred, a person is considered to be suffering from osteoporosis. Osteoporosis is an important health problem for older women both because of the debilitating effects of fracture and because among the very old complications of fracture can result in death.

Loss of bone mass increases following menopause, as evidenced by research comparing bone density in postmenopausal women and age-matched premenopausal controls and by research comparing women with hysterectomy alone to those having hysterectomy and bilateral oophorectomy (Gannon, 1990). Research has suggested that HRTs protect against loss of bone density following menopause, primarily by slowing the rate of resorption rather than by stimulating bone growth (Gannon, 1988; Matthews et al., 1993). However, there are individual differences in how effective HRTs or other interventions are. In addition, research results have varied depending on such factors as what bone is being measured and the health and age of subjects. In one study (Prince et al., 1991), for example, subjects selected on the basis of having low forearm bone density did, overall, show an increase in bone density following hormone treatment: Density increased 2.7% on the average at a distal forearm site. However, the standard deviation was 3.2%, suggesting that, although treatment was effective for some subjects, important individual differences also existed. Felson et al. (1993) have reported that HRT is less protective for women over 75 years of age than for younger women.

Research results on the protective effect of ERT and HRT have led to enthusiastic recommendations that these preparations be prescribed to women routinely to prevent heart disease and osteoporosis. Proponents have argued that because cardiovascular disease and osteoporosis are serious health risks, the protective effects of ERT and HRT should be welcomed. Felson et al. (1993) recommended a minimum of 7 years of hormone use, as their research demonstrated that this period of time was required for significant differences in bone density to appear, and this protection was not maintained when hormone use was discontinued. However, these recommendations have not gone undisputed. Researchers who are less enthusiastic have pointed out that exogenous estrogens are drugs, not a replacement therapy because they do not re-create the same endocrine environment as existed before menopause, as a different estrogen is used (Barrett-Connor & Bush, 1991). Furthermore, breast cancer risk may be elevated in HRT users, and other risks as yet unknown may exist. Some researchers have suggested that a treatment for osteoporosis that requires 7 years or more of drug treatment is less than ideal. Some dispute the idea that all healthy women should use hormones to reduce the risk that they become ill. Instead, the risk–benefit ratio may favor treatment for those showing high risk factors for disease, such as family history or physiological indicators such as low bone density. Even if menopause is causally related to changes in risk factors, it may nonetheless be true that nonpharmacological interventions may be effective in controlling these factors. Along this line, exercise and diet continue to be important areas of research in cardiovascular disease and osteoporosis. For example, Matthews et al. (1994) found that exercise was effective in maintaining levels of high-density lipoproteins among their population of healthy menopausal women.

Clearly, additional research is needed into what subgroups are at risk for heart disease or osteoporosis or who might appropriately benefit from hormone treatments, as is continued research on the efficacy of other treatments, such as exercise or diet regimens, stress management, and cognitive interventions. Additional research on risk factors, especially behavioral risk factors, is also needed.

Two large studies are underway that address some of these issues. The Women's Health Initiative is a massive study, initiated at the National Institutes of Health shortly after Bernardine Healy was named director, that examines cardiovascular disease and osteoporosis. A randomized, controlled trial will be conducted to evaluate the benefits and risks of HRT, adopting a low fat diet, and calcium and vitamin-D supplementation. This study will include over 50,000 women, who will be followed for 9 years. A second component is an observational study that will explore risk factors and biological markers for disease in women. A third component will examine how to enhance women's adoption of healthful behaviors. The second large study is the Postmenopausal Estrogen and Progestin Interventions trial. This study is a doubleblind, randomized clinical trial to study the effects of different hormone treatments on cardiovascular and osteoporotic risk factors (such as high-density lipoprotein levels), rather than actual incidence of disease. This study will take 3 years; data collection is almost completed.

Other Methodological Issues

In the past, researchers have varied in how they defined menopause and have sometimes combined peri- and postmenopausal women into one group. As stated above, a currently recommended standard for defining menopause is a lack of menstruation for 12 months (sometimes in combination with an FSH level elevated to above 30 IU), and the distinction between postmenopausal and perimenopausal (irregular menstruation) women is made. A standard definition is necessary to allow for comparable data across studies. However, these definitions are approximations. For example, there is great variability among women in perimenopause: Schmidt and Rubinow (1991) cite research stating that the duration of the climacteric based on menstrual cycle phase irregularity may vary between 1 and 10 years. The postmenopausal phase is ambiguous even physiologically: these authors also cite research that 3 of 12 women without periods and the elevated FSH levels typical of menopause nontheless had serum estrogen levels within the premenstrual range. For both psychological and physical effects, the number of years peri- or postmenopause is typically not measured but may be an important variable. Hot flashes, for example, appear to follow a time line following menopause, and correlates of them may vary depending on how many years postmenopausal women are. Psychological response to perimenopause may vary over time (e.g., if initial uncertainty leads to stress, but is resolved).

Asking whether a woman defines herself as menopausal is also a recent addition to the methodology. To the degree that the effects of menopause are psychosocial, it is important to know whether the woman defines herself as menopausal and, if so, what criteria she uses and what this means to her. The variability in definitions of menopause has been highlighted most in cross-cultural studies (e.g., Kaufert et al., 1985), where cessation of menses may not be the only factor defining one as menopausal and attitudes toward menopause may vary in culturally predictable ways. Although postmenopause is defined by researchers as 12 months without one's period, this may not correspond to every subject's definition. This raises an interesting question: At what point does a woman realize that the symptoms she is experiencing are those of perimenopause, or that her period is really not going to return and she is postmenopausal? When psychosocial effects are studied, anticipation of change, as well as change that has occurred, becomes important. This suggests the need to know what a woman expects will occur during menopause.

Although at one time researchers combined women with surgically induced menopause and natural menopause into one group, the two conditions are now known to vary in such psychological factors as history of and risk for depression that require that they be considered separately.

Whether or not women who have had different surgeries (e.g., hysterectomy with or without removal of the ovaries) can be combined into a single group is an unresolved question and may vary with the research question. J. McKinlay et al. (1987), for example, reported that women who had hysterectomies (with and without removal of the ovaries) and women who had bilateral oophorectomies (with the uterus left intact) were similar to each other in such facts as risk of depression, while all differed from women with natural menopause. However, given the lack of current knowledge concerning correlations between the different surgeries, keeping the groups separate would seem the most informative option.

In the past, studies did not always control for age when examining such variables as sexual interest or mood, which may be age related. In fact, age and menopausal status were often confounded, with one sometimes being used as an operational definition of the other. In recent research there has usually been at least a recognition that the two should be separated. Matthews et al. (1990), for example, used age-matched controls who were premenopausal for the menopausal women studied.

Depression, although frequently studied, has been assessed with a variety of measures that are not comparable. Often, measures have involved self-ratings of depressive feelings on a general checklist of menopausal symptoms rather than measures specific to depression. In more recent studies, well-validated measures of severity of depressive symptoms, such as the Center for Epidemiological Studies Depression Scale (Radloff, 1977) and the Beck Depression Inventory (Beck, 1967), have been used.

Finally, questionable statistical inferences remain a methodological issue, even in studies controlling for other problems. Ditkoff, Crary, Cristo, and Lobo (1991), for example, concluded from their study that estrogen improved psychological function in asymptomatic postmenopausal women. Their double-blind study included well-validated measures, namely, the Beck Depression Inventory and the MMPI, as well as less well known scales. They concluded that estrogen was effective in altering mood because scores of the group receiving hormones decreased significantly on the Beck Depression Inventory. However, these authors did multiple analyses without controlling for the fact that some would be expected to be significant by chance. Furthermore, the overall pattern of results did not support that the results for the inventory were psychologically meaningful. The only other significant findings were an increase in income management on a scale measuring adaptation to life and a decrease in the Schizophrenia scale on the MMPI. There were no significant changes on MMPI scales indicating dysphoria or scales on the adaptation to life measure indicating negative emotion. Furthermore, even if the Beck Inventory results were statistically reliable, they were clinically insignificant: The scores decreased approximately two points, but the means were well within the normal range to begin with. One wonders which inventory items were endorsed to produce this change.

CONCLUSION

The psychosocial context is a relatively recent focus of study in research on menarche, PMS, and menopause. The accumulation of findings seems more advanced for menarche and menopause than for PMS, where one is often confronted with disjointed, equivocal, or contradictory findings that are difficult to integrate. There continues to be definitional, measurement, and methodological issues in each of these areas, but, again, the most problematical issues generate from the research on PMS. Prospective, epidemiological studies of menopause and longitudinal cohort studies of menarche have provided valuable information on the role of psychosocial factors and their interface with biological variables. There are no comparable studies of PMS, yet these are needed to provide a stronger basis for examining causal hypotheses relating to psychosocial variables and for sorting out the interplay of these variables with biological factors.

To best study menstrual-related health issues, a clearer articulation of both psychosocial and biomedical methods, as well as an integration of biomedical and psychosocial perspectives, is needed. Researchers have critiqued the traditional biomedical models of PMS and menopause for their "disease state" conceptualization and lack of attention to social variables. An important recent development has been an increasing emphasis on broadening the biomedical model itself, which would facilitate integrating approaches. In the traditional medical model, the concept of what constitutes biological research has been overly narrow. Although a tenet of biology is that physiological systems exist in complex feedback loops, the traditional medical model has discouraged researchers from attending to physiological mechanisms other than hormonal changes that might be involved in these complex loops and that contribute to the production of premenstrual- and menopause-related symptoms. Another tenet of biology concerns the complex interplay between the behavior of an organism and its physiology. Again, the possible relationship of such lifestyle factors as diet, physical activity, and stress to physiological or psychological symptoms of PMS and menopause is outside the traditional medical model and only recently has been an object of research. Evolutionary theory is also at the heart of biology. However, notwithstanding the use of animal models, the comparative approach is not honored. For example, if female humans are compared with female animals rather than with male humans, what is most striking is not that female humans reproduce but the independence of human sexual responsiveness from hormonal cycles and its integration instead with social variables.

The integration of biomedical and psychosocial perspectives is underway in research on menarche, PMS, and menopause. It will bring not only new research on etiology but also research addressing treatments that minimize health risks and take into account the interplay of biological and psychosocial factors in women's health.

REFERENCES

Abraham, G. E. (1980). Premenstrual tension. *Current Problems in Obstetrics and Gynecology, 12,* 4–39.

American Psychiatric Association. (1987). *Diagnostic and statistical manual of mental disorders* (3rd ed., rev.). Washington, DC: Author.

Ashby, C. R., Carr, L. A., Cook, C. L., Steptoe, M. M., & Franks, D. D. (1988). Alteration of platelet serotonergic mechanisms and monoamine oxidase activity in premenstrual syndrome. *Biological Psychiatry, 24,* 225–233.

Asso, D. (1983). *The real menstrual cycle.* New York: Wiley.

AuBuchon, P. G., & Calhoun, K. S. (1985). Menstrual cycle symptomatology: The role of social expectancy and experimental demand characteristics. *Psychosomatic Medicine, 47,* 35–45.

Bains, G. K., & Slade, P. (1988). Attributional patterns, moods, and the menstrual cycle. *Psychosomatic Medicine, 20,* 469–476.

Ballinger, C. (1975). Psychiatric morbidity and the menopause. *British Medical Journal, 3,* 344–346.

Ballinger, C., Browning, M., & Smith, A. (1987). Hormone profiles and psychological symptoms in peri-menopausal women. *Maturitas, 9,* 235–251.

Bancroft, J. (1994). The premenstrual syndrome: A reappraisal of the concept and the evidence. *Psychological Medicine* (monograph supplement 24, pp. 1–47).

Bancroft, J., & Backstrom, T. (1985). Premenstrual syndrome. *Clinical Endocrinology, 22,* 313–336.

Bancroft, J., Williamson, L., Warner, P., Rennie, D., & Smith, S. K. (1993). Perimenstrual complaints in women complaining of PMS, menorrhagia, and dysmenorrhea: Toward a dismantling of the premenstrual syndrome. *Psychosomatic Medicine, 55,* 133–145.

Barrett-Connor, E., & Bush, T. (1991). Estrogen and coronary heart disease in women. *Journal of the American Medical Association, 265,* 1861–1866.

Beck, A. (1967). *Depression: Clinical, experimental and theoretical aspects* . New York: Hoeber.

Beck, L. E., Gevirtz, R., & Mortola, J. F. (1990). The predictive role of psychosocial stress on symptom severity in premenstrual syndrome. *Psychosomatic Medicine, 52,* 536–543.

Belsky, J., Steinberg, L., & Draper, P. (1991). Childhood experience, interpersonal development, and reproductive strategy: An evolutionary theory of socialization. *Child Development, 62,* 647–670.

Beyenne, Y. (1986). Cultural significance and physiological manifestations of menopause. *Cultural Medicine and Psychiatry, 10,* 47–71.

Brooks-Gunn, J. (1988). Antecedents and consequences of variations in girls' menstrual timing. *Journal of Adolescent Health Care, 9,* 365–373.

Brooks-Gunn, J. (1991a). Maturational timing variations in adolescent girls, consequences of. In R. Lerner, A. Peterson, & J. Brooks-Gunn (Eds.), *Encyclopedia of Adolescence* (pp. 614–618). New York: Garland.

Brooks-Gunn, J. (1991b). Menstrual timing variations in adolescent girls, antecedent of. In R. Lerner, A. Peterson, & J. Brooks-Gunn (Eds.), *Encyclopedia of Adolescence* (pp. 609–613). New York: Garland.

Brooks-Gunn, J., Petersen, A. C., & Eichorn, D. (1985). The study of maturational timing effects in adolescence. *Journal of Youth and Adolescence, 14,* 149–161.

Brooks-Gunn, J., & Reiter, E. O. (1990). The role of pubertal processes in the early adolescent transition. In S. Feldman & G. Elliott (Eds.), *At the threshold: The developing adolescent* (pp. 16–53). Cambridge, MA: Harvard University Press.

Brooks-Gunn, J., & Ruble, D. N. (1980). The menstrual attitude questionnaire. *Psychosomatic Medicine, 42,* 503–511.

Brooks-Gunn, J., & Ruble, D. N. (1982). The development of menstrual-related beliefs and behaviors during early adolescence. *Child Development, 53,* 1567–1577.

Brooks-Gunn, J., & Warren, M. P. (1985). Effects of delayed menarche in different contexts: Dance and nondance students. *Journal of Youth and Adolescence, 14,* 285–300.

Brooks-Gunn, J., Warren, M. P., & Hamilton, L. H. (1987). The relationship of eating disorders to amenorrhea in ballet dancers. *Medical Science in Sports and Exercise, 19,* 41–44.

Brown, M. A., & Zimmer, P. A. (1986). Personal and family impact of premenstrual symptoms. *Journal of Obstetrical and Gynecological Nursing* (Jan/Feb), 31–38.

Brown, M. A., & Zimmer, P. A. (1987, June). *Marital quality and partner support in women with varying levels of premenstrual symptomatology.* Paper presented at the 7th conference of the Society for Menstrual Cycle Research, Ann Arbor, MI.

Casper, R., Yen, S., & Wilkes, M. (1979). Menopausal flushes: A neuroendocrine link with pulsatile luteinizing hormone secretion. *Science, 205,* 823–825.

Caspi, A., & Moffitt, T. E. (1991). Individual differences are accentuated during periods of social change: The sample case of girls at puberty. *Journal of Personality and Social Psychology, 61,* 157–168.

Christensen, A. P., Board, B. J., & Oei, T. P. S. (1992). A psychosocial profile of women with premenstrual dysphoria. *Journal of Affective Disorders, 25,* 251–260.

Chuong, C. J., Colligan, R. C., Coulom, C. B., & Bergstralh, E. J. (1991). The MMPI as an aid in evaluating patients with premenstrual syndrome. In D. L. Taylor & N. F. Woods (Eds.), *Menstruation, health, and illness* (pp. 119–128). Washington, DC: Hemisphere.

Cohen, M. G. (1986). The relationship between premenstrual distress and marital satisfaction. Doctoral Dissertation, Yeshiva University, New York. (University Microfilms No. DA 874003).

Collins, J., & Propert, D. (1983). A developmental study of body recognition in adolescent girls. *Adolescence, 18,* 767–774.

Cooksey, S., Imle, M., & Smith, C. (1991). An inductive study of the transition to menopause. In A. Voda & R. Conover (Eds.), *Proceedings, 8th Conference, Society for Menstrual Cycle Research* (pp. 75–111). Scottsdale, AZ: Society for Menstrual Cycle Research.

Corney, R. H., & Stanton, R. (1991). A survey of 658 women who report symptoms of premenstrual syndrome. *Journal of Psychosomatic Research, 35,* 471–482.

Costello, A., Edelbrock, C., Kalas, R., Kessler, M., & Klaric, S. (1982). *Diagnostic Interview Schedule for Children-Child Version.* Bethesda, MD: National Institute of Mental Health.

Coughlin, P. C. (1990). Premenstrual syndrome: How marital satisfaction and role choice affect symptom severity. *Social Work, 35,* 351–355.

Dalton, K. (1984). *The premenstrual syndrome and progesterone therapy.* Chicago: Yearbook Medical.

Danza, R. (1983). Menarche: Its effects on mother–daughter and father–daughter interactions. In S. Dolub (Ed.), *Menarche* (pp. 99–106). Lexington, MA: Heath.

DeJong, R., Rubinow, D. R., Roy-Byrne, P., Hoban, M. C., Grover, G. N., & Post, R. M. (1985). Premenstrual mood disorder and psychiatric illness. *American Journal of Psychiatry, 142,* 1359–1361.

Delaney, J., Lupton, M. J., & Toth, E. (1976). *The curse: A cultural history of menstruation.* New York: E. P. Dutton.

Dennerstein, L., Morse, C. A., & Varnanides, K. (1988). Premenstrual tension and depression—Is there a relationship? *Journal of Psychosomatic Obstetrics and Gynecology, 18,* 45–52.

Ditkoff, E., Crary, W., Cristo, M., & Lobo, R. (1991). Estrogen improves psychological function in asymptomatic postmenopausal women. *Obstetrics and Gynecology, 78,* 991–995.

Eaker, E., Packard, B., Werger, N., Clarkson, T., & Tyroler, N. (1986). Coronary heart disease in women. National Heart, Lung, and Blood Institute, Bethesda MD; Workshop on Coronary Heart Disease in Women, Administrative report.

Endicott, J., & Halbreich, U. (1988). Clinical significance of premenstrual dysphoric changes. *Journal of Clinical Psychiatry, 49,* 486–489.

Englander-Golden, P., Sonleiter, F. S., Whitmore, M. R., & Corbley, G. J. M. (1986). Social and menstrual cycles. In V. L. Olesen & N. F. Woods (Eds.), *Culture, society, and menstruation* (pp. 97–114). Washington, DC: Hemisphere.

Englander-Golden, P., Whitmore, M. R., & Dienstbier, R. A. (1978). Menstrual cycle as a focus of study and self-reports of moods and behavior. *Motivation and Emotion, 2,* 75–87.

Eveleth, P. B., & Tanner, J. M. (1990). *Worldwide variation in human growth* (2nd ed.). Cambridge, England: Cambridge University Press.

Facchinetti, F., Romano, G., Fava, M., & Genazzani, A. R. (1992). Lactate infusion induces panic attacks in patients with premenstrual syndrome. *Psychosomatic Medicine, 54,* 288–296.

Felson, D., Zhang, Y., Hannan, M., Kiel, D., Wilson, P., & Anderson, J. (1993). The effect of postmenopausal estrogen therapy on bone density in elderly women. *New England Journal of Medicine, 329,* 1141–1146.

Fradkin, B., & Firestone, P. (1986). Premenstrual tension, expectancy, and mother–child relations. *Journal of Behavioral Medicine, 2,* 245–259.

Freeman, E. W., Sondheimer, S. J., & Rickels, K. (1987). Effects of medical history factors on symptom severity in women meeting criteria for premenstrual syndrome. *Obstetrics and Gynecology, 72,* 236–239.

Friedman, R. C. (1982). *Behavior and the menstrual cycle.* New York: Marcel Dekker.

Frisch, R. E. (1983). Fatness, menarche and fertility. In S. Golub (Ed.), *Menarche* (pp. 5–20). Lexington, MA: Heath.

Frisch, R. E., Welbergen, A., McArthur, J. W., Albright, T., Witschi, J., Beillen, B., Birnholz, J., Reed, R., & Herman, H. (1981). Delayed menarche, irregular cycles and amenorrhea of college athletes in relation to age of onset of training. *Journal of the American Medical Association, 246,* 1559–1563.

Frisch, R. E., Wyshak, G., & Vincent, L. (1980). Delayed menarche and amenorrhea of ballet dancers. *New England Journal of Medicine, 302,* 17–19.

Futterman, L. A., Jones, J. E., Miccio-Fonseca, L. C., & Quigley, M. E. (1992). Severity of premenstrual symptoms in relation to medical/psychiatric problems and life experiences. *Perceptual and Motor Skills, 74,* 787–799.

Gallant, S. J., Hamilton, J. A., Popiel, D. A., Morokoff, P. J., & Chakraborty, P. K. (1991). Daily moods and symptoms: Effects of awareness of study focus, gender, menstrual-cycle phase, and day of the week. *Health Psychology, 10*(3), 180–189.

Gallant, S. J., Popiel, D. A., & Hoffman, D. M. (1994). The role of psychological variables in the experience of premenstrual symptoms. *Mind-body rhythmicity: A menstrual cycle perspective.* Proceedings of the Society for Menstrual Cycle Research, 9th conference, pp. 139–151.

Gallant, S., Popiel, D. A., Hoffman, D. M., Chakraborty, P. K., & Hamilton, J. A. (1992a). Using Daily Ratings to Confirm Premenstrual Syndrome/Late Luteal Phase Dysphoric Disorder Part I: Effects of Demand Characteristics and Expectations. *Psychosomatic Medicine, 54,* 149–166.

Gallant, S. J., Popiel, D. A., Hoffman, D. M., Chakraborty, P. K., & Hamilton, J. A. (1992b). Using daily ratings to confirm premenstrual syndrome/late luteal phase dysphoric disorder. Part II. What makes a "real" difference? *Psychosomatic Medicine, 54,* 167–181.

Gannon, L. (1988). The potential role of exercise in the alleviation of menstrual disorders and menopausal symptoms: A theoretical synthesis of recent research. *Women and Health, 14,* 105–127.

Gannon, L. (1990). The endocrinology of menopause. In R. Formanek (Ed.), *The meanings of menopause: Historical, medical, and clinical perspectives 179–237.* Hillsdale, NJ: Analytic Press.

Gannon, L., & Ekstrom, B. (1993). Attitudes toward menopause—The influence of sociocultural paradigms. *Psychology of Women Quarterly, 17,* 275–288.

Gath, P., & Iles, S. (1988). Treating the premenstrual syndrome. *British Medical Journal, 297,* 237–238.

Giannini, A. J., Price, W. A., Loiselle, R. H., & Giannini, M. D. (1985). Pseudo cholinesterase and trait anxiety in premenstrual tension syndrome. *Journal of Clinical Psychiatry, 46,* 139–140.

Golub, S. (1992). *Periods: From menarche to menopause.* Newbury Park, CA: Sage.

Halbreich, U., Alt, I. H., & Paul, L. (1988). Premenstrual changes: Impaired hormonal homeostatis. *Neurologic Clinics, 6,* 173–194.

Halbreich, U., & Kas, D. (1977). Variations in the Taylor MAS of women with premenstrual syndrome. *Journal of Psychosomatic Research, 21,* 391–393.

Hamilton, J. A., & Gallant, S. (1993). Premenstrual syndromes: A health psychology critique of biomedically oriented research. In R. J. Gatchel & E. B. Blanchard (Eds.), *Psychophysiological disorders: Research and clinical applications* (pp. 383–438). Washington, DC: American Psychological Association.

Hamilton, T. A. (1986). Marital adjustment and coping strategies among couples with premenstrual syndrome. (Doctoral dissertation, University of San Francisco) University Microfilms order # 8802J89.

Hammond, D. C., & Keye, W. R. (1985). Premenstrual syndrome. *New England Journal of Medicine, 312,* 920.

Harrison, M. (1982). *Self-help for premenstrual syndrome.* New York: Random House.

Harrison, W. M., Sandberg, D., Gorman, J. M., Fyer, M., Nee, J., Uy, J., & Endicott, J. (1989). Provocation of panic with carbon dioxide inhalation in patients with premenstrual dysphoria. *Psychiatry Research, 46,* 183–192.

Heilbrun, A. B., & Frank, M. E. (1989). Self-preoccupation and general stress level as sensitizing factors in premenstrual and menstrual distress. *Journal of Psychosomatic Research, 33,* 571–577.

Helm, P., & Lidegaard, O. (1989). The relationship between menarche and sexual, contraceptive, and reproductive life events. *Scandinavian Journal of Primary Health Care, 8,* 59–63.

Helson, R., & Wink, P. (1992). Personality change in women from the early 40s to the early 50s. *Psychology and Aging, 7,* 46–55.

Hill, J. P. (1988). Adapting to menarche: Familial control and conflict. In M. R. Gunner & W. A. Collins (Eds.), *21st Minnesota symposium on child psychology* (pp. 43–77). Hillsdale, NJ: Erlbaum.

Hill, J. P., Holmbeck, G. N., Marlow, L., Green, T. M., & Lynch, M. E. (1985). Menarcheal status and parent–child relations in families of seventh-grade girls. *Journal of Youth and Adolescence, 14,* 301–316.

Holmbeck, G. N., & Hill, J. P. (1991). Conflictive engagement, positive affect, and menarche in families with seventh-grade girls. *Child Development, 62,* 1030–1048.

Hunter, M. (1990). Somatic experience of the menopause: A perspective study. *Psychosomatic Medicine, 52,* 357–367.

Hurt, S. W., Williams, N. A., Severino, S. K., & Anderson, M. (1986). Premenstrual syndrome and psychiatric disorder. *New Research Abstracts* (p. 36). Washington, DC: American Psychiatric Association.

Jackson, B. (1992). Black women's responses to menarche and menopause. In A. J. Dan & L. L. Lewis (Eds.), *Menstrual health in women's lives* (pp. 178–190). Chicago: University of Illinois Press.

Kaufert, P., Gilbert, P., & Tate, R. (1992). The Manitoba project: A re-examination of the link between menopause and depression. *Maturitas, 14,* 143–155.

Kaufert, P., Lock, M., McKinlay, S., Bevenre, Y., Coope, J., Davis, D., Eliasson, M., Goanalong-Nicolet, M., Goodman, M., & Holte, A. (1985). *Menopause research: The Korpilampi Workshop.* Unpublished manuscript.

Kestenberg, J. S. (1967). Phases of Adolescence, Parts 1 and 2. *Journal of the American Academy of Child Psychiatry, 6,* 426–463, 577–611.

Keye, W. R., Hammond, D. C., & Strong, T. (1986). Medical and psychologic characteristics of women presenting with premenstrual symptoms. *Obstetrics and Gynecology, 68,* 634–637.

Keye, W. R., & Trunnell, E. P. (1986). A biopsychosocial model of premenstrual syndrome. *International Journal of Fertility, 31,* 259–262.

Klebanov, P. K., & Jemmott, J. B. (1992). Effects of expectations and bodily sensations on self-reports of premenstrual symptoms. *Psychology of Women Quarterly, 16,* 289–310.

Klebanov, P. K., & Ruble, D. N. (1994). Toward an understanding of women's experience of menstrual symptoms. In V. J. Adesso, D. M. Reddy, & R. Fleming (Eds.), *Psychological perspectives on women's health* (pp. 183–221). Washington, DC: Taylor & Francis.

Koeske, R. K. D. (1980). Theoretical perspectives in menstrual cycle research: The relevance of attributional approaches for the perception and explanation of premenstrual emotionality. In A. J. Dan, E. A. Graham, & C. P. Beecher (Eds.), *The menstrual cycle, volume 1: A synthesis of interdisciplinary research* (pp. 8–25). New York: Springer.

Koeske, R. K., & Koeske, G. F. (1975). An attributional approach to moods and the menstrual cycle. *Journal of Personality and Social Psychology, 31,* 473–478.

Koff, E. (1983). Through the looking glass of menarche: What the adolescent girl sees. In S. Golub (Ed.), *Menarche* (pp. 77–86). Lexington, MA: Heath.

Koff, E., & Rierdan, J. (1991). Menarche and body image. In R. Lerner, A. Peterson, & J. Brooks-Gunn (Eds.), *Encyclopedia of adolescence* (pp. 631–636). New York: Garland.

Koff, E., Rierdan, J., & Jacobson, S. (1981). The personal and interpersonal significances of menarche. *Journal of the American Academy of Child Psychiatry, 20,* 148–158.

Koff, E., Rierdan, J., & Silverstone, E. (1978). Changes in representation of body image as a function of menarcheal states. *Developmental Psychology, 14,* 635–642.

Kuczmierczyk, A. R., Labrum, A. H., & Johnson, C. C. (1992). Perception of family and work environments in women with premenstrual syndrome. *Journal of Psychosomatic Research, 36,* 787–795.

Maddocks, S. E., & Reid, R. L. (1992). The role of negative life stress and PMS: Some preliminary findings. In A. J. Dan & L. L. Lewis (Eds.), *Menstrual health in women's lives* (pp. 38–51). Chicago: University of Illinois Press.

Magnusson, D., Strattin, H., & Allen, V. L. (1985). Biological maturation and social development: A longitudinal study of some adjustment processes from mid-adolescence to adulthood. *Journal of Youth and Adolescence, 14,* 267–283.

Mansfield, P., Theisen, S., & Boyer, B. (1992). Midlife women and menopause: A challenge for the mental health counselor [Special issue]. *Journal of Mental Health Counseling, 14,* 73–83.

Martin, E. (1987). *The women in the body: A cultural analysis of reproduction.* Boston: Beacon Press.

Matthews, K. (1989). Interactive effects of behavior and reproductive hormones on sex differences in risk for coronary heart disease. *Health Psychology, 8,* 373–387.

Matthews, K. (1992). Myths and realities of the menopause. *Psychosomatic Medicine, 54,* 1–9.

Matthews, K., Kuller, L., Wing, R., & Meilahn, E. (1994). Biobehavioral aspects of menopause: Lessons from the healthy women study. *Experimental Gerontology, 29,* 337–342.

Matthews, K., Kuller, L., Wing, R., Meilahn, E., & Bromberger, J. (1993). Menopausal experience of users of hormone replacement therapy. In G. Berg & M. Hammar (Eds.), *The modern management of the menopause* (pp. 447–451). New York: Parthenon.

Matthews, K., Wing, R., Kuller, L., Meilahn, E., Kelsey, S., Costello, E., & Caggiula, A. (1990). Influences of natural menopause on psychological characteristics and symptoms of middle-aged healthy women. *Journal of Consulting and Clinical Psychology, 58,* 345–351.

McCrae, F. (1983). The politics of menopause: The "discovery" of a deficiency disease. *Social Problems, 31,* 111–123.

McFarlane, J., & Williams, T. M. (1994). Placing premenstrual syndrome in perspective. *Psychology of Women Quarterly, 18,* 339–373.

McGrory, A. (1990). Menarche: Responses of early adolescent females. *Adolescence, 25,* 266–270.

McKinlay, J., McKinlay, S., & Brambilla, D. (1987). The relative contributions of endocrine changes and social circumstances to depression in mid-aged women. *Journal of Health and Social Behavior, 28,* 345–356.

McKinlay, S., & Jeffreys, M. (1974). The menopause syndrome. *Journal of Preventative and Social Medicine, 28,* 108–115.

McKinlay, S., & McKinlay, J. (1973). Selected studies of the menopause: A methodological critique. *Journal of Biosocial Science, 5,* 533–555.

Metcalf, M. G., Braiden, V., Livesey, J. H., & Wells, J. E. (1992). The premenstrual syndrome: Amelioration of symptoms after hysterectomy. *Journal of Psychosomatic Research, 36,* 569–584.

Metcalf, M. G., Livesey, J. H., Wells, J. E., Braiden, V., Hudson, S. M., & Bamber, L. (1991). Premenstrual syndrome in hysterectomized women: Mood and physical symptom cyclicity. *Journal of Psychosomatic Research, 35,* 555–567.

Miller, L. C., Murphy, R., & Buss, A. H. (1981). Consciousness of body: Private and public. *Journal of Personality and Social Psychology, 41,* 397–406.

Mills, S. V. (1991). The effects of stress upon PMS severity in couple relationships. In A. M. Voda & R. Conover (Eds.), *Proceedings of the 8th Conference of the Society of Menstrual Cycle Research* (pp. 627–642). Salt Lake City, UT: Society for Menstrual Cycle Research.

Mira, M., Vizzard, J., & Abraham, S. (1985). Personality characteristics in the menstrual cycle. *Journal of Psychosomatic Obstetrics and Gynaecology, 4,* 329–334.

Moffitt, T. E., Caspi, A., Belsky, J., & Silva, P. A. (1992). Childhood experience and the onset of menarche: A test of a sociobiological model. *Child Development, 63,* 47–58.

Mohan, V., & Chopra, R. (1987). Personality variations as an effect of premenstrual tensions. *Personality and Individual Differences, 8,* 763–765.

Monroe, S. M., Bromet, E. J., Cornell, M. M., & Steiner, S. C. (1986). Social support, life events, and depressive symptoms: A one-year prospective study. *Journal of Consulting and Clinial Psychology, 54,* 424–431.

Mortola, J. F. (1992). Issues in the diagnosis and research of premenstrual syndrome. *Clinical Obstetrics and Gynecology, 35,* 587–598.

National Heart, Lung, and Blood Institute. (1992, January). Cardiovascular health and disease in women: Health promotion and disease prevention, optimal disease recognition and management. Bethesda, MD.

Norris, R. V., & Sullivan, C. (1983). *Premenstrual syndrome.* New York: Rawson Associates.

O'Boyle, M., Severino, S. K., & Hurt, S. H. (1988). Premenstrual syndrome and locus of control. *International Journal of Psychiatry in Medicine, 18,* 67–74.

Olasov, B., & Jackson, J. (1987). Effects of expectancies on women's reports of mood during the menstrual cycle. *Psychosomatic Medicine, 49,* 65–78.

Ornitz, A. W., & Brown, M. A. (1993). Family coping and premenstrual symptomatology. *Journal of Obstetric, Gynecologic, and Neonatal Nursing, 22,* 49–55.

Osborn, M. F., & Gath, D. H. (1990). Psychological and physical determinants of premenstrual symptoms before and after hysterectomy. *Psychological Medicine, 20,* 565–572.

Paikoff, R. L., & Brooks-Gunn, J. (1991). Do parent–child relationships change during puberty? *Psychological Bulletin, 110,* 47–66.

Paikoff, R. L., Brooks-Gunn, J., & Carlton-Ford, S. (1991). Effect of reproductive status changes on family functioning and well-being of mothers and daughters. *Journal of Early Adolescence, 11,* 201–220.

Parlee, M. B. (1983). Menstrual rhythms in sensory processes: A review of fluctuations in vision, olfaction, audition, taste, and touch. *Psychological Bulletin, 93,* 539–548.

Parlee, M. B. (1988). Menstrual cycle changes in moods and emotions: Causal and interpretive processes in the construction of emotions. In H. L. Wagner (Ed.), *Social psychophysiology and emotion: Theory and clinical applications* (pp. 151–174). New York: Wiley.

Parlee, M. B. (in press). Psychology of menstruation and premenstrual syndrome. In M. Paludi & F. Denmark (Eds.), *Handbook of Psychology of Women.* Westport, CT: Greenwood.

Parry, B. L. (1994). Biological correlates of premenstrual complaints. In J. H. Gold & S. K. Severino (Eds.), *Premenstrual dysphorias: Myths and realities* (pp. 47–66). Washington, DC: American Psychiatric Press.

Pearlstein, T. B., Frank, E., Rivera-Tovar, A., Thoft, J. S., Jacobs, E., & Mieczkowski, T. A. (1990). Prevalence of axis I and axis II disorders in women with late luteal phase dysphoric disorder. *Journal of Affective Disorders, 20,* 129–134.

Persons, J. B. (1986). The advantage of studying psychological phenomena rather than psychiatric diagnoses. *American Psychologist, 41,* 1252–1260.

Peterson, A. C., & Crockett, L. (1985). Pubertal timing and grade effects on adjustment. *Journal of Youth and Adolescence, 14,* 191–206.

Peterson, C., Semmel, A., Von Baeyer, C., Abramson, L. Y., Metalsky, G., & Seligman, M. E. P. (1982). The attributional style questionnaire. *Cognitive Therapy and Research, 6,* 287–300.

Peterson, R. A., & Reiss, S. (1987). *Anxiety sensitivity index manual.* Worthington, OH: International Diagnostic Systems.

Prince, R., Smith, M., Dick, I., Price, R., Webb, P., Henderson, N., & Harris, M. (1991). Prevention of postmenopausal osteoporosis. *New England Journal of Medicine, 325,* 1189–1195.

Quinn, A. (1991). The woman's view of menopause. In A. Voda & R. Conover (Eds.), *Proceedings, 8th conference, Society for Menstrual Cycle Research* (pp. 256–263). Scottsdale, AZ: Society for Menstrual Cycle Research.

Radloff, L. (1977). The CES–D Scale: A self-report depression scale for research in the general population. *Applied Psychological Measurement, 1,* 385–401.

Rapkin, A. J., Edelmuth, E., Chang, L. C., et al (1987). Whole-blood serotonin in premenstrual syndrome. *Obstetrics and Gynecology, 70,* 533–537.

Reid, R. L., & Yen, S. S. C. (1981). Premenstrual syndrome. *American Journal of Obstetrics and Gynecology, 139,* 85–104.

Rierdan, J. (1983). Variations in the experience of menarche and function of preparedness. In S. Golub (Ed.), *Menarche* (pp. 119–126). Lexington, MA: Heath.

Rierdan, J., & Koff, E. (1990). Premenarcheal predictors of the experience of menarche: A perspective study. *Journal of Adolescent Health Care, 11,* 404–407.

Rierdan, J., & Koff, E. (1991). Depressive symptomatology among very early maturing girls. *Journal of Youth and Early Adolescence, 20,* 415–425.

Rierdan, J., Koff, E., & Stubbs, M. L. (1989). Timing menarche, preparation, and initial menstrual experience: Replication and further analyses in a prospective study. *Journal of Youth and Adolescence, 18,* 413–426.

Rivera-Tovar, A., Rhodes, R., Pearlstein, T. B., & Frank, E. (1994). In J. H. Gold & S. K. Severino (Eds.), *Premenstrual dysphorias: Myths and realities* (pp. 99–148). Washington, DC: American Psychiatric Press.

Rubinow, D. R., Hoban, M. C., Grover, G. N., Galloway, D. S., Roy-Byrne, P., Andersen, R., & Merriam, G. R. (1988). Changes in plasma hormones across the menstrual cycle in patients with menstrually related mood disorder and in control subjects. *American Journal of Obstetrical Gynecology, 158,* 5–11.

Ruble, D. N. (1977). Premenstrual symptoms: A reinterpretation. *Science, 197,* 291–292.

Ruble, D. N., & Brooks-Gunn, J. (1979). Menstrual symptoms: A social cognition analysis. *Journal of Behavioral Medicine, 2,* 171–194.

Ruble, D. N., & Brooks-Gunn, J. (1982). The experience of menarche. *Child Development, 53,* 1557–1566.

Ruble, D. N., & Brooks-Gunn, J. (1987). Perceptions of menstrual and premenstrual symptoms: Self-definitional processes at menarche. In B. E. Ginsburg & B. F. Carter (Eds.), *Premenstrual syndrome: Ethnical and legal implications in a biomedical perspective* (pp. 237–251). New York: Plenum Press.

Schachter, D., Bachman, G. A., Vaitukaitis, J., Phillips, D., & Saperstein, D. (1989). Perimenstrual symptoms: Time course of symptom intensity in relation to endocrinologically defined segments of the menstrual cycle. *Psychosomatic Medicine, 51,* 173–194.

Schmidt, P. J., Grover, G. N., Hoban, M. C., & Rubinow, D. R. (1990). State-dependent alterations in the perceptions of life events in menstrual-related mood disorders. *American Journal of Psychiatry, 147,* 230–234.

Schmidt, P. J., Nieman, L. K., Grover, G. N., Muller, K. L., Merriam, G. R., & Rubinow, D. R. (1991). Lack of effect of induced menses on symptoms in women with premenstrual syndrome. *New England Journal of Medicine, 324,* 1174–1179.

Schmidt, P., & Rubinow, D. (1991). Menopause-related affective disorder: A justification for further study. *American Journal of Psychiatry, 148,* 844–852.

Schnurr, P. P. (1989). Measuring amount of symptom change in the diagnosis of premenstrual syndrome. *Psychological Assessment: A Journal of Consulting and Clinical Psychology, 1,* 277–283.

Scott, C. S., Arthur, D., Panizo, M. I., & Owen, R. (1989). Menarche: The Black American experience. *Journal of Adolescent Health Care, 10,* 363–368.

Severino, S. K., Hurt, S. W., & Shindledecker, R. D. (1989). Spectral analysis of cyclic symptoms in late luteal phase dysphoric disorder. *American Journal of Psychiatry, 146,* 1155–1160.

Severino, S. K., & Moline, M. L. (1989). *Premenstrual syndrome: A clinician's guide.* New York: Guilford Press.

Siegel, J. P. (1986). Marital dynamics of women with premenstrual tension syndrome. *Family System Medicine, 4,* 358–365.

Simmons, R. G., & Blyth, D. A. (1987). *Moving into adolescence: The impact of pubertal change and school context.* New York: Aldine de Gruyter.

Simmons, R., Blyth, D., & McKinney, K. (1983). The social and psychological effects of puberty on white females. In J. Brooks-Gunn & A. C. Petersen (Eds.), *Girls at puberty: Biological and psychosocial perspectives* (pp. 227–272). New York: Plenum Press.

Slade, P., & Jenner, F. A. (1980). Attitudes to female roles, aspects of menstruation and complaining of menstrual symptoms. *British Journal of Social and Clinical Psychology, 19,* 109–113.

Smith, W. (1971). Critical life-events and prevention strategies in mental health. *Archives of General Psychiatry, 25,* 103–109.

Snowden, R., & Christian, B. (1983). *Patterns and perceptions of menstruation: A World Health Organization study.* New York: St. Martin's Press.

Sommer, B. (1973). The effect of menstruation on cognitive and perceptual-motor behavior: A review. *Psychosomatic Medicine, 35,* 515–534.

Stager, J. M., Wigglesworth, J. K., & Hatler, L. K. (1990). Interpreting the relationship between age of menarche and prepubertal training. *Medicine and Science in Sports and Exercise, 22,* 54–58.

Stampfer, M., & Colditz, G. (1991). Estrogen replacement therapy and coronary heart disease: A quantitive assessment of the epidemiologic evidence. *Preventive Medicine, 20,* 47–63.

Strattin, H., & Magnusson, D. (1990). *Pubertal maturation in female development.* Hillsdale, NJ: Erlbaum.

Stout, A. L., & Steege, J. F. (1985). Psychological assessment of women seeking treatment for premenstrual syndrome. *Journal of Psychosomatic Research, 29,* 621–629.

Surbey, M. K. (1990). Family composition stress, and the timing of human menarche. In T. Ziegler & F. Bercovitch (Eds.), *Socioendocrinology of primate reproduction, monographs in primatology, vol. 13* (pp. 11–32). New York: Wiley–Liss.

Tanner, J. M. (1969). Growth and endocrinology of the adolescent. In L. I. Gardner (Ed.), *Endocrine and genetic diseases of childhood.* Philadelphia: Saunders.

Tanner, J. M. (1991). Secular trends in age of menarche. In R. Lerner, A. Peterson, & J. Brooks-Gunn (Eds.), *Encyclopedia of adolescence* 637–641. New York: Garland.

Taylor, D., Woods, N. F., Lentz, M. J., Mitchell, E. S., & Lee, K. A. (1991). Perimenstrual negative effect: Development and testing of an explanatory model. In D. Taylor & N. F. Woods (Eds.), *Menstruation, health, and illness* (pp. 103–118). New York: Hemisphere.

Tobin-Richards, M. H., Boyer, A. M., & Petersen, A. C. (1983). The psychological significance of pubertal change: Sex differences in perceptions of self during early adolescence. In J. Brooks-Gunn & A. C. Petersen (Eds.), *Girls at puberty: Biological and psychosocial perspectives.* New York: Plenum.

Trunnell, E. P., Turner, C. W., & Keye, W. R. (1988). A comparison of psychological and hormonal factors in women with and without premenstrual syndrome. *Journal of Abnormal Psychology, 97,* 429–436.

Udry, J. R., & Cliquet, R. L. (1982). A cross-cultural examination of the relationship between ages at menarche, marriage and first birth. *Demography, 19,* 53–63.

Ulman, K. (1992). The impact of menarche in family relationships. In A. J. Dan & L. L. Lewis (Eds.), *Menstrual health in women's lives* (pp. 236–245). Chicago: University of Illinois Press.

Vandenbroucke, J. P., Van Laar, A., & Valkenburg, H. A. (1982). Synergy between thinness and intensive sports activity in delaying menarche. *British Medical Journal, 284,* 1907–1908.

Voda, A. (1992). Menopause: A normal view. *Clinical Obstetrics and Gynecology, 35,* 923–933.

Warner, P., Bancroft, J., Dixson, A., & Hampson, M. (1991). The relationship between perimenstrual depressive mood and depressive illness. *Journal of Affective Disorders, 23,* 9–23.

Warner, P., & Bancroft, J. (1990). Factors related to self-reporting of the pre-menstrual syndrome. *British Journal of Psychiatry, 157,* 249–260.

Warren, C. J., & Baker, S. (1992). Coping resources of women with premenstrual syndrome. *Archives of Psychiatric Nursing, 6,* 48–53.

Warren, M. P. (1980). The effect of exercise on pubertal progression and reproductive function in girls. *Journal of Clinical Endocrinology and Metabolism, 51,* 1150–1157.

Warren, M. P. (1983). Physician and biological aspects of puberty. In J. Brooks-Gunn & A. C. Petersen (Eds.), *Girls at puberty: Biological and psychosocial perspectives* (pp. 3–28). New York: Plenum Press.

Whisnant, L., & Zegans, L. (1975). A study of attitudes toward menarche in White middle-class American adolescent girls. *American Journal of Psychiatry, 132,* 809–814.

Williams, L. R. (1983). Beliefs and attitudes of young girls regarding menstruation. In S. Golub (Ed.), *Menarche* (pp. 139–148). Lexington, MA: Heath.

Williams, N. A., Severino, S. K., Hurt, S., & Anderson, M. (1986). *Premenstrual syndromes: Relationship to stress.* Unpublished manuscript.

Wilson, R., & Wilson, T. (1963). The fate of the non-treated postmenopausal woman: A plea for the maintenance of adequate estrogen from puberty to the grave. *Journal of the American Geriatric Society, 11,* 327.

Woods, N. F., Mitchell, E. S., & Lentz, M. J. (1993, June). *Stressors, coping and psychological distress: Experiences of women with three perimenstrual symptom patterns.* Paper presented at the 10th conference of the Society of Menstrual Cycle Research, Boston.

Woods, N. F., Most, A., & Longnecker, G. D. (1985). Major life events, daily stressors, and perimenstrual symptoms. *Nursing Research, 34,* 236–267.

World Health Organization. (1981). Research on the menopause. Report of a WHO scientific group. *WHO Technical Report Series 670,* Geneva, Switzerland: Author.

Selected Issues in Women's Reproductive Health: Psychological Perspectives

Annette L. Stanton and Sharon Danoff-Burg

Biologically and temperamentally . . . women were made to be concerned first and foremost with child care, husband care and home care.

Benjamin Spock, *Redbook*, 1969.

Baby hunger is powerful, defying all laws of logic. . . . When a women has baby hunger, nothing else is as important to her as this inner drive to bear a child.

Lois Davitz, *Baby Hunger*, 1984.

We hardly need these words to remind us that motherhood has long been touted as the ultimate fulfillment for women and infertility as the ultimate tragedy. Indeed, early writers conceptualized the psychology of women's health as synonymous with the psychology of women's reproductive and gynecological health. As other chapters in this volume illustrate, women's health encompasses content far more wide-ranging than women's reproductive capacity. Nonetheless, the substantial majority of women intend to become mothers (Jacobson & Heaton, 1991), and over four million babies were born in the United States in 1991 (U.S. Bureau of the Census, 1993). Whether or not women experience motherhood, most repeatedly confront fertility-related issues. Most devote considerable energy to preventing or attempting conception, experiencing their own or others' pregnancies, and raising children or living in a pronatalist world. Thus, reproductive health is a notable concern in women's lives.

The literature concerning psychological factors in women's reproductive health is vast. In this chapter, we highlight three areas of study that we believe are representative of this literature. We focus specifically on the psychological experience of (a) pregnancy and the postpartum, with a focus on the postpartum depression construct; (b) infertility; and (c) reproductive and birth-related technologies. Research and theory in these three areas highlight the central themes in the psychology of reproductive health, illustrate the conceptual and methodological limitations in this literature, and point to directions for future empirical scrutiny and application. We refer the reader to other sources for analyses of additional important topics in reproductive health, such as abortion and contraception (Adler et al., 1992; O'Hara, Reiter, Johnson, Milburn, & Engeldinger, 1995), preparation for childbirth (Wideman & Singer, 1984), and stress and birth-outcomes (Lobel, 1994).

THE PSYCHOLOGICAL EXPERIENCE OF PREGNANCY AND THE POSTPARTUM

Perhaps more than any other single topic related to the experience of pregnancy and the postpartum, negative psychological symptomatology, and particularly depression, has garnered the greatest attention in the empirical literature in recent years. A computerized search of the psychological and medical literature over the past decade revealed approximately 150 empirical psychological articles and over 20 reviews in scientific journals, as well as three scholarly texts (Brockington & Kumar, 1982; Hamilton & Harberger, 1992; Kumar & Brockington, 1988) and one popular book (Dix, 1985) devoted to some aspect of depression surrounding pregnancy and the postpartum. In characterizing the postpartum psychiatric patient,

Hamilton (1989) illustrated the marked tendency to focus on women's difficulties during this time:

> The remarkable changeability of many patients, their impetuousness, and their explosive qualities create treatment problems and hazards of considerable magnitude. . . . The physician, and all those who treat or come in contact with postpartum patients, including families of patients, should be made aware of the likely mercurial qualities of symptoms and the varieties of thinking and behavior that may be expected. (p. 275)

What is the evidence that women are prone to distress surrounding pregnancy and the postpartum? In this section, we will examine this evidence, organizing our discussion around the consensus in the literature that postpartum distress comprises three distinct syndromes: postpartum psychosis, postpartum blues, and postpartum depression. We will review data on the nature and severity of these syndromes, etiological factors, and treatment.

Postpartum Psychosis

Conducted primarily in the United Kingdom and relying in large part on hospital admission data, research indicates that *postpartum psychosis* is rare, affecting 1 to 2 in 1000 women who give birth (Appleby, 1990; Harding, 1989; O'Hara, 1991). The first postpartum month appears to be a time of elevated risk for psychotic disorders, with estimates of incidence risk ranging from 10 to 20 times that of nonpuerperal women (Harding, 1989; Kendell, 1985; O'Hara, 1991). The symptoms of postpartum psychosis appear to differ little from those of other psychotic disorders, with gross impairment in reality testing, delusions, and hallucinations common (Gitlin & Pasnau, 1989; O'Hara, 1991; Steiner, 1990; Whiffen, 1992). The cognitive distortions may involve childbearing-related content, and affective symptoms (i.e., depression or mania) often are present (Gitlin & Pasnau, 1989; Harding, 1989; O'Hara, 1991).

With regard to risk factors, the best predictor of postpartum psychosis appears to be a history of psychological disorder (Gitlin & Pasnau, 1989; O'Hara, 1991). Stressful life events have not been shown to constitute a risk factor (e.g., Marks, Wieck, Checkley, & Kumar, 1991). Most researchers assume a biological etiology (Appleby, 1990; Brockington, Oates, & Rose, 1990), with a leading hypothesis involving the exposure of sensitive dopamine receptors when chorionic steroids decrease in the first few days postpartum (Brockington et al., 1990; Wieck et al., 1991). However, no strong evidence for an endocrine or biochemical etiology has emerged (Appleby, 1990; George & Sandler, 1988).

Postpartum psychosis can be severely debilitating and can necessitate hospitalization. Mother-and-baby treatment units and outreach programs have been established in the United Kingdom specifically for treatment of postpartum disorders. There are virtually no controlled studies of treatment for women experiencing postpartum psychosis (Gitlin & Pasnau, 1989; Nurnberg, 1989; O'Hara, 1991), and intervention historically has been similar to that for other psychoses, including neuroleptic and antidepressant medication, as well as electroconvulsive therapy (Nurnberg, 1989; O'Hara, 1991; Steiner, 1990). Although the prognosis for postpartum psychosis appears relatively positive compared with that for nonpuerperal psychosis (Harding, 1989; Platz & Kendell, 1988; Steiner, 1990), many researchers regard postpartum psychosis as virtually indistinguishable from nonpuerperal psychosis (Gitlin & Pasnau, 1989; Harding, 1989). Questions remain regarding what specific factors surrounding childbirth act to trigger the increased puerperal incidence and whether there are any differences between puerperal and nonpuerperal disorders that would carry implications for safe and effective prevention and treatment.

Postpartum Blues

Postpartum blues is a constellation of negative affective symptoms occurring most frequently in the first 10 days after parturition (O'Hara, 1991). The experience of depressed mood, tearfulness, affective lability, anxiety, and other symptoms appears common, affecting 26% to 85% of new mothers (O'Hara, Schlechte, Lewis, & Wright, 1991). Prevalence figures vary so widely in large part due to the use of various diagnostic criteria, ranging from the self-reported presence of a single symptom to presence of at least four symptoms.

The nature and severity of postpartum blues must be viewed in the context of several other findings. First, evidence suggests that postpartum symptoms indeed are more pronounced than are normal fluctuations in daily mood, as indicated by studies that compare mood ratings in puerperal women in the 10 days postpartum with those of nonpuerperal women (Knight & Thirkettle, 1986; O'Hara, Zekoski, Philipps, & Wright, 1990). However, these symptoms in general are milder than those arising after operative interventions such as elective gynecological surgery (Iles, Gath, & Kennerley, 1989; Levy, 1987). Furthermore, four of five studies we reviewed demonstrated that women's state depression scores were higher during the third trimester than during the 10 days postpartum (Ballinger, 1982; Buesching, Glasser, & Frate, 1986; Knight & Thirkettle, 1986; O'Hara et al., 1990; but see Manly, McMahon, Bradley, & Davidson, 1982). Finally, three studies in which both positive and negative mood were assessed revealed that positive mood ratings were consistently greater than ratings of negative mood during the postpartum period (Kendell, McGuire, Connor, & Cox, 1981; O'Hara et al., 1990; Rosenberg, Darby, & Robinson, 1984). Thus, postpartum blues symptoms appear milder than those experienced prepartum or in conjunction with surgical procedures, and they occur at a time when happiness predominates.

Few researchers have examined etiological factors for the postpartum blues, perhaps because of the relatively mild and transient quality of the symptoms, as well as the assumption that symptoms must be biologically based owing to the dramatic hormonal and biochemical changes that occur postpartum. Indeed, prepartum levels of estrogen and progesterone are over 100 times higher than at five days postpartum (Filer, 1992). In the largest study to date examining a number of hormonal assays, O'Hara, Schlechte, Lewis, and Wright (1991) found weak support for the role of estriol withdrawal in blues symptoms. Consistently demonstrated associations between blues symptoms and physiological parameters have yet to emerge (Hopkins, Marcus, & Campbell, 1984; O'Hara, 1991). Moreover, results regarding the relations of blues symptoms with pregnancy and birth complications, and with demographic and psychosocial factors, have been mixed, leading to the suggestion that the only reliable predictor of blues symptoms is women's mood during pregnancy (O'Hara, Schlechte, Lewis, & Wright, 1991; Thirkettle & Knight, 1985).

Currently, reassuring patients that blues symptoms are normal and monitoring for the onset of severe symptoms represent a typical intervention (O'Hara, 1991). Although the relation demonstrated between the postpartum blues and subsequent occurrence of postpartum depression suggests that early intervention may be promising (Cox, Connor, & Kendell, 1982; Hannah, Adams, Lee, Glover, & Sandler, 1992; Hapgood, Elkind, & Wright, 1988; O'Hara, Schlechte, Lewis, & Wright, 1991; but see Gard, Handley, Parsons, & Waldron, 1986; Kennerley & Gath, 1989), no systematic test has been conducted.

Postpartum Depression

The experience of depressive symptoms, typically of at least two weeks' duration, during the first postpartum year constitutes *postpartum depression* (Cutrona, 1982; O'Hara, 1991). Prevalence estimates vary as a function of the specific criteria required for diagnosis, and the use of self-report questionnaires versus diagnostic interviews to assess symptoms. Our review of 10 recent studies using standardized self-report measures to assess depression prevalence revealed an 8–26% prevalence of at least mild depression (e.g., ≥10 on the Beck Depression Inventory), assessed from one to six months postpartum (Atkinson & Rickel, 1984; Campbell & Cohn, 1991; Cutrona & Troutman, 1986; Fawcett & York, 1986; Gotlib, Whiffen, Mount, Milne, & Cordy, 1989; Harris, Huckle, Thomas, Johns, & Fung, 1989; O'Hara, 1985; O'Hara, Neunaber, & Zekoski, 1984; Raskin, Richman, & Gaines, 1990; Watson & Evans, 1986). Ten studies used structured interviews to yield diagnoses of minor or major depression according to Research Diagnostic Criteria (RDC; Spitzer, Endicott, & Robins, 1978) or criteria from the revised third edition of the *Diagnostic and Statistical Manual of Mental Disorders* (American Psychiatric Association,

1987). These yielded prevalence rates of 3% to 16.5%, assessed up to 14 weeks postpartum (Affonso et al., 1992; Campbell & Cohn, 1991; Carothers & Murray, 1990; Cutrona, 1984; Gotlib et al., 1989; Gotlib, Whiffen, Wallace, & Mount, 1991; Harris et al., 1989; O'Hara et al., 1984; O'Hara et al., 1990, Whiffen, 1988). Studies using both assessment methods typically evidenced higher depression rates for self-report than for interview assessments, although each method yielded somewhat distinct subsamples. For example, Campbell and Cohn (1991) found a 60% concordance rate for the two methods in identifying postpartum depression.

Several questions arise with regard to the distinctiveness and utility of postpartum depression as a construct. First, is the prevalence of depression different in postpartum versus nonpuerperal women? In the only study that included matched nonpuerperal controls, O'Hara et al. (1990) found that the rate of RDC-diagnosed depression was 10.4% in childbearing women at nine weeks postpartum and 7.8% in nonpuerperal women, a nonsignificant difference. O'Hara et al. pointed out that this rate of postpartum depression is not considerably different from that found in large scale studies of depression in women of similar ages (Myers et al., 1984). In a controlled study of adolescent females, Troutman and Cutrona (1990) also found no significant difference in rates of diagnosed depression in postpartum versus nonpuerperal females.

Second, is the rate of depression higher at postpartum than during pregnancy? Of the 13 studies using self-report measures, 12 demonstrated a significant or nonsignificant decrease in depression from the second or third trimester of pregnancy to 1–24 weeks postpartum (Atkinson & Rickel, 1984; Buesching et al., 1986; Carver & Gaines, 1987; Fawcett & York, 1986; Fink & Windt, 1984; Huffman, Lamour, Bryan, & Pederson, 1990; Lips, 1985; O'Hara, Rehm, & Campbell, 1982; O'Hara et al., 1984; Olioff & Aboud, 1991; Pfost, Lum, & Stevens, 1989; Richman, Raskin, & Gaines, 1991; but see Cutrona, 1984). None of the five interview studies revealed a significant increase in depression postpartum (Cutrona, 1984; Gotlib et al., 1989; Gotlib et al., 1991; O'Hara et al., 1984; O'Hara et al., 1990), and two of these (Gotlib et al., 1989; Gotlib et al., 1991) demonstrated a nonsignificant decrease in diagnosed depression from prepartum to four weeks postpartum, when women diagnosed during pregnancy were excluded. For example, Gotlib et al.'s (1989) study of 295 women yielded a prepartum 24- and 36-week cumulative depression rate of 10.2%. At four weeks postpartum the total rate was 6.8%, which included only 10 new cases and represented a point prevalence of 3.4%. These studies suggest that depressive symptoms are likely to be more prominent during pregnancy than at postpartum.

A third question regarding the distinctiveness of postpartum depression is whether symptom presentation differs for childbearing versus non-childbearing depressed women. Two studies comparing these two groups yielded somewhat different results. O'Hara et al. (1990) found that childbearing depressed women at nine weeks postpartum reported somewhat more depressive symptoms and more social and marital maladjustment than did nonchildbearing depressed women, but that the groups did not differ in mean length of depression ($M = 44$–46 days, respectively). By contrast, Whiffen and Gotlib (1993) found that childbearing depressed women at one month postpartum evidenced less severe depressive symptoms and similar psychosocial functioning compared with nonchildbearing depressed women, with the exception that childbearing women reported lower marital satisfaction. A difference between this and the O'Hara et al. study in the timing of the assessment may account for these somewhat disparate findings. However, as Whiffen and Gotlib (1993) pointed out, the utility of viewing postpartum depression as a unique diagnosis is questionable if severity is the primary distinction between depression occurring following childbirth versus depression occurring at other times.

A final question exists regarding whether a distinct etiology exists for postpartum depression. To date, no consistent evidence has emerged for a specific endocrine or biochemical etiology for postpartum depression (Cutrona, 1982; Deakin, 1988; George & Sandler, 1988; Hopkins et al., 1984; Kendell, 1985; O'Hara, 1991), nor have demographic characteristics been found to be significant (Hopkins et al., 1984; O'Hara, 1987). Three factors appear more promising in their ability to predict postpartum depression in prospective studies:[1] (a) the prior experience of depression,

---

[1]Listings of results of individual studies are available from the authors.

including both a history of depression and depression occurring during pregnancy; (b) stressful life events, including both general stressful events and pregnancy-related or childcare stress; and (c) interpersonal support, including general social and marital support. Research testing multifactorial etiological models has revealed that substantial variance in postpartum depression can be accounted for by these factors. For example, Cutrona and Troutman (1986) found that self-reported depression and social support during the third trimester, as well as parenting self-efficacy and infant difficulty as rated by the new mother, accounted for 55% of the variance in self-reported depression at three months postpartum. Self-rated postpartum depression is better predicted than diagnostic status determined through interviews (O'Hara et al., 1984; O'Hara, Schlechte, Lewis, & Varner, 1991; Whiffen, 1988), owing at least in part to the dichotomous nature of diagnostic status and the greater stability over time of self-rated symptoms (O'Hara, Schlechte, Lewis, & Varner, 1991).

Results of investigations regarding predictors of postpartum depression lead us to two conclusions. First, contributors to depression during the postpartum—including prior experience of depression, general and event-specific stressful events, and lack of general and marriage-specific social support—are not substantially different from factors predicting depression at other times (Gotlib et al., 1991; Whiffen, 1991, 1992). These findings suggest that a distinct etiology of postpartum depression has yet to be established. Second, these studies indicate that risk factors for postpartum depression can be identified successfully, thus implying that effective preventive strategies may be developed. This is important, given the finding that postpartum depression has been found to confer risk for a subsequent depressive episode (Philipps & O'Hara, 1991).

In light of the considerable empirical attention devoted to the study of postpartum depression, it is surprising that so few controlled studies of prevention or treatment have been conducted. Elliott, Sanjack, and Leverton (1988) provided suggestive evidence that an 11-session intervention focusing on issues during the transition to parenthood was effective in decreasing the likelihood of depression in primiparous women at high risk (e.g., poor marital relationship, history of psychological problems) compared with high-risk control women. In a controlled study, Halonen and Passman (1985) found that a two-session relaxation training intervention administered to women who had taken childbirth education classes produced decreased depressive symptoms, both in the first nine days postpartum and at one month. The authors suggested that relaxation alone, rather than specialized situational training, can be effective in preventing postpartum distress.

Conclusions From the Literature on Postpartum Disorders

Taken together, findings regarding the postpartum experience, including both transient negative mood and more enduring depressive symptoms, lead us to question the utility of the postpartum depression construct, as have others in this area (Campbell & Cohn, 1991; O'Hara, 1991; Troutman & Cutrona, 1990; Whiffen, 1991, 1992). First, the assumption that the postpartum months are a period of increased risk for depression in childbearing women has not received definitive support. Indeed, a number of studies indicate that depressive symptoms are more prominent during pregnancy than during the postpartum period, suggesting that the term *postpartum depression* is, at the least, a misnomer. The lack of distinctiveness with regard to symptom picture and etiological factors for postpartum depression also render the utility of this diagnosis questionable. We question why some continue to argue for its inclusion in formal diagnostic systems (Hamilton, 1992), and we are concerned when postpartum depression is portrayed in the lay media as "the hormonally and biochemically induced reaction to the body's upheaval in giving birth" (Dix, 1985, p. 8).

This is not to suggest that some women do not experience marked distress surrounding pregnancy and childbirth or that these women should not receive effective therapeutic attention. Rather, we would argue that the focus on postpartum depression as a disorder may overemphasize the negative aspects of women's reproductive experience to the point of characterizing it as pathological. Furthermore, we are concerned that a concomitant increased interest in the effect of maternal depression on infants (e.g., Cohn, Campbell, Matias, & Hopkins, 1990; Whiffen & Gotlib, 1989), although yielding potentially important findings, may carry the unintended consequences of a tendency toward mother-blaming (Caplan & Hall-McCorquodale, 1985) and toward deemphasizing the role of the father. A number of additional methodological and conceptual difficulties exist in this literature that are also apparent in the literature on psychological aspects of infertility. We turn to this literature before delineating its limitations.

THE PSYCHOLOGICAL EXPERIENCE OF INFERTILITY

Since 1965, four nationally representative samples of women aged 14 to 44 have been surveyed regarding fertility status. The 1988 survey (Mosher & Pratt, 1990) revealed that *infertility,* typically defined as the inability to conceive a pregnancy after one year of sexual intercourse, affects about 2.3 million women in the United States. An additional 2.6 million have *impaired fecundity,* which includes difficulty or danger carrying a pregnancy to term. Approximately 10.7% of married couples are estimated to have impaired fecundity. Although overall rates of infertility do not appear to be increasing, the number of couples with *primary infertility* (i.e., zero parity) has doubled, increasing from 500,000 in 1965 to one million in 1988 (Mosher & Pratt, 1990). Further, increasing numbers of people are seeking medical treatment of infertility, among whom approximately 50% can expect to achieve a viable pregnancy (U.S. Congress, Office of Technology Assessment [OTA], 1988).

Psychologists and other professionals have demonstrated long-standing interest in the causes and consequences of infertility. Three questions have provoked the greatest exploration: (a) Are psychological factors a cause of infertility? (b) Are infertile individuals more distressed than other adults? and (c) In infertile couples, do women or men experience greater distress? We will examine material pertinent to these questions in turn.

Psychological Conceptualizations of Infertility

Stanton and Dunkel-Schetter (1991) identified three psychological models of infertility represented in the literature. Prominent during the era when organic causes of infertility often could not be identified, the first model conceptualized infertility as a psychosomatic illness, residing primarily in the female. Such putative cases as conflict over the maternal role and feminine sexual identity were advanced (Allison, 1979; Eisner, 1963), as exemplified by Sandler (1968):

> Sterility can thus be a defence of the disturbed personality against the experience of pregnancy and motherhood. . . . The story so often demonstrates the failure of these women to adapt to the demands of a mature interpersonal relationship, not only in the sexual sphere but in every aspect of life. (p. 58)

Reviewers of the research on psychogenesis have concluded that neither studies of personality pathology in infertile women nor research examining the contention that adoption facilitates conception by relieving emotional difficulties provides consistent support for this model (e.g., Edelmann & Connolly, 1986). As diagnosis of infertility improved, such that an organic cause now can be identified in over 80% of infertility cases (OTA, 1988), the psychosomatic model waned. Although stress appears to impair spermatogenesis and ovulation in some cases (Domar & Seibel, 1990; Giblin, Poland, Moghissi, Ager, & Olson, 1988; Harrison, Callan, & Hennessey, 1987), models that blame infertility on women's psychopathology no longer receive serious consideration.

Conceptualizing distress as more a consequence than a cause of infertility, other writers have viewed infertility as a life crisis (e.g., Menning, 1977). They assumed that infertility catalyzes a predictable sequence of emotions, which must be actively processed before resolution can occur. Although this approach legitimized the psychological consequences of infertility as worthy of empirical and therapeutic attention, it minimized individual variability in responses to infertility. The general literature on loss and other undesirable life events contradicts the assumption of uniformity in content or sequence of reactions to these experiences (Wortman & Silver, 1987), and the life crisis model has contributed little to our understanding of which individuals might be at risk for adverse psychological reactions to infertility.

A current model conceptualizes infertility as a potentially stressful experience and uses established psychological theory to identify the conditions under which those who confront infertility either are vulnerable to extreme distress and life disruption or are likely to evidence adaptive functioning (Stanton & Dunkel-Schetter, 1991). For example, stress and coping theory (e.g., Lazarus & Folkman, 1984) points to cognitive appraisals and coping strategies initiated in stressor-management attempts as central determinants of subsequent adjustment. Research guided by these psychological theories has begun to specify factors important in enhancing or hindering psychological adjustment, including social support (Abbey, Andrews, & Halman, 1991), control appraisals (Campbell, Dunkel-Schetter, & Peplau, 1991; Tennen, Affleck, & Mendola, 1991), and avoidant coping (Litt, Tennen, Affleck, & Klock, 1992; Stanton, 1991). However, the preponderance of psychological research on infertility has examined the more basic question of whether infertile women as a group are more distressed than other adults.

Are Infertile Women More Distressed Than Other Women?

Substantial attention has been devoted to examining the realms of psychosocial functioning affected by the infertility experience. In an important review of psychological reactions to infertility, Dunkel-Schetter and Lobel (1991) contrasted the findings of the clinical and empirical literatures on this issue. Over 30 clinical, descriptive articles characterized infertility as a life crisis, citing psychological effects in several realms. These included (a) emotional effects, including depression, anger, guilt, shock, and anxiety; (b) loss of control over a number of aspects of one's life; (c) effects on self-esteem, identity, and core beliefs; and (d) social effects, including those on marital interaction, sexual functioning, and the familial and social network. The clinical literature typically portrayed the psychological consequences of infertility as profound, enduring, and disruptive to functioning.

Dunkel-Schetter and Lobel (1991) compared these findings with those of the empirical literature, concluding that the empirical literature yields no consistent evidence for strong negative psychological effects of infertility. We updated their review, focusing on studies published since 1982 that used self-report measures with established psychometric adequacy that the authors compared with available norms (20 studies) or with a control group (11 studies). We excluded psychological treatment studies because of the likelihood of elevated distress in those seeking treatment. Where multiple reports by common authors apparently used the same sample, we cited relevant findings only once. Dunkel-Schetter and Lobel found 12 studies that met these criteria, and we examined 19 additional reports.[2]

In general, measures used in these studies fell into four domains: marital satisfaction/quality (12 studies), sexual satisfaction/functioning (9 studies), self-esteem (9 studies), and distress/psychopathology (28 studies). Research regarding marital and sexual satisfaction yielded the most consistent findings. All 12 studies that assessed marital satisfaction revealed no difference between infertile women and controls (e.g., fertile women) or yielded satisfaction scores within the normal range. In fact, two controlled studies suggested that marital satisfaction was higher in infertile women than in control women (Callan & Hennessey, 1989; Downey & McKinney, 1992). Similarly, all nine studies that examined sexual satisfaction or functioning found scores for infertile women that were within the normal range or that did not differ significantly from those of a control group. Studies exploring self-esteem differences were nearly as uniform in their findings, with eight of nine studies yielding comparable self-esteem scores for infertile and other women (but see Abbey et al., 1991).

[2]Abbey et al., 1991; Adler & Boxley, 1985; Berg & Wilson, 1990, 1991; Boivin, Takefman, Brender, & Tulandi, 1992; Bromham, Bryce, & Balmer, 1989; Callan, 1987 and Callan & Hennessy, 1988, 1989; Campbell et al., 1991; Connolly, Edelmann, Cooke, & Robson, 1992 and Edelmann, Connolly, Cooke, & Robson, 1991; Cook, Parsons, Mason, & Golombok, 1989; Daniluk, 1988; Dennerstein & Morse, 1985; Domar, Broome, Zuttermeister, Seibel, & Friedman, 1992; Downey & McKinney, 1992; Draye, Woods, & Mitchell, 1988; Fagan et al., 1986; Fouad & Fahje, 1989; Freeman, Boxer, Rickels, Tureck, & Mastroianni, 1985; Freeman, Garcia, & Rickels, 1983 and Garcia et al., 1985; Haseltine et al., 1985; Hearn, Yuzpe, Brown, & Casper, 1987; Koropatnick, Daniluk, & Pattinson, 1993; Lalos, Lalos, Jacobsson, & Von Schoultz, 1985; Leiblum, Kemmann, & Lane, 1987; Link & Darling, 1986; McEwan, Costello, & Taylor, 1987; Newton, Hearn, & Yuzpe, 1990; Paulson, Haarmann, Salerno, & Asmar, 1988; Reading, Chang, & Kerin, 1989; Stanton, 1991; Tennen et al., 1991; Wright et al., 1991.
Studies joined by *and* are those that used a single sample. Listings of results of individual studies are available from the authors.

Findings regarding psychological symptomatology were somewhat more mixed. Of 28 studies, 12 revealed levels of distress and well-being comparable to control or normative samples, and 7 indicated greater levels of distress in infertile women, on average. Nine of these studies yielded mixed results, with infertile women evidencing greater distress on some measures but not others (e.g., Bromham et al., 1989) or having mean scores greater than a control group but still within the normal range (e.g., Domar et al., 1992). For example, Edelmann et al. (1991) found that women first attending an infertility specialty clinic reported significantly greater state anxiety than control or normative comparison women, but no greater levels of distress on other measures (e.g., Beck Depression Inventory). The samples for these studies varied widely both with regard to size (e.g., fewer than 30 to more than 400 women) and the point at which measures were administered (e.g., first visit to an infertility clinic versus participation in in vitro fertilization). Furthermore, many different measures were used, from traditional measures of psychopathology (e.g., Minnesota Multiphasic Personality Inventory) to indexes of life satisfaction.

It is important to note that even when infertile women did report significantly greater distress on the average, the difference between infertile and control or normative samples often was not very extreme, and considerable variability in infertile women's scores was evident. Thus, the conceptualization of infertility as a uniform life crisis was not supported in the empirical literature, and our examination of this expanded set of studies leads us to the same conclusion drawn by Dunkel-Schetter and Lobel (1991) that "methodologically rigorous research suggests that the majority of people with infertility do not experience clinically significant emotional reactions, loss of self-esteem, or adverse marital and sexual consequences" (p. 50).

How can we explain this discrepancy in findings between the empirical and clinical literatures? Perhaps the empirical literature underestimates the distress arising from infertility. For example, it is possible that the couples recruited for empirical studies are at points of particular optimism (e.g., the beginning of an in vitro fertilization cycle) or are attempting to present themselves in a positive light in order to be accepted for treatment.

Perhaps the measures used are too global to detect distress specific to infertility. On the other hand, the descriptive literature may overestimate the negative psychological impact of infertility, given the likelihood that the most distressed couples are overrepresented in clinical samples. Examining these possibilities, Dunkel-Schetter and Lobel (1991) suggested that the discrepancy serves to highlight the considerable variability in psychological reaction to infertility. Extreme distress may be experienced by some and only mild distress by others. In addition, it is likely that distress regarding infertility occurs in a context of general positive adjustment. To illustrate, Freeman et al. (1985) found that, in spite of normal MMPI profiles and anxiety within the normal range, 48% of women and 15% of men in infertile couples reported that infertility was the most upsetting event of their lives. Perhaps these findings serve to illustrate the general resilience of infertile couples in the face of adversity.

Are Women or Men More Distressed by Infertility?

Men and women are approximately equally likely to carry an infertility diagnosis (Davajan & Israel, 1991), and both members of couples experience the impact of infertility. A third question generating considerable attention is whether women or men in these couples experience more distress. Certainly, many clinical and qualitative reports suggest that infertility is more upsetting for women than for men. For example, Greil, Leitko, and Porter (1988), in a qualitative interview study, suggested that women experience infertility as a "cataclysmic role failure," whereas men view infertility as a "disconcerting event but not as a tragedy" (p. 172). Moreover, infertile women and men themselves believe that the sexes experience infertility differently. Stanton (1991) found that over 80% of women and men in infertile couples believed that either infertility is more distressing for women or that women are more likely than men to express their distress regarding infertility.

Fifteen of the previously cited empirical studies conducted comparisons between partners on various indexes of psychological functioning.[3]

---

[3]Listings of results of individual studies are available from the authors.

All six investigations using measures of marital satisfaction yielded no differences between partners, as did four of five studies of sexual satisfaction. Three of five studies assessing self-esteem found that women reported significantly lower self-esteem than their partners. In the 13 studies examining global psychological symptomatology or life-quality, 6 found no differences between infertile partners, 5 found indication of greater distress in women than men, and 2 obtained mixed results. In the four studies that used measures constructed to assess distress specific to infertility, women reported more distress than their partners.

Two caveats are important to consider in interpreting these results. Although some support for gender differences emerged on global measures of self-esteem and psychological functioning, it is important to note that scores on these measures typically were in the normal range for both women and men. Second, gender differences obtained on these measures within normative or comparison groups should be noted. For example, Abbey et al. (1991) found that women in both infertile and presumed-fertile couples reported lower self-esteem and more depressed affect than their partners. Thus, gender differences should not be interpreted as indicating distress that is necessarily clinically significant or exclusive to infertile women.

Although infertility does not appear to take a differential toll on partners with regard to marital or sexual satisfaction, these results suggest that it may evoke more general psychological distress in women than in their male partners. Potential explanations for this finding include the likelihood that women often bear the physical burdens of infertility, engaging in more diagnostic tests and treatments (Abbey et al., 1991) and monitoring their bodies for signs of pregnancy. It is also likely that parenthood is emphasized as a more central role for women than for men and thus that infertility may represent a more profound potential loss for women (Abbey et al., 1991; Stanton, 1991). Indeed, researchers have found that infertile women rate having a child as more important than do their partners (Abbey et al., 1991; Berg & Wilson, 1991). Although infertility does appear to have somewhat different effects than other stressors for women (Andrews, Abbey, & Halman, 1992), differential distress in women and men may in part reflect the more general tendency of women to appraise negative events as more stressful than do men (Kessler & McLeod, 1984; Miller & Kirsch, 1987). Perhaps this general tendency results from women's propensity to experience stress from events occurring in their larger social network or to take greater responsibility for negative events. These possibilities are consistent with findings in the infertility literature. For example, women have been found to take responsibility for the couple's infertility even when the cause is unknown or is not a female factor (Draye et al., 1988; McEwan et al., 1987; Tennen et al., 1991). If women take responsibility for infertility in order to protect their husbands from potential stigma (Miall, 1986; Tennen et al., 1991), then an unfortunate consequence may be a greater psychological burden.

Conclusions From the Literature on Infertility

To date, research suggests that distress is more likely a consequence than a cause of infertility, that this distress typically does not constitute clinically significant psychopathology, and that it may be more likely to be expressed by women than men in infertile couples. Continued investigation of the mechanisms for gender differences in distress, the factors that confer risk for disrupted psychological functioning, and psychological interventions to promote successful management of infertility-associated distress (e.g., Domar, Seibel, & Benson, 1990; Lukse, 1985; Stanton, McQueeney, & Sigmon, 1991; Stewart et al., 1992) is warranted.

THE PSYCHOLOGICAL EXPERIENCE OF REPRODUCTIVE AND BIRTH-RELATED TECHNOLOGIES

Contemporary health care for women is characterized by a high level of technological intervention in the processes of reproduction, pregnancy, and birth.[4] In fact, women increasingly are learning to conceptualize their experiences of these processes in the language of medicine (Collins &

---

[4]In this chapter, we used the term *reproductive technologies* to describe those technologies relevant to fertility, pregnancy, and birth.

Rodin, 1991). The impact of the established and rapidly expanding role of these technologies on women's physical and psychological health is a critical area for study as we enter the 21st century.

In this section, we will summarize arguments for and against the use of reproductive technologies and discuss research regarding the psychological impact on women of several technological interventions: (a) in vitro fertilization, (b) the prenatal diagnostic techniques of ultrasonography and amniocentesis, and (c) cesarean section. All of these carry the potential for medical benefit but also may engender medical and perhaps psychological risk.

Reproductive Technologies: Domination or Liberation?

The value of reproductive technologies is a divisive issue among those concerned with women's health and welfare. Technology has been perceived as both an instrument of patriarchal domination and as a key to women's liberation (Wajcman, 1991). In general, the perspectives of psychologists have not been dominant in this debate; many of the following positions have been expounded by feminist biologists, sociologists, and ethicists, as well as by professional and lay people within the health care and childbirth reform movements. In summarizing critiques of reproductive technologies we concur with Hubbard (1990) in that we do not mean to indict women who choose to use technology but to delineate some potential problems with the practical consequences or the ideology involved with such interventions.

Criticisms of Reproductive Technology
Potential for Exploitation

The strongest position against technology comes from those who have argued that technology is intrinsically exploitive of women and nature (Klein, 1991; Mies, 1987). Some theorists have contended that reproductive technologies serve to control women through medical appropriation of female reproductive potential (Corea et al., 1985). In contrast, others have criticized not technology per se but male-dominated systems that control the creation, implementation, and interpretation of technology (Rosser, 1986; Stanworth, 1987; see also Wertz & Fletcher, 1993). There has been concern that as human life becomes increasingly commodified, practices such as surrogacy and oocyte donation will result in the exploitation of women. Some fear that prenatal testing will be used for the purposes of sex selection and pressure to create the "perfect" product of conception, such as a child without mental or physical disabilities (Wertz & Wertz, 1989). The use of amniocentesis and other screening technologies for selective abortion of female fetuses in countries such as India is particular cause for alarm (Kishwar, 1987).

The Motherhood Mandate

The cultural ideology of motherhood as a biological imperative has led to ambivalence regarding the creation of new reproductive technologies for women. As Wajcman (1991) commented, "Whereas abortion and contraception were about challenging the traditional definition of femininity which equated it with motherhood, by contrast these new technologies are about fulfilling, rather than rejecting, the traditional feminine role" (p. 57). Infertility-related technologies may reinforce the *motherhood mandate,* which refers to the pervasive social pressure on women to bear children (Russo, 1979). Furthermore, these technologies may contribute to the extolment of biological over social parenthood.

Fetuses as Patients

Advances in medicine and the increasing medicalization of pregnancy and childbirth have contributed to the view of fetuses as unborn patients deserving of medical attention and prompting interests that may conflict with those of pregnant women. When pregnant women are pitted against fetuses, obstetricians may be placed in the role of adjudicating disputes over whose interest is primary (Ruzek, 1991). In such cases, the perceived needs of the fetus may override the needs of the pregnant woman. For example, a national survey revealed that courts in 11 states had ordered cesarean sections against the will of pregnant women (Kolder, Gallagher, & Parsons, 1987). In 81 percent of cases in which court orders for obstetrical intervention were sought, the women involved were Black, Asian, or

Hispanic; 44 percent were unmarried, and 24 percent did not speak English as their primary language (Kolder et al., 1987). It is important to note that the American Medical Association (1990) has argued against judicial intervention when women make informed refusal of medical treatment intended to benefit the fetus.

The Expanding Standard of Care

Because many obstetric technologies initially intended for high-risk patients have become routine, there has been concern that patients may have difficulty refusing unwanted interventions. Nelson (1981) found that birthing mothers received more technological interventions than they had desired. Women who choose not to use particular technologies may be blamed or punished. Some critics of the expanding standard of care have framed it as a safety issue, focusing on the routine adoption of procedures that have not been subjected to rigorous scientific evaluation. Ruzek (1991) observed that far more evidence of the efficacy and cost-effectiveness of services such as expanded prenatal care and WIC (Women, Infants, and Children's Supplemental Food Program) has been demanded than of surgical interventions that may present substantial risks. Similarly, Grimes (1993) called for the medical profession to demand the same scientific standards for new technologies as for new medicines, warning that "[t]he alternative is uncontrolled human experimentation" (p. 3032).

Advantages of Reproductive Technologies

Despite the risks of technologies for women, the potential benefits remain compelling. Reproductive technologies have been conceptualized not only as tools of domination, but also as a means to women's procreative freedom. The advent of technologies has enabled women to better plan their pregnancies, utilize alternative means of conception, elect whether or not to continue pregnancies, and choose among alternative labor and delivery methods. Fertility technologies increase reproductive options for many women, including lesbians and unmarried heterosexual women. Oocyte donation has enabled women in their menopausal years to bear children (Sauer, Paulson, & Lobo, 1992). Finally, the fact that medical technologies have served to improve pregnancy and birth outcomes must not be ignored. Perhaps most significant to psychologists, however, is not the question of whether technology is good or bad, but the question of which women in which circumstances will benefit from particular technological interventions (Rodin & Collins, 1991).

Psychological Impact of Reproductive Technologies

Relatively little empirical research has been conducted on the psychosocial consequences of fertility, pregnancy, and birth technologies. Existing research suggests that different technologies carry different risks and benefits for women. To illustrate this variability in impact, we will discuss the psychological consequences of in vitro fertilization, prenatal diagnostic testing, and cesarean section.

In Vitro Fertilization

Of the infertility-related technologies, in vitro fertilization (IVF) and its variants have been most widely publicized and researched. IVF involves the stimulation of follicles, recovery of oocytes for laboratory fertilization, and transfer of the preembryo into the uterus. The success rate of a single IVF attempt is typically less than 20% (Society for Assisted Reproductive Technology, 1994), and the process is costly to patients in terms of financial expense and life disruption. Such disruption is likely to arise from the invasive and time-consuming nature of the IVF process, as well as from distress experienced subsequent to a negative result (Leiblum et al., 1987; Newton et al., 1990; Reading et al., 1989). Further, both the short-term side effects of fertility drugs (Klein, 1991; Leiblum et al., 1987) and their relatively unexplored effects on long-term physical health (e.g., Spirtas, Kaufman, & Alexander, 1993) are reason for concern.

Although IVF may offer hope to infertile women and couples, there are at least three potential negative psychological consequences associated with its availability. First, women are likely to overestimate their chances of success and underestimate their negative responses to failed IVF treatment (Adler, Keyes, & Robertson, 1991). Second, the availability of pregnancy-inducing technologies may create pressures to use them and prolong distress for infertile couples by preventing resolution. For example, Leiblum et al. (1987) found that after unsuccessful IVF, 52% of couples studied felt resolved, yet 93% reported that they would try a new reproductive technology if it enhanced their chance of pregnancy. Third, little is known about the psychological adjustment of women who are financially unable to access IVF or of women who choose not to pursue treatment.

Prenatal Diagnostic Testing

Diagnostic procedures designed to detect fetal abnormalities include ultrasonography, amniocentesis, alpha-fetoprotein testing, and chorionic villus sampling. The development of these technologies has had a significant impact on the experience of pregnancy. As Green (1990) commented,

> The existence of fetal diagnosis has opened doors that cannot be closed again. Pregnancy will never be the same, even for mothers who decline to take part, because they will always know that they could have had that knowledge and could have acted on it. (p. 1076)

We will discuss some of the psychological sequelae of ultrasonography and amniocentesis—the prenatal diagnostic procedures that have been the subject of the most research.

Ultrasonography during pregnancy has become routine in the United States, though the associated risks and benefits have not been researched extensively. In a recent, randomized trial involving 15,151 pregnant women at low risk for perinatal problems, routine prenatal ultrasound screening did not reduce perinatal morbidity or mortality, compared with selective use of the procedure based on clinician judgment (Ewigman et al., 1993). Despite lack of data supporting the need for routine ultrasonography, emotional response to ultrasonography is generally positive. Several studies have found that ultrasonography increases positive attitudes toward pregnancy and the fetus (e.g., Langer, Ringler, & Reinhold, 1988; Reading & Cox, 1982; Tsoi, Hunter, Pearce, Chudleigh, & Campbell, 1987) and that neonatal outcome may also be improved (Field, Sandberg, Quetel, Garcia, & Rosario, 1985).

Women's reactions to amniocentesis seem less uniform, although retrospective reports of reactions to amniocentesis are generally positive. Women who are at high risk for adverse outcomes are likely to report greater anxiety than those not at high risk, but anxiety levels usually return to normal after test results are obtained (see Adler et al., 1991). Little is known, however, about the psychological consequences of receipt of unfavorable test results or of misdiagnosis.

There is some question as to whether prenatal diagnostic testing significantly facilitates or disrupts pregnant women's bonding to the fetus. Whereas some investigators have found that diagnostic testing may bolster commitment to the fetus (Lydon & Dunkel-Schetter, 1994; Phipps & Zinn, 1986), others have cautioned that pregnant women may suspend commitment to the fetus until test results are known (Rothman, 1986; Spencer & Cox, 1988). If prenatal diagnostic techniques increase commitment to the fetus, then women's positive health behaviors during pregnancy may increase. In contrast, delay in fetal attachment prompted by diagnostic testing could result in decreased adherence to prescribed early prenatal regimens (Adler et al., 1991). More research is needed to examine the influence of prenatal diagnostic procedures on commitment to the fetus and subsequent health behaviors during pregnancy.

Cesarean Section

Cesarean section rates in the United States have increased dramatically, rising from 4.5 percent of births in 1965 (Taffel, 1989) to 23.5 percent in 1991 (National Center for Health Statistics, 1993). A host of reasons for this trend have been suggested, many of them not medically justifiable. For example, higher cesarean section rates have been documented among patients of higher socioeconomic status (Gould, Davey, & Stafford, 1989) and those who are privately insured (Stafford, 1990). A recent study demonstrated that performance of cesarean section was positively associated with number of hospital malpractice claims and physician-perceived risk of suit (Localio et al., 1993). Marieskind (1982) discussed not only economic incentives as reasons for the recent rise in cesarean sections but also factors including repeat cesarean policy; obstetrical training emphasizing surgical deliveries; use of electronic fetal monitoring; belief in superior outcome from cesarean section; changing indications for the procedure; and shifts in age, parity, and fertility characteristics of the childbearing population.

Although the rise in cesarean sections has been associated with decreased neonatal mortality, the maternal mortality rate for cesarean section is four times higher than for vaginal delivery. At least one-third of all cesarean patients suffer postoperative infections, and almost all experience abdominal pain (Ruzek, 1991). In some cases, negative effects may be reduced through preparatory intervention. Greene, Zeichner, Roberts, Callahan, and Granados (1989) demonstrated that women scheduled for cesarean delivery who viewed a preparatory slide/tape program experienced lower physiological arousal during cesarean delivery and enhanced postoperative recovery compared with a control group who viewed a neutral tape (see also Tadmor, 1988).

In a study of women's psychological adjustment 24–48 hours following childbirth, Padawer, Fagan, Janoff-Bulman, and Strickland (1988) found that compared with women who delivered vaginally, women who had emergency cesareans were less satisfied with the delivery. However, the groups did not differ on spousal interaction during birth or satisfaction with physical appearance/sexuality. Nor did they differ on measures of depression, anxiety, or confidence in mothering. Because the women gave birth in a hospital with progressive obstetrical care policies, the investigators cautioned that the results may not be generalizable.

Conclusions From the Literature on Reproductive Technologies

The established and rapidly expanding role of technology in reproduction may be viewed as a double-edged sword. Whereas reproductive technologies may offer women more choices regarding if, when, and under what conditions to have children, they also increase the capacity of the medical profession to exert control over women's bodies and lives (Stanworth, 1987). Our review of illustrative technologies suggests that different procedures carry the potential for very different psychological and health-related consequences for women. Psychologists can work to make reproductive technology a source of empowerment rather than exploitation in several ways: (a) by illuminating potential costs and benefits that specific technologies pose for different women under particular circumstances, (b) by developing programs that enable women to make informed decisions about the use of technologies and to exercise their rights as patients to have these choices respected, and (c) by increasing comfort with elected technological procedures.

METHODOLOGICAL, CONCEPTUAL, AND APPLIED CONCERNS

A number of methodological, conceptual, and applied issues accompany the literatures we have reviewed. Consideration of these can lead to identification of gaps in the current empirical foundation on reproductive health and specification of directions for future research.

Sample Selection

Sample selection is the first methodological issue deserving consideration. Participants for research on postpartum depression and infertility are typically recruited from populations of those seeking prenatal health care or specialized infertility services. Recruitment through the health care system limits generalization to other samples. Thus, little is known about women who do not pursue such care or who terminate treatment. As with so many other areas, findings reviewed here apply primarily to White, middle class women. This is particularly disturbing, given that women from lower socioeconomic strata are at increased risk for infertility and poor birth outcomes, as are African American women (U.S. Congress, OTA, 1988; Schoendorf, Hogue, Kleinman, & Rowley, 1992). An important series of studies by Dunkel-Schetter and colleagues revealing associations of psychosocial resources with maternal and infant outcomes (e.g., Collins, Dunkel-Schetter, Lobel, & Scrimshaw, 1993; Lobel, Dunkel-Schetter, & Scrimshaw, 1992) may aid in illuminating psychosocial issues in pregnancy and birth for low-income women.

Another limitation in sample selection is the lack of adequate control and comparison groups. Only a few studies we reviewed included demographically matched comparison groups, and randomized controlled studies of the psychological impact of reproductive technologies are nearly nonexistent. We also would like to mention the relative lack of attention to men with regard to their experience of infertility and reproductive events. Certainly the physical exigencies of infertility and pregnancy are more central to women. However, the inclusion of men in this research, as has been accomplished in the literature on transition to parenthood (e.g., Michaels & Goldberg, 1988), would highlight the fact that reproductive health is an issue for both women and men.

Measurement Issues

We must question whether global measures of psychopathology and distress are the most appropriate for examining psychological aspects of women's reproductive health. For example, some researchers studying postpartum depression have failed to eliminate depression inventory items encompassing somatic changes that accompany pregnancy and childbirth (e.g., weight alterations). Another study revealed that infertile women scored higher than a normative comparison on a measure of psychoticism (Berg & Wilson, 1990). The researchers astutely pointed out that the test item, "The idea that something serious is wrong with your body," is likely to be endorsed by infertile women and that it is quite unlikely to indicate psychoticism in this context. Inclusion of such items without consideration of the normal experience of reproductive events is likely to result in an overestimation of pathology. Researchers should examine general measures of psychological functioning carefully for content relevant to reproduction and should initiate construction of psychometrically adequate instruments to assess adjustment specific to reproductive experiences (e.g., O'Hara, Hoffman, Philipps, & Wright, 1992).

A second issue is the tendency in the research we reviewed to restrict assessments to those measuring distress or psychopathology. It is well established that positive and negative affect comprise relatively independent dimensions (Diener & Emmons, 1984; Watson & Tellegen, 1985). Thus, distress and well-being may coexist and may have different determinants. For example, the finding that some women experience postpartum blues takes on different meaning when it is pointed out that this occurs in a context of positive affect. Furthermore, Stanton (1991) found that the coping strategies that significantly predicted well-being in infertile couples would have been neglected had distress been the sole dependent variable. If we wish to reach an understanding of factors that promote resilience in women, we must include measures that assess positive as well as negative psychological functioning.

In addition to examination of adaptive outcomes, expansion of dependent variables to encompass other areas of functioning is warranted. With the exception of the literature on associations between stressful experiences and pregnancy outcomes (e.g., Istvan, 1986), few studies have examined psychosocial contributors to women's physical health in conjunction with reproductive events. Gjerdingen, Froberg, and Kochevar (1991) found that women's self-reported illness days increased from pregnancy to six months postpartum. Psychosocial contributors to objective and subjective indicators of physical health surrounding fertility-related experiences require investigation. In addition, the impact of reproductive events on outcomes such as sexuality (Bogren, 1991), body image, and other aspects of individual and relational identity (e.g., Ruble et al., 1990) also deserve empirical scrutiny.

Conceptual Issues

In line with our discussion of measurement, we would like to discourage a unitary focus on negative outcomes associated with reproduction. Our review offers little support for the view that postpartum depression represents a distinct diagnosis and suggests instead that the term "postpartum depression" may be a misnomer. Whiffen (1992) has proposed the term "childbearing depression," but we contend that until distinctive etiological or treatment-related agents are identified, the term "depression" may suffice for those women whose experience warrants such a diagnosis. Furthermore, the social construction of infertile couples as desperate (Franklin, 1990) appears unjustified from the empirical data. A narrow focus on negative sequelae of reproductive events in the scientific literature may contribute to the pathologization of women's reproductive health.

The empirical foundation on women's reproductive health also would become more solid with the addition of theory-driven, multifactorial causal models (Cutrona, 1982; Hopkins et al., 1984; Stanton & Dunkel-Schetter, 1991; Whiffen, 1991). Many of the studies we reviewed appeared atheoretical. Established theories regarding depression, stress and coping, and adult development may be useful when coupled with consideration of event-specific factors. Specification of the unique aspects of particular reproductive experiences within the context of extant frameworks can prevent researchers from reinventing the wheel with regard to theory-building and can advance both general theories regarding psychological and physical functioning and those specific to reproductive health.

Applied Issues

Given the number of descriptive studies available to characterize the psychological experience of reproduction, the paucity of controlled investigations to enhance women's reproductive health is striking. Three types of applied investigations are imperative. First, studies of the efficacy of psychological assessment in particular realms are necessary. For example, psychologists are becoming the gatekeepers for access to particular fertility-related technologies such as in vitro fertilization and donor insemination (e.g., Micioni, Jeker, Zeeb, & Campana, 1987). This is in the absence of valid data on whether extant instruments can screen adequately for those for whom treatment would be excessively stressful or those who would be inadequate parents. Psychological consequences of delaying or denying technologies based on such assessments also are unexplored. Second, with the exception of research on efficacy of childbirth-preparation methods (Wideman & Singer, 1984), controlled studies of pharmacological and psychological interventions for women experiencing negative sequelae of reproductive events are few. Whether or not established therapeutic strategies require modification in order to be maximally effective is an unanswered question. Third, preventive strategies represent a potentially fruitful area for exploration. Because depression occurring during pregnancy and childbirth occurs infrequently, a high-risk approach targeting those most at risk for depression (e.g., previous history of depression, low social support) for preventive interventions may be useful. Further, prevention of some causes of infertility may be accomplished through behavior change (e.g., strategies to prevent sexually transmitted diseases).

CONCLUSIONS FROM THE EMPIRICAL LITERATURE ON REPRODUCTIVE HEALTH

Our review of the literature leads us to the conclusion that several assumptions about women have guided research on psychological aspects of their reproductive health. First, the portrayal of motherhood as a primary role has led medical and psychological researchers in reproductive health to focus on women more than on men. We do not wish to discourage research on women. However, a unitary focus may serve to perpetuate the motherhood mandate, and we call for a concomitant effort to study the reproductive health of men. Second, early research on infertility illustrates the historical emphasis on psychogenesis as a cause of gynecological problems. This theme also is evident in conceptualizations that cite women's psychopathology as a catalyst for negative menstrual and menopausal symptoms. Research repeatedly has failed to support this assumption, and we believe that it should be abandoned in favor of more sophisticated and less woman-blaming biopsychosocial models of reproductive health. Third, the assumption that women differ in fundamental ways from men is demonstrated in clinical descriptions of gender differences in responses to infertility. This contention receives some support in the empirical literature on infertile couples. However, very little empirical attention has been devoted to discerning the mechanisms that underlie these differences, and we should take care in interpreting them until such investigation is undertaken. A fourth assumption is that the White, relatively affluent, married woman is the norm. Investigation of psychological issues in reproductive health is also necessary in women of color, those in lower socioeconomic groups, single women, and lesbian women.

290

It is imperative that researchers and practitioners neither trivialize nor pathologize women's experiences with reproductive events. This requires recognition of the heterogeneity demonstrated in women's reactions to infertility, childbirth, and reproductive technologies. Research indicates that some women evidence considerable distress and life disruption in response to pregnancy and childbearing concerns. Theory development and study directed toward identifying women at high risk for adverse reactions and preventing or ameliorating distress are essential. Sound evidence also demonstrates that most women adjust positively to reproductive events, and continued examination of factors that bolster women's adjustment is crucial. In this way, women's resilience in the face of reproductive challenges can be recognized and promoted.

REFERENCES

Abbey, A., Andrews, F. M., & Halman, L. J. (1991). Gender's role in responses to infertility. *Psychology of Women Quarterly, 15,* 295–316.

Adler, J. D., & Boxley, R. L. (1985). The psychological reactions to infertility: Sex roles and coping styles. *Sex Roles, 12,* 271–279.

Adler, N. E., David, H. P., Major, B. N., Roth, S. H., Russo, N. F., & Wyatt, G. E. (1992). Psychological factors in abortion. *American Psychologist, 47,* 1194–1204.

Adler, N. E., Keyes, S., & Robertson, P. (1991). Psychological issues in new reproductive technologies: Pregnancy-inducing technology and diagnostic screening. In J. Rodin & A. Collins (Eds.), *Women and new reproductive technologies: Medical, psychosocial, legal, and ethical dilemmas* (pp. 111–133). Hillsdale, NJ: Erlbaum.

Affonso, D. D., Lovett, S., Paul, S., Sheptak, S., Nussbaum, R., Newman, L., & Johnson, B. (1992). Dysphoric distress in childbearing women. *Journal of Perinatology, 12,* 325–332.

Allison, J. R. (1979). Roles and role conflict of women in infertile couples. *Psychology of Women Quarterly, 4,* 97–113.

American Medical Association, Board of Trustees. (1990). Legal interventions during pregnancy: Court-ordered medical treatments and legal penalties for potentially harmful behavior by pregnant women. *Journal of the American Medical Association, 265,* 2663–2670.

American Psychiatric Association. (1987). *Diagnostic and statistical manual of mental disorders* (3rd ed., rev.). Washington, DC: Author.

Andrews, F. M., Abbey, A., & Halman, L. J. (1992). Is fertility-problem stress different? The dynamics of stress in fertile and infertile couples. *Fertility and Sterility, 57,* 1247–1253.

Appleby, L. (1990). The aetiology of postpartum psychosis: Why are there no answers? *Journal of Reproductive and Infant Psychology, 8,* 109–118.

Atkinson, A. K., & Rickel, A. U. (1984). Postpartum depression in primiparous parents. *Journal of Abnormal Psychology, 93,* 115–119.

Ballinger, C. B. (1982). Emotional disturbance during pregnancy and following delivery. *Journal of Psychosomatic Research, 26,* 629–634.

Berg, B. J., & Wilson, J. F. (1990). Psychiatric morbidity in the infertile population: A reconceptualization. *Fertility and Sterility, 53,* 654–661.

Berg, B. J., & Wilson, J. F. (1991). Psychological functioning across stages of treatment for infertility. *Journal of Behavioral Medicine, 14,* 11–26.

Bogren, L. Y. (1991). Changes in sexuality in women and men during pregnancy. *Archives of Sexual Behavior, 20,* 35–45.

Boivin, J., Takefman, J. E., Brender, W., & Tulandi, T. (1992). The effects of female sexual response in coitus on early reproductive processes. *Journal of Behavioral Medicine, 15,* 509–518.

Brockington, I. F., & Kumar, R. (Eds.). (1982). *Motherhood and mental illness.* London: Academic Press.

Brockington, I. F., Oates, M., & Rose, G. (1990). Prepartum psychosis. *Journal of Affective Disorders, 19,* 31–35.

Bromham, D. R., Bryce, F. C., & Balmer, B. (1989). Psychometric evaluation of infertile couples. (Preliminary findings.) *Journal of Reproductive and Infant Psychology, 7,* 195–202.

Buesching, D. P., Glasser, M. L., & Frate, D. A. (1986). Progression of depression in the prenatal and postpartum periods. *Women & Health, 11*(2), 61–78.

Callan, V. J. (1987). The personal and marital adjustment of mothers and of voluntarily and involuntarily childless wives. *Journal of Marriage and the Family, 49,* 847–856.

Callan, V. J., & Hennessey, J. F. (1988). The psychological adjustment of women experiencing infertility. *British Journal of Medical Psychology, 61,* 137–140.

Callan, V. J., & Hennessey, J. F. (1989). Psychological adjustment to infertility: A unique comparison of two groups of infertile women, mothers and women childless by choice. *Journal of Reproductive and Infant Psychology, 7,* 105–112.

Campbell, S. B., & Cohn, J. F. (1991). Prevalence and correlates of postpartum depression in first-time mothers. *Journal of Abnormal Psychology, 100,* 594–599.

Campbell, S. M., Dunkel-Schetter, C., & Peplau, L. (1991). Perceived control and adjustment to infertility among women undergoing *in vitro* fertilization. In A. L. Stanton & C. Dunkel-Schetter (Eds.), *Infertility: Perspectives from stress and coping research* (pp. 133–156). New York: Plenum.

Caplan, P. J., & Hall-McCorquodale, I. (1985). Mother-blaming in major clinical journals. *American Journal of Orthopsychiatry, 55,* 345–351.

Carothers, A. D., & Murray, L. (1990). Estimating psychiatric morbidity by logistic regression: Application to post-natal depression in a community sample. *Psychological Medicine, 20,* 695–702.

Carver, C. S., & Gaines, J. G. (1987). Optimism, pessimism, and postpartum depression. *Cognitive Therapy and Research, 11,* 449–462.

Cohn, J. F., Campbell, S. B., Matias, R., & Hopkins, J. (1990). Face-to-face interactions of postpartum depressed and nondepressed mother–infant pairs at 2 months. *Developmental Psychology, 26,* 15–23.

Collins, A., & Rodin, J. (1991). The new reproductive technologies: What have we learned? In J. Rodin & A. Collins (Eds.), *Women and new reproductive technologies: Medical, psychosocial, legal, and ethical dilemmas* (pp. 153–161). Hillsdale, NJ: Erlbaum.

Collins, N. L., Dunkel-Schetter, C., Lobel, M., & Scrimshaw, S. C. M. (1993). Social support in pregnancy: Psychosocial correlates of birth outcomes and postpartum depression. *Journal of Personality and Social Psychology, 65,* 1243–1258.

Connolly, K. J., Edelmann, R. J., Cooke, I. D., & Robson, J. (1992). The impact of infertility on psychological functioning. *Journal of Psychosomatic Research, 36,* 459–468.

Cook, R., Parsons, J., Mason, B., & Golombok, S. (1989). Emotional, marital and sexual functioning in patients embarking upon IVF and AID treatment for infertility. *Journal of Reproductive and Infant Psychology, 7,* 87–93.

Corea, G., Klein, R. D., Hanmer, J., Holmes, H. B., Hoskins, B., Kishwar, M., Raymond, J., Rowland, R., & Steinbacher, R. (Eds.). (1985). *Man-made women: How new reproductive technologies affect women.* London: Hutchinson.

Cox, J. L., Connor, Y., & Kendell, R. E. (1982). Prospective study of the psychiatric disorders of childbirth. *British Journal of Psychiatry, 140,* 111–117.

Cutrona, C. E. (1982). Nonpsychotic postpartum depression: A review of recent research. *Clinical Psychology Review, 2,* 487–503.

Cutrona, C. E. (1984). Social support and stress in the transition to parenthood. *Journal of Abnormal Psychology, 93,* 378–390.

Cutrona, C. E., & Troutman, B. R. (1986). Social support, infant temperament, and parenting self-efficacy: A mediational model of postpartum depression. *Child Development, 57,* 1507–1518.

Daniluk, J. C. (1988). Infertility: Intrapersonal and interpersonal impact. *Fertility and Sterility, 49,* 982–990.

Davajan, V., & Israel, R. (1991). Diagnosis and medical treatment of infertility. In A. L. Stanton & C. Dunkel-Schetter (Eds.), *Infertility: Perspectives from stress and coping research* (pp. 17–28). New York: Plenum.

Davitz, L. J. (1984). *Baby Hunger: Every woman's longing for a baby.* Minneapolis, MN: Winston Press.

Deakin, J. F. W. (1988). Relevance of hormone–CNS interactions to psychological changes in the puerperium. In R. Kumar & I. F. Brockington (Eds.), *Motherhood and mental illness 2: Causes and consequences* (pp. 113–132). London: Wright.

Dennerstein, L., & Morse, C. (1985). Psychological issues in IVF. *Clinics in Obstetrics and Gynaecology, 12,* 835–846.

Diener, E., & Emmons, R. A. (1984). The independence of positive and negative affect. *Journal of Personality and Social Psychology, 47,* 1105–1117.

Dix, C. (1985). *The new mother syndrome.* Garden City, NY: Doubleday.

Domar, A. D., Broome, A., Zuttermeister, P. C., Seibel, M., & Friedman, R. (1992). The prevalence and predictability of depression in infertile women. *Fertility and Sterility, 58,* 1158–1163.

Domar, A. D., & Seibel, M. (1990). The emotional aspects of infertility. In M. Seibel (Ed.), *Infertility: A comprehensive text* (pp. 23–35). Norwalk, CT: Appleton–Lange.

Domar, A. D., Seibel, M. M., & Benson, H. (1990). The Mind/Body Program for Infertility: A new behavioral treatment approach for women with infertility. *Fertility and Sterility, 53,* 246–249.

Downey, J., & McKinney, M. (1992). The psychiatric status of women presenting for infertility evaluation. *American Journal of Orthopsychiatry, 62,* 196–205.

Draye, M. A., Woods, N. F., & Mitchell, E. (1988). Coping with infertility in couples: Gender differences. *Health Care for Women International, 9,* 163–175.

Dunkel-Schetter, C., & Lobel, M. (1991). Psychological reactions to infertility. In A. L. Stanton & C. Dunkel-Schetter (Eds.), *Infertility: Perspectives from stress and coping research* (pp. 29–57). New York: Plenum.

Edelmann, R. J., & Connolly, K. J. (1986). Psychological aspects of infertility. *British Journal of Medical Psychology, 59,* 209–219.

Edelmann, R. J., Connolly, K. J., Cooke, I. D., & Robson, J. (1991). Psychogenic infertility: Some findings. *Journal of Psychosomatic Obstetrics and Gynaecology, 12,* 163–168.

Eisner, B. G. (1963). Some psychological differences between fertile and infertile women. *Journal of Clinical Psychology, 19,* 391–395.

Elliott, S. A., Sanjack, M., & Leverton, T. J. (1988). Parents groups in pregnancy: A preventive intervention for postnatal depression? In B. H. Gottlieb (Ed.), *Marshaling social support: Formats, processes, and effects* (pp. 87–110). Newbury Park, CA: Sage.

Ewigman, B. G., Crane, J. P., Frigoletto, F. D., LeFevre, M. L., Bain, R. P., McNellis, D., & the RADIUS Study Group. (1993). Effect of prenatal ultrasound screening on perinatal outcome. *New England Journal of Medicine, 329,* 821–827.

Fagan, P. J., Schmidt, C. W., Rock, J. A., Damewood, M. D., Halle, E., & Wise, T. N. (1986). Sexual functioning and psychologic evaluation of in vitro fertilization couples. *Fertility and Sterility, 46,* 668–672.

Fawcett, J., & York, R. (1986). Spouses' physical and psychological symptoms during pregnancy and the postpartum. *Nursing Research, 35,* 144–148.

Field, T., Sandberg, D., Quetel, T. A., Garcia, R., & Rosario, M. (1985). Effects of ultrasound feedback on pregnancy anxiety, fetal activity, and neonatal outcome. *Obstetrics and Gynecology, 66,* 525–528.

Filer, R. B. (1992). Endocrinology of the postpartum period. In J. A. Hamilton & P. N. Harberger (Eds.), *Postpartum psychiatric illness: A picture puzzle* (pp. 153–163). Philadelphia: University of Pennsylvania Press.

Fink, R. M., & Windt, A. (1984). Depression during the prepartum and postpartum period. *Birth Psychology Bulletin, 5*(2), 1–22.

Fouad, N. A., & Fahje, K. K. (1989). An exploratory study of the psychological correlates of infertility on women. *Journal of Counseling and Development, 68,* 97–101.

Franklin, S. (1990). Deconstructing "desperateness": The social construction of infertility in popular representations of new reproductive technologies. In M. McNeil, I. Varcoe, & S. Yearley (Eds.), *The new reproductive technologies* (pp. 200–229). New York: St. Martin's Press.

Freeman, E. W., Boxer, A. S., Rickels, K., Tureck, R., & Mastroianni, L. (1985). Psychological evaluation and support in a program of in vitro fertilization and embryo transfer. *Fertility and Sterility, 43,* 48–53.

Freeman, E. W., Garcia, C., & Rickels, K. (1983). Behavioral and emotional factors: Comparisons of anovulatory infertile women with fertile and other infertile women. *Fertility and Sterility, 40,* 195–201.

Garcia, C., Freeman, E. W., Rickels, K., Wu, C., Scholl, G., Galle, P. C., & Boxer, A. S. (1985). Behavioral and emotional factors and treatment responses in a study of anovulatory infertile women. *Fertility and Sterility, 44,* 478–483.

Gard, P. R., Handley, S. L., Parsons, A. D., & Waldron, G. (1986). A multivariate investigation of postpartum mood disturbance. *British Journal of Psychiatry, 148,* 567–575.

George, A., & Sandler, M. (1988). Endocrine and biochemical studies in puerperal mental disorders. In R. Kumar & I. F. Brockington (Eds.), *Motherhood and mental illness 2: Causes and consequences* (pp. 78–112). London: Wright.

Giblin, P. T., Poland, M. L., Moghissi, K. S., Ager, J. W., & Olson, J. M. (1988). Effects of stress and characteristic adaptability on semen quality in healthy men. *Fertility and Sterility, 49,* 127–132.

Gitlin, M. J., & Pasnau, R. O. (1989). Psychiatric syndromes linked to reproductive function in women: A review of current knowledge. *American Journal of Psychiatry, 146,* 1413–1422.

Gjerdingen, D. K., Froberg, D. G., & Kochevar, L. (1991). Changes in women's mental and physical health from pregnancy through six months postpartum. *Journal of Family Practice, 32,* 161–166.

Gotlib, I. H., Whiffen, V. E., Mount, J. H., Milne, K., & Cordy, N. I. (1989). Prevalence rates and demographic characteristics associated with depression in pregnancy and the postpartum. *Journal of Consulting and Clinical Psychology, 57,* 269–274.

Gotlib, I. H., Whiffen, V. E., Wallace, P. M., & Mount, J. H. (1991). Prospective investigation of postpartum depression: Factors involved in onset and recovery. *Journal of Abnormal Psychology, 100,* 122–132.

Gould, J. B., Davey, B., & Stafford, R. S. (1989). Socioeconomic differences in rates of cesarean section. *New England Journal of Medicine, 321,* 233–239.

Green, J. M. (1990). Prenatal screening and diagnosis: Some psychological and social issues. *British Journal of Obstetrics and Gynaecology, 97,* 1074–1076.

Greene, P. G., Zeichner, A., Roberts, N. L., Callahan, E. J., & Granados, J. (1989). Preparation for cesarean delivery: A multicomponent analysis of treatment outcome. *Journal of Consulting and Clinical Psychology, 57,* 484–487.

Greil, A. L., Leitko, T. A., & Porter, K. L. (1988). Infertility: His and hers. *Gender and Society, 2,* 172–199.

Grimes, D. A. (1993). Technology follies: The uncritical acceptance of medical innovation. *Journal of the American Medical Association, 269,* 3030–3033.

Halonen, J. S., & Passman, R. H. (1985). Relaxation training and expectation in the treatment of postpartum distress. *Journal of Consulting and Clinical Psychology, 53,* 839–845.

Hamilton, J. A. (1989). Psychiatric illness after childbearing. In J. G. Howells (Ed.), *Modern perspectives in the psychiatry of affective disorders,* (Vol. 13, pp. 275–291). New York: Brunner/Mazel.

Hamilton, J. A. (1992). The issue of unique qualities. In J. A. Hamilton & P. N. Harberger (Eds.), *Postpartum psychiatric illness: A picture puzzle* (pp. 15–32). Philadelphia: University of Pennsylvania Press.

Hamilton, J. A., & Harberger, P. N. (1992). *Postpartum psychiatric illness: A picture puzzle.* Philadelphia: University of Pennsylvania Press.

Hannah, P., Adams, D., Lee, A., Glover, V., & Sandler, M. (1992). Links between early post-partum mood and post-natal depression. *British Journal of Psychiatry, 160,* 777–780.

Hapgood, C. C., Elkind, G. S., & Wright, J. J. (1988). Maternity blues: Phenomena and relationship to later post partum depression. *Australian and New Zealand Journal of Psychiatry, 22,* 299–306.

Harding, J. J. (1989). Postpartum psychiatric disorders: A review. *Comprehensive Psychiatry, 30,* 109–112.

Harris, B., Huckle, P., Thomas, R., Johns, S., & Fung, H. (1989). The use of ratings scales to identify post-natal depression. *British Journal of Psychiatry, 154,* 813–817.

Harrison, K. L., Callan, V. J., & Hennessey, J. F. (1987). Stress and semen quality in an in vitro fertilization program. *Fertility and Sterility, 48,* 633–636.

Haseltine, F. P., Mazure, C., De L'aune, W., Greenfeld, D., Laufer, N., Tarlatzis, B., Polan, M. L., Jones, E. E., Graebe, R., Nero, F., D'Lugi, A., Fazio, D., Masters, J., & DeCherney, A. H. (1985). Psychological interviews in screening couples undergoing *in vitro* fertilization. *Annals of the New York Academy of Sciences, 442,* 504–522.

Hearn, M. T., Yuzpe, A. A., Brown, S. E., & Casper, R. F. (1987). Psychological characteristics of in vitro fertilization participants. *American Journal of Obstetrics and Gynecology, 156,* 269–274.

Hopkins, J., Marcus, M., & Campbell, S. B. (1984). Postpartum depression: A critical review. *Psychological Bulletin, 95,* 489–515.

Hubbard, R. (1990). *The politics of women's biology.* New Brunswick, NJ: Rutgers University Press.

Huffman, L. C., Lamour, M., Bryan, Y. E., & Pederson, F. A. (1990). Depressive symptomatology during pregnancy and the postpartum period: Is the Beck Depression Inventory applicable? *Journal of Reproductive and Infant Psychology, 8,* 87–97.

Iles, S., Gath, D., & Kennerley, H. (1989). Maternity blues II. A comparison between post-operative women and post-natal women. *British Journal of Psychiatry, 155,* 363–366.

Istvan, J. (1986). Stress, anxiety, and birth outcomes: A critical review of the evidence. *Psychological Bulletin, 100,* 331–348.

Jacobson, C. K., & Heaton, T. B. (1991). Voluntary childlessness among American men and women in the late 1980's. *Social Biology, 38*(1/2), 79–93.

Kendell, R. E. (1985). Emotional and physical factors in the genesis of puerperal mental disorders. *Journal of Psychosomatic Research, 29,* 3–11.

Kendell, R. E., McGuire, R. J., Connor, Y., & Cox, J. L. (1981). Mood changes in the first three weeks after childbirth. *Journal of Affective Disorders, 3,* 317–326.

Kennerley, H., & Gath, D. (1989). Maternity blues III. Associations with obstetric, psychological, and psychiatric factors. *British Journal of Psychiatry, 155,* 367–373.

Kessler, R. C., & McLeod, J. D. (1984). Sex differences in vulnerability to undesirable life events. *American Sociological Review, 49,* 620–631.

Kishwar, M. (1987). The continuing deficit of women in India and the impact of amniocentesis. In G. Corea, R. D. Klein, J. Hanmer, H. B. Holmes, B. Hoskins, M. Kishwar, J. Raymond, R. Rowland, & R. Steinbacher (Eds.), *Man-made women: How new reproductive technologies affect women* (pp. 30–37). London: Hutchinson.

Klein, R. (1991). Women as body parts in the era of reproductive and genetic engineering. *Health Care for Women International, 12,* 393–405.

Knight, R. G., & Thirkettle, J. A. (1986). Anxiety and depression in the immediate post-partum period: A controlled investigation of a primiparous sample. *Australian and New Zealand Journal of Psychiatry, 20,* 430–436.

Kolder, V. E. B., Gallagher, J., & Parsons, M. T. (1987). Court-ordered obstetrical interventions. *New England Journal of Medicine, 316,* 1192–1196.

Koropatnick, S., Daniluk, J., & Pattinson, H. A. (1993). Infertility: A non-event transition. *Fertility and Sterility, 59,* 163–171.

Kumar, R., & Brockington, I. F. (Eds.). (1988). *Motherhood and mental illness 2: Causes and consequences.* London: Wright.

Lalos, A., Lalos, O., Jacobsson, L., & Von Schoultz, B. (1985). A psychosocial characterization of infertile couples before surgical treatment of the female. *Journal of Psychosomatic Obstetrics and Gynaecology, 4,* 83–93.

Langer, M., Ringler, M., & Reinold, E. (1988). Psychological effects of ultrasound examinations: Changes of body perception and child image in pregnancy. *Journal of Psychosomatic Obstetrics and Gynaecology, 8,* 199–208.

Lazarus, R. S., & Folkman, S. (1984). *Stress, appraisal, and coping.* New York: Springer.

Leiblum, S. R., Kemmann, E., & Lane, M. K. (1987). The psychological concomitants of in vitro fertilization. *Journal of Psychosomatic Obstetrics and Gynaecology, 6,* 165–178.

Levy, V. (1987). The maternity blues in post-partum and post-operative women. *British Journal of Psychiatry, 151,* 368–372.

Link, P. W., & Darling, C. A. (1986). Couples undergoing treatment for infertility: Dimensions of life satisfaction. *Journal of Sex and Marital Therapy, 12,* 46–59.

Lips, H. M. (1985). A longitudinal study of the reporting of emotional and somatic symptoms during and after pregnancy. *Social Science and Medicine, 21,* 631–640.

Litt, M. D., Tennen, H., Affleck, G., & Klock, S. (1992). Coping and cognitive factors in adaptation to *in vitro* fertilization failure. *Journal of Behavioral Medicine, 15,* 171–187.

Lobel, M. (1994). Conceptualizations, measurement, and effects of prenatal maternal stress on birth outcomes. *Journal of Behavioral Medicine, 17,* 225–272.

Lobel, M., Dunkel-Schetter, C., & Scrimshaw, S. C. M. (1992). The role of prenatal maternal stress in infant prematurity. *Health Psychology, 11,* 32–40.

Localio, A. R., Lawthers, A. G., Bengtson, J. M., Hebert, L. E., Weaver, S. L., Brennan, T. A., & Landis, J. R. (1993). Relationship between malpractice claims and cesarean delivery. *Journal of the American Medical Association, 269,* 366–373.

Lukse, M. P. (1985). The effect of group counseling on the frequency of grief reported by infertile couples. *Journal of Obstetric, Gynecologic, and Neonatal Nursing, 14,* 67–70.

Lydon, J., & Dunkel-Schetter, C. (1994). Seeing is committing: A longitudinal study of bolstering commitment in amniocentesis patients. *Journal of Personality and Social Psychology, 20,* 218–227.

Manly, P. C., McMahon, R. J., Bradley, C. F., & Davidson, P. O. (1982). Depressive attributional style and depression following childbirth. *Journal of Abnormal Psychology, 91,* 245–254.

Marieskind, H. I. (1982). Cesarean section. *Women and Health, 7*(3/4), 179–198.

Marks, M. N., Wieck, A., Checkley, S. A., & Kumar, R. (1991). Life stress and post-partum psychosis: A preliminary report. *British Journal of Psychiatry, 158*(Suppl. 10), 45–49.

McEwan, K. L., Costello, C. G., & Taylor, P. J. (1987). Adjustment to infertility. *Journal of Abnormal Psychology, 96,* 108–116.

Menning, B. E. (1977). *Infertility: A guide for the childless couple.* Englewood Cliffs, NJ: Prentice–Hall.

Miall, C. E. (1986). The stigma of involuntary childlessness. *Social Problems, 33,* 268–282.

Michaels, G. Y., & Goldberg, W. A. (Eds.). (1988). *The transition to parenthood: Current theory and research.* New York: Cambridge University Press.

Micioni, G., Jeker, L., Zeeb, M., & Campana, A. (1987). Doubtful and negative psychological indications for A.I.D. A study of 835 couples. Treatment outcome in couples with doubtful indication. *Journal of Psychosomatic Obstetrics and Gynaecology, 6,* 89–99.

Mies, M. (1987). Why do we need all this? A call against genetic engineering and reproductive technology. In P. Spallone & D. L. Steinberg (Eds.), *Made to order: The myth of reproductive and genetic progress* (pp. 34–47). Oxford: Pergamon Press.

Miller, S. M., & Kirsch, N. (1987). Sex differences in cognitive coping with stress. In R. C. Barnett, L. Biener, & G. K. Baruch (Eds.), *Gender and stress* (pp. 278–307). New York: Free Press.

Mosher, W. D., & Pratt, W. F. (1990). Fecundity and infertility in the United States, 1965–1988. *Advance Data from Vital and Health Statistics,* no. 192. Hyattsville, MD: National Center for Health Statistics.

Myers, J. K., Weissman, M. M., Tischler, G. L., Holzer, C. E., Leaf, P. J., Orvaschel, H., Anthony, J. C., Boyd, J. H., Burke, J. D., Kramer, M., & Stoltzman, R. (1984). Six-month prevalence of psychiatric disorders in three communities. *Archives of General Psychiatry, 41,* 959–967.

National Center for Health Statistics. (1993). Rates of cesarean delivery—United States, 1991. *Morbidity and Mortality Weekly Report, 482,* 285–289.

Nelson, M. K. (1981). Client responses to a discrepancy between the care they want and the care they receive. *Women & Health, 6*(3/4), 135–152.

Newton, C. R., Hearn, M. T., & Yuzpe, A. A. (1990). Psychological assessment and follow-up after in vitro fertilization: Assessing the impact of failure. *Fertility and Sterility, 54,* 879–886.

WOMEN'S REPRODUCTIVE HEALTH

Nurnberg, H. G. (1989). An overview of somatic treatment of psychosis during pregnancy and postpartum. General Hospital Psychiatry, 11, 328–338.
O'Hara, M. W. (1985). Depression and marital adjustment during pregnancy and after delivery. American Journal of Family Therapy, 13(4), 49–55.
O'Hara, M. W. (1987). Post-partum "blues," depression, and psychosis: A review. Journal of Psychosomatic Obstetrics and Gynaecology, 7, 205–227.
O'Hara, M. W. (1991). Postpartum mental disorders. In J. J. Sciarra (Ed.), Gynecology and Obstetrics (Vol. 6). Philadelphia: Harper & Row.
O'Hara, M. W., Hoffman, J. G., Philipps, L. H. C., & Wright, E. J. (1992). Adjustment in childbearing women: The Postpartum Adjustment Questionnaire. Psychological Assessment, 4, 160–169.
O'Hara, M. W., Neunaber, D. J., & Zekoski, E. M. (1984). Prospective study of postpartum depression: Prevalence, course, and predictive factors. Journal of Abnormal Psychology, 93, 158–171.
O'Hara, M. W., Rehm, L. P., & Campbell, S. B. (1982). Predicting depressive symptomatology: Cognitive–behavioral models and postpartum depression. Journal of Abnormal Psychology, 91, 457–461.
O'Hara, M. W., Reiter, R. C., Johnson, S. R., Milburn, A., & Engeldinger, J. (1995). Psychological aspects of women's reproductive health. New York: Springer.
O'Hara, M. W., Schlechte, J. A., Lewis, D. A., & Varner, M. W. (1991). Controlled prospective study of postpartum mood disorders: Psychological, environmental, and hormonal variables. Journal of Abnormal Psychology, 100, 63–73.
O'Hara, M. W., Schlechte, J. A., Lewis, D. A., & Wright, E. J. (1991). Prospective study of postpartum blues: Biologic and psychosocial factors. Archives of General Psychiatry, 48, 801–806.
O'Hara, M. W., Zekoski, E. M., Philipps, L. H., & Wright, E. J. (1990). Controlled prospective study of postpartum mood disorders: Comparison of childbearing and nonchildbearing women. Journal of Abnormal Psychology, 99, 3–15.
Olioff, M., & Aboud, F. E. (1991). Predicting postpartum dysphoria in primiparous mothers: Roles of perceived parenting self-efficacy and self-esteem. Journal of Cognitive Psychotherapy: An International Quarterly, 5, 3–14.
Padawer, J. A., Fagan, C., Janoff-Bulman, R., & Strickland, B. R. (1988). Women's psychological adjustment following emergency cesarean versus vaginal delivery. Psychology of Women Quarterly, 12, 25–34.
Paulson, J. D., Haarmann, B. S., Salerno, R. L., & Asmar, P. (1988). An investigation

301

of the relationship between emotional maladjustment and infertility. *Fertility and Sterility, 49,* 258–262.

Pfost, K. S., Lum, C. U., & Stevens, M. J. (1989). Femininity and work plans protect women against postpartum dysphoria. *Sex Roles, 21,* 423–431.

Philipps, L. H. C., & O'Hara, M. W. (1991). Prospective study of postpartum depression: $4^1/_2$-year follow-up of women and children. *Journal of Abnormal Psychology, 100,* 151–155.

Phipps, S., & Zinn, A. B. (1986). Psychological response to amniocentesis: I. Mood state and adaptation to pregnancy. *American Journal of Medical Genetics, 25,* 131–142.

Platz, C., & Kendell, R. E. (1988). A matched-control follow-up and family study of "puerperal psychoses." *British Journal of Psychiatry, 153,* 90–94.

Raskin, V. D., Richman, J. A., & Gaines, C. (1990). Patterns of depressive symptoms in expectant and new parents. *American Journal of Psychiatry, 147,* 658–660.

Reading, A. E., Chang, L. C., & Kerin, J. F. (1989). Psychological state and coping styles across an IVF treatment cycle. *Journal of Reproductive and Infant Psychology, 7,* 95–103.

Reading, A. E., & Cox, D. N. (1982). The effects of ultrasound examination on maternal anxiety levels. *Journal of Behavioral Medicine, 5,* 237–247.

Richman, J. A., Raskin, V. D., & Gaines, C. (1991). Gender roles, social support, and postpartum depression symptomatology: The benefits of caring. *Journal of Nervous and Mental Disease, 179,* 139–147.

Rodin, J., & Collins, A. (1991). The new reproductive technologies: Overview of the challenges and issues. In J. Rodin & A. Collins (Eds.), *Women and new reproductive technologies: Medical, psychosocial, legal, and ethical dilemmas* (pp. 1–10). Hillsdale, NJ: Erlbaum.

Rosenberg, S. A., Darby, J., & Robinson, C. C. (1984). Mothers' emotional responses to pregnancy and delivery. *Birth Psychology Bulletin, 5*(1), 1–8.

Rosser, S. V. (1986). *Teaching science and health from a feminist perspective.* New York: Pergamon.

Rothman, B. K. (1986). *The tentative pregnancy.* New York: Penguin.

Ruble, D. N., Brooks-Gunn, J., Fleming, A. J., Fitzmaurice, G., Stangor, C., & Deutsch, F. (1990). Transition to motherhood and the self: Measurement, stability, and change. *Journal of Personality and Social Psychology, 58,* 450–463.

Russo, N. F. (1979). Overview: Sex roles, fertility, and the motherhood mandate. *Psychology of Women Quarterly, 4,* 7–15.

Ruzek, S. (1991). Women's reproductive rights: The impact of technology. In J. Rodin & A. Collins (Eds.), *Women and new reproductive technologies: Medical, psychosocial, legal, and ethical dilemmas* (pp. 65–87). Hillsdale, NJ: Erlbaum.

Sandler, B. (1968). Emotional stress and infertility. *Journal of Psychosomatic Research, 12*, 51–59.

Sauer, M. V., Paulson, R. J., & Lobo, R. A. (1992). Reversing the natural decline in human fertility: An extended clinical trial of oocyte donation to women of advanced reproductive age. *Journal of the American Medical Association, 268*, 1275–1279.

Schoendorf, K. C., Hogue, C. J. R., Kleinman, J. C., & Rowley, D. (1992). Mortality among infants of black as compared with white college-educated parents. *New England Journal of Medicine, 326*, 1522–1526.

Society for Assisted Reproductive Technology, The American Fertility Society. (1994). Assisted reproductive technology in the United States and Canada: 1992 results from The American Fertility Society/Society for Assisted Reproductive Technology Registry. *Fertility and Sterility, 62*, 1121–1128.

Spencer, J. W., & Cox, D. N. (1988). A comparison of chorionic villi sampling and amniocentesis: Acceptability of procedure and maternal attachment to pregnancy. *Obstetrics and Gynecology, 72*, 714–718.

Spirtas, R., Kaufman, S. C., & Alexander, N. J. (1993). Fertility drugs and ovarian cancer: Red alert or red herring? *Fertility and Sterility, 59*, 291–293.

Spitzer, R. L., Endicott, J., & Robins, E. (1978). Research diagnostic criteria: Rationale and reliability. *Archives and General Psychiatry, 36*, 773–782.

Spock, B. (1969). Mothers who try to be all things. *Redbook, 132*(5), 60–65.

Stafford, R. S. (1990). Cesarean section use and source of payment: An analysis of California hospital discharge abstracts. *American Journal of Public Health, 80*, 313–315.

Stanton, A. L. (1991). Cognitive appraisals, coping processes, and adjustment to infertility. In A. L. Stanton & C. Dunkel-Schetter (Eds.), *Infertility: Perspectives from stress and coping research* (pp. 87–108). New York: Plenum.

Stanton, A. L., & Dunkel-Schetter, C. (Eds.). (1991). *Infertility: Perspectives from stress and coping research*. New York: Plenum.

Stanton, A. L., McQueeney, D. A., & Sigmon, S. T. (1991, August). Efficacy of emotion-focused and problem-focused group therapies for infertile women. In A. L. Stanton & A. Abbey (Chairs), *Infertility: Psychosocial influences on adjustment and coping skills interventions*. Symposium conducted at the annual meeting of the American Psychological Association, San Francisco.

Stanworth, M. (1987). Reproductive technologies and the deconstruction of motherhood. In M. Stanworth (Ed.), *Reproductive technologies: Gender, motherhood and medicine* (pp. 10–35). Minneapolis: University of Minnesota Press.

Steiner, M. (1990). Postpartum psychiatric disorders. *Canadian Journal of Psychiatry, 35,* 89–95.

Stewart, D. E., Boydell, K. M., McCarthy, K., Swerdlyk, S., Redmond, C., & Cohrs, W. (1992). A prospective study of the effectiveness of brief professionally-led support groups for infertility patients. *International Journal of Psychiatry in Medicine, 22,* 173–182.

Tadmor, C. S. (1988). The perceived personal control preventive intervention for a caesarean birth population. In R. H. Price, E. L. Cowan, R. P. Lorion, & J. Ramos-McKay (Eds.), *14 ounces of prevention: A casebook for practitioners* (pp. 141–152). Washington, DC: American Psychological Association.

Taffel, S. M. (1989). Cesarean section in America: Dramatic trends, 1970 to 1987. *Statistical Bulletin, 70,* 2–11.

Tennen, H., Affleck, G., & Mendola, R. (1991). Causal explanations for infertility: Their relation to control appraisals and psychological adjustment. In A. L. Stanton & C. Dunkel-Schetter (Eds.), *Infertility: Perspectives from stress and coping research* (pp. 109–131). New York: Plenum.

Thirkettle, J. A., & Knight, R. G. (1985). The psychological precipitants of transient postpartum depression: A review. *Current Psychological Research and Reviews, 4,* 143–166.

Troutman, B. R., & Cutrona, C. E. (1990). Nonpsychotic postpartum depression among adolescent mothers. *Journal of Abnormal Psychology, 99,* 69–78.

Tsoi, M. M., Hunter, M., Pearce, M., Chudleigh, P., & Campbell, S. (1987). Ultrasound scanning in women with raised serum alpha fetoprotein: Short term psychological effect. *Journal of Psychosomatic Research, 31*(1), 35–39.

U.S. Bureau of the Census. (1993). *Statistical abstract of the United States: 1993* (13th ed.). Washington, DC: Author.

U.S. Congress, Office of Technology Assessment. (1988). *Infertility: Medical and social choices,* OTA-BA-358. Washington, DC: U.S. Government Printing Office.

Wajcman, J. (1991). *Feminism confronts technology.* University Park: Pennsylvania State University Press.

Watson, D., & Tellegen, A. (1985). Toward a consensual structure of mood. *Psychological Bulletin, 98,* 219–235.

Watson, E., & Evans, S. J. W. (1986). An example of cross-cultural measurement of psychological symptoms in post-partum mothers. *Social Science and Medicine, 23,* 869–874.

Wertz, D. C., & Fletcher, J. C. (1993). A critique of some feminist challenges to prenatal diagnosis. *Journal of Women's Health, 2*(2), 173–188.

Wertz, R. W., & Wertz, D. C. (1989). *Lying-in: A history of childbirth in America.* New Haven: Yale University Press.

Whiffen, V. E. (1988). Screening for postpartum depression: A methodological note. *Journal of Clinical Psychology, 44,* 367–371.

Whiffen, V. E. (1991). The comparison of postpartum with non-postpartum depression: A rose by any other name. *Journal of Psychiatry and Neuroscience, 16,* 160–165.

Whiffen, V. E. (1992). Is postpartum depression a distinct diagnosis? *Clinical Psychology Review, 12,* 485–508.

Whiffen, V. E., & Gotlib, I. H. (1989). Infants of postpartum depressed mothers: Temperament and cognitive status. *Journal of Abnormal Psychology, 98,* 274–279.

Whiffen, V. E., & Gotlib, I. H. (1993). A comparison of postpartum and non-postpartum depression: Clinical presentation, psychiatric history, and psychosocial functioning. *Journal of Consulting and Clinical Psychology, 61,* 485–494.

Wideman, M. V., & Singer, J. E. (1984). The role of psychological mechanisms in preparation for childbirth. *American Psychologist, 39,* 1357–1371.

Wieck, A., Kumar, R., Hirst, A. D., Marks, M. N., Campbell, I. C., & Checkley, S. A. (1991). Increased sensitivity of dopamine receptors and recurrence of affective psychosis after birth. *British Medical Journal, 303,* 613–616.

Wortman, C., & Silver, R. (1987). Coping with irrevocable loss. In G. R. VandenBos & B. K. Bryant (Eds.), *Cataclysms, crises, and catastrophes: Psychology in action* (pp. 189–235). Washington, DC: American Psychological Association.

Wright, J., Duchesne, C., Sabourin, S., Bissonnette, F., Benoit, J., & Girard, Y. (1991). Psychosocial distress and infertility: Men and women respond differently. *Fertility and Sterility, 55,* 100–108.

PART FOUR

Health-Related Behaviors

9

Women and Smoking

Robin J. Mermelstein and Belinda Borrelli

I n the United States today, more women die from smoking-related diseases than from any other cause. Lung cancer now surpasses breast cancer as the leading cause of cancer death in women (American Cancer Society, 1993). Compared with nonsmokers, both male and female smokers
have an increased risk for a variety of cancers, coronary heart disease,
stroke, emphysema, bronchitis, and respiratory infections (U. S. Department of Health and Human Services [USDHHS], 1989). Women smokers have some additional, unique concerns, including increased risks of
cervical cancer, early menopause, decreased fertility, osteoporosis, and
complications of oral contraceptive use (USDHHS, 1980; 1989). A
woman's smoking affects not only her own health, but that of her fetus
and children as well. Smoking during pregnancy is a risk factor for low
birthweight and infant mortality, including sudden infant death syndrome
(USDHHS, 1980). Maternal smoking during pregnancy may also adversely affect the child's long-term growth and intellectual development
(USDHHS, 1980).

The writing of this chapter was supported in part by NHLBI grant HL42485 and NCI grant CA 42760.

Few everyday behaviors have such far-reaching and devastating con-sequences as smoking. This chapter reviews patterns of women's smoking: why women start to smoke, continue to smoke, stop smoking, or fail to do so. We discuss whether treatments need to be tailored to women and to special subpopulations of women, and areas where there may be gen-der differences in treatments or outcomes. In two excellent recent review papers, Grunberg, Winders, and Wewers (1991) and Waldron (1991) clearly documented that gender differences in tobacco use do exist, and reviewed possible reasons for these differences, including psychosocial and biological reasons. We will not duplicate those reviews, but instead, will focus on more recent research not covered in their reviews and the im-plication of gender differences for intervention and policy.

PATTERNS AND PREVALENCE OF SMOKING

Until the 1970s, there was a common misconception that women were im-mune to the damaging effects of smoking that were already well-documented for men (USDHHS, 1980). This illusion of immunity re-flected gender differences in patterns of smoking behavior and related problematic sampling strategies in studies of smoking-related health risks. Early studies examining the relative mortality risks between male and fe-male smokers were compromised by their comparisons of men who were long-term, relatively heavy smokers with women who were more recent, lighter smokers. As women's and men's smoking patterns started to con-verge, so did their health risks.

Prior to World War II, relatively few women in the United States smoked. Men, though, started smoking in large numbers at the beginning of the twentieth century, and by the early 1950s, more than 60 percent of adult men smoked (USDHHS, 1980). In 1964, the first Surgeon General's report concluded that cigarette smoking is a major health hazard. Fol-lowing that report, smoking prevalence among adult males started a steady fall from 50 percent in 1965 to 28.1 percent in 1991 (Centers for Disease Control [CDC], 1993).

Women's smoking has lagged behind that of men's both in its growth and its subsequent decline. Women started smoking in significant numbers at the start of World War II, when 25 percent of adult women smoked (USDHHS, 1980). Smoking prevalence among women peaked at 32 percent in the mid-60s and stayed level through the mid-70s, rather than declining as did the prevalence rates among men (USDHHS, 1989). Since the mid-70s, smoking rates have declined for women, although not as rapidly as they have for men. In 1990, 22.8 percent of adult women in the United States smoked, and in 1991, smoking prevalence among adult women was 23.5 percent (CDC, 1993). This leveling of prevalence rates may be due, in part, to the growth in discount cigarettes.

The overall prevalence rates for women are misleading because they mask important ethnic, educational, and economic differences. The prevalence of smoking among women in the United States is highest among Native Americans (35.2% in 1991; CDC, 1993) and lowest among Asians and Pacific Islanders (7.5% in 1991). Hispanic women in the United States also have a relatively low prevalence of smoking (15.5% in 1991), although among different Hispanic groups, prevalence varies greatly (Escobedo, Remington, & Anda, 1989). Differences in prevalence rates between Black and White women are much less (24.4% versus 23.8% in 1991). Smoking prevalence also varies significantly by education and economic status. Among women, smoking is most prevalent among those with no more than a high school education and those who live below the poverty level (CDC, 1993). These differences in smoking prevalence are important to understanding why women smoke and to developing and targeting interventions to address the diverse needs of population subgroups. Future interventions need to target specifically women with lower educational levels and poorer economic status. Future research also needs to try to disentangle the effects of education, ethnicity, and economic status on smoking prevalence.

Smoking prevalence rates are a function of two factors: the number of individuals who stop smoking each year and the number who start. Initiation rates are especially important because projections can be made from them about who will comprise the smoking population of the future. Since most smoking initiation occurs by age 21 (Geronimus, Neidert,

& Bound, 1993), surveys of high school seniors provide a good picture of initiation rates. Prevalence of daily smoking among female high school seniors equaled that of males in 1976 (Johnston, O'Malley, & Bachman, 1993). Between 1977 and 1981, daily smoking prevalence declined for both male and female adolescents, although as with adults, the decline was greater among males. Thus, female adolescents had a higher rate of smoking from 1977 to 1988. Since 1988, though, there have been no sex differences in smoking prevalence among high school seniors. In 1991, slightly over 17 percent of high school seniors smoked every day (Johnston et al., 1992), and these rates were essentially the same for males and females. However, these prevalence rates reflect a lower risk group: teenagers who were still in high school. Among teenagers who drop out of school, both males and females, the prevalence of smoking is much higher (CDC, 1991).

As with adults, though, the overall prevalence rates and changes in rates for adolescents mask important subpopulation differences and trends. Since 1981, there has been a consistent and significant decline in smoking among Blacks, and virtually no decline among Whites (Bachman et al., 1991; Johnston et al., 1993). Differences in smoking prevalence between those with and without college aspirations still remain large, though. Extrapolating from these trends, White women with no more than a high school education will make up a significant proportion of the future smoking population. It is not yet clear why this gap exists between Black and White youth smoking patterns, and more research is needed exploring why prevalence rates among White youths are not declining as rapidly as among Blacks.

One major gender difference still exists in tobacco use among teenagers: the rate of use of smokeless tobacco. Smokeless tobacco use has increased rapidly among teenage males, but its use among teenage girls has remained low, about 1 to 3 percent (USDHHS, 1992).

In sum, there are several important conclusions when we consider the trends in smoking prevalence over the past decade. First, smoking is equally prevalent among boys and girls. Second, educational aspirations remain a major predictor of who smokes. Third, although smoking rates have declined significantly among Blacks, Whites are not showing the same progress. It is now estimated that given these trends, males will continue to have higher prevalence rates than females through 2000, and any crossover in rates that might occur, would not happen until after then (Giovino, Shelton, & Schooley, in press). As the sociodemographic characteristics of women smokers change toward less-educated and lower-socioeconomic groups, new approaches to reach these target populations may be needed.

These prevalence rates remain unacceptably high when one considers the significant health hazards associated with smoking. Why, then, do so many women, and particularly White women, still smoke? To answer this question, we need to look at why women start to smoke, continue to smoke, and may have trouble quitting.

INITIATION: WHY WOMEN START TO SMOKE

Smoking initiation is a gradual process, beginning very early in adolescence and progressing through several stages, starting with thinking about smoking cigarettes and then for some, moving on to experimenting with cigarettes (Flay, d'Avernas, Best, Kersell, & Ryan, 1983). At the experimenter stage, adolescents may decide to quit or to continue experimenting often enough to become regular smokers. The progression from experimentation to regular use is a critical transition, since dependency rapidly develops (USDHHS, 1988). Boys and girls differ somewhat in their patterns of initiation. Boys experiment with cigarettes at earlier ages than do girls, but about the middle of junior high school, girls start to experiment more frequently than boys (Cohen, Brownell, & Felix, 1990). Among females, there are important racial differences in age of initiation. Black women start smoking at much older ages than do White women (Geronimus et al., 1993). Girls' experimentation needs to be taken seriously since they are almost twice as likely as boys to become regular smokers within the first year of initial experimentation and are also twice as likely to continue smoking four years later (Ershler, Leventhal, Fleming, & Glynn, 1989). Thus, reasons for starting to smoke and reactions to smoking (both psychological and physiological) are likely to differ for boys and girls.

Adolescents start to smoke for a multitude of reasons, including social influences, personality factors, and perceived benefits of smoking (e.g.,
weight control, affect regulation, and coping). Conrad and Flay (1992) reviewed findings from 27 prospective studies and found strong support for
the expected relationships between smoking onset and the following variables: (a) lower socioeconomic status; (b) social bonding variables, particularly peer and school bonding; (c) social learning variables, especially
peer smoking and approval, subjective prevalence estimates, and offers or
availability of cigarettes; (d) self-efficacy for refusing cigarettes; (e) knowledge, attitudes, and intentions; and (f) broad indicators of self-esteem.
Each of these factors may be differentially important for males and females, though relatively few studies have specifically examined the relative
importance of these variables separately by gender.

Social influence processes are among the best predictors of adolescent
smoking and also may have differential effects by gender. Adolescents'
smoking is strongly associated with peer smoking (Friedman, Lichtenstein,
& Biglan, 1985), and most notably, with having close friends who smoke
(Santi, Best, Brown, & Cargo, 1990–1991). The relative influence of peer
smoking on males and females may vary with age. Studies with younger
adolescents have found either no gender differences in peer influence (Mc-
Caul, Glasgow, O'Neill, Freeborn, & Pump, 1982) or that boys are more
influenced by their friends than girls (van Roosmalen & McDaniel, 1989).
However, the role of peers in facilitating female adolescent smoking may
become stronger over time. Chassin and her colleagues (Chassin, Presson,
Sherman, Montello, & McGrew, 1986) found that peer influences were significant for girls but not for boys between the 6th and 11th grades. Among
6th to 11th graders, the number of friends who smoked was related to
smoking intentions for girls, but not for boys (Presson et al., 1984). Hover
and Gaffney (1988) found that adolescent female smokers had significantly
lower levels of social skills than female nonsmokers, thus suggesting one
possible mechanism by which adolescent females may be susceptible to
the influence of smoking peers.

Parental smoking also plays a significant role in smoking initiation in
female adolescents. Some studies have found that females are more influ-

enced by familial smoking than males (Aaro, Hauknes, & Berglund, 1981; Charlton & Blair, 1989). Other studies, though, have found that the influence of other smokers in the family may vary by the gender match and age. Across a variety of ages, Murray, Kiryluk, and Swan (1985) found that boys were more likely to smoke if their fathers smoked, and girls were more likely to smoke if their mothers smoked. Similarly, Gottlieb (1982) found that maternal smoking was related to older adolescents' smoking, but smoking by a father or brother was not.

Studies by Kandel and her colleagues indicate that mothers may influence their children's smoking more than fathers (Kandel, Wu, & Davies, 1994). Kandel, Wu, and Davies (1994) examined the consequences of maternal smoking during pregnancy on children's smoking during adolescence. In two longitudinal samples, Kandel et al. found a significant association between maternal smoking during pregnancy and the child's smoking 13 years later. Importantly, the maternal effect of smoking during pregnancy was stronger on daughters than on sons, and especially for the child's continued smoking beyond experimentation. Thus, maternal smoking during pregnancy may pose a serious risk for smoking dependence in female children. Kandel and colleagues note that it is not clear why the intergenerational transmission of smoking from mother to child is stronger for daughters than sons, but hypothesize that perhaps the distinct gender differences in the fetal development of the brain, including hormonal and structural factors, may contribute to this sex difference.

Social influence processes affecting initiation go beyond the normative influences of direct peer pressure or modeling presented by family members and also include informational processes that affect the attitudes and values of children and adolescents. Of particular concern is the role of cigarette advertising in promoting female smoking. There is a growing body of literature describing children's awareness of and attitudes about cigarette advertisements, and the association of that awareness and attitudes to the children's smoking intentions and behaviors (Aitken, Eadie, Hastings, & Haywood, 1991; Fischer, Schwartz, Richards, Goldstein, & Rojas, 1991; Pierce et al., 1991). In the late 1960s, tobacco companies specifically started to target women, and tobacco advertising increased greatly in women's magazines (Warner & Goldenhar, 1992). Cigarette advertising emphasizes themes that are potent for female adolescents: body image, slimness, popularity, success, fashion, and "the good life" (Ernster, 1993; Gritz, 1993). The pervasiveness of cigarette advertising, especially in women's magazines and at women's sports, fashion, and political events, may contribute to adolescents' overestimation of the prevalence of cigarette smoking. Overestimates of smoking prevalence are among the strongest predictors of smoking initiation (Chassin, Presson, Sherman, Corty, & Olshavsky, 1984; Sussman, Dent, Mestel-Rauch, Johnson, Hansen, & Flay, 1988). Cigarette advertising may also influence adolescents' smoking in another way. To the extent that advertisements portray ideal self-images of adolescents, the adolescent might strive to be more like the individuals in the ads; that is, to be a smoker.

Work by Pierce and his colleagues adds strong evidence to the link between advertising and female adolescents' smoking. Pierce, Lee, and Gilpin (1994) examined the correspondence between trends in smoking initiation among adolescents and the specific targeting of tobacco advertising to women. There was a rapid growth in tobacco advertising targeting women from 1967 through 1975. By examining data from the National Health Interview Surveys, the authors found that the initiation rates for all 11 to 17-year old girls rose rapidly from 1967 through 1974. Boys, however, did not show the same pattern of increase. As the study documents, sales of women's cigarette brands coincided with the peak in smoking initiation among underaged girls. There was no evidence that initiation increased among males or among young women over age 18 during the same time period. These findings clearly demonstrate an association between tobacco advertising and smoking initiation among young girls.

The fact that many cigarette advertisements associate smoking with being slim and glamorous is not just coincidence. As Camp, Klesges, and Reylea (1993) note, most adolescents are concerned with appearance, and the weight control benefits of smoking may influence some youths to begin smoking. Adolescent females may be especially vulnerable to succumbing to the weight control aspects of smoking. Camp et al. (1993) found that belief in smoking as a weight-control strategy distinguished between adolescents who were regular smokers and those who were ex-perimenters (those who tried and quit), even when other important pre-dictors of smoking were in the equation. Most interesting, though, was their finding that belief in smoking as a weight-control strategy varied as a function of gender and race. White girls were much more likely to re-port that smoking can help control weight than White boys, Black boys, and Black girls. Among their sample of regular adolescent smokers, none of the Blacks of either sex reported smoking for weight control reasons.

The Camp et al. (1993) study highlights the importance of examin-ing potential predictors of smoking initiation by both gender and race. As we discussed above, smoking initiation among females may be particu-larly influenced by the presence of smokers in their social networks and for Whites, beliefs in the weight control benefits of smoking. Unfortu-nately, we do not yet know enough about consistent gender differences in predictors of adolescent smoking. To the extent that these differences ex-ist, prevention programs may need to address gender-specific issues.

PREVENTION PROGRAMS

There have been numerous evaluations of school-based smoking preven-tion programs (e.g., Flay, 1985; Hansen, 1992), with the general conclu-sion that those with social influence curricula are somewhat effective at delaying the onset of smoking, at least within the first year or two of the intervention. Unfortunately, we know little about the possibility of differ-ential effects of these curricula on males and females. In general, although evaluations of interventions often examine the possibility of differential program effects by gender, most find no gender differences, and thus re-port results with males and females combined (e.g., Elder et al., 1993; Flynn et al., 1992; Perry, Kelder, Murray, & Klepp, 1992). Even when main effects for gender differences in prevalence are found, there are not differential condition effects by gender (e.g., Sussman et al., 1993). Thus, despite some suggestions of gender differences in reasons for smoking among adoles-cents, there is not yet evidence for differential responses to prevention pro-grams for males and females. It would be interesting for future research to evaluate more specifically the need for or relative benefit of tailoring prevention programs. For example, Geronimus et al. (1993) suggested that given the delayed initiation of smoking among Black women, school-based prevention programs may not be enough to reach this target audience, and prevention interventions may need to extend beyond the traditional school-based domain. In addition, White adolescent girls may benefit from programs that address issues of smoking, weight and body image. It is striking how little is known about the effects of tailoring treatments among youth, and clearly, more research is needed in this area.

MAINTENANCE OF SMOKING: WHY WOMEN CONTINUE TO SMOKE

Both women and men smoke for a variety of complex and interacting psychosocial and pharmacological reasons. Lack of knowledge about the health hazards of smoking, though not a major reason, may nevertheless contribute to some women's smoking. In general, the vast majority of adults (88%) believe that smoking is harmful to health (Brownson et al., 1992). However, Brownson and colleagues (1992) also recently found that knowledge about the health effects of smoking and passive smoking are lower among women, less educated adults, and as one would expect, current smokers. Manfredi and colleagues (Manfredi, Lacey, Warnecke, & Buis, 1992) surveyed young Black women smokers living in subsidized public housing in Chicago and found that the message about smoking and lung cancer either had not reached them or had not been accepted by them. Sorenson and Pechacek (1987) also found that women were less likely than men to feel vulnerable to the negative health consequences of smoking or to endorse the health benefits of quitting smoking. However, as Grunberg et al. (1991) noted, several other studies have found no gender differences in level of concern about the health hazards of smoking. Regardless of whether there are gender differences in levels of concern, given the changing demographics of women smokers towards those with less education, it may be especially important for future interventions to include personalized messages to women about the relevant health hazards of smoking.

Lack of knowledge alone, though, does not explain women's smoking. Women and men continue to smoke, in part, because of the addictive properties of nicotine. The 1988 Surgeon General's Report (USDHHS, 1988) documented that smoking meets all the criteria for an addiction, including highly controlled or compulsive use, psychoactive effects, physical dependency, and drug-reinforced behavior. Like other psychoactive substances of abuse, nicotine produces effects that smokers often consider beneficial. Nicotine may enhance feelings of well-being, produce arousal or relaxation, help maintain attention, help control appetite and weight, and reduce anxiety (Benowitz, 1988). Several of these "benefits" of smoking may be especially relevant to women, most notably those of mood management and weight control.

There is now a growing body of evidence linking depressed mood to smoking (e.g., Anda et al., 1990; Frederick, Frerichs, & Clark, 1988; Glassman et al., 1990). Using data from a large-scale national community-based survey, Anda and colleagues (1990) found that the prevalence of smoking increased as depression scores increased. Furthermore, depressed smokers were significantly less likely to quit than nondepressed smokers. Anda et al. also found that women, as compared with men, were significantly more likely to have higher depression scores and significantly less likely to quit. In another large, community-based survey, Glassman et al. (1990) found similar relationships between continued smoking and depression. Several other studies have shown a prospective relationship between depressed mood and a failure to stop smoking (Glassman et al., 1988; Hall, Rugg, Tunstall, & Jones, 1984; Rausch, Nichinson, Lamke, & Matloff, 1990). Hughes (1988) suggested at least two mechanisms by which smoking and depression might be linked. First, certain personality characteristics, such as low self-esteem, may predispose individuals to both the development of depression and smoking. Second, smokers may use nicotine to self-medicate their depressed mood.

It is well documented that women have substantially higher rates of depression than men (Weissman & Klerman, 1977), and that depression is more common among less educated groups (Anda et al., 1990). Thus, as the smoking population shifts toward women of lower socioeconomic groups, it may reflect women who are more psychologically distressed than either ex-smokers or the general population (Glassman et al., 1988) and who have fewer resources with which to manage their distress. These smokers may be likely to use smoking more often to regulate affect because they possess few alternative coping mechanisms (Carmody, 1989). Smoking may provide a source of pleasure or a brief escape from feelings of stress or dysphoria.

Urban, low-income Black women may be a high risk group for continuing to smoke for the mood management benefits. Lacey et al. (1993) documented that a foremost concern for these women was living under very stressful conditions, and that for many of them, particularly the younger women, smoking-related health problems were of low importance. The authors noted that a consistent theme among this group of women was the feeling that smoking helped them to manage the overwhelming pressures in their lives and to stay calm. These women also perceived smoking as an attainable pleasure, far preferable to other alternatives, such as drugs, alcohol abuse, or loss of self-control. In sum, for these women and many others, the perceived mood benefits of smoking are a primary reason for continuing to smoke.

Women also continue to smoke for the weight control benefits and are more likely than men to cite weight control as a reason for smoking (Brandon & Baker, 1991; Klesges & Klesges, 1988). Klesges, Meyers, Klesges, and LaVasque (1989) reviewed 70 cross-sectional and longitudinal studies of smoking and body weight and found that 79% of the studies reported that smokers weigh less than nonsmokers and that those who quit smoking gain weight. Women may accrue greater weight control benefits than men while smoking, and then gain more weight upon quitting, in part because the metabolic effects of nicotine may last longer in women (Grunberg et al., 1991). Using data from the first National Health and Nutrition Examination Survey (NHANES I) and its follow-up study, Williamson et al. (1991) found that men gained an average of 2.8 kg after stopping smoking, whereas women gained an average of 3.8 kg.

There are two important and distinct questions of interest related to concerns about weight gain and cessation. First, do these concerns prevent women from trying to quit, and second, among those trying to quit, do weight concerns hinder cessation? In order to answer the first question, we need to look at community-based surveys of smokers and their quitting history or quitting intentions. To answer the second question, we can examine the relation of weight concerns to cessation among smokers trying to quit. In two community-based surveys (Klesges et al., 1988; Weekley, Klesges, & Reylea, 1992), smokers who had never tried to quit or who had no intention of quitting were more concerned about weight control than those who had made attempts to quit or those who planned to quit. Similarly, both Pirie, Murray, and Luepker (1991) and Sorensen and Pechacek (1987) found that women smokers reported substantially more concern about weight gain after quitting than did men. Thus, the data from several large studies suggest that concern about postcessation weight gain is more common in women than men, and that concern is associated with lower desire to quit.

The data about the effects of weight concern on cessation, though, are more equivocal. Klesges and colleagues (Klesges et al., 1988) found that concerns about postcessation weight gain prospectively predicted failure to quit. However, their sample was small ($N = 44$), and their power to examine the potential for interactions of gender with weight concern and cessation was thus limited. In two larger studies limited to women, weight concern did not predict cessation (French, Jeffery, Pirie, & McBride, 1992; Gritz, Berman, Read, Marcus, & Siau, 1990). Thus, it may be that weight concerns interfere with the initial decision to stop smoking, but once a serious attempt is made, concerns about postcessation weight gain do not hinder quitting.

Actual weight gain following cessation also may not hinder the maintenance of abstinence. Several studies have found no relationship between weight gain and relapse (Gritz et al., 1990; Hall, Ginsberg, & Jones, 1986; Pirie et al., 1992; Swan & Denk, 1987), although women may retrospectively attribute their relapses to weight gain (Klesges & Klesges, 1988). Weight gain may serve as a protective factor against relapse (Hall et al., 1986; Swan & Denk, 1987). For example, eating sweets may decrease withdrawal symptoms (West, Hajek, & Belcher, 1989), or eating may serve as an alternative coping mechanism for negative mood states.

In sum, women continue to smoke in part because of the perceived benefits of smoking, including mood management, the pleasure of smoking, and weight control. Women may also continue to smoke, though, because, like men, they have difficulty quitting and staying quit.

CESSATION

Why Do Women Want to Stop Smoking?

Both women and men have multiple reasons for wanting to stop smoking, including health concerns, social pressures, to demonstrate self-control, and to save money, among other reasons (Curry, Wagner, & Grothaus, 1990). In a study examining motivations for quitting, Curry et al. (1990) found no gender differences. Overall, health concerns were rated as most important and social influences as the least. Data from a large-scale national survey do, however, show some sex differences in reasons for quitting. Gilpin, Pierce, Goodman, Burns, and Shopland (1992) used the 1987 National Health Interview Survey to examine reasons for quitting. Both men and women mentioned health related reasons most frequently (62% of the sample). Social reasons for stopping, especially pressure from family and friends, were mentioned more often by women than men, although the difference was not large (23.9% versus 19.3%). Gilpin et al. suggest that women may experience more social pressure to quit or that women may be more responsive to that pressure. It may be that part of the social pressure women experience is due to smoking-related pregnancy risks or to having young children at home; for many women, these may be strong reasons for wanting to stop smoking.

Do Women Quit When Pregnant?

Given the significant risks of smoking during pregnancy (Abel, 1984), it would seem that pregnancy would be a powerful motivator for women to stop smoking. However, significant numbers of pregnant women still smoke. Williamson, Serdula, Kendrick, and Binken (1989) used data collected from the Behavioral Risk Factor Surveillance System surveys of 1985 and 1986 to determine the prevalence of smoking during pregnancy. The prevalence varied by age; as few as 14% of pregnant women in the 30 to 34 year age range smoked, and as many as 26% of pregnant women between 35 and 45 years of age smoked. Smoking during pregnancy tends to be higher among unmarried women (Haug, Aaro, & Fugelli, 1992; Williamson et al., 1989), especially among White unmarried women (Williamson et al., 1989), those who were heavy smokers prior to pregnancy (Cnattingius, 1989; Fingerhut, Kleinman, & Kendrick, 1990; Quinn, Mullen, & Ershoff, 1991; Williamson et al., 1989), those with less education (Fingerhut, Kleinman, & Kendrick, 1990; O'Campo, Brown, Faden, & Gielen, 1992; Williamson et al., 1989), those living with smokers (Cnattingius, 1989), and those who had previously given birth (Cnattingius, 1989).

Recent studies have found that approximately 40% of women who smoke prior to pregnancy quit when pregnant (Fingerhut et al., 1990; O'Campo, Brown, Fader, & Gielen, 1992; Quinn, Mullen, & Ershoff, 1991). Thus, more than half of women who smoke prior to pregnancy continue to smoke during their pregnancies. Unfortunately, both prepartum and postpartum relapse is common among those who quit during pregnancy. Quinn et al. (1991) found that about 20% of the women who spontaneously quit early in their pregnancies, relapsed while they were still pregnant. McBride and Pirie (1990) found that 65% of the women who quit during pregnancy had relapsed by six months. Similarly, Fingerhut et al. (1990) reported that in their national sample, 70% of the women relapsed within one year of delivery, and that 87% of the women who were smoking prior to pregnancy were smoking one year after delivery. Predictors of postpartum relapse include a spouse's smoking, lower social support, and types of coping strategies used (McBride, Pirie, & Curry, 1992). McBride et al. (1992) found that women who frequently thought about the negative health consequences of smoking and those who did not snack to cope with smoking urges were less likely to relapse. Lower levels of self-efficacy (McBride et al., 1992; Quinn et al., 1991), previous pregnancy, and lower levels of belief in the harmful effects of maternal smoking on fetal health

(Quinn et al., 1991) also have predicted postpartum relapse. The relatively low quit rates during pregnancy and the high postpartum relapse rates may well speak both to the reasons women continue to smoke and to the difficulty that women may have in stopping.

Are Women Ready to Quit?

Current conceptualizations of smoking view cessation as a developmental process and not as an all-or-nothing or one-step phenomenon (Prochaska, DiClemente, & Norcross, 1992). Smokers move from precontemplation, a stage in which smokers have no intention to change their behavior in the foreseeable future; to contemplation, when smokers start to think seriously about making a change and weigh the pros and cons of changing; through to preparation, when smokers intend to stop smoking soon and have made some recent attempts; to action; and lastly, to maintenance. As Prochaska and his colleagues (1992) note, movement through the stages of change is not necessarily linear, but is better characterized by a spiral progression, often with setbacks along the way and relapses to earlier stages. When considering women's smoking cessation patterns, it may be useful to think about the distribution of women smokers across the stages of change and how their patterns compare to those of men. For example, are women, compared with men, more or less likely to be precontemplators? Or, are women less likely than men to move from action into maintenance?

DiClemente and his colleagues (DiClemente et al., 1991) examined the early stages of change (precontemplation, contemplation, and preparation) among a large sample of smokers ($N = 1466$) who volunteered for a minimal intervention cessation research program. They found no significant differences in the sex distribution for these stages, although they reported a tendency (but not significant) for a greater percentage of women to be in the precontemplation (66.1%) and contemplation (65.6%) groups than in the preparation stage (57.7%). Given that their sample was composed of volunteers for a research project, however, these results may not be representative of the population of smokers as a whole.

There are only a few population-based surveys that examine gender differences in the distribution of stages. Owen, Wakefield, Roberts, and Esterman (1992) examined the population prevalence of the precontemplation, contemplation, and preparation stages of change in an Australian sample and found no differences between the stages for men and women. Pierce, Giovino, Hatziandreu, and Shopland (1989) classified respondents to the 1986 Adult Use of Tobacco Survey along a 10 category continuum, and some of their categories are similar to the stages of change. Approximately equal proportions of men (17.4%) and women (18.7%) who were current smokers could be considered precontemplators; that is, they never thought about quitting or would do so only if it were easy. Of the men and women who were smoking in the past year, 34% had made a quit attempt. However, of these attempters, fewer women (41.8%) than men (50.7%) were still not smoking at the time of the interview. Biener and Abrams (1991) also found no sex differences on either a measure of readiness or a question about intention to quit. However, Sorensen and Pechachek (1987) and Blake et al. (1989) found that men had greater intentions to quit than women. In one of the few studies examining intentions to quit among Black adults, Orleans and her colleagues (1989) found that female smokers were more likely than male smokers to have a strong desire to quit. Thus, several studies suggest that women and men seem to be equally represented among the early stages of change, but data from Pierce et al. (1989) suggest that fewer women make it from action into maintenance.

Do Women Have Trouble Quitting?

One of the controversies in the smoking cessation literature is whether women are less successful at quitting than men. The 1980 Surgeon General's Report (USDHHS, 1980) concluded that women have more difficulty both achieving and maintaining abstinence than do men. However, since that report, there have been substantial data refuting that claim, including much cross-cultural data indicating that women have higher quit rates than men (Waldron, 1991). Jarvis (1984) has argued that earlier reports claiming that women have a harder time quitting failed to take into account the tendency of men to switch to other forms of tobacco, such as cigars or pipes. Jarvis examined data from general population surveys in Great Britain and the United States and found that when adjustments are made for men's switching to other forms of tobacco, there are no gender differences in smoking cessation rates in the United States. The data from Great Britain also show that although there are no sex differences in cessation rates below the age of 50, in older age groups men are somewhat more likely to quit than women. More recent data from the United States (Salive et al., 1992) have shown no gender differences in either cessation or relapse rates among adults older than 65 years of age.

Fiore and his colleagues (1989) also addressed the question of differential quit rates in women and men using data from the National Health Interview Surveys. Fiore et al. calculated quit ratios, defined as the proportion of ever smokers who are former smokers at the time of the survey. The quit ratio is a point prevalence measure and does not reflect success at maintaining abstinence. Between 1974 and 1985, the estimated quit ratio for men increased from 38.5% to 45.8%, at a mean rate of change of +0.67 percentage points per year. During the same time, the quit ratio for women increased from 29.9% to 39.8%, at a mean rate of change of +0.90 percentage points per year, somewhat higher than that observed for men. The rate of change over time may be more important for determining future trends in smoking and quitting than absolute percentages. Thus, these data do not support the hypothesis that men and women differ in rates of quitting over time. However, they do not address the question of differences in maintaining abstinence, or long-term success. Data from the Framingham Heart Study, which has followed changes in smoking in a community-based cohort for over 30 years, also provide a comparison of quit rates for men and women. In this study, women were as likely to quit as men: After 32 years of follow-up, 42% of women smokers had successfully quit smoking all tobacco products, compared with 41% of men (Freund, D'Agostino, Belanger, Kannel, & Stokes, 1992). Pirie, Murray, and Luepker (1991) also found that both quitting attempts and successes were equally common among men and women.

Thus, when one examines the published data since 1980 from large-scale surveys, it appears that there are no gender differences either in the stages of change leading up to quitting or in initial quit rates. The data from treatment outcome studies, however, are equivocal or lacking. Most treatment outcome studies over the past few years have found either no gender differences in quitting (e.g., Curry, Marlatt, Gordon, & Baer, 1988; Curry, Wagner, & Grothaus, 1991; Gruder et al., 1993; Killen, Fortmann, Newman, & Varady, 1990), or unfortunately, have not specifically reported their data in a manner that would allow for comparisons of sex differences in outcomes (e.g., Hall, Tunstall, Vila, & Duffy, 1992; Hughes et al., 1992; Hymowitz, Campbell, & Feuerman, 1991; Lando, Hellerstedt, Pirie, & McGovern, 1992; Orleans et al., 1991; Ossip-Klein et al., 1991; Zelman, Brandon, Jorenby, & Baker, 1992).

There are, however, a few studies that have reported sex differences in outcome. Although not a treatment outcome study, Marlatt, Curry, and Gordon (1988) followed a sample of self-quitters and found that the men were more likely than the women to quit for at least 24 hours (82% of the men quit versus 73% of the women). However, the women were not less likely than the men to maintain their abstinence. Warnecke and colleagues (Warnecke, Langenberg, Wong, Flay, & Cook, 1992) found that following a minimal assistance televised cessation program, men were more likely than women to be abstinent at all measurement waves up to, but not including a 24-month follow-up. In a more intensive, multicomponent cessation program, Ockene et al. (1992) found that among a sample of smokers with coronary artery disease, men were more likely than women to be abstinent at a 6-month follow-up (42% of the women versus 62% of the men), but not significantly so by the 12-month follow-up (44% of the women were abstinent compared with 56% of the men). In sum, it is difficult to draw conclusions about differential success rates for men and women from outcome studies. Although most recent studies have found no sex differences in outcome, or unfortunately failed to present data addressing outcome by gender, a few have found some quitting advantage for men. It is rare, though, to find any that have reported better success for women.

Similarly, no clear-cut conclusions can be drawn about differential rates of success in maintaining abstinence for men and women. As we noted earlier, there is some suggestion (Pierce et al., 1989) that fewer women than men maintain abstinence. Blake et al. (1989), for example, found that women were less likely than men to sustain their abstinence for more than one week. However, in a study examining the rates of relapse and recycling (return to abstinence after relapse) separately for men and women, Swan and Denk (1987) found no gender differences. They did, though, find different predictors for relapse and recycling for men and women. These researchers argue that relapse should not be conceptualized independent of gender and that interventions may need to tailor efforts specifically to men and women.

Unique to women are findings that their withdrawal experiences after cessation, and perhaps their success in maintaining abstinence, may vary with their menstrual phase. O'Hara, Portser, and Anderson (1989), for example, found that women who quit smoking in the last phase of their menstrual cycle had greater withdrawal than those who quit in the early phase, or male quitters. These more intense withdrawal symptoms experienced by premenstrual women may also have an effect on treatment outcome (Craig, Parrott, & Coomber, 1992). Averaging across the phases of the menstrual cycle, though, women do not appear to have different withdrawal experiences than men (Svikis, Hatsukami, Hughes, Carroll, & Pickens, 1986).

GENDER BY TREATMENT INTERACTIONS

Differential success rates in quitting for men and women, if they do exist, may reflect the possibility that women and men respond differently to treatments. There are data suggesting that men and women prefer and use different cessation approaches. Fiore and colleagues (1990) found that women were more likely than men to express a preference for formal cessation programs and groups. Women may also be more likely to try to reduce the number of cigarettes smoked, whereas men may be more likely to try to quit completely (Blake et al., 1989). Flaxman (1978) evaluated different approaches to quitting and found that delayed quitting (i.e., setting a quit date a couple of weeks after the start of treatment) was more effective than immediately quitting for women, but immediate quitting was more effective for men. Flaxman also found that aversive conditioning procedures helped men to quit, but hindered women. More recently, Curry, Marlatt, Gordon, and Baer (1988) found that women and men responded very differently to alternative treatment approaches to preventing relapse. Women were significantly more likely to quit in a program that followed a relapse prevention model and focused on the gradual acquisition of nonsmoking skills than a more traditional program that used contingency contracting and emphasized the necessity for absolute abstinence. Men, however, had greater success with the latter approach. Ossip-Klein and her colleagues (Ossip-Klein, Carosella, & Krusch, 1994) also recently found a gender by condition interaction in a self-help cessation program. Men had higher abstinence rates with an intervention that used letters as reminders to call a cessation hotline as compared with an intervention that used proactive telephone counseling. Women, however, had higher abstinence rates with the phone calls than with the letter. In sum, women may prefer and do better with a stepped approach to quitting that emphasizes gradual skill building, increasing in self-efficacy, and personal contact. However, very few smoking cessation evaluations have had sufficient statistical power to detect gender by treatment interaction effects, even if they were there. Thus, conclusions about treatment interactions may need to be guarded at best.

Pharmacological treatments for smoking cessation also show gender by treatment interactions. Killen et al. (1990) evaluated different combinations of pharmacologic (nicotine gum, placebo, or no gum) and behavioral treatments (relapse prevention). Although the nicotine gum was better than the placebo or no gum for men, no treatment was significantly better among the women. Conversely, Glassman et al. (1988) found that clonidine was effective in promoting cessation for women, but not for men. Serotonin-enhancing substances, such as d-fenfluramine or tryptophan, also may be relatively more beneficial for women because of their ability to help prevent dysphoric mood or weight gain after cessation (Bowen, Spring, & Fox, 1991; Spring, Wurtman, Gleason, Wurtman, & Kessler, 1991). Thus, pharmacologic agents that address concerns that women have with quitting, such as weight gain or depressed mood, may show more promise for them.

TREATMENTS TARGETED TO WOMEN

Smoking cessation treatments targeted specifically to women have, for the most part, addressed one of two issues: smoking during pregnancy and preventing weight gain following cessation. Effective cessation programs for pregnant smokers are clearly needed given the continued high rates of smoking during pregnancy. Windsor and Orleans (1986) reviewed eight pregnancy-focused smoking cessation treatments and concluded that simply providing information about the risks of smoking during pregnancy is not enough; pregnant smokers need state-of-the-art cessation techniques. Windsor and Orleans suggest, though, that treatment should fit into the prenatal care routine, as pregnant smokers are unlikely to attend separate programs. They also note that, in general, there is room for improved methodologies in many studies. Of particular importance is the need for verification of self-reported quitting. Windsor et al. (1993) reported a 28% rate of misreporting. The demand characteristics for pregnant smokers to report cessation are obviously high.

In general, smoking cessation programs with pregnant women have been modestly successful in producing short-term cessation. For example, Windsor and colleagues (1993) have found that public health clinics can achieve a 6% to 12% quit rate improvement over usual care (i.e., advice to quit) with the addition of self-help materials, one-session counseling advice, reinforcement letters, and social support. Importantly, Windsor et al. found a large difference in quit rates between Black and White patients, with Black pregnant smokers having a significantly higher quit rate. Burling, Bigelow, Robinson, and Mead (1991) also found similar levels of improvement (7 to 10%) over usual care with the addition of other cost-effective minimal intervention approaches: the use of a personalized letter to patients with feedback about their carbon monoxide elevations and a recommendation to quit. Slightly higher cessation rates (27–28%) have been achieved in private, rather than public health care settings, and more intensive interventions (Ershoff, Mullen, & Quinn, 1989; Sexton & Hebel, 1984).

Smoking cessation interventions that address weight gain have had mixed outcomes. Pirie and colleagues (1992) conducted a randomized trial testing nicotine gum and a behavioral weight control program alone and in combination, for women who had weight concerns. Although Pirie et al. found significant differences among the treatment conditions, with the group receiving the gum achieving the highest abstinence rates (31.5% continuous abstinence at 12 months) and the group receiving only a basic cessation program having the lowest success (14.3% continuous abstinence at 12 months), there were no significant differences in weight changes among the treatment groups. The weight control component neither detracted from nor added to cessation rates.

Hall and her colleagues (1992), however, have provided a cautionary note to adding weight control interventions to cessation programs. They compared three interventions: (a) an innovative weight gain prevention program, comprised of daily self-monitoring of weight and calories, an individualized exercise plan, and behavioral self-management; (b) a nonspecific control including some nutritional and exercise information, along with group support and therapeutic attention; and (c) a standard treatment control, including just an information packet on nutrition and exercise. Subjects were mostly women (73%). There were no differences among the conditions on weight change. However, there were significant differences in abstinence in an unexpected direction. Subjects in both the innovative and nonspecific conditions had a higher risk of smoking relapse than did subjects in the control. Hall et al. conclude that the two active interventions may have been so complicated that they detracted from subjects' attempts to maintain abstinence. Furthermore, the caloric restrictions recommended by these two conditions may have encouraged smoking by increasing the reinforcing value of nicotine. Hall and her colleagues suggest that attitude changes about postcessation weight gain may be more beneficial than interventions focused on preventing the small gains that most smokers experience.

A study by Marcus and her colleagues (Marcus, Albrecht, Niaura, Abrams, & Thompson, 1991) is along similar lines to the interventions that have added weight control components, but instead focused on the relative benefits of adding an exercise component to a basic smoking cessation treatment for women smokers. Marcus et al. found that the women who exercised were more likely to maintain their abstinence, at least in the short-term, than women who did not exercise. Although this study had a very small sample size, it is suggestive that exercise training may improve quit rates for women.

Other interventions have attempted to reach a broader audience of women smokers and not just those who self-select into cessation programs or who are pregnant. Gritz, Berman, Bastani, and Wu (1992) attempted to reach nonvolunteer female smokers through a health maintenance organization. A random sample of female smokers were sent unsolicited, self-help materials that focused on particular concerns of women trying to stop smoking, including weight gain, social support, stress, and coping mechanisms. The mailed booklets contained content appropriate for precontemplators and then progressed through the stages of change to maintenance. The materials carried an attractive female motif and the theme, "Now is the time." However, these materials neither enhanced movement through the stages of change nor cessation rates relative to a control group. Gritz et al. concluded that targeting women by addressing their concerns in a self-help and unsolicited format may not be effective and suggested that personal contact as an adjunct to self-help programs might be more beneficial.

Davis, Cummings, Rimer, Sciandra, and Stone (1992) also tested the value of a self-help guide tailored specifically for women with young children. Women were recruited through a media campaign encouraging them to call a number to receive help in stopping smoking. Women in the target audience received tailored telephone counseling on quitting and one of three self-help guides, one of which ("Quitting Times") was developed specifically for them. There were no significant differences between the three groups in satisfaction with the guides, use of the guides, methods used to try to quit, or cessation rates. However, given that the women received tailored counseling, the tailored guides may have had no additional beneficial effect over the counseling. Davis et al. suggest that tailoring might be more useful for precontemplators rather than those already thinking about quitting.

Manfredi, Mermelstein, and Jones (1991) used the Chicago public schools Head Start program to reach low-income Black women smokers. Manfredi et al. developed an eight session smoking cessation program that was delivered as part of the Head Start parent education activities and included topics relevant for women, such as mood management, weight control, and social support. Participation in the stop smoking program helped fulfill the parent participation requirement of Head Start. Smokers in the intervention schools had a significantly higher cessation rate (11%) than those in control schools (3%). On average, most smokers attended only a few of the classes, and participation was due primarily to allegiance to the Head Start program and the opportunity for attending a support group, and not necessarily because of desire to stop smoking. Nevertheless, the cessation rates are respectable given that they include more than only self-selected smokers who are motivated to quit. Thus, this program was relatively successful in part because of the opportunistic setting and use of personal contact.

Mass media approaches are another way to reach a large audience of women smokers, especially those who may be unable to attend formal cessation programs. Currently, a study funded by the National Cancer Institute ("Strategies for Smoking Cessation Among Lower Educated Women;" R. Warnecke, R. Mermelstein, C. Manfredi, and D. Burton, Principal Investigators on this program project) is underway in Chicago to evaluate the effectiveness of a televised cessation program and self-help manual that specifically target women smokers who have no more than a high school education. This intervention is unique in being population-based and in its use of a motivation building intervention. The intervention attempts to motivate smokers to quit by associating nonsmoking with positive personality attributes to which women in the target audience aspire, rather than by focusing only on the negative aspects of smoking. The program emphasizes women working together to improve their lives, whether by quitting smoking or achieving another goal. The use of television to show women like themselves either who have been successful in quitting or who are currently trying to quit may bridge the gap between minimal assistance and more formal programs with group support. This program is likely to be more accessible to less educated women because of its use of television and self-help materials written at a low literacy level (fourth grade).

Although not specifically targeted to women smokers, Hall and her colleagues (Hall, Munoz, & Reus, 1994) recently evaluated a smoking cessation program that could clearly address another concern of women smokers: the problem of smoking and negative mood. Hall et al. evaluated the effectiveness of a cognitive–behavioral intervention designed to prevent the occurrence of negative mood in smoking treatment clients, and thereby reduce the probability of continued smoking. The intervention, which included a depression prevention program in addition to a standard smoking cessation component, was compared with standard cessation treatment alone. Hall et al. found that smokers who had a history of major depressive disorder were more likely to be abstinent when treated with the mood management program. However, smokers without a history of depression were not helped by the mood management program. Unfortunately, Hall et al. did not report whether they found any gender differences, although their relatively small sample size (total $N = 149$, with approximately half women) may have precluded their finding any significant differences. Hall et al.'s results point to the role of patient-treatment matching in smoking programs.

SUMMARY AND CONCLUSIONS

Despite the increased attention to the dangers of smoking over the past two decades and more intensive and broad-based efforts to encourage smokers to stop smoking, almost one in four women in the United States still smoke. The characteristics of smokers have changed, however. More and more, the smoking population is overrepresented by women with no more than a high school education, who live below the poverty level, and who may be more psychologically distressed than the population as a whole.

The changing demographics of women smokers have several important implications. First, results of studies of more than a decade ago, using subjects with potentially very different characteristics, may not hold for smokers today. To the extent that socioeconomic factors contribute to reasons for starting to smoke, stopping, and success at doing so, results of studies with better educated and more economically advantaged women of different ethnic backgrounds may not generalize to today's female smoker. Second, prevention and cessation approaches that can reach this audience are needed. For example, primary reliance on school-based prevention programs may be insufficient to reach adolescents who may have high dropout rates or who, as do Blacks, start smoking at older ages (Geronimus et al., 1993). Less educated adults may seek information and help from very different sources than do college-educated smokers. Thus, messages about smoking and resources for quitting need to be available and accessible to these women. Programs that use mass media, proactive outreach, or incorporate cessation information into routine health care visits for women (especially family planning and prenatal care) may show promise for reaching the smoking audience. Alternatively, more active legislation (e.g., taxation), policy and environmental approaches (e.g., location of advertising) may be useful. Third, beyond finding new avenues to reach women smokers, we may need different approaches and techniques to help them to quit. Equally important will be finding effective strategies both to motivate these women to quit, given that a significant percent-age may be in the precontemplation stage (e.g., DiClemente et al., 1991; Owen et al., 1992), and then, to move them through action into maintenance.

It is still equivocal whether women are more or less successful at quitting than men. The literature is marred by small sample sizes, selection bias, and contradictory and variable results. We need some large-scale studies directly addressing this issue, as well as addressing whether racial and SES variables interact with gender and success rates. Interventions need to focus on women, though, not because they may or may not have more difficulty quitting than men, but because women need to stop smoking, and their smoking may influence others more than does men's smoking. Women's smoking affects not only their own health, but the health of their children, and also increases the probability of their daughters' starting to smoke (Gottlieb, 1982; Kandel et al., 1994; Murray et al., 1985). Unfortunately, it is not clear that we know the effective strategies for helping women to stop smoking. There is some support for the notion that women prefer and do better with different strategies than men. For example, women may prefer personal contact, whether it is provided in the form of a group, telephone counseling, or in-person advice. Women may also do better with a more stepped approach, starting with a clear preparation phase prior to a target quit date and followed by relapse prevention training. Pharmacological approaches also may have differential patterns of success with men and women, although too few studies have examined this possibility for us to draw any firm conclusions.

The jury is also still out on whether tailoring programs specifically to women provides much, if any, advantage over multicomponent programs that are not specifically tailored to women. Both the Gritz et al. (1992) and Davis et al. (1992) studies provided excellent tests of a tailored versus nontailored approach and found no advantage for tailoring using a self-help format. It may be that thematic tailoring (i.e., clearly emphasizing a program for women) is less important in enhancing quit rates than strategic tailoring (i.e., emphasizing certain strategies and techniques). However, the results of studies attempting to enhance quitting among women by addressing relevant concerns, such as postcessation weight gain, have also been disappointing (Hall et al., 1992; Pirie et al., 1992). Besides increasing treatment complexity or the reinforcing qualities of nicotine, the addition of weight control components may not have facilitated cessation because weight concerns may play less of a role in achieving cessation than in deciding to try. Thus, it is still possible that programs that offer weight management components might encourage more women to think about quitting. The benefits of adding mood management components to cessation programs for women have not yet been sufficiently addressed, although Hall et al.'s study (1994) is an important first step. Even if tailoring does not improve quit rates per se, it may still be useful in moving women from the precontemplation or contemplation stages further along to preparation or action.

It is notable that there are still very little data about what women want from a cessation program. Smoking researchers are increasingly using focus groups to help develop and refine program materials and topics, but unfortunately, reports of the results of these focus groups rarely reach the literature. Given the emphasis of most journals on quantitative versus qualitative methodologies, this lack of reporting may not be surprising, however. Nevertheless, more formative research directed at answering questions such as whether women prefer certain treatment settings, gender-specific treatments, type and length of contacts, and different components may be useful. As we noted above, though, we still need to know whether women actually achieve higher cessation rates when given such tailored programs.

Programs that tailor their approach or treatment to women need to be cautious, though, about the potential messages they implicitly or explicitly convey. For example, pregnant smokers are often encouraged to quit for the health of their baby and to show that they care about their children. However, that message should not be interpreted to mean that the smoker who is unable to quit or has difficulty quitting is a "bad" or "uncaring" mother. These messages also might undermine intrinsic motivation for quitting unless supplemented with messages about quitting for the smoker's sake as well. Similarly, programs targeted to women need to be cautious about their rationales. Targeting women because they may be less successful at quitting than men or need more help in quitting than do men may lead to lowered self-efficacy expectations among women. Instead, targeting women because they have different concerns about quitting or paths to success does not necessarily imply that they are less capable than men.

In sum, smoking remains a significant problem among women and one for which effective approaches are still needed. Although there is a growing body of literature documenting gender differences in patterns of smoking and biological and psychosocial aspects of smoking (e.g., Grunberg et al., 1991; Waldron, 1991), there are relatively little data on gender differences in prevention and treatment approaches. Our review of interventions was hindered by a common problem of researchers' not reporting whether they examined the possibility of either main effects for gender or gender by treatment interactions. Failure to find main effects does not necessarily rule out the possibility of interaction effects. Thus, an obvious recommendation is for future studies to test for these effects and to report those outcomes routinely. Second, we need to know more about the relative advantages and disadvantages of tailoring and targeting treatments to women and whether the smoker's stage of change (e.g., precontemplation versus action) interacts with gender-specific tailoring. Third, we need to explore race and age as important factors to consider in treating women smokers. As we noted earlier, there are suggestions of racial differences in reasons for smoking (e.g., Camp et al., 1993) and success in quitting (e.g., Windsor et al., 1993), and these differences may have important treatment implications. Age, too, has been a relatively neglected issue with women smokers. Many of the efforts to reach women smokers have focused primarily on women of child-bearing age and used avenues that are appropriate for younger women (e.g., prenatal care clinics). Older women smokers may need different treatment approaches as well, perhaps because they may be more dependent smokers, have less successful quitting histories, or consider smoking to be a part of their self-images (Orleans, Rimer, Cristinzio, Keintz, & Fleisher, 1991). Fourth, the problems of comorbidity among smokers are increasing. There is a critical need to develop programs for women smokers with other substance use or psychological problems (e.g., depression). Fifth, research exploring the effects of policy or legislative changes on women's smoking is also needed. For example, do increases in cigarette taxes lead more women to stop smoking or simply to change to lower cost generic and discount brands? Thus, although much as been learned since the 1980 Surgeon General's report focusing on women, the research agenda for women and smoking still remains long.

REFERENCES

Aaro, L. E., Hauknes, A., & Berglund, E. L. (1981). Smoking among Norwegian schoolchildren 1975–1980: II. The influence of the social environment. *Scandinavian Journal of Psychology, 22,* 297–309.

Abel, E. L. (1984). Smoking and pregnancy. *Journal of Psychoactive Drugs, 16,* 327–338.

Aitken, P. P., Eadie, D. R., Hastings, G. B., & Haywood, A. J. (1991). Predisposing effects of cigarette advertising on children's intentions to smoke when older. *British Journal of Addiction, 86,* 383–390.

American Cancer Society. (1993). *Cancer Facts and Figures: 1993.* Atlanta, GA: Author.

Anda, R. F., Williamson, D. F., Escobedo, L. G., Mast, E. E., Giovino, G. A., & Remington, P. L. (1990). Depression and the dynamics of smoking: A national perspective. *Journal of the American Medical Association, 264,* 1541–1545.

Bachman, J. G., Wallace, J. M., O'Malley, P. M., Johnston, L. D., Kurth, C. L., & Neighbors, H. W. (1991). Racial/ethnic differences in smoking, drinking, and illicit drug use among American high school seniors, 1976–1989. *American Journal of Public Health, 81,* 372–377.

Benowitz, N. L. (1988). Pharmacologic aspects of cigarette smoking and nicotine addiction. *New England Journal of Medicine, 319,* 1318–1330.

Biener, L., & Abrams, D. B. (1991). The Contemplation Ladder: Validation of a measure of readiness to consider smoking cessation. *Health Psychology, 10,* 360–365.

Blake, S. M., Klepp, K., Pechacek, T. F., Folsom, A. R., Luepker, R. V., Jacobs, D. R., & Mittlemark, M. B. (1989). Differences in smoking cessation strategies between men and women. *Addictive Behaviors, 14,* 409–418.

Bowen, D. J., Spring, B., & Fox, E. (1991). Tryptophan and high-carbohydrate diet as adjuncts to smoking cessation therapy. *Journal of Behavioral Medicine, 14,* 97–110.

Brandon, T. H., & Baker, T. B. (1991). The Smoking Consequences Questionnaire: The subjective expected utility of smoking in college students. *Psychological Assessment, 3,* 484–491.

Brownson, R. C., Jackson-Thompson, J., Wilkerson, J. C., Davis, J. R., Owens, N. W., & Fisher, E. B. (1992). Demographic and socioeconomic differences in beliefs about the health effects of smoking. *American Journal of Public Health, 82,* 99–103.

Burling, T. A., Bigelow, G. E., Robinson, J. C., & Mead, A. M. (1991). Smoking during pregnancy: Reduction via objective assessment and directive advice. *Behavior Therapy, 22,* 31–40.

Camp, D. E., Klesges, R. C., & Reylea, G. (1993). The relationship between body weight concerns and adolescent smoking. *Health Psychology, 12,* 24–32.

Carmody, T. P. (1989). Affect regulation, nicotine addiction, and smoking cessation. *Journal of Psychoactive Drugs, 21,* 331–342.

Centers for Disease Control. (1991). Cigarette smoking among youth: United States, 1989. *Morbidity and Mortality Weekly Report, 40,* 712–715.

Centers for Disease Control. (1993). Cigarette smoking among adults: United States, 1991. *Morbidity and Mortality Weekly Report, 42,* 230–233.

Charlton, A., & Blair, V. (1989). Predicting the onset of smoking in boys and girls. *Social Science and Medicine, 29,* 813–818.

Chassin, L., Presson, C. C., Sherman, S. J., Corty, E., & Olshavsky, R. W. (1984). Predicting the onset of cigarette smoking in adolescents: A longitudinal study. *Journal of Applied Social Psychology, 14,* 224–243.

Chassin, L., Presson, C. C., Sherman, S. J., Montello, D., & McGrew, J. (1986). Changes in peer and parent influence during adolescence: Longitudinal versus cross sectional perspectives on smoking initiation. *Developmental Psychology, 22,* 327–334.

Cnattingius, S. (1989). Smoking habits early in pregnancy. *Addictive Behaviors, 14,* 453–457.

Cohen, R. Y., Brownell, K. D., & Felix, M. R. (1990). Age and sex differences in health habits and beliefs of schoolchildren. *Health Psychology, 9,* 208–224.

Conrad, K. M., & Flay, B. R. (1992). Why children start smoking cigarettes: Prediction of onset. *British Journal of Addiction, 87,* 1711–1724.

Craig, D., Parrott, A., & Coomber, J. (1992). Smoking cessation in women: Effects on the menstrual cycle. *The International Journal of the Addictions, 27,* 697–706.

Curry, S. J., Marlatt, G. A., Gordon, J., & Baer, J. S. (1988). A comparison of alternative theoretical approaches to smoking cessation and relapse. *Health Psychology, 7,* 545–556.

Curry, S. J., Wagner, E. H., & Grothaus, L. C. (1990). Intrinsic and extrinsic motivation for smoking cessation. *Journal of Consulting and Clinical Psychology, 58,* 310–316.

Curry, S. J., Wagner, E. H., & Grothaus, L. C. (1991). Evaluation of intrinsic and extrinsic motivation interventions with a self-help smoking cessation program. *Journal of Consulting and Clinical Psychology, 59,* 318–324.

Davis, S. W., Cummings, K. M., Rimer, B. K., Sciandra, R., & Stone, J. C. (1992). The impact of tailored self-help smoking cessation guides on young mothers. *Health Education Quarterly, 19,* 495–504.

DiClemente, C. C., Prochaska, J. O., Fairhurst, S. K., Velicer, W. F., Velasquez, M. M., & Rossi, J. S. (1991). The process of smoking cessation: An analysis of precontemplation, contemplation, and preparation stages of change. *Journal of Consulting and Clinical Psychology, 59,* 295–304.

Elder, J. P., Wildley, M., de Moor, C., Sallis, J. F., Eckhardt, L., Edwards, C., Erickson, A., Golbeck, A., Hovell, M., Johnston, D., Levitz, M. D., Molgaard, C., Young, R., Vito, D., & Woodruff, S. I. (1993). The long-term prevention of tobacco use among junior high school students: Classroom and telephone interventions. *American Journal of Public Health, 83,* 1239–1244.

Ernster, V. L. (1993). Women and smoking. *American Journal of Public Health, 83,* 1202–1204.

Ershler, J., Leventhal, H., Fleming, R., & Glynn, K. (1989). The quitting experience for smokers in sixth through twelfth grades. *Addictive Behaviors, 14,* 365–378.

Ershoff, D. H., Mullen, P. D., & Quinn, V. P. (1989). A randomized trial of a serialized self-help smoking cessation program for preganant women in an HMO. *American Journal of Public Health, 79*(2), 182–187.

Escobedo, L. G., Remington, P. L., & Anda, R. F. (1989). Long-term age-specific prevalence of cigarette smoking among Hispanics in the United States. *Journal of Psychoactive Drugs, 21,* 307–318.

Fingerhut, L., Kleinman, J., & Kendrick, J. (1990). Smoking before, during, and after pregnancy. *American Journal of Public Health, 80,* 541–545.

Fiore, M. C., Novotny, T. E., Pierce, J. P., Giovino, G. A., Hatziandreu, E. J., Newcomb, P. A., Surawicz, T. S., & Davis, R. M. (1990). Methods used to quit smoking in the United States: Do cessation programs help? *Journal of the American Medical Association, 263,* 2760–2765.

Fiore, M. C., Novotny, T. E., Pierce, J. P., Hatziandreu, E. J., Patel, K. M., & Davis, R. M. (1989). Trends in cigarette smoking in the United States. *Journal of the American Medical Association, 261,* 49–55.

Fischer, P. M., Schwartz, M. P., Richards, J. W., Goldstein, A. O., & Rojas, T. H. (1991). Brief logo recognition by children aged 3 to 6 years. *Journal of the American Medical Association, 266,* 3145–3153.

Flaxman, J. (1978). Quitting smoking now or later: Gradual, abrupt, immediate, and delayed quitting. *Behavior Therapy, 9,* 260–270.

Flay, B. R. (1985). Psychosocial approaches to smoking prevention: A review of findings. *Health Psychology, 4,* 449–488.

Flay, B. R., d'Avernas, J. R., Best, J. A., Kersell, M. W., & Ryan, K. B. (1983). Cigarette smoking: Why young people do it and ways of preventing it. In P. McGrath &

P. Firestone (Eds.), *Pediatric and adolescent behavioral medicine.* New York: Springer-Verlag.

Flynn, B. S., Worden, J. K., Secker-Walker, R. H., Badger, G. J., Geller, B. M., & Costanza, M. C. (1992). Prevention of cigarette smoking through mass media intervention and school programs. *American Journal of Public Health, 82,* 827–834.

Frederick, T., Frerichs, R., & Clark, V. A. (1988). Personal health habits and symptoms of depression at the community level. *Preventive Medicine, 17,* 173–182.

French, S. A., Jeffery, R. W., Pirie, P. L., & McBride, C. M. (1992). Do weight concerns hinder smoking cessation efforts? *Addictive Behaviors, 17,* 219–226.

Freund, K. M., D'Agostino, R. B., Belanger, A. J., Kannel, W. B., & Stokes, J. (1992). Predictors of cessation: The Framington Study. *American Journal of Epidemiology, 135,* 957–964.

Friedman, L. S., Lichtenstein, E., & Biglan, A. (1985). Smoking onset among teens: An empirical analysis of initial situations. *Addictive Behaviors, 10,* 1–13.

Geronimus, A. T., Neidert, L. J. & Bound, J. (1993). Age patterns of smoking in US Black and White women of childbearing age. *American Journal of Public Health, 83,* 1258–1264.

Gilpin, E., Pierce, J. P., Goodman, J., Burns, D., & Shopland, D. (1992). Reasons smokers give for stopping smoking: Do they relate to success in stopping? *Tobacco Control, 1,* 256–263.

Giovino, G. A., Shelton, D., & Schooley, M. W. (in press). Trends in cigarette smoking cessation among adults in the United States. *Tobacco Control.*

Glassman, A. H., Helzer, J. E., Covey, L. S., Cottler, L. B., Stetner, F., Tipp, J. E., & Johnson, J. (1990). Smoking, smoking cessation, and major depression. *Journal of the American Medical Association, 264,* 1546–1549.

Glassman, A. H., Stetner, F., Walsh, B. T., Raizman, P. S., Fleiss, J. L., Cooper, T. B., & Covey, L. S. (1988). Heavy smokers, smoking cessation, and clonidine. *Journal of the American Medical Association, 259,* 2863–2866.

Gottlieb, N. H. (1982). The effects of peer and parental smoking and age on the smoking careers of college women: A sex-related phenomenon. *Social Science and Medicine, 16,* 595–600.

Gritz, E. R. (1993). Lung Cancer: Now, more than ever, a feminist issue. *CA, A Cancer Journal for Clinicians, 43,* 197–199.

Gritz, E. R., Berman, B. A., Bastani, R., & Wu, M. (1992). A randomized trial of a self-help smoking cessation intervention in a nonvolunteer female population: Testing the limits of the public health model. *Health Psychology, 11,* 280–289.

Gritz, E. R., Berman, B. A., Read, L. L., Marcus, A. C., & Siau, J. (1990). Weight change among registered nurses in a self-help smoking cessation program. *American Journal of Health Promotion, 5,* 155–121.

Gruder, C. L., Mermelstein, R. J., Kirkendol, S., Hedeker, D., Wong, S. C., Schreckengost, J., Warnecke, R. B., Burzette, R., & Miller, T. Q. (1993). Effects of social support and relapse prevention training as adjuncts to a televised smoking-cessation intervention. *Journal of Consulting and Clinical Psychology, 61,* 113–120.

Grunberg, N. E., Winders, S. E., & Wewers, M. E. (1991). Gender differences in tobacco use. *Health Psychology, 10,* 143–153.

Hall, S. M., Ginsberg, D., & Jones, R. T. (1986). Smoking cessation and weight gain. *Journal of Consulting and Clinical Psychology, 54,* 342–346.

Hall, S. M., Munoz, R. F., & Reus, V. I. (1994). Cognitive–behavioral program increases abstinence rates for depressive-history smokers. *Journal of Consulting and Clinical Psychology, 62,* 141–146.

Hall, S. M., Rugg, D., Tunstall, C., & Jones, R. T. (1984). Preventing relapse to cigarette smoking by behavioral skill training. *Journal of Consulting and Clinical Psychology, 52,* 372–382.

Hall, S. M., Tunstall, C. D., Vila, K. L., & Duffy, J. (1992). Weight gain prevention and smoking cessation: Cautionary findings. *American Journal of Public Health, 82,* 799–803.

Hansen, W. B. (1992). School-based substance abuse prevention: A review of the state of the art in curriculum, 1980–1990. *Health Education Research, 7,* 403–430.

Haug, K., Aaro, L. E., & Fugelli, P. (1992). Smoking habits early in pregnancy and attitudes towards smoking cessation among pregnant women and their partners. *Family Practice, 9,* 494–499.

Hover, S. J., & Gaffney, L. R. (1988). Factors associated with smoking behavior in adolescent girls. *Addictive Behaviors, 13,* 139–145.

Hughes, J. R. (1988). Clonidine, depression, and smoking cessation. *Journal of the American Medical Association, 259,* 2901–2902.

Hughes, J. R., Gulliver, S. B., Fenwick, J. W., Valliere, W. A., Cruser, K., Pepper, S., Shea, P., Solomon, L. J., & Flynn, B. S. (1992). Smoking cessation among self-quitters. *Health Psychology, 11,* 331–334.

Hymowitz, N., Campbell, K., & Feuerman, M. (1991). Long-term smoking intervention at the worksite: Effects of quit-smoking groups and an "enriched milieu" on smoking cessation in adult and white collar employees. *Health Psychology, 10,* 366–369.

Jarvis, M. J. (1984). Gender and smoking: Do women really find it harder to give up? *British Journal of Addiction, 79,* 383–387.

Johnston, L. D., O'Malley, P. M., & Bachman, J. G. (1993). *National survey results on drug use from the Monitoring the Future Study, 1975–1992. Volume I, secondary school students.* U.S. Department of Health and Human Services. Rockville, MD: National Institute on Drug Abuse.

Kandel, D. B., Wu, P., & Davies, M. (1994). Maternal smoking during pregnancy and smoking by adolescent daughters. *American Journal of Public Health, 84,* 1407–1413.

Killen, J. D., Fortmann, S. P., Newman, B., & Varady, A. (1990). Evaluation of a treatment approach combining nicotine gum with self-guided behavioral treatments for smoking relapse prevention. *Journal of Consulting and Clinical Psychology, 58,* 85–92.

Klesges, R. C., Brown, K., Pascale, R. W., Murphy, M., Williams, E., & Cigrang, J. (1988). Factors associated with participation, attrition, and outcome in a smoking cessation program at the workplace. *Health Psychology, 7,* 575–590.

Klesges, R. C., & Klesges, L. M. (1988). Cigarette smoking as a weight loss strategy in a university population. *International Journal of Eating Disorders, 7,* 413–419.

Klesges, R. C., Meyers, A. W., Klesges, L. M., & LaVasque, M. E. (1989). Smoking, body weight, and their effects on smoking behavior: A comprehensive review of the literature. *Psychological Bulletin, 106,* 204–230.

Klesges, R. C., Somes, G. W., Pascale, R., Klesges, L. M., Murphy, M., Brown, K., & Williams, E. (1988). Knowledge and beliefs regarding the consequences of cigarette smoking and their relationships to smoking status in a biracial sample. *Health Psychology, 7,* 387–401.

Lacey, L., Manfredi, C., Balch, G., Warnecke, R. B., Allen, K., & Edwards, C. (1993). Social support in smoking cessation among black women in Chicago public housing. *Public Health Reports, 108,* 387–394.

Lando, H. A., Hellerstedt, W. L., Pirie, P. L., & McGovern, P. G. (1992). Brief supportive telephone outreach as a recruitment and intervention strategy for smoking cessation. *American Journal of Public Health, 82,* 41–46.

Manfredi, C., Lacey, L., Warnecke, R., & Buis, M. (1992). Smoking-related behavior, beliefs, and social environment of young black women in subsidized public housing in Chicago. *American Journal of Public Health, 82,* 267–272.

Manfredi, C., Mermelstein, R., & Jones, R. (1991, November). *The Chicago Public School Head Start Smoking Cessation Project: Implementation and results.* Paper presented at the annual meeting of the American Public Health Association, Atlanta, GA.

Marcus, B. H., Albrecht, A., Niaura, R., Abrams, D., & Thompson, P. (1991). Usefulness of physical exercise for maintaining smoking cessation in women. *American Journal of Cardiology, 68,* 406–407.

Marlatt, G. A., Curry, S., & Gordon, J. R. (1988). A longitudinal analysis of unaided smoking cessation. *Journal of Consulting and Clinical Psychology, 56,* 715–720.

McBride, C. M., & Pirie, P. L. (1990). Postpartum smoking relapse. *Addictive Behaviors, 15,* 165–168.

McBride, C. M., Pirie, P. L., & Curry, S. J. (1992). Postpartum relapse to smoking—A prospective study. *Health Education Research, 7,* 381–390.

McCaul, K., Glasgow, R., O'Neill, H. K., Freeborn, V., & Pump, B. S. (1982). Predicting adolescent smoking. *The Journal of School Health, 52,* 342–346.

Murray, M., Kiryluk, S., & Swan, A. V. (1985). Relation between parents' and children's smoking behaviour and attitudes. *Journal of Epidemiology and Community Health, 39,* 168–174.

O'Campo, P., Brown, H., Faden, R. R., & Gielen, A. C. (1992). The impact of pregnancy on women's prenatal and postpartum smoking behavior. *American Journal of Preventive Medicine, 8,* 8–13.

Ockene, J., Kristeller, J. L., Goldberg, R., Ockene, I., Merriam, P., Barrett, S., Pekow, P., Hosmer, D., & Gianelly, R. (1992). Smoking cessation and severity of disease: The coronary artery smoking intervention study. *Health Psychology, 11,* 119–126.

O'Hara, P., Portser, S. A., & Anderson, B. P. (1989). The influence of menstrual cycle changes on the tobacco withdrawal syndrome in women. *Addictive Behaviors, 14*(6), 595–600.

Orleans, T. C., Rimer, B. K., Cristinzio, S., Keintz, M. K., & Fleisher, L. (1991). A national survey of older smokers: Treatment needs of a growing population. *Health Psychology, 10,* 343–351.

Orleans, T. C., Schoenbach, V. J., Salmon, M. A., Strecher, V. J., Kalsbeek, W., Quade, D., Broods, E. F., Konrad, R. T., Blackmon, C., & Watts, C. (1989). A survey of smoking and quitting patterns among Black Americans. *American Journal of Public Health, 79,* 176–181.

Orleans, T. C., Schoenbach, V. J., Wagner, E. H., Quade, D., Salmon, M. A., Pearson, D. C., Fiedler, J., Porter, C. Q., & Kaplan, B. H. (1991). Self-help quit smoking interventions: Effects of self-help materials, social support instructions, and telephone counseling. *Journal of Consulting and Clinical Psychology, 59,* 439–448.

Ossip-Klein, D. J., Carosella, A. M., & Krusch, D. A. (1994, April). Smoking cessation in older populations. Paper presented at the Annual Meeting of the Society of Behavioral Medicine, Boston.

Ossip-Klein, D. J., Giovino, G. A., Megahed, N., Black, P. M., Emont, S. L., Stiggins, J., Shulman, E., & Moore, L. (1991). Effects of smokers' hotline: Results of a 10 county self-help trial. *Journal of Consulting and Clinical Psychology, 59*, 325–332.

Owen, N., Wakefield, M., Roberts, L., & Esterman, A. (1992). Stages of readiness to quit smoking: Population prevalence and correlates. *Health Psychology, 11*, 413–417.

Perry, C. L, Kelder, S. H., Murray, D. M., & Klepp, K. I. (1992). Community-wide smoking prevention: Long-term outcomes of the Minnesota Heart Health Program and the Class of 1989 study. *American Journal of Public Health, 82*, 1210–1216.

Pierce, J. P., Gilpin, E., Burns, D. M., Whalen, E., Rosbrook, B., Shopland, D., & Johnson, M. (1991). Does tobacco advertising target young people to start smoking? Evidence from California. *Journal of the American Medical Association, 266*, 3154–3158.

Pierce, J. P., Giovino, G., Hatziandreu, E., & Shopland, D. (1989). National age and sex differences in quitting smoking. *Journal of Psychoactive Drugs, 21*, 293–298.

Pierce, J. P., Lee, L., & Gilpin, E. (1994). Smoking initiation by adolescent girls, 1944 through 1988: An association with targeted advertising. *Journal of the American Medical Association, 271*, 608–611.

Pirie, P. L., McBride, C., Hellerstedt, W., Jeffery, R. W., Hatsukami, D., Allen, S., & Lando, H. (1992). Smoking cessation in women concerned about weight. *American Journal of Public Health, 82*, 1238–1243.

Pirie, P. L., Murray, D. M., & Luepker, R. V. (1991). Gender differences in cigarette smoking and quitting in a cohort of young adults. *American Journal of Public Health, 81*, 324–327.

Presson, C. C., Chassin, L., Sherman, S. J., Olshavsky, R., Bensenberg, M., & Corty, E. (1984). Predictors of adolescent's intentions to smoke: Age, sex, race, and regional differences. *The International Journal of Addictions, 19*, 503–519.

Prochaska, J. O., DiClemente, C. C., & Norcross, J. C. (1992). In search of how people change: Applications to addictive behaviors. *American Psychologist, 47*, 1102–1114.

Quinn, V. P., Mullen, P. D., & Ershoff, D. H. (1991). Women who stop smoking spontaneously prior to prenatal care and predictors of relapse before delivery. *Addictive Behaviors, 16*, 29–40.

Rausch, J. L., Nichinson, B., Lamke, C., & Matloff, J. (1990). Influence of negative affect on smoking cessation treatment outcome: A pilot study. *British Journal of Addiction, 85,* 929–933.

Salive, M. E., Cornoni-Huntley, J., LaCroix, A. Z., Ostfeld, A. M., Wallace, R. B., & Hennekens, C. H. (1992). Predictor of smoking cessation and relapse in older adults. *American Journal of Public Health, 82,* 1268–1271.

Santi, S., Best, A. J., Brown, S. K., & Cargo, M. (1990–91). Social environment and smoking initiation. *International Journal of the Addictions, 25*(7A-8A), 881–903.

Sexton, M., & Hebel, J. (1984). A clinical trial of change in maternal smoking and its effect on birth weight. *Journal of the American Medical Association, 25,* 911–935.

Sorenson, G., & Pechacek, T. F. (1987). Attitudes toward smoking cessation among men and women. *Journal of Behavioral Medicine, 10,* 129–137.

Spring, B., Wurtman, J., Gleason, R., Wurtman, R., & Kessler, K. (1991). Weight gain and withdrawal symptoms after smoking cessation: A preventive intervention using d-Fenfluramine. *Health Psychology, 10,* 216–223.

Sussman, S., Dent, C. W., Mestel-Rauch, J., Johnson, C. A., Hansen, W. B., & Flay, B. R. (1988). Adolescent nonsmokers, triers, and regular smokers' estimates of cigarette smoking prevalence: When do overestimations occur and by whom? *Journal of Applied Social Psychology, 18,* 537–551.

Sussman, S., Dent, C. W., Stacey, A. W., Sun, P., Simon, T. R., Burton, D., & Flay, B. R. (1993). Project towards no tobacco use: 1-year behavior outcomes. *American Journal of Public Health, 83,* 1245–1250.

Swan, G. E., & Denk, C. E. (1987). Dynamic models for the maintenance of smoking cessation: Event history and analysis of late relapse. *Journal of Behavioral Medicine, 10,* 527–554.

Svikis, D. S., Hatsukami, D. K., Hughes, J. R., Carroll, K. M., & Pickens, R. W. (1986). Sex differences in tobacco withdrawal syndrome. *Addictive Behaviors, 11,* 459–462.

U. S. Department of Health and Human Services. (1980). *The health consequences of smoking for women. A report of the Surgeon General.* Rockville, MD: U. S. Department of Health and Human Services, Office on Smoking and Health, Public Health Service.

U. S. Department of Health and Human Services. (1988). *The health consequences of smoking: Nicotine addiction. A report of the Surgeon General.* (CDC Publication No. 88-8406). Rockville, MD: U. S. Department of Health and Human Services, Public Health Services, Center for Disease Control.

U. S. Department of Health and Human Services. (1989). *Reducing the health consequences of smoking: 25 years of progress. A report of the Surgeon General.* (DHHS Publication No. CDC 89-8411). Washington, DC: U. S. Goverment Printing Office.

U. S. Department of Health and Human Services. (1992). *Smokeless Tobacco and Health. An International Perspective.* (Smoking and Tobacco Control Monographs No. 2; National Institutes of Health Publication No. 93-3461).

van Roosemalen, E. H., & McDaniel, S. A. (1989). Peer group influence as a factor in smoking behavior of adolescents. *Adolescence, 24,* 801–816.

Waldron, I. (1991). Patterns and causes of gender differences in smoking. *Social Science & Medicine, 32*(9), 989–1005.

Warnecke, R. B., Langenberg, P., Wong, S. C., Flay, B. R., & Cook, T. D. (1992). The second Chicago televised smoking cessation program: A 24-month follow-up. *American Journal of Public Health, 82,* 835–840.

Warner, K. E., & Goldenhar, L. M. (1992). Targeting of cigarette advertising in US magazines, 1959–1986. *Tobacco Control, 1,* 25–30.

Weekley, C. K., Klesges, R. C., & Reylea, G. (1992). Smoking as a weight-control strategy and its relationship to smoking status. *Addictive Behaviors, 17,* 259–271.

Weissman, M. M., & Klerman, G. L. (1977). Sex differences and the epidemiology of depression. *Archives of General Psychiatry, 34,* 98–111.

West, R. J., Hajek, P., & Belcher, S. (1989). Time course of cigarette withdrawal symptoms while using nicotine gum, *Psychopharmacology, 99,* 143–145.

Williamson, D. F., Madans, J., Anda, R. F., Kleinman, J. C., Giovino, G. A., & Byers, T. (1991). Smoking cessation and severity of weight gain in a national cohort. *New England Journal of Medicine, 324,* 739–745.

Williamson, D. R., Serdula, M. K., Kendrick, J. S., & Binkin, N. J. (1989). Comparing the prevalence of smoking in pregnant and nonpregnant women, 1985 to 1986. *Journal of the American Medical Association, 261,* 70–74.

Windsor, R. A., Lowe, J. B., Perkins, L. L., Smith-Yoder, D., Artz, L., Crawford, M., Amburgy, K., & Boyd, N. (1993). Health education for pregnant smokers: Its behavioral impact and cost benefit. *American Journal of Public Health, 83,* 201–206.

Windsor, R. A., & Orleans, T. C. (1986). Guidelines and methodological standards for smoking cessation intervention research among pregnant women: Improving the science and the art. *Health Education Quarterly, 13,* 131–161.

Zelman, D. C., Brandon, T. H., Jorenby, D. E., & Baker, T. B. (1992). Measures of affect and nicotine dependence predict differential response to smoking cessation treatments. *Journal of Consulting and Clinical Psychology, 60,* 943–952.

10

Physical Activity in Women: Current Status and Future Directions

Bess H. Marcus, Patricia M. Dubbert, Abby C. King, and Bernardine M. Pinto

INTRODUCTION

Historically, studies on physical activity and physical fitness, particularly in the domain of cardiovascular health and disease, did not include adequate samples of women, especially older and minority women. However, this has improved in recent years (e.g., Blair et al., 1989; Cauley et al., 1986; Owens, Matthews, Wing, & Kuller, 1990), and there is increasing evidence that physical activity holds the promise of improved physical and mental health for both women and men. For women, the potential benefits include improvement in cardiovascular health (Bovens et al., 1993; Cowan & Gregory, 1985; Jette, Sidney, & Campbell, 1988; Juneau et al., 1987; Owens et al., 1990), attenuation or reversal of mineral loss from bones (R. Marcus et al., 1992), improved immune function (Nieman et al., 1993), and possibly reduced risk for certain types of cancer (Frisch et al., 1985; Pinto & Marcus, 1994). Data suggest that exercise can serve as a primary or adjunctive therapy in mood disorders such as anxiety and depression (see reviews by de Coverley Veale, 1987; Martinsen, 1990; Plante & Rodin, 1990; Raglin, 1990), in middle-aged women (Doyne, Chambless, & Beutler, 1983; Ossip-Klein et al., 1989; Pappas, Golin, & Meyer, 1990), as well as helping to enhance mental well-being in older healthy women (King, Taylor, & Haskell, 1993; Moses, Steptoe, Mathews, & Edwards, 1989), and older women with physical or emotional impairments (Blumenthal et al., 1991). Available evidence suggests that participation in physical activity, rather than increased cardiovascular fitness, may be the factor associated with better health and mood (see review by LaFontaine et al., 1992).

The U.S. Centers for Disease Control and Prevention and the American College of Sports Medicine (1993) have recommended that every American adult should accumulate at least 30 min of moderate physical activity (e.g., brisk walking, gardening) on a daily basis. Despite increasing evidence of the benefits of physical activity, 58.5% of women in the United States remain largely sedentary (Pate et al., 1995), and 64.9% of minority women are reported to be inactive. Demographic factors associated with sedentary lifestyle include being older, African American, female, poorly educated, overweight, or having a history of being physically inactive (Blair et al., 1993). Given the low prevalence of regular activity in healthy women, it is no surprise that women with health problems such as obesity are less likely to participate in physical activity, even slow walking (King, Blair, et al., 1992).

Beyond adolescence and early adulthood, both national samples and community studies reveal a decrease in participation in regular activity (Gartside, Khoury, & Glueck, 1984; Schoenborn, 1986). Limited data on older adults suggest that this decline continues through age 80 with progressively larger proportions of women and men reporting that they get no leisure-time physical activity (Caspersen & Dipietro, 1991; Caspersen, Merritt, Heath, & Yeager, 1990). Even among adults who take up exercise, 50% of men and women are likely to drop out within 6 months (Dishman, 1990; Sallis et al., 1986). The decline in activity with age is particularly disappointing, given the evidence suggesting that people who increase their activity during adulthood can reduce their risk for cardiovascular disease to the level of those who have been active for many years (Paffenbarger et al., 1993).

When type of activity is examined, there is a trend for women to report lower participation in vigorous activity compared with men (Hovell et al., 1989; Sallis et al., 1986; Sidney et al., 1991). In a community sample of California adults, Sallis and colleagues (1986) found that 5% of women adopted vigorous activity versus 11% of men; but 34% of women adopted moderate activity versus 26% of men. Traditionally, assessments of physical activity were developed for male samples and this bias may account partially for the gender differences favoring greater activity in men (Young, King, Oka, & Haskell, in press). When light and moderate activities are considered in the determination of regular leisure-time physical activity levels, the gender difference diminishes or disappears. Besides sex differences related to intensity of exercise, women show a greater preference than men for aerobic dance and videotaped exercise programs (King, Taylor, Haskell, & DeBusk, 1990). If the intensity of the activity is standardized for declining cardiovascular fitness, the proportion of men reporting regular and intense activity increases around retirement and remains relatively stable through age 80 (Caspersen et al., 1990; Caspersen, Pollard, & Pratt, 1987). In contrast, the proportion of women reporting regular and intense activity continues to decline in older age groups. The U.S. Centers for Disease Control and Prevention report that 64.9% of older women are sedentary versus 59.1% of older men (1993). Hence, although participation in regular activity could improve cardiovascular status, and perhaps reduce risk of osteoporosis in middle-aged and older women, these subgroups are less likely to be active and have also been neglected in public health interventions to improve activity levels.

In this chapter, we examine barriers to women's adoption of regular physical activity, and then discuss interventions for the adoption and maintenance of exercise behavior. This is not an exhaustive review but one in which critical issues are highlighted. Finally, we present a research and a policy agenda for future exploration of efforts to promote adoption of an active lifestyle in women.

WHY ARE SO MANY WOMEN SEDENTARY?

Because we know that data showing that women are less active than men may not reflect women's true activity levels, perhaps the correct question to ask is "Why are women not as active as they need to be for optimal health and well-being?" Even if we had measures appropriate for women's lives, they would undoubtedly show that many women are very sedentary or are not performing the kinds and amounts of activity for optimal health and fitness.

The design of better intervention strategies to increase physical activity for women depends in part on an adequate understanding of what prevents them from being more active. Perceived barriers consistently predict amount of vigorous exercise in women and men (Sallis et al., 1989), and failure to overcome existing barriers may be an important reason for the high relapse rate observed in many intervention studies. It is important to look at gender differences because even though many barriers to increased activity are not unique to women, they may be more important or operate differently for women than for men. We discuss several types of barriers to optimal physical activity, which for many women are often closely interrelated.

Biologic and Physical Health Barriers

Differences in female and male anatomy and physiology are appropriate considerations in selecting the types and intensities of optimal activity, but they still too often serve as cues for limiting women's exercise and sports opportunities. Compared with men on average, women are at a strength and speed disadvantage in many activities due to their smaller size, higher body fat, and lower muscle mass. It is likely, however, that much of the increased risk for injury observed in adolescents and women engaged in rigorous training programs is due not to estrogens, but to lack of experience and lower levels of initial fitness (Brandt, 1991). More than 50% of women in their 70's find it difficult to carry 25 pounds and 75% are limited in their physical ability; much of this can be attributed to years of disuse (O'Brien & Vertinsky, 1991). When women and men train together and are equally challenged, their responses to exercise are quite similar (Drinkwater, 1984).

The importance of physical health barriers to exercise for women and men should not be underestimated. A study of female community exercisers found health problems second only to social and work demands as reasons for missed exercise (Dubbert et al., 1994), and a community survey in southern California revealed the most frequent reason for exercise relapses of three months or longer was injury (Hovell et al., 1990). Questions about the possible adverse effects of exercise on women's reproductive health also continue to be raised. High levels of physical activity have been associated with later menarche and menstrual dysfunction, which can lead to possible failure to achieve or maintain optimal bone mass, increased risk of stress fractures, osteoporosis, infertility, and even increased cardiovascular disease risk associated with low estrogen levels (Loucks, 1994). These are legitimate concerns, but primarily for the minority of adolescent and adult women who are very active, such as elite athletes and dancers (Loucks, 1994; Malina, 1994). It is important to note that the effects of physical activity on menstrual function have thus far been confounded with genetic factors (mothers and sisters of athletes also tend to have later menarche), dietary practices used to maintain a thin physique, and the psychological stress of training and competition (Loucks, 1994; Malina, 1994). Clinical observations suggest that most menstrual cycle abnormalities associated with heavy exercise training can be reversed with reduced training, rest, and/or weight gain (Constantine & Warren, 1994). Although untrained women may perceive maximal exercise as more stressful during the premenstrual phase and menses, trained athletes show no differences in maximal or submaximal exercise performance, perceived exertion, or time to fatigue when tested during the follicular and luteal phases of their cycles (DeSouza, Maguire, Rubin, & Maresh, 1990).

Current data suggest that exercise does not cause adverse outcomes in low-risk pregnancies and may even be associated with increased infant weight in women who are already fit (Hatch et al., 1993). However, the female anatomy and reproductive role can result in another type of barrier which is only now beginning to receive attention. A survey of women in private gynecologic clinics found that almost one third of exercisers had experienced urinary incontinence with at least one form of exercise (Nygaard, DeLancey, Arnsdorf, & Murphy, 1990). While 22% of nulliparous women reported problems, incontinence was significantly associated with number of vaginal (but not Caesarean) births. The respondents reported a variety of coping methods: 20% stopped the exercise, 18% changed the way they exercised, and 55% wore a pad as protection. Only 35% of the women had discussed this problem with a physician.

Psychosocial Barriers

There is now a considerable amount of evidence that psychological and social factors are important determinants of exercise (King, Blair, et al., 1992). Lack of interest and lack of enjoyment were identified as important barriers to vigorous exercise for women and men in a community exercise survey (Sallis et al., 1989). Perceived lack of knowledge about how to exercise and lack of exercise skills were also significant predictors. Since this survey was most representative of Caucasian, well-educated, middle and upper income adults, these perceived barriers may be even more important in less advantaged populations. Although women may not be more disadvantaged than men in this regard, it is probably difficult for many to get adequate information or training to guide their physical activity. Few physicians give routine advice about physical activity (King, Blair, et al., 1992), and most women do not have peer role models for appropriate physical activity.

Although it is not clear that participation in physical activity and sports during childhood and adolescent years influences activity throughout one's lifetime (Dishman & Sallis, 1994), most physical activity promotion advocates feel it is important to provide equitable opportunities to boys and girls during these formative years. This may not be easy to do in practice. Even grade school coaches and teachers notice that boys tend to get involved in organized activities earlier while girls tend to be less fit and lack even basic skills, such as how to throw a ball (Raithel, 1987). Most of today's mothers and grandmothers grew up in a time of very limited opportunities for organized sports for females of any age group. The passage of Title IX legislation 20 years ago, prohibiting sex discrimination at institutions that receive federal funds, facilitated many new opportunities for women's sports at educational institutions. In many cases, though, significant inequities remain at the high school and college level because men's sports still bring in and receive the largest share of the available funds. Title IX is also seen as a mixed blessing by those who are concerned that its major effect has been to provide opportunities for the few girls and women with exceptional talent, with little or no increased opportunities for those without unusual abilities (Raithel, 1987).

Lack of time has been reported by women as an important barrier to increased vigorous activity. A survey of African-American and Caucasian women found that women of different racial backgrounds but similar socioeconomic status agreed on the importance of exercise but cited competing demands for time as the major barrier to initiating or increasing physical activity (Johnson, Corrigan, Dubbert, & Gramling, 1990). Work demands, lack of time, and family demands were frequently cited reasons for exercise relapse in a southern California community survey (Hovell et al., 1990). Although many men are trying to expand their traditional roles in families where both partners work, women still usually assume more of the child care and household tasks than men (Rodin & Ickovics, 1990). In a random sample of urban Canadian women, Verhoef, Love, and Rose (1992) found that having children was the best negative predictor of vigorous exercise; employment and marital status were relatively unimportant once age and education were controlled. Among employed women, those with young children (less than 5 years old) are less likely to report exercise participation (Marcus, Pinto, Simkin, Audrain, & Taylor, 1994).

Convenient access to facilities has also consistently emerged as a predictor of exercise in community populations (Sallis et al., 1990), but physical proximity may not increase access equally for men and women. At worksites that provide exercise programs, women with children or elder care responsibilities may not be able to utilize the facilities as easily as men outside of regular working hours. While both women and men may have access to public parks, playgrounds, bicycle paths, sidewalks, and streets, these places may not be as safe for women as they are for men. Recent studies have also begun to evaluate another factor that may be an important barrier for some women: the social anxiety experienced by many individuals related to having to display their physique in an activity setting (O'Leary, 1992). Self-related athletic coordination (compared with same age and gender peers) was a significant predictor of vigorous exercise change in women in a community survey (Sallis et al., 1992).

355

Although there is little doubt that attitudes and expectations about women's participation in sport and exercise have changed significantly over the course of the past few decades, barriers of this type still remain to be overcome. Women are no longer regarded as too fragile to run an Olympic marathon; today's fathers can be seen cheering on their daughter's as well as son's tee-ball and soccer teams; even beauty pageants tout the physical fitness of their contestants. In many women's daily lives, however, social and business customs and fashions often tend to restrict rather than encourage physical activity. High-heeled shoes and tight-fitting skirts make it difficult to walk quickly; carefully coifed hairstyles and cosmetics deteriorate when women begin to perspire. Women may feel pressured to work longer hours to succeed in professions which once were open mainly to men. Concerns about competing with males or feeling that any kind of competition is not "feminine" may also continue to serve as barriers to exercise for some adolescents and adult women. Even four- and five-year-olds, asked to finish a story about a bike race between a boy and a girl, think the boy will win (Raithel, 1987).

Summary: Barriers to Physical Activity for Women

There is as yet very little empirical data to substantiate many of our notions about the multiple and complex factors that facilitate or interfere with healthful physical activity in women. Many studies have not reported findings separately by gender, but available evidence from community surveys suggests that correlates of exercise adoption and maintenance are different for women and men (Sallis, Hovell, & Hofstetter, 1992). It is likely that there are also important differences within gender in individuals with different ethnic backgrounds, income level, and education (Dishman & Sallis, 1994). Additional research examining gender differences is important because, even though many barriers to increased physical activity—low self-efficacy, limited access, health problems, lack of support from family and friends, conflicting demands or lack of time, perceived lack of knowledge or skill, social physique anxiety—are not unique to women, they may be more or less important or operate differently for women than for men.

WHAT HAS BEEN DONE TO INCREASE WOMEN'S PHYSICAL ACTIVITY?

Although much progress has been made in the past 10 years, the study of interventions to increase physical activity behavior in women and men remains at an earlier stage of development than interventions for other major health behaviors such as smoking. The results from currently available studies indicate that a variety of cognitive–behavioral interventions can increase adherence to exercise recommendations in health promotion and rehabilitation programs. One recent review (Dishman, 1991) estimated that adherence improvements averaged 10% to 25% in intervention when compared with control groups, but noted that the absolute levels of exercise usually fell below the frequency, duration, and intensity required for increased cardiorespiratory fitness. In addition, few of the studies reviewed in this article used physiologic measures or health outcomes to substantiate increased participation in exercise. Further, longer-term physical activity maintenance, as reflected in representative intervention studies, has often been poor. Although women have been included in many of the existing cognitive–behavioral health promotion studies, gender differences in response to these interventions have not been examined systematically.

Thus far, intervention studies have focused primarily on the individual or personal level (i.e., health risk appraisal and fitness testing), using behavioral and cognitive-behavioral strategies (see Table 1 for examples of psychological interventions), and utilizing various channels for intervention (i.e., family unit, worksite, physician office, institution, society). Some of these studies have examined the utility of using exercise as an adjunct to treatments for other chronic disease risk factors (i.e., smoking, obesity), and have also attempted to integrate activity interventions into large scale community programs (see review by King et al., 1992). Many of these interventions have shown short-term benefits and some have shown longer-term effects. However, there has been great variability in the scientific rigor of these studies, with few randomized, controlled trials. As mentioned earlier, much of the existing research has neglected women (both majority and minority).

Table 1

Psychological and Cognitive-Behavioral Interventions Used to Increase Women's Activity (Selected Studies)

Type of Intervention	Study	Description/Methods	Outcome
Stimulus control (environmental prompt)	Brownell, Stunkard, & Albaum, 1980	Observed commuters' (women and men) use of escalator vs. stairs using an ABA design to evaluate the effect of a sign encouraging taking stairs for heart health.	Stair use increased for women and men when the sign was present, but women were less responsive and decreased stair use more rapidly after the sign was withdrawn.
Decision balance sheet	Hoyt & Janis, 1975	During a 15-minute phone interview, women enrolled in an exercise class were asked to write down personal benefits, losses, gains and losses to important others, disapproval from self and others, and self approval for taking the exercise class. A control group was not interviewed, and a third group was asked to go through the same process but in regard to reducing smoking.	Attendance through the 7 weeks was almost twice as good for the exercise balance-sheet group relative to the other groups.
Perceived choice	Thompson & Wankel, 1980	Thirty-six adult women were matched by activity preference and were then randomized to one of two groups. Although all exercise programs were based on the women's choices, one group was told their program was based on the choices they had made, while the other was told the instructor decided to disregard their choices.	Attendance was significantly better for the women in the perceived choice group; these women maintained their program while the others dropped out.

Self-monitoring and exercise program staff attention	Weber & Wertheim, 1988	Fifty-five community women were randomized to one of three groups: self-monitoring, self-monitoring plus extra staff attention or control.	The self-monitoring group had the best class attendance, followed by the group which also received extra attention.
Phone call prompts and encouragement from staff for a home-based program	King et al., 1990	In an exercise adoption study, 26 women (and 26 men) were given instructions and a portable heart rate monitor. Subjects mailed daily logs to program staff and about 60% of the women and men also received 10 phone contacts during the 6-month study.	Women and men made equal fitness gains which were significantly greater for the phone and logging portion of the group. No significant difference in amount of exercise recorded by the two group portions.
		In an exercise maintenance study, one group received instructions and another group received phone calls to help them maintain established exercise.	Maintenance was significantly better in the group which received phone calls.
Exercise program staff feedback and type of goals	Martin et al., 1984	Twenty-nine women and four men in a community jogging course were randomized in a factorial design study to either time or distance goals, and to either personal or group encouragement and feedback.	Attendance was significantly better or similar in three of the groups but significantly worse in the group feedback and distance goals combination.
Contracting and exercise program supervision	Craighead & Blum, 1989	Sixty-two obese women enrolled in a university-based weight loss program were randomized to one of three levels of supervision: exercise contracting, exercise contracting plus supervised sessions, and minimal contact.	At one-year follow-up, women in the supervised exercise group maintained a significantly greater weight loss and were the only group which demonstrated fitness changes.

(Table continues)

359

Table 1 (cont.)

Type of Intervention	Study	Description/Methods	Outcome
Cognitive distraction and goal-setting strategy	Martin et al., 1984	Twelve women and five men in a community jogging course were randomized to one of two groups: either attend to internal body sensations or attend to pleasant external stimuli and set high standards for exercise performance and set flexible realistic standards.	The dissociative-cognitive, realistic goal-setting group had significantly better class attendance; fitness improvement correlated with attendance.
Stage-matched manuals to initiate or increase activity	Marcus, Banspach, Lefebvre, Rossi, Carleton, & Abrams, 1992	During a 6-week intervention, a community sample of 610 adults (77% women), whose stage of readiness for exercise was assessed by questionnaire, received a stage-matched manual (based on responses to the questionnaire) for exercise adoption and maintenance.	Subjects were significantly more active after the 6-week program. 62% of subjects in Contemplation became more active and 61% of those in Preparation became more active.
Relapse prevention	Belisle, Roskies, & Levesque, 1987	Participants in a university-based sports center program (60% female) were randomized as classes to receive either the standard training or an experimental one including discussion of obstacles to exercise and means of coping with these.	Experimental condition participants showed better adherence and maintenance to a 3 month follow-up in two studies.

Whereas most interventions have focused on the individual, the family unit offers an important avenue for intervention. The family unit may be important in influencing both the acquisition of exercise behavior as well as exercise maintenance (King, 1991). There are now a number of studies showing concordance of activity patterns among family members (Bouchard, 1990). This similarity may be due in part to genetic contributions to activity patterns, and the genetic predispositions may interact with the family environment to influence activity patterns. Similarly, the family environment may have an independent effect on activity patterns. Some of the factors in the family environment that have been studied include the presence of young children (Marcus, Pinto, et al., 1994), the modeling of exercise behavior among family members, common access to sedentary or active behavioral alternatives, and support of family members for exercising (Epstein, Wing, Koeske, Ossip, & Beck, 1982). It is possible that modifying the family environment, such as reducing access to television, may influence some family members' activity behavior (Epstein, 1992).

Many of the individual and community-level interventions evaluated thus far were inspired by Bandura's social learning/social–cognitive theories (1977, 1986), Marlatt and Gordon's relapse prevention model (1980) and, more recently, the transtheoretical model (Prochaska & DiClemente, 1983). Social learning/social–cognitive theories, broadly defined, view behavior, including health behaviors such as physical activity, as being acquired and maintained through a complex set of behavioral, cognitive, and environmental conditions (Bandura, 1986). These theories emphasize that participation in a health behavior such as physical activity is influenced by a variety of antecedents (both cognitive and environmental) that may facilitate or impede initial adoption of the behavior, as well as a variety of consequences (positive and negative) affecting subsequent participation or adherence. Success in being able to initiate and maintain increases in physical activity is determined by a person's ongoing ability to regulate his or her own behavior through personal strategies (e.g., applying realistic expectations for change, setting goals, monitoring progress toward goals) as well as environmental approaches (e.g., utilization of social support or environmental prompts for physical activity).

Central to social learning theory is the importance of self-efficacy (i.e., confidence in one's ability to successfully perform a specific behavior such as physical activity) as a mediator of attempts to adopt a new behavior as well as in the maintenance of behavior change. Self-efficacy is in turn affected by a variety of factors including personal experience, vicarious experience, and verbal persuasion. Interventions derived from social learning theory have proven to be effective for increasing regular physical activity participation in a variety of healthy as well as clinical populations (Martin et al., 1984; Oldridge & Jones, 1983).

The transtheoretical model integrates current behavioral status with a person's intention to maintain or change his or her pattern of behavior (Prochaska & DiClemente, 1983). Prochaska and DiClemente proposed that individuals who adopt new behaviors move through the stages of Precontemplation (not intending to make changes), Contemplation (considering making changes), Preparation (making small change), Action (engaging in the new behavior), and Maintenance (sustaining the behavior change over time). This model was initially proposed as a general model of intentional behavior change and has been applied to a variety of negative health behaviors, such as smoking (Prochaska & DiClemente, 1983), and more recently to positive health behaviors, such as physical activity (Marcus & Owen, 1992). Instruments have been developed to measure all of the core constructs and these measures have been shown to be reliable and valid (Marcus, Rakowski, & Rossi, 1992; Marcus, Rossi, Selby, Niaura, & Abrams, 1992; Marcus, Selby, Niaura, & Rossi, 1992; Marcus & Simkin, 1993). Moreover, two intervention studies have demonstrated the utility of this model by using stage-matched activity interventions to maximally reach the at-risk population of sedentary individuals (Marcus, Banspach, et al., 1992; Marcus, Emmons, Simkin, Taylor, et al., 1994). Interventions based on the transtheoretical model appear to be efficacious for women and men.

The relapse prevention model was originally designed to enhance maintenance of abstinence in addictive behaviors (Marlatt, 1985; Marlatt & Gordon, 1980). The goal of the model is to teach individuals that a lapse from abstinence (e.g., smoking a cigarette) need not lead to a relapse and that a lapse can be prevented from escalating into a complete relapse (e.g., return to the smoking habit). Cognitive and behavioral strategies are utilized to attenuate the abstinence violation effect associated with a lapse. The relapse prevention model has been applied to positive health behaviors such as weight control (e.g., Brownell, 1988) and exercise participation (e.g., Belisle, Roskies, & Levesque, 1987; King & Frederiksen, 1984; Marcus & Stanton, 1993; Martin et al., 1984). While the relapse prevention model and strategies could contribute to maintenance of exercise, there are difficulties in developing operational definitions of the constructs (e.g., definition of lapse) when the model is applied to the adoption of a positive behavior such as exercise.

WHAT HAS SUCCEEDED AND WHY?

In general, it appears that interventions that emphasize vigorous physical activity may lead to short-term increases in frequency of programmed leisure time activity, but such gains are not likely to be maintained compared with moderate physical activity. With increasing evidence that an extended bout of vigorous exercise 3–4 times per week may not be required for cardiovascular benefits, health promotion guidelines have been altered to promote moderate levels of physical activity and the integration of activity into daily routine (Blair et al., 1993). Moderate activities such as brisk walking, stair climbing, gardening, and recreational sports (3–4 metabolic equivalents) are associated with lower risk of orthopedic injury and it is likely that women could engage in short bouts of such activity (Sallis et al., 1986). King et al. (1991), in their study of middle-aged women and men, found that moderate exercise produced fitness effects that were comparable to changes associated with more intense exercise. Data also suggest that certain dosages of exercise (for example, moderate-intensity home-based activity, of 30 minutes duration) may not only be easier to adopt and maintain, but may produce equivalent or more pronounced psychological benefits compared with more vigorous, supervised group exercise (King, Taylor, et al., 1993).

As seen in Table 1, health researchers have attempted to promote the adoption of activity by investigating the effects of interventions (e.g., self-monitoring, decisional balance sheet, telephone call reminders) that were hypothesized to be equally applicable to all sedentary individuals. The prevalent theoretical trend, however, views behavior change as a dynamic process with individuals at different stages in the adoption of exercise. Development of effective interventions will require an assessment of individual variables (including exercise history, biomedical status, self-regulatory skills, misconceptions about exercise, self-efficacy, and outcome expectancies) and environmental factors that pertain to an individual's readiness to adopt exercise, and then tailoring the activity training (type of activity, frequency, intensity, duration, and locale) to address these factors.

It is also clear that the adoption of physical activity involves variables that differ from those contributing to exercise adherence. Studies evaluating adherence to exercise indicate that women may have a significantly greater number of lapses compared with men during an equivalent period (Dubbert, Stetson, & Corrigan, 1991). Many of the barriers that operate in a woman's attempt to incorporate activity into her lifestyle have been relatively unexplored in interventions at the individual and community level. For example, role overload and parenthood (Marcus, Pinto, et al., 1994; Verhoef & Love, 1992; Verhoef, Love, & Rose, 1992) may interfere with attendance at supervised exercise classes and these variables may moderate the effects of training. Interventions that incorporate social support or that increase program convenience could be particularly helpful for adoption of physical activity, especially among those groups of women (e.g., single parents) who are more likely to experience role overload. Our knowledge of exercise promotion has been derived chiefly from studies on male or mixed gender samples. Definitive conclusions about interventions that facilitate adoption and maintenance of exercise are limited by methodological drawbacks that include the lack of randomization and absence of control groups in some studies (Dishman, 1991).

Control groups are particularly necessary to examine the role of social variables operating in adoption of and adherence to behavior change. In general, subject samples have consisted of healthy volunteers, and hence results are not generalizable to men and women with health problems (such as obesity, arthritis, and angina). Studies are also limited by the use of physical activity questionnaires that were developed and standardized on male samples and, hence, may not be sensitive to the less intense, routine activities that are more characteristic of a woman's daily lifestyle. Thus far, the use of physical fitness measures (e.g., maximum oxygen uptake) for validation of training effects has been the gold standard for intervention studies. However, with the change in health recommendations favoring moderate activity, it may be worthwhile to incorporate behavioral measures (such as direct observations, electronic or self report of activity) and other health outcomes in exercise promotion efforts. Finally, there has been an encouraging trend in the increasing use of follow-up measures to explore maintenance effects of intervention studies.

RECOMMENDATIONS

The dearth of research on physical activity in women, coupled with the substantial prevalence of underactivity among most groups of American women, underscores the need for a coordinated effort on a number of fronts, if significant strides toward the Year 2000 Objectives for the Nation are to be achieved. Given the current pattern of physical inactivity, the Year 2000 goal of no more than 15% of the U.S. population age 6 and older being completely sedentary will not be met until 2024. Given the failure to make progress in this and other areas related to physical activity participation, it is perhaps not surprising that physical activity is listed as the first of the 22 priority areas noted in Healthy People 2000. For maximum effectiveness, such an effort needs to occur with respect to both research and public policy agendas over the next decade.

The Research Agenda

Determine the Effects of Physical Activity on Physical and Mental Health and Functioning

Although the gender gap for research related to physical activity outcomes has begun to close over the past decade, much remains to be learned in determining the specific effects of regular physical activity for women of different ages, health status, as well as socioeconomic circumstances and ethnic/racial backgrounds. The study of outcomes in addition needs to be extended beyond laboratory-based training studies focused on physical performance in highly selected subjects to studies of the longer-term health effects of physical activity in more representative groups of initially sedentary women (Blair et al., 1989; King et al., 1991). A greater emphasis on

365

research to better delineate the types of psychological and related effects of regular levels of physical activity on an individual's quality of life is strongly warranted. To date, relatively little is known about the effects of physical activity on the broad array of factors constituting a person's day-to-day levels of functioning and well-being, often referred to as health-related quality of life (Stewart & King, 1991).

Research in both physical and mental health areas needs to include a focus on delineating the type, format, and 'dose' of physical activity required to achieve minimal as well as optimal levels of a desired outcome. For instance, recent investigations have demonstrated that extended, uninterrupted bouts of exercise are not essential to obtain significant increases in physical fitness in men. In one such study, previously sedentary men who were assigned to undertake three separate 10-minute episodes of exercise per day, five days per week, were compared with men undertaking one sustained 30-minute episode per day, five days per week (De-Busk et al., 1990). Both groups showed comparable increases in cardiorespiratory fitness at the end of the eight-week study period. Similar studies, however, have not been undertaken in women. In addition, studies focusing on shorter bouts of activity (e.g., six five-minute bouts throughout a day) have not been undertaken for women or men. Similarly, exploring the comparative physical and psychological effects of undertaking different types of physical activity (e.g., gardening, brisk walking, swimming) or exercise formats (e.g., exercising in a class or at home, exercising alone or with others) remains in its infancy, particularly when the populations under study are women.

Develop Physical Activity Assessment Instruments Sensitive to the Types and Levels of Physical Activity Engaged in by Women

As noted previously, although national surveys typically report lower physical activity levels in women compared with men across all age ranges (USCDCP, 1993), it has been increasingly recognized that most physical activity assessment instruments are relatively insensitive to the lighter and more diverse forms of daily activities (e.g., walking, child care) engaged in by many women. Recent studies of physical activity that have used more objective measures of physical activity participation, such as physical performance measures or ambulatory heart rate and motion monitors (Blair et al., 1989; Young, King, Oka, & Haskell, in press) suggest that women may be more active than is typically reflected by current measurement instruments. Clearly, if knowledge is to be significantly advanced in this area, more accurate and sensitive instruments need to be developed.

Investigate Processes of Change as They Apply to Physical Activity in Women

Recent investigations underscore the utility of applications of the transtheoretical model and similar process-oriented approaches to the understanding of the stages and processes applicable to women's decisions to consider, prepare for, initiate, and maintain increases in physical activity (Marcus, Eaton, Rossi, & Harlow, 1994; Marcus, Rossi, et al., 1992). Clearly, however, much more work is needed in formulating the most effective interventions for women at these different stages of participation. In particular, investigations of those groups of women remaining in the precontemplation and contemplation stages of physical activity participation are scarce and are especially indicated (Blair et al., 1993; Marcus, Banspach, et al., 1992; Marcus & Simkin, 1994).

Similarly, the developmental stages and milestones that confront a woman throughout her life present potential challenges as well as opportunities for increasing physical activity levels (King et al., 1991). For instance, puberty has been associated with decreases in physical activity levels in young women (Fitness Profile in American Youth, 1983). Other potentially important transitional periods for women that deserve further exploration include entry into college or the workforce, pregnancy, parenthood, menopause, retirement, and family caregiving situations often faced by middle-aged and older women (King, 1991). The systematic investigation of how such milestones can enhance or inhibit physical activity participation is indicated.

Study How Physical Activity Interacts With Other Health Behaviors in Promoting Health

Although there is evidence for both behavioral and physiological synergy between physical activity and the other prominent health behaviors influencing chronic disease—most notably, cigarette smoking and dietary patterns (Wood et al., 1991)—these three health behaviors typically have been studied in isolation. The evidence to date suggests that there is much to be gained by studying the ways in which systematically intervening in one health behavior can have positive consequences on another health behavior. For instance, the planned introduction of a carefully supervised exercise program as part of a formal smoking cessation program has been shown to positively affect women's efforts to quit smoking and remain abstinent through a 12 month period (Marcus, Albrecht, et al., in press; Marcus, Albrecht, Niaura, Thompson, & Abrams, 1991). Similarly, participation in any of three moderate-intensity physical activity programs was found to result in significant reductions in perceived stress levels among initially sedentary smokers (King, Taylor, & Haskell, 1993), thereby reducing one frequently reported barrier to quitting smoking.

The Policy Agenda

In addition to increased scientific activity in the physical activity area for women, a concerted effort to define and disseminate an effective public policy agenda for the promotion of physical activity participation is strongly indicated. This is especially the case in light of the broad array of physical and psychological benefits attributed to regular physical activity participation and the currently low levels of participation by most American women. Formulations of a formal policy agenda in this area have lagged behind those of other health behaviors such as smoking, alcohol, and nutrition (King, Jeffery, & Fridinger, 1993). Two points should be considered in the development of policy-level activities in the physical activity area: Support for nonleisure exercise and the targeting of those members of the population in greatest need.

Support for Nonleisure Exercise

Most efforts to intervene in the physical activity area have focused on programmed or structured activities occurring during leisure-time. Yet, many women spend a large proportion of their day at work, undertaking tasks in or around the home, such as childcare, and in transportation activities. Intervention approaches need to be expanded to take into account these other potential avenues for energy expenditure. For instance, worksites can facilitate increases in activity through a variety of policy and environmental-based approaches, including flexible work hours that permit exercise, availability of showering or changing facilities on-site or close by, point-of-choice prompts and other incentives that encourage employees to use the stairs rather than elevators, and availability of nearby childcare facilities that reduce time and scheduling barriers that may interfere with the ability to exercise. The promotion of family-oriented physical activities may be helpful for women who have young children. In the transportation area, the development of policies that facilitate safe, convenient strategies for incorporating walking, bicycling, and related forms of physical activity into commuting behavior offers a potentially attractive means for encouraging the promotion of physical activity while at the same time helping to conserve natural resources (King, Jeffery, & Fridinger, 1993).

The development of policies that enhance access to recreational facilities in the community for all groups of women and that ensure that such settings will provide a safe and attractive location for families to engage in physical activities together also represents a useful approach for encouraging increases in physical activity across the population as a whole.

Target Those Members of the Population in Greatest Need

The health and functioning benefits of regular physical activity can be most keenly felt by those segments of the American public that are currently least active. A large percentage of such individuals are middle-aged and older women (USCDCP, 1993). It is becoming increasingly clear, however, that successfully involving such groups in regular levels of physical activity will require the development of alternatives to the higher-intensity, class-based approaches to physical activity that constitute the usual programming fare in most U.S. communities (King, in press–a). An example of one such alternative is the development of programs that can be undertaken in the individual's house or work environments, rather than requiring persons to travel to another venue to exercise (King, in press–b). This makes particular sense in light of the preference on the part of most adult women and men to undertake physical activity programs outside of a structured class or group (Iverson et al., 1985; King, in press–a). Systematic efforts to develop supervised home-based exercise programs of either lower or higher intensity have been found to be extremely promising for a variety of groups of women as well as men (King et al. 1991; King, in press–a). Ongoing instruction and support are carried out through the use of regular staff-initiated contacts via telephone and mail. These strategies have resulted in adequate exercise participation rates for periods of up to two years (King, Blair, et al., 1992). Such forms of supervised activity may be particularly useful for women taking care of either children or ailing relatives, many of whom are unable to attend exercise classes in the community on a regular basis (King, in press–b).

Ethnic and racial minorities and the economically disadvantaged represent other groups of women for whom programs tailored specifically to their needs and circumstances are particularly indicated. Those programs reported in the literature that have utilized formative research and other social marketing perspectives in developing interventions that meet the particular needs of such subgroups of women have met with at least some success (Community Health Assessment and Promotion Project [CHAPPS], 1989). Unfortunately, few such programs with disadvantaged populations are currently available. Those that are suggest that physical activity, rather than being perceived as superfluous or of low priority to groups struggling with urban crime, poverty, and related social issues, may be seen as a positive, health enhancing, controllable activity that can bring family and a community together (CHAPPS, 1989; King, 1991).

REFERENCES

Bandura, A. (1977). Self-efficacy: Toward a unifying theory of behavioral change. *Psychology Review, 84,* 191–215.

Bandura, A. (1986). *Social Foundations of Thought and Action: A Social Cognitive Theory.* Englewood Cliffs, NJ: Prentice Hall.

Belisle, M., Roskies, E., & Levesque, J.-M. (1987). Improving adherence to physical activity. *Health Psychology, 6,* 159–172.

Blair, S. N., Kohl, H. W., Paffenbarger, R. S., Clark, D., Cooper, K. H., & Gibbons, L. W.

(1989). Physical fitness and all-cause mortality: A prospective study of healthy men and women. *Journal of the American Medical Association, 262,* 2395–2401.

Blair, S. N., Powell, K. E., Bazzarre, T. L., Early, J. L., Epstein, L. H., Green, L. W., Harris, S. S., Haskell, W. L., King, A. C., Koplan, J., Marcus, B. H., Paffenbarger, R. S., & Yeager, K. K. (1993). Physical inactivity workshop V. *Circulation, 88,* 1402–1405.

Blumenthal, J. A., Emery, C. F., Madden, D. J., Schneibolk, S., Walsh-Riddle, M., George, L. K., McKee, D. C., Higginbotham, M. B., Cobb, F. R., & Coleman, R. E. (1991). Long-term effects of exercise on psychological functioning in older men and women. *Journal of Gerontology, 46,* 352–361.

Bouchard, C. (1990). Discussion: Heredity, fitness, and health. In C. Bouchard, R. J. Shephard, T. Stephens, J. R. Sutton, & B. D. McPherson (Eds.), *Exercise, fitness, and health: A consensus of current knowledge* (pp. 147–153). Champaign, IL: Human Kinetics.

Bovens, A. M., Van Baak, M. A., Vrencken, J. G., Wijnen, J. A., Saris, W. H., & Verstappen, F. T. (1993). Physical activity, fitness, and selected risk factors for CHD in active men and women. *Medicine and Science in Sports and Exercise, 25,* 572–576.

Brandt, E. B. (1991). Coed sports. *The Physician and Sports Medicine,* 19(9), 121–126.

Brownell, K. D. (1988). Weight management and body composition. In *American College of Sport Medicine, Resource manual for exercise testing and prescription* (3rd ed., pp. 355–366). Philadelphia: Lea & Febinger.

Brownell, K. D., Stunkard, A. J., & Albaum, J. M. (1980). Evaluation and modification of exercise patterns in the natural environment. *American Journal of Psychiatry, 137,* 1540–1545.

Caspersen, C. J., & Dipietro, L. (1991). National estimates of physical activity among older adults [Abstract]. *Medicine and Science in Sports and Exercise, 23,* S106.

Caspersen, C. J., Merritt, R. K., Heath, G. W., & Yeager, K. K. (1990). Physical activity patterns of adults aged 60 years and older. *Medicine and Science in Sports and Exercise, 22,* S79.

Caspersen, C. J., Pollard, R. A., & Pratt, S. O. (1987). Scoring physical activity data with special consideration for elderly populations. *Proceedings of the 1987 Public Health Conference on Records and Statistics: Data for an aging population.* (DHHS Publication No. PHS 88-1214, pp. 30–34). Washington, DC: U.S. Department of Health and Human Services.

Cauley, J. A., LaPorte, R. E., Black-Sandler, R., Orchard, T. J., Slemenda, C. W., & Petrini, A. M. (1986). The relationship of physical activity to high density lipoprotein cholesterol in postmenopausal women. *Journal of Chronic Disease, 39,* 687–697.

Community Health Assessment and Promotion Project (CHAPPS). (1989). *Mobilizing a minority community to reduce risk factors for cardiovascular disease: An exercise nutrition handbook.* Atlanta, GA: U.S. Centers for Disease Control.

Constantine, N. W., & Warren, M. P. (1994). Physical activity, fitness, and reproductive health in women: Clinical observations. In C. Bouchard, R. J. Shephard, & T. Stephens (Eds.), *Physical activity, fitness, and health* (pp. 955–966). Champaign, IL: Human Kinetics

Cowan, M. M., & Gregory, L. W. (1985). Responses of pre- and post-menopausal females to aerobic conditioning. *Medicine and Science in Sports and Exercise, 17,* 138–143.

Craighead, L. W., & Blum, M. D. (1989). Supervised exercise in behavioral treatment for moderate obesity. *Behavior Therapy, 20,* 49–59.

DeBusk, R. F., Hakansson, U., Sheehan, M., & Haskell, W. L. (1990). Training effects of long vs. short bouts of exercise. *American Journal of Cardiology, 65,* 1010–1013.

de Coverley Veale, D. M. (1987). Exercise and mental health. *Acta Psychiatrica Scandinavica, 76,* 113–120.

DeSouza, M. J., Maguire, M. S., Rubin, K. R., & Maresh, C. M. (1990). Effects of menstrual phase and amenorrhea on exercise performance in runners. *Medicine and Science in Sports and Exercise, 22,* 575–580.

Dishman, R. K. (1990). Determinants of participation in physical activity. In C. Bouchard, R. J. Shephard, T. Stephens, J. R. Sutton, & B. D. McPherson (Eds.), *Exercise, fitness and health* (pp. 75–102). Champaign, IL: Human Kinetics.

Dishman, R. K. (1991). Increasing and maintaining exercise and physical activity. *Behavior Therapy, 22,* 345–378.

Dishman, R. K., & Sallis, J. F. (1994). Determinants and interventions for physical activity and exercise. In C. Bouchard, R. J. Shephard, & T. Stephens (Eds.), *Physical activity, fitness, and health* (pp. 214–238). Champaign, IL: Human Kinetics.

Doyne, E. J., Chambless, D. L., & Beutler, L. E. (1983). Aerobic exercise as a treatment for depression in women. *Behavior Therapy, 14,* 434–440.

Drinkwater, B. L. (1984). Women and exercise: Physiological aspects. *Exercise and Sports Science Review, 12,* 21–51.

Dubbert, P. M., Stetson, B. A., & Britt, D. (1994, August). Why people don't exercise? A prospective study. Paper presented at the American Psychological Association Annual Convention, Los Angeles, CA.

Dubbert, P. M., Stetson, B., & Corrigan, S. A. (1991, August). Predictors of exercise maintenance in community women. In Marcus, B. H., & King, A. C. (Chairs), *Women and exercise: Community and special populations*. Symposium conducted at the American Psychological Association Annual Convention, San Francisco.

Epstein, L. H. (1992). Role of behavior theory in behavioral medicine. *Journal of Consulting and Clinical Psychology, 60*, 493–498.

Epstein, L. H., Wing, R. R., Koeske, R., Ossip, D. J., & Beck, S. (1982). A comparison of lifestyle change and programmed aerobic exercise on weight and fitness changes in obese children. *Behavior Therapy, 13*, 651–665.

Fitness Profile in American Youth (1983). *A report on 1981–1983 Fitness Test involving more than four million boys and girls in over 10,000 schools*. East Hanover, NJ: Nabisco Brands.

Frisch, R. E., Wyshak, G., Albright, N. L., Albright, T. E., Schiff, I., Jones, K. P., Witschi, J., Shian, E., Koff, E., & Marguglio, M. (1985). Lower prevalence of breast cancer and cancers of the reproductive system among former college athletes compared to non-athletes. *British Journal of Cancer, 52*, 885–891.

Gartside, P. S., Khoury, P., & Glueck, C. J. (1984). Determinants of high-density lipoprotein cholesterol in blacks and whites: The Second National Health and Nutrition Examination Survey. *American Heart Journal, 108*, 641.

Hatch, M. C., Shu, X., McLean, D. E., Levin, B., Begg, M., Reuss, L., & Sussen, M. (1993). Maternal exercise during pregnancy, physical fitness, and fetal growth. *American Journal of Epidemiology, 137*, 1105–1114.

Hovell, M. F., Hofstetter, C. R., Elder, J. P., Faucher, P., Spry, V. M., Barrington, E., & Hackley, M. (1990). Lifetime history of relapse from exercise. *Addictive Behaviors, 15*, 573–579.

Hovell, M. F., Sallis, J. F., Hofstetter, C. R., Spry, V. M., Faucher, P., & Caspersen, C. J. (1989). Identifying correlates of walking for exercise: An epidemiologic prerequisite for physical activity promotion. *Preventive Medicine, 18*, 856–866.

Hoyt, M. F., & Janis, I. L. (1975). Increasing adherence to a stressful decision via a motivational balance-sheet procedure: A field experiment. *Journal of Personality and Social Psychology, 31*, 833–839.

Iverson, D. C., Fielding, M. E., Crow, R. S., & Cristenson, G. (1985). The promotion of physical activity in the United States population: The status of programs in medical, worksite, community, and school settings. *Public Health Reports, 100*, 212–224.

Jette, M., Sidney, K., & Campbell, J. (1988). Effects of a twelve-week walking programme on maximal and submaximal work output indices in sedentary middle-aged men and women. *Journal of Sports Medicine, 28*, 59–66.

Johnson, C. A., Corrigan, S. A., Dubbert, P. M., & Gramling, S. E. (1990). Perceived barriers to exercise and weight control practices in community women. *Women and Health, 16,* 177–191.

Juneau, M., Rogers, F., De Santos, V., Yee, M., Evans, A., Bohn, A., Haskell, W. L., Taylor, C. B., & DeBusk, R. F. (1987). Effectiveness of self-monitored, home-based, moderate-intensity exercise training in middle-aged men and women. *American Journal of Cardiology, 60,* 66–70.

King, A. C. (1991). Community intervention for promotion of physical activity and fitness. *Exercise and Sport Sciences Reviews, 19,* 211–259.

King, A. C. (in press–a). Clinical and community interventions for exercise promotion. In R. K. Dishman (Ed.), *Exercise adherence: Its impact on public health* (2nd ed.). Champaign, IL: Human Kinetics.

King, A. C. (in press–b). Biobehavioral variables, exercise, and cardiovascular disease in women. Proceedings from the NHLBI Conference on Women, Behavior, and Cardiovascular Disease, Sept. 25–27, 1991. Washington, DC: National Institutes of Health.

King, A. C., Blair, S. N., Bild, D. E., Dishman, R. K., Dubbert, P. M., Marcus, B. H., Oldridge, N. B., Paffenbarger, R. S., Powell, K. E., & Yeager, K. K. (1992). Determinants of physical activity and interventions in adults. *Medicine and Science in Sports and Exercise, 24,* S221–S236.

King, A. C., & Frederiksen, L. W. (1984). Low cost strategies for increasing exercise behavior: Relapse preparation training and social support. *Behavior Modification, 8,* 3–21.

King, A. C., Haskell, W. L., Taylor, C. B., Kraemer, H. C., & DeBusk, R. F. (1991). Group- vs. home-based exercise training in healthy older men and women. *Journal of the American Medical Association, 266,* 1535–1542.

King, A. C., Jeffrey, R., & Fridinger, F. (1993). Environmental and policy approaches to intervention in the area of physical activity. *Proceedings from the U.S. Centers for Disease Control and Prevention Conference on Environmental and Policy Approaches to the Prevention of Cardiovascular Disease.* Atlanta, GA: U.S. Centers for Disease Control and Prevention.

King, A. C., Taylor, C. B., & Haskell, W. L. (1993). Effects of differing intensities and formats of 12 months of exercise training on physical outcomes in older adults. *Health Psychology, 12,* 292–300.

King, A. C., Taylor, C. B., Haskell, W. L., & DeBusk, R. F. (1990). Identifying strategies for increasing employee physical activity levels: Findings from the Stanford/Lockheed exercise survey. *Health Education Quarterly, 17,* 269–285.

LaFontaine, T. P., DiLorenzo, T. M., Frensch, P. A., Stucky-Ropp, R. C., Bargman, E. P., & McDonald, D. G. (1992). Aerobic exercise and mood: A brief review, 1985–1990. *Sports Medicine, 13,* 160–170.

Loucks, A. B. (1994). Physical activity, fitness, and female reproductive morbidity. In C. Bouchard, R. J. Shephard, & T. Stephens (Eds.), *Physical activity, fitness, and health* (pp. 943–954). Champaign, IL: Human Kinetics.

Malina, R. M. (1994). Physical activity: Relationship to growth, maturation, and fitness. In C. Bouchard, R. J. Shephard, & T. Stephens (Eds.), *Physical activity, fitness, and health.* (pp. 918–930) Champaign, IL: Human Kinetics.

Marcus, B. H., Albrecht, A. E., Niaura, R. S., Taylor, E. R., Simkin, L. R., Feder, S. I., Abrams, D. B., & Thompson, P. D. (in press). Exercise enhances the maintenance of smoking cessation in women. *Addictive Behaviors.*

Marcus, B. H., Albrecht, A. E., Niaura, R. S., Thompson, P. D., & Abrams, D. B. (1991). Usefulness of physical exercise for maintaining smoking cessation in women. *American Journal of Cardiology, 68,* 406–407.

Marcus, B. H., Banspach, S. W., Lefebvre, R. C., Rossi, J. S., Carleton, R. A., & Abrams, D. B. (1992). Using the stages of change model to increase the adoption of physical activity among community participants. *American Journal of Health Promotion, 6,* 424–429.

Marcus, B. H., Eaton, C. A., Rossi, J. S., & Harlow, L. L. (1994). Self-efficacy, decision-making, and stages of change: An integrative model of physical exercise. *Journal of Applied Social Psychology, 24* (6), 489–508.

Marcus, B. H., Emmons, K. M., Simkin, L. R., Taylor, E. R., Rossi, J. S., Linnan, L., & Abrams, D. B. (1994). Evaluation of stage-matched versus standard self-help physical activity interventions at the workplace. *Annals of Behavioral Medicine, 16,* S035.

Marcus, B. H., & Owen, N. (1992). Motivational readiness, self-efficacy and decision-making for exercise. *Journal of Applied Social Psychology, 22* (1), 3–16.

Marcus, B. H., Pinto, B. M., Simkin, L. R., Audrain, J. E., & Taylor, E. R. (1994). Application of theoretical models to exercise behavior among employed women. *American Journal of Health Promotion, 9,* 49–55.

Marcus, B. H., Rakowski, W., & Rossi, J. S. (1992). Assessing motivational readiness and decision-making for exercise. *Health Psychology, 11,* 257–261.

Marcus, B. H., Rossi, J. S., Selby, V. C., Niaura, R. S., & Abrams, D. B. (1992). The stages and processes of exercise adoption and maintenance in a worksite sample. *Health Psychology, 11,* 386–395.

Marcus, B. H., Selby, V. C., Niaura, R. S., & Rossi, J. S. (1992). Self-efficacy and the stages of exercise behavior change. *Research Quarterly for Exercise and Sport, 63,* 60–66.

Marcus, B. H., & Simkin, L. R. (1993). The stages of exercise behavior. *The Journal of Sports Medicine and Physical Fitness, 33,* 83–88.

Marcus, B. H., & Simkin, L. R. (1994). The transtheoretical model: Applications to the initiation, adoption and maintenance of exercise behavior. *Medicine and Science in Sports and Exercise.*

Marcus, B. H., & Stanton, A. L. (1993). Evaluation of relapse prevention and reinforcement interventions to promote exercise adherence in sedentary females. *Research Quarterly for Exercise and Sport, 64,* 447–452.

Marcus, R., Drinkwater, B., Dalsky, G., Dufek, J., Raab, D., Slemenda, C., & Snow-Harter, C. (1992). Osteoporosis and exercise in women. *Medicine and Science in Sports and Exercise, 24,* S301–S307.

Marlatt, G. A. (1985). Relapse prevention: Theoretical rationale and overview of the model. In G. A. Marlatt & J. R. Gordon (Eds.), *Relapse prevention: Maintenance strategies in the treatment of addictive behaviors* (pp. 3–70). New York: Guilford.

Marlatt, G. A., & Gordon, J. R. (1980). Determinants of relapse: Implications for the maintenance of behavior change. In P. O. Davidson & S. M. Davidson (Eds.), *Behavioral medicine: Changing health lifestyles* (pp. 410–452). Elmsford, NY: Pergamon.

Martin, J. E., Dubbert, P. M., Katell, A. D., Thompson, J. D., Raczynski, J. R., Lake, M., Smith, P. O., Webster, J. S., Sikora, T., & Cohen, R. E. (1984). Behavioral control of exercise in sedentary adults: Studies 1 through 6. *Journal of Consulting and Clinical Psychology, 52,* 795–811.

Martinsen, G. W. (1990). Benefits of exercise for the treatment of depression. *Sports Medicine, 9,* 380–389.

Moses, J., Steptoe, A., Mathews, A., & Edwards, S. (1989). The effects of exercise training on mental well-being in the normal population: A controlled trial. *Journal of Psychosomatic Research, 33,* 47–61.

Nieman, D. C., Henson, D. A., Gusewitch, G., Warren, B. J., Dotson, R. C., Butterworth, D. E., & Nehlsen-Cannarella, S. L. (1993). Physical activity and immune function in elderly women. *Medicine and Science in Sports and Exercise, 25,* 823–831.

Nygaard, I., DeLancey, J. O. L., Arnsdorf, L., & Murphy, E. (1990). Exercise and incontinence. *Obstetrics and Gynecology, 75,* 848–851.

O'Brien, S. J., & Vertinsky, P. A. (1991). Unfit survivors: Exercise as a resource for aging women. *The Gerontologist, 31,* 347–357.

Oldridge, N. B., & Jones, N. L. (1983). Improving patient compliance in cardiac rehabilitation. Effects of written agreements and self-monitoring. *Journal of Cardiopulmonary Rehabilitation, 3,* 257–262.

O'Leary, M. R. (1992). Self-presentational processes in exercise and sport. *Journal of Sport and Exercise Psychology, 14,* 339–351.

Ossip-Klein, D. J., Doyne, E. J., Bowman, E. D., Osborn, K. M., McDougall-Wilson, J. B., & Neimeyer, R. A. (1989). Effects of running or weight lifting on self-concept in clinically depressed women. *Journal of Consulting and Clinical Psychology, 57,* 158–161.

Owens, J. F., Matthews, K. A., Wing, R. R., & Kuller, L. H. (1990). Physical activity and cardiovascular risk: A cross-sectional study of middle-aged premenopausal women. *Preventive Medicine, 19,* 147–157.

Paffenbarger, R. S., Hyde, R. T., Wing, A. L., Lee, I. M., Jung, D. L., & Kambert, J. B. (1993). The association of changes in physical-activity level and other lifestyle characteristics with mortality among men. *New England Journal of Medicine, 328,* 538–545.

Pappas, G. P., Golin, S., & Meyer, D. L. (1990). Reducing symptoms of depression with exercise. *Psychosomatics, 31,* 112–113.

Pate, R. R., Pratt, M., Blair, S. N., Haskell, W. L., Macera, C. A., Bouchard, C., Buchner, D., Caspersen, C. J., Ettinger, W., Heath, G. W., King, A. C., Kriska, A., Leon, A. S., Marcus, B. H., Morris, J., Paffenbarger, R. S., Patrick, K., Pollock, M. L., Rippe, J. M., Sallis, J., & Wilmore, J. H. (1995). Physical activity and public health: A recommendation from the Centers for Disease Control and Prevention and the American College of Sports Medicine. *Journal of the American Medical Association, 273,* 402–407.

Pinto, B. M., & Marcus, B. H. (1994). Physical activity, exercise and cancer in women. *Medicine, Exercise, Nutrition and Health, 3,* 102–111.

Plante, T. G., & Rodin, J. (1990). Physical fitness and enhanced psychological health. *Current Psychology: Research and Reviews, 9,* 3–24.

Prochaska, J. O., & DiClemente, C. C. (1983). Stages and processes of self-change in smoking: Towards an integrative model of change. *Journal of Consulting and Clinical Psychology, 51,* 390–395.

Raglin, J. S. (1990). Exercise and mental health: Beneficial and detrimental effects. *Sports Medicine, 9,* 323–329.

Raithel, K. S. (1987). Are girls less fit than boys? *The Physician and Sports Medicine, 15* (11), 157–163.

Rodin, J., & Ickovics, J. (1990). Women's health: Review and research agenda as we approach the 21st century. *American Psychologist, 45,* 1018–1034.

Sallis, J. F., Haskell, W. L., Fortmann, S. P., Vranizan, K. M., Taylor, C. B., & Solomon, D. S. (1986). Predictors of adoption and maintenance of physical activity in a community sample. *Preventive Medicine, 15,* 331–341.

Sallis, J. F., Hovell, M. F., & Hofstetter, C. R. (1992). Predictors of adoption and maintenance of vigorous physical activity in men and women. *Preventive Medicine, 21,* 237–251.

Sallis, J. F., Hovell, M. F., Hofstetter, C. R., Elder, J. P., Hackley, M., Caspersen, C. J., & Powell, K. E. (1990). Distance between homes and exercise facilities related to frequency of exercise among San Diego residents. *Public Health Reports, 105,* 179–185.

Sallis, J. F., Hovell, M. F., Hofstetter, C. R., Faucher, P., Elder, J. P., Blanchard, J., Caspersen, C. J., Powell, K. E., & Christenson, G. M. (1989). A multivariate study of determinants of vigorous exercise in a community sample. *Preventive Medicine, 18,* 20–34.

Sallis, J. F., Simons-Morton, B. G., Stone, E. J., Corbin, C. B., Epstein, L. H., Faucette, N., Iannotti, R. J., Killen, J. D., Klesges, R. C., Petray, C. K., Rowland, T. W., & Taylor, W. C. (1992). Determinants of physical activity and interventions in youth. *Medicine and Science in Sports and Exercise, 24,* S248–S257.

Schoenborn, C. A. (1986). Health habits of U.S. adults: The "Alameda 7" revisited. *Public Health Reports, 101,* 571–580.

Sidney, S., Jacobs, D. R., Haskell, W. L., Armstrong, M. A., Dimicco, A., Oberman, A., Savage, P. J., Slattery, M. L., Sternfeld, B., & Van Horn, L. (1991). Comparison of two methods of assessing physical activity in the Coronary Artery Risk Development in Young Adults (CARDIA) study. *American Journal of Epidemiology, 133,* 1231–1245.

Stewart, A. L., & King, A. C. (1991). Evaluating the efficacy of physical activity for influencing quality-of-life outcomes in older adults. *Annals of Behavioral Medicine, 13,* 108–116.

Thompson, C. E., & Wankel, L. M. (1980). The effects of perceived activity choice upon frequency of exercise behavior. *Journal of Applied Social Behavior, 10,* 436–443.

U.S. Centers for Disease Control and Prevention. (1993). Prevalence of sedentary lifestyle—behavioral risk factor surveillance system, United States, 1991. *Morbidity and Mortality Weekly Report, 42,* 576–579.

Verhoef, M. J., & Love, E. J. (1992). Women's exercise participation: The relevance of social roles compared to non-role related determinants. *Canadian Journal of Public Health, 83,* 367–370.

Verhoef, M. J., Love, E. J., & Rose, M. S. (1992). Women's social roles and their exercise participation. *Women and Health, 19,* 15–29.

Weber, J., & Wertheim, E. H. (1988). Relationships of self-monitoring, special attention, body fat percent, and self-motivation to attendance at a community gymnasium. *Journal of Sport and Exercise Psychology, 11,* 105–114.

Wood, P. D., Stefanick, M. L., Williams, P. T., & Haskell, W. L. (1991). The effects on plasma lipoproteins of a prudent weight-reducing diet, with or without exercise, in overweight men and women. *New England Journal of Medicine, 325,* 461–466.

Young, D. R., King, A. C., Oka, R. K., & Haskell, W. L. (in press). Patterns of physical activity in older men and women: Are women really less active than men? *Medicine, Exercise, Nutrition, and Health.*

11

Alcohol Use and Alcohol Problems in Women

Sharon C. Wilsnack

Although scientific research on human alcohol consumption dates back at least to studies of psychomotor and cognitive effects of alcohol conducted in the mid-1800s, research that focused specifically on women's drinking was relatively rare before the 1970s. A comprehensive literature search in the early 1970s (Sandmaier, 1980) found only 28 English-language articles on alcohol use or alcohol problems in women, compared with hundreds of published studies of male drinking. Reasons for the early neglect of women in alcohol research most likely included the higher prevalence of drinking and problem drinking among men than among women, the fact that men's problems with alcohol (e.g., alcohol-related crime, accidents, or work problems) tended to be more visible than those of women, and the greater accessibility of men alcoholics as research subjects (e.g., in predominantly male Veterans Administration hospitals

The 1981–1991 national longitudinal study of women's drinking reported in this chapter was supported by Research Grant 5 R37 AA04610 from the National Institute on Alcohol Abuse and Alcoholism, National Institutes of Health. Other senior project staff are Richard W. Wilsnack, Nancy D. Vogeltanz, and T. Robert Harris. I am grateful to Nancy Vogeltanz and Richard Wilsnack for helpful comments on an earlier version of this chapter.

or state hospitals). Another contributing factor may have been the long-standing sexual double standard and stigma surrounding alcohol use in women, which historians have traced back as far as ancient Rome where the Law of Romulus allowed women to be put to death for drinking (Blume, in press). The greater social stigma of alcohol abuse for women may reflect deep-seated cultural fears that excessive drinking by women will threaten their successful performance of traditional wife–mother roles and will result in unrestrained sexual activity that will upset the traditional male-dominated sexual balance of power (Blume, 1991; Sandmaier, 1980). Whatever its source, the stigmatization of women's drinking has clearly contributed to the greater "invisibility" of women's alcohol abuse, by causing both women and their significant others to deny or minimize signs of women's alcohol abuse, and by discouraging women abusers from seeking help for alcohol problems they do acknowledge.

Public interest in and scientific attention to alcohol problems in women increased dramatically during the 1970s, due in part to the "rediscovery" and naming of the fetal alcohol syndrome in 1973 as one distinctive alcohol problem of women (Jones & Smith, 1973) and in part to the heightened awareness of women's health issues raised by the women's movement of the 1960s. Not only was women's drinking now acknowledged by the general public, but an epidemic increase in alcohol problems in women was reported by the popular media, despite the fact that epidemiological research indicated a relative stability of women's drinking during that period (S. Wilsnack, R. Wilsnack, & Klassen, 1986). This tendency to maximize the extent of women's drinking problems during the 1970s may represent a delayed reaction to a long-neglected problem (the assumption that the problem must have increased dramatically if it is just now coming to public attention) or may reflect a more general societal discomfort with changing gender roles and the expanding roles of women (Fillmore, 1984; Morrissey, 1986b).

Accompanying the increased public concern about women's drinking in the 1970s, scientific research on women and alcohol also increased substantially. In the early 1980s, a leading alcohol journal abstracted in one year nearly twice as many research articles on women as had been published between 1929 and 1970 (S. Wilsnack & Beckman, 1984), and studies of women have continued to proliferate since that time. The present chapter provides an overview of current knowledge about women's alcohol use and alcohol problems. Although the chapter assumes that alcohol abuse in women (as in men) reflects complex interactions among biological, psychological, and sociocultural factors, because of this volume's overall concern with psychological research on women's health, the chapter gives somewhat greater emphasis to psychosocial and behavioral aspects of women's drinking than to biological antecedents and consequences.

CONCEPTUAL AND METHODOLOGICAL ISSUES
Some Definitions

Much of the epidemiological research reported in this chapter uses an alcohol problems framework for conceptualizing and measuring drinking behavior and its consequences: Respondents are asked about a large number of specific drinking-related problems (e.g., with work, family, friends, or health), and distributions and correlates are reported either for individual alcohol problems or for specified levels on summary measures of multiple alcohol problems. Some epidemiological studies, and most clinical studies, use diagnostic or quasi-diagnostic measures of alcohol abuse and alcohol dependence. These measures are typically based on diagnostic criteria from the American Psychiatric Association's (1980) *Diagnostic and Statistical Manual of Mental Disorders,* Third Edition (*DSM–III*) or Third Edition, Revised (1987; *DSM–III–R*) in most recent studies. One study to date (Grant et al., 1994) has used *DSM–IV* criteria. In the *DSM–III–R,* alcohol abuse is defined as a maladaptive pattern of alcohol use indicated either by continued use despite persistent adverse personal or social consequences, or by recurrent use that is physically hazardous (e.g., driving while intoxicated). *DSM–III–R* alcohol dependence requires that at least three of nine criteria be met, including impairment of social role performance, unsuccessful attempts to cut down, physical tolerance to alcohol, and withdrawal symptoms. In the present chapter, the terms *alcohol problem* and *drinking problem* are used interchangeably to describe specific physical, behavioral, or social consequences of alcohol use; the focus is on the problem consequence itself (e.g., alcohol-related problems with work, health, or relationships). *Alcohol abuse* or *problem drinking* refers to a pattern of alcohol use that creates adverse consequences for the drinker in one or more major life areas (health, relationships, work, or others). *Alcohol dependence,* or the earlier term *alcoholism,* is used only where studies have included diagnostic measures of alcohol disorders.

Gender Bias in Measurement of Drinking Behavior
Drinking Levels

As discussed in a later section, the same amount of alcohol consumed by a woman and a man of the same weight will produce a higher blood alcohol concentration in the woman. Despite this gender difference in physiological alcohol effects, most surveys use the same definitions of drinking levels for women and men. (For example, *heavy drinking* is defined in many general population surveys as average consumption of two or more drinks per day, or 14 or more drinks per week, regardless of gender.)

Use of gender-specific drinking measures that take into account female–male differences in body weight and body fluid substantially reduces gender differences in reported alcohol consumption (York & Welte, 1994) but may not entirely eliminate men's higher rates of heavy drinking. In analyses of the 1988 National Health Interview Survey (Dawson & Archer, 1992), for example, male respondents continued to exceed female respondents in levels of alcohol consumption (especially at the highest levels of consumption) even after adjustments for gender differences in body weight and total body water. One issue not yet addressed in efforts to develop gender-specific drinking measures is possible gender differences in the rate of drinking: Some evidence suggests that men are more likely than women to drink rapidly, possibly counterbalancing to some extent women's tendency to attain higher blood alcohol levels from similar amounts of consumption (S. Wilsnack et al., 1986). Given the high rate of multiple substance use and abuse by women (see below), it is possible that survey measures of alcohol consumption should also be adjusted to take into account the synergistic effects of concurrent use of alcohol and other drugs.

Drinking-Related Problems

Many of the drinking problems measured in early alcohol surveys (e.g., drinking-related fights, financial problems, or job impairment) were more closely associated with traditional male roles than with traditional female roles, and this masculine bias may have contributed to underidentification and underestimation of women's alcohol problems. However, including additional problem consequences thought to be more relevant to women does not necessarily produce dramatic changes in women's self-reports of problem drinking. In our 1981 national survey, for example, less than 3% of female drinkers reported drinking-related accidents in the home or problems with children, and relatively large numbers of men acknowledged these "new" alcohol problems (S. Wilsnack et al., 1986). It is possible that efforts such as these to identify female-specific drinking problems (see also Klee, Schmidt, & Ames, 1991) will have diminishing returns as women's and men's daily activities increasingly overlap and differences in the types of problem consequences drinking produces in women and men slowly diminish.

Multiple Substance Abuse in Women

Despite considerable clinical evidence of combined abuse of alcohol and other drugs by alcoholic women in treatment (e.g., Celentano & McQueen, 1984; Gomberg, 1993, in press; Lex, 1993), most research on women's substance use continues to focus on either alcohol or one other drug, with only secondary attention to concurrent or alternating use of other substances. Separate funding agencies for alcohol research and drug research at the federal level, as well as different legal issues and treatment traditions, contribute to this substance-specific approach to research and clinical practice.

Different combinations of alcohol and other drug use (e.g., alcohol in combination with tobacco, prescription psychoactive drugs, marijuana, or other illicit drugs) appear to have different distributions and correlates among women in the general population (e.g., Bobo, 1989; Graham, Carver, & Brett, in press; Lex, 1993). These differences may mean that specific combinations of alcohol and other drugs have distinctive antecedents and consequences that may require differentiated approaches to treatment and prevention. Due to space limitations, the present chapter focuses primarily on women's use of alcohol while also acknowledging the need for more research on patterns of multiple substance use and abuse in women.

Subgroup Variations in Women's Drinking

Major themes in the early literature on women and alcohol were the neglect of women in the available research and the need for sensitivity to special characteristics of women's drinking in sample design, measurement, and data analysis (e.g., National Institute on Alcohol Abuse and Alcoholism, 1980, 1986). The energy expended in advocating for the need to study women in general may have caused early investigators to overlook important differences among women: Most early studies treated women as a relatively homogeneous group to be compared with equally homogeneous men. More recent research has given increased attention to variations within the general population of women, across subgroups differentiated by age, employment, marital or family status, ethnicity, and sexual orientation. This chapter highlights recent findings—and gaps in knowledge—regarding these subgroup variations in women's drinking.

Women and Alcohol Versus Gender and Alcohol

The striking neglect of women in alcohol research prior to the 1970s required a strong and specific focus on women's drinking to correct the neglect and imbalance. Given the substantial increase in research on women's drinking in the past two decades, it is now time to ask whether research should give continued specific attention to women's drinking, or more general attention to gender as a powerful sociopsychological variable affecting the drinking behavior and drinking problems of both women and men.

The answer is that both approaches are valuable and necessary, with each best suited to addressing specific questions and filling specific research gaps. Continued studies of all-female samples are important for identifying differences between problem-drinking women and nonproblem-drinking women, whose similar socialization as women cannot explain very different patterns of alcohol use. As discussed in detail below, studies of all-female samples are also critical for explicating similarities and differences in drinking behavior and drinking problems across various subgroups of women. On the other hand, broader gender-based research on both women and men would allow us to evaluate whether some "new" risk factors that appear to strongly predict women's drinking (e.g., sexual abuse or problems of sexual adjustment; see below) are unique to women, more characteristic of women than men, or equally valid for both genders. Further, encouraging greater attention to gender similarities and differences in all alcohol research would allow knowledge of women's drinking to benefit from the rapidly expanding knowledge base concerning alcohol use and alcohol problems generally, not just from studies specifically targeting women. Ultimately, a combination of women-specific research and female-male comparisons could allow treatment and prevention programs to be targeted more precisely to both the shared characteristics and the unique characteristics of women and of men.

DRINKING PATTERNS AND DRINKING PROBLEMS IN WOMEN: EPIDEMIOLOGICAL FINDINGS

Drinking Levels and Drinking Problems

A majority of U.S. women drink alcohol at least occasionally, and the great majority of those who drink do so moderately and without problem consequences. In our 1991 national survey of 1,099 women age 21 and older, 58% of women reported drinking at least once during the past year; 44% of women reported light drinking (average consumption less than 4 drinks per week), 12% reported moderate drinking (4 to 13 drinks per week), and 3% reported heavy drinking (14 or more drinks per week). In this national sample, 13% of women reported experiencing one or more drinking-related problems in the past year, while 10% reported one or more symptoms of alcohol dependence.

Although men were not included in the 1991 national survey, data from other surveys show consistent gender differences in drinking levels and drinking problems: At all age levels, men are more likely than women to drink, to drink heavily, and to report drinking-related problems (e.g.,

Hilton, 1991; Williams & DeBakey, 1992; S. Wilsnack & R. Wilsnack, 1993). Similar gender differences are also reported for other countries and historical periods: Meta-analyses of longitudinal survey data from 15 countries show that in every country and age group represented, adult women were less likely than their male counterparts to drink, to drink frequently or heavily, and to report drinking-related problems (Fillmore et al., in press).

Alcohol Disorders

General population surveys that assess symptoms of alcohol abuse and alcohol dependence find that more men than women meet diagnostic criteria for these alcohol disorders, with a male–female ratio between 2 to 1 and 3 to 1 in recent studies. Williams, Grant, Harford, and Noble (1989) used data from a 1984 national survey to approximate *DSM–III* criteria for alcohol abuse and dependence. The prevalence of these two alcohol disorders in males 18 and older was estimated to be 12.5% and in females 5.1%, a male–female ratio of 2.5 to 1. Using data from a 1988 national survey, Grant et al. (1991) estimated the 12-month prevalence of *DSM–III–R* alcohol abuse and dependence in males 18 and older to be 13.4% and the prevalence in females 18 and older 4.4%, a male–female ratio of 3.0 to 1. The 1990–92 National Comorbidity Survey, the first survey to administer a structured psychiatric interview to a U. S. national sample, found the 12-month prevalence of *DSM–III–R* alcohol abuse and dependence to be 14.1% among males age 15–54 and 5.3% among females, a male–female ratio of 2.7 to 1 (Kessler et al., 1994). The same gender ratio—2.7 males to 1 female—was found in a 1992 national survey of adults, age 18 and older (Grant et al., 1994). Using *DSM–IV* definitions, that survey identified 11.0% of males and 4.1% of females as meeting diagnostic criteria for alcohol abuse or dependence.

Changes in Women's Drinking and Drinking Problems

We have recently evaluated 20-year changes in women's drinking, using data from 15 U.S. national drinking surveys conducted between 1971 and 1991 (R. Wilsnack, Harris, & S. Wilsnack, 1993; S. Wilsnack, R. Wilsnack, & Hiller-Sturmhöfel, 1994). The combined survey evidence suggests that the prevalence of drinking and heavy drinking may have increased slightly during the 1970s but tended to decline after the early 1980s. A downward trend in women's drinking during the 1980s is consistent with reports of drinking declines among both women and men between 1983 and 1988 (Williams & DeBakey, 1992) and between 1984 and 1990 (Midanik & Clark, 1994) and with declining per capita alcohol sales in the United States during the same period (Williams, Stinson, Clem, & Noble, 1992).

Results of our own 10-year followup (1981–1991) of a national sample of 696 women indicated no significant changes in women's rates of drinking problems or alcohol dependence symptoms over the 10-year period (S. Wilsnack, R. Wilsnack, & Hiller-Sturmhöfel, 1994). However, among women drinkers, both the frequency of drinking and the quantity consumed per occasion declined between 1981 and 1991 in most age groups. Although women drinkers in most age groups reported fewer occasions of having six or more drinks in 1991 than in 1981, women drinkers under age 40 also reported an increased frequency of feeling drunk. The apparent paradox that women reported more intoxication despite fewer occasions of heavy episodic drinking may indicate an effect of alcohol awareness campaigns, as well as general increases in health consciousness: Women may now be alert to intoxicating effects from relatively few drinks, and this heightened awareness may cause them to curtail heavier consumption.

BIOLOGICAL ASPECTS OF ALCOHOL USE IN WOMEN

Gender Differences in Alcohol Metabolism

Studies conducted as early as the 1970s (e.g., Jones & Jones, 1976) demonstrated that women attain higher levels of blood alcohol concentration (BAC) than men when consuming the same amount of alcohol, even when effects of gender differences in body weight are controlled. Until recently, women's higher BACs were explained by the smaller proportion of women's bodies that is composed of water, making a smaller volume of fluid available for distribution of the alcohol consumed (e.g., Marshall, Kingstone, Boss, & Morgan, 1983). In 1990, Frezza et al. reported that gender differences in gastric metabolism of alcohol, regulated by the enzyme alcohol dehydrogenase (ADH), also appear to contribute to higher BACS in women. Nonalcoholic women had lower levels of gastric ADH activity than nonalcoholic men, and correspondingly lower proportions of alcohol metabolized in the stomach. Interestingly, alcoholic women and men had lower gastric ADH activity than their nonalcoholic counterparts, with the differences greatest for alcoholic women (who had virtually no gastric metabolism of alcohol).

Thus, there appear to be at least three reasons why women attain higher blood alcohol concentrations than men if they consume the same amount of alcohol: (a) their tendency, on average, to weigh less than men; (b) the smaller proportion of water available in women's bodies for distribution of the alcohol consumed; and (c) the smaller proportion of alcohol that is metabolized in women's stomachs in comparison with men's. These differences have been acknowledged in gender-specific guidelines for alcohol consumption, such as the U.S. Department of Agriculture's definition of "moderate" drinking as not more than two standard drinks (12 ounces beer, 5 ounces wine, 1 1/2 ounces liquor) per day for men and not more than one standard drink per day for women (Dietary Guidelines, 1990).

Biomedical Consequences of Alcohol Use in Women
Adverse Effects of Alcohol Consumption

The fact that women reach higher blood alcohol concentrations than men when consuming the same amounts of alcohol may help explain women's greater vulnerability to certain medical consequences of alcohol abuse. Gender differences in susceptibility are particularly pronounced for alcohol-related liver disease, including alcoholic cirrhosis, which is more likely to develop in alcohol abusing women than men and which tends to occur in women at an earlier stage of problem drinking and at lower levels of alcohol consumption (e.g., Deal & Gavaler, 1994; Hill, 1984, 1995). In addition to the increased bioavailability of alcohol in women, biochemical gender differences and interactions between alcohol effects and female hormones may contribute to the increased liver toxicity of alcohol in women (Lieber, 1993).

Other consequences of heavy alcohol consumption for which women may be at special risk include gastric ulcer (Rabinovitz, Van Thiel, Dindzans, & Gavaler, 1989), menstrual disturbances and impaired fertility (Becker, Tonnesen, Kaas-Claesson, & Gluud, 1989), and breast cancer. Several larger epidemiological studies have reported a modest positive association between alcohol consumption and breast cancer risk. Risks of developing breast cancer appear to be approximately twice as high (relative risk of 2.0) among women consuming two or more standard drinks per day as among women who do not drink; relative risks for women consuming fewer than two drinks per day are between 1.2 and 1.5 in most studies (Hiatt, 1990; Rosenberg, Metzger, & Palmer, 1993). The causal role of alcohol in these associations is unclear at present, and research on possible mechanisms (including alcohol-induced elevations of estrogen levels) is currently underway (Reichman, 1994).

Protective Effects of Moderate Consumption

There has been considerable scientific and public interest recently in the possible health benefits of moderate alcohol consumption (e.g., Ashley, Ferrence, Room, Rankin, & Single, 1994). Protective effects of moderate alcohol consumption on risk of coronary heart disease have been demonstrated in a number of studies of both women and men (e.g., Gaziano et al., 1993; Razay, Heaton, Bolton, & Hughes, 1992; Stampfer, Colditz, Willett, Speizer, & Hennekens, 1988). As with studies of alcohol and breast cancer, specific thresholds and upper limits of consumption that confer protective effects differ across studies. Among 2,599 women in the Framingham heart disease study (Gordon & Kannel, 1983), significant reductions in coronary heart disease deaths were observed for women who reported consuming between 0.7 drinks and 4.3 drinks daily, while in a more recent study of more than 87,000 women (Stampfer et al., 1988) risks of myocardial infarction were reduced among women consuming 0.1 to 1.5 drinks daily (Gavaler, 1993). Other evidence indicates that moderate alcohol consumption increases estradiol levels in healthy postmenopausal women (Gavaler & Van Thiel, 1992), suggesting one possible mechanism for alcohol's protective cardiovascular effects.

For individual women deciding whether to drink, evidence suggesting modest benefits of moderate drinking for cardiovascular health may conflict with other evidence of increased health risks (e.g., accidents, breast cancer) from less than excessive levels of drinking. Further research is needed to evaluate the risk–benefit ratios of moderate alcohol consumption within subpopulations of women. For example, Rehm and Sempos (1994) reported that positive effects of moderate alcohol consumption on all-cause mortality in a U.S. national sample were evident only among women and men over age 60, which suggests that cardiovascular benefits may not be great enough among younger persons to offset the increased risks of injury or death from alcohol-related traffic and other accidents.

Drinking in Pregnancy and Fetal Alcohol Syndrome

Although deleterious effects of drinking during pregnancy have been observed and recorded since Old Testament times, the fetal effects of heavy alcohol consumption in pregnancy have been identified as a medical syndrome for only the past 25 years. A distinctive cluster of fetal abnormalities (growth retardation, characteristic facial abnormalities, and central nervous system dysfunction) associated with heavy drinking in pregnancy was first reported in the medical literature by a French research group (Lemoine, Harouseau, Borteryu, & Menuet) in 1968 and independently in 1973 by American researchers (Jones & Smith) who first used the name "fetal alcohol syndrome" (FAS). Prevalence of FAS was estimated in 1987 to be 1.9 cases per 1,000 live births (Abel & Sokol, 1987); a more recent, revised estimate by the same authors is 0.33 cases per 1,000 live births (Abel & Sokol, 1991).

Although there is little disagreement that very heavy alcohol consumption during pregnancy can produce FAS and other milder fetal effects, there is less consensus about effects of light and moderate consumption. Differences in study populations, definitions of moderate drinking, patterns of drinking behavior assessed, and other methodological differences across studies have contributed to the inconsistent findings of research on moderate drinking in pregnancy (Day, 1992; Tolo & Little, in press). Also inconclusive are the much smaller number of studies investigating possible adverse effects of paternal drinking on pregnancy outcome (e.g., Cicero, 1994; Little & Sing, 1987; Savitz, Zhang, Schwingl, & John, 1992). Legal and sociopolitical aspects of alcohol use in pregnancy are discussed in a later section on social policy issues.

Familial and Genetic Contributions

One of the most consistent findings in the alcohol research literature is the association between a positive family history of alcohol dependence and an individual's increased risk for alcohol disorders. Cotton's (1979) frequently cited review of 39 family studies found that family histories of alcoholism were four to six times more common among alcoholics than among non-alcoholics, and were more common among women than men alcoholics.

Familial contributions to alcohol disorders can include both genetic and environmental factors, and a substantial body of behavioral genetic research conducted during the past two decades has attempted to disentangle the two types of influences. Most of this research supports a genetic contribution of moderate strength for alcohol dependence in men, particularly for dependence that is severe and develops early in life (Goodwin, Schulsinger, Hermansen, Guze, & Winokur, 1973; Hill & Smith, 1991; McGue, 1993). A recent review (McGue & Slutske, 1993) found support for genetic inheritance of male alcoholism in four of five adoption studies (comparing rates of alcohol disorders in adopted-away offspring of biological alcoholic and nonalcoholic parents) and in five of six twin studies (comparing alcohol disorders in monozygotic and dizygotic twins).

Genetic research on alcohol disorders in women is more limited, both in the number of available studies and in the smaller numbers of female subjects in most studies. Of the four adoption studies of women published at the time this chapter was written, two (Goodwin et al., 1977; Roe, 1944) found no significant differences between adopted-away daughters of biological alcoholic and nonalcoholic parents, while two (Bohman, Sigvardsson, & Cloninger, 1981; Cadoret, O'Gorman, Troughton, & Heywood, 1985) reported significant increases in risk for adopted-away daughters of biological alcoholic parents (only mothers in Bohman et al.). In five published studies of female twin pairs summarized by McGue and Slutske (1993), only two reported significantly higher concordance for alcohol dependence among monozygotic as compared with dizygotic twins. In one of the two published studies (Pickens et al., 1991), the higher concordance for female monozygotic twins occurred only for diagnoses of alcohol dependence (not alcohol abuse), suggesting greater heritability for more severe alcohol disorders. The second published twin study with positive findings is the largest reported to date (Kendler, Heath, Neale, Kessler, & Eaves, 1992): In 160 female twin pairs with one or both members alcohol dependent, the concordance rate was significantly higher for monozygotic twins (.32) than for dizygotic twins (.24). Other large-sample genetic studies that include female twin pairs were underway at the time of writing this chapter, and several unpublished reports (e.g., Heath et al., 1993) indicate significantly higher concordance for alcohol dependence in monozygotic than in dizygotic female twins.

Methodological limitations of earlier genetic studies of women (in particular, their small samples), as well as differences in sample characteristics and statistical assumptions across studies, make it difficult to draw firm conclusions. Indeed, behavioral genetic researchers themselves disagree about whether the inconsistent findings of available studies do (e.g., McGue & Slutske, 1993) or do not (e.g., Heath, Slutske, & Madden, in press; Hill, 1993) suggest a weaker genetic contribution to alcohol disorders in women than in men. What is clear, however, is that the available data do support a major contribution of environmental factors to women's risk of alcohol disorders. Some sense of the possible balance between genetic and environmental contributions is conveyed by an observation of McGue and Slutske's (1993): Of the 408 adopted-away daughters of alcohol abusers in the four adoption studies published to date, only 4.7% (compared with 3.1% of adopted-away daughters of non-alcohol abusers) themselves met diagnostic criteria for alcohol abuse. Obviously, a large amount of variance in women's risks of developing alcohol problems is yet to be explained, by familial and nonfamilial environmental factors or by combinations of genetic and environmental conditions too complex or subtle to be identified in behavioral genetic research conducted to date.

PSYCHOSOCIAL RISK FACTORS FOR ALCOHOL ABUSE IN WOMEN

Recent research on women and alcohol has identified a number of individual–psychological and social–environmental factors that correlate with (in cross-sectional analyses) or predict (in longitudinal studies) heavier drinking and adverse drinking consequences in women. Although in this section we use the term *risk factors,* in some cases the predictive significance of the variables has not yet been evaluated in longitudinal research. Where longitudinal data are available (and thus the "risk factor" terminology is precisely accurate), this fact is noted.

Demographic Characteristics and Social Roles

Age

Younger women. Women in their 20s and early 30s consistently show higher rates of drinking-related problems and alcohol dependence symptoms than do women in older age groups (e.g., Hilton, 1991; R. Wilsnack, S. Wilsnack, & Klassen, 1984). In the 1991 national survey, for example, 26% of women aged 21–30 reported experiencing at least one drinking problem and 22% reported experiencing at least one alcohol dependence symptom in the past 12 months; rates of drinking problems ranged from 2% to 17%, and rates of alcohol dependence symptoms from 1% to 10%, in older age groups (S. Wilsnack, R. Wilsnack, & Hiller-Sturmhöfel 1994). One reason for younger women's higher rates of problem consequences may be their greater tendency to engage in heavy episodic drinking (defined in our surveys as 6 or more drinks on a drinking day). A single "burst" of heavy drinking by a young woman may pose substantially greater risks of adverse social and behavioral consequences (e.g., impaired driving or being more vulnerable to sexual assault) than does the same number of drinks consumed by an older woman who spaces them more regularly over a longer period of time.

In addition to their higher rates of alcohol problems in cross-sectional analyses, young women are also the most likely to show fluctuation in their drinking problems over time (Fillmore et al., 1991). Longitudinal analyses of a subsample of 1981 problem drinkers and nonproblem drinkers who were reinterviewed in 1986 (S. Wilsnack, Klassen, Schur, & R. Wilsnack, 1991) found that women aged 21–34 were the most likely of any age group to show movement both into problem drinking (27% of 1981 nonproblem drinkers in this youngest age group reported at least one problem drinking indicator by 1986) and out of problem drinking (38% of young women reporting two or more problem drinking indicators in 1981 reported no such indicators in 1986). Women may move into and out of problem drinking more often in their twenties because their drinking contexts, drinking partners, and social roles (employment, marriage, parenthood)—all potentially important influences on drinking behavior—are more likely to change then than later in life.

Like general population surveys, clinical studies of alcoholic women in treatment also show age-related differences. In comparisons of three age groups of alcoholic women (approximately 100 women each in their 20s, 30s, and 40s), Gomberg (1991, 1993) found that alcoholic women in their 20s were more likely than older alcoholic women to report childhood histories of impulsive behavior, use of illicit drugs, drinking in public places, violent victimization, legal problems and arrests, and suicide attempts. These patterns suggest that early onset of alcohol problems in women, as in men, may be linked to impulsive behavior and antisocial personality disorder (Gomberg, in press).

Older women. Although women over age 65 consistently report the lowest rates of drinking and drinking problems of any age group, attention to older women's drinking is important for several reasons. These include the heightened physiological effects of alcohol in elderly persons; the prevalence of prescription drug use among older women, creating increased risks of alcohol–drug interactions; and the fact that sexist and ageist stereotypes combine to discourage identification of and intervention with older problem drinking women (Dufour, Archer, & Gordis, 1992; Finney, Moos, & Brennan, 1991; Graham et al., in press). Although recent survey data do not indicate a cohort increase in rates of drinking or drinking problems among older women socialized to alcohol after the era of Prohibition, the increasing numbers of women living to older ages means that the absolute numbers of older women with alcohol problems will likely increase. A recent review concluded that research is needed but lacking on at least three important issues: (a) reasons for older women's relatively low rates of drinking-related problems and relatively high rates of problem drinking remission; (b) influences of partner's drinking and other aspects of close relationships on older women's drinking; and (c) age- as well as gender-sensitive assessment and treatment for older problem drinking women (S. Wilsnack, Vogeltanz, Diers, & R. Wilsnack, in press).

Employment

Paid employment and multiple roles. As in other areas of women's health research, investigators studying women and alcohol have been interested in associations between employment status and women's drinking and drinking problems. Although women employed outside the home do report higher rates of drinking (nonabstention) or more frequent drinking than homemakers in most studies, rates of heavy drinking and drinking problems generally do not differ for employed women and homemakers (Shore, 1985, 1992; R. Wilsnack & S. Wilsnack, 1992).

There has been some concern that women might use alcohol to cope with stresses of trying to do too much, for example, taking on paid employment in addition to family roles. One early study (Johnson, 1982) reported increased alcohol abuse among women in a 1975 national sample who combined paid employment and marriage. However, more recent research suggests that having too few social roles may pose more risks for women's drinking than having too many. In our own 1981 national sample, women who lacked social roles (e.g., being unmarried or without a full-time work role) or who had lost social roles (e.g., through divorce, separation, or children's departure) reported more problem drinking indicators than did women with multiple roles (R. Wilsnack & Cheloha, 1987). Other findings consistent with role deprivation as a risk factor for women's alcohol abuse have been reported by Hammer and Vaglum (1989) in Norway, Romans-Clarkson, Walton, Herbison, and Mullen (1992) in New Zealand, Shore (1990) and Gomberg (in press) in the United States, and in longitudinal analyses of our 1981 and 1986 surveys (S. Wilsnack et al., 1991). Multiple roles may reduce women's alcohol use because of the increased self-esteem and social support gained from employment and family roles, because of increased responsibilities and performance demands, and because of the greater social monitoring and feedback that may discourage excessive drinking behavior. The degree to which women experience their multiple social roles as voluntary or involuntary may also mediate the roles' effects on drinking behavior: Analyses of our 1981 and 1986 survey data (R. Wilsnack, 1992) indicate that heavier drinking and adverse drinking consequences in women were associated both with not having roles that were desired (e.g., involuntarily being unmarried, unemployed, or childless) and with having roles that were not desired (e.g., an unwanted marriage, job, or family).

Nontraditional employment. Studies in Finland (Haavio-Mannila, 1991), Norway (Hammer & Vaglum, 1989), and the Czech Republic (Kubicka, Csemy, & Kozeny, 1991) have found that drinking and heavier drinking are more prevalent among women working in traditionally male-dominated occupations. In the United States, LaRosa (1990) found that high-ranking women executives were more likely to be drinkers, and among drinkers to drink moderately or heavily, than other employed women of comparable age and education; and R. Wilsnack and Wright (1991) found that women drinkers employed in occupations that were more than 50% male scored higher on a problem drinking index than women drinkers in occupations that were more than 50% female. As-yet-untested hypotheses are that predominantly male occupations may encourage women to drink more heavily or instrumentally because of the presence of heavier-drinking peers and increased drinking opportunities, stress related to women's minority status, obligations to conform to gendered occupational cultures that include drinking norms, and the possible symbolic use of drinking by women in traditionally male jobs as a way to assert or express power and gender equality.

Marital Status

Cohabitation. In both the 1981 and 1991 national surveys, unmarried women who lived with a partner were more likely than all other marital status groups to report heavy drinking, drinking problems, and alcohol dependence symptoms (R. Wilsnack et al., 1984; S. Wilsnack, in press). Cohabitation was also a longitudinal predictor of the onset of several problem drinking indicators in analyses of the 1981 and 1986 survey data (S. Wilsnack et al., 1991). Factors that may affect the drinking of cohabiting women include specific stresses or tensions (e.g., related to ambiguity, uncertainty, and lack of institutional support of nonmarital cohabitation), and the possibility that cohabiting male partners are more likely than husbands to provide women with models and encouragement for heavier drinking. In addition, women who live with a partner outside of marriage may be less conventional than other women, experiencing greater freedom from traditional norms that have limited both drinking behavior and nonmarital sexual behavior in women.

Divorce and separation. Most cross-sectional drinking surveys have found higher rates of heavy drinking or adverse drinking consequences among divorced and separated women than among married women (e.g., Clark & Midanik, 1982; Johnson, 1982; R. Wilsnack et al., 1984), although these patterns may be somewhat weaker in more recent surveys (Health & Welfare Canada, 1990; Hilton, 1991; S. Wilsnack & R. Wilsnack, 1993).

In longitudinal analyses of 1981 and 1986 survey data, nonproblem drinkers who divorced or separated between 1981 and 1986 were slightly more likely to report problem drinking indicators in 1986, but numbers of cases were too small to attain statistical significance. However, among women already showing signs of problem drinking in 1981, divorce or separation during the followup interval predicted a reduction in alcohol dependence symptoms (S. Wilsnack et al., 1991). Other analyses showed that associations between divorce or separation and problem drinking remission were particularly strong among problem drinking women whose marriages in 1981 were characterized by either a frequent-drinking partner, sexual dysfunction, or both (Klassen, Wilsnack, Harris, & Wilsnack, 1991). These patterns suggest that divorce may have several different relationships with women's problem drinking. Following divorce or separation, women not previously problem drinkers may experience some increased risk of problem drinking (see also Hanna, Faden, & Harford, 1993; Temple et al.,

1991). On the other hand, for women already experiencing problems with alcohol, one effect of divorce or separation may be to provide an escape from distressed relationships which may have contributed to their alcohol abuse, thus improving their chances of problem drinking remission.

Ethnicity

Among the three largest ethnic categories in the United States, national drinking surveys generally find that White non-Hispanic women and men are most likely to be drinkers, Black non-Hispanic women and men are least likely to drink, and Hispanic women and men are intermediate (e.g., Caetano, 1991; Grant et al., 1991; Herd, 1991). Within all ethnic subgroups and at all adult age levels, men exceed women in rates of drinking, heavier drinking, drinking problems, and alcohol disorders.

Research on ethnic variations in women's drinking has suffered from several methodological limitations. Even in national drinking surveys that oversample ethnic minority respondents (e.g., Clark & Hilton, 1991), the low rates of heavier drinking among African-American and Hispanic women mean that too few African-American and Hispanic women problem drinkers are available for reliable statistical analysis. An additional problem is the striking heterogeneity within broad ethnic categories such as "Asian," "Latino," "African American," and "American Indian," making the study of intragroup heterogeneity as important as the study of intergroup heterogeneity (Gilbert & Collins, in press). As one example, women's drinking patterns vary widely across American Indian tribal groups, with women in tribes with gender-differentiated behavior norms (e.g., the Pueblo Indians of the Southwest) typically drinking little if at all, while women of tribes with less differentiated gender roles (e.g., Plains Indian tribes such as the Apache, Ute, or Sioux) show much greater variation in drinking levels (May, 1991). Although African American and American Indian women appear to be at higher risk than White women for certain biomedical consequences of alcohol abuse, such as cirrhosis and fetal alcohol syndrome (Aase, 1994; Leland, 1984), uncontrolled environmental and health variables (e.g., poverty, malnutrition, other health problems) and ethnic stereotypes may exaggerate the extent of actual racial or ethnic differences in biological vulnerability to some alcohol effects.

One strong predictor of women's drinking across various ethnic subgroups is *acculturation,* the process by which an immigrant population adopts the attitudes, values, and behavior of the society they have entered (Gilbert & Collins, in press). Effects of acculturation are particularly striking in second- and third-generation Mexican-American women (e.g., Caetano & Medina Mora, 1988) but have also been reported for Japanese-American women (Kitano, Chi, Rhee, Law, & Lubben, 1992) and for Puerto Rican and Cuban-American women (Black & Markides, 1993). Recent reports of heavier drinking and increased smoking among younger and more highly acculturated Hispanic women (Berman & Gritz, 1993; Gilbert, 1991) suggest that subgroups of women experiencing rapid acculturation may be important target groups for health promotion efforts.

Individual–Psychological Risk Factors
Other Psychiatric Disorders

Depression. A sizable literature based on clinical studies of alcoholics in treatment describes co-occurrence or comorbidity of alcohol abuse and dependence with other psychiatric disorders. The most consistent findings regarding gender are that depression is more commonly diagnosed in alcoholic women, while antisocial personality disorder and other substance use disorders are more common in alcoholic men (e.g., Hesselbrock & Hesselbrock, in press; Hill, 1995). Although stronger associations between alcohol problems and depression among women than among men have also been reported in cross-sectional general population surveys (e.g., Midanik, 1983), neither clinical studies nor cross-sectional surveys permit firm conclusions about the temporal and causal sequences of alcohol abuse and depression.

Longitudinal analyses of a large international data set suggest that depression may indeed be a risk factor that precedes and increases the likelihood of problem drinking in women. In meta-analyses of eight longitudinal general population surveys in the U. S., Canada, and Scotland (Hartka et al., 1991), higher levels of depression at the first measurement point predicted higher alcohol consumption at the final measurement point for women but not for men. The reciprocal pattern also occurred: Depression at the final measurement point was significantly predicted by both alcohol consumption and level of depression at the first measurement point, with these relationships stronger among women than among men. This bidirectional association between alcohol consumption and depression has been reported in other studies of social drinkers and alcoholics (Hesselbrock & Hesselbrock, in press) and in our national longitudinal survey of women's drinking (S. Wilsnack et al., 1991).

Anxiety. The comorbidity of alcohol abuse and anxiety disorders has been described as "startlingly high," with the prevalence of severe anxiety disorders among alcoholics in treatment ranging as high as 50% (Barlow, 1988). As with depression, relationships between heavy alcohol use and anxiety may be reciprocal, and may vary across subtypes of anxiety disorders. A comprehensive review of clinical and epidemiological studies (Kushner, Sher, & Beitman, 1990) concluded that for agoraphobia and social phobia, alcohol abuse is more likely to follow, and represent an attempt to self-medicate, anxiety symptoms, whereas panic disorder and generalized anxiety disorder may more often be consequences of excessive alcohol consumption. Most studies do not provide gender-specific comorbidity rates for alcohol abuse and anxiety disorders. However, the higher rates of phobias and other anxiety disorders among women than among men (Kessler et al., 1994)—and the associations discussed below among sexual assault, posttraumatic stress disorder (PTSD), and alcohol abuse in women (e.g., Calhoun & Atkeson, 1991)—suggest that PTSD and the phobias may be significant contributors to the etiology of alcohol abuse among women.

Negative emotionality. McGue and Slutske (1993) recently summarized four studies of personality characteristics of women at risk for alcoholism by virtue of having an alcoholic parent. Three broad personality dimensions were measured in the four studies: positive emotionality (the tendency toward active and pleasurable engagement with one's environment), negative emotionality (the tendency to experience negative mood states and psychological distress), and behavioral control (the capacity to inhibit behavior and conform to conventional social norms). Average effect sizes for the three personality dimensions across the four high-risk studies suggested that positive emotionality was unrelated to alcoholism risk status in women, while negative emotionality and low behavioral control were significantly associated with alcoholism risk. Thus, findings of these high-risk studies are consistent with clinical-retrospective and longitudinal data suggesting that depression, anxiety, and other negative emotionality may be risk factors for subsequent problem drinking in women, perhaps to a greater extent than they are in men.

Eating disorders. Possibly because eating disorders are relatively rare in men, most studies of alcoholic samples until recently gave little attention to the co-occurrence of alcohol abuse and eating disorders. In the past decade, however, both clinical studies and general population surveys have documented an increased prevalence of alcohol and other drug abuse among eating disorder patients and of eating disorders among substance abuse patients. In a review of recent studies, Krahn (1993) concluded that there is support for two possible explanations of the comorbidity of eating disorders and substance abuse: the presence of a common, genetically influenced predisposition to both substance abuse and disordered eating behavior; and a tendency for food deprivation (i.e., from dieting) to increase the consumption, and possibly the reward value, of other reinforcing substances such as alcohol or other drugs. Other possible mechanisms might include long-term affective disregulation and profoundly damaged self-image and self-esteem resulting from traumatic early experiences such as childhood sexual abuse, increasing the risks of both alcohol abuse and disturbed eating behavior (e.g., Wonderlich, Wilsnack, & Wilsnack, 1995). The comorbidity of eating disorders and alcohol abuse in women suggests that professionals working with eating disorders need to be aware that these problems may contribute to alcohol abuse that could otherwise go unnoticed, as well as being alert to possible exacerbation of the health consequences of severe eating disorders by heavy alcohol intake.

Stress and Coping Styles

The tension reduction theory—that people drink alcohol for its tension-reducing properties—has a long history in the field of alcohol research (e.g., Cappell & Greeley, 1987; Pohorecky, 1991). According to this theory, stressful life events produce negative emotions such as anxiety, fear, or distress, which in turn motivate alcohol use to reduce the negative emotions. Not all people cope, or attempt to cope, with stressful life experiences in the same way, and different coping styles may carry different risks of alcohol abuse. In particular, *avoidant* coping styles, which deny or minimize problems and avoid direct attempts at solutions, appear linked to heavier alcohol use, perhaps both because alcohol can be used to avoid or escape problems and because a failure to cope actively with problems often results in further negative emotions which can then motivate further alcohol use (see Cooper, Frone, Russell, & Peirce, in press).

Recent analyses of gender similarities and differences in relationships among stress, coping, and alcohol use suggest that these relationships are complex. For example, in a New York state community sample of adults (Cooper, Russell, Skinner, Frone, & Mudar, 1992), both acutely stressful life events and avoidant coping styles were more strongly related to drinking behavior among males than among females. However, in other analyses of more chronic stressors, such as work-related stress or conflict between work and family, there were few differences between women and men in associations between work–family conflicts (Frone, Russell, & Cooper, 1993) or work stressors (House, Strecher, Metzner, & Robbins, 1986; Parker & Farmer, 1988) and drinking behavior. Gender differences in socialization—women socialized to internalize stress (e.g., becoming depressed) and men to externalize it (e.g., in aggressive or intoxicated behavior)—might help to explain men's greater vulnerability to effects of acute life stressors on drinking behavior (Cooper et al., 1992, in press). However, it is not clear why similar gender differences were not found in several studies of chronic life stressors and drinking.

Interpersonal and Relational Risk Factors
Partner's Drinking

Numerous studies of both clinical alcoholic samples (e.g., Dahlgren, 1979; Gomberg, in press; Jacob & Bremer, 1986) and general population samples (e.g., Corbett, Mora, & Ames, 1991; Hammer & Vaglum, 1989; Kolonel & Lee, 1981) have reported strong positive associations between women's drinking behavior and that of their husbands or partners. However, it is not clear whether husbands have a stronger influence on wives' drinking (Haer, 1955; R. Wilsnack & S. Wilsnack, 1990), wives have a stronger influence on husbands' drinking (Cronkite & Moos, 1984), or both partners influence each other roughly equally (Roberts & Leonard, in press). It is also unclear how much of the matching of drinking patterns between marital partners may result from assortative mating (drinkers choosing similar drinkers as partners; e.g., Jacob & Bremer, 1986). It does seem clear that marriage affects how women drink, whether through modeling, social pressures, or changes in drinking opportunities. For example, a study of 1,690 adult female twin pairs in Australia (Heath, Jardine, & Martin, 1989) found that marital status significantly modified the genetic contribution to women's patterns of alcohol consumption. Genetic differences (assessed by comparing monozygotic and dizygotic twins) explained substantially more variance in the drinking patterns of unmarried respondents than of married respondents.

If marriage tends to produce an alignment of partners' drinking, then it should not be surprising that discrepancies in how marital partners drink may predict drinking-related problems. Cross-sectional and longitudinal analyses of the 1981 and 1986 survey data indicated that discrepant drinking patterns (e.g., a frequent-drinking wife and an infrequent-drinking husband, or the reverse) were associated with more frequent heavy drinking by the wife and more adverse consequences of the wife's drinking than would otherwise have been expected (R. Wilsnack & S. Wilsnack, 1990), as well as with several indicators of marital distress (S. Wilsnack & R. Wilsnack, 1990). Similar findings were reported by Roberts and Leonard (in press), who found that discrepant drinking patterns in recently married couples were associated with poorer marital functioning and more problematic drinking behavior; and by Miller (in press), who found in a sample of male parolees and their wives that higher levels of alcohol problems in the wife predicted increased marital violence only in couples where the husband's alcohol problems were low. It may be that mismatched drinking patterns between spouses or partners serve to express or symbolize conflicts in the relationship, function as a source of distress and conflict, or do both. If women who drink very differently from their partners—as well as women involved with heavy-drinking partners—are at increased risk for problem drinking, such women may merit special attention in alcohol education and health promotion efforts.

Violent Victimization and Women's Drinking

Physical and sexual victimization in childhood. Clinical studies have found elevated rates of both physical abuse and childhood sexual abuse in the histories of alcoholic women in treatment (Miller & Downs, 1993; Rohsenow, Corbett, & Devine, 1988; Russell & Wilsnack, 1991), and elevated rates of alcohol abuse and dependence in mental health clients with histories of childhood sexual abuse (Pribor & Dinwiddie, 1992). In a recent series of studies, women in treatment for alcohol problems had significantly higher rates of both physical and sexual abuse in childhood than did women in a general household sample, or women without alcohol problems but receiving other mental health services (Miller, Downs, & Testa, 1993). Relationships between childhood victimization and adult alcohol abuse persisted after controlling for demographic characteristics and parental alcohol problems. These patterns suggest a specific link between physical and sexual victimization in childhood and women's risks of subsequent alcohol abuse, a risk not explained by family history of alcohol problems or other background characteristics.

Data from our 1991 national survey suggest that associations between childhood sexual abuse and problem drinking are also strong among women in the general, nonclinical population. Using definitions of childhood sexual abuse adapted from the work of Russell (1983) and Wyatt (1985) and controlling for age, we found significant relationships between sexual abuse before age 18 and heavy episodic drinking and intoxication, drinking-related problems and alcohol dependence symptoms, lifetime use of drugs other than alcohol, depression, binge eating, and vaginismus (S. Wilsnack, Klassen, Vogeltanz, & Harris, 1994; Wonderlich et al., 1995). These nationally representative data strongly support the impression from clinical studies that experiences of childhood sexual abuse may be an important risk factor for problem drinking and a variety of other long-term adverse consequences in women.

Relationship violence and other victimization in adulthood. Early studies of relationship violence and drinking used primarily treatment samples (e.g., of battered wives or abusive husbands) and focused largely on increased risks of victimization of women by intoxicated or alcoholic partners (e.g., Frieze & Schafer, 1984; Leonard & Jacob, 1988). A smaller number of clinical studies that also examined women's own drinking behavior generally found increased marital or relationship violence when the woman herself was drinking or a problem drinker (e.g., Miller, Downs, & Gondoli, 1989). General population surveys have reported similar findings for marital or other relationship violence (Amaro, Fried, Cabral, & Zuckerman, 1990; Kaufman Kantor & Asdigian, in press) and for sexual assault and violent assault in general (Fillmore, 1985; Martin, 1992): A woman's risks of being physically or sexually assaulted are increased when the perpetrator of the assault has been drinking or when the woman victim herself is a problem drinker or has been drinking.

Possible reasons for these links between women's drinking and increased risks of victimization include the likelihood that men will perceive women who have been drinking as more sexually accessible and more vulnerable to dominance (e.g., George, Gournic, & McAfee, 1988), and the likelihood that women who have been drinking may be less alert to interpersonal cues that would ordinarily enable them to avoid or deflect conflicts with male partners. In addition, drinking or problem drinking women may be seen as deviating from traditionally feminine sex role behavior, and societal norms may be more tolerant of male aggression toward women who are not behaving in an expected feminine manner (Miller, in press).

As with childhood victimization, physical and sexual assault in adulthood may increase women's risks of subsequent alcohol or other drug abuse. A recent national survey conducted telephone interviews with 4,009 adult women about their experiences of violent victimization, including sexual assault and rape, aggravated assault, and homicide of a family member or close friend (Kilpatrick, 1990; Kilpatrick, Edmonds, & Seymour, 1992). Women reporting any such experiences were more than four times as likely (6.6%) as nonvictims (1.5%) to report two or more serious al-

SHARON C. WILSNACK

cohol-related problems. When victims were grouped according to whether they had ever experienced posttraumatic stress disorder (PTSD), crime victims with PTSD were much more likely (14.5%) than nonvictims (1.5%) to report two or more alcohol problems. Although a majority (54%) of victims in this cross-sectional study retrospectively reported a later age for their first alcohol intoxication than for their first victimization, additional longitudinal data are needed to fully explicate the effects of violent victimization on adult women's subsequent risks of alcohol abuse.

Sexual Experience and Women's Drinking

Research in the past decade has reported important linkages between aspects of women's sexual experience and their drinking behavior. Indeed, among the large number of variables included in our own national longitudinal study of women's drinking, sexuality-related variables were among the strongest cross-sectional correlates and longitudinal predictors of women's alcohol use and alcohol problems (S. Wilsnack, 1991b).

Sexuality-related alcohol expectancies and high-risk sexual behavior. In contrast to laboratory evidence that alcohol consumption decreases physiological sexual arousal in both women and men (Lang, 1985; Wilson, 1981), there is considerable evidence that both genders subjectively expect drinking to have positive facilitative effects on sexual experience. In our 1981 national sample, 60% of women drinkers reported that drinking reduces their sexual inhibitions (Klassen & Wilsnack, 1986); the same proportion (60%) of women drinkers in the 1991 survey reported these effects. In both surveys, heavier drinkers were more likely than lighter drinkers to report these positive effects, suggesting that such beliefs may be one motivation for heavier drinking among women.

The high prevalence of positive expectancies about drinking and sexuality suggests that alcohol consumption might increase women's likelihood of engaging in sexual activity, including high-risk sexual activity (i.e., unprotected, with multiple partners, or with partners at high risk for HIV/AIDS). However, in several studies only a minority of women reported that drinking strongly facilitates their sexual behavior (Fillmore,

408

Bacon, & Hyman, 1979; Klassen & Wilsnack, 1986), and several studies using diary methods have failed to demonstrate links between drinking and risky sex on specific occasions of sexual activity (Harvey & Beckman, 1986; Leigh, 1993). Associations between women's drinking and women's sexual behavior—including high-risk sexual behavior—may be more complex than any simple theory that drinking disinhibits women sexually. The associations may depend on individual characteristics of the woman, her partner, and their relationship; the degree to which a given sexual behavior would have been inhibited by other factors without the effects of alcohol; and the degree to which drinking facilitates participation in social situations that lead to sexual activity or high-risk sexual activity (Cooper, 1992).

Sexual orientation. Early studies of alcohol use and sexual orientation reported high rates of alcohol problems—generally around 30%—among both lesbians and gay men (e.g., Fifield, Latham, & Phillips, 1977; Saghir & Robins, 1973). However, many of these early studies obtained their samples at least in part through gay bars, almost certainly overrepresenting heavier drinking homosexual persons. Although the AIDS epidemic has stimulated several well-designed probability surveys of communities of gay men (Paul, Stall, & Bloomfield, 1991), the increased concern for systematic sampling of gay men has for the most part not extended to lesbians.

Three studies are available which have asked somewhat more representative samples of lesbians about their drinking behavior and drinking problems. McKirnan and Peterson (1989a) recruited 3,400 respondents (748 women) from several sources in Chicago, including readers of a gay newspaper, community and health organizations, and gay cultural events. Although lesbians in the Chicago sample were no more likely (9%) than women in a 1979 national survey (7%) to be heavy drinkers, lesbians were more likely (23%) than women in the national sample (8%) to report alcohol problems. A comparison of 55 lesbian and bisexual women and 373 heterosexual women in a random household sample of San Francisco residents ages 18–50 (Bloomfield, 1993) found no significant differences between the two groups in drinking levels or drinking patterns. However, a higher proportion of lesbian and bisexual women (13%) than of heterosexual women (3%) described themselves as recovered or recovering alcoholics. In a national study of lesbian health concerns conducted in 1984–85 (Bradford & Ryan, 1987), 83% of the 1,917 lesbian respondents reported drinking at least occasionally, 6% reported daily drinking, and 14% indicated that they were worried about their alcohol use. These rates are only slightly higher than those for all women in our 1981 national survey, a small difference that may be accounted for by the higher educational and occupational level of the lesbian sample. Interestingly, in both the Chicago and the national lesbian samples, drinking did not decline with age as it does in the general population of women. Rather, daily drinking in the national lesbian sample increased steadily with age, from 3% of respondents ages 17–24 to 21% of respondents age 55 and older.

Empirical information about risk factors for alcohol abuse among lesbians is very limited. Isolation and alienation in response to societal homophobia and discrimination are generally believed to contribute to alcohol abuse in both lesbians and gay men (e.g., Fifield et al., 1977). However, among Chicago respondents who frequented bars and who reported expectancies that drinking would reduce tension, measures of social discrimination and alienation were significantly related to alcohol problems among gay men but not among lesbians (McKirnan & Peterson, 1989b; Norris, in press). Other risk factors for alcohol abuse in lesbians may include underemployment, a heavy-drinking partner, physical or sexual abuse, and relationship violence (Hughes & S. Wilsnack, 1994; Schilit, Lie, & Montagne, 1990; Underhill & Wolverton, 1993).

Sexual dysfunction and problem drinking. Problems of sexual adjustment may show a curvilinear relationship to drinking levels among women in the general population: In our 1981 national sample, moderate drinkers (who reported consuming 4 to 13 drinks per week) scored lower than either lighter or heavier drinkers on an index of female sexual dysfunctions (Klassen & Wilsnack, 1986). It is possible that societal suppression and personal inhibition affect both drinking and sexual functioning for women who drink little or not at all. At the highest levels of consumption, heavy drinking may be both an attempt to self-medicate sexual problems and the cause of worsened sexual difficulties.

Clinical studies of alcoholic women in treatment typically report elevated rates of sexual dysfunction (Covington & Kohen, 1984; Schaefer & Evans, 1987; S. Wilsnack, 1984), although temporal sequences of heavy drinking and sexual problems are generally ambiguous. The available longitudinal data suggest that sexual dysfunction may contribute to the chronicity of problem drinking in women: In longitudinal analyses of five-year followup data from women showing signs of problem drinking in 1981, a higher level of sexual dysfunction in 1981 was the single strongest predictor of continued problem drinking in 1986 (S. Wilsnack et al., 1991). Also supporting a link between sexual difficulties and women's problem drinking is the finding that 1981 problem drinkers who divorced or separated between 1981 and 1986 were more likely to experience remission of problem drinking if their 1981 marriages had been sexually dysfunctional (Klassen et al., 1991).

TREATMENT OF ALCOHOL DISORDERS IN WOMEN

Until the 1970s, most treatment programs for alcohol abuse and dependence were oriented primarily toward men, who made up the large majority of patients in typical alcoholism treatment settings such as VA hospitals and state hospitals. Most treatment was based on a medical model which gave relatively little attention to social and environmental contributions to alcohol abuse. Participation in Alcoholics Anonymous was stressed, and considerable emphasis was placed on confronting the patient's denial and helping him admit his powerlessness over his use of alcohol. Women who did enter treatment were generally treated together with men (e.g., in mixed-gender groups where disclosure of sensitive issues such as sexuality or abuse might be difficult), with little or no attention to their special characteristics or needs (Curlee, 1971).

In the late 1970s, both the National Institute on Alcohol Abuse and Alcoholism (NIAAA) and the National Institute on Drug Abuse (NIDA) expressed interest in substance abuse treatment models for women, and both agencies funded treatment demonstration projects to encourage new approaches to intervention and treatment for women. Although the demonstration grant program produced a number of innovative programs designed specifically for women (e.g., Finkelstein, Duncan, Derman, & Smeltz, 1990; Underhill, 1986), virtually no controlled outcome evaluations were conducted. Progress since that time in introducing specialized services for women into the mainstream of alcoholism treatment programs has been slow. In a 1989 national survey of alcohol and drug treatment units (NIDA/NIAAA, 1990), only one in three of the 2,500 treatment units surveyed had any specialized services (e.g., all-women therapy groups) for women substance abusers. Some writers have speculated that the very existence of a small number of treatment programs designed specifically to serve women may actually reduce pressure on the larger treatment system to increase its sensitivity to the needs of women clients (Reed, 1987).

Identification and Casefinding

Although the proportion of women in alcohol treatment has increased in recent years—from 22% of alcohol clients in 1982 to 28% in 1990 (Schmidt & Weisner, 1993)—women have traditionally been underrepresented in alcohol and drug abuse treatment, with male-to-female ratios as high as 10 to 1 or higher in some treatment settings (Blume, in press; Reed, 1987). One reason for this underrepresentation is that most of the common casefinding systems that serve alcoholism treatment programs have traditionally been male-oriented. Employee assistance programs (EAPs) have often been more effective in identifying and referring male workers than female workers, although there is some evidence that specialized supervisor training can increase EAPs' ability to successfully refer women employees (Cahill, Volicer, & Neuberger, 1982). Drinking-driver programs in particular, and the criminal justice system more generally, have been much more likely to identify and refer male offenders than female offenders (Popkin, 1994; Wells-Parker, Popkin, & Ashley, in press).

Women alcohol abusers are more likely than men to seek help in medical settings, which therefore offer important opportunities for identification and referral. Unfortunately, medical professionals often lack the education and awareness to identify alcohol problems in women patients, perhaps another indication of the stigma surrounding alcohol abuse in women and the stereotype of alcoholism as a "man's disease." In a large study of physicians' effectiveness in identifying alcohol abuse in their hospitalized patients (Moore et al., 1989), physicians were significantly less likely to identify problem drinking in women and older patients than in men and younger patients.

Concern about risks of drinking in pregnancy has triggered research on screening instruments that can identify high-risk drinking patterns in obstetric-gynecologic patients. Combinations of gender-sensitive brief screening questionnaires and laboratory tests that are especially sensitive to women's alcohol consumption levels are currently being evaluated in populations of pregnant women (e.g., Russell, 1994). Those screening instruments found to be most successful in obstetric-gynecology settings may eventually be used more widely in other medical settings, ideally increasing the effectiveness of the health care delivery system in the early identification of problem drinking women.

Barriers to Treatment for Women With Alcohol Problems

Beyond the lack of gender-specific treatment programming and the limitations of traditional casefinding systems, problem drinking women face a number of other barriers to accessing treatment for their alcohol problems. Many of these barriers involve the attitudes and behavior of women's partners, family, and friends. In a 1985–1988 survey of alcohol treatment programs and community caregivers, denial of women's alcohol problems by family members was identified by all groups interviewed as a major obstacle to treatment for problem drinking women (S. Wilsnack, 1991a). Similarly, Beckman and Amaro (1984) found that women entering alcoholism treatment were significantly more likely than men entering treatment to report that their partners, family, or friends had actively opposed their efforts to seek treatment. It is unclear whether such opposition derives from the reflected stigma of acknowledging female alcohol abuse in one's wife, partner, or other family member; from economic circumstances that make it difficult for many women to leave their family responsibilities to enter treatment; or from other factors. In any case, the findings suggest that the partners and other significant persons in the lives of problem drinking women may be appropriate targets of alcohol education efforts designed to reduce negative attitudes and increase support for women's help-seeking efforts.

Research and clinical experience have found that lack of childcare is a highly significant barrier to treatment for many problem drinking women. In addition to practical concerns about children's safety and welfare during a mother's absence for treatment, the social stigma of female alcohol abuse causes many women to fear that they will be seen as "unfit mothers" and even lose custody of their children if they seek alcoholism treatment (Blume, in press). Beyond childcare, programs that offer treatment services for children appear to be more successful in recruiting and retaining female clients (Beckman & Amaro, 1984). By evaluating and intervening early in children's physical and behavioral problems, child treatment services can help reduce the heavy burden of guilt most alcoholic mothers experience with regard to effects of their drinking on their children, as well as maximizing the chances of successful intervention with the children's problems.

Treatment Issues for Women Who Are Problem Drinkers

A few major themes of recent clinical literature on treatment of women's problem drinking are highlighted here from detailed reviews available elsewhere (Bepko, 1991; Braiker, 1984; Finkelstein et al., 1990; McCrady & Raytek, 1993). The first is the need for a comprehensive, multidisciplinary, and coordinated range of services for problem-drinking women and their families. As discussed in previous sections, possible risk factors for women's alcohol abuse include not only individual–psychological characteristics but also a broad range of interpersonal and social–environmental factors, including lack of access to social roles, heavy-drinking partners and environments, abuse and violence, and others. In addition, women who lack basic physical and economic security will find it difficult to marshall the personal resources needed to change longstanding patterns of self-destructive substance use. For these reasons, most specialists in the treatment of alcoholic women agree that the most successful programs are those that address the full range of women's needs, including not only psychological–therapeutic services but also assistance with such practical issues as employment, housing, physical health, childcare, legal issues, and others (Finkelstein et al., 1990; Reed, 1987). The question of whether such comprehensive services are more critical to women's recovery from substance abuse than to men's has not been addressed by empirical research.

Many influences on women's alcohol abuse (e.g., violence toward women, women's limited economic resources, stigmatization of alcohol problems in women) directly or indirectly derive from women's lower status and power in a male-dominated society. Incorporating these sociopolitical issues into substance abuse treatment (e.g., through education about gender roles and gender socialization and their contributions to substance abuse) can give problem-drinking women a new perspective on societal factors contributing to their alcohol or drug abuse, and can help to reduce the internalized stigma and self-blame experienced by many problem-drinking women (Bepko, 1991; Reed, 1987).

Recent literature on treatment of women's alcohol abuse emphasizes the importance of relational issues. Like traditional models of (male) psychological development, which stress autonomy and separation as hallmarks of psychological health, traditional models of alcoholism treatment have had an individual, "medical model" focus that paid little attention to important relationships in the alcoholic's life. Drawing on newer models of women's psychological development that focus on the growth of the self in the context of intimate relationships with others (e.g., Gilligan, 1982; Jordan, Kaplan, Miller, Stiver, & Surrey, 1991), feminist therapists have recently called for increased attention to the relational contexts of substance abusing women's lives. Covington and Surrey (in press) discuss a number of "relational disconnections" which increase the risks of substance abuse in women, including culturally determined nonmutuality of female–male relationships, "shaming" of women for problematic relationships, distorted or limiting images of female attractiveness and health, and personal and systemic abuse and violence toward women. Finkelstein (1993a) discusses substance abuse treatment issues related to women's roles as daughters (e.g., effects of growing up in an alcoholic home), as partners (including sexuality and violence), and as parents, arguing that effective treatment of women's alcohol and drug abuse must aid women in learning to negotiate more mutually satisfying and supportive relationships.

The relationships that most strongly influence treatment for many women are with their children and partners. Women's children can be both powerful positive motivators for change and equally powerful disincentives if childcare responsibilities interfere with treatment-seeking (Reed, 1987). As noted earlier, women's partners can play several important roles in the development of women's alcohol or drug problems: by providing models and incentives for heavier substance use, by contributing to sexual problems or relationship violence that increases women's risks of substance abuse, and by failing to support (or actively opposing) women's entry into treatment. Conversely, treatment that helps women improve the quality of their intimate relationships with partners—or that helps them leave problematic or abusive relationships—can have potentially powerful positive effects on their recovery.

Associations discussed earlier between sexual problems and women's drinking suggest the value of sex education, sexual enhancement training, and sex therapy as components of comprehensive alcohol treatment programs for women (Covington & Surrey, in press; Schaefer & Evans, 1987). Specific treatment for long-term consequences of sexual abuse and sexual assault is also critical in light of the large numbers of substance abusing women who have been sexually victimized (Root, 1989; Turner & Colao, 1985). Additionally, there is a need for professional education of both alcoholism therapists and marital and sex therapists about the complex interactions between women's alcohol use and sexual functioning.

Outcome of Alcohol Treatment for Women

Because treatment of alcohol abuse and alcoholism has focused predominantly on male drinkers, women are seriously underrepresented in research on treatment outcome. In a comprehensive review of treatment outcome research conducted before 1980, Vannicelli (1984) found that 57% of the available studies used all-male or gender-unspecified samples, 2% used all-female samples, and only 11% included both females and males and reported gender-specific outcomes. A more recent selective review of treatment outcome studies published since 1980 (McCrady & Raytek, 1993) reported only limited improvement: Of the post-1980 treatment studies sampled, 27% had male subjects only, 10% had female subjects only, and 18% had both female and male subjects and reported outcome rates separately by gender. Among the 42% of studies that included both genders but did not provide gender-specific outcomes, roughly one third had less than 20% female subjects.

A few generalizations are possible based on the small number of studies that have compared women's and men's treatment outcomes. Of 23 such outcome studies reviewed by Vannicelli (1984), only five showed significant gender differences; in four of these, women had superior outcomes. A more recent study of adult alcohol abusers receiving inpatient treatment (Filstead, 1990) reported no gender differences. Two studies of adolescent inpatients (Alford, Koehler, & Leonard, 1991; Filstead, 1990) reported significantly better outcomes for females. A well-designed study comparing three levels of intensity of behaviorally oriented treatment for problem drinking (Sanchez-Craig, Leigh, Spivak, & Lei, 1989) found that at one-year followup women had significantly better outcomes than men in all three intensity conditions. Thus, among the minority of studies that show any gender differences in treatment outcome, there is little support for the view expressed in much of the early clinical literature (see Beckman, 1976; Blume, 1980) that women alcoholics have substantially worse treatment outcomes than men.

Although most specialists in alcoholism treatment for women favor women-only programs over mixed-gender programs, empirical data to support (or refute) this preference are very limited. A Swedish study (Dahlgren & Willander, 1989) randomly assigned 200 early-stage women problem drinkers to either a women-only or a mixed-gender treatment program. The women-only program was designed to provide close supportive contact with staff, cooperation from relatives, exchange of experiences with other women, and a therapeutic focus on "female perspectives" and problems common to women. At two-year follow-up, participants in the women-only program showed superior outcomes not only on measures of drinking behavior but also on indices of social, occupational, and family functioning. A recent Australian study (Copeland, Hall, Didcott, & Biggs, 1993) suggests that the woman-focused content of the Swedish program was important, not just the all-female gender composition of the treatment population. In the Australian research on women clients in three comparably traditional substance abuse programs (all based on a traditional disease model and the 12–step philosophy of Alcoholics Anonymous), clients in a women-only program did not differ significantly in treatment outcome from women clients in two mixed-gender programs.

PREVENTION AND SOCIAL POLICY ISSUES

Theory and research on the prevention of alcohol problems have increased substantially in the past 10 years, both in general (e.g., Holder & Howard, 1992; Miller & Nirenberg, 1984; Watson, 1990) and specifically with regard to women (e.g., Ferrence, 1984; Morrissey, 1986a; Nirenberg & Gomberg, 1993; S. Wilsnack, 1982). Prevention approaches can be broadly divided into those *individualistic* strategies that typically attempt to reduce the demand for alcohol by altering the values, attitudes, and behavior of the individual drinker, and those *situational* or environmental strategies that attempt to reduce the supply of alcohol through social, economic, and legal interventions. The sections that follow highlight several issues of particular relevance to women within these two broad approaches to prevention. Since secondary prevention strategies (which attempt to intervene with individuals in early stages of problem drinking) were covered to some extent in the earlier discussion of casefinding and early intervention, this section focuses somewhat more on primary prevention: attempts to prevent the onset of alcohol problems in women who presently experience no drinking-related problems.

Individualistic Prevention Strategies
Women-Specific Alcohol Education Programs

A number of alcohol education programs and media campaigns targeting women individually have been implemented in recent years. One early program was "Reflections in a Glass," a structured eight-session course designed to be taught to groups of women by a lay facilitator (National Institute on Alcohol Abuse and Alcoholism, 1981). The Woman to Woman program of the Association of Junior Leagues International was an ambitious national alcohol education campaign that included development of educational materials incorporating current research findings on women's drinking, a major national radio and television alcohol awareness campaign, surveys of alcohol treatment programs and community gatekeeper groups by trained Junior League volunteers in more than 100 cities, and the development of community-based alcohol abuse prevention programs by Junior Leagues nationwide (Association of Junior Leagues, 1986; S. Wilsnack, 1991a). The Women's Alcohol and Drug Education Project (WADEP) is an equally ambitious program designed by the Women's Action Alliance to reach underserved low-income and ethnic minority women by educating staff of women's centers about the interconnections between alcohol and drug abuse and many other problems faced by women (e.g., unemployment, sexual abuse, and other violence) (Roth, 1991). Although none of these educational programs have been subjected to a controlled outcome evaluation, anecdotal evidence and process evaluation data suggest that the educational materials and messages have been well received by women in the target audiences. Certainly, the sheer numbers of women reached nationwide by the Woman to Woman and WADEP projects are impressive, including both the many thousands of women who were recipients of the educational messages and the many hundreds of women who worked as prevention agents, helping to deliver the educational programs to the target groups.

Prevention To Reduce Specific Risk Factors

Occasional prevention programs have attempted to prevent alcohol misuse in specific high-risk groups of women. For example, California-based Project Breakthrough targeted recently divorced and separated women and offered workshops in life and career planning and stress management, in addition to basic alcohol education and education about the women's at-risk status. A randomized outcome evaluation with a no-treatment control group indicated positive effects of the intervention, including increased self-esteem and decreased use of alcohol and other drugs (California Women's Commission on Alcoholism, 1984).

Further research is needed to design and evaluate new prevention approaches for other at-risk groups of women. For many of these groups, a broader prevention approach addressing a number of interrelated problems may be more effective than a narrowly alcohol-specific approach. For example, among female adolescents and young women, a combined approach might be particularly effective in reducing a cluster of associated behaviors, including alcohol or other drug use, sexually transmitted diseases, unwanted pregnancy, and alcohol-related sexual assault (Nirenberg & Gomberg, 1993).

Because of the strong associations between childhood sexual abuse and a variety of long-term adverse consequences, this apparent risk factor may merit special attention. Primary and secondary prevention efforts might include education and advocacy to reduce the societal incidence of sexual abuse, alcohol and sex education to reduce the use of alcohol to cope with psychological and sexual distress, and innovative models for the early identification of and intervention with sexually abused children and adolescents. High priority should also be given to further research on resiliency and protective factors which allow some women to resist the destructive effects of traumatic sexual victimization.

Resiliency Factors and Predictors of "Spontaneous" Remission

Much remains to be learned about personal and environmental resiliency factors that predict the absence of alcohol disorders among high-risk women more generally. Research on children of alcoholic parents is giving some attention to gender similarities and differences in both risk and resiliency factors (e.g., Neff, 1994; Sher, Walitzer, Wood, & Brent, 1991). Other high-risk groups for whom greater knowledge of resiliency factors would be particularly valuable are women in heavy-drinking environments and women who have experienced violent victimization.

Similarly, longitudinal findings cited earlier showing considerable fluctuation in women's problem drinking over time (Fillmore et al., 1991; S. Wilsnack et al., 1991) suggest the need to understand better what factors predict women's movement out of problem drinking. Possible candidates include changes in drinking environments, drinking partners, number and quality of social roles, and characteristics of women's close personal relationships. Like research on resiliency factors, increased knowledge of predictors of "spontaneous" remission might find application in specific prevention strategies to nurture and strengthen those personal and social–environmental factors that predict movement out of hazardous drinking behavior.

Environmental Prevention Strategies

Alcohol Control Strategies

A variety of economic and legal measures have been used and proposed in an attempt to limit the availability of alcohol and reduce per capita alcohol consumption in the general population. These include laws regulating drinking age and locations of alcohol outlets, taxation of alcoholic beverages, and restrictions on alcohol sales and marketing. Although some of these strategies specifically affect women (e.g., restrictions on special sales promotions, such as "ladies' nights," that target women), for the most part research and policy discussions surrounding these strategies have not been gender-specific. There is some evidence that women in general are more likely than men to support public policy measures to reduce alcohol problems, including those designed to restrict alcohol availability (Blume, in press; Whitehead, 1978).

Criminal Sanctions Against Pregnant Substance Abusers

A currently controversial alcohol policy issue is the use of the criminal justice system to attempt to control alcohol and other drug use by pregnant women. Between 1985 and 1992, more than 150 women in 24 states were charged with criminal offenses (including child abuse or neglect, child endangerment, delivery of drugs to a minor, and others) related to their alcohol or other drug use during pregnancy (Blume, in press). Despite the clear and urgent need for services for pregnant substance abusing women, there is a strong consensus among health professionals concerned with substance abuse in women that criminalization of alcohol and drug use in pregnancy is misguided and counterproductive. Jailing pregnant substance abusers does not assure them adequate care for either their pregnancy or their substance abuse problem; it further stigmatizes sick and suffering women, thus reducing even further the likelihood that they will voluntarily seek treatment; it deters pregnant abusers from seeking either prenatal care or substance abuse treatment, for fear of criminal prosecution; and it does nothing to remedy the serious dearth of treatment programs for pregnant substance-abusing women (e.g., Blume, in press; Finkelstein, 1993b). An important challenge for future policy and advocacy efforts is to reduce the prevailing punitive and stigmatizing attitudes toward pregnant substance abusers, while also working to increase the availability of appropriate and sensitive treatment services for this underserved population.

Changing Societal Images of Women and Alcohol

In addition to reducing punitive attitudes toward pregnant substance abusers, a broader prevention goal might be to reduce the negative stereotypes and social stigma of alcohol abuse for women in general. Some might argue that society's sexual double standard regarding alcohol use, and even the stigmatization of women's alcohol abuse, provide a certain "protection" against heavy drinking for many women. Probably outweighing any such protective effect, reducing or eliminating the negative cultural images of problem-drinking women could have powerful positive effects in helping women, and their significant others, to more readily acknowledge women's alcohol problems, and to seek help more quickly for these problems.

Prevention efforts might also be directed at other cultural images of alcohol. These include associations between drinking and enhanced intimacy and sexuality, and associations between drinking and masculinity, power, and "liberation." Although these are long-standing, deeply rooted symbolic images, smoking prevention efforts in recent decades have had considerable success in altering powerful public perceptions, norms, and images of smoking and smokers (e.g., Berman & Gritz, 1993). Perhaps the alcohol prevention field can learn some lessons from research on smoking, and design new approaches to altering destructive cultural and media images of women and alcohol.

CONCLUSIONS: SOME DIRECTIONS FOR THE FUTURE

Among the numerous physical diseases and mental disorders, alcohol abuse and dependence provide one of the clearest illustrations of the biopsychosocial etiology of disease, with relatively well-documented biological, psychological, interpersonal, and sociocultural influences. Nonetheless, most research on alcohol problems in general, and on women's alcohol problems specifically, employs the theories and methods of a single discipline, while sometimes paying lip service to the complex multifactorial causation of the problems being studied. One clear need for future research on women's drinking is for truly interdisciplinary studies that conceptualize, measure, and analyze interactions among variables from multiple domains and levels of analysis. As one example, the intriguing finding cited earlier that married female twins showed lower concordance of drinking behavior than unmarried twins (Heath et al., 1989) appears to illustrate an important interaction between a biological etiological factor (genetic predisposition) and a psychosocial etiological factor (husband's drinking behavior and other features of the marital relationship). Measuring both types of variables in the same study would allow complex interactions of biological and psychosocial variables to be analyzed, greatly increasing the predictive power of the models developed.

If separate, discipline-specific study of biological variables, psychological variables, and sociological variables has limited research on women's drinking, so also has substance-specific research that focuses on either alcohol or some other drug(s) of abuse. Although it is not practical to conduct detailed investigations of the antecedents and consequences of a large number of highly specific combinations of alcohol and individual other drugs, research on women would be improved by measuring and analyzing relatively broad combinations of multiple substances (e.g., women abusing alcohol alone vs. alcohol in combination with psychoactive prescription drugs or over-the-counter medications vs. alcohol in combination with one or more illicit drugs). Greater attention to patterns of multiple substance abuse—as well as increased coordination and collaboration among researchers studying women's alcohol use, smoking behavior, other drug use, and perhaps eating behavior—could help to clarify similarities and differences across these various categories of behaviors, perhaps suggesting broader biopsychosocial models relevant to a range of compulsive or addictive behaviors.

Without minimizing the significance of biological–genetic factors and gender differences in physiological alcohol effects, one clear conclusion from recent research on women and alcohol is the powerful contribution of interpersonal and sociocultural influences. These include not only aspects of women's important interpersonal relationships (e.g., mutuality–nonmutuality, partner's substance abuse, sexual adjustment, conflict and violence) but also features of the larger sociopolitical environment (e.g., lack of access to valued social roles, systemic violence toward women, stigmatization of female substance use). Clearly, continued attention to the interpersonal and sociocultural context of women's lives will be critical for a fuller understanding of women's use of alcohol and other substances, and ultimately for the development of effective approaches to preventing women's substance use disorders.

Research described in this chapter has identified a number of possible individual and environmental risk factors for alcohol abuse in women. If confirmed by other studies, these risk factors may suggest specific strategies for preventing and treating alcohol abuse in women. As examples, risks associated with childhood sexual abuse or heavy-drinking partnerships might be reduced respectively by early intervention with sexually abused girls and adolescents, and by preventive education and skills training for women with heavy-drinking partners. Accumulating knowledge about how sexual dysfunction and depression are associated with women's drinking might be translated into treatment modules for problem drinking women. The dearth of empirical evaluations of prevention and treatment components specifically designed for women reflects the difficulty of conducting controlled research in these areas, but accentuates the need for such research. Empirical data on the efficacy of specific research-based prevention and treatment components, for subgroups of women, and for women in comparison with men, will become increasingly important amid growing concerns about health care cost containment and cost-effective matching of clients and intervention strategies (e.g., Institute of Medicine, 1990; Schmidt & Weisner, 1993).

Finally, although considerable progress has been made in the past two decades, research on women's alcohol use and abuse still lags significantly behind research on men. As one example, a recent plethora of studies of neurobiological and behavioral characteristics of offspring of alcoholic parents has involved almost exclusively male samples (e.g., Pihl, Peterson, & Finn, 1990) . In addition to continued support of studies focused specifically on women, inclusion of female subjects in all alcohol research (animal and human), and attention to gender similarities and differences in data analysis and reporting, will pay substantial dividends toward understanding human drinking behavior and reducing the enormous personal and social costs of alcohol problems in both women and men.

REFERENCES

Aase, J. M. (1994). Clinical recognition of FAS: Difficulties of detection and diagnosis. *Alcohol Health and Research World, 18,* 5–9.

Abel, E. L., & Sokol, R. J. (1987). Incidence of fetal alcohol syndrome and economic impact of FAS-related anomalies. *Drug and Alcohol Dependence, 19,* 51–70.

Abel, E. L., & Sokol, R. J. (1991). A revised conservative estimate of the incidence of FAS and its economic impact. *Alcoholism: Clinical and Experimental Research, 15,* 514–524.

Alford, G. S., Koehler, R. A., & Leonard, J. (1991). Alcoholics Anonymous–Narcotics Anonymous model inpatient treatment of chemically dependent adolescents: A 2-year outcome study. *Journal of Studies on Alcohol, 52,* 118–126.

Amaro, H., Fried, L. E., Cabral, H., & Zuckerman, B. (1990). Violence during pregnancy and substance use. *American Journal of Public Health, 80,* 575–579.

American Psychiatric Association. (1980). *Diagnostic and statistical manual of mental disorders* (3rd ed.). Washington, DC: Author.

American Psychiatric Association. (1987). *Diagnostic and statistical manual of mental disorders* (3rd ed., rev.). Washington, DC: Author.

American Psychiatric Association. (1994). *Diagnostic and statistical manual of mental disorders* (4th ed.). Washington, DC: Author.

Ashley, M. J., Ferrence, R. G., Room, R., Rankin, J., & Single, E. (1994). Moderate drinking and health: Report of an international symposium. *Canadian Medical Association Journal, 151,* 1–20.

Association of Junior Leagues. (1986). *Summary of findings: Woman to Woman Community Services Survey.* New York: Author.

Barlow, D. H. (1988). *Anxiety and its disorders: The nature and treatment of anxiety and panic.* New York: Guilford.

Becker, U., Tonnesen, H., Kaas-Claesson, N., & Gluud, C. (1989). Menstrual disturbances and fertility in chronic alcoholic women. *Drug and Alcohol Dependence, 24,* 75–82.

Beckman, L. J. (1976). Alcoholism problems and women: An overview. In M. Greenblatt & M. A. Schuckit (Eds.), *Alcoholism problems in women and children* (pp. 65–96). New York: Grune & Stratton.

Beckman, L. J., & Amaro, H. (1984). Patterns of women's use of alcohol treatment agencies. In S. C. Wilsnack & L. J. Beckman (Eds.), *Alcohol problems in women: Antecedents, consequences, and intervention* (pp. 319–348). New York: Guilford Press.

Bepko, C. (Ed.). (1991). *Feminism and addiction.* New York: Haworth.

Berman, B. A., & Gritz, E. R. (1993). Women and smoking: Toward the year 2000. In E. S. L. Gomberg & T. D. Nirenberg (Eds.), *Women and substance abuse* (pp. 258–285). Norwood, NJ: Ablex.

Black, S. A., & Markides, K. S. (1993). Acculturation and alcohol consumption in Puerto Rican, Cuban-American, and Mexican-American women in the United States. *American Journal of Public Health, 83,* 890–893.

Bloomfield, K. (1993). A comparison of alcohol consumption between lesbians and heterosexual women in an urban population. *Drug and Alcohol Dependence, 33,* 257–269.

Blume, S. B. (1980). Researches on women and alcohol. In National Institute on Alcohol Abuse and Alcoholism, *Alcoholism and alcohol abuse among women: Research issues* (NIAAA Research Monograph No. 1, Department of Health, Education, and Welfare Publication No. ADM 80-835, pp. 121–151). Washington, DC: U. S. Government Printing Office.

Blume, S. B. (1991). Sexuality and stigma: The alcoholic woman. *Alcohol Health and Research World, 15,* 139–146.

Blume, S. B. (in press). Women and alcohol: Issues in social policy. In R. W. Wilsnack & S. C. Wilsnack (Eds.), *Gender and alcohol.* New Brunswick, NJ: Rutgers University Center of Alcohol Studies.

Bobo, J. K. (1989). Nicotine dependence and alcoholism epidemiology and treatment. *Journal of Psychoactive Drugs, 21,* 323–329.

Bohman, M., Sigvardsson, S., & Cloninger, C. R. (1981). Maternal inheritance of alcohol abuse. *Archives of General Psychiatry, 38,* 965–969.

Bradford, J., & Ryan, C. (1987). *The National Health Care Survey: Final report.* Washington, DC: National Lesbian and Gay Health Foundation.

Braiker, H. B. (1984). Therapeutic issues in the treatment of alcoholic women. In S. C. Wilsnack & L. J. Beckman (Eds.), *Alcohol problems in women: Antecedents, consequences, and intervention* (pp. 349–368). New York: Guilford Press.

Cadoret, R. J., O'Gorman, T., Troughton, E., & Heywood, E. (1985). Alcoholism and antisocial personality: Interrelationships, genetic and environmental factors. *Archives of General Psychiatry, 42,* 161–167.

Caetano, R. (1991). Findings from the 1984 National Survey of Alcohol Use among U. S. Hispanics. In W. B. Clark & M. E. Hilton (Eds.), *Alcohol in America: Drinking practices and problems* (pp. 293–307). Albany, NY: State University of New York Press.

Caetano, R., & Medina Mora, M. E. (1988). Acculturation and drinking among people of Mexican descent in Mexico and the United States. *Journal of Studies on Alcohol, 49,* 462–471.

Cahill, M. H., Volicer, B. J., & Neuberger, E. (1982). Female referral to employees assistance programs: The impact of specialized intervention. *Drug and Alcohol Dependence, 10,* 223–233.

Calhoun, K. S., & Atkeson, B. M. (1991). *Treatment of rape victims: Facilitating psychosocial adjustment.* New York: Pergamon.

California Women's Commission on Alcoholism. (1984). *Project Breakthrough: Executive summary.* Inglewood, CA: California Women's Commission on Alcoholism.

Cappell, H., & Greeley, J. (1987). Alcohol and tension reduction: An update on research and theory. In H. T. Blane & K. E. Leonard (Eds.), *Psychological theories of drinking and alcoholism* (pp. 15–54). New York: Guilford.

Celentano, D. D., & McQueen, D. V. (1984). Multiple substance abuse among women with alcohol-related problems. In S. C. Wilsnack & L. J. Beckman (Eds.), *Alcohol problems in women: Antecedents, consequences, and intervention* (pp. 97–116). New York: Guilford Press.

Cicero, T. J. (1994). Effects of paternal exposure to alcohol on offspring development. *Alcohol Health and Research World, 18,* 37–41.

Clark, W. B., & Hilton, M. E. (Eds.). (1991). *Alcohol in America: Drinking practices and problems.* Albany, NY: State University of New York Press.

Clark, W. B., & Midanik, L. (1982). Alcohol use and alcohol problems among U. S. adults: Results of the 1979 national survey. In National Institute on Alcohol Abuse and Alcoholism, *Alcohol consumption and related problems* (Alcohol and Health Monograph No. 1, Department of Health and Human Services Publication No. ADM 82-1190, pp. 3–52). Washington, DC: U. S. Government Printing Office.

Cooper, M. L. (1992). Alcohol and increased behavioral risk for AIDS. *Alcohol Health and Research World, 16*(1), 64–72.

Cooper, M. L., Frone, M. R., Russell, M., & Peirce, R. S. (in press). Gender, stress, coping, and alcohol use. In R. W. Wilsnack & S. C. Wilsnack (Eds.), *Gender and alcohol.* New Brunswick, NJ: Rutgers University Center of Alcohol Studies.

Cooper, M. L., Russell, M., Skinner, J. B., Frone, M. R., & Mudar, P. (1992). Stress and alcohol use: Moderating effects of gender, coping, and alcohol expectancies. *Journal of Abnormal Psychology, 101,* 139–152.

Copeland, J., Hall, W., Didcott, P., & Biggs, V. (1993). A comparison of a specialist women's alcohol and other drug treatment service with two traditional mixed-sex services: Client characteristics and treatment outcome. *Drug and Alcohol Dependence, 32,* 81–92.

Corbett, K., Mora, J., & Ames, G. (1991). Drinking patterns and drinking-related problems of Mexican-American husbands and wives. *Journal of Studies on Alcohol, 52,* 215–223.

Cotton, N. S. (1979). The familial incidence of alcoholism: A review. *Journal of Studies on Alcohol, 40,* 89–116.

Covington, S. S., & Kohen, J. (1984). Women, alcohol, and sexuality. *Advances in Alcohol and Substance Abuse, 4*(1), 41–56.

Covington, S. S., & Surrey, J. L. (in press). The relational model of women's psychological development: Implications for substance abuse. In R. W. Wilsnack & S. C. Wilsnack (Eds.), *Gender and alcohol.* New Brunswick, NJ: Rutgers University Center of Alcohol Studies.

Cronkite, R. C., & Moos, R. H. (1984). The role of predisposing and moderating factors in the stress-illness relationship. *Journal of Health and Social Behavior, 25,* 372–393.

Curlee, J. (1971). Sex differences in patients' attitudes toward alcoholism treatment. *Quarterly Journal of Studies on Alcohol, 32,* 643–650.

Dahlgren, L. (1979). *Female alcoholics: A psychiatric and social study.* Stockholm: Karolinska Institute.

Dahlgren, L., & Willander, A. (1989). Are special treatment facilities for female alcoholics needed? A controlled 2-year follow-up study from a specialized female unit (EWA) versus a mixed male/female treatment facility. *Alcoholism: Clinical and Experimental Research, 13,* 499–504.

Dawson, D. A., & Archer, L. (1992). Gender differences in alcohol consumption: Effects of measurement. *British Journal of Addiction, 87,* 119–123.

Day, N. L. (1992). The effects of prenatal exposure to alcohol. *Alcohol Health and Research World, 16,* 238–244.

Deal, S. R., & Gavaler, J. S. (1994). Are women more susceptible than men to alcohol-induced cirrhosis? *Alcohol, Health and Research World, 18,* 189–191.

Dietary Guidelines. (1990). *Nutrition and your health: Dietary guidelines for Americans* (3rd ed.). Washington, DC: U. S. Department of Agriculture, U. S. Department of Health and Human Services.

Dufour, M. C., Archer, L., & Gordis, E. (1992). Alcohol and the elderly. *Clinics in Geriatric Medicine, 8*(1), 127–141.

Ferrence, R. G. (1984). Prevention of alcohol problems in women. In S. C. Wilsnack & L. J. Beckman (Eds.), *Alcohol problems in women: Antecedents, consequences, and intervention* (pp. 413–442). New York: Guilford.

Fifield, L. H., Latham, J. D., & Phillips, C. (1977). *Alcoholism in the gay community: The price of alienation, isolation, and oppression.* Los Angeles: Gay Community Services Center.

Fillmore, K. M. (1984). "When angels fall": Women's drinking as cultural preoccupation and as reality. In S. C. Wilsnack & L. J. Beckman (Eds.), *Alcohol problems in women: Antecedents, consequences, and intervention* (pp. 7–36). New York: Guilford Press.

Fillmore, K. M. (1985). The social victims of drinking. *British Journal of Addiction, 80,* 307–314.

Fillmore, K. M., Bacon, S. D., & Hyman, M. (1979). *The 27-year longitudinal panel study of drinking by students in college, 1949–1976.* (Final Report to NIAAA, Contract No. ADM-281-76-0015). Berkeley, CA: University of California at Berkeley, School of Public Health, Social Research Group.

Fillmore, K. M., Golding, J. M., Leino, E. V., Motoyoshi, M., Shoemaker, C., Terry, H., Ager, C. R., & Ferrer, H. P. (in press). Patterns and trends in women's and men's drinking. In R. W. Wilsnack & S. C. Wilsnack (Eds.), *Gender and alcohol.* New Brunswick, NJ: Rutgers University Center of Alcohol Studies.

Fillmore, K. M., Hartka, E., Johnstone, B. M., Leino, E. V., Motoyoshi, M., & Temple, M. T. (1991). A meta-analysis of life course variation in drinking. *British Journal of Addiction, 86,* 1221–1268.

Filstead, W. J. (1990). *Treatment outcome: An evaluation of adult and youth treatment services.* Park Ridge, IL: Parkside Medical Services Corporation. (As cited in Mc-Crady & Raytek, 1993.)

Finkelstein, N. (1993a). The relational model. In D. Kronstadt, P. F. Green, & C. Marcus (Eds.), *Pregnancy and exposure to alcohol and other drug use* (pp. 126–163). Washington, DC: U. S. Department of Health and Human Services, Center for Substance Abuse Prevention.

Finkelstein, N. (1993b). Treatment programming for alcohol and drug-dependent pregnant women. *International Journal of the Addictions, 28,* 1275–1309.

Finkelstein, N., Duncan, S., Derman, L., & Smeltz, J. (1990). *Getting sober, getting well: A treatment guide for caregivers who work with women.* Cambridge, MA: Women's Alcoholism Program/CASPAR, Inc.

Finney, J. W., Moos, R. H., & Brennan, P. L. (1991). The Drinking Problems Index: A measure to assess alcohol-related problems among older adults. *Journal of Substance Abuse, 3,* 395–404.

Frezza, M., Di Padova, C., Pozzato, G., Terpin, M., Baraona, E., & Lieber, C. S. (1990). High blood alcohol levels in women: The role of decreased gastric alcohol dehydrogenase activity and first-pass metabolism. *New England Journal of Medicine, 322,* 95–99.

Frieze, I. H., & Schafer, P. C. (1984). Alcohol use and marital violence: Female and male differences in reactions to alcohol. In S. C. Wilsnack & L. J. Beckman (Eds.), *Alcohol problems in women: Antecedents, consequences, and intervention* (pp. 260–279). New York: Guilford Press.

Frone, M. R., Russell, M., & Cooper, M. L. (1993). Relationship of work-family conflict, gender, and alcohol expectancies to alcohol use/abuse. *Journal of Organizational Behavior, 14,* 545–558.

Gavaler, J. S. (1993). Alcoholic beverage consumption and estrogenization in normal postmenopausal women. In E. S. L. Gomberg & T. D. Nirenberg (Eds.), *Women and substance abuse* (pp. 18–41). Norwood, NJ: Ablex.

Gavaler, J. S., & Van Thiel, D. H. (1992). The association between moderate alcoholic beverage consumption and serum estradiol and testosterone levels in normal postmenopausal women: Relationship to the literature. *Alcoholism: Clinical and Experimental Research, 16,* 87–92.

Gaziano, J. M., Buring, J. E., Breslow, J. L., Goldhaber, S. Z., Rosner, B., VanDenburgh, M., Willett, W., & Hennekens, C. H. (1993). Moderate alcohol intake, increased levels of high-density lipoprotein and its subfractions, and decreased risk of myocardial infarction. *New England Journal of Medicine, 329,* 1829–1834.

George, W. H., Gournic, S. J., & McAfee, M. P. (1988). Perceptions of postdrinking female sexuality: Effects of gender, beverage choice, and drink payment. *Journal of Applied Social Psychology, 18,* 1295–1317.

Gilbert, M. J. (1991). Acculturation and changes in drinking patterns among Mexican-American women. *Alcohol Health and Research World, 15,* 234–238.

Gilbert, M. J., & Collins, R. L. (in press). Ethnic variation in women and men's drinking. In R. W. Wilsnack & S. C. Wilsnack (Eds.), *Gender and alcohol.* New Brunswick, NJ: Rutgers University Center of Alcohol Studies.

Gilligan, C. (1982). *In a different voice: Psychological theory and women's development.* Cambridge, MA: Harvard University Press.

Gomberg, E. S. L. (1991). Women and alcohol: Psychosocial aspects. In D. J. Pittman & H. R. White (Eds.), *Society, culture, and drinking patterns reexamined* (pp. 263–283). New Brunswick, NJ: Rutgers University Center of Alcohol Studies.

Gomberg, E. S. L. (1993). Women and alcohol: Use and abuse. *Journal of Nervous and Mental Disease, 181,* 211–219.

Gomberg, E. S. L. (in press). Alcohol abuse: Age and gender differences. In R. W. Wilsnack & S. C. Wilsnack (Eds.), *Gender and alcohol.* New Brunswick, NJ: Rutgers University Center of Alcohol Studies.

Goodwin, D. W., Schulsinger, F., Hermansen, L., Guze, S. B., & Winokur, G. (1973). Alcohol problems in adoptees raised apart from alcoholic biological parents. *Archives of General Psychiatry, 28,* 238–243.

Goodwin, D. W., Schulsinger, F., Knop, J., Mednick, S., & Guze, S. B. (1977). Alcoholism and depression in adopted-out daughters of alcoholics. *Archives of General Psychiatry, 34,* 751–755.

Gordon, T., & Kannel, W. B. (1983). Drinking habits and cardiovascular disease: The Framingham Study. *American Heart Journal, 105,* 667–673.

Graham, K., Carver, V., & Brett, P. J. (in press). Alcohol and drug use by older women: Results of a national survey. *Canadian Journal on Aging, 14.*

Grant, B. F., Harford, T. C., Chou, P., Pickering, R., Dawson, D. A., Stinson, F. S., & Noble, J. (1991). Epidemiologic Bulletin No. 27: Prevalence of DSM–III–R alcohol abuse and dependence: United States, 1988. *Alcohol Health and Research World, 15*(1), 91–96.

Grant, B. F., Harford, T. C., Dawson, D. A., Chau, P., DuFour, M., & Pickering, R.

(1994). Prevalence of DSM–IV alcohol abuse and dependence, United States, 1992. *Alcohol Health and Research World, 18,* 243–248.

Haavio-Mannila, E. (1991, March). *Impact of colleagues and family members on female alcohol use.* Paper presented at the Symposium on Alcohol, Family and Significant Others, Social Research Institute of Alcohol Studies and Nordic Council for Alcohol and Drug Research, Helsinki, Finland.

Haer, J. L. (1955). Drinking patterns and the influence of friends and family. *Quarterly Journal of Studies on Alcohol, 16,* 178–185.

Hammer, T., & Vaglum, P. (1989). The increase in alcohol consumption among women: A phenomenon related to accessibility or stress? A general population study. *British Journal of Addiction, 84,* 767–775.

Hanna, E., Faden, V., & Harford, T. (1993). Marriage: Does it protect young women from alcoholism? *Journal of Substance Abuse, 5,* 1–14.

Hartka, E., Johnstone, B. M., Leino, V., Motoyoshi, M., Temple, M., & Fillmore, K. M. (1991). A meta-analysis of depressive symptomatology and alcohol consumption over time. *British Journal of Addiction, 86,* 1283–1298.

Harvey, S. M., & Beckman, L. J. (1986). Alcohol consumption, female sexual behavior, and contraceptive use. *Journal of Studies on Alcohol, 47,* 327–332.

Health and Welfare Canada. (1990). *National Alcohol and Other Drugs Survey (1989): Highlights report.* Catalogue No. H39-175/1990E. Ottawa, Canada: Author.

Heath, A. C., Bucholz, K. K., Dinwiddie, S. H., Madden, P. A. F., Dunne, M. P., Statham, D., & Martin, N. G. (1993, July). *The contribution of genetic factors to risk of alcohol problems in women.* Paper presented at the Behavior Genetics Association Annual Meeting, Sydney, Australia.

Heath, A. C., Jardine, R., & Martin, N. G. (1989). Interactive effects of genotype and social environment on alcohol consumption in female twins. *Journal of Studies on Alcohol, 50,* 38–48.

Heath, A. C., Slutske, W. S., & Madden, P. A. F. (in press). Gender differences in the genetic contribution to alcoholism risk and to alcohol consumption patterns. In R. W. Wilsnack & S. C. Wilsnack (Eds.), *Gender and alcohol.* New Brunswick, NJ: Rutgers University Center of Alcohol Studies.

Herd, D. (1991). Drinking problems in the black population. In W. B. Clark & M. E. Hilton (Eds.), *Alcohol in America: Drinking practices and problems* (pp. 308–328). Albany, NY: State University of New York Press.

Hesselbrock, M. N., & Hesselbrock, V. M. (in press). Gender, alcoholism, and psychiatric comorbidity in alcoholic women. In R. W. Wilsnack & S. C. Wilsnack

(Eds.), *Gender and alcohol.* New Brunswick, NJ: Rutgers Center of Alcohol Studies.

Hiatt, R. A. (1990). Alcohol consumption and breast cancer. *Medical Oncology and Tumor Psychotherapy, 7,*(2/3), 143–151.

Hill, S. Y. (1984). Vulnerability to the biomedical consequences of alcoholism and alcohol-related problems among women. In S. C. Wilsnack & L. J. Beckman (Eds.), *Alcohol problems in women: Antecedents, consequences, and intervention* (pp. 121–154). New York: Guilford Press.

Hill, S. Y. (1993). Genetic vulnerability to alcoholism in women. In E. S. L. Gomberg & T. D. Nirenberg (Eds.), *Women and substance abuse* (pp. 42–61). Norwood, NJ: Ablex.

Hill, S. Y. (1995). Mental and physical health consequences of alcohol use in women. In M. Galanter (Ed.), *Recent developments in alcoholism, Volume 12: Alcoholism and women.* (pp. 181–197). New York: Plenum Press.

Hill, S. Y., & Smith, T. R. (1991). Evidence for genetic mediation of alcoholism in women. *Journal of Substance Abuse, 3,* 159–174.

Hilton, M. E. (1991). The demographic distribution of drinking patterns in 1984. In W. B. Clark & M. E. Hilton (Eds.), *Alcohol in America: Drinking practices and problems* (pp. 73–86). Albany, NY: State University of New York Press.

Holder, H. D., & Howard, J. M. (Eds.). (1992). *Community prevention trials for alcohol problems: Methodological issues.* New York: Praeger.

House, J. S., Strecher, V., Metzner, H. L., & Robbins, C. A. (1986). Occupational stress and health among men and women in the Tecumseh Community Health Study. *Journal of Health and Social Behavior, 27,* 62–77.

Hughes, T. L., & Wilsnack, S. C. (1994). Research on lesbians and alcohol: Gaps and implications. *Alcohol Health and Research World, 18,* 202–205.

Institute of Medicine. (1990). Populations defined by structural characteristics. In *Broadening the base of treatment for alcohol problems* (pp. 356–380). Washington, DC: National Academy Press.

Jacob, T., & Bremer, D. A. (1986). Assortative mating among men and women alcoholics. *Journal of Studies on Alcohol, 47,* 219–222.

Johnson, P. B. (1982). Sex differences, women's roles and alcohol use: Preliminary national data. *Journal of Social Issues, 2,* 93–116.

Jones, B. M., & Jones, M. K. (1976). Women and alcohol: Intoxication, metabolism, and the menstrual cycle. In M. Greenblatt & M. A. Schuckit (Eds.), *Alcoholism problems in women and children* (pp. 103–136). New York: Grune & Stratton.

Jones, K. L., & Smith, D. W. (1973). Recognition of the fetal alcohol syndrome in early infancy. *Lancet, II,* 999–1001.

Jordan, J. V., Kaplan, A. G., Miller, J. B., Stiver, I. P., & Surrey, J. L. (1991). *Women's growth in connection: Writings from the Stone Center.* New York: Guilford Press.

Kaufman Kantor, G., & Asdigian, N. L. (in press). Gender differences in alcohol-related spousal aggression. In R. W. Wilsnack & S. C. Wilsnack (Eds.), *Gender and alcohol.* New Brunswick, NJ: Rutgers University Center of Alcohol Studies.

Kendler, K. S., Heath, A. C., Neale, M. C., Kessler, R. C., & Eaves, L. J. (1992). A population-based twin study of alcoholism in women. *Journal of the American Medical Association, 268,* 1877–1882.

Kessler, R. C., McGonagle, K. A., Zhao, S., Nelson, C. B., Hughes, M., Eshleman, S., Wittchen, H., & Kendler, K. S. (1994). Lifetime and 12-month prevalence of DSM–III–R psychiatric disorders in the United States: Results from the National Comorbidity Survey. *Archives of General Psychiatry, 51,* 8–19.

Kilpatrick, D. G. (1990, August). *Violence as a precursor of women's substance abuse: The rest of the drugs–violence story.* Paper presented at Topical Mini-Convention on Substance Abuse and Violence, 98th Annual Convention, American Psychological Association, Boston.

Kilpatrick, D. G., Edmonds, C. N., & Seymour, A. K. (1992). *Rape in America: A report to the nation.* Arlington, VA: National Victim Center.

Kitano, H. H. L., Chi, I., Rhee, S., Law, C. K., & Lubben, J. E. (1992). Norms and alcohol consumption: Japanese in Japan, Hawaii, and California. *Journal of Studies on Alcohol, 53,* 33–39.

Klassen, A. D., & Wilsnack, S. C. (1986). Sexual experience and drinking among women in a U. S. national survey. *Archives of Sexual Behavior, 15,* 363–392.

Klassen, A. D., Wilsnack, S. C., Harris, T. R., & Wilsnack, R. W. (1991, March). *Partnership dissolution and remission of problem drinking in women: Findings from a U. S. longitudinal survey.* Paper presented at the Symposium on Alcohol, Family and Significant Others, Social Research Institute of Alcohol Studies and Nordic Council for Alcohol and Drug Research, Helsinki, Finland.

Klee, L., Schmidt, C., & Ames, G. (1991). Indicators of women's alcohol problems: What women themselves report. *International Journal of Addictions, 26,* 885–901.

Kolonel, L. N., & Lee, J. (1981). Husband–wife correspondence in smoking, drinking, and dietary habits. *American Journal of Clinical Nutrition, 34,* 99–104.

Krahn, D. D. (1993). The relationship of eating disorders and substance abuse. In

E. S. L. Gomberg & T. D. Nirenberg (Eds.), *Women and substance abuse* (pp. 286–313). Norwood, NJ: Ablex.

Kubicka, L., Csemy, L., & Kozeny, J. (1991, March). *The sociodemographic, microsocial, and attitudinal context of Czech women's drinking.* Paper presented at the Symposium on Alcohol, Family and Significant Others, Social Research Institute of Alcohol Studies and Nordic Council for Alcohol and Drug Research, Helsinki, Finland.

Kushner, M. G., Sher, K. J., & Beitman, B. D. (1990). The relation between alcohol problems and the anxiety disorders. *American Journal of Psychiatry, 147,* 685–695.

Lang, A. R. (1985). The social psychology of drinking and human sexuality. *Journal of Drug Issues, 15,* 273–289.

LaRosa, J. H. (1990). Executive women and health: Perceptions and practices. *American Journal of Public Health, 80,* 1450–1454.

Leigh, B. C. (1993). Alcohol consumption and sexual activity as reported with a diary technique. *Journal of Abnormal Psychology, 102,* 490–493.

Leland, J. (1984). Alcohol use and abuse in ethnic minority women. In S. C. Wilsnack & L. J. Beckman (Eds.), *Alcohol problems in women: Antecedents, consequences, and intervention* (pp. 66–96). New York: Guilford Press.

Lemoine, P., Harouseau, H., Borteryu, J. T., & Menuet, J. C. (1968). Les enfants des parents alcooliques: Anomalies observees a propos de 127 cas. [Children of alcoholic parents: Observed anomalies in 127 cases.] *Ouest Medical, 21,* 476–482.

Leonard, K. E., & Jacob, T. (1988). Alcohol, alcoholism, and family violence. In V. B. Van Hasselt, R. L. Morrison, A. S. Bellack, & M. Hersen (Eds.), *Handbook of family violence* (pp. 383–406). New York: Plenum Press.

Lex, B. W. (1993). Women and illicit drugs: Marijuana, heroin, and cocaine. In E. S. L. Gomberg & T. D. Nirenberg (Eds.), *Women and substance abuse* (pp. 162–190). Norwood, NJ: Ablex.

Lieber, C. S. (1993). Women and alcohol: Gender differences in metabolism and susceptibility. In E. S. L. Gomberg & T. D. Nirenberg (Eds.), *Women and substance abuse* (pp. 1–17). Norwood, NJ: Ablex.

Little, R. E., & Sing, C. F. (1987). Father's drinking and infant birth weight: Report of an association. *Teratology, 36,* 59–65.

Marshall, A. W., Kingstone, D., Boss, M., & Morgan, M. Y. (1983). Ethanol elimination in males and females: Relationship to menstrual cycle and body composition. *Hepatology, 3,* 701–706.

435

Martin, S. E. (1992). The epidemiology of alcohol-related interpersonal violence. *Alcohol Health and Research World, 16,* 230–237.

May, P. A. (1991). Fetal alcohol effects among North American Indians: Evidence and implications for society. *Alcohol Health and Research World, 15,* 239–248.

McCrady, B. S., & Raytek, H. (1993). Women and substance abuse: Treatment modalities and outcomes. In E. S. L. Gomberg & T. D. Nirenberg (Eds.), *Women and substance abuse* (pp. 314–338). Norwood, NJ: Ablex.

McGue, M. (1993). From proteins to cognitions: The behavioral genetics of alcoholism. In R. Plomin & G. E. McClearn (Eds.), *Nature, nurture, and psychology* (pp. 245–268). Washington, DC: American Psychological Association.

McGue, M., & Slutske, W. (1993, September). *The inheritance of alcoholism in women.* Paper presented to the Working Group for Prevention Research on Women and Alcohol, National Institute on Alcohol Abuse and Alcoholism, National Institutes of Health, Bethesda, MD.

McKirnan, D. J., & Peterson, P. L. (1989a). Alcohol and drug use among homosexual men and women: Epidemiology and population characteristics. *Addictive Behaviors, 14,* 545–553.

McKirnan, D. J., & Peterson, P. L. (1989b). Psychosocial and cultural factors in alcohol and drug abuse: An analysis of a homosexual community. *Addictive Behaviors, 14,* 555–563.

Midanik, L. (1983). Alcohol problems and depressive symptoms in a national survey. *Advances in Alcohol and Substance Abuse, 2,* 9–28.

Midanik, L. T., & Clark, W. B. (1994). The demographic distribution of U. S. drinking patterns in 1990: Description and trends from 1984. *American Journal of Public Health, 84,* 1218–1222.

Miller, B. A. (in press). Women's alcohol use and the connections to violent victimization. In E. Taylor, J. Howard, P. Mail, & M. Hilton (Eds.), *Prevention research on women and alcohol.* Washington, DC: U. S. Government Printing Office.

Miller, B. A., & Downs, W. R. (1993). The impact of family violence on the use of alcohol by women. *Alcohol Health and Research World, 17,* 137–143.

Miller, B. A., Downs, W. R., & Gondoli, D. M. (1989). Spousal violence among alcoholic women as compared to a random household sample of women. *Journal of Studies on Alcohol, 50,* 533–540.

Miller, B. A., Downs, W. R., & Testa, M. (1993). Interrelationships between victimization experiences and women's alcohol use. *Journal of Studies on Alcohol* (Suppl. 11), 109–117.

Miller, P. M., & Nirenberg, T. D. (Eds.). (1984). *Prevention of alcohol abuse.* New York: Plenum Press.

Moore, R. D., Bone, L. R., Geller, G., Mamon, J. A., Stokes, E. J., & Levine, D. M. (1989). Prevalence, detection, and treatment of alcoholism in hospitalized patients. *Journal of the American Medical Association, 261,* 403–407.

Morrissey, E. R. (1986a). Of women, by women or for women? Selected issues in the primary prevention of drinking problems. In National Institute on Alcohol Abuse and Alcoholism, *Women and alcohol: Health-related issues* (NIAAA Research Monograph No. 16, Department of Health and Human Services Publication No. ADM 86-1139, pp. 226–259). Washington, DC: U.S. Government Printing Office.

Morrissey, E. R. (1986b). Power and control through discourse: The case of drinking and drinking problems among women. *Contemporary Crises, 10,* 157–179.

National Institute on Alcohol Abuse and Alcoholism. (1980). *Alcoholism and alcohol abuse among women: Research issues* (NIAAA Research Monograph No. 1, U.S. Department of Health, Education and Welfare Publication No. ADM 80-835). Washington, DC: U.S. Government Printing Office.

National Institute on Alcohol Abuse and Alcoholism. (1981). *SPECTRUM: Alcohol problem prevention projects for women by women.* Rockville, MD: Author, Division of Prevention.

National Institute on Alcohol Abuse and Alcoholism. (1986). *Women and alcohol: Health-related issues* (NIAAA Research Monograph No. 16, Department of Health and Human Services Publication No. ADM 86-1139). Washington, DC: U.S. Government Printing Office.

National Institute on Drug Abuse & National Institute on Alcohol Abuse and Alcoholism. (1990). *National Drug and Alcoholism Treatment Unit Survey (NDATUS): 1989 Main Findings Report.* Washington, DC: U.S. Government Printing Office.

Neff, J. A. (1994). Adult children of alcoholic or mentally ill parents: Alcohol consumption and psychological distress in a tri-ethnic community. *Addictive Behaviors, 19,* 185–197.

Nirenberg, T. D., & Gomberg, E. S. L. (1993). Prevention of alcohol and drug problems in women. In E. S. L. Gomberg & T. D. Nirenberg (Eds.), *Women and substance abuse* (pp. 339–359). Norwood, NJ: Ablex.

Norris, J. (in press). Alcohol consumption and female sexuality: A review. In E. Taylor, J. Howard, P. Mail, & M. Hilton (Eds.), *Prevention research on women and alcohol.* Washington, DC: U.S. Government Printing Office.

Parker, D. A., & Farmer, G. C. (1988). The epidemiology of alcohol abuse among employed men and women. In M. Galanter (Ed.), *Recent developments in alcoholism, Vol. 6* (pp. 113–130). New York: Plenum Press.

Paul, J. P., Stall, R., & Bloomfield, K. A. (1991). Gay and alcoholic: Epidemiologic and clinical issues. *Alcohol Health and Research World, 15,* 151–160.

Pickens, R. W., Svikis, D. S., McGue, M., Lykken, D. T., Heston, L. L., & Clayton, P. J. (1991). Heterogeneity in the inheritance of alcoholism: A study of male and female twins. *Archives of General Psychiatry, 48,* 19–28.

Pihl, R. O., Peterson, J., & Finn, P. (1990). Inherited predisposition to alcoholism: Characteristics of sons of male alcoholics. *Journal of Abnormal Psychology, 99,* 291–301.

Pohorecky, L. A. (1991). Stress and alcohol interaction: An update of human research. *Alcoholism: Clinical and Experimental Research, 15,* 438–459.

Popkin, C. L. (1994). A consideration of factors influencing drinking and driving by women. *Alcohol, Drugs, and Driving, 9,* 197–210.

Pribor, E. F., & Dinwiddie, S. H. (1992). Psychiatric correlates of incest in childhood. *American Journal of Psychiatry, 149*(1), 52–56.

Rabinovitz, M., Van Thiel, D. H., Dindzans, V., & Gavaler, J. S. (1989). Endoscopic findings in alcoholic liver disease: Does gender make a difference? *Alcohol, 6,* 465–468.

Razay, G., Heaton, K. W., Bolton, C. H., & Hughes, A. O. (1992). Alcohol consumption and its relation to cardiovascular risk factors in British women. *British Medical Journal, 304,* 80–82.

Reed, B. G. (1987). Developing women-sensitive drug dependence treatment services: Why so difficult? *Journal of Psychoactive Drugs, 19,* 151–164.

Rehm, J., & Sempos, C. T. (1994, June). *Alcohol consumption and all cause mortality.* Paper presented at the 20th Annual Alcohol Epidemiology Symposium of the Kettil Bruun Society for Social and Epidemiological Research on Alcohol, Ruschlikon, Switzerland.

Roberts, L. J., & Leonard, K. E. (in press). Gender differences and similarities in the alcohol and marriage relationship. In R. W. Wilsnack & S. C. Wilsnack (Eds.), *Gender and alcohol.* New Brunswick, NJ: Rutgers University Center of Alcohol Studies.

Roe, A. (1944). The adult adjustment of children of alcoholic parents raised in foster homes. *Quarterly Journal of Studies on Alcohol, 5,* 378–393.

Rohsenow, D. J., Corbett, R., & Devine, D. (1988). Molested as children: A hidden contribution to substance abuse? *Journal of Substance Abuse Treatment, 5,* 13–18.

Romans-Clarkson, S. E., Walton, V. A., Herbison, G. P., & Mullen, P. E. (1992). Alcohol-related problems in New Zealand women. *Australian and New Zealand Journal of Psychiatry, 26,* 175–182.

Root, M. P. P. (1989). Treatment failures: The role of sexual victimization in women's addictive behavior. *American Journal of Orthopsychiatry, 59,* 542–549.

Rosenberg, L., Metzger, L. S., & Palmer, J. R. (1993). Alcohol consumption and risk of breast cancer: A review of the epidemiologic evidence. *Epidemiologic Reviews, 15,* 133–144.

Roth, P. (Ed.). (1991). *Alcohol and drugs are women's issues. Vol. 1: A review of the issues. Vol. 2: The model program guide.* New York: Women's Action Alliance; Metuchen, NJ: Scarecrow Press.

Russell, D. E. H. (1983). The incidence and prevalence of intrafamilial and extrafamilial sexual abuse of female children. *Child Abuse and Neglect: The International Journal, 7,* 133–146.

Russell, M. (1994). New assessment tools for risk drinking during pregnancy: T-ACE, TWEAK, and others. *Alcohol Health and Research World, 18,* 55–61.

Russell, S. A., & Wilsnack, S. C. (1991). Adult survivors of childhood sexual abuse: Substance abuse and other consequences. In P. Roth (Ed.), *Alcohol and drugs are women's issues. Vol. 1: A review of the issues* (pp. 61–70). New York: Women's Action Alliance; Metuchen, NJ: Scarecrow Press.

Saghir, M. T., & Robins, E. (1973). *Male and female homosexuality: A comprehensive investigation.* Baltimore: Williams & Wilkins.

Sanchez-Craig, M., Leigh, G., Spivak, K., & Lei, H. (1989). Superior outcome of females over males after brief treatment for the reduction of heavy drinking. *British Journal of Addiction, 84,* 395–404.

Sandmaier, M. (1980). *The invisible alcoholics: Women and alcohol abuse in America.* New York: McGraw-Hill.

Savitz, D. A., Zhang, J., Schwingl, P., & John, E. M. (1992). Association of paternal alcohol use with gestational age and birth weight. *Teratology, 46,* 465–471.

Schaefer, S., & Evans, S. (1987). Women, sexuality and the process of recovery. In E. Coleman (Ed.), *Chemical dependency and intimacy dysfunction* (pp. 91–120). New York: Haworth Press.

Schilit, R., Lie, G., & Montagne, M. (1990). Substance abuse as a correlate of violence in intimate lesbian relationships. *Journal of Homosexuality, 19*(3), 51–65.

Schmidt, L., & Weisner, C. (1993). Developments in alcoholism treatment. In M. Galanter (Ed.), *Recent developments in alcoholism. Vol. 11: Ten years of progress* (pp. 369–396). New York: Plenum Press.

Sher, K. J., Walitzer, K. S., Wood, P. K., & Brent, E. E. (1991). Characteristics of children of alcoholics: Putative risk factors, substance use and abuse, and psychopathology. *Journal of Abnormal Psychology, 100,* 427–448.

Shore, E. R. (1985). Alcohol consumption rates among managers and professionals. *Journal of Studies on Alcohol, 46,* 153–156.

Shore, E. R. (1990). Business and professional women: Primary prevention for new role incumbents. In P. M. Roman (Ed.), *Alcohol problem intervention in the workplace: Employee assistance programs and strategic alternatives* (pp. 113–124). New York: Quorum.

Shore, E. R. (1992). Drinking patterns and problems among women in paid employment. *Alcohol Health and Research World, 16,* 160–164.

Stampfer, M. J., Colditz, G. A., Willett, W. C., Speizer, F. E., & Hennekens, C. H. (1988). A prospective study of moderate alcohol consumption and the risk of coronary heart disease and stroke in women. *New England Journal of Medicine, 319,* 267–273.

Temple, M., Fillmore, K. M., Hartka, E., Johnstone, B. M., Leino, V., & Motoyoshi, M. (1991). A meta-analysis of change in marital and employment status as predictors of consumption of alcohol on a typical occasion. *British Journal of Addiction, 86,* 1269–1281.

Tolo, K., & Little, R. E. (in press). The epidemiology of alcohol consumption and pregnancy. In R. W. Wilsnack & S. C. Wilsnack (Eds.), *Gender and alcohol.* New Brunswick, NJ: Rutgers University Center of Alcohol Studies.

Turner, S., & Colao, F. (1985). Alcoholism and sexual assault: A treatment approach for women exploring both issues. In Cook, D., Straussner, S. L. A., & Fewell, C. H. (Eds.), *Psychosocial issues in the treatment of alcoholism* (pp. 91–103). New York: Haworth Press.

Underhill, B. L. (1986). Issues relevant to aftercare programs for women. *Alcohol Health and Research World, 11,* 46–47.

Underhill, B. L., & Wolverton, T. (1993). *Creating visibility: Providing lesbian-sensitive and lesbian-specific alcoholism recovery services.* Los Angeles: Alcoholism Center for Women.

Vannicelli, M. (1984). Treatment outcome of alcoholic women: The state of the art in relation to sex bias and expectancy effects. In S. C. Wilsnack & L. J. Beckman (Eds.), *Alcohol problems in women: Antecedents, consequences, and intervention* (pp. 369–412). New York: Guilford Press.

Watson, R. R. (Ed.). (1990). *Drug and alcohol abuse prevention.* Clifton, NJ: Humana Press.

Wells-Parker, E., Popkin, C. L., & Ashley, M. (in press). Alcohol issues for prevention research among women: Drinking and driving. In E. Taylor, J. Howard, P. Mail, & M. Hilton (Eds.), *Prevention research on women and alcohol.* Washington, DC: U.S. Government Printing Office.

Whitehead, P. C. (1978). *Evaluation of a media campaign: The AWARE program and attitudes toward alcohol.* Regina, Canada: Department of Health, Province of Saskatchewan.

Williams, G. D., & DeBakey, S. F. (1992). Changes in levels of alcohol consumption: United States, 1983–1988. *British Journal of Addiction, 87,* 643–648.

Williams, G. D., Grant, B. F., Harford, T. C., & Noble, J. (1989). Epidemiologic Bulletin No. 23: Population projections using DSM–III criteria: Alcohol abuse and dependence, 1990–2000. *Alcohol Health and Research World, 13,* 366–370.

Williams, G. D., Stinson, F. S., Clem, D., & Noble, J. (1992, December). *Apparent per capita alcohol consumption: National, state, and regional trends, 1977–1990.* (Surveillance Report No. 23). Rockville, MD: National Institute on Alcohol Abuse and Alcoholism.

Wilsnack, R. W. (1992). Unwanted statuses and women's drinking. *Journal of Employee Assistance Research, 1,* 239–270.

Wilsnack, R. W., & Cheloha, R. (1987). Women's roles and problem drinking across the lifespan. *Social Problems, 34,* 231–248.

Wilsnack, R. W., Harris, T. R., & Wilsnack, S. C. (1993, June). *Changes in U. S. women's drinking: 1981–1991.* Paper presented at the 19th Annual Alcohol Epidemiology Symposium of the Kettil Bruun Society for Social and Epidemiological Research on Alcohol, Krakow, Poland.

Wilsnack, R. W., & Wilsnack, S. C. (1990, June). *Husbands and wives as drinking partners.* Paper presented at the 16th Annual Alcohol Epidemiology Symposium of the Kettil Bruun Society for Social and Epidemiological Research on Alcohol, Budapest, Hungary.

Wilsnack, R. W., & Wilsnack, S. C. (1992). Women, work, and alcohol: Failures of simple theories. *Alcoholism: Clinical and Experimental Research, 16,* 172–179.

Wilsnack, R. W., Wilsnack, S. C., & Klassen, A. D. (1984). Women's drinking and drinking problems: Patterns from a 1981 national survey. *American Journal of Public Health, 74,* 1231–1238.

Wilsnack, R. W., & Wright, S. I. (August, 1991). *Women in predominantly male occupations: Relationships to problem drinking*. Paper presented at the Annual Meeting of the Society for the Study of Social Problems, Cincinnati, OH.

Wilsnack, S. C. (1982). Prevention of alcohol problems in women. In National Institute on Alcohol Abuse and Alcoholism, *Special population issues* (NIAAA Alcohol and Health Monograph No. 4, Department of Health and Human Services Publication No. ADM 82-1193, pp. 77–108). Washington, DC: U.S. Government Printing Office.

Wilsnack, S. C. (1984). Drinking, sexuality, and sexual dysfunction in women. In S. C. Wilsnack & L. J. Beckman (Eds.), *Alcohol problems in women: Antecedents, consequences, and intervention* (pp. 189–227). New York: Guilford Press.

Wilsnack, S. C. (1991a). Barriers to treatment for alcoholic women. *Addiction and Recovery, 11*(4), 10–12.

Wilsnack, S. C. (1991b). Sexuality and women's drinking: Findings from a U. S. national study. *Alcohol Health and Research World, 15*, 147–150.

Wilsnack, S. C. (in press). Patterns and trends in women's drinking: Recent findings and some implications for prevention. In E. Taylor, J. Howard, P. Mail, & M. Hilton (Eds.), *Prevention research on women and alcohol*. Washington, DC: U.S. Government Printing Office.

Wilsnack, S. C., & Beckman, L. J. (Eds.). (1984). *Alcohol problems in women: Antecedents, consequences, and intervention*. New York: Guilford Press.

Wilsnack, S. C., Klassen, A. D., Schur, B. E., & Wilsnack, R. W. (1991). Predicting onset and chronicity of women's problem drinking: A five-year longitudinal analysis. *American Journal of Public Health, 81*, 305–318.

Wilsnack, S. C., Klassen, A. D., Vogeltanz, N. D., & Harris, T. R. (1994, May). *Childhood sexual abuse and women's substance abuse: National survey findings*. Paper presented at the Conference on Psychosocial and Behavioral Factors in Women's Health, American Psychological Association, Washington, DC.

Wilsnack, S. C., Vogeltanz, N. D., Diers, L. E., & Wilsnack, R. W. (in press). Drinking and problem drinking in older women. In T. P. Beresford & E. S. L. Gomberg (Eds.), *Alcohol and aging*. London: Oxford University Press.

Wilsnack, S. C., & Wilsnack, R. W. (1990, June). *Marital drinking and the quality of marital relationships: Patterns from a U. S. longitudinal survey*. Paper presented at the 35th International Institute on the Prevention and Treatment of Alcoholism and Drug Dependence, International Council on Alcohol and Addictions, Berlin, Germany.

Wilsnack, S. C., & Wilsnack, R. W. (1993). Epidemiological research on women's drinking: Recent progress and directions for the 1990s. In E. S. L. Gomberg & T. D. Nirenberg (Eds.), *Women and substance abuse* (pp. 62–99). Norwood, NJ: Ablex.

Wilsnack, S. C., Wilsnack, R. W., & Hiller-Sturmhöfel, S. (1994). How women drink: Epidemiology of women's drinking and problem drinking. *Alcohol Health and Research World, 18,* 173–181.

Wilsnack, S. C., Wilsnack, R. W., & Klassen, A. D. (1986). Epidemiological research on women's drinking, 1978–1984. In National Institute on Alcohol Abuse and Alcoholism, *Women and alcohol: Health-related issues* (NIAAA Research Monograph No. 16, Department of Health and Human Services Publication No. ADM 86-1139, pp. 1–68). Washington, DC: U.S. Government Printing Office.

Wilson, G. T. (1981). The effects of alcohol on human sexual behavior. In N. K. Mello (Ed.), *Advances in substance abuse: Behavioral and biological research* (Vol. 2.) Greenwich, CT: JAI Press.

Wonderlich, S. A., Wilsnack, R. W., & Wilsnack, S. C. The relationship of sexual abuse and bulimic behavior: Results of a U.S. national survey. Submitted for publication.

Wyatt, G. E. (1985). The sexual abuse of Afro-American and white women in childhood. *Child Abuse and Neglect: The International Journal, 9,* 507–519.

York, J. L., & Welte, J. W. (1994). Gender comparisons of alcohol consumption in alcoholic and nonalcoholic populations. *Journal of Studies on Alcohol, 55,* 743–750.

12

Eating Disorders in Women: Current Issues and Debates

Ruth H. Striegel-Moore and Marsha D. Marcus

In western societies, eating disorders represent a significant threat to women's health: In studies of point prevalence, as many as 2% of adult women meet diagnostic criteria for anorexia nervosa (AN) or bulimia nervosa (BN) (Fairburn & Beglin, 1990; Hall & Hay, 1991), and even greater prevalence rates have been reported for adolescent girls (Lucas, Beard, O'Fallon, & Kurland, 1991; Whitaker et al., 1990). It is further estimated that approximately 2% of women meet diagnostic criteria for binge eating disorder (BED) (Yanovski, 1993), a syndrome listed in the appendix of *DSM–IV* (American Psychiatric Association, 1994) as a disorder in need of further study. In addition, a sizeable number of women exhibit a clinically significant syndrome of disordered eating that does not fit current criteria for any of the eating disorders (e.g., persistent purging without binge eating), presently termed *eating disorder not otherwise specified* (EDNOS). Epidemiologic studies suggest that individuals with EDNOS outnumber individuals with AN or BN by a factor of 2 (Kendler et al., 1991; Killen et al., 1994; Striegel-Moore & Huydic, 1993; Whitehouse, Cooper, Vize, Hill, & Vogel, 1992).

The profoundly negative impact of an eating disorder on physical and psychological health and on social and vocational functioning has been documented extensively (Keller, Herzog, Lavori, Bradburn, & Mahoney, 1992; Sharp & Freeman, 1993). Individuals with an eating disorder report a wide variety of concurrent somatic and psychological symptoms, including dizziness, sleep disturbance, gastrointestinal complaints, anxiety, depression, and substance abuse (Mitchell, 1984; Mitchell, Soll, Eckert, Pyle, & Hatsukami, 1989). Furthermore, these individuals often experience interpersonal difficulties, including conflicted relationships with family members, social alienation, interpersonal distrust, and impaired sexual functioning (Coovert, Kinder, & Thompson, 1989; Grissett & Norvell, 1992; Strober & Humphrey, 1987; Thelen, Farmer, Mann, & Pruitt, 1990). Because research on the natural course of eating disorders is still in an early stage, it is unclear to what extent the various comorbid symptoms are merely a part of the eating disorder syndrome and to what extent they are caused by the eating disorder.

Few studies have examined the long-term consequences of an eating disorder. In many cases, the eating disorder takes a chronic course (Deter & Herzog, 1994; Herzog, Keller, & Lavori, 1988). A small but growing literature has begun to describe the impact of an eating disorder on women's reproductive health and on their role as mothers. This research has shown that a significant number of women seeking treatment for unexplained infertility have an eating disorder. In a majority of cases, these women underwent extensive medical evaluation and treatment before the eating disorder was properly diagnosed (Stewart, 1992). Similarly, women who are able to conceive despite their eating disorder are at increased risk for premature births and for delivering low birthweight babies (Stewart, 1992). Little is known about the impact of a mother's eating disorder on her children. Preliminary studies suggest, however, that these children are more likely to receive inadequate nutrition than children of mothers who do not have an eating disorder (Fahy & Treasure, 1989; Stein & Fairburn, 1989; Van Wezel-Meijler & Wit, 1989).

Eating disorders may have a lasting impact on physical health, even in women whose eating-related symptoms improve. For example, prolonged poor nutritional practices and emaciation that accompany AN are risk factors for osteoporosis (Putukian, 1994). Based on initial studies of women with BED, some investigators have argued that recurrent binge eating in the absence of compensatory behaviors may be a risk factor for obesity (Yanovski, 1993). The long-term impact of an eating disorder on a woman's psychological and social development is unclear. We do not know, for example, how much these women recover from the disruption of normative developmental tasks (e.g., individuation/separation) caused by their disorder.

Eating disorders are a feminist issue. Prevalence studies have found that women with eating disorders outnumber men by a factor of 10 (Fairburn & Beglin, 1990). Although the etiology of these disorders is unknown, cultural factors have been implicated, including the definition of femininity, the female beauty ideal of extreme thinness, normative developmental challenges girls encounter, and gender-related stressful life events (Striegel-Moore, 1993). Two components of Western culture's construction of femininity appear particularly relevant for an understanding of women's heightened risk for eating disorders. One, women are socialized to be more *interpersonally oriented* than men—to develop an identity that is organized around one's relationships with others; to value, seek out, and nurture social relationships; and to assume responsibility for the success of these relationships. Girls learn at an early age that physical attractiveness plays an important role in interpersonal success, and girls make deliberate attempts to improve their appearance in efforts to increase their popularity (Rodin, Silberstein, & Striegel-Moore, 1985). Two, beauty is inextricably linked with femininity, and efforts to enhance attractiveness serve to affirm one's feminine identity to oneself and to others.

Eating disorders typically emerge during adolescence. Initial research has linked both the particular nature of the psychosocial tasks and the numerous, stress-inducing normative life changes of female adolescence with the increased risk for eating disorders in adolescent girls (Striegel-Moore, 1993). For example, in the context of contemporary cultural norms of female beauty, the fat spurt associated with puberty poses a particular challenge to young girls. In light of these biological processes, it is not surprising that weight dissatisfaction and dieting emerge as major concerns for girls during puberty (Killen et al., 1992). Initial research has shown that adolescent girls are at increased risk when they are confronted with multiple developmental tasks in a short time span. For example, girls who experience onset of puberty at the same time that they enter junior high school are at greater risk for developing symptoms of an eating disorder than girls who experience these normative events sequentially (Levine, Smolak, Moodey, Shuman, & Hessen, 1994).

The role of childhood sexual abuse in the etiology of eating disorders is a hotly debated topic among eating disorder experts (Kearney-Cooke & Striegel-Moore, 1994). Consistently, controlled studies have found that childhood sexual abuse is associated with a significantly increased risk for a wide range of psychiatric disorders, including eating disorders (Pope & Hudson, 1992; Welch & Fairburn, 1994). Therefore, few experts would argue that sexual abuse is unrelated to the etiology of eating disorders. Disagreement centers around specificity of risk. Proponents of the *specific link* hypothesis describe complex, multiple mediating mechanisms between sexual abuse and disordered eating. They emphasize the adverse effects of sexual victimization on body esteem, self-esteem, identity, and interpersonal functioning (Kearney-Cooke & Striegel-Moore, 1994; Pribor & Dinwiddie, 1992; Root, 1991). Opponents of this hypothesis point out that epidemiological studies have failed to show disproportionately higher rates of sexual victimization among eating disordered women compared with women with other forms of psychopathology (Pope & Hudson, 1992; Welch & Fairburn, 1994). We agree with Wonderlich (1994) that too many methodological issues remain unresolved to permit a conclusive judgement about the specific impact of sexual abuse on women's mental health. This debate should not (but often does) obscure the fact that a history of sexual abuse has important implications for the treatment of an eating disorder (Kearney-Cooke & Striegel-Moore, 1994; Root, 1991). Its implications for diagnosis require further investigation.

Feminist scholarly efforts in the area of eating disorders have focused primarily on theoretical analyses of eating disorders (e.g., Bordo, 1993) and on developing treatment approaches (e.g., Fallon, Katzman, & Wooley, 1993). Feminist scholars have focused much less on classification. This chapter will begin to address this gap. Our exploration of the definitions of eating disorders will show that the question of how to best define and classify eating disorders is still unresolved. We believe that it is important for feminist researchers to have a voice in the classification of eating disorders. Describing and naming a problem occur at the first stage of any scientific investigation. Classification has a profound impact on how a disorder is conceptualized; it becomes inseparably entwined with shaping research agendas, with defining populations in need of therapeutic or preventive interventions, and with determining payment policies of insurance companies. Referring to the *DSM,* Millon (1991) wrote "In great part, clinically based taxa gain their import and prominence by virtue of consensus and authority. Cumulative experience and tradition are crystallized and subsequently confirmed by official bodies" (p. 256). Feminist researchers and scholars need to bring their experience and critical thinking to bear on this process so that feminist voices enter the dialogue that shapes taxonomies.

The chapter is organized into three sections. The first section introduces challenges involved in classification. The second and major section offers a detailed review of diagnostic criteria for eating disorders as specified in the *DSM–IV* (American Psychiatric Association, 1994) and provides specific suggestions for revisions. In the concluding section, we delineate several areas in need of further conceptual and empirical work. We recognize that a chapter cannot do justice to the complexities of the topic and our focus is selective—reflecting at best our expertise, and at worst our ignorance.

CLASSIFICATION SYSTEMS CHALLENGES AND QUESTIONS

Psychiatric Classification

Classification systems are inevitably limited and limiting in that they never can fully capture the complexity of a clinical syndrome, and they ultimately require a decision about presence or absence of the disorder. They reflect accumulated knowledge about human functioning and value judgments about "normal" and "abnormal" behavior (Wakefield, 1992). Whether a behavior is regarded as a symptom is determined in part by a culture's tolerance for deviance and for suffering. For example, in our society, vomiting to achieve thinness is seen as a pathological behavior whereas undergoing liposuction is not. Because scientific knowledge about human functioning does not remain static and because cultural norms about the acceptability of deviance and of suffering change over time, psychiatric taxonomy needs to be understood as work-in-progress, subject to frequent revisions.

Several elements are usually cited as reflecting good quality of a taxonomy, including reliability (e.g., across time, across reporting sources); internal consistency (i.e., individuals receiving the same diagnosis evidence a similar clinical picture); specificity (i.e., the diagnostic elements tell what the diagnosis is and what it is not); external validity (e.g., the diagnosis conveys meaningful information about etiology, prognosis, and treatment); and utility (e.g., scientific heuristics) (Werry, 1992). With these criteria in mind, we approach the classification of eating disorders.

Classification of Eating Disorders

Some feminist researchers and clinicians have argued against a medical classification of disordered eating altogether, because such a practice is thought to pathologize and to reduce to an individual problem what is fundamentally a social problem rooted in the particular ways by which our culture constructs femininity (Bordo, 1993; Orbach, 1986). A majority of researchers and clinicians accept the utility of classification, yet find it difficult to agree on the specific types of eating disorders to be recognized and on the particular criteria that define these disorders. Ideally, diagnostic schemes reflect an understanding of the etiology of the disorder and thus guide therapeutic interventions. *DSM–IV* classification of eating disorders (as is the case in psychiatry in general) is based on descriptive clinical information rather than on etiological factors, and poses problems because the defining characteristics are *polythetic* (i.e., defined by more than one criterion) and occur on a continuum (Kendell, 1975). Yet, an operational definition requires that symptoms be converted into dichotomous variables, for example by imposing severity or frequency thresholds. The challenge of classification involves striking a balance between selecting criteria that are not so restrictive as to exclude cases that may not evidence all features of the prototypical expression of the disorder, yet share its essential features. The challenge also involves selecting criteria that are not so inclusive as to encompass cases where the symptom picture does not appear to be clinically significant.

It is important to note that a discussion of how to define *clinical significance* is almost completely absent from the eating disorder literature. In part, this omission may be due to the fact that the *DSM* offers a definition of clinical significance in its introductory explanation of the concept of mental disorder. Specifically, the *DSM–IV* uses the criteria of "present distress (a painful symptom) or disability (impairment in one or more important areas of functioning) or . . . a significant increase in risk of suffering death, pain, disability, or an important loss of freedom" (American Psychiatric Association, 1994, p. A8). In justifying diagnostic criteria, experts typically refer to associated physical and psychological functioning which, in turn, are defined not by absolute values but in relative terms. There has been a growing concern among eating disorder experts that the current classification system may exclude from research and treatment a large number of individuals whose clinical picture is serious enough to warrant a diagnosis of an eating disorder (Bruce & Agras, 1992; King, 1990; Williamson, Gleaves, & Savin, 1992). These individuals either do not evidence all of the symptoms required to fit the prototypical picture, and/or they do not meet certain severity criteria for key clinical symptoms. We need to evaluate the costs and benefits of both narrowly and broadly defined diagnostic criteria.

Another major unresolved question concerns differentiation among the eating disorders. For example, significant overlap in symptoms and high rates of comorbidity between AN and BN raise questions about the specificity and utility of these diagnoses (Brumberg & Striegel-Moore, 1993). In fact, the recent proposal of a new disorder, BED, has been criticized in part because the relationship between BN and BED has not yet been clearly articulated (Fairburn, Welch, & Hay, 1993).

To date, diagnostic criteria have been based on the clinical picture of individuals presenting for treatment, even though concerns have been raised that clinically derived classification schemes are inappropriate for community-based cases (Fairburn & Beglin, 1990; Szmukler, 1985). Although there is an extensive base of literature documenting the prevalence of various eating disorder symptoms in community-based samples, efforts to capture the full spectrum of eating disorders and to develop an empirically derived classification of eating disorders have only just begun (Fairburn et al., 1993; Hay, Fairburn, & Doll, 1994; Strober, 1983).

Criteria derived from clinic samples reflect the most salient features of these cases, such as presence of serious emaciation in AN or purging in BN. Many studies create a tautological dilemma: By studying clients or patients meeting diagnostic criteria to see whether these individuals exhibit the key features of the disorder, it is inevitable that in a majority of cases the key features in question are present. This problem may be magnified by the fact that many studies are conducted at specialty treatment centers. It is plausible that these clinics or hospitals get referrals for individuals whose clinical picture fits established norms for a particular disorder. Similarly, many study protocols limit study samples not only by using narrowly defined diagnostic criteria but also by specifying additional inclusion criteria such as gender (e.g., women only), age (e.g., only young adults), or associated psychopathology (e.g., no comorbid substance abuse disorder). Classification schemes developed from such highly selective study samples are bound to be inadequate when applied to a broader population.

Clinic-based samples are not representative of all women with an eating disorder. Only a minority of women with an eating disorder seek medical or psychological help specifically for their eating disorder (Welch & Fairburn, 1994). In one study, women who requested treatment were significantly more depressed than women who did not request treatment but shared similar levels of eating related symptoms (Mitchell, Pyle, Eckert, Pomeroy, & Hatsukami, 1988). Overreliance on clinic-based samples may be responsible for the widely held belief that eating disorders only affect affluent Caucasian women. Several recent studies in the United States suggest that risk for an eating disorder is unrelated to socioeconomic status (Striegel-Moore, Schreiber, Pike, Wilfley, & Rodin, in press; Wilfley, Schreiber, Rodin, Pike, & Striegel-Moore, 1994). A recent British study found diagnostic bias, favoring the accurate diagnosis of BN among wealthier women and interfering with the detection of the disorder in working-class women (Welch & Fairburn, 1992).

Studies using clinic-based samples often comprise exclusively Caucasian women, fostering the impression that minority women do not exhibit disordered eating. A few studies of community-based samples have found, however, that women of color are not immune to developing eating disorders (for reviews, see Pate, Pumariega, Hester, & Garner, 1992; Root, 1990). Because of the omission of racial minority groups in studies of eating disorders, it is not known whether there are racial differences in the expression (or *symptom language;* Brumberg, 1988) of an eating disorder. Therefore, even those studies in which members of racial minority groups are included cannot fully answer the question of how common eating disorders are among these groups, because the criteria used to identify such disorders may be racially biased.

We will now review diagnostic criteria for anorexia nervosa, bulimia nervosa, and binge eating disorder to begin to examine what is at stake in the debate about classification of eating disorders. *DSM–IV* diagnostic criteria for these disorders are listed in the appendix to this chapter. For each disorder we discuss key features and explore how thresholds have been defined. Next, we examine subtypes of clinical syndromes. We then consider the similarities and differences among the three eating disorders to evaluate specificity of the diagnostic criteria.

CLASSIFICATION OF ANOREXIA NERVOSA

Essential Features of Anorexia Nervosa

The core feature of AN is the relentless pursuit of thinness with a complete disregard for the potential or actual negative health consequences associated with weight loss. Current diagnostic criteria for AN and the other disorders discussed in this chapter are shown in the appendix to this chapter. The criteria for AN include physical symptoms (low body weight; amenorrhea); affective symptoms (fear of fatness); and cognitive symptoms (body image disturbance). In contrast to BN and BED, behavioral symptoms (e.g., dieting or purging) are not essential for the diagnosis. If any one of the four symptoms is absent or insufficiently severe, a diagnosis of anorexia nervosa cannot be given, regardless of the presence or severity of the remaining symptoms. Each of the criteria for AN will be discussed individually.

Criterion A: Failure to Maintain Minimum Weight

Failure to maintain minimum body weight is the most prominent symptom of AN. The emphasis on this feature has its historical origin in the importance of differential diagnosis of wasting diseases which were common at the time when anorexia nervosa was first recognized as a medical illness (Brumberg, 1988). Moreover, this emphasis has been justified with research documenting the severe health risks associated with emaciation (Sharp & Freeman, 1993). It is important to note, however, that no consensus has been achieved concerning at what point low weight represents a serious health risk (Pirke & Ploog, 1987). Although the importance of low weight as a clinical symptom is indisputable, the narrow focus on this symptom without explicit consideration of the behavioral means by which the goal of weight loss is pursued likely excludes from diagnostic consideration women whose weight loss efforts are not "successful" enough to meet diagnostic criteria for AN, yet who evidence all other anorexic symptoms. Moreover, weight recovery is the primary criterion of treatment success, even though many weight-recovered individuals with AN still report a wide range of eating-related symptoms (e.g., highly restrictive eating) and associated psychopathology (e.g., Windauer, Lennerts, Talbot, Touyz, & Beumont, 1993).

Criterion B: Fear of Gaining Weight

Although most experts maintain that weight or shape concerns form the motivational core from which all other symptoms develop in modern AN, a few dissenting voices have suggested that AN should be recognized in individuals whose weight loss efforts do not appear to be motivated by fear of fatness or a desire to be thin (Palmer, 1993). Historical accounts of the disorder in Victorian girls fail to include observations on fear of fatness (Brumberg, 1988; Hsu & Lee, 1993), yet it is widely accepted that the syndrome described by Lasegue (1964) and Gull (1964) is the same as modern AN. Fear of weight gain is also absent in many patients from nonwestern societies (Hsu & Lee, 1993). For example, in a series of 70 patients treated for AN in Hong Kong, 41 (59%) did not report fear of fatness (Lee, Ho, & Hsu, 1993). It is notable that these patients did not differ from patients with fear of fatness on other clinical features central to the diagnosis of AN. By insisting on a definition for which fear of weight gain is an essential feature, we may misdiagnose AN in individuals from cultures where obesity is uncommon and where there is little emphasis on slimness. However, the motivation for food refusal remains critical in distinguishing AN from other types of mental illnesses where food restriction or weight loss is part of the clinical picture (Palmer, 1993). For example, food refusal may be present in individuals suffering from paranoid ideation who believe that their food has been poisoned. To avoid misdiagnosis, refusal to eat due solely to another psychiatric or organic disorder could be added as an exclusion criterion for AN.

Considering the importance of fear of fatness in classification of AN, surprisingly few studies have examined this symptom. Research suggests that fear of fatness is common among girls and women in western societies. In fact, in prepubertal girls whose bodies still conform to the contemporary beauty ideal of the prepubescent female body, fear of fatness is much more common than feeling fat or dissatisfied with one's body weight (Striegel-Moore, Nicholson, & Tamborlane, 1992). Because most studies of body image concerns among women with AN have not differentiated between fear of fatness and other aspects of body image disturbance such as body dissatisfaction (e.g., feeling fat), it is unclear how well fear of fatness allows for discrimination between healthy women and women with AN.

Our clinical experience suggests that some women deny weight-related concerns as a strategy of denying the symptomatic nature of their eating behavior. These women's insistence that their food refusal is not motivated by weight concerns is part of the very syndrome the fear of weight gain criterion aims to define. It may not be possible to elicit fear of weight gain prior to initiation of a period of refeeding. One study found that fear of fatness remained a significant concern particularly among those women whose treatment resulted in successful weight restoration; in contrast, fear of fatness was less common among those women who had failed to gain weight (Walford & McCune, 1991).

Criterion C: Body Image Disturbance

Bruch (1962) is widely credited with first highlighting body image disturbance as a salient clinical feature of AN. Describing women with AN, Bruch noted, for example, "the absence of concern about emaciation, even when advanced, and the rigor and stubbornness with which the often gruesome appearance is defended as normal and right" (p. 189). In its deliberations of diagnostic criteria, however, the Eating Disorders Work Group for *DSM–IV* debated whether to drop body image disturbance as an essential feature because this feature is not uniformly found among individuals with AN, and it is not always readily admitted by women who do experience such concerns (Wilson & Walsh, 1991). Body image disturbance is a multidimensional construct, encompassing perceptual distortion (e.g., claiming to be grossly overweight when emaciated); body image dissatisfaction (e.g., feeling fat); overvalued ideas about the body (e.g., weight is the most important determinant of self-worth); and fear of fatness. To date, these components have often been investigated either as interchangeable aspects of the same phenomenon, or in isolation from each other. Of these components, perceptual distortion in the form of body-size overestimation has been studied the most. These research efforts have been justified by the importance afforded to perceptual distortions in etiological models of AN. Bruch (1962), for example, proposed that fear of fatness was fueled in part by the perception of being fat even when seriously emaciated. It is noteworthy that these intense research efforts have continued even after several authoritative reviews concluded that size overestimation was not limited to individuals with AN, that different methodologies produced differing results, and that size overestimation was not uniformly present in AN (Garner, Garfinkel, Stancer, & Moldolfsky, 1976; Hsu & Sobkiewicz, 1991; Slade & Brodie, 1994).

Consistently, research has shown that women with AN report more negative attitudes about their body image than healthy controls (Hsu & Sobkiewicz, 1991; Williamson, Cubic, & Gleaves, 1993). However, body image dissatisfaction, particularly feeling fat, is so common among women in western societies that it has been dubbed a "normative discontent" (Rodin, Silberstein, & Striegel-Moore, 1985). Not all individuals with AN acknowledge body image dissatisfaction and, similar to fear of weight gain, failure to do so has been interpreted as denial of their disorder. Recently, attention has shifted away from perceptual distortion and body image dissatisfaction to the overvaluation of shape or weight. This shift is reflected in the wording of Criterion C. Research has yet to explore this concept in people with AN.

Despite a large body of literature on the assessment of body image disturbance in AN, few treatment studies have assessed improvement of body image disturbance as an outcome variable. Body image disturbance remains a persistent feature, even in individuals who have successfully participated in treatment programs (Ratnasuriya, Eisler, Szmukler, & Russell, 1991; Sohlberg, Norring, Holmgren, & Rosmark, 1989; Walford & McCune, 1991; Windauer et al., 1993). Bruch (1962) considered improvement of body image disturbance essential to achieving lasting therapeutic success. Whether interventions specifically aimed at reducing body image disturbance will improve outcome of AN therapy still needs to be studied.

Criterion D: Amenorrhea

When *DSM–IV* criteria were developed, inclusion of the amenorrhea criterion was debated. Given the fact that menstrual functioning is influenced by nutritional status and body weight, women who meet the below-minimum-weight criterion are likely to be amenorrheic. Therefore, some experts considered Criterion D redundant. Because research has not yet fully examined the relationship between minimal weight and amenorrhea, data are not available concerning the number of women who fail to meet full syndrome criteria solely on the basis of not meeting the criterion of amenorrhea.

Debate about amenorrhea as a diagnostic criterion is fueled further by the fact that, for obvious reasons, this criterion is restricted to women. Given that diagnosis in men is based on the remaining three key features, decision to retain amenorrhea as an additional criterion in women may appear arbitrary. Without question, amenorrhea is associated with considerable health risk and therefore has important prognostic value (Highet, 1989; Sharp & Freeman, 1993; Wilmore, 1991). In a number of cases, amenorrhea is an early symptom of AN, which may be present well before the required threshold of low body weight has been reached. It thus may aid in early identification of disordered eating. Moreover, given our culture's strong bias toward thinness, amenorrhea may be more readily recognized as a medical problem than being below minimum weight. By making it a diagnostic criterion, amenorrhea is recognized as an important symptom. Clearly, research is needed regarding the clinical and prognostic significance of amenorrhea.

Defining Thresholds

Whether the current diagnostic criteria are based on an optimal demarcation on the continuum of weight concerns and related weight control behaviors remains to be determined. Fear of fatness, body image disturbance, and efforts to achieve significant weight loss (e.g., restrictive dieting) are widely prevalent among women; however, the clinical syndrome of AN is rare (Hoek, 1991; Rastam, 1992; Whitaker et al., 1990; Whitehouse et al., 1992). For two of the four key symptoms—amenorrhea and refusal to maintain a minimal body weight—severity thresholds are provided. In studies of individuals requesting treatment for an eating disorder, *subthreshold* cases of AN outnumbered full syndrome cases of AN (Bunnell, Shenker, Nussbaum, Jacobson, & Cooper, 1990; Clinton & Glant, 1992; Herzog, Hopkins, & Burns, 1993; Williamson et al., 1992). Typically, subthreshold AN was defined in these studies as meeting all but one criterion for AN; the two most commonly reported reasons for a subthreshold diagnosis were insufficient weight loss and insufficient abnormality of menstrual functioning.

The fact that a considerable number of women with subthreshold AN enter eating disorder clinics suggests that even though their symptom picture may not warrant a full syndrome diagnosis, these women (or their families) experience levels of distress severe enough to motivate them to seek medical help. Recent clinic-based studies found patients who met all but the weight-loss criteria for AN to be indistinguishable from full syndrome patients on measures of eating disorder symptoms and of general psychiatric distress. For example, subthreshold anorexia cases were similar to full syndrome cases on measures of weight dissatisfaction, preoccupation with thinness and dieting, and anxiety or depression (Bunnell et al., 1990; Williamson et al., 1992).

More research is needed to determine the clinical significance of subthreshold symptomatology. In clinic-based samples, one-year follow-up data of subthreshold cases suggest that these women's eating pathology is likely to be persistent (Herzog et al., 1993). Initial data suggest that some women with subthreshold AN simply may not have been ill long enough to reach the weight loss necessary for a full syndrome diagnosis, and some appear to be in transition between AN and BN (Bunnell et al., 1990). Whether those with subthreshold diagnoses respond more favorably to treatment than is usual in full syndrome cases remains to be investigated. Virtually no study has examined the clinical significance, natural course, and prognosis of subthreshold cases of AN in community samples. We would argue that subthreshold AN has not received sufficient scientific attention because of our culture's strong positive evaluation of thinness and its acceptance of chronic dieting as a way of life for women. Furthermore, we believe that more emphasis should be placed on inappropriate weight loss behaviors.

Subtyping Anorexia Nervosa

The most noteworthy change in the diagnostic criteria for AN in *DSM–IV* is the introduction of two subtypes of the disorder, which are based on behavioral symptoms. Depending on the presence of recurrent binge eating, individuals with AN are classified as *restricting type* or *binge-eating/ purging type*. An important implication of subtyping is that a diagnosis of AN will now supersede BN. Individuals who meet criteria for both disorders will no longer receive two separate diagnoses, as was the practice with the *DSM–III–R*; rather, they will be diagnosed AN–BN subtype.

Subtyping by the presence or absence of binge eating has been justified on the basis of numerous studies comparing individuals with AN who binge with those who do not binge. This research suggests marked group differences in impulsivity: substance abuse, suicide attempts, self-mutilatory behavior, labile mood, and stealing are significantly more common among individuals with AN whose symptom pictures include binge eating (Bunnell et al., 1990; Casper, Hedeker, & McClough, 1992; DaCosta & Halmi, 1992).

Challenging this scheme, Garner and colleagues have argued that purging rather than binging determines the subtype (Garner, 1993; Garner, Shafer, & Rosen, 1992). These researchers compared three groups of patients: 116 AN-diagnosed individuals, who neither binged nor purged (*restricting nonpurgers*); 74 who purged but did not binge (*restricting purgers*); and 190 who binged (*bulimic anorexics*). Importantly, only a small minority among the bulimic anorexics (12%) did not engage in any form of purging behavior. Measures of general psychopathology revealed striking differences between the restricting nonpurgers and the other two groups: The restricting nonpurgers exhibited less psychiatric distress, less depression, and fewer suicide attempts. These findings are consistent with results of several other recent studies (Casper et al., 1992; Shisslak, Pazda, & Crago, 1990; Whitaker et al., 1990). In practice, subtyping based on purging will result in a more homogeneous subgroup of restricting nonpurgers. Because most binging anorexics also purge (Clinton & Glant, 1992; Garner, 1993; Viesselman & Roig, 1985), an additional subdivision of binging anorexics that is based on purging appears to be unnecessary. The resulting emphasis on purging is consistent with data of the serious health consequences associated with purging (Mitchell, Pomeroy, & Huber, 1988; Sharp & Freeman, 1993). The comparison of restricting nonpurgers, restricting purgers, bulimic anorexics, and purging or binging anorexics yielded another interesting finding. The three groups had a similar age of onset, but the restricting purgers and the bulimic anorexics had been ill twice as long as the restricting nonpurgers. Thus, it has been proposed that purging and/or binging represent symptoms that emerge later in the course of AN in most patients (Garner, Garner, & Rosen, 1993; Rastam, 1992). Such a developmental course is consistent with observations that a considerable number of anorexic patients eventually develop BN (Kassett, Gwirtsman, Kaye, Brandt, & Jimerson, 1988; Mitchell et al., 1989). The pattern of a progression from AN to BN raises questions about the relationship between these disorders that we will consider after the discussion of BN.

CLASSIFICATION OF BULIMIA NERVOSA

Essential Features of Bulimia Nervosa

Bulimia nervosa (BN) received formal recognition as a psychiatric illness in the *DSM–III* (American Psychiatric Association, 1980); however, there are numerous historical records of clinical descriptions of patients who today would be diagnosed to suffer from BN (e.g., Stunkard, 1993). As shown in the appendix to this chapter, BN is defined by a behavioral pattern of recurrent binge eating followed by recurrent inappropriate compensatory behaviors (e.g., severely restrictive dieting, or purging in the form of vomiting or abuse of substances thought to promote weight loss). Frequency thresholds specify that binge eating and compensatory behaviors occur at a minimum average frequency of twice a week over a 3 month period. In addition to these behaviorally defined criteria, for a full syndrome diagnosis, the presence of an undue emphasis on weight or shape in self-evaluation is required.

Criterion A: Recurrent Episodes of Binge Eating

Much like failure to maintain minimum weight is the central criterion for AN, *binge eating* represents the core criterion for BN. However, the definition of binge eating remains problematic. In the *DSM–IV*, binge eating involves two components: eating an objectively large amount of food, and experiencing the eating episode as out of one's volitional control. This definition is consistent with how women with BN view their binge eating (Beglin & Fairburn, 1992), and with the lay public's understanding of the term (Striegel-Moore, Brownell, Wilfley, & Vaughn, 1993).

461

In normal eating behavior there is considerable variability in the size, frequency, and composition of eating episodes. Thus, a particular individual's deviation from what is normal is difficult to assess. For example, what constitutes an "objectively large" number of cookies? Although most clinicians would agree that 20 cookies is a "large number," what about 10 or 8? Laboratory studies of binge eating in women with BN have found considerable intra- and intersubject variability in the size and composition of binge episodes (Kaye et al., 1992; Walsh, Kissileff, Cassidy, & Dantzic, 1989). A recent analysis of 225 self-reported binge episodes among women with nonpurging BN yielded a range of calories ingested from a low of 25 calories to a high of more than 6,000 calories (Rossiter, Agras, Telch, & Bruce, 1992). Moreover, many women with BN report smaller binges as they improve in treatment. Whether *subjective bulimic episodes* (eating a normal amount of food and experiencing such an episode as out of control; Fairburn & Cooper, 1993) represent a clinically significant symptom that should count toward diagnosis needs to be tested.

The requirement of loss of control is equally problematic. In our clinical experience, many women with BN describe that they experience a control paradox in their deliberate surrender of control over eating (e.g., binge episodes are carefully planned). In this context, overeating appears to represent a form of protest or acting-out in an otherwise tightly controlled life (Johnson & Connors, 1987). Thus, unlike individuals with brain abnormalities that may interfere with voluntary control of eating, individuals with BN are quite capable of regulating their eating behavior (e.g., they will often stop binge eating in response to social interruption).

Criterion B: Recurrent Inappropriate Compensatory Behaviors

Some of these behaviors are more readily quantifiable than others. For example, vomiting and the use of laxatives or diuretics represent discrete events that can be reported in terms of their frequency and, in the case of laxative use, in terms of the amount of the substance involved. It is considerably more difficult to quantify and determine as symptomatic behaviors such as exercising (Beumont, Arthur, Russell, & Touyz, 1994). We recommend, for example, that deliberately exercising at a frequency or at intensity levels that result in injury or that ignore already existing injuries or health problems should be considered symptomatic behavior and count towards diagnosis of an eating disorder. Such a practice may result in an increase in the number of men who meet diagnostic criteria for an eating disorder.

Criterion C: Frequency Criterion for Binge Eating and Purging

We will discuss Criterion C in the section devoted to defining thresholds.

Criterion D: Undue Importance of Shape or Weight

Persistent overconcern with body weight and shape has long been considered a central feature of BN (Russell, 1979). Unlike the debates about the diagnostic utility of body image disturbance in AN, experts agree that overvalued ideas about shape and weight are a necessary diagnostic feature of BN. The selection of this particular aspect of body image disturbance over other components, such as fear of weight gain or body image dissatisfaction (components emphasized in AN), appears justified on the basis of the prognostic validity of overvaluation of weight (Fairburn & Garner, 1986).

The extensive literature documents that most individuals with BN fear fatness and experience profound body image dissatisfaction (Garfinkel, 1992). However, these symptoms are not unique to BN, but are reported by a large number of non-eating-disordered individuals as well (Cooper & Fairburn, 1993; Garfinkel et al., 1992). Body image dissatisfaction was absent in 20% of 524 individuals in treatment for BN; in contrast, only 3% of these individuals did not evidence overconcern with weight or shape (Garfinkel et al., 1992). These results are consistent with data reported by other research groups (Cooper, Cooper, & Fairburn, 1989; Hadigan & Walsh, 1991; Rosen, Vara, Wendt, & Leitenberg, 1990; Wilson & Smith, 1989). Garfinkel's group found that overconcern with weight/shape was closely associated with degree of body image satisfaction, although not in a linear fashion. Highly weight-dissatisfied women have typically overvalued weight and shape, whereas women who attributed great importance to weight/shape for their self-evaluation were not necessarily dissatisfied with their bodies.

Criterion E: Disturbance Does Not Occur Exclusively During Anorexic Episodes

This criterion raises issues concerning the relationship between AN and BN and will be addressed in the following section.

Defining Thresholds

Two questions have interested experts from the moment BN was formally recognized: Which behavioral symptoms best capture the disorder, and at what level of severity do these symptoms warrant a psychiatric diagnosis? Studies reporting that occasional binge eating was acknowledged by a large number of women provided the impetus for a narrowing of criteria for BN by means of frequency thresholds, a practice that resulted in a significant reduction of the number of cases of BN. Based on a review of some 50 epidemiological studies, Fairburn and Beglin (1990) reported a mean prevalence of bulimia (*DSM–III*) of 10%, compared to a mean prevalence of BN (*DSM–III–R*) of less than 3%. Research is not yet available to determine the impact on prevalence rates of the newly introduced frequency criterion for compensatory behaviors (*DSM–IV*).

The frequency criterion of binge eating has been a matter of considerable debate (Wilson, 1992). Several studies have shown a significant positive association between frequency of binge eating and degree of associated psychopathology (Lancelot, Brooks-Gunn, Warren, & Newman, 1991; Whitehouse et al., 1992); however, other studies have found that frequency of binge eating was unrelated to concurrent psychopathology (Kendler et al., 1991) or to treatment outcome (Wilson & Eldredge, 1991). In a large community-based study of twins, women with BN were compared with women who did not binge twice a week but met all other criteria for BN. These subthreshold bulimic women did not differ from full syndrome cases on measures of concurrent psychopathology or on measures of putative risk factors (Kendler et al., 1991).

As has been observed among women with subthreshold AN, a large number of women with subthreshold BN have been found to evidence a chronic course of their eating disorder (Herzog et al., 1993). Moreover, a majority of subthreshold BN cases can be expected to meet full syndrome criteria for either AN or BN at some point in their lives (Herzog et al., 1993; Yager, Landsverk, & Edelstein, 1987). This considerable crossover between subthreshold classification and full syndrome classification has led some experts to conclude that a subthreshold diagnosis might be largely an artifact of the timing of the diagnostic assessment (Herzog et al., 1993). More research is needed to determine the clinical significance of varying levels of frequency of binge eating.

Subtyping Bulimia Nervosa

Like the new practice of subtyping AN, in the *DSM–IV* BN is now classified into two subtypes: purging and nonpurging BN. Purging BN refers to individuals who regularly vomit or use laxatives or diuretics to control their weight. The introduction of subtypes of BN has been justified in part on the basis of established research practice: Most epidemiological studies and treatment outcome studies have been limited to individuals with purging BN (Mitchell, 1992; Wilson & Walsh, 1991). Further justification of subtyping of BN derives from findings of significant differences between individuals with BN who purge versus individuals with BN who do not purge, on various indices of eating related pathology and associated psychopathology (for review, see Mitchell, 1992). For example, in a controlled comparison women with BN who purged reported significantly greater anxiety about eating, and more severe body image disturbance than nonpurging women with BN (Willmuth, Leitenberg, Rosen, & Cado, 1988). On the other hand, in a community-based sample of purging and nonpurging individuals with BN, no significant differences were found on a wide range of variables including body image disturbance, self-esteem, and psychopathology (Walters et al., 1993).

The Relationship of Anorexia Nervosa to Bulimia Nervosa

Despite the early understanding of BN as closely related to AN (Russell, 1979, 1985), the disorder was entered into the *DSM–III* as *bulimia*, a syndrome distinct from AN (American Psychiatric Association, 1980). Signaling recognition of similarities between AN and BN, bulimia was renamed *bulimia nervosa* in *DSM–III–R* (American Psychiatric Association, 1987; Fairburn & Garner, 1986). However, the two syndromes were maintained as distinct and separate disorders. The convention of assigning a dual diagnosis to individuals who meet criteria for both disorders has been abandoned in *DSM–IV*, and a diagnosis of AN now supersedes a diagnosis of BN: Individuals who meet criteria for both AN and BN now receive a diagnosis of AN/binge eating type. This suggests that the major distinguishing feature between AN and BN is weight.

Several studies have noted similarities between individuals with AN who binge and individuals with BN who purge on personality traits and on associated psychopathology (for review, see DaCosta & Halmi, 1992). Some experts therefore conclude that it is the behavioral symptom of purging that underlies these similarities (Garner et al., 1993) but have not gone so far as to suggest that BN/purging subtype and AN/binge-eating type represent the same clinical syndrome. Several observations raise questions about the wisdom of conceptualizing these syndromes as separate disorders. In clinic-based samples, a significant number of women with AN have been found to develop BN during the course of their illness (Halmi et al., 1991; Herzog et al., 1988; Rastam, 1992; Ratnasuriya et al., 1991; Sohlberg et al., 1989). Similarly, a sizeable subgroup of women with BN reports a history of AN (for review, see Mitchell, 1992). In a majority of individuals who meet lifetime criteria for both disorders, AN precedes the onset of BN (Herzog et al., 1988; Rastam, 1992; Russell, 1985), a pattern consistent with etiological explanations of binge eating that emphasize dietary restriction as a major risk factor for BN (Striegel-Moore, Silberstein, & Rodin, 1986). However, the reverse pattern has also been found (Herzog et al., 1988). One study suggested that crossover from BN to AN may be on the increase (Kassett et al., 1988).

An extensive literature describes differences between anorexic individuals who neither binge nor purge (nonpurging restricters), binging and/or purging anorexics, and bulimics on measures of personality and general psychopathology. Consistently, nonpurging restricters score significantly lower on indicators of impulsivity such as substance abuse, suicidality, self-mutilating behaviors, and stealing while they score higher on measures of social alienation (DaCosta & Halmi, 1992; Fahy & Eisler, 1993). These group differences have been found in a variety of cultures (e.g., Higuchi, Suzuki, Yamada, Parrish, & Kono, 1993). Treatment of underweight women includes weight restoration as a central goal; however, other aspects of the treatment of AN and BN do not differ significantly. Research is needed to determine whether the current separate classification of AN and BN can be supported in light of different etiological factors or different outcomes.

CLASSIFICATION OF BINGE EATING DISORDER

It has been well documented that there is a group of individuals who report persistent and frequent binge-eating in the absence of the regular compensatory behaviors (i.e., purge behaviors, severe calorie restriction, or excessive exercise) seen in BN. For example, 20–30% of obese individuals seeking treatment in university centers report clinically significant problems with binge eating. A significant minority of these individuals is male. In these clinic samples, when compared to equally obese non-binge-eaters, obese binge-eaters report significantly higher rates of psychiatric morbidity and poorer social functioning. Recently, a collaborative research group (Spitzer et al., 1992, 1993) has developed criteria for a new diagnosis, *binge eating disorder* (BED) to describe noncompensating binge-eaters. The BED criteria are included in the *DSM–IV* as an example of ED-NOS, and in an appendix as an example of a proposed diagnosis requiring further study (see chapter appendix). Two multisite field trials have provided preliminary reliability and validity data for the BED criteria. Available information indicates that BED occurs in approximately 2% of community samples and in 5–8% of obese individuals in the general community. Further, a diagnosis of BED is associated with obesity, early onset of dieting behavior, body image dissatisfaction, frequent episodes of weight loss and regain, and general psychiatric distress (Yanovski, 1993).

Essential Features of Binge Eating Disorder

The essential feature of BED is a frequent (minimum average of two episodes per week) and persistent (duration of six months or more) pattern of binge eating, accompanied by marked distress. The presence of at least three of five associated behaviors (e.g., eating rapidly, overeating when not hungry) is also required for the diagnosis. Finally, the binge eating must not be associated with regular inappropriate compensatory behaviors or occur exclusively during the course of AN or BN. BED is not divided into subtypes.

Criterion A: Recurrent Episodes of Binge Eating

It is important to note that binge-eating in BED is defined identically to the way it is in BN, namely as the recurrent intake of a large amount of food given the circumstances with an associated sense of loss of control over eating. Not surprisingly, the definition of binge eating in BED is problematic, as it is in BN. The regular purge behavior seen in individuals with BN often serves to punctuate binge episodes and thus purging aides in the demarcation of discrete episodes. In contrast, the absence of regular compensatory behavior in BED renders the assessment of the length and size of episodes difficult, particularly because an episode of loss of control over eating may span several hours. In fact, Marcus found that 24% of binge episodes reported by women with BED lasted an entire day (Marcus, Smith, Santelli, & Kaye, 1992). Most researchers, therefore, have decided to report the number of binge days per week or month rather than of discrete episodes for BED; this practice is reflected in the BED criteria.

The assessment of loss of control over eating is also difficult in individuals with BED. In our clinical experience, many of these individuals insist that once they have overeaten on a given day, their eating is out of control for the rest of the day. However, these out-of-control days often include long periods of time when there is no food intake (e.g., at work). Can eating be really considered out of control for the entire day? Moreover, clinical experience suggests that many individuals with BED deny any loss of control because they have given up all efforts to manage what they regard as a hopeless eating problem.

Criterion B: External Validators of Loss of Control

The BED criteria stipulate that three of the five behaviors associated with binge eating be present for a diagnosis. These behaviors include rapid eating, eating until uncomfortably full, overeating in the absence of hunger, solitary eating, and strong negative affect after overeating. Data from the BED field trials have indicated that few participants with clinically significant binge eating did not report at least three of five associated features (Spitzer et al., 1993). This suggests that inclusion of this criterion may be redundant. However, Criterion B was retained to generate a fuller description of the syndrome in the diagnostic criteria.

Criterion C: Marked Distress Regarding Binge Eating

In individuals who engage in recurrent binge eating, almost all report significant distress associated with the behavior; thus distress might be more appropriately considered as secondary to the disorder rather than a core feature. Furthermore, significant impairment and/or marked distress is implied in the diagnosis of any *DSM* disorder. Spitzer and colleagues recommended to retain Criterion C in the proposed BED criteria to ensure a high threshold for the diagnosis: Without this criterion, the number of individuals meeting BED criteria would have increased by 10% among individuals requesting weight control therapy and by 50% in a community sample (Spitzer et al., 1992, 1993).

Criterion D: Frequency and Duration Criterion

Because Criterion D establishes a threshold, it will be described below.

Criterion E: Absence of Regular Inappropriate Compensatory Behaviors; Does Not Occur Exclusively During the Course of AN or BN

By definition, individuals with BED fail to compensate for the effects of binge-eating by the regular use of purging, severe caloric restriction, or excessive exercise. The failure to compensate for binge-eating may in fact be related to obesity in many individuals with BED. Nevertheless, it is clear that purging behaviors are not uncommon among individuals with BED. For example, Marcus and colleagues reported that approximately 13% of one group of obese binge eaters induced vomiting at least occasionally, and 6.7% reported some laxative misuse (Marcus, Wing, & Hopkins, 1988). It may be that efforts to compensate for binge behaviors in women with BED are insufficiently frequent to allow these women to maintain a normal body weight. However, this conjecture requires empirical verification. In light of this, it has become critical to clarify what, if anything, discriminates between subthreshold and threshold levels of purging among individuals with BED, and how purging in BED differs from purging in BN.

Defining Thresholds

The BED collaborative group adopted the frequency criterion to be consistent with the threshold criterion adopted for BN. To our knowledge, there are no data that shed light on the utility of the twice-weekly binge frequency criterion. Similarly, the adoption of the six-month duration criterion was not based on theoretical or empirical grounds, but rather represented a pragmatic decision aimed at avoiding the over-diagnosis of BED. Research is needed to determine optimal frequency and duration criteria for binge-eating in BED.

Binge Eating Disorder and Bulimia Nervosa: Are they Related?

Future work is needed to clarify the differences between nonpurging BN and BED. Initial data indicate that women with nonpurging BN closely resemble women with purging BN on measures of eating-related pathology, and significantly differ from women with BED. The latter individuals are heavier, and although they are weight-dissatisfied, do not report strict dieting between binge episodes (Williamson et al., 1992). Similarly, research has shown a continuum in the severity of associated psychiatric symptomatology from purging BN (most severe) and nonpurging BN (moderately severe) to obese binge-eaters (least severe) (Clinton & Glant, 1992; De Zwaan et al., 1994; Fichter, Quadflieg, & Brandl, 1993; Kirkley, Kolotkin, Hernandez, & Gallagher, 1992; Prather & Williamson, 1988). At present it is unclear whether individuals with BED who purge at subthreshold levels should be excluded from BED. Also unexamined is the question of cross-over between BED and BN.

The present taxonomy does not include differences in body weight as a relevant dimension in BN and BED. How weight factors into course, outcome, and treatment has not yet been explored sufficiently in theoretical or empirical work. In a theoretical paper on dieting, Lowe (1993) has argued that the physiological and psychological sequelae of dieting depend on the dieter's weight status. In our treatment of obese women with BN and of normal weight women with BED, we have found significant differences in the perceived credibility and acceptability of the treatment.

CONCLUSIONS

The preceding analysis of *DSM–IV* diagnostic criteria for eating disorders revealed several contradictions that have far-reaching implications for research, treatment and prevention. Although the goal of the *DSM–IV* is to permit classification of clinically significant syndromes, the representative scope (Millon, 1991) of the present taxonomy is too narrow to capture the majority of individuals with a clinically significant pattern of disordered eating. The exclusion of a significant range of the spectrum of eating disorders interferes with the acquisition of knowledge about these conditions that, until now, have not been classified with any precision. For example, to date, individuals experiencing EDNOS are systematically excluded from controlled treatment trials; consequently, little is known about the appropriate choice of treatment for EDNOS. Even though in theory all mental disorders listed in the *DSM–IV* meet the criteria of dysfunction and harm (Wakefield, 1992) and individuals presenting for treatment with a diagnosable condition should be entitled to receive therapy, in practice the "left over" or "waste basket" categories of *not otherwise specified* (NOS) are often perceived as less severe and therefore as less worthy of treatment than the named disorders. Individuals requesting treatment are faced with the risk of being denied insurance reimbursement for treatment expenses if their condition does not fit the narrow criteria of AN or BN. The narrow definition of eating disorders also affects primary prevention efforts. If eating disorders are seen as relatively rare phenomena, their inclusion among the list of health or mental health problems to be targeted for prevention efforts may not be perceived as urgent.

Research is needed to evaluate the full spectrum of eating-related symptoms in community-based samples. We believe that a major reason for the poor fit between the current taxonomy and the types of syndromes experienced in our society derives from the fact that diagnostic criteria have been developed with data derived from clinic-based populations. At present, we have an extremely limited data base to determine whether factors such as race or ethnicity, socioeconomic status, or sexual orientation play a role in risk for and symptom expression of eating disorders. Research has shown that clinical services use-patterns are influenced by variables such as race, ethnicity, socioeconomic status, or sexual orientation (e.g., Bradford & Ryan, 1987). Initial efforts at developing an empirically based taxonomy are currently underway in England (Hay et al., 1994). This work represents an important step toward a more comprehensive description of disordered eating; however, cross-cultural psychiatry has provided ample examples of the necessity to investigate a particular disorder within its cultural context for a culturally valid understanding of the disorder. Therefore, research using study samples that more adequately reflect the diversity of the U.S. population is urgently needed.

Broadening the scope of the eating disorder taxonomy should not occur in the absence of a critical evaluation of the concept of clinical significance. Such an evaluation needs to be conducted using multidisciplinary teams of experts because clinical significance inherently is a context-bound concept. Hence, historians, ethicists and sociologists will provide useful perspectives, as will psychopathologists and clinicians. These deliberations will be enhanced by a more extended empirical data base of normal and symptomatic behavior. Little empirical evidence has been accumulated on normative concerns that adolescent girls experience; in this relative vacuum, it is difficult to determine which body image concerns or eating behaviors should be considered clinically significant symptoms. Systematic research into the objectively measurable correlates and outcomes of specific symptoms (e.g., vomiting) and into various syndromes of eating disorders is needed. It is also important to incorporate continuous measures of eating-related symptoms and of subthreshold cases, thus permitting a more empirically based establishment of threshold criteria. Lastly, examination of how gender-role expectations influence experts' judgments of clinical significance is needed.

Researchers need a fuller discussion of the costs and benefits of defining a set of symptoms as a clinical syndrome, and a better understanding of the subjective experience of individuals who exhibit such symptoms and syndromes in terms of concepts such as *harm* and *suffering*. Similarly, individuals with an eating disorder presently have no formal forum to influence classification. Although a number of self-help organizations and advocacy groups exist, there has been little dialogue between these groups and those experts who ultimately influence or make classification decisions.

Another problem involves the systematic effort of categorizing symptoms into narrowly defined, nonoverlapping categories, and the clinical reality that individuals appear to "move in and out of" diagnostic categories. The dilemma behind classifying eating disorders into several distinct types mirrors the dilemma involved in classification in general. Multiple specific categories promise greater accuracy of the description of a phenomenon and may aid in identifying underlying causes and successful treatments. Emphasis on subgroup characteristics may detract from identifying shared etiological factors, and from developing therapeutic or preventive interventions that may apply to all types of eating disorders (see also Garner et al., 1993).

The current taxonomy does not fully consider the clinical course of eating disorders, which results in certain inconsistencies. Due in part to the narrowly defined thresholds, a large number of individuals with EDNOS vacillate between full-syndrome criteria and subthreshold criteria. However, their shifting status may simply reflect different stages of the same disorder (e.g., Herzog et al., 1993; Striegel-Moore, Silberstein, Frensch, & Rodin, 1989). Moreover, developmental psychopathology suggests multiple pathways into a disorder. For example, a 45-year-old woman who develops AN for the first time following a divorce has successfully negotiated developmental challenges that women with an earlier onset of the disorder have failed to meet. Symptom expression may change across the developmental spectrum, resulting in a different set of key features of the same underlying disorder. Similarly, the treatment needs of an adolescent girl are likely to differ from the needs experienced by an older woman, yet this issue has not yet been explored empirically.

Ultimately, classification of eating disorders should reflect an understanding of etiology. Although there is considerable consensus that eating disorders involve a multifactorial etiology, agreement has not yet been reached about the relative importance of the various etiological factors that have been proposed (Striegel-Moore et al., 1986). Our theoretical views of eating disorders, along with our attitudes and beliefs about these disorders in particular and about healthy or normal functioning in women in general, strongly determine what evidence we look for when classifying these disorders. Therefore, it is paramountly important for feminists to contribute to the dialogue on classification. For example, feminist scholars have spearheaded efforts to include consideration of variables such as attachment-style or history of sexual victimization as potential causal factors in the etiology of eating disorders. These efforts have contributed to a vigorous scientific debate about etiology and are likely to become incorporated into future taxonomies.

APPENDIX

DSM–IV DIAGNOSTIC CRITERIA FOR EATING DISORDERS (AMERICAN PSYCHIATRIC ASSOCIATION, 1994)

Anorexia Nervosa

A. Refusal to maintain body weight at or above a minimally normal weight for age and height (e.g., weight loss leading to maintenance of body weight less than 85% of that expected; or failure to make expected weight gain during period of growth, leading to body weight less than 85% of that expected).

B. Intense fear of gaining weight or becoming fat, even though underweight.

C. Disturbance in the way in which one's body weight or shape is experienced, undue influence of body weight or shape on self-evaluation, or denial of the seriousness of the current low body weight.

D. In postmenarcheal females, amenorrhea, i.e., the absence of at least three consecutive menstrual cycles. (A woman is considered to have amenorrhea if her periods occur only following hormone, e.g., estrogen, administration.)

Specify type:

Restricting Type: during the current episode of Anorexia Nervosa, the person has not regularly engaged in binge eating or purging behavior (i.e., self-induced vomiting or the misuse of laxatives, diuretics, or enemas).

Binge Eating/Purging Type: during the episode of Anorexia Nervosa, the person has regularly engaged in binge eating or purging behavior (i.e., self-induced vomiting or the misuse of laxatives, diuretics, or enemas).

Bulimia Nervosa

A. Recurrent episodes of binge eating. An episode of binge eating is characterized by both of the following:

From *Diagnostic and Statistical Manual of Mental Disorders, Fourth Edition.* Copyright 1994 by the American Psychiatric Association. Reprinted with permission of the publisher.

(1) eating, in a discrete period of time (e.g., within any 2-hour period), an amount of food that is definitely larger than most people would eat during a similar period of time and under similar circumstances.

(2) a sense of lack of control over eating during the episode (e.g., a feeling that one cannot stop eating or control what or how much one is eating).

B. Recurrent inappropriate compensatory behavior in order to prevent weight gain, such as self-induced vomiting; misuse of laxatives, diuretics, enemas, or other medications; fasting; or excessive exercise.

C. The binge eating and inappropriate compensatory behaviors both occur, on average, at least twice a week for three months.

D. Self-evaluation is unduly influenced by body shape and weight.

E. The disturbance does not occur exclusively during episodes of Anorexia Nervosa.

Specify type:

Purging type: during the current episode of Bulimia Nervosa, the person regularly engages in self-induced vomiting or the misuse of laxatives, diuretics, or enemas.

Nonpurging type: during the current episode of Bulimia Nervosa, the person has used other inappropriate compensatory behaviors, such as fasting or excessive exercise, but has not regularly engaged in self-induced vomiting or the misuse of laxatives, diuretics, or enemas.

Research Criteria for Binge Eating Disorders

A. Recurrent episodes of binge eating. An episode of binge eating is characterized by both of the following:

(1) eating, in a discrete period of time (e.g., within any 2-hour period), an amount of food that is definitely larger than most people would eat during a similar period of time under similar circumstances;

(2) a sense of lack of control over eating during the episode (e.g., a feeling that one cannot stop eating or control what or how much one is eating).

B. The binge eating episodes are associated with three (or more) of the following:

(1) eating much more rapidly than normal

(2) eating until feeling uncomfortably full

(3) eating large amounts of food when not feeling physically hungry

(4) eating alone because of being embarrassed by how much one is eating

(5) feeling disgusted with oneself, depressed, or very guilty after overeating

C. Marked distress regarding binge eating is present.

D. The binge eating occurs, on average, at least two days a week for six months.

Note: The method of determining frequency differs from that used for Bulimia Nervosa; future research should address whether the preferred method of setting a frequency threshold is counting the number of days on which binges occur or counting the number of episodes of binge eating.

E. The binge eating is not associated with the regular use of inappropriate compensatory behaviors (e.g., purging, fasting, excessive exercise) and does not occur exclusively during the course of Anorexia Nervosa or Bulimia Nervosa.

Eating Disorders Not Otherwise Specified

Disorders of eating that do not meet the criteria for a specific Eating Disorder. Examples include:

(1) all of the criteria for Anorexia Nervosa are met except the individual has regular menses.

(2) all the criteria for Anorexia Nervosa are met except, despite significant weight loss, the individual's current weight is in the normal range.

(3) all of the criteria for Bulimia Nervosa are met except binges occur at a frequency of less than twice a week or a duration of less than three months.

(4) an individual of normal body weight regularly engages in inappropriate compensatory behavior after eating small amounts of food (e.g., self-induced vomiting after eating small amounts of food (e.g., self-induced vomiting after the consumption of two cookies).

(5) an individual who repeatedly chews and spits out, but does not swallow, large amounts of food.

(6) binge eating disorder: recurrent episodes of binge eating in the absence of the regular use of inappropriate compensatory behaviors characteristic of bulimia nervosa (see page 729 [of the *DSM-IV*] for suggested criteria).

REFERENCES

American Psychiatric Association. (1980). *Diagnostic and statistical manual of mental disorders* (3rd ed.). Washington, DC: Author.

American Psychiatric Association. (1987). *Diagnostic and statistical manual of mental disorders* (3rd ed., rev.). Washington, DC: Author.

American Psychiatric Association. (1994). *Diagnostic and statistical manual of mental disorders* (4th ed). Washington, DC: Author.

Beglin, S. J., & Fairburn, C. G. (1992). What is meant by the term "binge"? *American Journal of Psychiatry, 149,* 123–124.

Beumont, P. J. V., Arthur, B., Russell, J. D., & Touyz, S. W. (1994). Excessive physical activity in dieting disorder patients: Proposals for a supervised exercise program. *International Journal of Eating Disorders, 15,* 21–36.

Bordo, S. (1993). *Unbearable weight: Feminism, western culture, and the body.* Berkeley, CA: University of California Press.

Bradford, J., & Ryan, C. (1987). *The national lesbian health care survey.* (Available from the National Lesbian and Gay Foundation, P.O. Box 65472, Washington, DC 20035).

Bruce, B., & Agras, W. S. (1992). Binge eating in females: A population-based investigation. *International Journal of Eating Disorders, 12,* 365–373.

Bruch, H. (1962). Perceptual and conceptual disturbances in anorexia nervosa. *Psychosomatic Medicine, 24,* 187–194.

Brumberg, J. J. (1988). *Fasting girls.* Cambridge, MA: Harvard University Press.

Brumberg, J. J., & Striegel-Moore, R. H. (1993). Continuity and change in symptom choice: Anorexia. In R. D. Parke, G. Elder, & J. Modell (Eds.), *Children in time and place* (pp. 131–146). Cambridge, England: Cambridge University Press.

Bunnell, D. W., Shenker, I. R., Nussbaum, M. P., Jacobson, M. S., & Cooper, P. (1990). Subclinical versus formal eating disorders: Differentiating psychological features. *International Journal of Eating Disorders, 9,* 357–362.

Casper, R. C., Hedeker, D., & McClough, J. F. (1992). Personality dimensions in eating disorders and their relevance for subtyping. *Journal of the American Academy of Child and Adolescent Psychiatry, 31,* 830–840.

Clinton, D. N., & Glant, R. (1992). The eating-disorders spectrum of DSM–III–R: Clinical features and psychological concomitant of 86 consecutive cases from a Swedish urban catchment area. *The Journal of Nervous and Mental Disease, 180,* 244–250.

Cooper, P. J., & Fairburn, C. G. (1993). Confusion over the core psychopathology of bulimia nervosa. *International Journal of Eating Disorders, 13,* 385–390.

Cooper, Z., Cooper, P. J., & Fairburn, C. G. (1989). The validity of the Eating Disorder Examination and its subscales. *British Journal of Psychiatry, 154,* 807–812.

Coovert, D. L., Kinder, B. N., & Thompson, J. K. (1989). The psychosexual aspects of anorexia nervosa and bulimia nervosa: A review of the literature. *Clinical Psychology Review, 9,* 169–180.

DaCosta, M., & Halmi, K. A. (1992). Classification of anorexia nervosa: Question of subtypes. *International Journal of Eating Disorders, 11,* 305–314.

Deter, H. C., & Herzog, W. (1994). Anorexia nervosa in a long-term perspective: Results of the Heidelberg–Mannheim study. *Psychosomatic Medicine, 56,* 20–27.

De Zwaan, M., Mitchell, J. E., Seim, H. C., Specker S. M., Pyle, R. L., Raymond, N. C., & Crosby, R. B. (1994). Eating related and general psychopathology in obese females with binge eating disorder. *International Journal of Eating Disorders, 15,* 43–52.

Fahy, T., & Eisler, I. (1993). Impulsivity and eating disorders. *British Journal of Psychiatry, 162,* 193–197.

Fahy, T., & Treasure, J. (1989). Children of the mothers with bulimia nervosa. *British Medical Journal, 299,* 1031.

Fairburn, C. G., & Beglin, S. J. (1990). Studies of the epidemiology of bulimia nervosa. *American Journal of Psychiatry, 147,* 401–408.

Fairburn, C. G., & Cooper, Z. (1993). The Eating Disorder Examination (12th ed.). In C. G. Fairburn & G. T. Wilson (Eds.), *Binge eating: Nature, assessment, and treatment* (pp. 317–360). New York: Guilford Press.

Fairburn, C. G., & Garner, D. M. (1986). The diagnosis of bulimia nervosa. *International Journal of Eating Disorders, 5,* 403–420.

Fairburn, C. G., Welch, S. L., & Hay, P. J. (1993). The classification of recurrent overeating: The "Binge Eating Disorder" proposal. *International Journal of Eating Disorders, 13,* 155–160.

Fallon, P., Katzman, M. A., & Wooley, S. C. (1993). *Feminist perspectives on eating disorders.* New York: Guilford Press.

Fichter, M. M., Quadflieg, N., & Brandl, B. (1993). Recurrent overeating: An empirical comparison of binge eating disorder, bulimia nervosa, and obesity. *International Journal of Eating Disorders, 14,* 1–16.

Garfinkel, P. E. (1992). Evidence in support of attitudes to shape and weight as a diagnostic criterion of bulimia nervosa. *International Journal of Eating Disorders, 11,* 321–325.

Garfinkel, P. E., Goldbloom, D., Davis, R., Olmsted, M. P., Garner, D. M., & Halmi, K. A. (1992). Body dissatisfaction in bulimia nervosa: Relationship to weight and shape concerns and psychological functioning. *International Journal of Eating Disorders, 11,* 151–161.

Garner, D. M. (1993). Binge eating in anorexia nervosa. In C. G. Fairburn & G. T. Wilson (Eds.), *Binge eating: Nature, assessment, and treatment* (pp. 50–76). New York: Guilford Press.

Garner, D. M., Garfinkel, P. E., Stancer, H. C., & Moldofsky, H. (1976). Body image disturbances in anorexia nervosa and obesity. *Psychosomatic Medicine, 38,* 327–336.

Garner, D. M., Garner, M. V., & Rosen, L. W. (1993). Anorexia nervosa "restricters" who purge: Implications for subtyping anorexia nervosa. *International Journal of Eating Disorders, 13,* 171–186.

Garner, D. M., Shafer, C. L., & Rosen, L. W. (1992). Critical appraisal of the DSM–III–R diagnostic criteria for eating disorders. In S. R. Hooper, G. W. Hynd, & R. E. Mattison (Eds.), *Child psychopathology. Diagnostic criteria and clinical assessment* (pp. 261–303). Hillsdale, NJ: Erlbaum.

Grissett, N. I., & Norvell, N. K. (1992). Perceived social support, social skills, and quality of relationship in bulimic women. *Journal of Consulting and Clinical Psychology, 60,* 293–299.

Gull, W. W. (1964). Anorexia nervosa. In R. M. Kaufman & M. Heiman (Eds.), *Evolution of psychosomatic concepts* (pp. 132–139). New York: International Universities Press. (Originally published in 1874).

Hadigan, C. M., & Walsh, B. T. (1991). Body shape concerns in bulimia nervosa. *International Journal of Eating Disorders, 10,* 323–331.

Hall, A., & Hay, P. J. (1991). Eating disorder patient referrals from a population region 1977–1986. *Psychological Medicine, 21,* 697–701.

Halmi, K. A., Eckert, E., Marchi, P., Sampugnaro, V., Apple, R., & Cohen, J. (1991).

Comorbidity of psychiatric diagnoses in anorexia nervosa. *Archives of General Psychiatry, 48,* 712–718.

Hay, P. J., Fairburn, C. G., & Doll, H. (1994, April). *Towards the reclassification of bulimic eating disorders: A community based cluster analytic study.* Paper presented at the International Conference on Eating Disorders, New York, NY.

Herzog, D. B., Hopkins, J. D., & Burns, C. D. (1993). A follow-up study of 33 subdiagnostic eating disordered women. *International Journal of Eating Disorders, 14,* 261–267.

Herzog, D. B., Keller, M. B., & Lavori, P. W. (1988). Outcome in anorexia nervosa and bulimia nervosa: A review of the literature. *The Journal of Nervous and Mental Disease, 176,* 131–143.

Highet, R. (1989). Athletic amenorrhea. An update on aetiology, complications and management. *Sports Medicine, 7,* 82–108.

Higuchi, S., Suzuki, K., Yamada, K., Parrish, K., & Kono, H. (1993). Alcoholics with eating disorders: Prevalence and clinical course. A study from Japan. *British Journal of Psychiatry, 162,* 403–406.

Hoek, H. W. (1991). The incidence and prevalence of anorexia nervosa and bulimia nervosa in primary care. *Psychological Medicine, 21,* 455–460.

Hsu, L. K. G., & Lee, S. (1993). Is weight phobia always necessary for a diagnosis of anorexia nervosa? *American Journal of Psychiatry, 150,* 1466–1471.

Hsu, L. K. G., & Sobkiewicz, T. A. (1991). Body image disturbance: Time to abandon the concept for eating disorders? *International Journal of Eating Disorders, 10,* 15–30.

Johnson, C., & Connors, M. E. (1987). *The etiology and treatment of bulimia nervosa: A biopsychosocial perspective.* New York: Basic Books.

Kassett, J. A., Gwirtsman, H. E., Kaye, W. H., Brandt, H. A., & Jimerson, D. C. (1988). Pattern of onset of bulimic symptoms in anorexia nervosa. *American Journal of Psychiatry, 145,* 1287–1288.

Kaye, W. H., Weltzin, T. E., McKee, M., McConaha, C., Hansen, D., & Hsu, L. K. G. (1992). Laboratory assessment of feeding behavior in bulimia nervosa and healthy women: Methods for developing a human-feeding laboratory. *American Journal of Clinical Nutrition, 55,* 372–380.

Kearney-Cooke, A., & Striegel-Moore, R. H. (1994). Treatment of childhood sexual abuse in anorexia nervosa and bulimia nervosa: A feminist psychodynamic approach. *International Journal of Eating Disorders, 15,* 305–319.

Keller, M. B., Herzog, D. B., Lavori, P. W., Bradburn, I. S., & Mahoney, E. M. (1992).

The naturalistic history of bulimia nervosa: Extraordinarily high rates of chronicity, relapse, recurrence, and psychosocial morbidity. *International Journal of Eating Disorders, 12,* 1–9.

Kendell, R. E. (1975). *The role of diagnosis in psychiatry.* Aberdeen, Scotland: Aberdeen University Press.

Kendler, K. S., MacLean, C., Neale, M., Kessler, R., Heath, A., & Eaves, L. (1991). The genetic epidemiology of bulimia nervosa. *The American Journal of Psychiatry, 148,* 1627–1637.

Killen, J. D., Hayward, C., Litt, L., Hammer, L. D., Wilson, D. D., Miner, B., Taylor, C. B., Varady, A., & Shisslak, C. (1992). Is puberty a risk factor for eating disorders? *American Journal of Diseases of Children, 146,* 323–325.

Killen, J. D., Taylor, C. B., Hayward, C., Wilson, D. M., Hammer, L. D., Robinson, T. N., Litt, I., Simmonds, B. A., Haydel, F., Varady, A., & Kramer, H. (1994). The pursuit of thinness and onset of eating disorder symptoms in a community sample of adolescent girls: A three year prospective analysis. *International Journal of Eating Disorders, 16,* 227–228.

King, M. B. (1990). Eating disorders in general practice. *Journal of the Royal Society of Medicine, 83,* 229–232.

Kirkley, B. G., Kolotkin, R. L., Hernandez, J. T., & Gallagher, P. N. (1992). A comparison of binge-purgers, obese binge eaters, and obese nonbinge eaters on the MMPI. *International Journal of Eating Disorders, 12,* 221–228.

Lancelot, C., Brooks-Gunn, J., Warren, M. P., & Newman, D. L. (1991). Comparison of DSM-III and DSM-III-R bulimia nervosa classifications for psychopathology and other eating behaviors. *International Journal of Eating Disorders, 10,* 57–66.

Lasegue, G. (1964). De l'anorexie hysterique. In R. M. Kaufman & M. Heiman (Eds.), *Evolution of psychosomatic concepts* (pp. 141–155). New York: International University Press. (Originally published 1873).

Lee, S., Ho, T. P., & Hsu, L. K. G. (1993). Fat phobia and non-fat phobic anorexia nervosa; a study of 70 Chinese patients in Hong Kong. *Psychological Medicine, 23,* 999–1017.

Levine, M. P., Smolak, L., Moodey, A. F., Shuman, M. D., & Hessen, L. D. (1994). Normative developmental challenges and dieting and eating disturbances in middle school girls. *International Journal of Eating Disorders, 15,* 11–20.

Lowe, M. R. (1993). The effects of dieting on eating behavior: A three-year factor model. *Psychological Bulletin, 114,* 100–121.

Lucas, A. R., Beard, C. M., O'Fallon, W. M., & Kurland, L. T. (1991). 50-year trends in the incidence of anorexia nervosa in Rochester, Minnesota: A population-based study. *American Journal of Psychiatry, 148,* 917–922.

Marcus, M. D., Smith, D., Santelli, R., & Kaye, W. (1992). Characterization of eating disordered behavior in obese binge eaters. *International Journal of Eating Disorders, 12,* 249–255.

Marcus, M. D., Wing, R. R., & Hopkins, J. (1988). Obese binge eaters: Affect, cognitions, and response to behavioral weight control. *Journal of Consulting and Clinical Psychology, 56,* 433–439.

Millon, T. (1991). Classification in psychopathology: Rationale, alternatives, and standards. *Journal of Abnormal Psychology, 100,* 245–261.

Mitchell, J. E. (1984). Medical complications of anorexia nervosa and bulimia. *Psychiatric Medicine, 1,* 229–255.

Mitchell, J. E. (1992). Subtyping of bulimia nervosa. *International Journal of Eating Disorders, 11,* 327–332.

Mitchell, J. E., Pomeroy, C., & Huber, M. (1988). A clinician's guide to the eating disorders medicine cabinet. *International Journal of Eating Disorders, 7,* 211–223.

Mitchell, J. E., Pyle, R., Eckert, E. D., Pomeroy, C., & Hatsukami, D. (1988). Patients versus symptomatic volunteers in bulimia nervosa research. *International Journal of Eating Disorders, 7,* 837–843.

Mitchell, J. E., Soll, E., Eckert, E. D., Pyle, R. L., & Hatsukami, D. (1989). The changing population of bulimia nervosa patients in an eating disorders program. *Hospital and Community Psychiatry, 40,* 1188–1189.

Orbach, S. (1986). *Hunger strike: The anorectic's struggle as a metaphor for our age.* New York: Norton.

Palmer, R. L. (1993). Weight concern should not be a necessary criterion for the eating disorders: A polemic. *International Journal of Eating Disorders, 14,* 459–465.

Pate, J. E., Pumariega, A. J., Hester, C., & Garner, D. M. (1992). Cross-cultural patterns in eating disorders: A review. *Journal of the American Academy of Child and Adolescent Psychiatry, 31,* 802–809.

Pirke, K. M., & Ploog, D. (1987). Biology of human starvation. In P. J. V. Beumont, G. D. Burrows, & R. C. Casper (Eds.), *Handbook of Eating Disorders* (pp. 79–102). Amsterdam: Elsevier.

Pope, H. G., & Hudson, J. I. (1992). Is childhood sexual abuse a risk factor for bulimia nervosa? *American Journal of Psychiatry, 149,* 455–463.

Prather, R. C., & Williamson, D. A. (1988). Psychopathology associated with bulimia, binge eating, and obesity. *International Journal of Eating Disorders, 7,* 177–184.

Pribor, E. F., & Dinwiddie, S. H. (1992). Psychiatric correlates of incest in childhood. *American Journal of Psychiatry, 149,* 52–56.

Putukian, M. (1994). The female triad: Eating disorders, amenorrhea, and osteoporosis. *Medical Clinics of North America, 78,* 345–356.

Rastam, M. (1992). Anorexia nervosa in 51 Swedish adolescents: Premorbid problems and comorbidity. *Journal of the American Academy of Child and Adolescent Psychiatry, 31,* 819–829.

Ratnasuriya, R. H., Eisler, I., Szmukler, G. I., & Russell, G. F. M. (1991). Anorexia nervosa: Outcome and prognostic factors after 20 years. *British Journal of Psychiatry, 158,* 495–502.

Rodin, J., Silberstein, L. R., & Striegel-Moore, R. H. (1985). Women and weight: A normative discontent. In T. B. Sonderegger (Ed.), *Nebraska Symposium on Motivation* (pp. 267–308). Lincoln: University of Nebraska Press.

Root, M. P. (1990). Disordered eating in women of color. *Sex Roles, 22,* 525–536.

Root, M. P. (1991). Persistent, disordered eating as a gender-specific, post-traumatic stress response to sexual assault. *Psychotherapy: Theory, Practice, and Research, 28,* 96–102.

Rosen, J. C., Vara, L., Wendt, S., & Leitenberg, H. (1990). Validity studies of the Eating Disorder Examination. *International Journal of Eating Disorders, 9,* 519–528.

Rossiter, E. M., Agras, W. S., Telch, C. F., & Bruce, B. (1992). The eating patterns of non-purging bulimic subjects. *International Journal of Eating Disorders, 11,* 111–120.

Russell, G. F. M. (1979). Bulimia nervosa: An ominous variant of anorexia nervosa. *Psychological Medicine, 9,* 429–448.

Russell, G. F. M. (1985). Premenarchal anorexia nervosa and its sequelae. *Journal of Psychiatric Reviews, 19,* 363–369.

Sharp, C. W., & Freeman, C. P. L. (1993). The medical complications of anorexia nervosa. *British Journal of Psychiatry, 162,* 452–462.

Shisslak, C. M., Pazda, S. L. K., & Crago, M. (1990). Body weight and bulimia as discriminators of psychological characteristics among anorexic, bulimic, and obese women. *Journal of Abnormal Psychology, 99,* 380–384.

Slade, P., & Brodie, D. (1994). Body-image distortion and eating disorder: A reconceptualization based on the recent literature. *Eating Disorders Review, 2,* 32–46.

Sohlberg, S., Norring, C., Holmgren, S., & Rosmark, B. (1989). Impulsivity and long-term prognosis of psychiatric patients with anorexia nervosa/bulimia nervosa. *Journal of Nervous & Mental Disease, 177,* 249–258.

Spitzer, R. L., Devlin, M., Walsh, B. T., Hasin, D., Wing, R., Marcus, M., Stunkard, A., Wadden, T., Yanovski, S., Agras, S., Mitchell, J., & Nonas, C. (1992). Binge eating disorder: A multisite field trial of the diagnostic criteria. *International Journal of Eating Disorders, 11,* 191–204.

Spitzer, R. L., Yanovski, S., Wadden, T., Wing, R., Marcus, M. D., Stunkard, A., Devlin, M., Mitchell, J., Hasin, D., & Horne, R. L. (1993). Binge eating disorder: Its further validation in a multisite study. *International Journal of Eating Disorders, 13,* 137–154.

Stein, A., & Fairburn, C. (1989). Children of mothers with bulimia nervosa. *British Medical Journal, 299,* 777–778.

Stewart, D. E. (1992). Reproductive functions in eating disorders. *Annals of Medicine, 24,* 287–291.

Striegel-Moore, R. H. (1993). Etiology of binge eating: A developmental perspective. In C. G. Fairburn & G. T. Wilson (Eds.), *Binge eating: Nature, assessment and treatment* (pp. 144–172). New York: Guilford Press.

Striegel-Moore, R. H., Brownell, K., Wilfley, D., & Vaughn, L. (1993). *Definition of binge eating.* Unpublished manuscript, Wesleyan University, Middletown, CT.

Striegel-Moore, R. H., & Huydic, E. S. (1993). Problem drinking and symptoms of disordered eating in female high school students. *International Journal of Eating Disorders, 14,* 417–425.

Striegel-Moore, R. H., Nicholson, T. J., & Tamborlane, W. V. (1992). Prevalence of eating disorder symptoms in preadolescent and adolescent girls with IDDM. *Diabetes Care, 15,* 1361–1368.

Striegel-Moore, R. H., Schreiber, G. B., Pike, K. M., Wilfley, D. E., & Rodin, R. (in press). Drive for thinness in black and white preadolescent girls. *International Journal of Eating Disorders.*

Striegel-Moore, R. H., Silberstein, L. R., Frensch, P., & Rodin, J. (1989). A prospective study of disordered eating among college students. *International Journal of Eating Disoders, 8,* 499–509.

Striegel-Moore, R. H., Silberstein, L. R., & Rodin, J. (1986). Toward an understanding of risk factors for bulimia. *American Psychologist, 41,* 246–263.

Strober, M. (1983). *An empirically derived topology of anorexia nervosa. Anorexia nervosa: Recent developments in research.* New York: Alan R. Liss.

Strober, M., & Humphrey, L. L. (1987). Familial contributions to the etiology and course of anorexia nervosa and bulimia. *Journal of Consulting and Clinical Psychology, 55,* 654–659.

Stunkard, A. J. (1993). A history of binge eating. In C. G. Fairburn & G. T. Wilson (Eds.), *Binge eating: Nature, assessment, and treatment* (pp. 15–34). New York: Guilford Press.

Szmukler, G. I. (1985). The epidemiology of anorexia nervosa and bulimia. *Journal of Psychiatric Reviews, 19,* 143–153.

Thelen, M. H., Farmer, J., Mann, L. M., & Pruitt, J. (1990). Bulimia and interpersonal relationships: A longitudinal study. *Journal of Counseling Psychology, 37,* 85–90.

Van Wezel-Meijler, G., & Wit, J. M. (1989). The offspring of mothers with anorexia nervosa: A high-risk group for undernutrition and stunting? *European Journal of Pediatrics, 149,* 130–135.

Viesselman, J. O., & Roig, M. (1985). Depression and suicidality in eating disorders. *Journal of Clinical Psychiatry, 46,* 118–124.

Wakefield, J. C. (1992). The concept of mental disorder: On the boundary between biological facts and social values. *American Psychologist, 47,* 373–388.

Walford, G., & McCune, N. (1991). Long-term outcome in early-onset anorexia nervosa. *British Journal of Psychiatry, 159,* 383–389.

Walsh, B. T., Kissileff, M. R., Cassidy, S. M., & Dantzic, S. (1989). Eating behavior of women with bulimia. *Archives of General Psychiatry, 46,* 54–58.

Walters, E. E., Neale, M. C., Eaves, L. J., Heath, A. C., Kessler, R. C., & Kendler, K. S. (1993). Bulimia nervosa: A population-based study of purgers versus non-purgers. *International Journal of Eating Disorders, 13,* 265–272.

Welch, S. L., & Fairburn, C. G. (1992, April). *Bias and bulimia nervosa.* Paper presented at the 5th International Conference on Eating Disorders, New York.

Welch, S. L., & Fairburn, C. G. (1994). Sexual abuse and bulimia nervosa: Three integrated case control comparisons. *American Journal of Psychiatry, 151,* 402–407.

Werry, J. S. (1992). Child psychiatric disorders: Are they classifiable? *British Journal of Psychiatry, 161,* 472–480.

Whitaker, A., Johnson, J., Schaffer, D., Rapoport, J., Kalizow, K., Walsh, J., Davies, M., Braman, S., & Dolinsky, A. (1990). Uncommon troubles in young people. *Archives of General Psychiatry, 47,* 487.

Whitehouse, A. M., Cooper, P. J., Vize, C. V., Hill, C., & Vogel, L. (1992). Prevalence of eating disorders in three Cambridge general practices: Hidden and conspicuous morbidity. *British Journal of General Practice, 42,* 57–60.

Wilfley, D. E., Schreiber, G., Rodin, J., Pike, K., & Striegel-Moore, R. H. (1994). *Similarities in eating disturbances among black and white women.* Unpublished manuscript, Yale University, New Haven, CT.

Williamson, D. A., Cubic, B. A., & Gleaves, D. H. (1993). Equivalence of body image disturbances in anorexia and bulimia nervosa. *Journal of Abnormal Psychology, 102,* 177–180.

Williamson, D. A., Gleaves, D. H., & Savin, S. S. (1992). Empirical classification of eating disorder not otherwise specified: Support for DSM–IV changes. *Journal of Psychopathology and Behavioral Assessment, 14,* 201–216.

Willmuth, M. E., Leitenberg, H., Rosen, J. C., & Cado, S. (1988). A comparison of purging and non-purging normal weight bulimics. *International Journal of Eating Disorders, 7,* 825–835.

Wilmore, J. H. (1991). Eating and weight disorders in the female athlete. *International Journal of Sports Nutrition, 1,* 104–117.

Wilson, G. T. (1992). Diagnostic criteria for bulimia nervosa. *International Journal of Eating Disorders, 11,* 315–319.

Wilson, G. T., & Eldredge, K. L. (1991). Frequency of binge eating in bulimic patients: Diagnosis validity. *International Journal of Eating Disorders, 10,* 557–561.

Wilson, G. T., & Smith, D. (1989). Assessment of bulimia nervosa: An evaluation of the Eating Disorders Examination. *International Journal of Eating Disorders, 8,* 173–179.

Wilson, G. T., & Walsh, B. T. (1991). Eating disorders in the DSM–IV. *Journal of Abnormal Psychology, 100,* 362–365.

Windauer, U., Lennerts, W., Talbot, P., Touyz, S. W., & Beumont, P. J. V. (1993). How well are 'cured' anorexia nervosa patients? An investigation of 16 weight-recovered anorexic patients. *British Journal of Psychiatry, 163,* 195–200.

Wonderlich, S. (1994). *Sexual abuse and eating disorders: A review.* Presented at the International Conference on Eating Disorders, New York, NY, April 30.

Yager, J., Landsverk, J., & Edelstein, C. K. (1987). A 20-month follow-up study of 628 women with eating disorders. I: Course and severity. *American Journal of Psychiatry, 144,* 1172–1177.

Yanovski, S. Z. (1993). Binge eating disorder: Current knowledge and future directions. *Obesity Research, 1,* 306–318.

PART FIVE

Toward the Future

13

The Meaning of Health for Older Women

Margaret Gatz, Jennifer R. Harris,
and Susan Turk-Charles

INTRODUCTION

S cholars interested in health issues and gender inequities are virtually
obliged to include aging in their arguments and studies. On the one
hand, most women who are sick are old. For the majority of illnesses and
chronic conditions, such as cardiovascular disease and breast cancer, prevalence increases with age. On the other hand, most old people are women.
There is a difference in life expectancy between men and women, with
women out-surviving men. As a consequence, old age is disproportionately inhabited by women.

Two paradoxes, perhaps interrelated, highlight older women's situation. First, older women experience a higher prevalence of chronic disease
and report more doctor visits than do older men, but men have more
lethal illnesses. Second, although 80% of older adults have at least one
chronic health condition (Ory, Abeles, & Lipman, 1992), older people do

The authors thank Donna Polisar and Christopher Hilgeman for their assistance with graphics and bib-
liographies, and Marcia Ory, Ilene Siegler, and the editors for their input on an earlier draft. We acknowledge the support of NIA Grants R01-AG04563, R37-AG0797, and R01-AG08724, the MacArthur
Foundation Research Network on Successful Aging, and the Swedish Council for Social Research.

not perceive themselves as being universally in poor health. Compared with younger groups, elderly rate their health as more positive than their objective health status would indicate. These observations raise the question: What does it mean to be healthy for older women?

In this chapter, we review the existing knowledge base organized around six "healths"—physical, functional, cognitive, psychological, social, and economic—each reflecting a domain of functioning that has its own characteristics and interacts with the other domains. The choice of six areas elaborates upon the World Health Organization's (WHO) classical definition of health as encompassing complete physical, mental, and social well-being (World Health Organization, 1958). Physical health encompasses the dimension from physiological well-being to pathology. While we will allude to a number of diseases, the intent is not to be disease-specific. We differentiate functional health from physical health because functional level is pivotal to independent living in old age. We separate mental health into cognitive and psychological functioning, reflecting their dissimilar life-span trajectories and implications. Lastly, we specify economic health as a distinct area because of its singular relevance to the well-being of older women. After reviewing these six domains, we then turn to self-rated health. We regard self-rated health as having a distinct status separate from the six domains, because this variable is fundamentally an index of the subjective meaning of "being healthy."[1]

Prior to starting the body of the chapter, we will provide a demographic and theoretical context for the literature that follows. We briefly summarize information concerning longevity and distribution of the pop-

[1]These domains can be compared with other systems that have been devised for measurement of health status or for assessing the service needs of older adults. For instance, Stewart (1992) divided the WHO definition into five categories: clinical status (presence and severity of physical and mental diseases), physical functioning and well-being (including functional health, mobility, pain, and other symptoms), mental functioning and well-being (including both cognitive disorders and psychological distress), social and role functioning and well-being (limitations on performance of daily social and role activities due to health), and general health perceptions and satisfaction (that is, one's outlook on one's own health, including whether one feels "healthy" and satisfied with one's own health). The Older Americans Resources and Services (OARS) multi-dimensional assessment strategy continues to be popular (Pfeiffer, 1978). The OARS instrument includes social resources, economic resources, mental health (divided into cognitive and psychiatric status), physical health, and performance of activities of daily living. The conceptual domains in the present chapter converge well with the OARS scheme, while reflecting the WHO definition that is also embodied in the Stewart categories.

ulation by age and gender. We then introduce the need to take a life-span developmental perspective to understanding health in older women.

Demography

Demographers bring several points that help to frame the topic. Age 65 is usually taken to delimit "old age." In 1990, persons aged 65 and older represented 12.5% of the U.S. population (U.S. Bureau of the Census, 1992c). To be more concrete, one in every eight Americans was aged 65 or older. The Census Bureau projects that around 2010 a sharp increase in older persons relative to other age groups will begin, as the leading edge of the baby-boom generation approaches age 65 (U.S. Bureau of the Census, 1992c). Further, the elderly population is getting older, and the fastest growing segment of the U.S. population is the very old. Just between 1980 and 1990, there was a nearly 38% increase in the population aged 85 and older (U.S. Bureau of the Census, 1992c).

Longevity has improved such that the average life expectancy at birth is just over 79 for women and some seven years less for men (U.S. Bureau of the Census, 1992b). Those who survive to age 65 can now expect to live beyond 80. Life expectancy at age 65 is 19 years for women and 15 years for men, a marked difference by gender that has persisted over three decades (U.S. Bureau of the Census, 1992c). It is unknown whether the gender difference in life expectancy is due to accumulated effects that manifest themselves in old age, or whether there are genetic or other types of effects that become expressed in late life. One viewpoint is that women are healthier than men at all ages, and that the basis for the survival advantage of older women was established well before old age (Hazzard, 1986; Smith & Warner, 1989). In addition to differences in biology and in external stressors, others note that women may have a more constructive attitude toward taking care of their health (Rakowski, 1992). Regardless of its source, a further implication of the gender difference in life expectancy is that older women outnumber older men three to two. Among those aged 85 and older, there are five women for every two men (U.S. Bureau of the Census, 1992c).

Among women, of the expected years of life after age 65, only about the first 80% can be viewed as healthy, with substantial assistance needed for everyday activities during the latter 20% (Ory, Cox, Gift, & Abeles, 1994). Reflecting this phenomenon, in *Healthy People 2000* (U.S. Department of Health and Human Services, 1991), which sets out priorities for the nation's health and guides the research strategies of the National Institutes of Health, the target for older adults is not altering life expectancy, but increasing the span of healthy life. A corollary emphasis is making preventive services more available.

Theory and Methodology: Life Span Development

All health psychology, whether or not explicitly recognized, is developmental health psychology because age is an inextricable aspect of all our research subjects and all our clients. Thinking developmentally necessitates considering four concepts: Continuity, cohort, diversity, and sampling. The first is *continuity.* That is, one cannot understand any particular life stage without an overview of the entire life in which it is embedded. Phrased alternatively, it is the same self who passes through the entire life span.

In relation to health, an example of the need to consider the entire life span is osteoporosis. The life history of menstrual cycles, calcium intake, and exercise interacts with genetic propensity in determining peak bone mass, which in turn describes the risk for osteoporosis in later life (Berg & Cassells, 1990).

Moreover, the best predictor of a woman's physical and mental well-being in old age is how healthy she was when she was younger. Thus, how people approach their own health, such as responses to symptoms or commitment to engage in preventive health behaviors shows substantial continuity over time (Ory, Abeles, & Lipman, 1992). It further follows that from a life-span viewpoint, it is shortsighted to establish prevention goals only within age groups. Rather, preventive efforts at one age can affect health outcomes later in life; for example, smoking in young adulthood is related to chronic obstructive pulmonary disease in older adults.

Second, age and *cohort* are inextricably linked. That is, one is born, matures, and ages within a given generation; thus, it is always impossible to know precisely what influence is traceable to age per se, and what to the cohort into which one was born. It is especially important not to attribute differences to age that more convincingly can be linked to cohort. For example, should one generally conclude that people begin to like Big Band music when they turn 70? Or would it be more accurate to infer that those born in 1920 and shortly thereafter learned as youth to like Big Band music and have always liked Big Band music? Examples of cohort influences directly relevant to health would be immunization programs in effect when the individual was a child (e.g., vaccination for polio), media attention to the importance of exercise, and childbearing practices, such as age at birth of first child (a putative risk for breast cancer) or not having children (which can have profound effects on social support or economic status).

Figure 1 illustrates the cohorts represented by those now old. Women who reached their eighth decade in the 1980s were born between 1900 and 1909; for the most part they were youngsters during World War I, it was rare for them to progress far through the educational system, they were of the age to start families during the Great Depression and World War II, and they and their husbands reached retirement age during the Great Society and national debate over Vietnam. Those who turned 65 in the 1980s were born between 1915 and 1924. Most were youngsters during the Great Depression; many of the women went to work in defense-related industries during World War II; they were rearing families while Eisenhower was President. Attitudes toward reliance on governmental services, views about family values, and use of the health care system all are shaped earlier in the life span, and in many instances older women's attitudes seem less likely to reflect their age, and more likely to have been influenced by the historical period in which the attitudes were formed.

The third consideration is the *diversity* of older adults. Diversity is, of course, present at birth, and is generally thought to amplify throughout the life span. It would be a mistake to refer to older women as a monolithic category. First, consider the diversity of ages within old age. For example, the number of years between age 62 and age 85 is the same as the number of years between age 15 and age 38. Women in their 60s, 70s, 80s, and 90s will likely have distinctively different physical and psychosocial is-

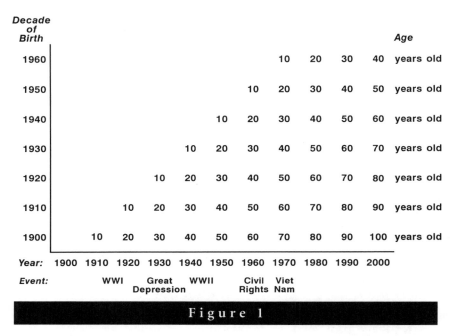

Decade of Birth											Age
1960							10	20	30	40	years old
1950						10	20	30	40	50	years old
1940					10	20	30	40	50	60	years old
1930				10	20	30	40	50	60	70	years old
1920			10	20	30	40	50	60	70	80	years old
1910		10	20	30	40	50	60	70	80	90	years old
1900	10	20	30	40	50	60	70	80	90	100	years old

Year:	1900	1910	1920	1930	1940	1950	1960	1970	1980	1990	2000
Event:		WWI		Great Depression	WWII		Civil Rights	Viet Nam			

Figure 1

Schematic depiction of birth cohorts. The diagram illustrates ages of different birth cohorts during different historical decades, and associated historical events.

sues. Maggie Kuhn, founder of the Gray Panthers, wrote in her autobiography,

> Life at eighty-five years is very different. Different, of course, from twenty-five and thirty-five, but also different from sixty-five and seventy-five. The losses accumulate: the bones weaken, the eyes grow dim, the ears disappoint. (Kuhn, 1991, p. 211)

Other important dimensions on which older women will differ include socioeconomic status, marital status and history, labor force participation, and ethnicity. The elderly population is increasing in racial and ethnic diversity: for example, the elderly Latino population is expected to more than double between 1990 and 2010 (U.S. Bureau of the Census, 1992c). There are pronounced ethnic group differences in longevity, but with women consistently surviving longer than men. For example, the average life expectancy from birth for Whites is 80 for women and 73 for men, compared to African-

Americans at 74 for women and 66 for men (U.S. Bureau of the Census, 1992b). There is evidence that in very old age, there is a crossover, with African-Americans gaining an advantage, such that life expectancy for African-American women at age 85 outstrips Whites (Guralnik, Land, Blazer, Fillenbaum, & Branch, 1993). Maya Angelou wrote:

> The fact that the adult American Negro female emerges a formidable character is often met with amazement, distaste and even belligerence. It is seldom accepted as an inevitable outcome of the struggle won by survivors and deserves respect if not enthusiastic acceptance. (Angelou, 1969, p. 265)

In studying health over the life span, the fourth key consideration is *sampling*. Because illness is distributed differentially by age, care must be taken in drawing comparisons across ages. Siegler, Nowlin, and Blumenthal (1980) present hypothetical data, shown in Figure 2, to illustrate the

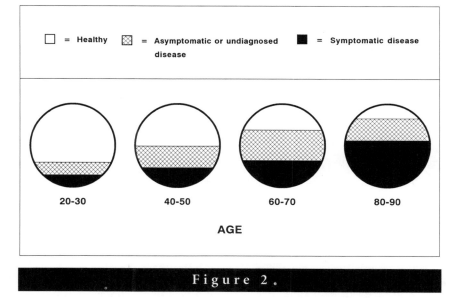

Figure 2.

Schematic representation of four hypothetical populations. From Siegler, Nowlin, and Blumenthal (1980, p. 601). Copyright 1980 by the American Psychological Association. Adapted with permission of the authors.

497

dilemma in securing representative samples for age comparisons. At increasingly older ages, there will be greater proportions of individuals who have significant health problems. The four circles represent women at four different decades. The bottom of each circle are those who have a disease. The middle area are those who would report no disease, but for whom physical examination would show some indication of changes, such as hypertension. The top of each circle represents those who have no clinical disease.

Some cross-sectional research, either explicitly or in effect, limits recruitment of subjects to those who are healthy. For example, a study of cognitive function in normal adults of different ages might exclude those who have a significant physical illness, in order to be certain that the effects are due to age rather than to the disease entity. Or, recruitment of older adult participants from groups of older volunteers might inadvertently exclude the less healthy, in part because the least healthy may be in institutions. As is evident from the figure, adopting such a sampling strategy would result in an increasingly select (or elite) subset of the population, with over 80% of the youngest decade eligible and under 20% of the oldest decade eligible.

Even if the experimenter intends to obtain a representative subset from each age group, with no exclusion criteria related to health status, sampling biases can still occur. In a cross-sectional study, it is likely that those who are most ill will refuse (selection bias), while in a longitudinal study they will drop out (selective attrition). In essence, one would be studying different samples at different ages. Elias, Elias, and Elias (1990), Schaie, Campbell, Meredith, and Rawlings (1988), and Siegler et al. (1980) offer sensible suggestions for those embarking on research in aging.

Comorbidity further complicates the issue of finding representative samples of older adults. In recruiting subjects for the study of any one disease, it will be increasingly difficult with age to find subjects who are free of other conditions. In short, the design challenges are formidable, but this factor should not be used to exclude older adults, particularly elderly women, from clinical trials or only to include those who are physiologically select (Berg & Cassells, 1990; Gurwitz, Col, & Avorn, 1992; Yates & Yancik, 1987).

OVERVIEW OF AGE AND GENDER DIFFERENCES IN HEALTH

The Six Healths

Physical and Physiological Health

There is decline in every organ system with age, following early phases of growth during which all of the physiologic systems reach a peak in functional capacity. What varies across organ systems and among individuals is the point of onset and rate of decline (Arking, 1991). Older adults have lower immunocompetence levels and more rigid organ and muscle tissue, making them more susceptible to disease or disability and less able to rebound after illness or injury (Kenney, 1989). Changes do not suddenly begin in old age; past health habits, exposure to toxic agents, and wear and tear accumulate throughout adulthood.

Disease, of course, occurs throughout the life span. Some diseases are specific to younger groups and are relatively rare in old age, such as lupus erythematosus. Some of the same illnesses occur in older and younger adults, although they may be observed with greater frequency as people age, for example, cancer, or with greater severity, such as pneumonia. Other illnesses or disorders occur predominantly in older age groups and are uncommon at younger ages, for example, urinary incontinence, dementia, and systolic hypertension. For instance, the prevalence of urinary incontinence has been estimated at 38% in noninstitutionalized elderly women, while it is relatively rare for younger women (Diokno, Brock, Brown, & Herzog, 1986).

An example of gradual decline manifesting as health problems in later life is loss of bone mass. Women experience greater loss of bone mass than men, with decrease beginning in the twenties and thirties. By the time they are elderly, women typically experience a 25% bone loss, compared with about 12% in men (Arking, 1991; Garn, 1975). This differential is even more impressive, given that men start with a three to two advantage over women. Women are therefore more likely to suffer from disease processes associated with bone loss, such as osteoporosis.

Illnesses in old age vary for men and women. For older women, the top five chronic conditions, in order are (a) arthritis, (b) hypertension,

(c) hearing impairment, (d) heart conditions, and (e) orthopaedic problems (U.S. National Center for Health Statistics, 1994). Diseases and conditions more likely in women aged 75 and older than in their male age peers include spinal degeneration, colitis, anemia, migraines, bladder infection, varicose veins, high blood pressure, and stomach ulcers (U.S. National Center for Health Statistics, 1994).

Generally speaking, women and men die from the same diseases, with the leading causes of death being heart disease, cancer, stroke, chronic obstructive pulmonary disease, pneumonia, and influenza (U.S. National Center for Health Statistics, 1994). However, older men tend to live for a longer time with serious problems related to life-threatening conditions (such as heart disease and cancer) relative to women (Manton, 1990). In contrast, women report more chronic, non-life-threatening impairments than men, and spend more years with chronic, debilitating diseases (Strawbridge, Kaplan, Camacho, & Cohen, 1992). For instance, 63% of women indicate having arthritis, compared with 38% of men (U.S. National Center for Health Statistics, 1994).

Two important topics in representing the complexity of health in older women are comorbidity and the difficulty of distinguishing where normal aging ends and disease begins. Comorbidity is the rule rather than the exception in old age, and women tend to have more comorbidity than men (Guralnik, LaCroix, Everett, & Kovar, 1989). In other words, older women tend to have multiple chronic conditions, which can increase the severity of a major health condition and can impose limitations on treatment strategies. For example, diabetes not only is a risk factor for onset of, but also reduces survival following, heart disease or stroke (Wallace & Lemke, 1991).

Data from a large survey in Sweden,[2] shown in Figure 3, give some idea of the extent of comorbidity. For women under age 55, more than half have either no chronic condition or only one condition from a list of 13 categories, encompassing an illness in any of 11 major organ systems (e.g., cardiovascular, respiratory, neurologic, metabolic), cancer, and aller-

---

[2]Unpublished data from the Swedish Adoption/Twin Study of Aging.

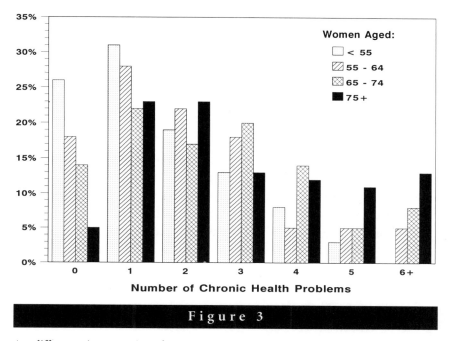

Figure 3

Age differences in proportion of women reporting coexisting chronic health problems. Unpublished data from the Swedish Adoption/Twin Study of Aging.

gies. In increasingly older groups, there are fewer women with no chronic disorders, achieving 5% in those aged 75 and older. There are correspondingly more women with multiple conditions in the older age groups. For example, among those aged 75 and older, nearly 50% have at least three chronic conditions.

The importance of distinguishing between age and disease has been highlighted in the literature because of the strong wish not to perpetuate the myth that aging equates with inevitable decline (cf. Elias et al., 1990). While it is generally accepted that the changes that characterize normal aging are separable from disease processes (Rowe & Kahn, 1987), it is also postulated that aging is a risk factor for illness. Here, a distinction can be drawn between age-dependent and age-related mechanisms (Brody & Schneider, 1986). An example of an age-related change in the lung is the gradual decrease in the number of alveoli, resulting in a smaller surface area for gas exchange, and greater difficulty oxygenating the blood. An age-dependent disease for the lung is emphysema, in which airflow is restricted by cumulative assault on the bronchial tree by such irritants as smoke or repeated infection (Arking, 1991).

The difficulty is that the boundary between normal age-related decline and disease entity is probably *not* entirely clear, and health and disease are not opposites (Caplan, 1990). As described above, the aging process is marked by a decline of the vital organs, with the rate of decline reducing each organ's reserve capacity. Since multiple organ systems all register declines to various extents, in very old age there is a backdrop of frailty that contributes to making the individual vulnerable to a variety of diseases. This decline might be termed "normal aging." Gradual decline of a specific system eventually manifests as a health problem when the extent of loss passes a clinical threshold, beyond which the severity of the illness leads to its being diagnosed (Fries, 1989). This line of thinking is applicable to the diagnosis of such illnesses as Parkinson's disease, which is diagnosed when there has been an 80% loss of dopamine receptors, or hypertension, for which cut-off scores are typically employed (Elias et al., 1990). For other diseases (for example, pneumonia), general vulnerability is simply a risk factor. Such a threshold approach redefines the distinction between aging and disease, makes age of onset difficult to pinpoint, and implies that there is an intermediate level of health (as was shown in Figure 2) when the extent of symptomatology is preclinical. For example, systolic hypertension is now being treated at levels previously thought to be asymptomatic (Howard, 1994). A more sophisticated screening tool may, for that matter, detect pathology that was previously hidden, long before the symptoms reach a significant level (Elias et al., 1990). For example, Morris et al. (1991) found Alzheimer's type lesions in neuropathological examination of brains of older adults whose performance on neuropsychological tests was within normal range.

There is debate about the implications of this threshold approach to defining disease. Fries (1989) projected a compression of morbidity, based on the argument that preventive interventions to modify risk factors would push back age of onset nearer to death. The controversial issue concerns whether Fries was correct in positing that the healthy life span—sometimes called active life expectancy (Katz, Branch, Branson, Papsidero, Beck, & Greer, 1983)—could be extended to accompany the increased length of life (See Figure 4). Currently, data are inconclusive. Arguing for expansion rather than for compression of morbidity, Guralnik (1991) demonstrated that as life expectancy continued to increase, most of the gain was in years of disability. Supportive of this position, others established that age of onset for various impairments was, if anything, decreasing, perhaps due to better detection (Haan, Rice, Satariano, & Selby, 1991; G. A. Kaplan, 1991). On the other hand, particularly strong evidence for the compression of morbidity has recently been provided from a study of prevalence and incidence of chronic disability (Manton, Corder, & Stallard, 1993). Using a longitudinal methodology that accounts for mortality and changes in the age structure of the population, this group of investigators found a proportional decrease over time in the percent of older individuals who were disabled. Further, although women have both higher rates of disability and greater longevity than men, most analyses indicate that the ratio of disability-free years to disabled years is the same across men and women (Branch et al., 1991), translating to no gender differences in the compression of morbidity phenomenon.

There are important implications for intervention stemming from the greater predominance of chronic conditions in old age compared with acute disorders. The concept of curing disease is less applicable (Caplan, 1990; Ory et al., 1992); as well, physicians must consider normal physical changes and comorbidity in planning treatment. For example, older adults are more responsive to medications because the renal system is less efficient in eliminating drugs. The effects of medications can be further magnified in older women due to differences in body fat, which retains certain drugs (Berg & Cassells, 1990). Consequently, older women are especially susceptible to medication side effects, and it is all too easy to imagine a health care provider being dismissive about the patient's legitimate complaints.

In relation to preventive intervention, reflecting the nature of chronic disorders and the threshold model of disease onset, many behaviors are not related to just one disease entity. Examples would include smoking

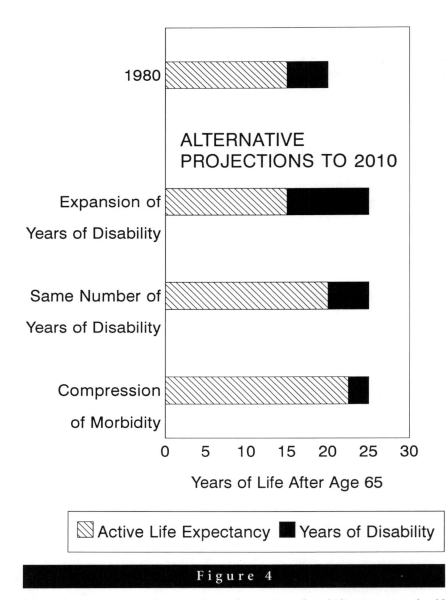

Figure 4

Schematic representation of compression and expansion of morbidity. Exact ages should not be inferred from this diagram, which is intended only to illustrate the concepts of active life expectancy and compression of morbidity.

cessation, diet modifications, and exercise. There is some debate about whether preventive health behaviors are as potent in later life, and whether there are gender differences in effectiveness of particular preventive interventions, but with the conclusion that there are detectable effects from health habit improvements for men and women at almost any age (Kane, 1988; Strawbridge, Camacho, Cohen, & Kaplan, 1993).

Functional Health

Functional health refers to degree of impairment in activities due to physical frailty, which in turn affects the ability to live independently. Accordingly, changes in functional health typically are more directly related to quality of life than are particular diseases, and functional health scales may be the most appropriate metric for the effects of nonfatal conditions that accumulate in later life. As Berg and Cassells (1990) pointed out, disability cannot be classified in diagnostic systems meant for categorizing physical diseases.

Functional and physical health assessments may be rather poorly correlated for a number of reasons. First, as noted, impaired functioning can occur with no particular disease process accounting for the difficulties, or someone with a serious life-threatening illness may not necessarily experience interference with most activities. Second, perception of impairment—which is measured by self-reported functional health—reflects individual differences in life demands and in ability to overcome health problems as well as actual differences in health.

Activities of daily living (ADL) scales continue to be one of the most commonly used indices of functional health. These scales typically encompass personal care items such as dressing and putting on shoes, bathing, toileting, transferring, and feeding. The items are scored for degree of independence versus dependence on another person. Instrumental activities of daily living go beyond personal care to include cooking, cleaning, shopping, attending social activities such as a movie or church, using the telephone, and managing personal finances. Sometimes mobility is measured separately, including ability to go out of doors, climb stairs, and walk half a mile (see review by Guralnik & Simonsick, 1993). Some gender bias is built into these lists. Inability assumes a rather different status depending on whether the individual ever could perform the activity, for example, older men who had never cooked their own meals or older women who had never managed the family's finances. Other measurement problems are introduced for individuals in institutional settings. For example, the opportunity to perform functional activities may be limited by the environment rather than by physical status.

ADL scales, however, are most relevant for assessing functional level among relatively disabled individuals, and many studies of normal aging report little variation in ADL scores. Interest in assessing a broader spectrum of functional ability has led to the development and use of performance measures rather than proxy or self-report indices (Guralnik & Simonsick, 1993). Performance measures are based on independent observer evaluations of the individual's ability to perform a particular task. The battery typically includes tests of upper body movement, manual dexterity, balance, and gait. Amount of time for completion is also figured into the scoring procedure. Such protocols offer the advantages of better face validity and reproducibility. Additionally, physical performance tests have been revealed to be more highly associated with measures of physical health status than are self-reports (Rozzini, Frisoni, Bianchetti, Zanetti, & Trabucchi, 1993). For instance, performance-based measures of mobility appear to be the best single predictor of recurrent falls (Tinetti, Williams, & Mayewski, 1986).

Generally, functional health problems are more pronounced among women than men, as indicated by performance tests (Seeman et al., 1994), self-reports (Strawbridge et al., 1992), and concerns about decline (Holahan, Holahan, & Belk, 1984), with longitudinal decline rates also greater among women than men (Strawbridge et al., 1992). This gender difference is probably attributable, at least in part, to gender differences in longevity (Manton, 1988).

Only recently has the medical profession begun to recognize functional assessment as a fundamental aspect of geriatric practice. Falls provide an example of the convergence of functional and physical health. Falls often occur in relation to environmental hazards encountered during daily activities. Parkinson's disease, abnormal gait, and impaired balance all predict risk of falling. Also, medications (e.g., anxiolytics) can cause dizziness and postural hypotension. Physically, muscle weakness and impaired postural reflexes can lead to failure to stop the fall once it has begun. Those with osteoporosis are in particular danger of incurring fractures when they fall, including hip fracture. Hip fracture is then associated with other medical complications such as urinary tract infections, and further decrease in functional health. Moreover, approximately 12% excess mortality can be attributed to hip fracture, especially over age 75, although less in women than in men (Berg & Cassells, 1990). Finally, fear of falling can itself lead to reduced independence (Tinetti & Powell, 1993). Thus, functional abilities reflect (albeit imperfectly) physiological health, index active life expectancy, and betoken future health outcomes.

Cognitive Health

Dementia—defined as progressive impairment of memory and other cognitive abilities—is not a normal part of aging. While some decline with age in certain areas of cognitive functioning may be expected, any steep decline suggests a pathological process. Prevalence of moderate to severe dementias in those aged 65 and older has typically been estimated to be around five to six percent (Mortimer & Hutton, 1985; Regier et al., 1988). Incidence of dementia escalates with age, making age-specific rates more informative. Across several studies, rates of moderate to severe dementia have been found to be about 2–3% in those aged 65–74, 7–8% in those aged 75–84, and 24% in those aged 85 and older (Bachman et al., 1992; Jorm, Korten, & Henderson, 1987; Regier et al., 1988), although Evans et al. (1989) found rates in excess of 40% among those aged 85 and older. Dementia of the Alzheimer's type accounts for the majority of dementia cases, followed by the vascular dementias. Detailed discussions of diagnostic and epidemiological issues regarding dementia may be found in Cummings and Benson (1992), Mortimer (1994), and Raskind and Peskind (1992).

Dementia is a major risk factor for institutionalization. According to the 1985 National Nursing Home Survey (U.S. National Center for Health Statistics, 1989), 22% were admitted with diagnosed organic brain disorders (senile dementia, organic psychotic conditions, nonpsychotic disorders due to organic brain disease).

Recent meta-analyses reveal that it is probably inaccurate that women are more susceptible to dementia than men (Anthony & Aboraya, 1992). However, there are more women than men with dementia, if only by virtue of the fact that age is the greatest risk factor. Following a similar logic, the number of persons with dementia is projected to expand in the future, in conjunction with the increased number of elderly aged 85 and older.

A classic differential diagnostic problem in older adults is to distinguish dementia from depression, and dementia from delirium, and all of the three from normal aging. Delirium in particular is often missed or misdiagnosed. Delirium is an acute disruption of brain physiology, involving confusion, and often accompanied by disorientation, delusions, and agitation. Possible causes include any disruption of oxygen supply to the brain, such as toxic effects of medications, infections and fever, and postanaesthesia reactions (Caine & Grossman, 1992; Raskind & Peskind, 1992). In the very elderly, the brain has less cerebral reserve, so that insults that would not formerly have been sufficiently severe, now push the patient over a clinical threshold (Mortimer, 1994). Up to half of hip surgery patients have been reported to develop delirium (Cummings & Benson, 1992). It is easy to imagine older women with delirium being dismissed as crazy old ladies or inappropriately medicated for psychosis.

Psychological Well-being

Psychological health refers not only to the absence of functional mental disorders but also to positive mental health; in other words, what are the psychological processes through which the older woman maintains a sense of psychological well-being despite physical health limitations?

The two most frequent categories of functional mental disorders in older adults are depression and anxiety, with the former having received more attention.[3] Prevalence of depressive disorders (major depressive episode and dysthymia) has been found to be markedly lower in adults

---

[3]For reviews of depression and anxiety, respectively, see Schneider, Reynolds, Lebowitz, and Friedhoff (1994) and Sheikh (1992). For paranoid disorders see Post (1987). For an overview of aging and mental disorders, see LaRue, Dessonville, and Jarvik (1985).

aged 65 and older than in 25–64 year olds, with rates of current disorder from 1.5% to 4% (Bliwise, McCall, & Swan, 1987; Regier et al., 1988).

A great deal of effort has gone into questioning epidemiological figures which suggest that older adults have low rates of depression. These clinicians and researchers typically note the high rate of subclinical depressive symptoms in older adults, and express concern about underdiagnosis and hence deprivation of sufferers from treatment (NIH Consensus Development Panel on Depression in Late Life, 1992). While it is important not to minimize genuine distress, it is also important to be careful not to argue that rates of depression should be higher in older women, primarily on the basis of an observer's thinking that the aged should be more depressed, due to the variety of stress in their lives (Jarvik, 1976).

Furthermore, these epidemiological figures characterize those who are now old. Although it is possible that only the nondepressed survive to be old, there may be a historical effect, with successive birth cohorts having higher rates of depression (Klerman et al., 1985). If this explanation is correct, rates of depression among older adults will be far greater in 2020 than they are in 1990.

A distinct exception to the patterns of age differences in depression discussed above is that rates of depression are elevated in older adults with medical disorders, suggesting that depression may occur in reaction to illness. Depression can also be a side-effect of medical disease, such as metabolic disorders, or of medications (e.g., for hypertension) (Cohen, 1992).

There is a well-known gender difference in levels of self-reported depressive symptoms, with women more depressed than men, but this difference is not universally observed in older adults. For instance, no gender differences were found by Rodin, McAvay, and Timko (1988), and several large cross-sectional surveys have found either convergence or crossover in the oldest group, with men at the very oldest ages reporting more depressive symptomatology than women (e.g., Berkman et al., 1986; Murrell, Himmelfarb, & Wright, 1983).

Another psychological disorder often attributed to older women is hypochondriasis. Indeed, complaints about vague physical symptoms can be a feature of depression (Koenig & Blazer, 1992). However, given the

509

pattern of chronic illnesses characteristic of older women, it would not be surprising to experience nonspecific symptoms. E.M. Brody (1985) and Ory, Abeles, and Lipman (1992) suggest that older women may actually underreport potentially serious symptoms (perhaps mistakenly attributing them to aging, rather than to illness), but overuse physicians for nonserious—but troublesome—complaints.

Importantly, not all older adults with physical health or other problems become depressed, anxious, or hypochondriacal. As Maggie Kuhn explains:

> Old age is not a disaster. It is a triumph over disappointment, failure, loss, illness. When we reach this point in life, we have great experience with failure. I always know that if one of the things that I've initiated falters and fails, it won't be the end. I'll find a way to learn from it and begin again. When I was younger, I took failure much more seriously. (Kuhn, 1991, p. 214)

Siegler and Costa (1985) raised the question of whether coping with illness is a special situation best handled with particular mechanisms, or whether the general techniques for coping with other life events can be extended to coping with illness. Social comparisons may be one important general coping mechanism (Cooper & Goethals, 1981; Ryff, 1991). Thus, a woman of eighty might say, "Look at Virginia. She had to move into a life care community because she couldn't take care of her house any longer. Her older daughter has MS, and her younger daughter has gone to live with a cult. I guess I shouldn't feel sorry for myself."

Perceptions of control may be another critical link in relating coping and illness in older adults. It seems obvious to design interventions that create greater control, but the architect of the intervention faces several dilemmas. Dimensions to consider include accurate recognition of which situations are modifiable and which are not, the role of information and how information is provided, and the design of methods of empowerment that are sensitive to individual preferences.

Social Well-being

Older women generally have larger social networks of family members and friends than older men (Depner & Ingersoll-Dayton, 1988), but are far more likely to live alone compared to same-aged older men (U.S. Bureau of the Census, 1992a). For older persons of both genders, diminished social activity typically occurs.

A large literature substantiates that social network and social contacts have a significant effect on mortality (literature reviewed by House, Landis, & Umberson, 1988). Gender differences have also been suggested. For women in particular, Blazer (1982) found higher rates of mortality associated with lower perceived social support, restricted availability of social roles, and less frequent social interaction. Notably, quality of social interaction may be the critical consideration rather than its quantity.

To integrate the empirical literature and offer a life-span theory of social well-being, Carstensen (1993) has proposed socioemotional selectivity theory: As people age, they become more selective in choosing social partners, tending more toward people to whom they already feel close. Being more selective helps to conserve physical energy and regulate affect, increasing the probability of positive emotions and limiting the risk of negative feelings.

For older women, caregiving becomes an increasingly significant part of their social interactions. Women outnumber men 2.5 to 1 as caregivers for older family members (Stoller, 1990). A variety of explanations for this gender imbalance has been advanced, from gender-role socialization to sociobiology (Lee, 1992; Miller & Cafasso, 1992). Regardless, the result is that those caring for frail older adults are predominantly their wives and daughters. Caregivers face emotional and physical strain, that may be even greater for women, according to results from a meta-analysis of this literature (Miller & Cafasso, 1992). Social contact with friends and family may be constricted due to role engulfment (Skaff & Pearlin, 1992). Older adults, both women and men, receive less social support than younger adults in attempting to maintain reciprocity with their friends and family members (Antonucci & Akiyama, 1991). Therefore, older caregivers may find themselves in isolation with their responsibilities.

Bereavement is a social loss that occurs with greater frequency in later life. Mortality has been shown to be higher in the recently bereaved than in the general population (Mellström, Nilsson, Odén, Rundgren, & Svanborg, 1982). Although the association between bereavement and mortality tends to be stronger in younger than in older persons, and men have been shown to be more adversely affected by bereavement than women (Stroebe & Stroebe, 1983), older women are still the most likely group to become widowed. For women aged 75 and older, 26% are married, 65% are widowed, and the rest are either single (5%) or divorced (4%). These figures contrast with men aged 75 and older, of whom 70% are married, 24% are widowed, and the remaining are either single (3%) or divorced (3%) (U.S. Bureau of the Census, 1992a). Moreover, widowhood is among the reasons for living alone; and living alone is a risk factor for negative health consequences and for institutionalization (Steinbach, 1992). Thus, bereavement remains a women's issue.

In sum, older women's social networks are under trial from caregiving and bereavement. Yet, properly conceptualized, social ties are a key protective factor.

Economic Well-Being

Health and economics are coupled by virtue of poverty being a risk factor for health problems (e.g., hypertension and diabetes) and health care costs representing the largest threat to older adults' economic viability. Marked differences in mortality rates have been shown according to socioeconomic status, with education conferring a major advantage in terms of survival (Guralnik et al., 1993). Income has been demonstrated to have an impressive effect on a variety of physical and functional health measures, with 55 to 75 year-olds of lower socioeconomic status far more likely to experience health problems than those who are more advantaged (House et al., 1990).

Although in general the economic status of older adults has improved over the past several decades, in danger of being overlooked is that an unacceptably high proportion of elderly women remain in the ranks of the poor or near poor. Older women living alone have five times the rate of poverty compared with older men living alone (with the poverty rate defined as $6,268 in 1990). Thus, nearly a quarter of White women aged 65 and older who do not live with relatives are below the poverty level. In an example of cumulative inequity, six out of ten elderly African-American women—and nearly half of elderly Latino women—who do not live with relatives live in poverty (U.S. Bureau of the Census, 1992c).

Furthermore, due to the federal budget deficit and to other pressing social concerns, the last decade has seen a fresh debate concerning generational equity, that is, the argument that federal programs to assist older adults were depriving future generations. The driving concern has been the large proportion of dollars in the federal domestic budget attributed to people aged 65 and older. For instance, one third of national health expenditures are accounted for by older adults (Estes & Rundall, 1992). A major factor in accounting for this budgetary pattern is Medicare, much of which funds are channeled not to the older adult, but to physicians, hospitals, clinical laboratories, and other health care providers. Thus, pressure for health care reform is highly germane to the well-being of older adults.

Neugarten and Neugarten (1989) suggested that the intergenerational equity argument is misstated, because it neglects the point that aged and children who live in poverty are shared evidence of the failure of broader economic and social policies affecting both groups. However, this viewpoint has not found its way into policy, possibly reflecting the lack of tradition in the United States of collectivist responsibility of the society for the basic welfare of its members (Clark, 1991).

The economic issues facing older adults—Medicare, Social Security, and nursing home placement and costs—are not advertised as women's issues. Nonetheless, as Carstensen and Pasupathi (1993) point out, fundamentally they are. The age at which these economic concerns become more pressing are the years past age 75, when women account for an increasing proportion of older adults. Moreover, women disproportionately are subject to key risk factors for financial difficulties:

1. They more often live alone, which may necessitate paid in-home assistance and often puts the woman at risk for placement in a nursing home. Only after becoming impoverished is an older individual eligible for Medicaid, as Medicare excludes coverage for long term care.

2. Women more often have responsibilities to care for an impaired relative. A wife must often contend first with her husband's nursing home costs and then with her own, at which point she has no remaining eco-

nomic resources. Thus, as George (1993) pointed out, being fearful about the adequacy of one's future financial resources is entirely reasonable.

3. Women more often have reduced social security and retirement benefits due to events earlier in their lives: nonpayment for household work, intermittent employment, and lower pay while working. Carstensen and Pasupathi (1993) warned against assuming that this gender difference will change: One must consider the number of women in poverty today, often single parents dependent upon public assistance, who will ultimately move into the ranks of the elderly poor.

It does seem possible that health care reform is in the wings. It remains to be seen whether the reforms will reorient the system to eliminate the bias toward an acute care model, which does not fit the chronic nature of health problems in older adults (Estes & Rundall, 1992), and whether the reforms will be linked with social policies assuring adequate income and housing.

Self-Rated Health

Self-rated health (e.g., "Overall, would you rate your health as excellent, good, fair, or poor?" asked alone or in combination with similar questions) has received a great deal of attention by gerontologists for two reasons.

First, the cumulative literature on the topic suggests that experiences inherent to aging may mediate perceptions of health in ways that are not captured by other measures. Perceptions of health and physical health outcomes have generally been found to be modestly related. For example, self-rated health has been shown to correlate with number of symptoms, physician ratings of health, days in the hospital, and extent of functional disability (Cockerham, Sharp, & Wilcox, 1983; Liang, 1986; Markides & Lee, 1990). While the causal mechanisms have not been fully clarified, the emergence of health psychology attests to the individual's impact on her own health status and the role of beliefs in behavior. For instance, Leventhal, Leventhal, and Schaefer (1992) have shown that older adults are unusually vigilant with respect to perceiving health problems, leading them to better adherence with treatment and prevention activities. At the same time, self-rated health is more strongly associated with life satisfaction and well-being than are objective measures of health (Zautra & Hempel, 1984), showing its close affiliation with conceptualizations of quality of life.

Subjective health evaluations among older adults tend to be more favorable than would be expected based on their objective health status (Johnson, Mullooly, & Greenlick, 1990) and more positive than physician ratings (LaRue, Bank, Jarvik, & Hetland, 1979). Thus, although older respondents are somewhat less likely to claim excellent health and somewhat more likely to claim poor health in comparison with younger adults, there is an optimistic bias. For instance, in survey data from Sweden,[2] among women aged 65 and older, only 6.3% rated their health status as bad, although 27.2% indicated that their current health compared unfavorably to five years previously. Furthermore, 32% of women aged 65 and older indicated that their health was better compared with same-aged peers, while only 18% of women under age 65 saw their health as better than their peers.

The second, and perhaps more provocative, reason for interest in self-rated health is that it is strongly and independently associated with mortality. Self-rated health is a better predictor of survival than are objective measures of health (Kaplan, Barell, & Lusky, 1988). Moreover, across a large number of epidemiological studies, self-rated health has remained a significant predictor of survival beyond the statistical influence of other factors, such as objective health status, life satisfaction, health practices, social networks, health service use, religious involvement, socioeconomic status, and functional abilities (Idler & Kasl, 1991; G. A. Kaplan & Camacho, 1983; Mossey & Shapiro, 1982; Wolinsky & Johnson, 1992). Although reasons for the link between perceptions of health and mortality are largely unknown, these findings highlight the possibility that other factors, aside from physical health status, influence survival.

The power of perceived health as a predictor is illustrated by data from the longitudinal Gothenburg H-70 study, a large Swedish population study of normal aging (Rinder, Roupe, Steen, & Svanborg, 1975). Participants were from a representative sample born 1901–1902 and identified through the population register. The first data collection point at age 70 included 449 men and 525 women. In a set of analyses by Harris, Berg, and Ljungqvist (1994), first, simple survival for men and for women was examined. For women who participated at age 70, 27% were still alive at age 90, whereas only 11% of the original sample of men were alive. Using this same sample, self-rated health collected when participants were age 70, 75, and 79 was used to predict survival at age 90. These results, shown in Figure 5, strikingly illustrate the pertinence of self-rated health. Self-rated health measured at age 70 predicts survival at age 90 for both women and men. The same is true for self-rated health at age 75 and at age 79 for men, although perceptions of health collected at age 79 no longer significantly predict survival at age 90 for women. Notably, the survival advantage of women outweighs self-rated health, in that women who perceived themselves as unhealthy still had significantly better survival than men who rated themselves as healthy.

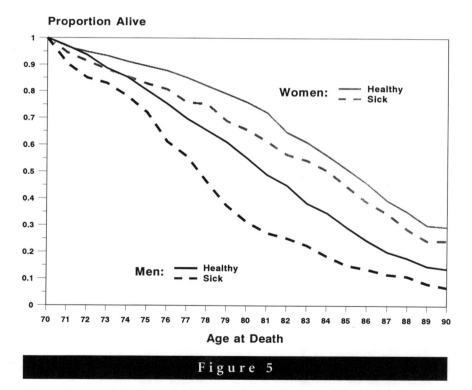

Figure 5

Differential survival for men and women over 20 years based on self-rated health at age 70. From Harris, Berg, & Ljungqvist (1994).

Further analyses of physical health indicated that the amount of decline in health was significantly less among those who had stable perceptions of themselves as "healthy." The results suggest a process whereby age-associated physical symptoms are not immediately reflected in subjective health ratings; rather, it is necessary for some threshold of physical decline to be reached, after which the woman modifies her self-perceived health to accommodate the actual changes that had taken place. Supportive of this hypothesized process, Rodin and McAvay (1992) also have reported self-rated health at a subsequent time of measurement to be predicted by actual changes in health, which include more new illnesses, worsening of previously existing conditions, increased visits to the doctor, and more medications than at the previous interview.

Some investigators have found no mean differences in self-rated health between men and women (Harris, 1988), although gender differences have been reported by Idler (1993), with women being more positive than men. Along similar lines, Siegler, Nowlin, and Blumenthal (1980) cite results showing that, when women were matched with men on self-rated health, the women reported more objective health problems relative to the men. Several studies find that self-rated health is a stronger predictor of mortality in men than in women of comparable ages (Harris et al., 1994; Idler & Kasl, 1991).

These accumulated research results demonstrate that perceptions of health are an integral part of people's system of self-conceptions; perceptions constitute a synopsis of their objective health conditions, yet people continue to regard themselves as healthy even when they have disabilities that limit their functioning. In short, self-rated health seemingly represents the individual's beliefs concerning what it means to be "healthy", an interpretation corroborated by evidence that people do have a very good sense of their own vitality.

CONCLUSION

What can be done to improve the health of older women? Specifically, what are some lessons to be derived for health services provision, prevention, and research?

Regarding the health care system, there will be an inevitable rise in the number of older adults in need of long term care. Because older women suffer from more functional limitations than do older men, they will place the greatest demand on long term care. The configuration of disabilities most characteristic of older women forms a backdrop of frailty, often without a single specific disease predominating.

This profile of impairments often is best answered with social supportive services and technical aids to facilitate in-home living, rather than with institutional care. At present, however, funding sources favor biomedical services (Estes, Swan, & Associates, 1993). Informal caregiving tends to be regarded as a family problem rather than as an issue for the service provision system, despite the fact that "home health care remains one of the most empowering of the health services" (Estes et al., 1993, p. 82). Especially with changing family configurations and the likelihood that older women will live alone, it cannot simply be assumed that family can handle community-based care for their older relatives.

In relation to medical practitioners, examples of older women and older men receiving disparate care for the same conditions, with no basis in research, have been demonstrated by Belgrave (1993). For example, men were more likely to receive cardiac catheterization, bypass surgery, renal dialysis, and renal transplant; whereas women were more often prescribed tranquilizers and hypnotic drugs.

Thus, within the health care system, the kinds of solutions that would best improve health and combat dependency include entitlement to services, such as nursing care and community-based long term care; communal options that move beyond traditional notions of family; and increased dignity, choice, and symmetry in relation to health care professionals.

Regarding research, inferences about appropriate treatments are often made to older women based on results for older men, despite differences in their physiology. For instance, Gurwitz et al. (1992) found a significantly increased likelihood of excluding older adults from clinical trials for acute myocardial infarction over the past three decades, combined with protocols often designed to recruit only men. Given the seriousness of this health concern for older women, these biases are a real threat to their well-being.

Research is also needed to tease apart implications for older women's distinctive profiles of risk factors and reserves so that prevention can be targeted more effectively. Preventive behaviors available to the older person encompass controlling blood pressure, exercise, smoking cessation, weight management, self-examination and other early detection of cancer, control of dietary fat and cholesterol, vision care, stress management, knowledgeable use of prescribed medications, and moderation with respect to alcohol (Rakowski, 1992). These are, of course, quite general suggestions that would be applicable across the life span, and—indeed—prevention must be construed as a life-span affair. However, complications arise in old age. For example, the level of activity necessary to make a difference is unclear and may differ by gender (Strawbridge et al., 1993), and the level of activity that is possible to maintain may be curtailed by age-related changes (Rakowski, 1992). Furthermore, research results present quandaries about the best course of action. For instance, osteoporosis is a major source of morbidity in older women. Some protection against osteoporosis, which is known to result from estrogen deficiency that occurs postmenopausally, may be afforded by estrogen replacement therapy (F. S. Kaplan, 1985). Another positive factor is some indication that estrogen replacement therapy may be a protective factor with regard to Alzheimer's disease (Henderson, Paganini-Hill, Emanuel, Dunn, & Buckwalter, 1994). At the same time, an increased occurrence of endometrial carcinoma in postmenopausal women who are on estrogen replacement therapy has been reported (Mann, 1985). What is required is more specific assistance with regard to prevention regimens given age, gender, and health history.

In sum, the research agenda for older women needs to include evaluation of methods to reduce dependency, establishment of empirical bases for preventive behaviors, and inclusion of women in treatment trials. Research and policy must concern itself with improvements at multiple levels, from diet and exercise to social and economic policies that can influence health in later life.

What have we learned about what it means to be healthy for older women? We proposed a multidimensional framework for applying the WHO definition of health to older women. That is, we suggested that health encompasses physical, functional, cognitive, emotional, social, and economic well-being. Especially in older adults, an increasingly relevant index is functional health, which can be used to measure the healthy life span, that is, the number of years without significant impairment. Preventive and treatment efforts can therefore be aimed at improving the healthy life span.

We submitted that two incongruities are particularly relevant to understanding the situation of older women. First, women live longer than men, although they also face more morbidity and more comorbidity than older men. Second, many women with notable disabilities still report good self-rated health and positive well-being. There is some possibility that inequalities confronting women throughout their life spans are embodied in these incongruities, fostering both greater exposure to psychosocial risk factors known to affect physical health, and greater adaptive strengths.

In summary, we emphasize the interrelatedness of the various dimensions of health. Being healthy appears to represent maintaining an ability to compensate for inevitable physical health problems, drawing on psychological, social, and economic resources. Addressing psychosocial risk factors on a societal level, combined with incorporation of new knowledge based on greater research attention to older women, should bring about further improvements in their health, especially given how well older women are now doing, despite barriers.

REFERENCES

Angelou, M. (1969). *I know why the caged bird sings.* New York: Random House.

Anthony, J. C., & Aboraya, A. (1992). The epidemiology of selected mental disorders in later life. In J. E. Birren, R. B. Sloane, & G. D. Cohen (Eds.), *Handbook of mental health and aging,* (2nd ed., pp. 26–73). San Diego, CA: Academic Press.

Antonucci, T. C., & Akiyama, H. (1991). Convoys of social support: Generational issues. *Marriage and Family Review, 16,* 103–123.

Arking, R. (1991). *Biology of aging: Observations and principles.* Englewood Cliffs, NJ: Prentice–Hall.

Bachman, D. L., Wolf, P. A., Linn, R., Knoefel, J. E., Cobb, J., Belanger, A., D'Agostino, R. B., & White, L. R. (1992). Prevalence of dementia and probable senile dementia of the Alzheimer type in the Framingham Study. *Neurology, 42,* 115–119.

Belgrave, L. L. (1993). Discrimination against older women in health care. In J. D. Garner & A. A. Young (Eds.), *Women and healthy aging: Living productively in spite of it all* (pp. 181–199). Binghamton, NY: Haworth.

Berg, R. L., & Cassells, J. S. (Eds.). (1990). *The second fifty years: Promoting health and preventing disability.* Washington, DC: National Academy Press.

Berkman, L. F., Berkman, C. S., Kasl, S., Freeman, D. H., Leo, L., Ostfeld, A. M., Cornoni-Huntley, J., & Brody, J. A. (1986). Depressive symptoms in relation to physical health and function in the elderly. *American Journal of Epidemiology, 124,* 372–388.

Blazer, D. G. (1982). Social support and mortality in an elderly community population. *American Journal of Epidemiology, 115,* 684–694.

Bliwise, N. G., McCall, M. E., & Swan, S. J. (1987). The epidemiology of mental illness in late life. In E. E. Lurie, J. H. Swan, & Associates (Eds.), *Serving the mentally ill elderly* (pp. 1–38). Lexington, MA: Lexington.

Branch, L. G., Guralnik, J. M., Foley, D. J., Kohout, F. J., Wetle, T. T., Ostfeld, A., & Katz, S. (1991). Active life expectancy for 10,000 caucasian men and women in three communities. *Journal of Gerontology: Medical Sciences, 46,* M145–150.

Brody, E. M. (1985). *Mental and physical health practices of older people.* New York: Springer.

Brody, J. A., & Schneider, E. L. (1986). Diseases and disorders of aging: An hypothesis. *Journal of Chronic Diseases, 39,* 871–876.

Caine, E. D., & Grossman, H. T. (1992). Neuropsychiatric assessment. In J. E. Birren, R. B. Sloane, & G. D. Cohen (Eds.), *Handbook of mental health and aging* (2nd ed., pp. 603–642). San Diego, CA: Academic Press.

Caplan, A. (1990). Can philosophy cure what ails the medical model? In R. L. Berg & J. S. Cassells (Eds.), *The second fifty years: Promoting health and preventing disability* (pp. 291–310). Washington, DC: National Academy Press.

Carstensen, L. L. (1993). Motivation for social contact across the life span: A theory of socioemotional selectivity. In J. Jacobs (Ed.), *Nebraska symposium on motivation: 1992. Developmental perspectives on motivation, Vol. 40* (pp. 209–254). Lincoln, NE: University of Nebraska Press.

Carstensen, L. L., & Pasupathi, M. (1993). Women of a certain age. In S. Matteo (Ed.), *American women in the nineties: Today's critical issues* (pp. 66–78). Boston: Northeastern University Press.

Clark, P. G. (1991). Ethical dimensions of quality of life in aging: Autonomy vs. collectivism in the United States and in Canada. *Gerontologist, 31*, 631–639.

Cockerham, W. C., Sharp, K., & Wilcox, J. A. (1983). Aging and perceived health status. *Journal of Gerontology, 38*, 349–355.

Cohen, G. D. (1992). The future of mental health and aging. In J. E. Birren, R. B. Sloane, & G. D. Cohen (Eds.), *Handbook of mental health and aging* (2nd ed., pp. 893–912). San Diego, CA: Academic Press.

Cooper, J., & Goethals, G. R. (1981). The self-concept and old age. In S. B. Kiesler, J. N. Morgan, & V. K. Oppenheimer (Eds.), *Aging: Social change* (pp. 431–452). New York: Academic Press.

Cummings, J. L., & Benson, D. F. (1992). *Dementia: A clinical approach* (2nd ed.). Boston: Butterworth–Heinemann.

Depner, C. E., & Ingersoll-Dayton, B. (1988). Supportive relationships in later life. *Psychology and Aging, 3*, 348–357.

Diokno, A. C., Brock, B. M., Brown, M. B., & Herzog, A. R. (1986). Prevalence of urinary incontinence and other urological symptoms in the noninstitutionalized elderly. *Journal of Urology, 136*, 1022–1025.

Elias, M. F., Elias, J. W., & Elias, P. K. (1990). Biological and health influences on behavior. In J. E. Birren & K. W. Schaie (Eds.), *Handbook of the psychology of aging* (3rd ed., pp. 79–102). San Diego, CA: Academic Press.

Estes, C. L., & Rundall, T. G. (1992). Social characteristics, social structure, and health in the aging population. In M. G. Ory, R. P. Abeles, & P. D. Lipman (Eds.), *Aging, health, and behavior* (pp. 299–326). Newbury Park, CA: Sage.

Estes, C. L., Swan, J. H., & Associates (1993). *The long term care crisis: Elders trapped in the no-care zone.* Newbury Park, CA: Sage.

Evans, D. A., Funkenstein, H. H., Albert, M. S., Scherr, P. A., Cook, N. R., Chown, M. J., Hebert, L. E., Hennekens, C. H., & Taylor, J. O. (1989). Prevalence of Alzheimer's disease in a community population of older persons: Higher than previously reported. *Journal of the American Medical Association, 262*, 2551–2556.

Fries, J. (1989). The compression of morbidity: Near or far? *The Milbank Quarterly, 67*, 208–232.

Garn, S. M. (1975). Bone-loss and aging. In R. Goldman & M. Rockstine (Eds.), *The physiology and pathology of human aging* (pp. 39–57). New York: Academic Press.

George, L. K. (1993). *Financial security in later life: The subjective side.* Philadelphia, PA: Boettner Institute of Financial Gerontology.

Guralnik, J. M. (1991). Prospects for the compression of morbidity: The challenge posed by increasing disability in the years prior to death. *Journal of Aging and Health, 3,* 138–154.

Guralnik, J. M., Land, K. C., Blazer, D., Fillenbaum, G. G., & Branch, L. G. (1993). Educational status and active life expectancy among older Blacks and whites. *New England Journal of Medicine, 329,* 110–116.

Guralnik, J. M., LaCroix, A. Z., Everett, M. S., & Kovar, M. G. (1989). *Aging in the eighties: The prevalence of comorbidity and its association with disability.* Advance data from Vital and Health Statistics of the National Center for Health Statistics. No. 170. (DHHS Publication No. PHS 89-1250). Hyattsville, MD: National Center for Health Statistics.

Guralnik, J. M., & Simonsick, E. M. (1993). Physical disability in older Americans. *Journal of Gerontology, 48* [Special Issue], 3–10.

Gurwitz, J. H., Col, N. F., & Avorn, J. (1992). The exclusion of the elderly and women from clinical trials in acute myocardial infarction. *Journal of the American Medical Association, 268,* 1417–1422.

Haan, H. M., Rice, D. P., Satariano, W. A., & Selby, J. V. (1991). Living longer and doing worse? Present and future trends in the health of the elderly. *Journal of Aging and Health, 3,* 133–137.

Harris, J. R. (1988). *The etiology of individual differences in health and anthropometric measures: A developmental study of adult twins.* Unpublished doctoral dissertation, Pennsylvania State University, University Park, PA.

Harris, J. R., Berg, S., & Ljungqvist, B. (1994). More perceptions on perceived health. Manuscript in preparation.

Hazzard, W. R. (1986). Biological basis of the sex differential in longevity. *Journal of the American Geriatrics Society, 34,* 455–471.

Henderson, V., Paganini-Hill, A., Emanuel, C., Dunn, M., & Buckwalter, J. (1994). Estrogen replacement therapy in older women: Comparisons between Alzheimer's disease cases and nondemented controls. *Archives of Neurology, 51,* 896–900.

Holahan, C. K., Holahan, C. J., & Belk, S. S. (1984). Adjustment in aging: The roles of life stress, hassles, and self-efficacy. *Health Psychology, 3,* 315–328.

House, J. S., Kessler, R. C., Herzog, A. R., Mero, R. P., Kinney, A. M., & Breslow, M. J. (1990). Age, socioeconomic status, and health. *Milbank Quarterly, 68,* 383–411.

House, J. S., Landis, K. R., & Umberson, D. (1988). Social relationships and health. *Science, 241,* 540–545.

Howard, P. A. (1994). Treating isolated systolic hypertension in the elderly. *Annals of Pharmacotherapy, 28,* 367–372.

Idler, E. L. (1993). Age differences in self-assessments of health: Age changes, cohort differences, or survivorship? *Journal of Gerontology: Social Sciences, 48,* S289–300.

Idler, E., & Kasl, S. (1991). Health perceptions and survival: Do global evaluations of health status really predict mortality? *Journal of Gerontology: Social Sciences, 46,* S55–65.

Jarvik, L. F. (1976). Aging and depression: Some unanswered questions. *Journal of Gerontology, 31,* 324–326.

Johnson, R. E., Mullooly, J. P., & Greenlick, M. R. (1990). Morbidity and medical care utilization of old and very old persons. *Health Services Research, 25,* 639–665.

Jorm, A. F., Korten, A. E., & Henderson, A. S. (1987). The prevalence of dementia: A quantitative integration of the literature. *Acta Psychiatrica Scandinavia, 76,* 465–479.

Kane, R. L. (1988). Empiric approaches to prevention in the elderly: Are we promoting too much? In R. Chernoff & D. A. Lipschitz (Eds.), *Health promotion and disease prevention in the elderly* (pp. 161–168). New York: Raven.

Kaplan, F. S. (1985). Osteoporosis. *Women and Health, 10* [Special Issue], 95–114.

Kaplan, G., Barell, V., & Lusky, A. (1988). Subjective state of health and survival in elderly adults. *Journal of Gerontology: Social Sciences, 43,* S114–120.

Kaplan, G. A. (1991). Epidemiologic observations on the compression of morbidity: Evidence from the Alameda County study. *Journal of Aging and Health, 3,* 155–171.

Kaplan, G. A., & Camacho, T. (1983). Perceived health and mortality: A nine-year follow-up of the human population laboratory cohort. *American Journal of Epidemiology, 117,* 292–304.

Katz, S., Branch, L. G., Branson, M. H., Papsidero, J. A., Beck, J. C., & Greer, D. S. (1983). Active life expectancy. *New England Journal of Medicine, 309,* 1218–1224.

Kenney, R. A. (1989). *Physiology of aging: A synopsis* (2nd ed.). Chicago: Yearbook Medical Publications.

Klerman, G. L., Lavori, P. W., Rice, J., Reich, T., Endicott, J., Andreasen, N. C., Keller, M. B., & Hirschfield, R. M. A. (1985). Birth-cohort trends in rates of major depressive disorder among relatives of patients with affective disorder. *Archives of General Psychiatry, 42,* 689–693.

Koenig, H. G., & Blazer D. G. (1992). Mood disorders and suicide. In J. E. Birren, R. B. Sloane, & G. D. Cohen (Eds.), *Handbook of mental health and aging* (2nd ed., pp. 379–407). San Diego, CA: Academic Press.

Kuhn, M. (1991). *No stone unturned.* New York: Ballantine Books.

LaRue, A., Bank, L., Jarvik, L., & Hetland, M. (1979). Health in old age: How do physicians' and self-ratings compare? *Journal of Gerontology, 34,* 687–691.

LaRue, A., Dessonville, C., & Jarvik, L. F. (1985). Aging and mental disorders. In J. E. Birren & K. W. Schaie (Eds.), *Handbook of the psychology of aging* (2nd ed., pp. 664–702). New York: Van Nostrand Reinhold.

Lee, G. R. (1992). Gender differences in family caregiving: A fact in search of a theory. In J. W. Dwyer & R. T. Coward (Eds.), *Gender, families, and elder care* (pp. 120–131). Newbury Park, CA: Sage.

Leventhal, H., Leventhal, E. A., & Schaefer, P. M. (1992). Vigilant coping and health behavior. In M. G. Ory, R. P. Abeles, & P. D. Lipman (Eds.), *Aging, health, and behavior* (pp. 109–140). Newbury Park, CA: Sage.

Liang, J. (1986). Self-reported physical health among aged adults. *Journal of Gerontology, 41,* 248–260.

Mann, W. J. (1985). Reproductive cancer. *Women and Health, 10* [Special Issue]. 63–73.

Manton, K. G. (1988). A longitudinal study of functional change and mortality in the United States. *Journal of Gerontology: Social Sciences, 43,* S153–161.

Manton, K. G. (1990). Population models of gender differences in mortality, morbidity, and disability risks. In M. G. Ory & H. R. Warner (Eds.), *Gender, health, and longevity* (pp. 201–255). New York: Springer.

Manton, K. G., Corder, L. S., & Stallard, E. (1993). Estimates of change in chronic disability and institutional incidence and prevalence rates in the U.S. elderly populations from 1982, 1984, and 1989 National Long Term Care Survey. *Journal of Gerontology: Social Sciences, 48,* S153–166.

Markides, K. S., & Lee, D. J. (1990). Predictors of well-being and functioning in older Mexican-Americans and Anglos: An eight-year follow-up. *Journal of Gerontology: Social Sciences, 45,* S69–73.

Mellström, D., Nilsson, Å., Odén, A., Rundgren, Å., & Svanborg, A. (1982). Mortality among the widowed in Sweden. *Scandinavian Journal of Social Medicine, 10,* 33–41.

Miller, B., & Cafasso, L. (1992). Gender differences in caregiving: Fact or artifact? *Gerontologist, 32,* 498–507.

Morris, J. C., McKeel, D. W., Jr., Storandt, M., Rubin, E. H., Price, J. L., Grant, E. A., Ball, M. J., & Berg, L. (1991). Very mild Alzheimer's disease: Informant-based clinical, psychometric, and pathologic distinction from normal aging. *Neurology, 41,* 469–478.

Mortimer, J. (1994). What are the risk factors for dementia. In F. Huppert, C. Brayne, & D. O'Connor (Eds.), *Dementia and normal aging* (pp. 208–229). Cambridge, MA: Cambridge University Press.

Mortimer, J. A., & Hutton, J. T. (1985). Epidemiology and etiology of Alzheimer's disease. In J. T. Hutton & A. D. Kenny (Eds.), *Senile dementia of the Alzheimer's type* (pp. 177–196). New York: Alan R. Liss.

Mossey, J. M., & Shapiro, E. (1982). Self-rated health: A predictor of mortality among the elderly. *American Journal of Public Health, 7,* 800–808.

Murrell, S. A., Himmelfarb, S., & Wright, K. (1983). Prevalence of depression and its correlates in older adults. *American Journal of Epidemiology, 117,* 173–185.

Neugarten, B. L., & Neugarten, D. A. (1989). Policy issues in an aging society. In M. Storandt & G. R. VandenBos (Eds.), *The adult years: Continuity and change* (pp. 143–167). Washington, DC: American Psychological Association.

NIH Consensus Development Panel on Depression in Late Life. (1992). Diagnosis and treatment of depression in late life. *Journal of the American Medical Association, 268,* 1018–1024.

Ory, M. G., Abeles, R. P., & Lipman, P. D. (1992) Introduction: An overview of research on aging, health, and behavior. In M. G. Ory, R. P. Abeles, & P. D. Lipman (Eds.), *Aging, health, and behavior* (pp. 1–23). Newbury Park, CA: Sage.

Ory, M. G., Cox, D. M., Gift, H. C., & Abeles, R. P. (1994). Aging and quality of life: Celebrating new research discoveries. In R. P. Abeles, H. C. Gift, & M. G. Ory (Eds.), *Aging and quality of life: Charting new territories in behavioral sciences research* (pp. 1–16). New York: Springer.

Pfeiffer, E. (Ed.). (1978). *Multidimensional functional assessment: The OARS methodology* (2nd ed.). Durham, NC: Duke University, Center for the Study of Aging and Human Development.

Post, F. (1987). Paranoid and schizophrenic disorders among the aging. In L. L. Carstensen & B. A. Edelstein (Eds.), *Handbook of clinical gerontology* (pp. 43–56). New York: Pergamon.

Rakowski, W. (1992). Disease prevention and health promotion with older adults. In M. G. Ory, R. P. Abeles, & P. D. Lipman (Eds.), *Aging, health, and behavior* (pp. 239–275). Newbury Park, CA: Sage.

Raskind, M. A., & Peskind, E. R. (1992). Alzheimer's disease and other dementing disorders. In J. E. Birren, R. B. Sloane, & G. D. Cohen (Eds.), *Handbook of mental health and aging* (2nd ed., pp. 478–515). San Diego, CA: Academic Press.

Regier, D. A., Boyd, J. H., Burke, J. D., Rae, D. S., Myers, J. K., Kramer, M., Robins, L. N., George, L. K., Karno, M., & Locke, B. Z. (1988). One-month prevalence of mental disorders in the United States. *Archives of General Psychiatry, 45,* 977–986.

Rinder, L., Roupe, S., Steen, B., & Svanborg, A. (1975). Seventy year-old people in Gothenburg: A population study in an industrialized Swedish city. I. General presentation of the study. *Acta Medicae Scandinavia, 198,* 397–407.

Rodin, J., & McAvay, G. (1992). Determinants of change in perceived health in a longitudinal study of older adults. *Journal of Gerontology: Psychological Sciences, 47,* P373–384.

Rodin, J., McAvay, G., & Timko, C. (1988). A longitudinal study of depressed mood and sleep disturbances in elderly adults. *Journal of Gerontology: Psychological Sciences, 43,* P45–53.

Rowe, J. W., & Kahn, R. L. (1987). Human aging: Usual and successful. *Science, 237,* 143–149.

Rozzini, R., Frisoni, G. B., Bianchetti, A., Zanetti, O., & Trabucchi, M. (1993). Physical performance test and activities of daily living scales in the assessment of health status in elderly people. *Journal of the American Geriatrics Society, 41,* 1109–1113.

Ryff, C. D. (1991). Possible selves in adulthood and old age: A tale of shifting horizons. *Psychology and Aging, 6,* 286–295.

Schaie, K. W., Campbell, R. T., Meredith, W., & Rawlings, S. C. (Eds.). (1988). *Methodological issues in aging research.* New York: Springer.

Schneider, L. S., Reynolds, C. F., III, Lebowitz, B. D., & Friedhoff, A. J. (Eds.). (1994). *Diagnosis and treatment of depression in late life* (pp. 55–59). Washington, DC: American Psychiatric Press.

Seeman, T. E., Charpentier, P. A., Berkman, L. F., Tinetti, M. E., Guralnik, J. M., Albert, M., Blazer, D., & Rowe, J. W. (1994). Predicting changes in physical performance in a high-functioning elderly cohort: MacArthur studies of successful aging. *Journal of Gerontology: Medical Sciences, 49,* M97–108.

Sheikh, J. I. (1992). Anxiety and its disorders in old age. In J. E. Birren, R. B. Sloane, & G. D. Cohen (Eds.), *Handbook of mental health and aging* (2nd ed.) (pp. 409–432). San Diego, CA: Academic Press.

Siegler, I. C., & Costa, P. T., Jr. (1985). Health behavior relationships. In J. E. Birren & K. W. Schaie (Eds.), *Handbook of the psychology of aging* (2nd ed., pp. 144–166). New York: Van Nostrand Reinhold.

Siegler, I. C., Nowlin, J. B., & Blumenthal, J. A. (1980). Health and behavior: Methodological considerations for adult development and aging. In L. W. Poon (Ed.), *Aging in the 1980s* (pp. 599–612). Washington, DC: American Psychological Association.

Skaff, M. M., & Pearlin, L. I. (1992). Caregiving: Role engulfment and the loss of self. *Gerontologist, 32,* 656–664.

Smith, D. W. E., & Warner, H. R. (1989). Does genotypic sex have a direct effect on longevity? *Experimental Gerontology, 24,* 277–288.

Steinbach, U. (1992). Social networks, institutionalization, and mortality among elderly people in the United States. *Journal of Gerontology: Social Sciences, 47,* S183–190.

Stewart, A. L. (1992). The Medical Outcomes Study: Framework of health indicators. In A. L. Stewart & J. E. Ware (Eds.), *Measuring functioning and well-being* (pp. 12–24). Durham, NC: Duke University Press.

Stoller, E. P. (1990). Males as helpers: The role of sons, relatives, and friends. *Gerontologist, 30,* 228–235.

Strawbridge, W. J., Camacho, B. A., Cohen, R. D., & Kaplan, G. A. (1993). Gender differences in factors associated with change in physical functioning in old age: A 6-year longitudinal study. *Gerontologist, 33,* 603–609.

Strawbridge, W. J., Kaplan, G. A., Camacho, B. A., & Cohen, R. D. (1992). The dynamics of disability and functional change in an elderly cohort: Results from the Alameda county study. *Journal of the American Geriatrics Society, 40,* 799–806.

Stroebe, M., & Stroebe, W. (1983). Who suffers more? Sex differences in health risks of the widowed. *Psychological Bulletin, 93,* 297–301.

Tinetti, M. E., & Powell, L. (1993). Fear of falling and low self-efficacy: A cause of dependence in elderly persons. *Journal of Gerontology, 48* [Special Issue], 35–38.

Tinetti, M. E., Williams, T. F., & Mayewski, R. (1986). Fall risk index for elderly patients based on number of chronic disabilities. *American Journal of Medicine, 80,* 429–434.

U.S. Bureau of the Census. (1992a). *Marital status and living arrangements.* Current Population Reports. Series P20-468. Washington, DC: U.S. Government Printing Office.

U.S. Bureau of the Census. (1992b). *Population projections of the U.S. by age, sex, race, and Hispanic origin: 1992 to 2050.* Current Population Reports. Series P25-1092. Washington, DC: U.S. Government Printing Office.

U.S. Bureau of the Census. (1992c). *Sixty-five plus in America.* Current Population Reports, Special Studies, P23-178RV. Washington, DC: U.S. Government Printing Office.

U.S. Department of Health and Human Services. (1991). *Healthy people 2000.* (DHHS Publication No. PHS 91-50212). Washington, DC: U.S. Government Printing Office.

U.S. National Center for Health Statistics. (1989). *National nursing home survey.* (DHHS Publication No. PHS 89-1758). (Series 13, No. 97). Washington, DC: U.S. Government Printing Office.

U.S. National Center for Health Statistics. (1994). *Current estimates from the National Health Interview Survey, 1992.* (DHHS Publication No. PHS 94-1517) (Series 10, No. 189). Washington, DC: U.S. Government Printing Office.

Wallace, R. B., & Lemke, J. H. (1991). The compression of comorbidity. *Journal of Aging and Health, 3,* 237–246.

Wolinsky, F. D., & Johnson, R. J. (1992). Perceived health status and mortality among older men and women. *Journal of Gerontology: Social Sciences, 47,* S304–312.

World Health Organization. (1958). *The first ten years of the World Health Organization.* Geneva: World Health Organization.

Yates, J. W., & Yancik, R. (1987). Cancer management issues. In L. L. Carstensen & B. A. Edelstein (Eds.), *Handbook of clinical gerontology* (pp. 123–131). New York: Pergamon Press.

Zautra, A., & Hempel, A. (1984). Subjective well-being and physical health: A narrative literature review with suggestions for future research. *International Journal of Aging and Human Development, 19,* 95–110.

14

Health Care Policy and Practice for Women's Health

Cheryl B. Travis, Diane L. Gressley, and
Patricia L. Adams

INTRODUCTION

Health care has a colorful (and somewhat checkered) history in western Anglo culture. Initially, providers were as likely to be herbalists, priests, barbers, or midwives as nurses and physicians. The emergence of a licensed and trained professional class has been a relatively recent phenomenon. In addition, philosophies of intervention have shifted on a number of dimensions, for example, from a relatively gentle, homeopathic approach to a more invasive, allopathic approach. Other changes have included a shift from a predominance of general family doctors to a growing number of specialists, from an emphasis on inpatient treatment to one of outpatient care, and from tertiary care to prevention. A similar spectrum of change has occurred in technology, greatly increasing the possibilities for intervention (e.g. nuclear medicine imaging). Most of this emerged without an overarching plan or the explicit voicing of a political will. On the whole, Americans have only limited experience in constructing national plans for the delivery of health care. The question then becomes, what principles and priorities ought to inform efforts to enact national health care reform?

This chapter discusses general systems issues involving the administration and delivery of health care and the policies that underlie them,
particularly as they relate to women's health issues. Three major sections
address the topics of (a) problems in health care, (b) national objectives
in health care, and (c) strategies for reform in health care. Our thinking
was influenced by three principles outlined in this introduction. First, legitimacy in health care is socially constructed; second, individual empowerment is of central importance; and third, inclusiveness, equity, and
diversity are essential (Travis, Gressley, & Crumpler, 1991).

Social Construction of Legitimacy

The first tenet that shaped our thinking is the proposition that much of
the understanding of health care problems and solutions is socially constructed. The core of this idea is the assumption that the identification of
a problem worthy of remediation is ultimately a political process. The initial identification and characterization of a problem, for example, as medical rather than social, frames the nature of proposed solutions, the priority attached to the problem, and the resources allocated to it. Whether
or not certain conditions and treatments are covered in regular benefits,
the location at which care is delivered (e.g., hospital or home), and the
range of providers eligible for reimbursement (e.g., obstetrician or nurse
midwife) are all subject to review and revision by political processes.

These issues may be formulated as debates about legitimacy. What is
a "real" problem; who is an "authentic" provider; and what are the "proper"
procedures? The answers to these questions vary depending on one's point
of view, the availability of relevant information, vested interests, and other
often politicized factors. Questions of legitimacy are particularly relevant
in the area of health care, and that which has been designated as legitimate medicine has varied greatly in the history of health care. For example, some of the witches of the 1600s and 1700s were burned primarily
for practicing medicine, an enterprise that was restricted to men (Ehrenreich & English, 1973). Women have been excluded because in the view
of the patriarchy they could not be legitimate providers of health care.
Women consumers have been further excluded because only male

providers had the legitimate authority to know about treatments and choose among alternatives. The women's health movement was founded on the idea that a woman's right to her body is the right to her life (Boston Women's Health Collective, 1973; Dreifus, 1977), and that the expropriation of women's health has been historically based on who was legitimized to control knowledge and choice (Sandelowski, 1981).

Once women began to take initiative in defining problems and exploring potential new treatments, the boundaries of orthodox medicine were necessarily challenged. The women's health movement has always been amenable to the consideration of alternative forms of health care, such as holistic medicine, herbal treatments, meditation, and self-healing (Weiss, 1984). Some of the alternative forms practiced today were predated by the work of women of the nineteenth century who argued for the benefits of dietary moderation, mind–body synergisms, and other self-healing techniques (Butler & Schoepflin, 1990). However, because the legitimate avenues of medicine were at the time defined in a more orthodox manner, the contributions of these women often were expressed within the context of religious belief rather than authoritative health care.

For example, Ellen White's views about dietary moderation were developed in the Seventh Day Adventist church; Mary Baker Eddy, who advocated mind–body synergism, founded the Christian Scientist church; and Aimee Semple McPherson inspired the International Church of the Foursquare Gospel. Had legitimate medicine been conceptualized more broadly at that time, the principles of dietary prevention of disease, imagery in healing, and psychosocial elements of health might have been introduced much earlier as a part of legitimate medicine. While not all the details of their ideas have been adopted or proved effective, it is certainly the case that attention to diet and nutrition, for example, has become well recognized in the prevention of heart disease and cancer. In addition, the emerging field of psychoneuroimmunology has incorporated the fundamental idea that a mind–body synergy has very real outcomes for health. Further, a recent study reported that surgery patients had less psychological distress, lower blood pressure, and shorter hospital stays when they roomed with patients who were nonsurgery or postoperative patients (Kulik, Moore, & Mahler, 1993). We suggest that such social factors might well have found their way into health research in a more timely fashion if women's experiences and alternative viewpoints had been admitted as legitimate. The possibility of alternative approaches to treatment recently has been accorded some limited stature in the form of the Office of Alternative Medicine within the office of the Director for the National Institutes of Health. Today, as national health care programs are revised, the types of providers and the services covered will have the effect of redefining what is legitimate in health care.

More recently, the process of defining health care problems has often not included women's health needs, or has defined them as falling within a very narrow realm of reproductive biology. The "important" problems typically have been identified as those key to the well-being of White, middle-class men. The fact that women, as well as men, die of heart disease, contract AIDS, and have chronic illnesses frequently has been ignored in the design of clinical trials and overlooked with respect to special treatment needs of women with these conditions. Health concerns that uniquely involve women have been given a relatively low priority for research, as has historically been the case with breast cancer, or have received limited funding for community interventions, as in the case of domestic violence. Thus, it is important from the outset that women's perspectives be included in the definition of problems and in the setting of priorities.

Moreover, we were concerned that the initial definition and characterization of problems would serve to construct potential solutions. Indeed, quite different solutions emerge to the extent that problems are defined as being primarily biomedical diseases, rather than matters of lifestyle or wellness. Not incidentally, the criteria and methods by which reforms and solutions are evaluated are also socially constructed. Only some solutions will be legitimatized as meeting the criteria of "efficacy" or as being "appropriate" or "cost effective." In the last section of this chapter we take a look at the various difficulties of cost–benefit analysis and complications in assessing cost effectiveness, and suggest that at least one criterion for evaluating reform should involve considerations of equity.

A critical feature of this debate involves not only the questions of what are considered legitimate health problems and solutions or who are considered legitimate health care providers, but who does the deciding on these issues. Clearly, it is Congress that drafts and votes on legislation. Nevertheless, groups that are already recognized and that hold strong vested interests are likely to be heavily involved in testifying before Congress, in lobbying, and in having direct discussions with legislators. Professional organizations, pharmaceutical and medical corporations, the nursing home industry, and insurance groups all will have ideas about these issues, and they are well represented before Congress and the president. One wonders who will be judged the relevant experts, and what kind of information these experts will invoke to shape the nature of the debate—economists, health administrators, grass roots groups? And finally, given the mix of players in the debate, what will be the implications for women's health care?

Individual Empowerment

A second principle that shaped our thinking holds that individual experience and choice are of central importance in any system of health reform. This principle has been developed in feminist scholarship in a variety of contexts. Women telling their own stories as oral history and in their own voices represents one variant (Bernhardt, 1980; Lebra-Chapman, 1991). The fundamental feature of this principle is that the individual's experience must be an essential basis for understanding and action. Smith (1991) has proposed that it is this first level of experience that is the beginning of knowledge about society, and we propose that it is equally true with respect to issues of health.

Individual empowerment is part of the process of raising consciousness with respect to gender as a class-variable, and of building a sense of entitlement that allows women to recognize their own efficacy in bringing about change. Empowerment authorizes the individual to recognize and name her (or his) own issues and to choose among solutions. Empowering those who do not have easy access to resources, conveniences, or information has become a major theme within the feminist movement as feminism has evolved in a number of settings (Sagaria, 1988). Making the emotional and cognitive connection between internal events (such as conflict, stress, and anger) and external institutions and social structures is the principal component necessary for the private realization that the personal is political (Gilbert, 1980; Worell & Remer, 1992). Certainly it is the case that access to care and the quality of care that one receives are shaped by political, as well as by social and biomedical factors.

Issues involving the importance of the individual are particularly evident in women's health care, and some of the initial feminist protest involving women's health care centered around the fact that women were often poorly and/or inappropriately treated by the established health care system. This is especially apparent in the history of childbirth. Throughout the 1800s, changes were made in medical technology that rendered the practice of midwifery virtually obsolete (Oakley, 1984; Rich, 1976). By the end of the Civil War, the introduction of new technologies found pregnant women relying on physicians who used chloroform and forceps, often resulting in physical damage to the woman, and lethargic neonates. This increased technology resulted in a general movement of ideas about birth from the realm of the normal to the realm of the abnormal and dangerous. In addition, the more recent trends of electronic fetal monitoring and high rates of Cesarean surgery have raised the question of women's choice (Butter, 1993; Rodin & Collins, 1991). Certainly, the fact that nearly one quarter of all births are now performed by Cesarean surgery is suspicious. The experiences of women and the voices of women have been very important in revising childbirth in the United States. Almost every hospital in the United States now allows the presence of fathers or coaches in labor and delivery rooms. Many also have options for rooming-in of newborns with their mothers and special birthing rooms, as opposed to surgical delivery rooms. The issues of choice and decision-making in all aspects of women's health care are as relevant today as they ever were.

Diversity, Inclusiveness, & Equity

Political influence on the personal has not been limited to women. Sexism shares qualities with the other major "isms"—ableism, ageism, heterosexism, racism, and classism. Early feminists recognized the fact that individual women shared their fate, not only with other women, but also with members of other minority groups (Hacker, 1951). More recent feminist scholarship contends that these shared outcomes are generated by a common process of power dynamics, in both political and personal arenas (Hyde, 1991; Kahn & Yoder, 1989; Yoder & Kahn, 1992).

Feminist critiques of psychological theory and research have provided a framework for understanding the value of diversity and inclusiveness in issues of health care. For example, early psychological theory viewed women as exceptions, or problems to be compared to a normative (male) prototype (Crawford & Marecek, 1989). Despite the fact that some might yearn for the "good ol' days" when sex was a neatly packaged biological variable, psychological theory, research, and applications have been enhanced by the inclusion of women. Moreover, there is increased recognition of diversity among women (Landrine, 1994; Unger & Crawford, 1993; Yoder & Kahn, 1993).

Contemporary thinking in feminist scholarship regarding diversity also provides a useful model for application to discussion of health care issues. Questions about equity in health care are intimately related to issues of diversity. These questions are concerned with who has access to care, which services are offered, which providers are available, and the quality of services extended to different groups. Particular attention should be accorded those groups that typically are overlooked or underserved—not only women, but also age groups, economic groups, and ethnic/cultural groups. Needs-assessments for these groups may suggest a picture somewhat different from that recommended for majority groups. Health needs for members of underserved groups may include a number of factors not regularly considered when planning for the health needs of more privileged populations (Kirschstein & Merritt, 1985).

Recognition of the growing number of aged persons also has implications for health care reform (Ginzberg, 1987). Specific health conditions associated more frequently with women and aging, such as osteoporosis and Alzheimer's disease, are now the topics of formal research, though at one time they were neglected (Catchen, 1988; Herzog, 1989; Roberto, 1988). In addition, the needs of minority women's mental and physical health have begun to be addressed as the impact of AIDS on these groups becomes more apparent (Amaro, 1988; Fullilove, Fullilove, Haynes, & Gross, 1990). Evidence suggesting that Black women are more likely to have problem or unwanted pregnancies is of equal concern. For example, the mean adjusted rate for abortion per 100,000 people is roughly 86 for Black women and only 19 among White women (Agency for Health Care Policy and Research, April 1994b).

The above points regarding legitimacy, empowerment, and diversity have organized our thinking and stimulated much of our analysis. In the next section we review some basic information about health care and why it is now being debated as in need of major reform. In the remaining sections we review nationally established objectives for health in the United States, proposals for health care reform, and the issues of particular relevance to women.

PROBLEMS IN HEALTH CARE

While there is a complex array of important considerations in health care, two problems almost universally recognized are the access to and cost of health care. The divorced mother of three who loses her health insurance because she was previously covered by a plan obtained through her husband's employment can explain very quickly that getting access is a major problem. The man who lost his original coverage because of a heart problem and now cannot obtain insurance because of his preexisting condition will come to the same conclusion. The self-employed contractor and the family-owned business manager will point out that even though eligible for insurance coverage, they simply can't afford it. Even major corporations are concerned that an increasing percentage of their operating overhead, and therefore the cost of their products, is expended on health insurance.

Access

Approximately 77% of people in the United States have private insurance; about 6% are covered by Medicaid, the largest government health care financing program, and about 15%, or 38 million, are not covered at all.

Almost 75% of the uninsured are under age 35 and are female (Short, 1990). Contrary to stereotypes, the majority of people lacking insurance have jobs, obligations, and family lives. In fact, over any two year period, approximately 25% of Americans will be without coverage for some period of time because they change jobs, move, or are dropped by their insurance company (Clinton, 1993). Most businesses that provide health insurance offer only one plan for their employees, and new employees may not be eligible for coverage because of preexisting health conditions. The current health care crisis also means that some people may experience "job-lock" because they are currently covered but would not be able to obtain coverage if they changed jobs, and it also means that there is more limited choice among providers. These conditions are especially problematic for women, minorities, migrants, homeless people, older people, and those with chronic illnesses. These groups are often uninsured or underinsured. Women—particularly minority women, single heads of households, and older women—are more likely to be underemployed, employed part-time, or employed in small businesses without health benefits.

The system of payment is another integral part of the access equation. Medicaid costs grew 10% per year throughout the 1980s, and in the early part of this decade increased even more dramatically. Nevertheless, an ongoing problem has been locating physicians who are willing to treat Medicaid patients. Traditionally, low reimbursement rates and additional administrative mandates were central issues for physician decisions to exclude Medicaid patients from their practices (U.S. General Accounting Office [USGAO], 1993). Because women and the children they support are a high percentage of Medicaid recipients, plans to restrict, limit, or restructure Medicaid have a disproportionate impact on women.

Economic barriers that block access to care are particularly offensive, but the possibility that economic gain might influence the quality of care patients receive should be carefully examined. While not definitive, there are some worrisome data suggesting that a patient's source of payment indeed may influence medical decision-making. In a study we currently are conducting of records for 400,000 heart disease patients, those patients with private insurance were twice as likely to receive bypass surgery as

Medicaid patients who had the same diagnoses. While these findings do not conclusively prove improper care, they do raise red flags about the subtle and sometimes not-so-subtle role of economics in treatment decisions (Adams, Travis, Gressley, & Adams, 1993).

Cost

Health care costs have led the consumer price index every year since 1980. There are higher out-of-pocket costs for those who seek care; and there are higher premiums for less coverage. The United States spends about 800 billion dollars annually on health care, a figure that has grown dramatically since 1980 and is continuing to grow (Eastaugh, 1992). By the year 2000, expenditures will reach trillions of dollars. These expenditures will constitute approximately 17% of the gross national product (Sonnefeld, Waldo, Lemieux, & McKusick, 1991).

As noted in the examples below, many of the conditions that contribute to the 145 billion dollar national bill (Agency for Health Care Policy and Research, 1994a) for inpatient health care within hospitals are prevalent in, if not exclusive to women; and women are heavily represented in the existing programs charged with providing or paying for these services—Medicare and Medicaid. Furthermore, the most costly hospital patient/group receiving treatment involves circulatory diseases, the leading cause of death among women, and three of the other most costly diagnostic categories involve pregnancy and delivery. Medicare and Medicaid, programs with a high percentage of women enrolled, had total bills of approximately 64 billion and 14 billion dollars respectively, compared to 50 billion dollars for private insurance. One of the top listed conditions requiring treatment under Medicare is fracture of the neck of the femur, an event that affects older women more than men. The largest primary payer for Medicaid services is Aid for Families with Dependent Children, again with women more likely than men to be single heads of families below the poverty line. Therefore, any plan to minimize or contain costs in these areas will necessarily have a direct impact on women's health.

A complex array of factors contribute to the escalating cost of health care. Two important factors are supply and demand. The supply factor is characterized by increasing specialization among practitioners. While there are fewer general family physicians, surgical specialties have risen dramatically (Eastaugh, 1992). The practice patterns of these specialists (as well as other general practice providers) have evolved as a major supply-side factor in health care access and cost. Physician practice patterns determine who gets hospitalized, which diagnostic tests are conducted, what surgical interventions are pursued, and the pharmaceuticals that are prescribed. In effect, 1% of the population determines how 10% of the nation's gross national product will be spent (Eisenberg, 1985). Under the present system, the majority of physicians practice under a fee-for-service scheme that encourages interventions. Further, the general culture encourages physicians to use the most modern technologies, even when these technologies are of uncertain effectiveness compared to alternative, and less expensive options (Anderson, 1994). Because there are few iron-clad rules about medical decisions, there is considerable variation in physician practice patterns. Such variation can (though does not necessarily) indicate flawed decision-making and potential overuse of some procedures. For example, in the case of hysterectomy, the most common major surgery in the United States, approximately 25% of the roughly 600,000 surgeries performed annually may be of questionable necessity (Travis, 1985).

A related issue that has become a growing concern among practitioners is the rising cost of malpractice. Providers assert that the cost of malpractice insurance is too high and awards are often excessive. In addition, the time involved in a legal battle prior to settlement is a consideration. These problems have led to continued reformation surrounding malpractice insurance (USGAO, 1986a, 1986b, 1992). The threat of malpractice litigation is pervasive, and providers have responded by practicing *defensive medicine*. Defensive medicine can involve a host of strategies such as increasing the number of follow-up visits and performing additional diagnostic tests or treatment procedures. In 1985, the American Medical Association estimated the cost of defensive medicine to be about $15 billion per year (USGAO, 1986a).

Another factor related to supply-side economics involves a changing social construction of illness as a uniquely medical phenomenon. The medicalization of illness has been highlighted by sociologists and anthropologists and defines how we view illness and health in terms of our history and culture. The concepts of illness and health are increasingly constructed in a way that is Cartesian, i.e., that person and body are distinct categories. In this formulation, the body, which is biomechanical, must be treated with interventions that are also biomechanical in nature. Furthermore, the knowledge and experience of the body are separate from the self. In true "scientific" formula, the knower and that which is known must be kept separate. Thus, the recognition and naming of symptoms, diagnosis, and decision making are placed in the realm of experts. And of course, if a little bit of expertise is good, then lots of experts must be better. To the extent that powerful others are thought to hold answers to illness, individuals may be comforted by thoughts of a kindly protector, but they also are likely to lose their sense of entitlement and choice.

The medicalization of disease has led to an increasing reliance on medical doctors and high technology. This presumption, confounded by a socio-cultural stratification of society, has led to an increasing level of expensive technologies available to only certain groups of patients, and to adoption of expensive interventions when behavioral and social interventions might have been equally effective (Ginzberg, 1987). The medicalization phenomenon is apparent in many areas of women's health, such as those Riessman (1983) has discussed in relation to childbirth, abortion, contraception, premenstrual syndrome, mental health issues, and menopause. For example, there is a distinct increase in the rate of tranquilizers and other psychotropic medications prescribed for women when they reach the age of menopause (National Center for Health Statistics & Koch, 1983).

Overall demand for care also has risen, and with it the costs of care. The way in which individuals access the health care system and the types of services and technologies they seek also drive up costs of care. The fact that many individuals are without a regular health care provider also means that hospital emergency rooms have become the source of primary care for many conditions that could be treated in less expensive settings. Increased demand for use of life support systems and other heroic efforts to sustain life is another major factor that drives cost.

In summary, health care problems of national importance include the high cost of care, total expenditure for health care as a percentage of the GNP, decreased access due to limited insurance sources, and restriction of choice in health care. Explanations for these trends include both economic and social factors. A major question involves whether costs can be contained while meeting national objectives for healthy people, and in particular, how women's needs will be addressed in these national objectives.

NATIONAL HEALTH OBJECTIVES

The objective of health care reform should be not only to develop a more accessible, cost effective system of care, but also to promote better health overall. Thus, any plan of reform should address issues of the substantive, day-to-day well-being of people. In contrast to plans for insurance that are activated once illness has been diagnosed, national objectives in health tend to emphasize antecedent conditions and events that might improve overall health status. In documents from the Surgeon General's office, such as *Healthy People 2000*, these health objectives are conceptualized in terms of protection, promotion, and prevention (USDHHS, 1991).

Protection

Occupational injury and disease constitute an important area in health protection. There are 10 million employment-related injuries each year (Muller, 1990). It is not only in dramatic settings such as high-rise construction, oil rigs, or coal mines that workers are at risk. The largest number of these employment-related injuries occur where there are the greatest number of workers—typically including restaurants, grocery stores, hospitals, and department stores, all of which are areas of high employment for women (Muller, 1990).

Employed women, whether in service-oriented, industrial, agricultural, or clerical and office occupations are continually at risk for injury (Stellman, 1987). Food service workers are subject to burns and scalding, while cleaning personnel may be exposed to harmful chemicals. Health service workers, the majority of whom are female, have substantial risk of exposure to hazardous substances and infectious disease. Assembly line workers, piece workers, and stitchers also have risks of injury and illness, particularly eye and hand injuries that may be permanently debilitating. And finally, clerical and office staff may suffer from joint disorders and eye strain.

Despite the still-prevalent sentiment in our society that women should be protected, some of the earliest documented cases of occupational illness were identified among women workers (Muller, 1990). In World War I, about 2,000 young women were hired to apply luminous paint containing radium to watch dials. In order to obtain fine points on their brushes the women licked their brush tips, with the result that many suffered from radiation poisoning, developed what was labeled "jaw rot", and some eventually died. From 1922 to 1925, workers succeeded in verifying the occupational disease through demands for on-site investigations, public appeals, and lawsuits (Stellman, 1987).[1]

Recently, the identification of health problems in workplace settings has received increased attention, especially risks posed by environmental toxins to reproductive health. However, regulations that protect women from harm may simultaneously bar them from better paying jobs, without providing protection to men, resulting in discrimination against women and the exploitation of men. Some companies (e.g., Dupont, General Motors, Johnson Controls, and Monsanto; Gilbert, 1991; Markus, 1990; Vobejda & Swoboda, 1991) have attempted to demand that only women who have been sterilized can work in areas where they may be exposed to mutagens or teratogens (Allen, 1991; Annas, 1991; Claus, Berzon, & Bertein, 1993; Scialli, 1993). However, recent U.S. Supreme Court rulings on these issues have determined that decisions regarding the priority accorded reproductive and economic roles must be left to the individual woman (Greenhouse, 1991). It is not incidental that the jobs where women were previously excluded on the basis of fetal protection are also typically the higher paying jobs.

---

[1]The women who led this effort were Katherine Schaub, one of the workers, Katherine Wiley, president of the National Consumer's League (a group concerned about working women), and Alice Hamilton, a toxicologist at Harvard.

Promotion

Health promotion also covers a wide variety of areas relevant to women. Topics that have been identified by national panels as needing attention are physical fitness and activity; the dangers of tobacco, alcohol, and drugs; family planning; nutrition; mental health; and prevention of violence and abusive behaviors (USDHHS, 1991). Each of these areas has special applications to women. Women often have specific needs that may not be effectively addressed if programs are simply established for men. This seems to be particularly true in the area of tobacco, alcohol, and drugs. For example, the percentage of men who smoke has declined nearly 50% since 1973 (the year of the first Surgeon General's statement on cancer risks), while the percentage of women who smoke has declined only slightly (Pierce, Fiore, Novotny, Hatziandreu, & Davis, 1989). Furthermore, some of the groups that show an increase in smoking include teenage girls.

Health promoting behaviors such as exercise have been continually stressed as beneficial to good psychological and physical health. Many original studies of the benefits of exercise were done in conjunction with promoting healthy cardiovascular systems as demonstrated in the San Francisco Longshoremen Study, the Harvard Alumni Study, and the Framingham Heart Study (Brannon & Feist, 1992). Because of the emphasis on cardiovascular health and because heart disease was viewed as a man's disease, men were often the focus of such studies. However, roughly equal numbers of women and men suffer from heart disease and programs designed to promote heart-friendly lifestyles need to include women as well as men. Women's inclusion in such programs can serve them in other health areas. For example, recent evidence indicates that exercise, recommended as a preventive measure against heart disease, also may prove beneficial in prevention of osteoporosis, a primary health concern for women (Harris, Caspersen, DeFriese, & Estes, 1989).

Prevention

Numerous objectives have been established for the nation in the area of prevention, and most of these objectives have relevance and special applications for women; for example, issues involving breast cancer and AIDS/HIV infection are particularly relevant for women. Breast cancer has received increased attention in recent years, due to its increasing incidence that now equals one in eight women (American Cancer Society, 1995). Health psychologists have relied on basic psychological theory to address the related problems of prevention and psychological adjustment. It has been estimated that breast cancer death rates could be reduced 30% if women were regularly screened, yet many women delay using screening services, often with fatal consequences. Community surveys among older women indicate that too few have had a mammogram within the past year. Behavioral scientists have worked to develop a growing body of knowledge about health behaviors involving breast self-exam and mammography (Alagna & Reddy, 1984; Champion, 1992; Grady, 1988). Variations in models of health beliefs, health locus-of-control, and reasoned action have been useful in guiding research in this area. Studies indicate that perceived susceptibility, cues to action, barriers, self-efficacy, and response efficacy are significantly related both to intentions and behaviors.

However, efforts in improved screening and early detection do not alter the fact that women with breast cancer face an assault on their psychological well-being and that of their loved ones. Thus, prevention is not the only issue of importance. In fact, Sandra Levy has argued that although much of the prevention literature is based on narrow assumptions about carcinogenesis, behavior and social–psychological factors need to be taken seriously (Levy, 1981, 1983). In this light, a number of researchers have examined coping strategies among breast cancer patients (Royak-Schaler, 1991; Stanton & Snider, 1993). Active (as opposed to passive) coping has been found to be positively related to quality of life among women with breast cancer, and in particular, a sense of personal control appears to reduce anxiety and depression. The relation of psychological aspects of coping and endocrine pathways that might mediate the cancer process remains unclear, but the possible interactions are receiving increased research in the field of psychoneuroimmunology.

AIDS/HIV infection also is a major issue of particular relevance to women; it is not just a problem affecting young gay men. Health care policies are needed to address the growing numbers of women with AIDS/HIV and those that give birth to babies with AIDS/HIV. Currently, over 2 million HIV-infected adults have developed AIDS, with over 400,000 new cases of AIDS identified in the United States by the end of 1993 (Merson, 1993). In the United States, women constitute approximately 11% of these cases, and African American women account for half of these cases (Keifer, 1990). However, case identification among women has been hampered by a narrow definition of signs and symptoms. The list of relevant signs and symptoms has now been expanded to be more appropriate for women; as the clinical definition of AIDS/HIV is enlarged to include conditions relevant to women, the number of cases among women will undoubtedly increase.

In addition to problems in case identification and treatment, the vertical transmission of AIDS from mothers to infants suggests that prevention efforts targeting women need to be modified. For a large percentage of women, positive HIV status is incurred through drug-related activities and not primarily because of sexual promiscuity or prostitution (Keifer, 1990). The pathway of transmission for these women is revealed in the analysis of pediatric AIDS. Approximately 1 million children have been infected perinatally (Keifer, 1990). Fifty percent of pediatric cases are among African American children. Black and Hispanic women make up 90% of the mothers who have AIDS-infected children in New York City (Joseph, 1988). The most common vertical transmission pathway of the mother's exposure category is that the mother is an intravenous-drug user (Keifer, 1990). Of the children in New York City who were infected with AIDS by their mothers, 80% of the mothers used intravenous drugs or had sex partners who used intravenous drugs (Joseph, 1988). For these women, AIDS/HIV is not so much tied to sexual behavior as it is to drug addiction.

Continued financial support for AIDS research, education, and community support groups is our best step toward preventing the spread of AIDS. Chu and Diaz (1993) suggest that access to care for many impoverished women is limited by inadequate social services. A national health care policy should include special provisions such as improved social services for women with AIDS and their children. Including a diversity of groups of sexually active adults or teenagers, and not just gay males, in attempts to solve this crisis will facilitate awareness and slow the spread of AIDS/HIV.

When discussing large-scale health issues and objectives like protection, promotion, and prevention, it is perhaps appropriate to assume a more general, abstract approach. However, when translated into specific programs, objectives are not always gender-neutral. For example, a program to lower blood pressure might include only men. It should also be pointed out that these national health objectives generally address the need to keep people from getting sick; they don't address therapeutic interventions or treatment issues. Objectives to lower the incidence of high blood pressure or reduce the number of low-birthweight infants do not suggest what to do once these conditions are manifested in a state of disease. In contrast to the Surgeon General's focus on prevention for improvement of the overall health profile of the United States, most of the national reform focus has been on treatment, illness expense and insurance, and types of treatment interventions to be included in benefits packages. While these strategies for reform can be presented in terms of broad principles, they may or may not be applied with an even hand where gender, race, and class are concerned. The following section presents basic goals and principles of reform currently under consideration, and highlights questions of special significance for women.

STRATEGIES FOR REFORM

While the United States has a limited history of health care reform, there have been innovations of historical significance, notably Medicare and Medicaid. However, these programs were designed for special groups in need. When Medicare and Medicaid were designed, there was belief that most Americans had access to the care they needed. Furthermore, the assumption was that the quality, quantity, and cost of health care in general was something to be determined largely by the medical community and insurers, along with some judicious federal support for provider training programs. Both of these assumptions have now been reexamined, and the general consensus is that health care is not readily available, is too expensive, and that coverage is precarious for most Americans. How to redress these problems has been a matter of furious debate.

Proposals have come forward from think-tanks such as the Heritage Foundation and the Brookings Institute, state governments, national commissions (e.g., the Pepper Commission), insurance-related groups, business–employer groups, and provider organizations, as well as from Congress. No less than a dozen bills dealing with health care reform were introduced in Congress during the 1991 session, while another dozen proposals were already being discussed.

Despite the numerous proposals and even more numerous advocates, three major conceptual strategies for reform are typically recognized: *single-payer government-based systems* like Canada's, *employer mandated plans,* and *market reform* combined with consumer tax incentives. All have the general objective of achieving broad coverage and reducing costs. Single-payer plans fund health care through general tax revenues, rather than through individual insurance premiums. In Canada, this approach has been characterized by global budgeting for hospitals, and in some cases the setting of physicians' fees. Total expenditures and fees are more easily monitored under a single-payer system. It is also thought that a single-payer system would reduce the plethora of forms and papers associated with multiple payers, thus reducing administrative costs.

During 1991, six bills based on a Canadian style system were officially introduced in Congress. Lead sponsors for these bills were Representatives Dingell, Gibbons, Oaker, Russo, and Stark, and Senator Kerrey. The general approaches of these plans called variously for states to administer federally approved plans, state administration of Medicare coverage to all residents, and administration of a compulsory national insurance program by the federally based Health Care Financing Administration. Even though all fell within the general single-payer strategy, the particulars between them varied. For example, some plans specified inpatient mental health benefits of 30 days per year, while other plans designated 190 days per lifetime. Coverage for preventive care was similarly spotty among these bills. For example, screening mammography and pap smears for cervical cancer were specifically covered in the Gibbons, Oaker, Stark, and Kerrey bills, but not mentioned in the Dingell or Russo bills. Details of these bills have continued to be discussed and debated.

Employer based plans, sometimes referred to as "pay or play," require all employers to provide a minimum health benefit to their employees (play) or to contribute to a general public pool of funds (pay), usually a specific percentage of the payroll. Since employers now broker the majority of health care plans, it is assumed that there would be less disruption in the providing of services if reform is built upon features of the system now in place. The real innovation in such employer based plans is that all employers, large and small, would be required to participate. Additionally, coverage typically is mandated for part-time as well as full-time employees. Currently, small businesses with relatively few employees are not required to offer health insurance; and even large companies, for example large fast food chains and nationally based supermarkets, are not required to offer insurance plans to their part-time employees, who may represent a large percentage of their employees, as is the case with McDonald's.

Market reforms and tax incentives allow a tax deduction, credit, or voucher to individuals. One feature of this approach is that self-employed individuals would be eligible for a credit or voucher. Market reforms typically involve some kind of managed competition and incorporate insurance industry reform along with general health reform. Market reform usually attempts to protect small groups of individuals, for example family businesses, by requiring insurers to offer a minimum benefit package, prohibiting the exclusion of individuals with preexisting conditions, and guaranteeing renewal of coverage. This approach allows for the formation of health insurance purchasing groups, rather than employers, to bargain collectively for a range of benefits packages. Theoretically these collectives or alliances would bargain to establish an array of insurance plans of varying comprehensiveness and cost. Individuals and small businesses, as well as large businesses, could then select from among the plans most suited to their needs and capacity to pay. All available plans, however, would meet some minimum standard of covered benefits. Since these collectives would be bargaining on behalf of large groups of recipients, they could ostensibly get insurance companies to offer better coverage at lower rates.

A number of bills introduced in Congress in 1991 had a mixture of employer mandates and health insurance reform. These included bills sponsored by Representatives Pease, Rostenkowski, Sabo, and Waxman, and Senators Mitchell and Rockefeller. As with the other bills, the exact nature of covered benefits varied. Only Senator Rockefeller's bill specifically covered family planning services, although the Mitchell bill did have provision for postnatal family planning services. None of the bills mentioned abortion.

Hawaii has taken initiative in health care reform and was the first state with employer mandated health care coverage, which was passed in 1974 and instituted in 1975. This law required employers to provide health insurance for any employee who worked a minimum of 20 hours a week. In 1989, a State Health Insurance Program (SHIP) was launched to extend coverage to people who fell into the gaps of existing programs. These two state programs work in concert with federal Medicare and Medicaid and private insurance programs. The entire constellation of programs has allowed Hawaii to achieve approximately 97% health coverage.

In terms of health status effects, the results are promising. Hawaii has been ranked first in studies of longevity, low infant mortality, lower premature morbidity, and lower mortality from heart and lung disease and cancer (Lewin & Sybinsky, 1993). However, the difference in health outcomes attributable specifically to these health programs is not clear. In addition, there are several unique features about Hawaii that may limit the ability to generalize the Hawaii experience to other states (Miike, 1993). For example, Hawaii has a relatively low unemployment rate, a unique geographic location, and tourist-based industry that is not really free to move to another state with less restrictive laws. Finally, the impact of the plan on particular subgroups, for example women, has not been fully evaluated, and it would seem appropriate that any health care reforms (state or national) should include provisions to evaluate the particular benefits and limitations with respect to major classes of users.

Other states, such as Oregon and Tennessee, have begun to reform their state plans in order to expand Medicaid coverage to the uninsured. The Tennessee plan, Tenncare, has only recently been instituted and may be modified further. The Oregon Medicaid Demonstration Project is designed to cover people below the federal poverty line through Medicaid and to cover others with employer mandates. The Health Services Commission of Oregon established a prioritized list of about 700 treatment benefits, 588 of which were adopted by the state legislature in July 1991 as part of standard benefits that would be covered through Medicaid funds or available in workplace plans (Fisher, Welch, & Wennberg, 1992). This excluded over a hundred other procedures that would not be eligible for reimbursement. Because such plans necessarily mean excluding coverage for some conditions (and thus the people who have the condition), there was much discussion about the rationing of health care and the basis for making such decisions.

A crescendo of activity was reached in September of 1993 when President Clinton introduced a plan for the Health Security Act. The Clinton plan, based on six principles (universal coverage, cost containment, quality, choice, reduced paper work, and responsibility), drew heavily on employer based mandates and market reform strategies, rather than a single payer system. It proposed that the federal government would define the set of guaranteed benefits, set limits in the growth of insurance premiums, and establish quality standards. States would establish health alliances, certify health plans, and monitor the availability of care. States also would negotiate premiums and coverage, and guarantee quality of care. States could opt to establish a single-payer system. Health alliances would operate under the aegis of states as nonprofit corporations or as agencies of the executive branch of state government. Under this plan, health alliances (operating under state government oversight) would solicit competitive bids from health plans, provide consumer information on these plans, collect premiums, and pay health plans. The vast majority of individuals would continue to choose their health care coverage through their employers, who would provide information on various available plans. Other bills continued to be debated, and shortly after the introduction of President Clinton's plan, Representative Jim Cooper introduced the Bipartisan Health Care Reform Act, and Representative Richard Gephardt introduced the Guaranteed Health Insurance Act. However, Senator

George Mitchell led negotiations and committee work on the Health Security Act derived from the president's plan. Alternative viewpoints and proposals continue to be debated, with active input from Senators Durenberger and Chafee. Clearly, in the 1995 session, no vote will occur on legislation that introduces comprehensive reform.

Regardless of which Congressional bill is passed, any attempt at reform must address a number of issues that include questions about universal coverage, the nature of payment systems, cost containment, quality, choice, preventive care, and the streamlining of bureaucracy. The needs and interests of women will not be met automatically by these reforms. We anticipate that issues of legitimacy, individual empowerment, and equity outlined at the beginning of the chapter will continue to be problematic. Trouble spots can be projected in attempts to provide secure coverage, cost containment, and benefits design.

Coverage

Secure, universal coverage is an admirable goal, but plans can differ on how well they would achieve this end. Most important for women, access to insurance should not depend upon full-time employment. Women who are self-employed in "cottage" occupations, who work in domestic services, run small businesses, have only part-time employment, or who are full-time homemakers need access to health insurance. Therefore, plans that rely entirely on an employer mandated system will undoubtedly fail to include women in a universal or secure fashion.

Most plans proposed in Congress include a provision whereby those now covered under Medicare would continue to be covered under that system. However, plans do vary with respect to the treatment of Medicaid recipients and eligibility requirements. Some plans would cover individuals whose income was 50% above the federally designated poverty level income, while other plans would encompass individuals whose annual income was up to twice that of the poverty level. Other approaches have moved in a direction to restrict the coverage of Medicaid to recipients of Aid to Families with Dependent Children or recipients of Supplemental Social Security Income. Individuals not covered by Medicare or Medicaid would choose a health plan through their area health purchasing alliance, with their employers paying a portion of the premium. Under these kinds of arrangements, individuals with incomes below a certain level, such as 150% of the poverty level, would be eligible for discounts to cover a portion of copayments and deductibles.

However, coverage itself may not solve the problem. While many women in need by virtue of poverty already are covered by Medicaid, they continue to have difficulty in obtaining the services they require, particularly reproductive services. For example, it has been reported that approximately 44% of obstetricians–gynecologists do not accept Medicaid patients (Braveman, Oliva, Miller, Schaff, & Reiter, 1988).

Managing Costs

There are a variety of ways to manage costs. One way is to promote competition among insurers, the rationale being that insurance companies will hold down fees, develop efficient claims processes, and carefully supervise providers. Plans that call for insurance cooperatives or alliances are based on the assumption that insurance corporations will compete to be included in the programs endorsed by such alliances and that these various alliances will compete for consumer subscriptions. These plans typically designate a list of preferred providers, pharmacies, and hospitals where claims will be honored. According to President Clinton's plan, a uniform package of basic benefits will be available through all health plans. However, different plans may be offered that cover selected additional services. Different plans would be priced according to the risk characteristic of each plan's participants.

Deductibles, copayments, and cost-sharing generally are proposed as features to control demand side costs. Deductibles that must be met before insurance coverage begins payment would vary under different plans, but might for example be set at $1,500 for individuals and $3,000 for families. Higher copayments typically would be required should an individual wish to see a provider not included in the accepted listing of their plan.

One factor that would contribute to overall health care costs involves the inclusion of the 38 million residents now without health insurance.

Just how much care these people need is unknown. Certainly, there would be increased demand for services, increased physician visits, and more hospital admissions. The difference in what is now sufficient in the way of health resources and what would be needed if universal coverage were instituted is known as the *access gap*. Paradoxically, there might be some reductions in health care costs associated with universal coverage, because some of the charges now imposed on insured patients are designed to compensate for care already received by uninsured patients.

However, managing costs per se does not address issues regarding the social construction of legitimacy and the quality and equity of care. We speculate that longstanding issues that underlie the definition of legitimate care—issues that ultimately limit choice—will continue to operate. Payment becomes the final division between that which is legitimate, "real" health care and that which is substitute or alternative health care. Often the only true health care is equated with orthodox medicine. However, there are a number of alternative options regarding the sites of care, providers, and scope of services. When these alternatives are explored, one becomes aware that legitimate health care has been constructed in a relatively narrow model. These limits are likely to be preserved in current proposals for reform. The pervasive medical model has defined what is legitimate medicine, and this social construction of medicine conveys to society that hospitals are the authorized centers of healing.

Simply managing costs will not resolve problems in equitable access and quality of care. As long as profits and fees associated with some patients, such as those covered through a private employer, are higher than those associated with the care of, for example, Medicaid patients, access to care will continue to be a major problem. Physicians will continue to refuse to accept Medicaid patients, and hospitals will accord fewer days of care for the same medical conditions. Studies have found, for example, that uninsured individuals are discharged from hospitals sooner than insured individuals admitted for the same conditions (Hadley, Steinberg, & Feder, 1991), and also that uninsured patients often have fewer procedures during their hospital stay (Weissman & Epstein, 1989). One large-scale California-based study found that privately insured women were 50%

more likely to have Cesarean sections than indigent or self-insured women (Stafford, 1990).

Benefits Design

What constitutes a minimum basic package of health benefits and, more to the point, what criteria should be used to determine the answer to this question? One reasonable approach would be to determine a benefits plan that included necessary and prudent services and technologies of established worth and excluded discretionary or unproven services. Unfortunately, large scale studies of technology effectiveness, relative benefits, and costs among alternative approaches, and long-term patient outcomes do not exist for the most part. Of particular relevance to women would be questions about whether or not "experimental" treatments like bone marrow transplant for breast cancer patients would be covered. Related questions concern the value of preventive care, such as whether or not general screening mammography or Pap smears would be covered.

Other benefits having special relevance for women come readily to mind, such as mental health, substance abuse, and expanded home health care. Because women are more likely to seek mental health care from their general provider (Shapiro et al., 1984) and to receive over 60% of psychotropic prescriptions (National Center for Health Statistics & Koch, 1983), mental health issues are particularly important for women. In contrast, women with alcoholism may be underdiagnosed. Furthermore, because women live longer than men, home health care is also particularly important. Additionally, an entire cadre of conditions particularly relevant for the growing number of older women need to be included, especially those involving chronic illnesses, such as arthritis, Alzheimer's, diabetes, asthma, and orthopedic and muscular problems, as well as vision, hearing, and speech impairments (Collins, 1993). Chronic illnesses become increasingly important as demographics change. Currently, 12% of the population is over 65 years of age, but in the year 2025, estimates are that 20% of the population will be over 65, and dramatic increases in the population over 85 will also be evident (Collins, 1993). Since women's life expectancies are higher than men's, the majority of these individuals will be women.

However, simply listing what is or what is not included in a benefits package does not address a number of larger issues. Is health care to be primarily therapeutic, or should it also encompass prevention of illness and the promotion of wellness? One of the most sensitive questions concerns the availability of family planning services and abortion, and many of the proposed plans are vague on these points. While abortion in the first trimester has been legal since 1973, the Hyde amendment forbids use of Medicaid funds for abortion counseling or abortion services. Furthermore, recent court decisions have opened the door for state-by-state policies and practices regarding abortion. This crucial issue is fundamental to the status of all women. The landmark guide *Our Bodies, Ourselves* (Boston Women's Health Collective, 1973) energized women with these principles, and many of today's feminists continue to align themselves with the right to control one's body (Dreifus, 1977). It is instructive to note that recent litigation has not been won on the basis of women's right to self-determination. The *Roe v. Wade* (1973) Supreme Court decision legalizing abortion was decided on the principle of privacy implied by the Constitution. The attack now developing on the right to abortion will probably hinge on the litigated constitutionality of a right to privacy.

Finally, covered benefits must be examined in the context of the delivery of care. Managed care does not automatically guarantee more effective care, better decision-making, or most importantly equitable care. The list of covered benefits and the extent of payments as they now exist in government health programs is not gender-neutral. For example, while Medicare covers about 81% of expenses for heart attack and 79% of expenses for enlarged prostate, it covers only 65% of care for breast cancer and only about 48% of costs for stroke (Sofaer & Abel, 1990).

Other problems that may or may not be affected by health care reform initiatives encompass the inclusion of women in clinical trials, breast cancer research, and AIDS case identification. Looking at these topics with respect to gender, poverty, race, geographic location, and socioeconomic status will give assurance that policy-makers can provide quality care for a diversity of individuals.

The possibility that treatment interventions may be shaped inappropriately by gender stereotypes is especially alarming. For example, recent data from the AIDS Cost and Services Utilization Survey (Hellinger, 1993) reveal that women and adolescent girls who test positive for HIV receive fewer medications, fewer hospital admissions, and fewer outpatient visits than men with the same diagnosis. Females with full AIDS diagnoses are significantly (20%) less likely than male IV-drug user, with AIDS to be admitted to a hospital for any AIDS-related condition. These findings continue to hold true even after the data have been controlled for income, race, insurance, and geographic differences.

Our own research on the diagnosis and treatment of coronary heart disease illustrates some of the complexities of evaluating the equity of care. Although heart disease is the leading cause of death among women and although more women than men die of coronary heart disease (CHD), there continues to be a tendency to view CHD as a man's disease (Wenger, 1994). Treatment interventions are not gender-neutral, and there is a very real possibility that some of the differential treatment could be due to bias. In a national sample of 711,068 males hospitalized with chronic ischemia, 27% received bypass, while 18% of 359,389 females hospitalized with the same diagnosis received bypass (Gressley, Travis, & Adams, 1993). A variety of judgment heuristics and flawed reasoning may contribute to such discrepancies (Travis, Gressley, & Phillippi, 1993). One explanation commonly offered in medical circles is that the disease process starts much later for females, and women are consequently more fragile and have acquired other health conditions that would place them at greater risk during surgery. However, when we examined the proportion of patients with chronic ischemia by gender and age we found that approximately 40% of men in their fifties had bypass, while less than 30% of women in their fifties with the diagnosis had bypass.

CONCLUSIONS

One way to keep the tangle of prevention objectives, payment plans, delivery systems, and treatment priorities in perspective is to remember that the market good of cost containment may not be the final or only criterion that should be applied to health care reform. In fact, social good is the ultimate long-term objective. As plans are being devised and designed, it is not only the containment of cost, but also the long term relationship of cost to social well-being that should be evaluated. The locus and type of care, and the identification and legitimacy of providers need to be examined carefully. Plans centralized around hospitals, or physicians, or communities will have quite different impacts. Similarly, focus on wellness, prevention, or tertiary care will produce distinct results.

We would like to point out that medical judgment can be flawed at times, and any system that goes into place, regardless of the particulars, needs to have a strong component that involves surveillance and evaluation. There is a pressing need to expand research on the delivery system itself, on patient outcomes, and treatment effectiveness in order to properly implement any health care plan that is considered.

In planning the future of health care, it is important that policymakers deliver a package that will incorporate the issues that we have outlined above. Focusing on women's health issues is just the beginning. We also need to carefully scrutinize the social construction of legitimacy, and to develop a system that will promote empowerment, equity, and inclusiveness. Interweaving basic feminist principles into policy planning may facilitate action and provide women with a sense of security in their individual health and well-being. In addition, a broad feminist agenda for health care policy can serve to promote the health and well-being of all individuals.

REFERENCES

Adams, P. L., Travis, C. B., Gressley, D. L., & Adams, J. M. (1993, April). *Heart disease: Which variables really play a role?* Presentation at Women's Psychological and Physical Health: A Scholarly and Social Agenda, Lawrence, KA.

Agency for Health Care Policy and Research. (1994a, February). *The national bill for diseases treated in U.S. hospitals: 1987.* (DHHS-PHS AHCPR Pub. No. 94-0002). Washington, DC: U.S. Government Printing Office.

Agency for Health Care Policy and Research. (1994b). *Trends in hospital procedures performed on black patients and white patients: 1980–1987* (Provider Studies Research Note 20. DHHS-PHS AHCPR Pub. No. 94-0003). Washington, DC: U.S. Government Printing Office.

Alagna, S. W., & Reddy, D. M. (1984). Predictors of proficient technique and successful lesion detection in breast self-examination. *Health Psychology, 3,* 113–127.

Allen, R. E. (1991). International Union, United Automobile, Aerospace and Agricultural Implement Workers of America, UAW, et al. vs. Johnson Controls, Inc.—Part I: Overview. *American Industrial Hygiene Association Journal, 52,* A440–441.

Amaro, H. (1988). Considerations for prevention of HIV infection among Hispanic women. *Psychology of Women Quarterly, 12,* 429–444.

American Cancer Society. (1995). *Cancer facts and figures.* New York: Author.

Anderson, C. (1994). Measuring what works in health care. *Science, 263,* 1080–1082.

Annas, G. J. (1991). Fetal protection and employment discrimination—the Johnson Controls case. *New England Journal of Medicine, 325,* 740–743.

Bernhardt, D. (1980). *Working women roots: An oral history primer.* Ann Arbor, MI: Institute of Labor and Industrial Relations, University of Michigan–Wayne State University.

Boston Women's Health Collective. (1973). *Our bodies, ourselves.* New York: Simon & Schuster.

Brannon, L., & Feist, J. (1992). *Health psychology.* Belmont, CA: Wadsworth.

Braveman, P., Oliva, G., Miller, M. G., Schaff, V. M., & Reiter, R. (1988). Women without health insurance: Links between access, poverty, ethnicity, and health. *Western Journal of Medicine, 149,* 708–711.

Butler, J. M., & Schoepflin, R. B. (1990). Charismatic women and health: Mary Baker Eddy, Ellen G. White, and Aimee Semple McPherson. In R. D. Apple (Ed.), *Women, health, and medicine in America.* New York: Garland.

Butter, I. H. (1993). Premature adoption and routinization of medical technology: Illustrations from childbirth technology. *Journal of Social Issues, 49*(2), 11–34.

Catchen, H. (1988). Generational equity: Issues of gender and race. *Women and Health, 14*(3/4), 31–38.

Champion, V. L. (1992). Relationship of age to factors influencing breast self-examination practice. *Health Care for Women International, 13,* 1–9.

Chu, S. Y., & Diaz, T. (1993). Living situation of women with AIDS. *Journal of Acquired Immune Deficiency Syndromes, 6*(4), 431–432.

Claus, C. A., Berzon, M., & Bertein, J. (1993). Litigating reproductive and developmental health in the aftermath of UAW vs. Johnson Controls. *Environmental Health Perspectives, 101* (Suppl. 2), 205–220.

Clinton, W. J. (1993, September). *Health security for all Americans.* Address before a joint session of the United States Congress, Washington, DC.

Collins, J. G. (1993). Prevalence of selected chronic conditions: United States, 1986–88. *Vital and Health Statistics 10* (82). DHHS Publication No. (PHS) 93-1510). Hyattsville, MD: National Center for Health Statistics.

Crawford, M., & Marecek, J. (1989). Psychology reconstructs the female 1968–1988. *Psychology of Women Quarterly, 13,* 147–165.

Dreifus, C. (1977). Abortion, this piece is for remembrance. In C. Dreifus (Ed.), *Seizing our bodies: The politics of women's health* (pp. 131–145). New York: Vintage.

Eastaugh, S. R. (1992). *Health economics: Efficiency, quality, and equity.* Westport, CT: Auburn House.

Ehrenreich, B., & English, D. (1973). *Witches, midwives, and nurses: A history of women healers,* New York: Feminist Press.

Eisenberg, J. M. (1985). Physician utilization: The state of research about physicians' practice patterns. *Medical Care, 23,* 461–483.

Fisher, E. S., Welch, H. G., & Wennberg, J. E. (1992). Prioritizing Oregon's hospital resources. *Journal of the American Medical Association, 267,* 1925–1931.

Fullilove, M., Fullilove, R. E., Haynes, K., & Gross, S. (1990). Black women and AIDS prevention: A view towards understanding gender roles. *Journal of Sex Research, 27,* 47–64.

Gilbert, E. (1991). Women sue to challenge fetal protection policies. *National Underwriting 95,* pp. 4, 16.

Gilbert, L. A. (1980). Feminist therapy. In A. M. Brodsky & R. T. Hare-Mustin (Eds.), *Women and psychotherapy* (pp. 245–265). New York: Guilford.

Ginzberg, E. (1987). *Medicine and society: Clinical decisions and societal values.* Boulder, CO: Westview Press.

Grady, K. E. (1988). Older women and the practice of breast self-examination [Special Issue: Women's health: Our minds, our bodies]. *Psychology of Women Quarterly, 12,* 473–487.

Greenhouse, L. (1991, March 21). Court backs right of women to jobs with health risks. *New York Times,* pp. 1, 12.

Gressley, D. L., Travis, C. B., & Adams, P. L. (1993, April). *Differential treatment of heart disease: Is there biased decision making?* Paper presented at Women's Psychological and Physical Health: A Scholarly and Social Agenda, Lawrence, KA.

Hacker, H. M. (1951). Women as a minority group. *Social Forces, 30,* 60–69.

Hadley, J., Steinberg, E. P., & Feder, J. (1991). Comparison of uninsured and privately insured hospital patients: Condition on admission, resource use and outcome. *Journal of the American Medical Association, 265,* 374–379.

Harris, S. S., Caspersen, C. J., DeFriese, G. H., & Estes, H. (1989). Physical activity counseling for healthy adults as a primary preventive intervention in the clinical setting: Report for the U.S. Preventive Services Task Force. *Journal of the American Medical Association, 261,* 3590–3598.

Hellinger, F. J. (1993). The use of health services by women with HIV infection. *Health Services Research, 28,* 543–561.

Herzog, A. R. (1989). Physical and mental health in older women: Selected research issues and data sources. In A. R. Herzog, K. C. Holden, & M. M. Seltzer (Eds.), *Health and economic status of older women* (pp. 35–91). Amityville, NY: Baywood.

Hyde, J. S. (1991). *Half the human experience: The psychology of women.* Lexington, MA: D.C. Heath and Company.

Joseph, S. C. (1988). Current issues concerning AIDS in New York City. *New York State Journal of Medicine, 88,* 253–258.

Kahn, A. S., & Yoder, J. D. (1989). The psychology of women and conservatism: Rediscovering social change. *Psychology of Women Quarterly, 12,* 417–432.

Keifer, R. (1990). Pediatric AIDS. *Multicultural Inquiry and Research on AIDS, 4*(3), 1–11.

Kirschstein, R. L., & Merritt, D. H. (1985). *Women's health: Report of the Public Health Service task force on women's health issues.* Washington, DC: U.S. Public Health Service.

Kulik, J. A., Moore, P. J., & Mahler, H. I. M. (1993). Stress and affiliation: Hospital roommate effects on preoperative anxiety and social interaction. *Health Psychology, 12,* 118–124.

Landrine, H. (Ed.). (1994). *Bringing cultural diversity to feminist psychology: Theory, research, and practice.* Washington, DC: American Psychological Association.

Lebra-Chapman, J. (1991). *Women's voices in Hawaii.* Ninot, CO: University Press of Colorado.

Levy, S. M. (1981). Psychology and cancer: A reply to Stachnik. *American Psychologist, 36,* 219–220.

Levy, S. M. (1983). Host differences in neoplastic risk: Behavioral and social contributors to disease. *Health Psychology, 2,* 21–44.

Lewin, J. C., & Sybinsky, P. A. (1993). Hawaii's employer mandate and its contribution to universal access. *Journal of the American Medical Association, 269* (19), 2538–2543.

Markus, R. (1990, March 27, final edition). Court to weigh workplace fetal safety: Sex discrimination issue raised in case. *The Washington Post,* p. A1.

Merson, M. H. (1993). Slowing the spread of HIV: Agenda for the 1990's. *Science, 260,* 1266–1268.

Miike, L. (1993). Background paper. *Health insurance: The Hawaii experience.* Washington, DC: Office of Technology Assessment.

Muller, C. F. (1990). *Health care and gender.* New York: Russell Sage Foundation.

National Center for Health Statistics & H. Koch. (1983). *Drug utilization in office practice by age and sex of the patient: National ambulatory medical care survery, 1980.* (Advanced Data from Vital and Health Statistics, No. 90 DHHS Pub. No. PHS 83-1250). Hyattsville, MD: Public Health Service.

Oakley, A. (1984). *The captured womb: A history of the medical care of pregnant women.* New York: Basil Blackwell.

Pierce, J. P., Fiore, M. C., Novotny, T. E., Hatziandreu, E. J., & Davis, R. M. (1989). Trends in cigarette smoking in the United States: Projections to the year 2000. *Journal of the American Medical Association, 261,* 61–65.

Rich, A. (1976). *Of woman born: Motherhood as experience and institution.* New York: W.W. Norton.

Riessman, C. K. (1983). Women and medicalization: A new perspective. *Social Policy, 14,* 3–18.

Roberto, K. A. (1988). Stress and adaptation patterns of older osteoporotic women. *Women and Health, 14*(3/4), 105–120.

Rodin, J., & Collins, A. (1991). *Women and the new reproductive technologies: Medical, psychosocial, legal, and ethical dilemmas.* Hillsdale, NJ: Erlbaum.

Royak-Schaler, R. (1991). Psychological processes in breast cancer: A review of selected research. *Journal of Psychosocial Oncology, 9,* 71–89.

Sagaria, M. A. D. (1988). *Empowering women: Leadership development strategies on campus.* San Francisco: Jossey–Bass.

Sandelowski, M. (1981). *Women health and choice.* Englewood Cliffs, NJ: Prentice Hall.

Scialli, A. R. (1993). Fetal protection policies in the United States. *Seminar in Perinatology, 17,* 50–57.

Shapiro, S., Skinner, E. A., Kessler, L. G., Korff, M. V., German, P. S., Tischler, G. L.,

Leaf, P. J., Benham, L., Cottler, L., & Regier, D. A. (1984). Utilization of health and mental health services. *Archives of General Psychiatry, 41*, 971–978.

Short, P. (1990). *Estimates of the uninsured population, calendar year 1987.* National Medical Expenditure Survey Data Summary 2, Agency for Health Care Policy and Research (DHHS Pub. No. PHS 90-3469). Rockville, MD: Public Health Service.

Smith, D. E. (1991). Writing women's experience into social science. *Feminism and Psychology, 1*(1), 155–169.

Sofaer, S., & Abel, E. (1990). Older women's health and financial vulnerability: Implications of the Medicare benefit structure. *Women and Health, 16*, 47–67.

Sonnefeld, S. T., Waldo, D. R., Lemieux, J. A., & McKusick, D. R. (1991). Projection of national health expenditures through the year 2000. *Health Care Financing Review, 13*, 1–15.

Stafford, R. S. (1990). Cesarean section use and source of payment: An analysis of California hospital discharge abstracts. *American Journal of Public Health, 80*, 313–315.

Stanton, A. L., & Snider, P. R. (1993). Coping with a breast cancer diagnosis: A prospective study. *Health Psychology, 12*, 16–23.

Stellman, J. M. (1987). The working environment of the working poor: An analysis based on workers' compensation claims, census data and known risk factors. *Women and Health, 12*(3/4), 83–101.

Travis, C. B. (1985). Medical decision making and elective surgery: The case of hysterectomy. *Risk Analysis, 5*, 241–251.

Travis, C. B., Gressley, D. L., & Crumpler, C. A. (1991). Feminist contributions to health psychology. *Psychology of Women Quarterly, 15*(4), 557–566.

Travis, C. B., Gressley, D. L., & Phillippi, R. (1993). Medical decision making, gender, and cardiovascular disease. *Journal of Women's Health, 2*(3), 269–279.

Unger, R., & Crawford, M. (1993). *Women and gender.* New York: McGraw–Hill.

U.S. Department of Health and Human Services. (1991). *Healthy people 2000: Full report with commentary* (DHHS Pub. No. PHS 91–50212). Washington, DC: U.S. Government Printing Office.

U.S. General Accounting Office. (1986a). *Medical malpractice: No agreement on the problems or solutions.* Gaithersburg, MD: Author.

U.S. General Accounting Office. (1986b). *Medical malpractice: Insurance costs increased but varied among physicians and hospitals.* Gaithersburg, MD: Author.

U.S. General Accounting Office. (1992). *Medical malpractice: Alternatives to litigation.* Gaithersburg, MD: Author.

U.S. General Accounting Office. (1993). *Medicaid: States turn to managed care to improve access and control costs.* Gaithersburg, MD: Author.

Weiss, K. (1984). *Women's health care: A guide to alternatives.* Reston, VA: Reston Publishing.

Weissman, J., & Epstein, A. M. (1989). Case mix and resource utilization by uninsured hospital patients in the Boston metropolitan area. *Journal of the American Medical Association, 261,* 3572–3576.

Wenger, N. K. (1994). Coronorary heart disease in women: Needs and opportunities. In S. M. Czajkowski, D. R. Hill, & T. B. Clarkson (Eds.), *Women, behavior and cardiovascular disease* (NIH pub. No. 94-3309, pp. 7–18). Washington, DC: U.S. Government Printing Office.

Worell, J., & Remer, P. (1992). *Feminist perspectives in therapy: An empowerment model for women.* New York: John Wiley & Sons.

Yoder, J. D., & Kahn, A. S. (1992). Toward a feminist understanding of women and power. *Psychology of Women Quarterly, 16*(4), 381–388.

Yoder, J. D., & Kahn, A. S. (1993). Working toward an inclusive psychology of women. *American Psychologist, 48*(7), 846–850.

15

Psychology of Women's Health: Challenges for the Future

Annette L. Stanton and Sheryle J. Gallant

As the foregoing chapters amply illustrate, the rapid expansion in knowledge concerning the role of psychosocial and behavioral factors in women's health is cause for optimism. Clearly, the chapters document the growing awareness among scientists that women's health concerns represent a crucial area for intensive study. It also is apparent that progress is uneven and that many questions remain. In some areas, findings have accumulated that carry specific implications for promoting women's health. In others, critical studies of women's experiences have yet to be conducted, or the extant research has suffered from conceptual and methodological problems that cast doubt on the utility of the findings. Certainly, research in psychological perspectives on women's health presents an array of challenges and must be considered work-in-progress. The authors of each chapter have offered specific suggestions for the direction of that work. Our goal in this chapter is not to reiterate those recommendations, but rather to delineate themes across substantive areas and challenges for future research and application in the psychology of women's health. We will consider issues in three domains: conceptual frameworks in women's health, methodological considerations, and issues in application.

CONCEPTUAL FRAMEWORKS IN
WOMEN'S HEALTH

What sorts of conceptual frameworks will be most useful in addressing questions regarding psychosocial issues in women's health? This question can be addressed by critically examining the organizational structure of the present volume. The structure reveals a focus on disease- or behavior-specific content. A disease-based model for psychosocial research has parallels with a traditional biomedical model and may carry similar potential advantages and drawbacks. The model's focus on a stepwise process of careful identification of characteristics of a discrete disorder, specification of the disorder's cause, and development of a specific treatment has led to significant advances in understanding and treating many diseases. Intensive study of diseases and related behaviors that represent leading causes of mortality and morbidity for women (e.g., cardiovascular disease, cancer) is essential for improving women's lives. Further, there are several practical realities that encourage a disease-specific focus on the part of psychosocial researchers. First, the existing federal and private funding structures, as evidenced in the National Institutes of Health or the American Cancer Society, for example, promote research on discrete diseases. Second, both physician collaborators, who often specialize in treating particular diseases, and research participants may expect researchers to be conversant in the language and knowledge base of a specific disease. Perhaps more important is the likelihood that the ability to conduct sound psychosocial research often necessitates knowledge on the part of the investigator of the determinants, course, and treatment of a specific disorder. The expertise required is considerable, and the exigencies only multiply when an investigator attempts research that cuts across several diseases or behaviors. Thus, it is not surprising that many who investigate psychosocial issues in women's health have specialized in discrete diseases or content problems (e.g., smoking) rather than examining psychosocial issues more broadly.

It is important, however, that researchers who adopt a disease-specific focus not fall prey to some of the traditional drawbacks of the biomedical model. These include biological reductionism, fragmentation in research and health care, a focus on pathology rather than on health, a tendency toward atheoretical research and conceptual frameworks that fail to address adequately the multiple contextual determinants of health outcomes, and a lack of attention to diversity among the subjects of study.

With regard to biological reductionism, the chapters in this volume render apparent the advantages of developing multifactorial and biopsychosocial models rather than engaging in reduction of a health issue to any single-factor biological cause. Furthermore, biological status need not be the gold standard with regard to health endpoints. As Gatz, Harris, and Turk-Charles pointed out, the many "healths" include physical, functional, and psychological health, among others, and even older women who are likely to have multiple chronic conditions perceive themselves as healthier than their physical status would predict. Although mortality and physical morbidities represent important endpoints for research, psychosocial outcomes also deserve increased theoretical and empirical attention.

A related potential disadvantage of a traditional biomedical approach results from its tendency to contribute to fragmentation in research and health care. Studying discrete psychosocial, biological, and behavioral factors may not produce an accurate and useful portrait of the contributors to women's health. Rather, examining links among these factors may better serve to advance research and application in women's health. For example, chapter authors referred to the need for scrutiny of the relations between depression and such health behaviors and outcomes as smoking maintenance, diabetes, and cardiovascular disease. Marcus, Dubbert, King, and Pinto cited research suggesting that participation in exercise may help women quit smoking. The traditional model also may promote the treatment of isolated organ systems rather than whole women with complex and interacting health care needs. For instance, how is a woman to decide on electing exogenous hormone administration when it may confer benefit with regard to preventing heart disease and risk with regard to developing cancer (Barrett-Connor, 1994; Hulka, 1994; Lobo & Speroff, 1994)? Is women's optimal health promoted when researchers construct protocols that provide incentives to women for attending cancer screening but do not offer simple blood pressure checks at the same appointment? Research that prevents such fragmentation through examination of multiple determinants of multifaceted health outcomes is needed.

We also would argue that the adequate conceptualization of multi-faceted health outcomes implies not only examination of pathological psychosocial and biological processes, but also of salutory health effects. A traditional biomedical approach often promotes a focus on pathology rather than health, and several chapters noted the history of viewing women's biology and health through a lens of difference and deficiency. Although it surely is important to explore what makes women sick, it is equally crucial to acknowledge women's health-related strengths and to examine factors that promote women's optimal health and well-being. O'Leary and Ickovics (1995) have advanced a model of resilience as applied to women's health, and other researchers have developed psychological constructs shown to be related to positive psychological and physical health outcomes in women and men, such as optimism (Scheier & Carver, 1992) and hope (Snyder et al., 1991). To date, far too little research has been conducted on factors related to resiliency and other potentially health-promoting attributes and behaviors.

Researchers also should be aware that maintaining a narrow focus on a specific disease or behavior may prove limiting with regard to theory-testing and development. For example, as discussed by Stanton and Danoff-Burg, much of the research on postpartum depression failed to benefit from established theories regarding depression in general. As Marcus and colleagues suggested, general theories of behavior change can serve as a foundation for understanding and promoting physical activity in women. Theoretically grounded work will advance the study of specific diseases, and work on psychosocial constructs and theories that cut across health outcomes and behaviors may prove even more beneficial.

We also observe that many of the theories and constructs applied to the psychology of women's health to date have centered on explanatory variables presumably residing within the individual rather than in the sociocultural context of women's and men's lives. Women's reluctance to encourage condom use by their partners has been assumed to reflect women's health beliefs or lack of assertiveness rather than power differentials in intimate relationships. Depression following childbearing often has been assumed to be a result of biological upheaval rather than the demands that accompany assumption of the role of primary caretaker. Programs designed to promote exercise participation have focused on enhancing self-regulatory or other individual skills rather than addressing such barriers to activity as women's caretaking responsibilities or lack of convenient access to safe exercise facilities.

Conceptual focus on intraindividual factors is useful in accounting for some of the variance in health-related variables and in developing interventions to foster individuals' control over their health. However, an isolated concentration on the individual woman and her internal attributes may result in misplaced blame for negative health behaviors and outcomes, as well as in limited conceptual models and applications (see Bohan, 1993; Hare-Mustin & Marecek, 1990; Kahn & Yoder, 1989; Mednick, 1989; Prilleltensky, 1989). Viewing a woman's "failure" to obtain a mammogram as reflecting her lack of interest in her own health, as opposed to attributing it to the absence of a physician's referral, or possibly a woman's desire to devote all extra funds to her children's education, provides a considerably different conceptual picture and carries very different implications for maximally effective intervention. Contextual factors such as socioeconomic conditions, exposure to violence, ethnic and cultural norms, organizational (e.g., workplace) involvement, physical environments and hazards, and the sociopolitical milieu warrant far more theoretical and empirical attention (see Revenson, 1990, for other recommendations regarding conceptualizing contexts). Several chapters also pointed to the positive and negative influences of interpersonal relationships on women's health. For example, authors cited interpersonal factors as potentially important determinants of women's drinking, smoking, exercise, and sexual behaviors. Women's roles as caretakers across the life span carry consequences for their own health as well as for that of others. Attitudes toward women held by health care providers translate into potentially differential treatment of women and men. Thus, the influences of relational contexts deserve increased consideration in conceptualizations of women's health.

To conceptualize women's health without regard for the contexts of women's lives will result in a partial and potentially distorted picture.

The recognition of contextual and individual differences among women highlights the need for considering issues of diversity in conceptual models for women's health. Traditional disease-based approaches often have concentrated on the disease process itself, with minimal consideration of factors promoting vulnerability or resilience within the host or within the host's environment. Up to this point, we have spoken of questions pertinent to conceptualizing "women's health." However, we do not mean to imply that women compose a homogeneous group. Indeed, many researchers have pointed out the likelihood that the within-group differences among women are greater in many domains than are average differences between women and men (e.g., Hyde, 1994; Worell & Etaugh, 1994). Thus, when one asks how best to conceptualize women's health, perhaps the question "which women with which characteristics in what contexts?" would provide a useful frame. To date, much of the documented psychology of women's health in the United States must be said to be a psychology of White, relatively affluent women. Chapter authors called repeatedly for consideration of women's health from more diverse perspectives. Inclusion in conceptual models of sociodemographic and lifestyle characteristics, such as age, ethnicity, socioeconomic status, sexual orientation, and family structure may serve as a starting point for capturing women's heterogeneity. However, like gender, these characteristics may act only as proxy variables for a host of other psychological and social mechanisms, and fine-grained analyses of these mechanisms are necessary.

In sum, we have noted several criticisms of the biomedical model, which traditionally has undergirded disease-specific approaches. We are not advocating that disease-focused research be stopped. Indeed, we believe that ample room exists for both keen empirical concentration on discrete diseases or behaviors and integration across health and psychosocial domains. Rather, our intention was to outline common disadvantages of the traditional model, so that researchers in the psychology of women's health can avoid them if they choose. Our view is that the most useful conceptual models for women's health will be those that (a) take into account potential interactions among biological, psychological, and social factors in determining women's health; (b) include multifaceted outcomes, including both pathological and optimal indicators of health in multiple realms (e.g., physical, psychological, social); and (c) are grounded in carefully developed theories that take into account the diverse contexts of women's lives. Of course, we do not expect that one comprehensive biopsychosocial theory will capture adequately the domain of the psychology of women's health (see also Chesney & Ozer, 1995). We hope that researchers will take on the challenge of developing and testing conceptual frameworks in their specific areas of interest, as well as those that cut across health behaviors or outcomes, with the goal of adequately characterizing and promoting health for women across the life span.

METHODOLOGICAL CONSIDERATIONS IN WOMEN'S HEALTH RESEARCH

What sorts of considerations merit attention in designing research to examine women's health issues? Of course, a first step is to devise questions that carry the potential to advance understanding and promotion of women's health, many of which were suggested by authors of the previous chapters. In doing so, we must examine our assumptions regarding women and the topic of interest, as well as asking what conceptual frameworks will be most useful, as has been discussed above. As Meyerowitz and Hart argued regarding psychosocial research on women and cancer, gender-biased assumptions may influence the nature of the questions and hypotheses advanced. In addition to questioning our own assumptions, involving colleagues and potential research participants in the initial stage of research conceptualization may prove beneficial. Several other sources also provide suggestions for examining assumptions and decreasing biases in conducting research, such as avoiding sexism (e.g., Denmark, Russo, Frieze, & Sechzer, 1988; McHugh, Koeske, & Frieze, 1986), heterosexism (e.g., Herek, Kimmel, Amaro, & Melton, 1991), ageism (e.g., Shaie, 1993), and ethnocentricism (e.g., Betancourt & López, 1993; Graham, 1992; Zuckerman, 1990).

Selecting the unit of analysis also is a crucial step in study conceptu-alization. As previously noted, selection of the individual as the unit of analysis has been most typical in women's health research, and perhaps in psychological research in general. For example, Felton and Shinn (1992; Shinn, 1989) have suggested that even in research on social support, the individual most often has been the focus of study. Greater attention to the relational and larger environmental context is necessary. The relatively small bodies of work on couples coping with health threats (see Reven-son, 1994, for a review) and women's daily transitions from paid employ-ment to home contexts (e.g., Frankenhaeuser, 1991) provide examples of research that transcends the individual level of analysis or examines mul-tiple contexts. Revenson (1990) offers an illustration in which a researcher might choose to study determinants of adherence to healthy dietary habits in an individual by examining characteristics of adjacent systems (e.g., the family's attitudes toward altering dietary patterns), the surrounding con-text (e.g., the availability of nutritious foods in one's work setting), and the larger social system (e.g., increased public awareness of the benefits of healthy diets). Characteristics of the sociocultural, interpersonal, situa-tional, and temporal contexts (Revenson, 1990) merit consideration as im-portant influences on women's health. Even when the investigator studies individuals in a single setting, considering the larger contextual picture is important.

A number of different methodologies have been useful in advancing women's health research. Qualitative strategies such as intensive interviews and focus groups directed toward exploring women's experience regard-ing a particular issue may be especially helpful in the stage of hypothesis generation. Careful descriptive research is necessary in many areas, and longitudinal studies have the advantage of allowing researchers to gauge effects over time in natural settings and to assess the interplay of etiolog-ical factors, as well as the long-term effects of interventions. Experimen-tal investigations, both to explore causal relationships and to devise health-promoting interventions that subsequently can be tested in natural settings, are also warranted. Feminist analyses have provided trenchant criticisms of the positivist, empirical tradition in science (e.g., Gergen,

1988; Harding, 1986; Keller, 1985; Riger, 1992) such as its assumption that science is value-neutral and its emphasis on experimental control over external validity and consequent tendency to decontextualize women's experience. We agree with Riger (1992) that no method is free of limitations and that, given awareness on the part of researchers of the value assumptions inherent in their research approach, a variety of methods can be of value in enabling understanding and improvement of women's lives (see also Peplau & Conrad, 1989).

How should researchers in women's health comprise their samples? Cogent arguments regarding the advantages and drawbacks of studying and reporting sex-related differences have been offered over the past several years (e.g., Baumeister, 1988; Eagly, 1990, 1995; Hare-Mustin & Marecek, 1990; Hyde & Plant, 1995; McHugh et al., 1986). We suggest that the researcher's choice of study participants, whether they be females and males, females (or males) only, or a specific subgroup of females (e.g., reservation-dwelling Native American women) should be guided by the questions and conceptual frameworks of interest. Certainly, study of underserved groups, such as poor women, older women, and women of color, is essential, as is inclusion of women participants in sufficient numbers for reliable analysis in research in which they have been underrepresented (e.g., psychosocial issues in cardiovascular disease). Of course, in research revealing group differences, whether it be between women and men or between African American and White women, for example, one should not confuse description with explanation. That is, sex or other immutable group characteristics should not be viewed as explanatory variables, but rather the finding of a group difference should be further explored to illuminate the mechanisms for the difference. In addition, effect sizes should be included in reports of group differences to indicate their magnitude. Furthermore, the history of applying results of studies on men to women illuminates the dangers of assumed generalization from any group to humans in general; careful description of our samples and specification of limitations on generalizability are critical.

Development of reliable and valid measures is crucial for women's health research. Consideration of the appropriateness of measures for women in particular contexts is essential. Several chapter authors noted the importance of establishing the validity of measures of such constructs as Type A behavior and quality of life (Shumaker & Smith), alcohol use (Wilsnack), exercise behaviors (Marcus et al.), and pregnancy-related adjustment (Stanton & Danoff-Burg) in women. It is vital to ensure that researchers not overestimate pathology in women by including as indicators of maladjustment items that characterize women's normative experiences (e.g., weight changes in pregnancy mistakenly counted as a symptom of depression). In addition, development of measures of positive health indicators is warranted, as is greater attention to measurement of dependent variables reflecting health outcomes more likely to affect women, such as various morbidities and comorbidity (Gatz et al., this volume; Verbrugge & Jette, 1994). Researchers in women's health also will wish to investigate links between psychosocial and physical health variables necessitating careful conceptualization and measurement of several sorts of indicators. This will require the researcher to cultivate knowledge in a number of realms or to initiate involvement in interdisciplinary research teams possessing expertise in psychological, social, and biological health domains.

APPLICATIONS IN WOMEN'S HEALTH

How should research be translated into interventions that will promote optimal health for women? A first question addresses the targets at which interventions should be directed. This question echoes themes of previous sections regarding appropriate units of analysis and consideration of context. Should interventions be designed to engender positive change in individual women, relationships, communities, or the larger sociopolitical context? Our answer is "yes." Certainly, removing structural barriers to and expanding resources for women's optimal health are important goals. As suggested by Travis, Gressley, and Adams, greater access to such resources as adequate income and education, a safe physical environment, and effective health care is needed. Many psychologists have been involved in research translating health care policy into interventions within the social system, and lessons learned from effective community action groups (e.g., Boston Women's Health Collective, advocacy groups for women with breast cancer and people with AIDS) can be used to mobilize social change. In addition, several chapter authors cited the need to be cognizant of structural impediments such as lack of child care or transportation and to provide such resources in order to allow women's participation in health-enhancing programs (e.g., Marcus et al.; Morokoff et al.; Wilsnack).

Considerably more research directed toward improving treatment of women in the health care system is warranted. Shumaker and Smith cited research that suggested that health care providers manage heart disease in women less aggressively than in men, and that women are less likely to attend rehabilitation programs after a cardiac event. Wilsnack indicated that physicians are less likely to identify problem-drinking in women than men. Determinants of differential treatment require study, and interventions directed toward enhancing health care providers' provision of effective treatment to women are necessary. In addition, there is a need to educate physicians in training about psychosocial and behavioral aspects of women's health in ways that will maximize their care of women.

Strategies designed to support change in health behaviors of individual women and men also are necessary, although they may not reach maximal success without attention to structural or relational barriers to change. Targeting men's behaviors, including drug use, smoking, condom use, and violence, will improve not only the health of men, but also of the women with whom they live. Programs to engender positive health behavior change in women, as well as their abilities to be informed and active consumers of health care, are necessary. Rather than a sole focus on treatment of problematic behaviors or conditions after they have developed, proactive approaches are essential. Research designed to identify contextual and individual attributes that place girls and women at risk for negative health outcomes and to specify effective methods for preventing those outcomes is merited. Moreover, programs aimed at promoting women's positive health behaviors require continued study. In general, illness prevention and health promotion for women require attention across the life span and at multiple levels of intervention.

In addition to considering appropriate targets for intervention, researchers must attend to the nature of the interventions. A primary challenge here is to determine the varieties of content, format, and structure that will be most useful. A question that emerged in several chapters addressed the differential effectiveness of psychosocial and behavioral interventions for women and men. Although authors noted that gender-related differences in efficacy were not tested in many cases, Butler and Wing demonstrated that women with diabetes may lose weight more successfully when treated with their partners and men may be more successful when treated alone. Mermelstein and Borelli found that women who smoke may prefer more formal smoking cessation programs and group treatment than men. What are the mechanisms by which some interventions may be more effective for women than for men? The question of what specific characteristics of health-promoting interventions render them most effective for which women (e.g., older women, women with young children) in which contexts is just beginning to be addressed. Again, meeting the diversity of women's health needs constitutes a central challenge.

Researchers and practitioners must also be concerned with the consequences of interventions. We strongly advocate the inclusion of measurable outcomes so that the efficacy of interventions can be evaluated adequately. Both short- and long-range outcomes for individuals and larger social systems require scrutiny. In addition, researchers should anticipate and attempt to minimize potential unintended, negative consequences of their interventions. For example, does instructing women in assertiveness with the aim of promoting condom use inadvertently misplace responsibility on women? Does encouraging the use of advanced reproductive technologies contribute to delayed resolution or option-seeking in women with fertility problems? The current impetus toward initiatives designed to promote women's health is exciting; it is important that this momentum not outstrip empirical support for the approaches being advocated. Careful consideration and assessment of the outcomes of interventions is essential.

Increasingly, those implementing interventions will be called upon to demonstrate their cost-effectiveness. Butler and Wing cited evidence that preconception health care for diabetic women is cost-effective, and Sobel (1994) provided evidence that an array of psychosocial and educational interventions can lower health care costs. Such documentation will provide strong argument for changes in health care policy and practice to promote women's health. Finally, dissemination of interventions that are shown to be effective is an important goal. Use of the media and other sources to communicate information regarding research and application in women's health to women themselves, as well as to the community of researchers and practitioners, is a responsibility of those working in this area.

CONCLUSIONS

The chapters in this volume highlight the considerable progress that has been made toward building a solid knowledge base in psychosocial aspects of women's health, and they specify issues that require attention if that progress is to continue. No single encompassing biopsychosocial paradigm emerges to characterize women's health; rather, the challenge is to scrutinize and build upon existing theories where possible, and to revise and reframe where needed to reflect more fully women's experience of health and well-being.

It is clear from the preceding chapters that health is not a univariate phenomenon, but rather is a function of the complex interplay of economic, sociopolitical, environmental, psychological, and biological determinants, the formula for which varies over the life course and across diverse groups of women. This complexity underscores the need for multivariate models and methods, as well as broadened interdisciplinary collaboration in research and application. It also highlights the need for continued intensive study of women's diversity and their commonality with regard to health. Along with the recognition that a range of important issues remains to be addressed, there is cause for optimism about the pace at which our understanding is increasing. We are confident that current lines of investigation will inspire a future generation of research and application that will pave the way for achievement of optimal health in women's lives.

REFERENCES

Barrett-Connor, E. (1994). Heart disease in women. *Fertility and Sterility, 62* (Suppl. 2), 127S–132S.

Baumeister, R. F. (1988). Should we stop studying sex differences altogether? *American Psychologist, 43,* 1092–1095.

Betancourt, H., & López, S. R. (1993). The study of culture, ethnicity, and race in American psychology. *American Psychologist, 48,* 629–637.

Bohan, J. S. (1993). Regarding gender: Essentialism, constructionism, and feminist psychology. *Psychology of Women Quarterly, 17,* 5–22.

Chesney, M. A., & Ozer, E. M. (1995). Women and health: In search of a paradigm. *Women's health: Research on gender, behavior, and policy, 1,* 3–26.

Denmark, F., Russo, N. F., Frieze, I. H., & Sechzer, J. A. (1988). Guidelines for avoiding sexism in psychological research: A report of the Ad Hoc Committee on Nonsexist Research. *American Psychologist, 43,* 582–585.

Eagly, A. H. (1990). On the advantages of reporting sex comparisons. *American Psychologist, 45,* 560–562.

Eagly, A. H. (1995). The science and politics of comparing women and men. *American Psychologist, 50,* 145–158.

Felton, B. J., & Shinn, M. (1992). Social integration and social support: Moving "social support" beyond the individual level. *Journal of Community Psychology, 20,* 103–115.

Frankenhaeuser, M. (1991). The psychophysiology of sex differences as related to occupational status. In M. Frankenhaeuser, U. Lundberg, & M. Chesney (Eds.), *Women, work, and health: Stress and opportunities* (pp. 39–61). New York: Plenum.

Gergen, M. M. (1988). Building a feminist methodology. *Contemporary Social Psychology, 13,* 47–53.

Graham, S. (1992). "Most of the subjects were white and middle class": Trends in published research on African Americans in selected APA journals, 1970–1989. *American Psychologist, 47,* 629–639.

Harding, S. (1986). *The science question in feminism.* Ithaca, NY: Cornell University Press.

Hare-Mustin, R. T., & Marecek, J. (Eds.). (1990). *Making a difference: Psychology and the construction of gender.* New Haven, CT: Yale University Press.

Herek, G. M., Kimmel, D. C., Amaro, H., & Melton, G. B. (1991). Avoiding heterosexist bias in psychological research. *American Psychologist, 46,* 957–963.

Hulka, B. S. (1994). Links between hormone replacement therapy and neoplasia. *Fertility and Sterility, 62* (Suppl. 2), 168S–175S.

Hyde, J. S. (1994). Can meta-analysis make feminist transformations in psychology? *Psychology of Women Quarterly, 18,* 451–462.

Hyde, J. S., & Plant, E. A. (1995). Magnitude of psychological gender differences: Another side of the story. *American Psychologist, 50,* 159–161.

Kahn, A. S., & Yoder, J. D. (1989). The psychology of women and conservatism: Rediscovering social change. *Psychology of Women Quarterly, 13,* 417–432.

Keller, E. F. (1985). *Reflections on gender and science.* New Haven, CT: Yale University Press.

Lobo, R. A., & Speroff, L. (1994). International consensus conference on postmenopausal hormone therapy and the cardiovascular system. *Fertility and Sterility, 62* (Suppl. 2), 176S–179S.

Mednick, M. T. (1989). On the politics of psychological constructs: Stop the bandwagon, I want to get off. *American Psychologist, 44,* 1118–1123.

McHugh, M. C., Koeske, R. D., & Frieze, I. H. (1986). Issues to consider in conducting nonsexist psychological research: A guide for researchers. *American Psychologist, 41,* 879–890.

O'Leary, V. E., & Ickovics, J. R. (1995) Resilience and thriving in response to challenge: An opportunity for a pardigm shift in women's health. *Women's Health: Research on Gender, Behavior, and Policy, 1,* 121–142.

Peplau, L. A., & Conrad, E. (1989). Beyond nonsexist research: The perils of feminist methods in psychology. *Psychology of Women Quarterly, 13,* 379–400.

Prilleltensky, I. (1989). Psychology and the status quo. *American Psychologist, 44,* 795–802.

Revenson, T. A. (1990). All other things are not equal: An ecological approach to personality and disease. In H. S. Friedman (Ed.), *Personality and disease* (pp. 65–94). New York: Wiley.

Revenson, T. A. (1994). Social support and marital coping with chronic illness. *Annals of Behavioral Medicine, 16,* 122–130.

Riger, S. (1992). Epistemological debates, feminist voices: Science, social values, and the study of women. *American Psychologist, 47,* 730–740.

Schaie, K. W. (1993). Ageist language in psychological research. *American Psychologist, 48,* 49–51.

Scheier, M. F., & Carver, C. S. (1992). Effects of optimism on psychological and physical well-being: Theoretical overview and empirical update. *Cognitive Therapy and Research, 16,* 201–228.

Shinn, M. (1989). Crossing substantive domains. *American Journal of Community Psychology, 17,* 565–570.

Snyder, C. R., Harris, C., Anderson, J. R., Holleran, S. A., Irving, L. M., Sigmon, S. T., Yoshinobu, L., Gibb, J., Langelle, C., & Harney, P. (1991). The will and the ways: Development and validation of an individual-differences measure of hope. *Journal of Personality and Social Psychology, 60,* 570–585.

Sobel, D. S. (1994). Mind matters, money matters: The cost-effectiveness of clinical behavioral medicine. In S. J. Blumenthal, K. Matthews, & S. M. Weiss (Eds.). *New frontiers in behavioral medicine: Proceedings of the national conference* (pp. 25–36). (NIH Publication No. 94-3772). Washington, DC: U.S. Government Printing Office.

Verbrugge, L. M., & Jette, A. M. (1994). The disablement process. *Social Science and Medicine, 38,* 1–14.

Worell, J., & Etaugh, C. (1994). Transforming theory and research with women: Themes and variations. *Psychology of Women Quarterly, 18,* 443–450.

Zuckerman, M. (1990). Some dubious premises in research and theory on racial differences: Scientific, social, and ethical issues. *American Psychologist, 45,* 1297–1303.

Author Index

Subject Index

Coronary heart disease (*continued*)
definition, 25
depression and, 40–41
diabetes and, 104
diagnosis, 25, 31, 32, 35
etiology, 28
gender differences, 25–27, 41, 558
hormone therapy for prevention of, 29
moderate alcohol consumption and, 391
mortality, 25, 26
nonpsychosocial risk factors, 36, 38
onset, 26
opportunities for research, 41–42
prevalence, 25–26
psychosocial aspects, 29–32, 34–35, 41
psychosocial risk factors, 36–41
recovery from, 25, 33–35
treatment, 28–29, 33, 35, 558
Cost of care, 540–543
gender disparities, 26
in health care reform strategies, 554–556, 558–559
research considerations, 578–579

Dementia, 507–508
Depression
AIDS and, 154
alcohol use and, 401–402
autoimmune disorders and, 179, 185
diabetes and, 108
in elderly people, 508–509
heart disease risk and, 40–41
hormone replacement therapy and, 231, 235, 237, 243–244
interpersonal loss and, 233
medical health and, 233
menopause and, 231–235, 243–244
postpartum, conceptualizations of, 262–271, 288

in pregnancy, preventive intervention for, 289–290
premenstrual syndrome and, 216–217, 227
smoking and, 319–320
tobacco use and, 334
vs. dementia, 508
vs. premenstrual syndrome, 227
Development, physical
aging processes, 499–505
life-span development model, 494–498
menarche, 200–201
Development, psychological
infertility and, 272, 273
life-span development model, 494–498
menarche, 201–203
menopause and midlife psychology, 235–237
Diabetes
associated disorders, 85, 108
atherosclerosis risk and, 28
clinical features, 85
concerns for women, 88, 108–109
contraception and, 98
depression risk, 108
economic costs, 85
heart disease risk and, 28, 36, 38
mortality, 85
pregnancy and preexisting, 94, 95–99
prevalence, 85
See also Gestational diabetes mellitus; Insulin-dependent diabetes
See also Non-insulin dependent (Type II) diabetes mellitus (NDDM)
Diet and nutrition, 12
coronary heart disease risk and, 38
gestational diabetes mellitus and, 100–101

About the Editors

An associate professor and coordinator of the Clinical Health and Rehabilitation Psychology Graduate Specialty at the University of Kansas, **Annette L. Stanton** also serves as associate editor for *Health Psychology*, an APA journal, and for *Women's Health: Research on Gender, Behavior, and Policy*. Her edited book (with Christine Dunkel-Schetter), titled *Infertility: Perspectives From Stress and Coping Research*, was published in 1991. Stanton has focused on stress and coping theory in her research, particularly as applied to individuals and couples coping with cancer and infertility. Currently, she is interested in the role of coping through emotional approach in adjustment to health-related adversity.

Sheryle J. Gallant is an associate professor of psychology at the University of Kansas. In her research she has focused on conceptual and methodological issues in the assessment of mood and behavior changes during the menstrual cycle and biopsychosocial correlates of premenstrual syndrome. In her most recent work, she examined problematic aspects of diagnosing premenstrual dysphoric disorder (PMDD), and the role of stress, coping, and relationship factors in the experience of PMDD. Gallant was chair of APA's 1994 national conference "Psychosocial and Behavioral Factors in Women's Health: Creating an Agenda for the 21st Century."